Public Sector Economics

Public Sector Economics

Theory and Applications

First Edition

Vivien Burrows

OXFORD
UNIVERSITY PRESS

OXFORD
UNIVERSITY PRESS

Great Clarendon Street, Oxford, OX2 6DP,
United Kingdom

Oxford University Press is a department of the University of Oxford.
It furthers the University's objective of excellence in research, scholarship,
and education by publishing worldwide. Oxford is a registered trade mark of
Oxford University Press in the UK and in certain other countries.

Published in the United States of America by Oxford University Press
546 Fifth Avenue, New York, NY 10036, United States of America

British Library Cataloguing in Publication Data
Data available

Library of Congress Control Number: 2026937359

ISBN 9780198869016

Printed and bound by CPI Group (UK) Ltd., Croydon, CR0 4YY

The manufacturer's authorized representative in the EU for product safety is
Oxford University Press España S.A. of Parque Empresarial San Fernando de Henares,
Avenida de Castilla, 2 – 28830 Madrid (www.oup.es/en or product.safety@oup.com).
OUP España S.A. also acts as importer into Spain of products made by the manufacturer.

MIX
Paper | Supporting responsible forestry
FSC® C013604
FSC www.fsc.org

About the author

Vivien Burrows is a Senior Research Economist at Nest Insight, a public-benefit research and innovation centre based in London. She previously worked as an Associate Professor in Economics at the University of Reading, where she taught a course on Public Economics for over ten years. This is where she first took inspiration to work on this book. She has a PhD in Economics from the University of York.

Acknowledgements

This book benefited from the input and support of a number of different people, but there are two in particular without whom I feel it would never have been finished. To Ali and Adam, I am immensely grateful for their unwavering encouragement and willingness to sense-check random pieces of writing at all hours of the day. I am also very grateful to Ali for proofreading and for some great suggestions. I would like to thank my parents, Jean and Hugh, and my brother and his partner, Chris and Ana, for always rooting for me. My Dad generously shared the trials and tribulations of book writing from his own experience—he always asked me how it was going and reassured me when I was feeling overwhelmed. And of course, I am grateful to my niblings Madalena (Leni) and Afonso (Alfie) for letting me borrow their names for the examples throughout the text.

I owe a special thank you to Simon Burke, who first planted the idea of writing a textbook on public economics in my head several years ago. I am also grateful to the various cohorts of students on the Public Economics module I taught at the University of Reading. Their interest and energy inspired me to find engaging ways to teach public economics to a diverse audience, which I hope to have incorporated into this book.

Bringing this book to life would not have been possible without the belief and patience of my editorial team at Oxford University Press. First and foremost, I am grateful to Felicity Boughton, with whom I began this journey. I would also like to thank Hayden Merrick, Makalah Moore, Caitlin Moreton-Lisle, Daminee Salahuddin and Emma Sheffield for continuing this process and eventually seeing me across the finish line. Last but not least, thank you to the reviewers for their time and invaluable feedback, which helped me refine the manuscript and undoubtedly contributed to a better book.

I would like to acknowledge some authors whose work particularly inspired me throughout this process: Nicholas Barr, Diane Coyle, and Mariana Mazzucato.

I have learnt so much from writing this book and I hope that it will be useful to those setting out on their own public economics journey.

Brief contents

Detailed contents

PART I INTRODUCTION TO PUBLIC ECONOMICS AND THE ROLE OF GOVERNMENT IN THE ECONOMY

PART III FINANCING THE GOVERNMENT

PART I

INTRODUCTION TO PUBLIC ECONOMICS AND THE ROLE OF GOVERNMENT IN THE ECONOMY

1
Introduction to public economics

Learning objectives

By the end of this chapter, you will be able to:

1.1 Explain the core questions of public economics and discuss the role of positive and normative analysis in public economics.
1.2 Explain the rationale for government intervention in the economy, the range of ways in which governments intervene, and the limits to government intervention.
1.3 Describe how the size and composition of the public sector varies across countries.
1.4 Discuss how perspectives on the role of government in the economy have changed over time and some of the factors which explain these changes.
1.5 Describe the theoretical and empirical tools that are used in public economics.

Introduction

Governments intervene in the economy in a variety of ways. They provide goods and services, such as defence and policing, roads and other physical infrastructure, education, healthcare, and pensions. They redistribute income through taxes and transfers, providing welfare benefits to individuals—including unemployment, sickness, and disability benefits—and subsidies to businesses. Governments are also responsible for a wide range of laws and regulations that affect virtually all areas of the economy, from health and safety and environmental regulations to minimum wages and employment law, competition policy, and consumer protection laws, even sometimes regulating the minimum quantity of sugar in jam. To finance their activities, governments levy taxes on goods and services, individual incomes, savings and wealth, and company profits. While the nature and extent of government intervention vary across countries, there is no doubt that governments play an important role in the economy.

Why do governments intervene in the economy? Is there a *right* level of government intervention? These questions are at the heart of **public economics**. To answer them, we need to think about the objectives that society wants to achieve and the best way of achieving them. These social objectives may include things like protecting individual freedoms, fostering social cohesion, or even promoting patriotism. Economists typically focus on two social objectives: **efficiency**; and **equity** or **social justice**. Government intervention is often presented as an alternative to the market mechanism as a way of achieving these social objectives, but governments and markets are not mutually exclusive. This simplistic view also ignores the important role that other institutions, such as community organizations, play in our economies.

This chapter provides an introduction to the field of public economics. We start by describing the core questions of public economics in section 1.1. Section 1.2 provides an overview of the economic role of government and the different ways in which governments intervene in the economy. In section 1.3 we look at how the size and composition of the public sector vary across countries, and section 1.4 explores how perspectives on the economic role of government have changed over time. Section 1.5 outlines some of the main theoretical and empirical tools of public economics, and section 1.6 concludes with an outline of the book and its scope.

1.1 What is public economics?

Public economics—or the economics of the public sector—is the study of the role of government in the economy. It is concerned with both government expenditures and how the government raises the revenues it needs to finance these expenditures. On the expenditure side, public economics explores questions like why some goods and services—such as education, healthcare, and old-age pensions—are often provided by the government, while others—such as food, clothing, internet, and home insurance—are provided by the private sector. On the revenue side, public economics looks at how the government raises revenues to finance its expenditure, particularly how it decides what activities or goods and services should be taxed and at what rates, and what impact these taxes have on individuals and the wider economy. Although public economics only emerged as a subject in its own right in the 1960s, its origins date back to the work of the early classical economists (see Box 1.1).

In this section, we review the key questions that public economics focuses on and explore the distinction between positive and normative analysis, before looking at why studying public economics is so important.

Box 1.1 A brief history of public economics

Public economics has its roots in the works of early political economists, such as Adam Smith and David Ricardo, who were concerned about issues of policy and the proper role of government in the economy. For Adam Smith, the government's role should be limited to safeguarding **property rights**, providing national defence, and maintaining certain public works, such as highways. He devoted Book V of *The Wealth of Nations*, published in 1776, to a historical analysis of government expenditures and revenues, and to questions of how the government could finance its activities, focusing on taxation and public borrowing, including the principles of good taxation and the risks of public debt.

Public economics started to emerge as a subject in its own right following the Second World War, a period of rapid government growth in the West. The term 'public economics' was first used in the mid-1960s (Kolm, 1987). However, prior to this, significant work had been carried out under the guise of **public finance**, including Richard Musgrave's seminal work, *The Theory of Public Finance*, published in 1959. Nowadays, the terms 'public finance' and 'public economics' (or sometimes 'public sector economics') tend to be used interchangeably.

1.1.1 The key questions of public economics

Public economics focuses on four key questions.[1]

1. When should governments intervene in the economy?

Traditionally, there are two main arguments for government intervention in the economy: to increase economic efficiency by addressing **market failures**—that is, instances where private markets fail to achieve an efficient allocation of resources—and to promote equity and social justice by redistributing resources.[2] These arguments are based on the assumption of the primacy of the market—in other words, that unfettered perfectly competitive markets will, in most cases, lead to an allocation of resources that maximizes the welfare of society. Critics of this approach argue that it provides an incomplete and biased picture, that it relies on a specific definition of competitive free markets and of what constitutes market failure.[3] In addition, as we will see in Chapter 2, individuals do not always behave in the way that traditional economic models assume. We do not always have access to all the information we need to make a fully informed choice, or there may be limits to our ability to process that information. This can lead to decisions that do not maximize individual welfare, thus providing a further argument for government intervention.

2. How can governments intervene?

Governments have a range of policy tools at their disposal: they can provide goods and services directly or pay for goods and services to be provided by the private sector (e.g. education, healthcare, or defence); they can use taxes and transfers to redistribute income and help tackle inequality and poverty, or to encourage or discourage certain types of behaviour; they can also use regulations to influence behaviour—for example, setting **price controls** such as minimum wages or limits on the amount of pollution cars can emit. We will explore these various tools in more detail in section 1.2.3 below. The way in which governments intervene in the economy varies across countries and over time. For example, in the UK, the majority of healthcare is publicly funded, through a combination of taxes and social security contributions, and provided by the government through the National Health Service (NHS).[4] In the Netherlands, on the other hand, healthcare is largely funded through mandatory private health insurance and the majority of hospitals are privately run, not-for-profit foundations, although the government plays an important role in setting healthcare priorities and regulating and monitoring private providers.

3. What impact do government interventions have?

Here it is important to consider both the direct and the indirect effects of government interventions. Direct effects are the predicted effects of a particular intervention if individuals and firms do not change their behaviour in response to that intervention. Indirect effects are the effects that arise because individuals and firms change their behaviour in response to government interventions. For example, imposing a higher tax on cigarettes should lead to a fall in consumption (direct effect), but it may also lead to the development of an underground

[1] Adapted from Gruber (2013).
[2] These arguments are explored in a bit more detail in section 1.2 and more thoroughly in Chapter 2.
[3] We return to these criticisms in Chapter 2.
[4] With the exception of **general practitioner (GP)** practices, the majority of which are private contractors.

market for cigarettes (indirect effect). We discuss the challenges involved in assessing both the direct and indirect effects of policies in Chapter 5.

4. How do governments decide when and how to intervene?

Public economics does not only look outside of government, at how government actions impact on the economy; it also looks at how decisions are made within government—this is the **political economy** or **public choice** aspect of public economics. One important question here is: how can governments aggregate the often conflicting preferences of millions of citizens and translate these into policy? As we will see in Chapter 4, there is no perfect mechanism for combining individual preferences into a collective choice. Public choice also acknowledges that governments are not always benevolent social planners, intent on maximizing the welfare of society; governments are made up of individuals who have their own interests and motivations, which may not always coincide with the best interests of society. Governments are also constrained by the information they have available, by their limited power to control how the market will respond, and by the constraints imposed by the electoral process. These are the leading sources of **government failure**, which can limit the effectiveness of government policies. We return to these points in section 1.2.4 below.

Box 1.2 illustrates how we might apply these four questions to a particular issue—the problem of housing affordability in the private rented sector.[5]

Box 1.2 The role of government in addressing problems of housing affordability

Across Europe, many countries are struggling with a housing affordability crisis, with housing costs taking up an increasing proportion of household incomes, particularly among low- and moderate-income households (UNECE, 2024). In England, problems of housing affordability have been particularly severe in the private rented sector, where households could expect to spend, on average, 36.3 per cent of their income on rent in 2025 (ONS, 2025a). In London, this figure is 41.6 per cent (ONS, 2025a). The proportion of households living in the private rented sector in England has been rising steadily for the past 20 years and currently around 20 per cent of households in England rent their homes from private landlords (ONS, 2025b). What is the role of government in supporting housing affordability in the private rented sector?

Should governments intervene?

Housing is an essential good—everyone needs somewhere to live. In fact, the right to adequate housing and shelter was recognized as a basic human right in the 1948 Universal Declaration of Human Rights. Most economic arguments for government intervention, however, are based on whether government intervention can improve on the market outcome, either by increasing efficiency or by promoting equity or social justice. So to answer this question, we need to think about the particular features of housing and housing markets.

[5] It is worth noting that the housing market is not a completely free market to begin with, as housing supply depends on a country's planning system and housebuilding is subject to many regulations. This issue highlights the wider difficulty in establishing what a market with no government intervention would look like in many contexts; this is a point we return to in Chapter 2.

Are there any market failures in housing markets? Can government intervention increase efficiency? Is government intervention justified on equity grounds?[6]

How can governments intervene?

There are a wide range of ways in which governments can, and do, intervene in housing markets. To support households in the private rented sector, governments can introduce rent controls, placing a cap on the maximum rent that landlords can charge. These policies have been in place in New York for several decades and were recently introduced in some cities in Germany. Alternative policies include providing rental subsidies to help households cover their housing costs, or to provide rental housing directly.[7]

What impact do government interventions have on the economy?

We can use economic theory and evidence to assess the impact of these three policies: rent control, rental subsidies, and the provision of social housing. In doing so, we want to consider both the direct effect of the policies and whether they will make rental housing more affordable, and any possible indirect effects, such as whether the policies will have an impact on housing supply or housing quality.

How do governments decide when and how to intervene?

This question brings us back to the political and social context in which policy decisions are made. In the UK, there has been a move away from providing social housing since the 1980s, when many council houses were sold to tenants under the government's Right to Buy scheme. While the scheme aimed to support homeownership, critics have argued that it has contributed to a housing shortage, particularly for lower-income households. Government policy has focused on alternative means of supporting the housing needs of low-income households.

1.1.2 Positive and normative analysis

Public economics involves both **positive analysis** and **normative analysis**. Positive analysis is concerned with statements of fact, of how things are, whereas normative analysis is concerned with how things should be. Positive statements are objective and can be tested, at least in theory. 'Raising the minimum wage will lead to an increase in unemployment' is an example of a positive statement. We can apply economic theory and use data to analyse the impact of an increase in the minimum wage on unemployment. Normative analysis involves statements that are subjective and cannot be tested, such as 'the government should increase the minimum wage to reduce poverty'. This statement involves a value judgement about what the government *should* do in order to reduce poverty. Normative economics relies on positive economics, since we need to have a clear understanding of what the likely impact of a policy will be before we can assess its desirability, and good normative economics should always be explicit about the values or objectives that underpin it.

[6] The concepts of market failure and equity are explored in more detail in Chapter 2.
[7] The social rented sector refers to rental housing that is provided by the government.

The attempt to separate positive and normative analysis within economics is relatively recent and it is not something we typically see in other social or natural sciences. Early economists working in the eighteenth and nineteenth centuries focused on studying society as a whole and addressing broad policy questions. Adam Smith, who is considered one of the fathers of modern economics, published *The Theory of Moral Sentiments* in 1759, where he embraced questions of ethics and morality (although he is best known for his later work, *The Wealth of Nations*). The distinction between positive and normative analysis in economics was largely motivated by the desire to make economics more like a 'proper' science—objective and value-free. In the twentieth century, economists came to view themselves as 'scientists of society', whose role was not to pass judgement on the workings of the economy and society, but rather to act as impartial analysts, using theory and data to examine economic problems and assess different policy solutions (Hausman, 2018).

However, at its heart, economics studies human interactions and it is difficult to do this in a value-free way. This is particularly true in the case of public economics, with its focus on government policy. The question about what the aim of policy should be is essentially a normative one, whereas the question about how best to achieve those aims is largely a positive one. Some would argue that there is no such thing as value-free economics. For example, modern **cost–benefit analysis (CBA)** is a tool which is widely used to assess different policies and which is generally assumed to be objective. However, it relies on underlying normative assumptions regarding what the goal of policy should be (i.e. maximizing individual welfare) and how this should be measured.[8]

1.1.3 Why study public economics?

Most countries in the world today are **mixed economies**, combining elements of free markets and government intervention. In mixed economies, there is no fixed boundary between the government and the private sector—there is no clear set of rules that stipulate what the government should do and what should be left to the private sector. This is why studying public economics is so important. Public economics provides a framework and a set of tools for analysing questions about what the role of government in the economy should be and what impact government interventions have on the economy. For example, in the UK, the government plays an important role in funding and providing healthcare, but a much less significant role in providing housing—both healthcare and housing are essential goods, so why should the government be responsible for providing one but not the other?

As we will see in Chapter 3, governments have also grown considerably since the early twentieth century and this pattern of growth has been common across countries with very different cultural, political, and institutional backgrounds. Across much of western Europe, North America, Australasia, and Japan, average government spending as a share of gross domestic product (GDP) increased from 10 per cent in 1890 to 47 per cent in 2022.[9] However, there are still big differences in the size of government across countries: public spending as a share of GDP is around 57 per cent in France and Finland, compared with 36 per cent in the USA and 23 per cent in Ireland.[10] Public economics can help explain why governments have

[8] We discuss these issues in Chapter 5, where we focus on tools for policy evaluation.
[9] Based on data from IMF (2023)—with minor processing by Our World in Data.
[10] Ibid.

grown, and why the size and composition of public spending varies across countries. Public economics can also help us understand the economic implications of different means of financing public expenditures—what types of taxes should governments use and what level should tax rates be set at? When should government borrow to finance its expenditure and what impact will this have on the economy?

The future is inherently unpredictable and we need the right skills and tools to respond to the ever-evolving challenges that society faces. Addressing today's growing income and wealth inequality, the rise in generative artificial intelligence, the climate crisis, food insecurity, and demographic change calls for a critical understanding of the role of government in the economy and the policy tools that governments have available. Studying public economics will equip you to analyse these and other emerging issues, to assess and compare the impacts of alternative policies, and to contribute to core debates about how some of the biggest societal challenges should be addressed.

1.2 The government and the economy

Before we can address the question of what the proper role of government in the economy is, we need to have a clear understanding of what we mean by the government and what government intervention looks like. In this section, we start by defining the concept of government and explore the rationale for government intervention in the economy. We then discuss some of the different ways in which governments intervene in the economy and the limits or barriers to these interventions.

1.2.1 What is the government?

Most of us have an intuitive understanding of what the government is: perhaps we associate this with the prime minister and/or the president, secretaries of state, ministers and members of parliament, the criminal justice system, or our local councils. These are all important parts of government in a democratic society. However, governments often extend beyond this to include a wide array of government agencies and public bodies. In the UK, these are generally referred to as arm's-length bodies (ALBs), which are public organizations that are responsible for delivering or managing public services and providing advice to the government. In 2022/3, the UK had a total of 305 ALBs, with a total budget of £353.3 billion (Modernisation and Reform Unit, 2024) (see Table 1.1 for a breakdown by type of organization). In addition to these organizations, there are a host of local-level government organizations, as well as public corporations, such as the British Broadcasting Corporation (BBC), the Civil Aviation Authority, and the Office for Nuclear Regulation.

The boundaries between public and private sector institutions are not always clear, particularly in the case of companies set up by the government and run on a for-profit basis. So what is it that defines the government and distinguishes it from private sector institutions?

There is no single undisputed definition of government. The German sociologist Max Weber defined the state or government as a polity or political entity which has a monopoly

Table 1.1 Types of arm's-length bodies in the UK

Type of arm's-length body	Total number	Examples
Executive agencies	38	Forestry England, UK Space Agency, Standards and Testing Agency
Non-departmental public bodies (NDPBs)[a]	247	British Council, Care Quality Commission, Environment Agency, Office for Budget Responsibility
Non-ministerial departments	20	The Charity Commission, Competition and Markets Authority, HM Revenue & Customs, Ofgem, UK Statistics Authority

[a] In the UK, non-departmental public bodies (NDPBs) are sometimes referred to as quasi-autonomous non-governmental organizations (quangos), although the latter is not an official term and has acquired more pejorative connotations. An NDPB is a public body which has some degree of independence from government and operates at arm's length from government departments.

over the legitimate use of physical force within a given territory. This definition highlights three key characteristics of the state in a democratic society:

- **Territoriality**: the state exerts its power and control over a given geographical area.
- **Monopoly over the use of physical force or compulsion**: the government has the power to compel or force people to pay their taxes and to restrict individual freedoms—for example, by sending people to prison if they break the law. In comparison, the majority of private sector exchanges are voluntary.
- **Accountability**: this is crucial to ensure that individuals in a given society comply willingly with the rules set by the state. In democratic societies, the government is elected by voters, and governments acquire their legitimacy from the electoral process, which acts as a constraint on state power, as governments are periodically held accountable to all voters.[11]

Some authors would also argue that the fundamental motivation of the government and public sector employees is different from what drives private sector organizations. Public sector employees are less likely to be driven by money or profits and more likely to be driven by a desire to serve the public interest. These public-spirited or non-selfish motives can also drive other institutions or organizations—for example, families or charities are typically motivated by a desire to help others. And, as we will see in section 1.2.4 below and in Chapter 4, government officials may be driven by self-interested motives. In fact, some authors would argue that there is no difference in the motives that drive individuals in the public and private sectors.[12]

The terms 'government', 'state', and 'public sector' will be used interchangeably in this book to refer to the political entity, as distinct from private corporations and individuals or civil society. However, when thinking about the role of government in the economy, it is important to keep in mind that the government is not a monolithic entity, but rather there are multiple levels of government: some decisions are made at the national or federal level, while others lie at the local or provincial level; and then there are supranational organizations, such as the European Union (EU) (see Box 1.3).

[11] Organizations in the private and voluntary sectors also face constraints—namely, from their shareholders or members of their board of trustees.

[12] See, for example, Buchanan (1962).

Box 1.3 The levels of government

Governments are not single, monolithic entities. Decision-making within government happens at various levels, which depend on the type of government system in place.

The majority of countries across the world have a **unitary government**, where the central government holds the majority or all of the power to govern, although some authority and the implementation of certain policy decisions are often delegated to subnational units. In these countries, the central government will typically be responsible for setting taxes and determining how public money will be allocated, making decisions regarding the delivery of public services such as health, policing, and welfare, as well as being responsible for decisions regarding defence and foreign policy. Local government authorities typically have very few legislative powers, although they may have some powers to set local taxes such as property taxes (e.g. council tax and business rates). They are usually responsible for providing community services, such as education, social services, parks and recreation services, and sanitation, but they operate within the legal framework set by the central government and Parliament.

Federal states, in contrast, combine a central or **federal government** authority and regional government authorities (e.g. provincial or state governments), and powers are shared between both levels of government. Examples of federal states include the USA, Canada, Brazil, India, and Russia. The central or federal government will typically be responsible for decisions regarding defence and foreign policy, whereas decisions concerning education, health, and welfare are delegated to provincial or state governments. Other decisions are made at lower local levels—for example, decisions regarding rubbish collection, street cleaning, and local parks and recreation facilities.

For many European countries, some governing power now lies at the supranational level, within the organizations of the EU, which has some of the characteristics of a federal system.

1.2.2 The economic role of government

The **market economy** is the predominant system for allocating resources in the world today. In a market economy, prices act as a coordinating mechanism, conveying information about the relative demand for different goods and services and the relative costs of producing them, thereby determining how resources are allocated. The main alternative to the market system is a **centrally planned** or **command economy**, where production, investment, and distribution decisions are determined by a central planner or decision-makers appointed by the government.[13] The extent of government intervention in market economies can vary significantly, ranging from more free market or **laissez-faire** systems where government intervention is limited, to more interventionist systems, where the state plays a more active role in the allocation of resources.

[13] Examples of centrally planned economies include the economies of the former Soviet Union, China, Cuba, and North Korea. However, with the exception of Cuba and North Korea, all of these countries have now moved towards a market system and dismantled their planned economies.

What should be the relative roles of the government and the market or other institutions in a market economy? The answer to this question will depend in part on the objectives that society wants to achieve. These social objectives are likely to vary across countries and to change over time. They may include things like promoting freedom, civic participation, social cohesion, or patriotism. Two objectives that are of particular interest to economists are efficiency and equity or social justice, which are the cornerstones of **social welfare**. These two objectives provide the main rationales for government intervention in the economy. Early work in public finance in fact highlighted three roles of government in the economy: allocation, which is related to the promotion of efficiency; distribution, which is related to the promotion of equity; and stabilization (see Box 1.4).

Economic efficiency is essentially about ensuring that scarce resources are used in the best way possible, to maximize **total welfare**, given individual preferences and the production technology available. Neoclassical economists work with a more precise concept known as **Pareto efficiency** or **allocative efficiency**.[14] An allocation of resources is Pareto efficient if there is no way to change this allocation to make at least one individual better off without making anyone else worse off.[15] How can efficiency be maximized? We can show that, under certain conditions, the competitive **market equilibrium** will lead to an efficient allocation of resources. This result is known as the **First Fundamental Theorem of Welfare Economics**. This is a very powerful result, and one which suggests that the role of government in the economy should be limited.

We explain this result and the conditions required for it to hold in Chapter 2. To understand the intuition behind this result, it is helpful to think about how resources are allocated

Box 1.4 The three branches of government

Richard Musgrave was an American economist who is seen by many as the founder of modern public finance. He is perhaps best known for his work *The Theory of Public Finance*, published in 1959, which lay the foundations for the development of the field of public finance. His work focused on answering the big questions in economics, including the question of what the proper role of government in the economy should be. He identified three branches of government intervention in the economy: allocation, distribution, and stabilization. The allocation branch involved government intervention in the allocation of resources, either by providing goods and services directly or through taxes and subsidies, to discourage or encourage production and consumption of certain goods and services. The distribution branch focused on equity and how the goods and services produced were distributed among the population. The stabilization branch focused on macroeconomic issues, including the role of government in promoting full employment and stabilizing prices.

[14] This concept takes its name from the Italian economist, sociologist and philosopher Vilfredo Pareto (1848–1923).

[15] Another important concept is the concept of **X-inefficiency**, which refers to situations where a firm's costs of production are higher than necessary. We will return to this concept in our discussion of the public ownership of production in Chapter 7.

by the market. In a market economy, all exchanges are voluntary, and individuals and businesses will participate in an exchange as long as the benefit to them from doing so is no greater than the cost incurred. In the market equilibrium, all mutually beneficial trades have taken place. At this point, the value placed on one additional unit of a good just equals the cost of producing it—that is, **social marginal benefit** equals **social marginal cost**, which is the condition required for the outcome to be efficient. If the marginal benefit were greater than the marginal cost, it would be possible to increase welfare (and make some people better off without making anyone else worse off) by increasing production, since the benefit of producing an additional unit of output would outweigh the cost. Since trades are voluntary, individuals would be willing to engage in further exchanges to increase their welfare. Conversely, if the marginal benefit were less than the marginal cost, then society would benefit if production were reduced. When social marginal benefit equals social marginal cost, the net gains from trade—the difference between total benefits and costs—are maximized.

However, this result will only hold under a set of fairly restrictive assumptions, which we discuss in Chapter 2. Instances when one or more of these assumptions fail to hold are often referred to as market failures—situations where the market outcome is not Pareto efficient. These market failures provide a rationale for government intervention in the economy to increase efficiency.

An efficient allocation is also not necessarily equitable or fair. This may seem counterintuitive, but it is possible to maximize total welfare and still have a highly unequal distribution of resources. This is because in order to be able to participate in trades, individuals must have something they can trade (their time/labour or other resources), and the individual benefits and costs of trades will depend on what they have available to trade, which in turn will depend on the initial allocation of resources. If society cares about equity and social justice, then government intervention in the economy may be necessary to redistribute resources. Equity is a multifaceted concept which incorporates notions of fairness, justice, and rewards for effort or merit, and different societies will have different concepts of equity. We discuss some particular concepts of equity in Chapter 2.

Efficiency and equity provide two reasons for government intervention in the economy. However, these are just two possible social objectives. Society may care about other objectives, such as promoting freedom or social cohesion, which may provide additional reasons for government intervention in the economy. It is also important to avoid a simplistic government versus market dichotomy. Governments and markets are not the only institutions for organizing collective choice; societies have a range of non-state collective institutions, such as community organizations, social networks, associations, and families.[16] Nor are states and markets necessarily mutually exclusive. The market is one of many institutions that make up our modern economies and markets are unlikely to be the right institution for all exchanges. Markets are not morally neutral: market values change the character of an exchange or relationship; creating markets for things, putting a price on things, changes their value and how they are perceived by society (Sandel, 2012).[17]

[16] See, for example, Coyle (2020), Ostrom (2010), and Raworth (2017) in the Further Reading at the end of the chapter.

[17] This is a point we return to in Chapter 2.

1.2.3 Types of government intervention

Government policies typically fall into three general categories:

1. **Taxes and subsidies**: governments can use taxes and subsidies to influence individual behaviour. For example, in many countries governments impose higher taxes on alcohol or cigarettes to discourage consumption of these products, or levy environmental taxes to reduce pollution. Subsidies can be used to encourage certain activities—for example, subsidized loans can support more people to invest in higher education. Taxes and transfers also play an important redistributive role and help to reduce poverty and inequality. This is particularly the case if the income tax system is progressive and higher-income individuals pay a larger proportion of their income in taxes than lower-income individuals.[18]
2. **Regulation**: this involves stipulating what activities can be carried out and what rules should govern those activities. Examples include minimum wages, public health programmes, health and safety legislation, and setting limits on the amount of pollution that cars can emit.
3. **Direct provision of goods and services**: governments can aim to achieve the desired allocation of resources by providing goods and services directly. Examples include the provision of healthcare, education, and social housing. In some cases, governments will produce these goods and services themselves, whereas in others they will finance the provision of the goods but leave production to the private sector.[19]

Insights from psychology and behavioural economics are increasingly being used in policy design, helping to broaden the range of policy tools available to governments. For example, evidence suggests that the way in which information is presented affects the choices individuals make. These **framing effects** have been used to encourage certain types of behaviour. **Inertia**, or the tendency of individuals to accept the status quo or default option, has also informed the development of policies, particularly in the context of retirement saving. One example is in the design of **automatic enrolment pension schemes**, where eligible individuals are enrolled into a pension scheme by their employer and monthly pension contributions are deducted from their salary automatically, although individuals can opt out of the scheme if they wish to. Automatic enrolment pension schemes have been introduced in countries including Italy, New Zealand, Turkey, and the UK, and have been found to have a positive impact on individual saving for retirement.[20]

When discussing different types of government policies it is also useful to draw a distinction between transfers in cash and transfers in kind. **Cash transfers**, as the name suggests, refer to programmes that provide cash benefits to recipients. Examples include old-age pensions, unemployment benefits, and sickness and disability benefits. **In-kind transfers** involve the provision of goods and services directly to recipients, such as healthcare, education, housing, and food stamps. In-kind transfers have the advantage of ensuring that support is targeted where it is considered most needed, guaranteeing the consumption of or access to a

[18] We discuss the impact of different types of taxes in Chapters 13, 14, and 15.

[19] This distinction between finance and production plays an important role in the classification of different healthcare systems, as we will see in Chapter 8.

[20] We discuss this policy in more detail in Chapter 11.

minimum level of education, healthcare, or housing. This can be particularly important when problems of **imperfect information** or **bounded willpower** (e.g. a lack of self-control)[21] may prevent individuals from making socially optimal choices if given transfers in cash. However, transfers in cash have the advantage of not restricting individual choice.

1.2.4 The limits to government intervention

Will government intervention always succeed in increasing social welfare? For government intervention to be effective in increasing social welfare, we would need governments that are: benevolent, in the sense of being driven solely by the desire to promote social welfare; omniscient, in the sense of having access to all the information necessary to design and implement effective policies; and omnipotent, in terms of having the ability to implement the necessary policies. In practice, governments are unlikely to satisfy all of these requirements perfectly in all situations, which leads to government failure. This term is used to refer to situations where government interventions cause or contribute to inefficiency. We can think of the main sources or causes of government failure as based on departures from these characteristics of an 'ideal' government.[22]

Developments in the field of public choice have highlighted how governments should not be assumed to be impartial and benevolent social planners, driven solely by a desire to promote social welfare.[23] Governments are made up of individuals who have their own interests and motivations, and these may not always align with the common good or promote the welfare of society. While some government officials may be motivated by a concern for the public interest, others may be motivated by a desire to be re-elected or secure lucrative positions in the private sector once their term in office is over, which may make them vulnerable to **lobbying** and corruption. Public officials are no different from ordinary citizens when it comes to their motivations, and therefore the pursuit of the public interest is just one among several goals that drive their behaviour.

We can also question whether governments are likely to have all the information they need to design and implement their policies effectively. For example, the government may want to introduce a policy providing cash grants to support low-income households who are struggling to meet their living costs. In practice, it is difficult for the government to accurately identify all households who need this support, leading to situations where some households who need support do not have access to it, while other households who perhaps do not need the support receive it. Governments are also unable to control—and in many cases fully anticipate—how the market will respond to its actions. Policies designed to encourage individuals to save more for their retirement through government-backed schemes may have the perverse result of reducing individual savings in other areas, so that the total level of individual saving is unchanged.

[21] See Chapter 2 for a review of these concepts.

[22] Ideal in the sense of meeting the requirements necessary to ensure government interventions will increase social welfare.

[23] Public choice theory focuses on applying economic methods to the analysis of decision-making within government and the political arena. Work by James Buchanan and Gordon Tullock, started in the 1950s and 1960s, played a seminal role in questioning the assumption of governments as benevolent dictators or benevolent social planners.

Governments do not have the power to singlehandedly implement their policies. They need to rely on other agents (individuals or organizations) to carry out their policies and these agents may not share the same goals as the government, or they may be lazy or corrupt. This lack of control over those responsible for implementing policies may result in policies being poorly implemented. There are other constraints on what governments can achieve which are a result of the political process. In democratic societies, there is no single government official who has the power to decide what policies should be implemented; these need the approval of Parliament or another legislative body. Different members of Parliament may have different objectives or priorities, which can lead to policies that might have increased social welfare not being adopted. The desire for re-election may also lead to **policy myopia**, where government policy interventions prioritize short-term gains over longer-term solutions.

While markets may not always lead to an efficient allocation of resources, there are also limits to what the government can achieve and government intervention will not always improve on the market outcome. Economists disagree over whether governments should adopt a more active or more limited role in the economy. Some, such as Milton Friedman, would argue that the scope for government failure is pervasive enough that government intervention in the economy should be kept to a minimum. Others would defend a more active role for governments, given the inability of markets to address fundamental societal problems, such as inequality or the climate crisis. Ultimately, we need to take into account the limitations of both markets and governments when assessing the need for and potential impact of government interventions. We return to these questions in Chapter 4, where we focus on public choice theory.

1.3 The size and composition of the public sector

The size of the public sector varies significantly across countries, but there is one common trend: across most of the world, the public sector has grown considerably since the end of the nineteenth century. The average level of government spending across much of western Europe, North America, Australasia, and Japan increased from 9.8 per cent of GDP in 1890 to 47 per cent in 2022.[24] The increase in the size of government in absolute terms has been even greater since GDP has increased in most countries over this period. The size of the public sector tends to be strongly correlated with a country's income level, with higher-income countries typically having a larger government. However, there is still quite a lot of variation in the size of government, even among countries with similar income levels.

Figure 1.1 shows how government spending as a share of GDP changed between 1950 and 2023 across a number of countries. In 1950, government spending ranged from just under 10 per cent of GDP in Portugal to 36 per cent in Austria. By 2023, the lowest level of government spending was in Ireland, at 23 per cent of GDP, but in countries including France, Finland, and Belgium, government spending was over 50 per cent of GDP. Among the countries illustrated, only in Ireland did government spending as a share of GDP not increase during this period.

[24] Based on data from IMF (2023)—with minor processing by Our World in Data. A similar pattern of public expenditure growth can also be seen in some Latin American countries, such as Argentina and Brazil. For the rest of the world, the patterns of public expenditure growth are more varied.

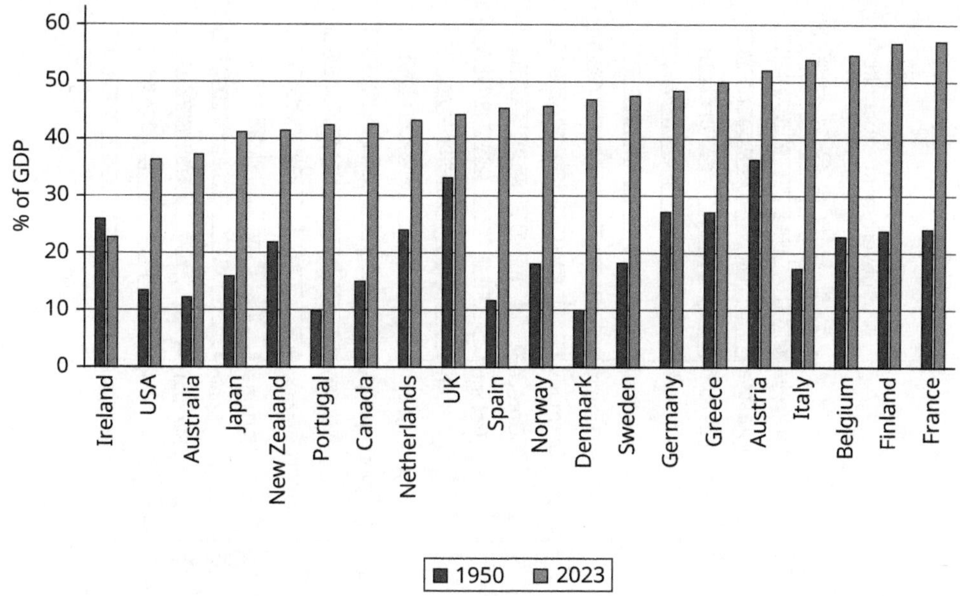

Figure 1.1 Government spending as a share of GDP for a sample of countries, 1950 and 2023
Source: IMF (2025)—with minor processing by Our World in Data.

The growth in government spending throughout most of the twentieth century has progressed in different stages, particularly among early industrialized countries. Government spending was generally low until the First World War. This was followed by a period of volatile growth between the wars, and then more rapid growth following the end of the Second World War, as many countries introduced or expanded social welfare programmes. Since the 1980s, government growth has slowed in most countries, and in some cases even decreased, at least until the onset of the Covid-19 pandemic. This is something we look at in more detail in Chapter 3, where we explore some of the theories that have been proposed to explain the growth of the public sector over time.

Government spending covers a wide range of areas. Figure 1.2 illustrates the proportion of total government expenditure allocated to different areas for a selection of countries in the Organization for Economic Cooperation and Development (OECD), which provides some insights into how spending priorities vary across countries. Spending on social protection is the largest area of expenditure for most countries, accounting for 35 per cent of all government spending on average across the OECD. However, there is some variation across countries, with Finland allocating 46 per cent of government spending to social protection, compared to 20 per cent in the USA. Spending on social protection includes various welfare payments—for example, sickness and disability benefits, and unemployment and old-age benefits.

Defence spending is highest in the USA, at 8 per cent of total government expenditure. This compares with an OECD average around half that value, at 4 per cent. The USA also has the highest spending on health, at 26 per cent of total government expenditure. This is particularly interesting given the structure of the US healthcare system, which is mainly privately financed and privately provided. The UK, on the other hand, has a mainly publicly financed and provided healthcare system, but allocates only 19 per cent of all government

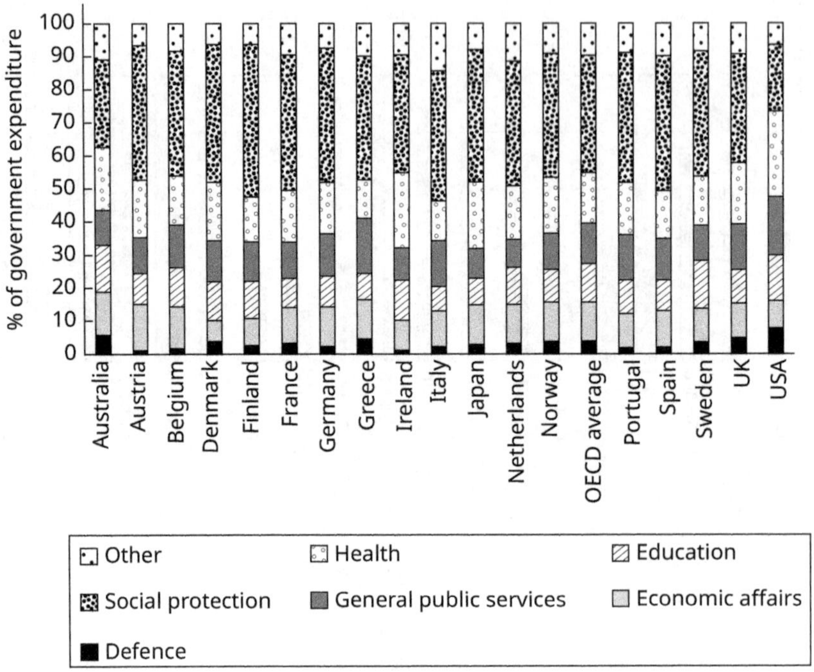

Figure 1.2 General government spending by function as a proportion of total government spending, 2023

Note: 'Other' includes spending on housing and community amenities, public order and safety, recreation, and environmental protection. 'OECD average' is average for all OECD countries.

Source: OECD (2025b).

spending to health. This is something we will explore in more detail when we look at the role of government in healthcare in Chapter 8.

The majority of government spending is financed through taxes. These include **direct taxes** on individuals and corporations (e.g. personal income tax, social security contributions, and corporation tax) and **indirect taxes** on goods and services (e.g. value-added tax or VAT, and sales taxes). Figure 1.3 shows how the importance of these different taxes for government revenue varies across countries. The majority of government tax revenue is collected through income taxes, social security contributions and taxes on goods and services, which together account for 80 per cent of all tax revenue raised on average across the OECD. Indirect taxes on goods and services are an important source of government revenues across virtually all countries, accounting for, on average, just over 30 per cent of total tax revenues across the OECD, and over 40 per cent in Greece. In the USA, however, these taxes account for only 16 per cent of revenues raised. The proportion of revenues raised from individual income taxes ranges from 14 per cent in Greece to over 55 per cent in Denmark.

Taxes are essential to finance public spending that will have a positive impact on welfare—for example, investing in roads, bridges, and cycle paths, or funding schools and hospitals. However, taxes also impose a significant cost on society. They reduce individual spending power and can affect individual incentives to work and save. We will explore the implications of taxes for efficiency and equity in Chapters 13, 14, and 15.

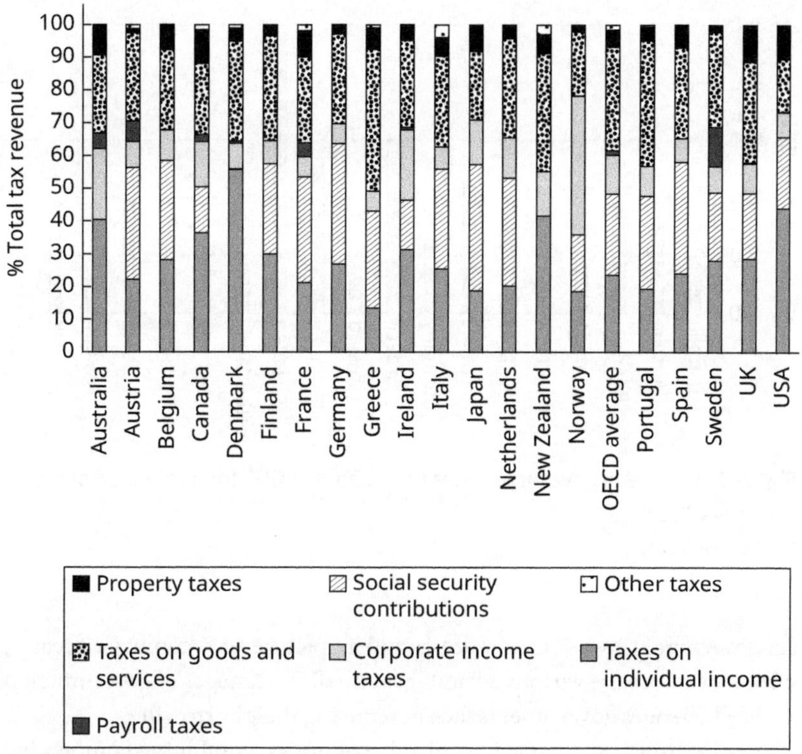

Figure 1.3 Sources of government tax revenue for selected OECD countries, 2022

Note: Figures as a % of total tax revenue for 2022. 'OECD average' represents average across all OECD countries.

Source: OECD (2025a).

Governments set tax rates rather than the level of tax revenue they need to finance their expenditure and any shortfall needs to be covered by government borrowing. Government borrowing is therefore sensitive to fluctuations in the economy: during an economic downturn, tax receipts inevitably fall, as unemployment increases and consumer demand dries up; at the same time, the need for government expenditure—for example, on unemployment and other welfare benefits—will increase. So when analysing government borrowing, it is important to do so in the context of the broader economic environment. It also important to draw a distinction between the **government deficit** and **government debt**. The government deficit measures the difference between government revenues and spending, typically over the course of a financial year. Government debt measures the total amount of money owed by the government at a particular point in time, accumulated from borrowing to cover budget deficits.

As Figure 1.4 shows, the level of government debt varies significantly across countries, ranging from 28 per cent of GDP in Denmark to 237 per cent of GDP in Japan. Government debt peaked in many countries during the Covid-19 pandemic, but has started to fall back since then. High levels of government debt raise concerns about the sustainability of public finances. However, it is important to consider government debt in the context of the

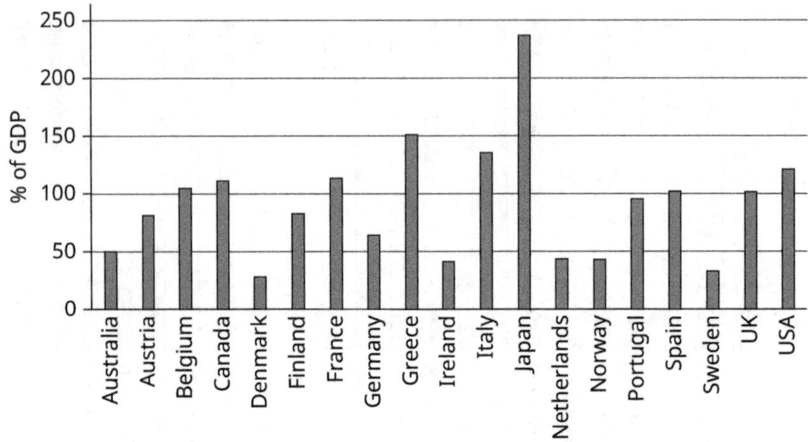

Figure 1.4 General government debt as a share of GDP for a selection of OECD countries, 2024
Source: IMF (2025).

assets the government owns for a more complete picture of a country's fiscal position. In Chapter 16, we explore the various advantages and disadvantages of government borrowing, as well as the challenges governments face in reducing their borrowing.

Most countries today are classed as mixed economies, combining competitive free markets with some government intervention. However, as these figures show, there is still a lot of variation in the size of government across countries. Across the world, governments have grown considerably since the end of the nineteenth century and government spending priorities have shifted over time. In the next section, we will explore how perspectives on the role of government in the economy have changed over time.

1.4 The changing role of government in the economy

The government as we know it today is a fairly recent phenomenon. For much of recorded history, we did not have governments that taxed their citizens and used these revenues to finance public spending programmes. But even in the last 100 years, views about the proper role of government in the economy have changed considerably. In this section, we will provide an overview of these evolving perspectives. As we will see, there has often been a lag between theory and ideology, and what governments have done in practice. Underpinning these changing perspectives are different theories of society or different frameworks for explaining how societies are structured and how they evolve (see Box 1.5).

It is important to note that this story is being told from a predominantly Western perspective, focusing in particular on the experience of the UK and the USA. It therefore does not provide a complete or comprehensive picture. However, it does help illustrate how perspectives on the role of government in the economy have changed over time and the role of external factors and events, as well as new theories, in driving this evolution.

Box 1.5 Theories of society

We can identify three broad types of theories of society, although in practice the distinction between different theories is not always clear cut. **Libertarian theories of society** are based on the primacy of individual liberty and advocate for private property and free markets, with very limited government intervention. Natural-rights libertarians, such as Robert Nozick, would argue that private property is a natural right and that government intervention is, in general, morally wrong, and can only be justified in very limited circumstances. Nozick popularized the idea of a night-watchman state, whose role was solely to defend individuals and their property (Nozick, 1974). Less stringent libertarians include authors such as Friedrich Hayek and Milton Friedman, who also argue for a limited role of government, not because it is deemed morally wrong, but because it will reduce social welfare. In this view, the state should not have any role in the distribution of resources, other than to provide certain **public goods**.

Liberal theories of society are also rooted in the principle of individual liberty and see private markets as an efficient mechanism for allocating resources. However, they acknowledge the significant inequalities inherent in the market system and would argue for a greater role for government intervention to address these inequalities. Within the liberal tradition, utilitarian theories are based on the view that resources should be distributed in a way that maximizes the well-being or utility of society as a whole, whereas the Rawlsian view of social justice (named after the US political philosopher John Rawls) argues for equal basic rights and the promotion of the interests of the least well-off members of society.

These two terms, 'libertarian' and 'liberal', can generate some confusion. The term 'liberal' was used in the nineteenth century to refer to thinkers who believed in free markets and the laissez-faire approach, and who would, under this classification, be better referred to as libertarians. There are also some differences in the way the terms are commonly used in the USA and Europe: in the USA, 'liberal' is typically used to describe more left-of-centre approaches, which in Europe would be referred to as social democratic; in Europe, 'liberal' is still largely used to refer to more right-of-centre approaches, which would be considered libertarian in the USA.

Collectivist or socialist theories of society view it through the lens of social classes. Society is more than the sum of its individuals. Humans are social animals and the pursuit of wider social concerns should override the pursuit of individual self-interest, putting the group or society ahead of the individual. These theories still share a concern for individual freedom, but the concept of freedom is closely intertwined with the notion of equality and economic security. Freedom cannot be said to exist if there is significant inequality in the distribution of economic and political power. Within collectivist theories, there is some disagreement over whether the goals of greater freedom and equality can be achieved within a mixed economy (a view shared by the democratic socialist theories) or whether this would require the abolition of private property and the imposition of state control over the allocation of resources (a view held by Marxist theories).

See Barr (2020: ch. 2) for a more in-depth discussion.

1.4.1 From mercantilism to laissez-faire economics

From the sixteenth century to the late eighteenth century, western European economic thought and policy was dominated by **mercantilism**, a doctrine that advocated that governments should play an active role in promoting industry and trade, supporting domestic industries through subsidies and restricting imports using tariffs and quotas. In 1700, Britain banned imports of Indian cotton textiles to protect its own textile industry, subsequently imposing its textile exports on India in the mid-nineteenth century, by which point mechanization of the industry in Britain had given it a clear competitive edge.

The publication of Adam Smith's *The Wealth of Nations* in 1776 marked a turning point, promoting the view that the pursuit of private interest would promote the public good. Adam Smith's work influenced nineteenth-century economists such as John Stuart Mill and Nassau Senior, who advocated for a laissez-faire approach. According to this view, the market allocation was generally efficient and therefore government intervention in the economy should be kept to a minimum. Governments should focus on developing and maintaining the institutions necessary for trade to flourish, providing national defence, policing, and administration. The role of the state in promoting education was also acknowledged. This was the dominant view among the classical economists and political philosophers during the nineteenth century, but governments continued to pursue protectionist policies until the late nineteenth century. In fact, in much of western Europe and the USA, trade protectionism actually increased between 1870 and 1913, although during this period many governments embraced the free market doctrine in relation to fiscal and monetary policies (e.g. through the pursuit of balanced budgets and the establishment of the Gold Standard).[25]

Not all nineteenth-century thinkers agreed with the laissez-faire approach. Karl Marx was perhaps one of the most influential political theorists writing during this period. He argued for greater state involvement in the distribution of resources and control over the means of production. His views had a significant influence on Vladimir Lenin, who led Soviet Russia from 1917 to 1924, following the Russian Revolution of 1917, turning it into a one-party socialist state, which eventually abolished private ownership of the means of production and became a fully fledged centrally planned economy. However, Marx's theories also influenced more moderate thinkers such as Eduard Bernstein and Karl Kautsky, who advocated for the regulation of working hours and the development of a **welfare state**. Even as the free market doctrine was spreading, the nineteenth century also saw the early beginnings of the welfare state, as Germany introduced a **social insurance** system in the 1880s which provided retirement benefits and disability benefits to workers.

1.4.2 The expanding role of the government in the twentieth century

In the West, it was after the end of the First World War that attitudes towards the role of the government in the economy started to change more profoundly. The Great Depression of 1929, triggered by the Wall Street Crash, further helped spur on greater government

[25] The Gold Standard was the basis of the international monetary system from the 1870s until 1971 (although it was suspended for a period in the 1920s and 1930s). Under this system, the value of national currencies was directly linked to a fixed quantity of gold.

involvement in the economy, even in countries which until then had seemed resistant or immune. The huge increase in unemployment and fall in economic output following the Wall Street Crash reverberated across the Western world, leading to significant increases in poverty and hardship, and highlighting the lack of any sort of social safety net.

The work of the economist John Maynard Keynes in the 1930s helped inspire a resurgence in the belief that governments should act to stabilize the level of economic activity and promote the welfare of disadvantaged groups in society. In practice, there was a widespread rejection of the laissez-faire doctrine, particularly in the USA and Sweden. The New Deal programmes in the USA introduced legislation separating the commercial and investment arms of banks,[26] increased the regulation of the stock market, and invested in large public infrastructure projects (e.g. the Hoover Dam). The US Social Security Act 1935 introduced old-age pensions and unemployment insurance. In Sweden, income tax was introduced and used to finance the expansion of the welfare state. In the UK, the government introduced a fully funded unemployment benefit system in 1931, building on the more meagre unemployment and health insurance programme introduced in 1911.

The aftermath of the Second World War saw a further expansion of government welfare programmes and a significant increase in government intervention in the economy across almost all countries. This period was marked by a wave of nationalizations or the setting up of new state-owned enterprises in key industries such as steel, coal, energy, and the railways in several European countries. In the UK, the Beveridge Report was published in 1942 and argued for greater government involvement to tackle the 'five giants on the road to post-war reconstruction': Want, Disease, Ignorance, Squalor and Idleness. This report laid the foundations of the welfare state in Britain, including an expansion of the National Insurance scheme and the creation of the NHS. Taxes were increased to pay for the additional government expenditures, and governments embraced Keynesian macroeconomic policies, increasing government spending during economic downturns and decreasing it during economic expansions. On the international trade front, the General Agreement on Tariffs and Trade—the precursor to today's World Trade Organization—was set up in 1947, encouraging reductions in tariffs to promote international trade.

1.4.3 A return to the market

The 1970s were a period of economic stagnation and rising inflation in many countries, driven in part by oil price shocks and the decision by the USA to end the convertibility of the US dollar to gold, which led to the collapse of the Gold Standard. The election of Margaret Thatcher in the UK in 1979 and Ronald Reagan in the USA in 1981 led to a wave of policies aimed at reducing state intervention in the economy throughout the 1980s: the higher rates of income tax were cut;[27] government spending in areas such as housing, education, and transport was cut back; in the UK, many previously state-owned enterprises were sold to private investors, including steel, gas, electricity, and water; and financial regulations were slashed. This shift towards increasing the role of market forces was not

[26] The Glass–Steagall Act 1933.

[27] For example, in the UK, in 1978, the top rate of income tax was 98 per cent; by 1988, this had been cut to 40 per cent.

restricted to the UK and the USA. During the 1990s alone, $1 trillion worth of state-owned enterprises were transferred from the public to the private sector across the world (OECD, 2002). This wave of **privatizations** was combined with extensive **deregulation**, particularly in financial markets.

This period saw the rise of **neoliberalism**, with the work of economists such as Milton Friedman advocating for less government involvement in the economy. With the collapse of socialism at the end of the 1980s, capitalism and the neoliberal agenda were hailed as the best economic system and brought in an era of free market triumphalism.

1.4.4 The Global Financial Crisis and beyond

The Global Financial Crisis of 2008 reignited the debate about the proper role of government in the economy.[28] The bankruptcy of the Bear Stearns and Lehmann Brothers investment banks in the USA led to a financial panic that swept across most of the world. Initially, most countries adopted Keynesian macroeconomic policies, and large financial institutions and firms were bailed out by the government.[29] However, these interventionist approaches were soon abandoned and austerity measures were adopted or imposed on countries, with governments cutting back on spending. Even though the crisis was triggered by a laxity in financial markets, financial reforms were slow to materialize. By 2010, many of the large banks had returned to earning large profits and paying out generous bonuses to their managers, as the losses caused by the financial crisis were effectively socialized. In 2013, the EU proposed a financial transaction tax and a cap on financial sector bonuses, but to date participating countries have been unable to reach an agreement.

More recently, the Covid-19 pandemic highlighted the vital role that governments play in supporting social welfare, as governments across the world were able to roll out mass vaccination programmes, subsidize businesses, and provide financial support to households at a time when tax revenues were falling. Although many of the forms of government support introduced during the pandemic were subsequently abandoned, this episode illustrated just how far government intervention can go.

The dominant perspectives on the appropriate role of government in the economy have changed over time. However, there have been few periods in recent history when governments have retreated completely from the economic arena. Supporters of the market argue that government interventions introduce distortions, moving the market further away from the efficient outcome. Supporters of government intervention, on the other hand, argue that its critics exaggerate government failings, and that the market cannot resolve many of the societal challenges facing the world today. These debates are ongoing and will probably never be resolved satisfactorily. It is perhaps more productive to invest in designing the most effective and meaningful policies for the particular challenges at hand.

[28] Prior to this, there had been the Asian Financial Crisis of the 1990s and the bursting of the dot.com bubble in the USA in 2000, although the impact of these crises was arguably more contained.

[29] In October 2008, the UK government made £20 billion of capital available to the Royal Bank of Scotland; this was followed by a second bailout in December 2009, which took the total to £46 billion and led to the government owning 84 per cent of the bank (Mor, 2018).

1.5 Doing public economics

Public economics involves three distinct but interrelated elements:

- **Descriptive**: at the most basic level, public economics involves describing what the government does. How are government revenues raised and what weight is given to different types of taxes? How are these revenues allocated across different areas and levels of government?
- **Analytical**: public economics is also concerned with analysing the impact of government policies. It involves going beyond describing how things are to examining the consequences of, for example, raising the tax on fuel on traffic congestion; or how providing free childcare for children under the age of five will affect female labour force participation.
- **Evaluative**: public economics also involves comparing and evaluating the outcomes of alternative policies. In order to do this, we need to analyse the consequences of different policies, but we also need to know what the objectives of government policy are; this will provide us with the criteria for evaluating different policies. We can then advise the government on what policy or policies it should adopt to achieve its intended goals. For example, if the government has set itself a goal of reducing child poverty, public economics can suggest what policies are likely to be most effective in achieving this goal.

In each of these elements, public economics relies on a range of theoretical and empirical tools. We discuss these below.

1.5.1 Theoretical tools of public economics

The theoretical tools of public economics provide the framework for understanding how individual economic agents—individuals or households, firms, and governments—make decisions. This is where economic models play an important role. Economic models are essentially simplified descriptions of reality. Unlike in most natural sciences, economic agents do not respond mechanically to changes in their environment; rather, their decisions and actions are guided by certain motivations. Economic models make assumptions about these motivations, about what drives the behaviour of individuals and firms, and therefore allow us to try and predict how economic agents will respond to government policies. For example, we could use a standard model of supply and demand to analyse how an increase in the tax on sugary drinks will affect demand for those drinks, and how the magnitude of this effect depends on the **elasticity of demand.**

We can also use models to analyse possible knock-on effects and to predict how changes in one market are likely to affect other markets. For example, how will an increase in the tax on sugary drinks affect demand for other types of drinks? This is where the distinction between partial equilibrium models and general equilibrium models is important. In **partial equilibrium analysis**, we focus on the impacts of changes in specific markets in isolation, whereas **general equilibrium analysis** considers how conditions in each market in a set of related markets affect equilibrium outcomes in other markets in that set.

Public economics draws heavily on **neoclassical economic theory**, which is based on a set of assumptions about how the economy operates and what drives the behaviour of individual consumers and producers. Consumers are assumed to have well-defined preferences about what goods and services they want to consume, and they choose the bundle of goods which maximizes their **utility** or welfare subject to what they can afford (the **rational choice model**). Producers make decisions about what to produce to minimize costs and maximize profits. The market plays a central role, coordinating the actions of rational and self-interested economic agents.

While the neoclassical framework is useful, like all theoretical frameworks it has its limitations. Recent work in public economics has built on work in behavioural economics, which brings together insights from economics and psychology to provide a more complete understanding of individual behaviour. **Behavioural public economics** emphasizes the normative implications of non-standard decision-making for designing policies that will increase social welfare.

Welfare economics is the branch of economics that focuses on defining and measuring the welfare of society as a whole. Welfare economics can be approached from both a neoclassical perspective and a behavioural perspective. An alternative approach to analysing the welfare of society is based on the capabilities approach proposed by Amartya Sen. For Sen, well-being is not just about wealth or happiness, but about having the freedom to choose a life we have reason to value, which depends on our capability to make choices regarding our education, health, employment, security, and participation (Sen, 1986). The **capability approach** highlights the importance of considering the impact of policies on all affected capabilities.

Models impose a logical structure on our arguments and help ensure their coherence, but a model is only ever as good as its underlying assumptions. Models are by definition incomplete. This is why it is important to make these assumptions explicit from the outset and to consider what would happen to our conclusions if we changed these assumptions. Any policy recommendations based on economic models should explicitly acknowledge their limitations.

1.5.2 Empirical tools of public economics

The empirical tools allow us to use data to test the predictions of our models and further help inform the design of policies. This may involve, for example, using observational data to estimate relationships between variables and to test specific hypotheses predicted by the theory. Building on our previous example, we could collect data on the consumption of sugary drinks to estimate how sensitive demand for sugary drinks is to changes in their price and, from here, predict how large an impact a tax on sugary drinks would have on consumption. Empirical public economics has advanced significantly in the last few decades, in part due to the wider availability of large-scale datasets.

One of the biggest challenges facing empirical work in economics involves establishing **causality**—that is, demonstrating that one variable is causing changes in other variables, rather than there simply being a **correlation** between them. **Randomized control trials (RCTs)** provide the gold standard for establishing causal relationships. RCTs involve randomly assigning individuals to two groups: one group receives a particular treatment, such as an increase in welfare benefits (this is the **treatment group**); the other group receives no treatment (the **control group**). The outcomes of the two groups can then be compared to assess the effectiveness of the treatment or intervention. RCTs are widely used in medicine to test the effectiveness of specific treatments. They have increasingly been used to test the impact of economic and social policies—for example, to evaluate different labour market and welfare programmes.

While RCTs have been growing in popularity, they have their limitations. They can be very costly to run and it is not always possible to extrapolate from the behaviour of people in the sample to wider society. **Quasi-experiments** offer a useful middle ground. These are situations where changes in the economic environment (e.g. the introduction of a new policy) create virtually identical control and treatment groups, allowing the impact of that policy to be assessed; in these cases, the randomization is created by external forces.

Laboratory experiments are also used as a source of data to test economic theories and evaluate policies. For example, participants in an experiment may be given an income and asked to decide how much of this income to report to the tax authorities. If they are found to have underreported their income, they will have to pay a fine. This process is often repeated for a number of rounds and, at the end of the experiment, individuals receive a payment that is proportional to their earnings in the experiment. Crucially, in a laboratory experiment, individuals know they are participating in an experiment. Participants are typically students, and therefore the results might not generalize to the wider population.

Public economists have a wealth of tools at their disposal, both theoretical and empirical. However, this does not prevent—and may even contribute to—disagreements among economists. Economists (and policymakers) may disagree over the consequences of particular policies and over what model is the most appropriate one to use. They can disagree over the magnitude of estimated impacts and what is the right empirical method to use in a particular situation. Economists also disagree about values; even if there were perfect agreement on the full impact of a policy, there might still be disagreement over its desirability, since policies will always involve trade-offs. But economists can also change their views over time.

1.6 Overview of this book

The aim of this book is to introduce students to the economic theory behind why governments intervene in the economy, as well as to equip them with the tools to assess government interventions in a wide range of policy areas. This textbook balances economic theory, presented in a rigorous yet accessible manner, with applications of the theory to real-world policies and policy problems, drawing on examples from a range of countries. The book will focus mainly on the experience of countries in western Europe, North America, Australasia, and Japan. However, where possible, suggestions for further reading that cover a broader range of countries are provided. The book draws on neoclassical economic theory, but this is presented through a critical lens and alternative approaches are also incorporated.

The book is divided into three parts. Part I, which includes this chapter, introduces public economics and discusses the role of government in the economy and some of the tools that are used for policy evaluation. Chapter 1 has provided an introduction to the subject of public economics and laid out the framework for thinking about the role of government in the economy. It has also reviewed how perspectives on the role of government in the economy have changed over time, and discussed some of the theoretical and empirical tools that are used in public economics. Chapter 2 expands on the theoretical framework for understanding the role of government in the economy, building on some of the concepts introduced in Chapter 1. Chapter 3 provides an overview of how the size and composition of government has changed over time and how it varies across countries, before discussing some of the theories that have been proposed to explain the evolution of the public sector. Chapter 4 introduces the field of public choice theory. It analyses how we can model the behaviour of voters, politicians, bureaucrats, and interest groups, and what this implies for the design and implementation of policy. Chapter 5 introduces the tools used to evaluate policies. It begins with a discussion of cost–benefit analysis, covering both the underlying theory and the steps involved in applying CBA in practice. Some of the limitations of CBA and alternative tools for policy evaluation are then discussed.

Part II of the book focuses on particular areas of government expenditure. In Chapter 6, it begins with a review of public goods and the role of government in their provision. Chapter 7 builds on these topics and discusses the arguments for and against public ownership and production of goods and services. The advantages and disadvantages of private ownership are then discussed, and the chapter concludes by reviewing the challenges involved in effectively regulating private companies. The following five chapters focus on specific areas of government expenditure: the role of government in healthcare and education is explored in Chapters 8 and 9; Chapter 10 focuses on the environment and the rationale for government intervention to address environmental problems; Chapter 11 analyses the role of government in the provision of retirement pensions and in supporting saving for retirement more broadly; and Chapter 12 looks at the problems of inequality and poverty, and how government intervention can help address them. In each case, we discuss the main arguments for government intervention, different ways in which governments can intervene, and the limitations of these interventions. Real-world examples of problems and policies are used throughout to illustrate applications of the theory.

Part III focuses on the revenue side of government, exploring what tools the government has available to raise the revenues required to finance its activities and what the implications of these various tools are. Chapters 13, 14, and 15 focus on taxation. Chapter 13 introduces taxation and covers some of the different types of taxes and their economic implications. Chapter 14 focuses on indirect taxes on goods and services, exploring the impact of these taxes for economic efficiency and equity, and ending with a detailed discussion of VAT. Chapter 15 looks at direct taxes on individual income, savings, and wealth. Chapter 16 focuses on the role of government borrowing, the economic impact of government deficits, and the challenges involved in reducing deficits. The final chapter, Chapter 17, explores two interrelated problems that have become a growing concern in many countries: tax evasion and tax avoidance. It reviews the theory and evidence on tax evasion, and discusses the implications for the design of policies to reduce it.

Questions to encourage discussion are provided at the end of each chapter, along with suggestions for further reading. For certain chapters, supplementary materials that expand on key concepts and develop the mathematics behind some of the results are included in the relevant chapter appendices.

Questions for discussion

1. 'Governments should take steps to reduce poverty and inequality, in order to promote economic growth.' What are the positive and normative components of this statement?
2. Equity and efficiency are two possible social objectives. What other objectives might society want to pursue? To what extent will the market system enable society to achieve these objectives?
3. 'The concept of efficiency is value-free, unlike the concept of equity.' Do you agree with this statement?
4. How do economists measure social welfare? What are the difficulties with implementing this concept in practice?
5. Discuss the possible direct and indirect consequences of the following policies:
    a. Minimum wage legislation;
    b. Regulations to limit vehicle emissions;
    c. Increased taxes on alcoholic drinks.

Further reading

For a critical discussion of the role of markets, the state and other institutions in modern economies:

Chang, Ha-Joon (2002). Breaking the mould: An institutionalist political economy alternative to the neo-liberal theory of the market and the state. *Cambridge Journal of Economics*, *26*, 539–559.

Coyle, D. (2020). *Markets, state and people: Economics for public policy*. Princeton University Press.

Mazzucato, M. (2019). *The value of everything: Making and taking in the global economy*. Penguin.

Ostrom, E. (2005). Policies that crowd out reciprocity and collective action. In G. Gintis Herbert, S. Bowles, R. Boyd, & E. Fehr (Eds.), *Moral sentiments and material interests: The foundations of cooperation in economic life* (pp. 253–275). MIT Press.

Ostrom, E. (2010). Beyond markets and states: Polycentric governance of complex economic systems. *American Economic Review*, *100*(3), 641–672.

Raworth, K. (2017). *Doughnut economics: Seven ways to think like a 21st-century economist*. Chelsea Green Publishing.

Sandel, M. J. (2012). *What money can't buy: The moral limits of markets*. New York: Farrar, Straus, & Giroux.

On the changing perspectives on the role of government in the economy:

Tanzi, V. (2011). *Government versus markets: The changing economic role of the state*. Cambridge University Press.

For a more in-depth discussion of the different theories of society:

Barr, N. (2020). *The economics of the welfare state* (6th ed.). Oxford University Press.

On behavioural economics and public policy:

Bernheim, B. D., & Taubinsky, D. (2018). *Behavioral public economics*. National Bureau of Economic Research working papers, no. w24828. Available at: https://doi.org/10.3386/w24828

Congdon, W., Kling, J. R., & Mullainathan, S. (2011). *Policy and choice: Public finance through the lens of behavioural economics*. Brookings Institution Press.

On the capability approach to measuring welfare:

Nussbaum, M. (2002). Capabilities and social justice. *International Studies Review*, *4*(2), 123–135. https://doi.org/10.1111/1521-9488.00258

Sen, A. K. (1986). The concept of well-being. In S. Guhan and M. Shroff (Eds.), *Essays on economic progress and welfare: In honour of I. G. Patel* (pp. 174–192). Oxford University Press.

Bibliography

Barr, N. (2020). *The economics of the welfare state* (6th ed.). Oxford University Press.

Buchanan, J. M. (1962). Politics, policy, and the Pigovian margins. *Economica*, *29*(113), 17–28. https://doi.org/10.2307/2601517

Congdon, W., Kling, J. R., & Mullainathan, S. (2011). *Policy and choice: Public finance through the lens of behavioural economics*. Brookings Institution Press.

Coyle, D. (2020). *Markets, state and people: Economics for public policy*. Princeton University Press.

Desmarais-Tremblay, M., Johnson, M., & Sturn, R. (2023). Mapping the history of public economics in the twentieth century: An introduction to the special issue. *European Journal of the History of Economic Thought*, *30*(5), 689–712. https://doi.org/10.1080/09672567.2023.2248319

Feldstein, M. (2002). The transformation of public economics research: 1970–2000. *Journal of Public Economics*, *86*(3), 319–326. https://doi.org/10.1016/S0047-2727(01)00190-6

Gruber, J. (2013). *Public finance and public policy* (4th ed.). Worth Publishers.

Hall, T. E. (2014). *Aftermath: The unintended consequences of public policies*. Cato Institute.

Hausman, D. M. (2018). The bond between positive and normative economics. *Revue d'économie politique*, *128*(2), 191–208. https://doi.org/10.3917/redp.282.0191

IMF (2023). *Government expenditure (% of GDP)* [data set]. *Public finances in modern history* [original data]. International Monetary Fund. Available at: https://ourworldindata.org/grapher/historical-gov-spending-gdp (accessed 13 March 2025).

IMF (2025). *Government spending as share of GDP* [data set]. International Monetary Fund, *Public finances in modern history* [original data]. Retrieved from https://archive.ourworldindata.org/20250909-093708/grapher/historical-gov-spending-gdp.html (archived 9 September 2025).

Keech, W. R., & Munger, M. C. (2015). The anatomy of government failure. *Public Choice*, *164*, 1–42. https://doi.org/10.1007/s11127-015-0262-y

Kolm, S.-C. (1987). Public economics. In *The new Palgrave dictionary of economics* (pp. 1–13). Palgrave Macmillan. https://doi.org/10.1057/978-1-349-95121-5_1832-1

Modernisation and Reform Unit (2024). *Understanding arm's length bodies: A fresh look at Britain's public sector*. Available at: https://moderncivilservice.blog.gov.uk/2024/12/18/understanding-arms-length-bodies-a-fresh-look-at-britains-public-sector/

Mor, F. (2018). *Royal Bank of Scotland bailout: 10 years and counting*. House of Commons Library. Available at: https://commonslibrary.parliament.uk/royal-bank-of-scotland-bailout-10-years-and-counting/

Nozick, R. (1974). *Anarchy, state and utopia*. Basil Blackwell.

OECD (2002). *OECD in figures 2002: Statistics on the member countries*. Organization for Economic Cooperation and Development. Observer 2002/supplement 1.

OECD (2025a). *A comparative table of countries in the global database*. Organization for Economic Cooperation and Development. Data explorer revenue statistics. Available at: https://data-explorer.oecd.org (accessed 11 August 2025).

OECD (2025b). *Public finance and procurement by function: Government at a glance indicator*. Organization for Economic Cooperation and Development. Data explorer. Available at: https://data-explorer.oecd.org (accessed 20 October 2025).

ONS (2025a). *Private rental affordability, England, Wales and Northern Ireland: 2024* (release date, 18 August). Office for National Statistics. Available at: https://www.ons.gov.uk/peoplepopulationandcommunity/housing/bulletins/privaterentalaffordabilityengland/2024

ONS (2025b). *Private rented sector statistics from across the UK: 2025* (release date, 25 September). Office for National Statistics. Available at: https://www.ons.gov.uk/peoplepopulationandcommunity/housing/articles/privaterentedsectorstatisticsfromacrosstheuk/2025

Ostrom, E. (2010). Beyond markets and states: Polycentric governance of complex economic systems. *American Economic Review*, *100*(3), 641–672.

Raworth, K. (2017). *Doughnut economics: Seven ways to think like a 21st-century economist*. Chelsea Green Publishing.

Sandel, M. J. (2012). *What money can't buy: The moral limits of markets*. New York: Farrar, Straus, & Giroux.

Sen, A. K. (1986). The concept of well-being. In S. Guhan and M. Shroff (Eds.), *Essays on economic progress and welfare: In honour of I. G. Patel* (pp. 174–192). Oxford University Press.

Stiglitz, J., E., & Rosengard, J. K. (2015). *Economics of the public sector* (4th ed.). W. W. Norton.

Tanzi, V. (2011). *Government versus markets: The changing economic role of the state*. Cambridge University Press.

UNECE (2024). *UN urges action to tackle persistent housing affordability crisis in Europe* (press release, 2 October). United Nations Economic Commission for Europe. Available at: https://unece.org/media/press/395067

2

The role of government in the economy

Learning objectives

By the end of this chapter, you will be able to:

- 2.1 Explain why a minimum level of government intervention is required to provide the foundations for economic activity to develop.
- 2.2 Explain why competitive markets will lead to an efficient allocation of resources.
- 2.3 Discuss why government intervention may be necessary to increase efficiency.
- 2.4 Discuss the role of government in promoting equity and social justice.
- 2.5 Critically evaluate the neoclassical theory of the role of government in the economy.

Introduction

In most countries today, most goods and services are produced and distributed by the private sector. The food we eat, our clothes and shoes, the mobile phones and laptops we rely on for work and leisure, our cars and bikes, the films we watch, the shops, cafés, and restaurants we visit, the medications we take—these are all typically provided by private businesses. In contrast, our healthcare, education, and defence—and in some cases basic utilities such as water, gas, and electricity—are often provided by the government. Governments also levy taxes, provide subsidies and income transfers, and regulate a range of private sector activities.

Why do governments intervene in some areas of the economy and not others? This is the focus of this chapter. Drawing on neoclassical economic theory, we will explore the rationale for government intervention in the economy.[1] The market plays a central role within this framework: under certain conditions, the market will lead to an efficient allocation of resources, where no individual can be made better off without making anyone else worse off. Government intervention is only justified in cases where the market fails to deliver an efficient outcome or where there is a desire to achieve a more equitable allocation.

We start in section 2.1 by exploring the basic level of government intervention required for economic activity to develop. We then analyse, in section 2.2, the properties of competitive markets and the circumstances under which they lead to an efficient allocation. This provides the basis for discussing two core arguments for government intervention: to increase efficiency, which we cover in section 2.3, and to promote equity and social justice, which we cover in section 2.4. In section 2.5, we discuss some of the criticisms of this approach.

[1] Governments also play an important role in stabilizing the economy, pursuing countercyclical policies during economic downturns to ensure the appropriate level of aggregate demand and promoting employment. We will not be covering this stabilization role of government in this book.

2.1 The minimal state

The first question we need to consider is: what are the basic conditions required for economic activity to thrive? In order for individuals to be willing to produce and exchange goods and services, they need to know that their rights over the fruits of their labour will be respected and that the terms of any exchange agreement they enter into will be respected. So at the most basic level, we need well-defined property rights, which establish the ownership of economic resources and how they can be used. Without these rights, the concept of theft becomes meaningless, the conditions for individuals to trade break down, and the incentives for individuals to produce at all are greatly diminished (since anything they own or produce can simply be appropriated by others). Alongside property rights, we also need **contract laws** that determine the rules of exchange and how trade is carried out. Contract laws reduce the uncertainty involved in economic transactions, by ensuring that individuals know or get what they expected from an exchange.

The existence of well-defined property rights and contract laws is an important starting point, but these rights and laws also need to be enforced. This requires some form of policing to monitor and enforce the laws, and courts where disputes can be resolved. Whether this enforcement can be carried out by individuals or private agencies, or whether a higher public entity is needed, is subject to some debate. However, even the libertarian political philosopher Robert Nozick believed that individuals would find it in their interests to take steps to set up a state or government to protect and enforce individual rights. In *Anarchy, State and Utopia* (1974), Nozick conceived of a minimal state that would function as a 'nightwatchman', responsible only for protecting citizens against violence, theft and fraud, and for enforcing contracts. The state, in Nozick's theory, would have a monopoly over the use of legitimate force in a country and would be responsible for providing protection to all citizens with that country. The state would also be responsible for defending the proceeds of economic activity from outsiders.

In order to provide national defence and policing, and enforce property rights and contract laws, the state would need to employ armies, police officers, and officers to staff the courts where disputes could be resolved, and these individuals would need to be paid. Therefore, even a minimal state would require revenues to be collected in order to finance its activities. The process of collecting and managing these government revenues would, in turn, require an administrative structure, which would also need to be financed.

So the first role of the government would be to create 'an environment in which trade can flourish' (Hindriks & Myles, 2013: 121), by establishing and enforcing property rights and contracts laws, and defending a country's economic gains from outsiders. Beyond this minimal state, the need for government intervention in the economy is subject to debate. We discuss some of the main arguments in the sections below.

2.2 Competitive market equilibrium and efficiency

Beyond the minimal state, the dominant rationale for government intervention in the economy is rooted in neoclassical economic theory. The neoclassical school is based on a set of assumptions about how the economy operates and what drives the behaviour of individual consumers and producers, and has become the dominant approach to economic theory (see Box 2.1). According to neoclassical theory, there are two reasons why government intervention in the economy may be justified:

1. when conditions in a particular market are such that the market cannot operate in a way that will lead to an efficient allocation of resources (the efficiency argument);
2. when the resulting distribution or allocation of resources achieved through the operation of the market is deemed to be unfair or inequitable (the equity argument).

Government intervention may therefore be justified either to increase efficiency or to promote greater equity or fairness in the allocation of resources. In Chapter 1, we saw briefly why efficiency and equity are two important social objectives/aims of policy. In this section, we are going to start by exploring the concept of efficiency in more detail, before we analyse the circumstances under which efficiency will be maximized. This will provide the basis for understanding when and how government intervention may be necessary to help promote efficiency, which we discuss in section 2.3.

Box 2.1 The neoclassical school

Neoclassical economics is a school of economic thought that emerged in the late nineteenth century and is rooted in the work of the economists William Jevons, Carl Menger, and Léon Walras. The market plays a central role, coordinating the actions of rational and self-interested economic agents. Competition in the market ensures that although individuals act in pursuit of their own interest, their actions lead to a socially beneficial outcome.

Consumers are assumed to have well-defined preferences over what goods and services they want to consume, and they choose the bundle of goods which maximizes their utility or welfare, subject to what they can afford (their **budget constraint**). Their utility-maximizing choice is given by the point where the gain they receive from consuming an extra unit of the good (their **marginal utility** or marginal benefit) just equals the cost of acquiring it. Individual preferences are assumed to satisfy a set of assumptions, including the assumption of non-satiation, or that more of a good is always preferred to less.

Producers make decisions about what to produce to minimize costs and maximize profits. They buy their inputs at the lowest possible cost and use inputs in the most cost-effective way to maximize their output. Producers will choose the level of output to produce so that the cost of producing one additional unit just equals the revenue they get from selling it.

The neoclassical school is still the dominant school of economic thought in most circles, so much so that it is often seen as synonymous with 'mainstream economics'. Other schools of economics thought include the Marxist school, the developmentalist tradition, the Austrian school, the Schumpeterian school, the Keynesian school, the institutionalist school, and the behaviouralist school.[2]

Sources: Chang (2014) and Neck (2022).

[2] Ha-Joon Chang provides a good overview of these different schools of economic thought in chapter 4 of his book, *Economics: A User's Guide* (2014).

2.2.1 Pareto efficiency and the two theorems of welfare economics

As we saw in Chapter 1, economic efficiency is essentially about ensuring that scarce resources are used in the best way possible, given individual tastes and the technology available. Neoclassical economists, however, tend to work with a more precise concept of efficiency, which was named after the Italian economist, sociologist, and philosopher Vilfredo Pareto (1848–1923). An allocation of resources is deemed to be Pareto efficient or **Pareto optimal** if there is no way in which this allocation can be changed to make at least one individual better off without making anyone else worse off. A change in the allocation of resources is considered a Pareto improvement if it makes at least one individual better off, without making anyone else worse off.

Intuitively, this is a fairly appealing concept: if there is a way to reallocate resources so that we can make at least one person better off without making anyone else worse off, then surely we should do this and our initial allocation would not have been optimal in any commonsense understanding of the concept. Alternatively, if resources in a society are allocated in such a way that it is impossible to redistribute them so that we make at least one person better off, but without making anyone else worse off, then it would seem that that we cannot improve on that allocation. However, the Pareto efficiency criterion does have its limitations, which we turn to in section 2.4. It is also quite a strict requirement, since it requires that *no* individual is made worse off by a change in the allocation of resources. One of the assumptions that underpins neoclassical consumer theory is that individual consumers always prefer more to less (see Box 2.1). This means that any reallocation which involved taking some resources away from one individual, without giving them any compensation in return, would always make them worse off, thus making the practical applicability of the concept of Pareto efficiency limited. A less stringent alternative to the Pareto criterion is the **Kaldor–Hicks efficiency criterion**, which focuses on *potential* Pareto improvements (see Box 2.2).

Box 2.2 The Kaldor–Hicks efficiency criterion and potential Pareto improvements

The Kaldor–Hicks efficiency criterion was proposed independently by Nicholas Kaldor (1939) and John Hicks (1939). This criterion focuses on the question of whether it is possible to reallocate resources in such a way that those who gain from the reallocation could hypothetically compensate those who lose out, and still be better off. In other words, would this reallocation lead to an increase in *net* welfare, even if some individuals lose out as a result? If the answer is yes, then the reallocation will increase efficiency under this definition. It is important to emphasize that this criterion is based on hypothetical compensations—that is, whether the gainers could compensate the losers *in theory*—and that no actual compensation is required. This criterion therefore overcomes one of the key shortcomings of the Pareto efficiency criterion. And it is not just an abstract concept; the Kaldor–Hicks criterion underpins much of modern cost-benefit analysis, which is widely used in policy decision-making (and which we discuss in detail in Chapter 5).

Under what conditions will efficiency be maximized? To answer this question, we need to turn to welfare economics. As we saw in Chapter 1, welfare economics is a branch of economics that focuses on defining and measuring the welfare of society as a whole. Two important results in welfare economics provide the foundation for understanding the relationship between Pareto efficiency and the market as an allocation mechanism. According to the First Fundamental Theorem of Welfare Economics, which we encountered in Chapter 1, the operation of perfectly competitive markets will lead to an equilibrium allocation of resources that is Pareto efficient. This is a powerful result: it tells us that, under certain conditions, markets will guarantee efficiency, suggesting a limited role for government intervention. This theorem is also known as the 'Invisible Hand Theorem', and it encapsulates the assumption of the primacy of the competitive market that underpins neoclassical theory.

However, as we have seen, governments do not just care about efficiency, but also about equity or fairness. There are many possible allocations that are Pareto efficient, but these might not all be equally desirable from society's point of view. An allocation in which 1 per cent of the population hold 90 per cent of an economy's resources would be Pareto efficient, since it would not be possible to make anyone better off without making someone (the 1 per cent of the population) worse off. This suggests another reason for government intervention in the economy—to achieve a more equitable allocation of resources. Can society achieve a more equitable allocation, without sacrificing efficiency? According to the **Second Fundamental Theorem of Welfare Economics**, if individual preferences and technology are **convex**, then *any* Pareto-efficient allocation can be sustained as a competitive equilibrium, for some initial allocation.

The Second Theorem of Welfare Economics essentially says that a more equitable allocation can be achieved by redistributing the initial resources in the economy and then allowing markets to operate, which will ensure the final allocation is Pareto efficient.

Both of these theorems rely on a set of fairly strong assumptions, which we discuss in section 2.2.4. Before we do this, it is helpful to dig a little deeper to understand why competitive markets will lead to a Pareto-efficient allocation of resources.

2.2.2 Efficiency in a single market

The simplest way to see why the competitive market equilibrium will maximize economic efficiency is by focusing on the case of a single market—for example, the market for trainers. This is known as partial equilibrium analysis and is distinct from general equilibrium analysis, which focuses on equilibrium across a number of interrelated markets.

Figure 2.1 illustrates the market supply and demand curves for a particular good. The market **supply curve** illustrates the total quantity of the good that the firms in the industry are willing to produce at each price. This is derived by adding up the individual supply curves for all firms in the industry, where each firm's supply curve depends on its costs of production. The market supply curve therefore also measures the **marginal cost (MC)** of production—that is, the cost of producing each additional unit. The market **demand curve** illustrates the total quantity of the goods that all individuals in the market are willing to buy at each price. This is derived by adding up the individual demand curves for all individuals in the market. The demand curve reflects individuals' **willingness to pay**,[3] the maximum amount that they are willing to spend

[3] This is sometimes abbreviated to WTP.

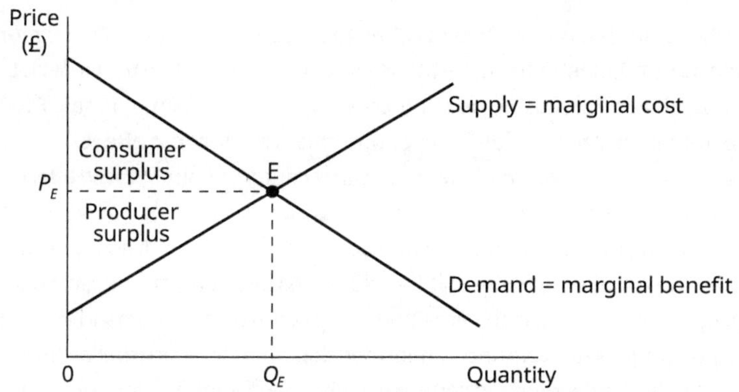

Figure 2.1 Efficiency of the competitive equilibrium in a single market

for an additional unit of the good. The market demand curve is a measure of the **marginal benefit (MB)** that individuals derive from buying each additional unit of the good.

The market equilibrium is given by point E, where the quantity demanded and quantity supplied are equal. The equilibrium quantity is Q_E and the equilibrium price is P_E. At point E, the marginal benefit of producing one additional unit of the good equals the marginal cost, so this equilibrium outcome is efficient. If the marginal benefit were greater than the marginal cost, it would be possible to increase social welfare (and make some people better off without making anyone else worse off) by increasing production, since the benefit of producing an additional unit of output would outweigh the cost. Conversely, if the marginal benefit were less than the marginal cost, then society would benefit if production were reduced.

The area below the demand curve and above the equilibrium price, P_E, is the **consumer surplus** (see Box 2.3). This captures the benefit to consumers from consuming a good, measured as the difference between the price they are willing to pay for a good and the price they actually pay. If you were willing to pay £50 for a new pair of trainers, but only pay £40, then your surplus from buying the trainers is £10. The area above the supply curve and below the equilibrium price is the **producer surplus**, which captures the benefit that producers derive from selling their goods in the market. This is measured as the difference between the price for which they were willing to sell their goods and the price at which the goods are sold. Together, consumer and producer surplus provide a measure of total welfare. The competitive market equilibrium is therefore efficient as it maximizes the sum of consumer and producer surplus.

Box 2.3 Consumer surplus and the compensated and uncompensated demand curve

Consumer surplus captures the benefit to individuals from buying goods in the market. It is measured as the difference between how much they are willing to pay for the good and how much they actually pay. How much an individual is willing to pay for each unit of a good is measured by the demand curve, which tells us how demand for the good changes as the price changes. The impact of a price change on demand can be broken down into two separate effects. Suppose the price of trainers falls from £40 a pair to £30. This means trainers have now become cheaper relative to other goods, so individuals will buy more of the good that has become relatively cheaper—this is known as the **substitution effect.** But as the price falls, an individual's purchasing power increases—a given income of, say, £100 will now buy you more trainers and more of all other goods; this is the **income effect**.

The regular (or uncompensated) demand curve captures both of these effects. The **compensated demand curve**, on the other hand, captures how demand for a good changes as the price changes, assuming that money is given or taken away from the individual to ensure their utility from buying the good is unchanged; it therefore measures only the substitution effect. Strictly speaking, consumer surplus is the area under the compensated demand curve. In most cases, however, the compensated and uncompensated demand curves are similar, therefore measuring the area under the regular demand curve is usually a good approximation for consumer surplus.

2.2.3 Efficiency across markets

Understanding the characteristics of the equilibrium in a single market is useful, but it provides an incomplete picture. In practice, markets are interdependent, and changes in one market will have an effect on prices and quantities in other markets. If the equilibrium price of wheat goes up, this is likely to have an impact on the price of bread. It may also affect the wages of bakery workers, if the bakery owners attempt to keep the price of bread down by cutting labour costs. It could also have an impact on the price of substitute goods, such as oatmeal or cornflour bread, if individuals switch their consumption to these different types of bread in response to the higher prices. With interdependent markets, the equilibrium prices and quantities in all markets are determined simultaneously.

Three conditions are required for the equilibrium across markets to be efficient:

1. **Efficiency in exchange or in consumption**: the goods and services being produced are going to the individuals who value them the most.
2. **Efficiency in production**: production must ensure that output is maximized given available resources (e.g. land, labour, and machinery), their prices, and the technology available.
3. **Efficiency in product mix**: the combination of goods and services being produced in the economy must be those that individuals value the most.

We explore each of these conditions below.

Efficiency in exchange

Efficiency in exchange is about how the goods and services produced in an economy are distributed among consumers. Efficiency in exchange requires that goods and services are allocated so that it is not possible to change this allocation in a way that would make at least one consumer better off without making anyone else worse off.

To analyse efficiency in exchange, we need to rely on the tools of neoclassical consumer theory.[4] Individual tastes or preferences over goods are represented by **indifference curves**,

[4] These concepts are covered in more detail in most intermediate microeconomics textbooks. See, for example, Frank and Cartwright (2021) or Varian (2014).

where each indifference curve tells us the different combinations of goods that provide the same level of satisfaction or utility. Individuals will choose the bundle of goods that maximizes their utility, given what they can afford, which will depend on the prices of the goods and the income they have available. Prices and income determine the individual's budget constraint.

The individual's utility maximization problem is illustrated in Figure 2.2 for any two goods, X and Y.[5] This consumer's preferences are represented by the indifference curves U_1, U_2, and U_3, with higher indifference curves implying a higher level of utility, since they involve more of both goods. The budget line tells us what combinations of the two goods the consumer can afford, given the prices of the goods, p_X and p_Y, and the consumer's income *M*, assuming they are spending all of their income.[6] The slope of the budget line is equal to the ratio of the prices of the two goods, $\frac{p_X}{p_Y}$.

The consumer will maximize their utility by choosing the most preferred bundle of goods that they can afford. This bundle must therefore be a point where their budget line is tangential to their highest possible indifference curve. This optimal or utility-maximizing bundle is given by point A in the figure. At this point, the slope of the budget line is equal to the slope of the indifference curve.[7] We have seen that the slope of the budget line is given by the ratio of the prices of the two goods. The slope of the indifference curve is given by the **marginal rate of substitution (MRS)**. This tells us how much of good Y the individual must give up to obtain one more unit of good X, while keeping their utility constant.[8] So at the optimal choice, the marginal rate of substitution between the two goods must equal the price ratio.

In a competitive market, all individuals face the same prices. If all individuals are choosing consumption bundles where their marginal rate of substitution equals the price ratio, then

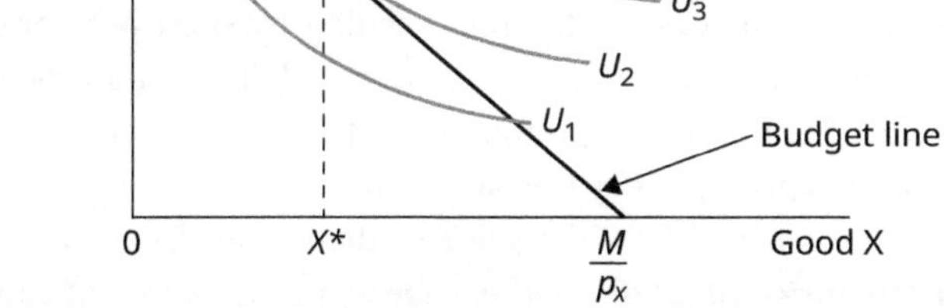

Figure 2.2 The consumer choice problem: maximizing utility subject to a budget constraint

[5] Focusing on choices involving two goods simplifies the analysis, but these results can be extended to any number of goods.

[6] Combinations of goods that lie inside the budget line are affordable, but they do not involve the individual spending all of their income. Only points on the budget line itself involve the individual spending all of their income.

[7] This follows from the tangency condition: if the indifference curve is tangential to the budget line at a particular point, the slope of the curve must equal the slope of the line at that point.

[8] Utility is constant along each indifference curve. To increase consumption of good X while keeping utility constant (e.g. in moving from point B to point A), the consumer must give up some of good Y because more is preferred to less.

the marginal rates of substitution must be equal across individuals. This is precisely what is required for efficiency in exchange. If the marginal rates of substitution between goods are equal across individuals, there is no way to make any one individual better off without making anyone else worse off.

Suppose we have two consumers, Alfie and Leni, and two goods, biscuits and cheese. Given the quantity of biscuits and cheese Alfie currently has, he would be willing to give up one piece of cheese in exchange for an extra biscuit—so his marginal rate of substitution between biscuits and cheese is 1. Leni would be willing to give up three pieces of cheese in exchange for an extra biscuit, so her marginal rate of substitution between biscuits and cheese is 3. There is scope for a mutually beneficial trade between Alfie and Leni, as Leni values biscuits more highly, given the quantity of the two goods she currently has. Leni could give Alfie two pieces of cheese in exchange for one of his biscuits, and they would both be better off. As they exchange biscuits and cheese, their marginal rates of substitution will change.[9] Once Alfie and Leni's marginal rates of substitution are equal, there will no longer be scope for further exchanges that will make at least one of them better off without making the other worse off—so efficiency in exchange will have been achieved.

Efficiency in production

For production to be efficient, it must not be possible to increase the amount of one good that is being produced without decreasing production of any other good. This means that the economy's resources must be used in the best way possible, so the level of output of all goods produced in the economy is maximized given the inputs and technology available.

To analyse production efficiency, we draw on the tools of neoclassical producer theory. The producers in an economy are assumed to buy their inputs at the lowest possible cost and to use these inputs in the most cost-effective way to maximize their output. We assume producers only use two inputs in production, labour and capital.[10] The producer's **isoquants** show the different combinations of inputs the producer can use to produce the same level of output; this is analogous to the consumer's indifference curves that we saw above. The slope of each isoquant measures the **marginal rate of technical substitution (MRTS)**: the amount by which the quantity of one input has to be reduced to increase the quantity of the other input by one unit, while keeping total output constant; or equivalently, the quantity by which one input has to be increased, if the quantity of the other input is reduced by one unit. The different combinations of the two inputs the producer can use for the same total cost is represented by the **isocost** line; this is analogous to the consumer's budget constraint that we saw above. The slope of the isocost line is given by the ratio of input prices, where the price of labour is the wage w and the price of capital is the rental cost of capital r.

The producer's cost-minimization or output-maximization problem is illustrated in Figure 2.3. The producer wants to choose the combination of inputs, labour L and capital K, that will allow it to maximize output for a given level of total expenditure on inputs, E. The production function is illustrated by the isoquants, Q_1, Q_2, and Q_3, where the level of

[9] See the chapter appendix for an explanation of why the MRS typically varies along an indifference curve.

[10] This is done in order to simplify the analysis, but as with our model of consumer choice, the results can be generalized to any number of inputs.

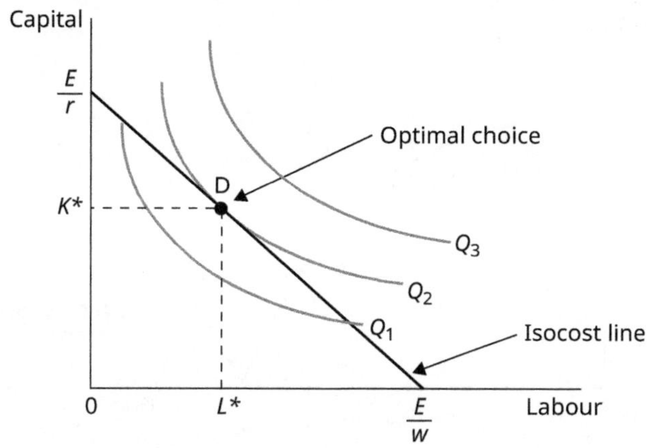

Figure 2.3 The producer's decision: maximizing output for a given level of input expenditure

output is constant along each isoquant and higher isoquants are associated with a higher level of output.

For a given level of expenditure on inputs, the producer will maximize the amount of output it can produce by selecting the input combination at the point where the isocost line is tangential to the highest possible isoquant. This is illustrated by point D in Figure 2.3. At this point, the slope of the isoquant and isocost line are equal, which means that the MRTS is equal to the ratio of input prices. In a perfectly competitive market, all producers face the same input prices. So if each producer is selecting the combination of inputs where the MRTS is equal to the ratio of input prices, in equilibrium the MRTS will be equal across all producers. This is the condition required for efficiency in production.

To see why, suppose that the MRTS in the production of biscuits is 1, and that in the production of cheese it is 2. This means that, given the quantity of labour and capital currently being used, the biscuit producer would need one more unit of capital if it reduced the quantity of labour by one unit. The cheese producer would need two more units of capital if it reduced labour by one unit; or equivalently, it could give up two units of capital in exchange for one additional unit of labour, and still produce the same level of output. If we moved one worker from producing biscuits to producing cheese, and moved one unit of capital from cheese production to biscuit production, the quantity of biscuits produced would not change (since we have just exchanged one unit of labour for one unit of capital), but the quantity of cheese produced would increase, since the cheese producer has only had to give up one unit of capital in exchange for one extra worker. When the marginal rates of technical substitution are equal across all producers, there is no way to increase production of one good without reducing the quantity of other goods being produced—so production is efficient.

Efficiency in product mix

Efficiency in product mix requires that the optimal combination of goods and services is being produced, given individual preferences and the technology available. First, we need to determine the maximum amount of each good that can be produced, for a given level of production of other goods. We then need to consider individuals' preferences for the various

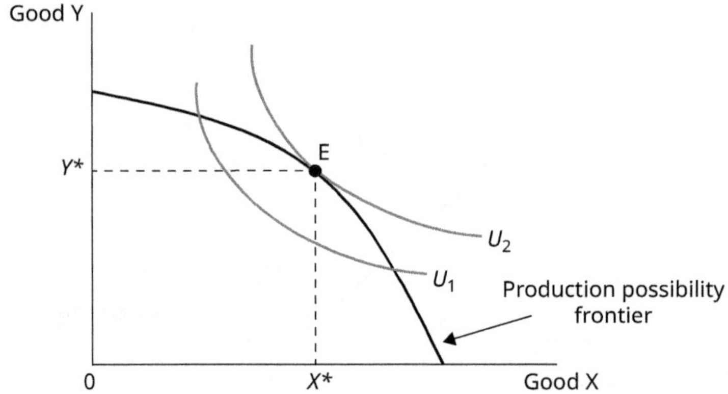

Figure 2.4 Efficiency in product mix

goods, to determine what combination of goods should be produced. How resources should be allocated to building schools and hospitals, for example, will depend on the different combinations of schools and hospitals that are technically feasible, and individuals' preferences over schools and hospitals.

The **production possibility frontier (PPF)** depicts the maximum feasible level of production of one good, for each level of production of another good. It is therefore the set of all possible output combinations that can be produced with a given level of inputs and for a given technology. The PPF for two goods is illustrated in Figure 2.4. The slope of the production possibility frontier is the **marginal rate of transformation (MRT)**, which measures the **opportunity cost** of producing one good in terms of the other. This just equals the ratio of the marginal cost of producing the two goods, $\frac{MC_X}{MC_Y}$.[11]

To determine whether the combination of goods being produced is the one that society values the most, we need to consider individual preferences. Assuming, for simplicity, that all individuals have identical preferences over these two goods, we can represent these using indifference curves, as shown in Figure 2.4. Utility is maximized at the point where the production possibility frontier is tangential to the highest possible indifference curve. This is illustrated by point E in Figure 2.4. At this point, the slope of the PPF is equal to the slope of the indifference curve—or equivalently, the MRT is equal to the MRS. This is the condition required for the economy to be efficient in terms of its product mix.

In a competitive market, firms will produce at the point where the price of their output equals the marginal cost of production. Since the MRT equals the ratio of the marginal cost of producing the two goods, this is equivalent to saying the MRT equals the ratio of the prices of the two goods. And, as we saw above, utility-maximizing consumers will choose a consumption bundle where their MRS equals the price ratio. Since the MRT and the MRS both equal the price ratio, this means the MRT must equal the MRS in a competitive equilibrium.

[11] The marginal cost is just the cost of producing one additional unit of a good. Suppose the marginal cost of producing good X is £100 and the marginal cost of producing good Y is £50. To produce one additional unit of good X, we would need to sacrifice $\frac{100}{50} = 2$ units of good Y.

The conditions that underpin the First Fundamental Theorem of Welfare Economics are summarized in Box 2.4.

We have demonstrated how the operation of perfectly competitive markets will lead to an equilibrium allocation of resources that is Pareto efficient (the First Fundamental Theorem of Welfare Economics). In addition, the Second Fundamental Theorem of Welfare Economics tells us that we do not need to sacrifice efficiency for equity, and that a more equitable allocation can be achieved by redistributing the initial resources in the economy and then allowing markets to operate. These are powerful results and would suggest a limited role for government intervention in the economy. However, they rely on a set of fairly strong requirements, known as the first-best conditions. We review these conditions in section 2.2.4 below.

Box 2.4 The First Fundamental Theorem of Welfare Economics

Efficiency in exchange

Consumers maximize their utility by selecting a consumption bundle where their budget constraint is tangential to their highest possible indifference curve. For two consumers, Ana and Ben, and two goods, X and Y, this implies their marginal rate of substitution (MRS) is equal to the price ratio at the utility-maximizing choice. Since all consumers face the same prices in competitive markets, this implies the marginal rates of substitution are equal for all consumers:

$$MRS_{XY}^{A} = \frac{p_X}{p_Y} = MRS_{XY}^{B}$$

Efficiency in production

Firms minimize costs—or maximize the level of output they can produce for a given level of expenditure—by choosing the combination of inputs such that the marginal rate of technical substitution between two inputs, labour and capital ($MRTS_{LK}$), equals the ratio of their prices, where the price of labour is the wage rate, w, and the price of capital is r. Since all firms face the same input prices in a perfectly competitive market:

$$MRTS_{LK}^{X} = \frac{w}{r} = MRTS_{LK}^{Y}$$

Efficiency in product mix

Profit-maximizing firms will produce where price equals marginal cost (MC):

$$p_X = MC_X$$

$$p_Y = MC_Y$$

The marginal rate of transformation (MRT) is equal to the ratio of the marginal cost of producing the two goods. So in equilibrium:

$$MRT_{XY} = \frac{MC_X}{MC_Y} = \frac{p_X}{p_Y} = MRS_{XY}$$

2.2.4 Under what conditions will the competitive market allocation be efficient?

The competitive market equilibrium will only be efficient if the conditions of a **first-best economy** are satisfied. These conditions include the following:

C1. Perfect competition: this requires a large number of buyers and sellers in the market, so that neither buyers nor sellers can affect the market price (buyers and sellers are **price-takers**). There can be no returns to scale and no barriers preventing buyers or sellers from entering or exiting the market.
C2. No externalities or public goods: private and social costs and benefits are equal, and all goods are **rival** and **excludable.**[12]
C3. Buyers and sellers have perfect and symmetric information.
C4. Consumers and producers are rational and self-interested. Consumers care about maximizing their utility and producers care about maximizing profits.
C5. Markets are complete, including for all future goods and services.
C6. There is no distortionary taxation.[13]

If one or more of these conditions fails to hold, the market allocation will no longer be efficient. This opens up the possibility for government intervention in the economy to increase efficiency. However, just because the market does not maximize efficiency this does not mean that government intervention will automatically improve on the market outcome—government intervention can also cause or contribute to inefficiency. This is the problem of government failure, which we introduced in Chapter 1 and which we discuss in more detail in Chapter 4. In some cases, if one or more of the conditions required for optimality fail to hold, the next-best solution may actually involve moving further away from what would otherwise be optimal (see Box 2.5).

Box 2.5 The theory of the second best

The theory of the second best (Lipsey & Lancaster, 1956) states that, if we cannot meet all of the conditions required for the competitive market outcome to be efficient, then the next-best solution may actually involve moving further away from what would otherwise be optimal. The classic example involves a polluting monopolist. Here there are two conditions of a first-best economy which are not satisfied: a failure of perfect competition (because

[12] Goods are rival if consumption by one individual reduces the amount available for others to consume—for example, an apple is rival in consumption, since if I eat an apple, no one else will be able to eat that same apple. Goods are excludable if it is possible to prevent or exclude people from consuming them. For example, you can be excluded from eating an apple unless you pay for it. We discuss these characteristics and different types of economic goods in more detail in Chapter 6 on public goods.

[13] A tax is non-distortionary if there is no way that individuals can change their behaviour to reduce the amount of tax they pay. Most taxes, as we will see in more detail in Chapter 13, are distortionary—for example, if you want to reduce the amount of income tax you pay, you could (in theory) choose to work fewer hours.

of monopoly power) and **externalities** (from the pollution). To move the economy closer to optimality, we might consider adopting a policy to reduce the power of the monopolist and promote competition. However, this could in fact make the pollution problem worse, since by encouraging more competition, output will increase, and if pollution is linked to the level of output, pollution will also increase. The key lesson here is that if we cannot eliminate *all* distortions in the economy, then eliminating just one distortion could either increase or reduce social welfare. The theory of the second best highlights the importance of not analysing policies in isolation and the need to take the broader economic context into account when designing policies.

2.3 Government intervention to increase efficiency

Instances when one or more of the first-best assumptions fail to hold are often referred to as market failures—situations where the market outcome is not Pareto efficient. These market failures provide a rationale for government intervention in the economy to improve efficiency. The classic categories of market failure covered in most microeconomics textbooks are: imperfect competition; public goods; externalities; and asymmetric information. In this section, the discussion is structured more broadly around departures from the conditions required for a first-best economy described above and what they imply for government intervention. A summary is provided in Table 2.1.

Table 2.1 Market failure and government intervention

Market failure	Definition	Examples	Possible government response
Imperfect competition	Buyers or sellers have market power	Natural monopoly (e.g. energy or water supply); oligopolies (e.g. mobile phone operators)	Regulation of private monopolies; state ownership
Public goods	Good which are non-rival and non-excludable	Streetlighting, defence	Public finance or provision
Externalities	Action of producers or consumers affects other economic agents and this effect is not reflected in the market price	Pollution, second-hand smoke, research and development (R&D) spillovers	Taxes (negative externalities) or subsidies (positive externalities)
Asymmetric information	One party to the transaction has more information than the other	Insurance, bank lending	Regulation
Bounded rationality, bounded willpower	Departures from the strict rationality requirements of neoclassical theory	Framing effects, loss aversion, hyperbolic discounting	Regulation, commitment devices, automatic enrolment

2.3.1 Imperfect competition and increasing returns to scale

Perfectly competitive markets are characterized by having a large number of buyers and sellers, which ensures that no individual buyer or seller has sufficient market power to influence market prices. It is in this sense that buyers and sellers are referred to as price-takers. In reality, there are many cases where the sellers—and sometimes the buyers—of a good or service have **market power or monopoly power**: that is, the ability to influence market prices.[14] A **monopoly** is a market where there is a single seller, which therefore has control over the market price and the quantity produced. In many countries, public utilities such as gas, electricity, and water, and train operators are examples of monopolies.[15] Examples of pure monopolies that operate on a global scale are rare. For a long time, the diamond company De Beers was considered a monopoly, although its market power has since decreased. Companies such as Microsoft and Google also have a significant degree of market power, although they would not be considered pure monopolies.

An **oligopoly** is another type of imperfect competition, where the market is characterized by a small number of sellers. Aerospace manufacturing, where the market is dominated by Boeing and Airbus, is a good example.[16] Other examples include mobile phone operators and energy suppliers in some countries.

Firms may have market power if they have exclusive control over key inputs or resources (e.g. oil or diamonds), if they benefit from a patent, government licence, or franchise, or if the production technology exhibits **increasing returns to scale**. Increasing returns to scale arise when output increases more than proportionately with the increase in inputs, so the firm's average cost of production is falling over a large output range. In all cases, a firm with market power will set its price above marginal cost and therefore the market outcome will no longer be efficient.

In the presence of imperfect competition, governments may intervene through regulation, to promote competitive practices, or by taking control of the production of certain goods and services. The latter is particularly prevalent in the case of natural monopolies, which often arise in the energy, water, and telecommunications markets. We will be exploring some of these arguments in Chapter 7.

2.3.2 Externalities and public goods

Externalities arise when an action by a producer or consumer affects other economic agents and this effect is not reflected in the market price. Externalities can arise in production or consumption, and can be positive or negative. A **negative externality** arises when the action of a consumer or producer imposes a cost on other economic agents—for example, pollution or second-hand smoke. A **positive externality** arises when the action of a consumer or producer imposes a benefit on other economic agents—for example, knowledge spillovers from R&D. Externalities cause a divergence between private and social costs and benefits, so the

[14] When a single buyer dominates the market for a particular good or input, this is referred to as a **monopsony**. An example would be where a single firm is the main employer in a particular region and therefore has the power to set wages in that market.

[15] These types of monopolies are known as **natural monopolies**; we discuss these in more detail in Chapter 7.

[16] When two companies dominate the market, this is known as a **duopoly**.

price of a good does not necessarily reflect its social value. Firms or consumers may therefore supply or consume too much or too little, and the market outcome is no longer efficient. In order to drive the market towards the efficient level of the good or service, governments may impose taxes, to raise the cost and reduce the level of a good generating a negative externality, or provide subsidies, to encourage production or consumption of a good generating positive externalities.[17]

Public goods are a particular type of economic commodity and are defined by the following two characteristics: they are **non-rival** in consumption, which means that consumption of the good by one person does not reduce the amount available for others to consume; and they are **non-excludable**, which means it is impossible—or extremely costly—to exclude or prevent any individual from consuming the good once it is provided. An example of a public good is street lighting: it is non-rival (up to a point) because the fact that I benefit from street lighting does not reduce the amount of street lighting that my neighbours can enjoy; it is also non-excludable because it would be very difficult to exclude any individual in a neighbourhood from enjoying the benefits of street lighting in that neighbourhood, once a decision had been made to provide this good. It is important to note that a public good, in the strict economic sense, is not the same as a publicly provided good—that is, any good provided by the state.

Full non-rivalry and non-excludability are fairly strict requirements. In practice, many goods exhibit these characteristics to some degree—these are known as **impure public goods**: goods that are rival but non-excludable, or non-rival but excludable. There are two types of impure public goods. **Common-pool resources** are non-excludable, but they are they are rival in consumption, which means the use or consumption of the resources by one individual reduces the amount available for others to consume. Examples of common-pool resources include fisheries, forests, grazing lands, and water systems.[18] **Club goods** are non-rival but excludable—for example, online movie-streaming providers.

Public goods are a problem for competitive markets because if individuals cannot be excluded from consuming a good, they have an incentive to understate their true valuation of the good so that they can enjoy its benefits without paying for it (or paying less)—essentially, they have an incentive to **free ride**. If every potential consumer of the good understates their true valuation in the hope of enjoying the good more cheaply or for free, then the public good will be underprovided or may not be provided at all—this is the **free rider problem**. This may require governments to intervene to provide the good directly or finance its provision. We discuss the properties of public goods and what they imply for government intervention in Chapter 6.

2.3.3 Imperfect and asymmetric information

The requirement that both consumers and producers have complete information is essential for the market outcome to be efficient. In order for consumers to maximize their utility subject to their budget constraint, they need to be well informed about the nature and quality of the goods and services available, and their prices. Similarly, producers need to

[17] The problem with externalities and how these can be addressed is discussed in detail in the context of the environment, in Chapter 10.

[18] The particular challenges associated with common-pool resources are discussed in Chapter 10.

have full information about the quality of the inputs available, their prices, and the production technology.

Imperfect information, introduced in Chapter 1, refers to situations in which consumers and producers do not have all of the information they need to make an informed decision. **Asymmetric information** is a slightly different concept, in that it refers to situations in which one party to a transaction has more information than the other.[19] Asymmetric information can affect both consumers and producers. An individual wanting to take out private health insurance will know more about their own health history and how healthy their lifestyle is than the insurance company; a second-hand car salesperson will have more information about the quality of the car they are trying to sell.

Both imperfect and asymmetric information can lead to a competitive market outcome that is no longer efficient. Asymmetric information gives rise to two particular problems:

1. **Adverse selection**: this is a problem of hidden information, which arises when either buyers or sellers have more information about some of aspect of the quality of the good. This can lead to lower-quality goods driving high-quality goods out of a market or, in the extreme, can cause a market to collapse.[20] In the context of health insurance, for example, the problem of adverse selection arises because it is difficult for insurance companies to identify good risks (healthier individuals) and bad risks (less healthy individuals). The insurance company will therefore charge an **insurance premium** that reflects the average risk in the pool of people it insures. Some of the healthier individuals may find this premium too high and decide not to take out insurance. This will then increase the proportion of bad risks being insured, which will drive up the insurance company's costs, leading it to charge a higher premium. This, in turn, may push further good risks out of the market, increasing the proportion of bad risks, and therefore the premiums, even further.
2. **Moral hazard**: this is a problem of hidden action, where one party to a transaction may take actions that the other cannot observe after they have entered into an agreement, which may lead the uninformed party to trade less than it otherwise would want. Moral hazard problems are common in insurance markets. An individual who has taken out home insurance may be less careful about protecting their property, which could increase the probability of being burgled, which will increase the insurance company's costs.[21]

Another type of problem associated with asymmetric information is the **principal–agent problem**. This arises when a principal (e.g. an employer) delegates a task to an agent (e.g. an employee), but cannot observe the actions of the agent, and therefore cannot ensure that the principal's objectives are maximized.[22] The agent will typically have more information than the principal and may not always act in the principal's best interest, particularly if this involves a cost.

[19] We can think of imperfect information as a situation in which everyone is equally ignorant, whereas with asymmetric information, one party is more ignorant than the other.

[20] The seminal paper outlining the nature of this problem was written by George Akerlof (1970) and focused on the problem of asymmetric information in the market for used cars.

[21] We discuss the problems of adverse selection and moral hazard in the context of healthcare in Chapter 8.

[22] The principal–agent problem is discussed in the context of state ownership in Chapter 7.

The requirement of perfect information also extends to information about the future. Many decisions we make involve **risk** or **uncertainty**—most of us do not know how much healthcare we will need to consume over the course of our lives, or how much money we will need to save for our retirement. Risk refers to situations where the probability distribution of future outcomes is known—for example, we can estimate the probability that it will rain tomorrow. Uncertainty refers to situations where the probability distribution of future outcomes is not known. Risk can be quantified, whereas uncertainty cannot.[23] The presence of risk and uncertainty creates a need for insurance, but markets will not always be able to provide insurance, or to provide the efficient level of insurance (see Box 2.6).[24] In some circumstances, government-provided social insurance may be needed to mitigate certain risks—for example, the risk of unemployment or poverty.[25]

In some cases, the market may be able to provide the necessary information—for example, through price comparison websites, product reviews, or consumer magazines.[26] In other

Box 2.6 The efficiency of private insurance markets

The market supply of insurance depends on the probability of a loss and the costs associated with that loss. Suppose a street has 100 residents and the probability that any house on that street will be broken into in a given year is 1 per cent. If a house is broken into, the cost to the individual will be £2,000. The expected loss is therefore 1%×£2,000=£20. If the insurance company charges each resident £20 per year, this will be just enough to cover the loss for the individual who has their house broken into.

The premium is the price that individuals will have to pay for an insurance policy in a competitive market. Formally, an actuarially fair premium is defined as:

$$P_i = (1+\alpha)\pi_i L$$

where α is a factor that covers the additional administrative costs of the insurance provider, π_i is the probability of a loss for individual i, and L is the value of that loss (so $\pi_i L$ represents the expected loss).

Private insurance markets will only operate efficiently if the following conditions hold:

1. The probabilities must be independent: the probability of one individual suffering a loss must be independent of the probability of anyone else suffering a loss.
2. The probability must be less than 1: if the probability is 1, there is certainty.
3. The probability must be known or it must be possible to estimate it from available information.
4. There can be no problems of adverse selection or moral hazard.

When one or more of these conditions fail to hold, this can lead to missing or incomplete markets for insurance.

[23] This distinction between risk and uncertainty was originally made by Frank Knight (1921).

[24] See Barr (2020: ch. 4) for a more detailed discussion of the issues that arise in the supply and demand for insurance.

[25] The topic of social insurance is discussed in more detail in Chapters 11 and 12.

[26] For example, in the UK, the consumer magazine *Which?* carries out detailed reviews of a range of consumer goods and services.

cases, dealing with problems of imperfect and asymmetric information may require government intervention through regulation (e.g. on food safety, minimum standards, or information disclosure requirements) or mandatory insurance (e.g. for car insurance). As we will see in Chapter 8, when we look at the arguments for government intervention in healthcare, compulsory health insurance is one of the main mechanisms for dealing with problems of adverse selection in the market for health insurance.

2.3.4 Departures from the strict rationality assumptions

One of the fundamental assumptions in neoclassical consumer theory is that individuals are rational, self-interested utility-maximizers. They are assumed to have well-defined preferences, are able to correctly identify the consumption bundle that will maximize their utility—given their preferences and budget constraint—and will choose that consumption bundle. Developments in the field of behavioural economics, which brings together insights from economics and psychology, have brought these assumptions into question. Are individuals really able to collect and process all the information required to make a utility-maximizing choice? Even if they are able to identify the optimal choice, can they then translate this choice into action?

Bounded rationality captures the idea that individual rationality is limited by the information people have available and their ability to process that information. This, in turn, will depend on factors including the complexity of the information, the time horizon of the decision problem, and individual cognitive and time limitations. Real-world decisions may therefore fall short of the utility-maximizing ideal. Problems of bounded rationality may manifest themselves in individuals adopting **rules of thumb** to guide their behaviour—for example, saving 20 per cent of their income, regardless of their level of income and their particular needs and wants. Framing effects, endowment effects, and loss aversion are some other examples of individual behaviour that fails to conform to the neoclassical ideal (see Box 2.7).

Box 2.7 Irrational behaviour?

The behavioural economics literature is vast. Here we describe a small selection of some of the 'behavioural biases' that have been identified, where individual behaviour does not conform with the assumptions or predictions of neoclassical consumer theory.[27]

- **Endowment effect**: individuals tend to value goods that they own more highly, which leads to a mismatch between the amount individuals are willing to pay for a good and the amount they are willing to accept to give up a good.
- **Framing effects**: the way in which a choice is described and how information is presented affects the choices individuals make. For example, whether information is presented as a loss or a gain will typically lead to different decisions.

[27] For a more detailed discussion, see some of the works on this topic provided in the Further Reading.

- **Anchoring effect**: individual choices or judgements are influenced by reference points, typically pieces of information which may be completely irrelevant to the decision being made.[28]
- **Loss aversion**: individuals treat losses and gains differently in their decisions—in particular, they tend to prefer avoiding losses to receiving a gain of the same magnitude.
- **Hyperbolic discounting**: hyperbolic **utility functions** involve a relatively high discount rate over short horizons (e.g. the present) and a relatively low discount rate over long horizons (e.g. in the future).[29] These types of preferences can explain seemingly inconsistent individual behaviour—for example, where an individual may state that they plan to start an aggressive saving plan next year, but once next year arrives, they decide to postpone their saving for another year.[30]

Bounded willpower refers to situations where, although individuals know what decision will maximize their welfare, they fail to act accordingly. We often face problems of self-control, where we fail to carry out plans we have made that we know are in our own best interests. This can help explain why many of us may fail to exercise as much or eat as healthily as we know we should, and why many people fail to save enough for our retirement.

Bounded rationality and bounded willpower imply a further role for government intervention. This could involve regulation to make the choices that individuals face simpler, establishing commitment devices (e.g. to encourage individual saving), or establishing automatic enrolment schemes (e.g. in some employer pension schemes).[31]

2.3.5 Missing markets

Under the first-best conditions, markets will provide any good or service for which individuals are willing to pay a price that covers the costs of production. In reality, there are many instances where, even though individual buyers would be willing to pay for a good or service and sellers would be willing to produce it, no such market exists—these are referred to as missing markets. We have already encountered one example above, in the case of public goods. In extreme cases, no market to provide such goods will exist because the producers cannot guarantee that consumers will pay for the good due to the free rider problem.

Markets may also fail to provide insurance for certain types of risks that are uninsurable (e.g. risks related to pandemics, house prices, or having children). In section 2.3.3, we reviewed the conditions required for private insurance markets to operate efficiently. When one or more of these conditions fail, governments may need to intervene to guarantee that

[28] In a classic study by Tversky and Kahneman (1974), individuals were asked to estimate the percentage of African countries that were members of the United Nations. Before giving their estimate, they were shown a number on a roulette wheel. Participants who saw the roulette wheel stop on the number 10 gave a much lower estimate (on average, they estimated 25 per cent) than participants who had seen the roulette wheel stop at 65 (who gave an estimate of 45 per cent, on average).

[29] The discount rate measures the value an individual places on consumption today versus consumption in the future.

[30] These types of preferences are particularly important in the context of saving for retirement, which we discuss in Chapter 11.

[31] The advantages of automatic enrolment into employer pension schemes are discussed in Chapter 11.

some form of insurance is provided. Capital market imperfections may mean that certain types of loans (e.g. student loans) are not provided.[32]

Instances of missing markets may require governments to intervene to provide the good or service directly or to finance or facilitate its provision by private firms.

2.3.6 Distortionary taxation

According to the Second Fundamental Theorem of Welfare Economics, a more equitable allocation can be achieved by redistributing the initial resources in the economy and then allowing markets to operate, which will ensure the final allocation is Pareto efficient. However, governments need to be able to use **non-distortionary taxation** to reallocate initial resources. A tax is non-distortionary if there is no way that individuals can change their behaviour to reduce the amount of tax they pay. In practice, most taxes, as we will see in more detail in Chapter 13, are distortionary. For example, if you want to reduce the amount of income tax you pay, you can (in theory) choose to work fewer hours. Individuals can reduce the amount of fuel taxes they pay by driving less and reducing their consumption of fuel. Distortionary taxes lead to inefficiency.

An example of a non-distortionary tax is a **lump-sum tax**. This is a type of fixed tax that does not depend on any characteristics of the entity being taxed. An example of a lump-sum tax was the Community Charge (or poll tax) introduced in the UK in the 1990s, which was a single, flat-rate per capita tax that all adults in the UK were required to pay. The tax was highly unpopular and was abolished three years later. Lump-sum taxes are highly inequitable, since everyone is required to pay the same amount, regardless of their income or other resources. They are therefore rarely used by governments in practice, which limits the practical applicability of the Second Fundamental Theorem of Welfare Economics.

In each of these cases, where the conditions of real-world markets deviate from the first-best assumptions, government intervention may be justified in order to help steer the market towards the efficient outcome. However, we should not assume that government intervention can always increase efficiency. Just as markets may fail, so can governments, and we discuss some of the sources of government failure in more detail in Chapter 4.

2.4 Government intervention to promote equity and social justice

The discussion so far has focused on the role of government in increasing economic efficiency. But governments and societies do not just care about efficiency or maximizing the size of the economic pie; they also care about equity or how the pie is distributed. Since the 1980s, inequality between countries has been falling, but inequality within countries has been increasing. Across the OECD, the richest 10 per cent now earn roughly 9.5 times the income of the poorest 10 per cent, whereas in the 1980s this ratio was 7.1 (Cingano, 2014). The government plays an important redistributive role, through tax and spending policies, as we will see in Chapter 12. In this section, we are going to introduce some of the different concepts of equity and how these can be incorporated into the framework we have been analysing. But first, we need to understand why an efficient allocation is not necessarily and equitable one.

[32] The challenge with market provision of student loans is discussed in Chapter 9.

2.4.1 Equity and the Second Fundamental Theorem of Welfare Economics

For an economy with a given set of resources, there are many possible allocations that are Pareto efficient. However, these may not all be equally desirable. To illustrate this point, consider a simple economy with two individuals, Ana and Ben. The **utility possibility frontier (UPF)** in Figure 2.5 illustrates the maximum level of utility that Ana can achieve, given Ben's utility. All points on the UPF are Pareto efficient, whereas all points within the curve are Pareto suboptimal.

Suppose that for a given initial allocation of resources and given individual preferences, the two individuals trade in the market and the market outcome is point F. This point is Pareto efficient, since it is located on the UPF, but we might feel it is not the 'best' outcome because person Ben's utility is so much higher than person Ana's. A point like E might be more desirable from society's point of view. The question is whether it is possible to change the final outcome from F to E—in other words, can this society achieve a more equitable outcome, without sacrificing efficiency? According to the Second Fundamental Theorem of Welfare Economics, the answer is yes.

The Second Fundamental Theorem of Welfare Economics essentially says that a more equitable allocation can be achieved by redistributing the initial resources in the economy and then allowing markets to operate, which will ensure the final allocation is Pareto efficient. As we saw in section 2.2.1 above, this relies on the condition that both individual preferences and the production technology are convex. Convexity means there are no increasing returns in production and that individual consumers will have a single utility-maximizing bundle for a given set of prices and income. In other words, it implies that for a given set of prices and resources, each consumer will be willing to buy a specific (unique) consumption bundle and firms will be willing to supply a specific (unique) bundle of goods.

The Second Fundamental Theorem of Welfare Economics implies that we do not need to sacrifice efficiency for greater equity. However, it relies on a set of fairly strong conditions, including the requirement that markets are perfectly competitive and that the government can use non-distortionary taxation to redistribute resources. In practice, it is generally assumed that in most situations there is likely to be an **equity–efficiency trade-off**: promoting greater equity implies sacrificing some efficiency. For example, a welfare programme that aims to reduce poverty may also have a negative impact on individuals' incentives to work and save, thus leading to inefficiency. But the goals of equity and efficiency need not be mutually incompatible (see Box 2.8).

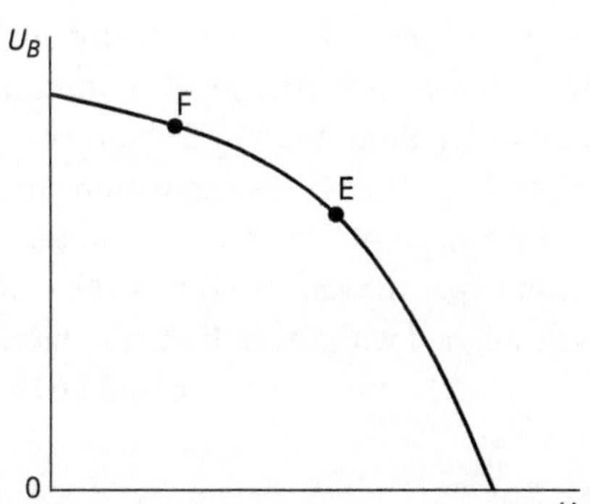

Figure 2.5 Utility possibility frontier

Box 2.8 Do policymakers need to sacrifice efficiency for greater equity?

The equity–efficiency trade-off is at the heart of many economic policy debates. But these two objectives are not always mutually incompatible: there are situations where promoting equity can also lead to an increase in efficiency.

Poverty is associated with higher crime rates across countries (Dunn, 2025) and crime imposes costs on society. Crimes such as theft and burglary, for example, involve a cost for individuals, including the time and money costs of replacing stolen items or filling out insurance claims, the costs of taking additional precautionary measures such as investing in alarm systems, and the emotional cost of the crime itself. Crime also imposes a wider cost on society, including the resources devoted to fighting crime (e.g. investing in policing). Policies that promote equity by reducing poverty will therefore increase efficiency as well.

Many social insurance schemes, designed to address risks that markets will typically fail to provide adequate insurance for (e.g. unemployment or poverty), can also increase both efficiency—by addressing market failures—and equity, redistributing resources from people who do not experience these risks to those who do.

More generally, if individuals have altruistic preferences and care about the well-being of others, then policies that increase other people's welfare, such as income **redistribution** policies, will also increase efficiency and social welfare.

The Second Fundamental Theorem of Welfare Economics is compatible with multiple conceptions of equity. This is part of its appeal: it does not require us to commit to a particular view of equity. While most of us have an intuitive understanding of what a fair and equitable society would look like, settling on a precise definition of equity is more challenging. This is the question we turn to below.

2.4.2 What do we mean by equity?

Equity is a multifaceted concept which incorporates notions of fairness or justice, and rewards for effort or merit. Different theories of society have different views about what equity means.[33] A detailed discussion of these different views is beyond the scope of this book. Instead, here we will focus on defining a few key concepts that will be useful for our analysis through the book.

One important distinction is between the concepts of **horizontal equity** and **vertical equity**. Horizontal equity is essentially about the equal treatment of individuals who are equal in all relevant respects, so there should be no discrimination based on characteristics such as gender, race, or ethnicity. In the context of taxation, for example, this implies that individuals who earn the same income should pay the same amount in taxes or face the same tax burdens. Vertical equity is more closely aligned with the notion of redistribution as it implies that individuals who are unequal in any relevant respects should be treated unequally. Individuals

[33] Three broad categories of theories of society were introduced in Chapter 1: libertarian, liberal, and collectivist or social. For a discussion of how these different theories conceive of equity, see, for example, Barr (2020).

with greater needs should receive more resources; or individuals with higher incomes should pay more taxes.

But what does it mean for individuals to be treated equally? One concept that we will draw on throughout this book is the concept of **equality of opportunity**. Equality of opportunity is closely related to the notion of social justice. It captures the idea that everyone, regardless of their own personal circumstances and socioeconomic background, should have fair and equal access to the same chances in life, whether in access to healthcare, education, security, etc. Equality of opportunity may not translate into equality of outcomes; this will depend, in part, on individual effort and the choices people make. The concept of equality of opportunity draws a distinction between effort or choice factors, which individuals have some control over, and chance or circumstance factors. The latter can lead to unfair differences in outcomes.[34]

2.4.3 Measuring social welfare

How can we measure the welfare of society? Within the neoclassical framework, social welfare depends on the total quantity of goods and services available in the economy (efficiency) and how these are distributed (equity). **Social welfare functions** provide a mechanism for incorporating both efficiency and equity into decision-making. A social welfare function summarizes the well-being or welfare of society as a function of the welfare of the individuals in that society.

Social welfare functions are compatible with different concepts of equity and the form of the social welfare function will reflect different attitudes towards inequality. Two special cases of social welfare functions are:

1. The **utilitarian social welfare function**: social welfare is defined as the sum of individual welfare or utilities,

$$W = U_1 + U_2 + \ldots + U_N$$

All individual utilities are given equal weight. This implies transfers between individuals should be made as long as the total utility gain outweighs the total utility loss.

2. The **Rawlsian social welfare function**: social welfare depends on the welfare of the worst-off member of society,

$$W = \min\{U_1, U_2, \ldots, U_N\}$$

This social welfare function is named after the American political philosopher, John Rawls. Rawls' theory of justice provides an alternative to the utilitarian approach. It is based on the ethical principles that free and rational individuals would agree to starting from an original position of equality. Behind what Rawls called the 'veil of ignorance', no one knows their position in society, their social class or status, what assets or wealth they will have, or their natural abilities (Rawls, 1971). Rawls argued that, from this starting point, individuals would want to ensure the welfare of the least well-off member of society was maximized.

[34] See, for example, Roemer (2000, 2002) for a discussion of the canonical normative model of inequality of opportunity.

One criticism of social welfare functions is their reliance on interpersonal comparisons of utility. In order to be able to aggregate individual utilities into a single function, we need to be able to make the utilities of different individuals comparable. But utility is traditionally an ordinal concept rather than a cardinal one, in the sense that utility values are only useful insofar as they provide a ranking of alternatives, but the actual level of utility itself is meaningless.[35]

Social welfare functions are based on individual preferences and therefore assume that individuals are the best judges of their own welfare. But individuals are notoriously bad at understanding the consequences of their decisions and often make choices that are not in their best long-term interest. Wearing a seatbelt in cars, for example, only became widespread once it was mandated by law. Some authors have argued against social welfare functions based on individual preferences in favour of more objective measures of well-being. Sen (1985, 1999) and Nussbaum (2001) advocate a capabilities-approach to measuring welfare, where capabilities are defined as the opportunities or real freedoms that individuals have to achieve their potential 'doings and beings' (Robeyns, 2021). Nussbaum's (2001) list of Central Human Functional Capabilities includes elements such as: bodily health and integrity; the development and expression of senses, imagination, and thought; emotional health; play; and control over one's environment.[36]

2.5 A critique of the neoclassical story of the role of government in the economy

Neoclassical economic theory provides a useful framework for thinking about the role of government in the economy. According to this school of thought, there are two reasons why government intervention in the economy may be justified: to increase efficiency and to promote equity and social justice. However, this theory is not without its critics. In this section, we are going to focus on two sets of criticisms: the first is based on the Pareto efficiency criterion; the second is based on the concept of markets within this framework.

2.5.1 Limitations of the Pareto efficiency criterion

Neoclassical economic theory tells us that, under certain conditions, competitive markets will lead to a Pareto-efficient allocation of resources, where it is not possible to make at least one person better off without making anyone else worse off. The Pareto criterion is intuitively appealing: if we could redistribute resources in a way that would make some people better off and no one would be made worse off, then surely we should do this? It is also seemingly value

[35] If the bundle of goods A gives Alfie five units of utility while the bundle of goods B gives him eight units of utility, this tells us that Alfie values bundle B more highly than bundle A. If bundle A gives Leni six units of utility, we cannot really say whether she values bundle A more highly than Alfie does, since a unit of utility may mean something different to Leni and Alfie.

[36] These Central Human Functional Capabilities provided the basis for the United Nations' Sustainable Development Goals.

neutral, in that it does not assume a particular view of equity or what a fair and just society would look like. However, there are three key criticisms:

1. The Pareto efficiency criterion is inherently individualistic, in the sense that individual welfare is the only thing that matters. It does not consider the welfare of other social entities, such as families or communities, or only insofar as they are made up of individuals—but there is no 'society' above individuals. Moreover, animals and the environment only have value insofar as they contribute to individual well-being. But as a society, we might feel that protecting animal welfare and the environment are important and have value over and above the value that individuals place on them.
2. Individuals are assumed to be the best judges of their own welfare. In this respect, the Pareto criterion embodies the principle of consumer sovereignty, the idea that individuals know their wants and needs, and how best to satisfy them. But do we always know what is best for us? There are many areas where individual knowledge may be lacking and where we may not be best placed to make sensible judgements about what would enhance our welfare. We mentioned the example of wearing seatbelts above, but we could think more broadly about choices we might make around our health or how much time (and effort) to devote to our education.[37] Even when we do know what is best for us or what would improve our welfare, we sometimes lack the willpower to actually do what's best. For example, we might not exercise as much, eat as healthily, or save as much as we feel we should.
3. Lastly, the Pareto efficiency criterion implies nothing about the distribution of income or resources. Social welfare is increased if the welfare of at least one individual has increased and no one else is made worse off. This implies that a reallocation that made the wealthiest people in society better off could be a Pareto improvement, as long as it did not make anyone else worse off. If we care about inequality, we might struggle to accept that this reallocation would in fact be considered an improvement in any sense. This limitation of the Pareto criterion is summed up perfectly in this quote by the Nobel Prize-winning economist, Amartya Sen:

> An economy can be [Pareto] optimal... even when some people are rolling in luxury and others are near starvation as long as the starvers cannot be made better off without cutting into the pleasures of the rich... In short, a society or an economy can be Pareto optimal and still be perfectly disgusting. (Sen, 1970: 22)

Does this mean we should abandon the Pareto criterion? Not necessarily. The Pareto criterion can still provide a useful tool for comparing policies, but it is important to keep in mind the implicit value judgements that underlie it. This suggests the Pareto criterion should not be used in isolation; rather, it should be combined with other criteria for evaluating the welfare impact of policies on society.

[37] Health and education are examples of what are known as **merit goods**. Merit goods are goods that individuals are likely to underconsume because they do not realize the full private benefits of doing so. Merit goods may also have wider social benefits (or positive externalities) associated with them.

2.5.2 Rethinking the nature of markets

How we think about the market will influence how we think about the role of government.[38] The market plays a central role within the neoclassical framework. The market mechanism facilitates the exchange of goods and services between consumers and producers; it is where the forces of demand and supply come together to determine the price and quantity of goods and services traded in the economy.

Chang (2002) criticizes this idea that market exchanges are in some sense the natural buildings blocks of human economic activity and that the market as an institution takes precedence over all other institutions—including the government. This is what he calls the 'market primacy assumption' that is embedded in neoclassical theory. Economic historians have shown that markets were not a dominant feature of society until the rise of capitalism. In fact, the government played a key role in the development and creation of markets, particularly during the early stages of capitalism (Polanyi, 2024). For example, enclosure laws were a necessary building block for the development of free markets in the UK.[39] In the USA, the government also played a crucial role in establishing property rights and supporting investment in critical infrastructure, such as railways and telegraphy, that enabled markets to develop (Chang, 2002). By assuming the market comes first, we are relegating other institutions—including the government, firms, and voluntary organizations—to a secondary role, rather than thinking about the role that each institution is best placed to play in the economy.

In neoclassical economic theory, the market is the economy. In reality, the market is one of many institutions that make up our modern economies, all of which have a role to play. And markets are unlikely to be the right institution for all exchanges. Markets are not morally neutral; market values change the character of an exchange or relationship. Putting a price on something not only has the potential to lead to unfairness; it also changes the value of the thing being marketized. This is the point made by the political philosopher Michael Sandel (2012). He provides several examples where imposing market values risks degrading the nature of the exchange or relationship, including organ donation and the growing trend to pay others to queue for us. Sandel discusses one example in particular that really illustrates the potential corrupting influence of markets. This example involved an Israeli daycare centre which, faced with the problem of parents arriving late to pick up their children, decided to introduce a fine. However, rather than the number of late pick-ups falling, these actually increased in response to the fine; the fine essentially turned the relationship between parents and the centre into a financial transaction and made the behaviour of turning up late acceptable. Eventually the centre reverted back to its old system without the fine, but the damage had been done: parents continued to turn up late because the introduction of market values (even if only briefly) had replaced a relationship based on shared values of collective responsibility with a transactional relationship.

Neoclassical economic theory is also based on a particular notion of what the ideal market is. The ideal market *is* the perfectly competitive market, with its large number of buyers and sellers—all of whom have full information—and no barriers to entry or exit. This definition of the ideal market then provides the basis for how we define 'market failures'.

[38] The discussion in this section summarizes some of the key criticisms laid out more fully in Chang (2002); this article is in the suggested Further Reading at the end of the chapter.

[39] The enclosure laws were a series of legal Acts introduced in England, starting in the seventeenth century. They enclosed what had been common land, which then became the property of individual landowners.

Massive inequality and environmental degradation are not considered market failures in the traditional sense, whereas imperfect competition is. However, as a society, we might feel that a mechanism that brings about significant inequalities and the destruction of environmental resources on which we rely for our health and well-being is in fact failing in some sense. At the same time, economists such as Joseph Schumpeter would argue that imperfect competition is necessary to foster innovation and could therefore be seen as a sign of a well-functioning market. Markets also do not operate in the mechanistic way the theory assumes; markets are complex, dynamic systems (Raworth, 2017). The neoclassical theory of the market is not the only legitimate theory.

Crucially, 'the market' is not an objective and impartial concept. No market is truly free: there are rules about who can participate and under what conditions, and these rules may vary across countries and over time. Establishing these rules is a political exercise. It is in this sense that markets are, as Chang argues, political constructs: 'they are defined by a range of formal and informal institutions that embody certain rights and obligations, whose legitimacy (and therefore whose contestability) is ultimately determined in the realm of politics' (Chang, 2002: 553). How we define competitive free markets will ultimately determine what we consider a government intervention. Chang (2002) gives the example of child labour and asks whether a ban on child labour should be considered a government intervention. Is a 'free market' one in which children are 'free' to supply their labour if the market wage exceeds their reservation wage? Or is child labour considered a violation of fundamental human rights, in which case questions about how banning child labour would impact on market efficiency would not even be considered?

Conclusion

Why do governments intervene in the economy? At a basic level, some form of government intervention is needed to establish and enforce property rights and the rules that govern exchanges between individuals, as well as to defend a country's economic gains from outsiders. Beyond this minimal state, the dominant rationale for government intervention in the economy is based on neoclassical economic theory, where the market plays a central role. In this chapter, we reviewed the conditions under which competitive markets will lead to a Pareto-efficient allocation of resources, where it is not possible to make at least one person better off without making anyone else worse off. We then analysed the two main arguments for government intervention offered by neoclassical economists: to increase efficiency and to promote equity and social justice. We also reviewed some of the criticisms of this approach, focusing in particular on the implicit assumptions that underlie the Pareto efficiency criterion and the concept of competitive markets.

So where does this leave our understanding of what the appropriate role of government in the economy is? As we saw in Chapter 1, the extent of government intervention varies across countries, and it has changed over time. Neoclassical economic theory does not tell us where the boundary between the market and the government should lie; ultimately, this will be shaped by historical, political, social, and institutional factors. But the theory can provide a framework for understanding why governments do what they do and, therefore, provide a benchmark against which to assess different policy interventions. We will be drawing on this framework in our analysis of specific areas of government intervention in subsequent chapters.

Questions for discussion

1. What does it mean to say an allocation is efficient? Under what conditions will efficiency be maximized?
2. 'No state more extensive than the minimal state is justified.' Do you agree with this statement? Why or why not?
3. Is Pareto efficiency a good criterion to use to evaluate different policy interventions?
4. Will a policy designed to promote equity always imply less efficiency?
5. Is it possible to evaluate a policy in a truly objective manner, without making any value judgements?

Further reading

On the equity–efficiency trade-off:

Fleurbaey, M. (2009). Beyond GDP: The quest for a measure of social welfare. *Journal of Economic Literature*, *47*(4), 1029–1075.

Le Grand, J. (1990). Equity versus efficiency: The elusive trade-off. *Ethics*, *100*(3), 554–568.

Le Grand, J. (1991). *Equity and choice: An essay in economics and applied philosophy*. Routledge.

Okun, A. M. (1975). *Equality and efficiency: The big trade-off*. Brookings Institution.

For a discussion of the theory of competitive markets, efficiency, and welfare economics:

Frank, R., & Cartwright, E. (2021). *Microeconomics and behaviour* (3rd ed.). McGraw-Hill.

Johansson, P. O. (1991). *An introduction to modern welfare economics*. Cambridge University Press. This book provides a non-technical discussion of the theory of modern welfare economics.

Hindriks, J., & Myles, G. (2013). *Intermediate public economics* (2nd ed.). MIT Press. Chapter 2 provides a more advanced discussion of the theory underlying the two theorems of welfare economics.

Varian, H. (2014). *Intermediate microeconomics: A modern approach* (9th ed.). W. W. Norton.

For a more detailed discussion of the failure of private markets and insurance:

Barr, N. (2020). *Economics of the welfare state*. Oxford University Press. See chapter 4.

On behavioural economics and policy:

Congdon, W., Kling, J. R., & Mullainathan, S. (2011). *Policy and choice: Public finance through the lens of behavioural economics*. Brookings Institution. See especially chapters 2 and 3.

Kahneman, D. (2003). Maps of bounded rationality: Psychology for behavioural economics. *American Economic Review*, *93*(5), 1449–1475.

Kahneman, D. (2012). *Thinking, fast and slow*. Penguin.

Leicester, A., Levell, P., & Rasul, I. (2012). *Tax and benefit policy: Insights from behavioural economics*. Institute for Fiscal Studies commentary C125. See especially chapters 2 and 3.

Thaler, R. H., & Sunstein, C. R. (2021). *Nudge: The final edition*. Penguin.

For a critique of neoclassical economic theory:

Chang, Ha-Joon (2002). Breaking the mould: An institutionalist political economy alternative to the neo-liberal theory of the market and the state. *Cambridge Journal of Economics*, *26*, 539–559.

Raworth, K. (2017). *Doughnut economics: Seven ways to think like a 21st-century economist*. Chelsea Green Publishing.

Sandel, M. J. (2012). *What money can't buy: The moral limits of markets*. Farrar, Straus, & Giroux.

Bibliography

Akerlof, G. A. (1970). The market for 'lemons': Quality uncertainty and the market mechanism. *Quarterly Journal of Economics, 84*(3), 488–500.

Chang, Ha-Joon (2002). Breaking the mould: An institutionalist political economy alternative to the neo-liberal theory of the market and the state. *Cambridge Journal of Economics, 26*, 539–559.

Chang, Ha-Joon (2014). *Economics: A user's guide*. Pelican.

Cingano, F. (2014). *Trends in income inequality and its impact on economic growth*. Organization for Economic Cooperation and Development. Social, employment and migration working papers, no. 163. Available at: https://doi.org/10.1787/5jxrjncwxv6j-en

Congdon, W., Kling, J. R., & Mullainathan, S. (2011). *Policy and choice: Public finance through the lens of behavioural economics*. Brookings Institution Press.

Desmarais-Tremblay, M., Johnson, M., & Sturn, R. (2023). Mapping the history of public economics in the twentieth century: An introduction to the special issue. *European Journal of the History of Economic Thought, 30*(5), 689–712. https://doi.org/10.1080/09672567.2023.2248319

Dunn, A. (2025). The poverty–crime nexus revisited: Absolute poverty, relative poverty, and crime rates in 105 countries. *International Journal of Comparative and Applied Criminal Justice, 49*(2), 107–123.

Feldstein, M. (2002). The transformation of public economics research: 1970–2000. *Journal of Public Economics, 86*(3), 319–326. https://doi.org/10.1016/S0047-2727(01)00190-6

Frank, R., & Cartwright, E. (2021). *Microeconomics and behaviour* (3rd ed.). McGraw-Hill.

Hall, T. E. (2014). *Aftermath: The unintended consequences of public policies*. Cato Institute.

Hicks, J. R. (1939). The foundations of welfare economics. *Economic Journal, 49*(196), 696–712.

Hindriks, J., & Myles, G. (2013). *Intermediate public economics* (2nd ed.). MIT Press.

Kaldor, N. (1939). Welfare propositions of economics and interpersonal comparisons of utility. *Economic Journal, 49*(195), 549–552.

Keech, W. R., & Munger, M. C. (2015). The anatomy of government failure. *Public Choice, 164*, 1–42. https://doi.org/10.1007/s11127-015-0262-y

Knight, F. (1921). *Risk, uncertainty and profit*. Houghton Mifflin.

Lipsey, R. G., & Lancaster, K. (1956). The general theory of second best. *Review of Economic Studies, 24*(1), 11–32.

Neck, R. (2022). Neoclassical economics: Origins, evolution, and critique. In D. McCallum (Ed.), *The Palgrave handbook of the history of human sciences* (pp. 1501–1540). Palgrave Macmillan. Available at: https://doi.org/10.1007/978-981-15-4106-3_5-1

Nozick, R. (1974). *Anarchy, state and utopia*. Basil Blackwell.

Nussbaum, M. C. (2001). *Women and human development: The capabilities approach*. Cambridge University Press.

Polanyi, K. (2024). *The great transformation: The political and economic origins of our time*. Penguin Random House.

Rawls, J. (1971). *A theory of justice*. Harvard University Press.

Raworth, K. (2017). *Doughnut economics: Seven ways to think like a 21st-century economist*. Chelsea Green Publishing.

Robeyns, I. (2021). The capability approach. In G. Berik & E. Kongar (Eds.), *The Routledge handbook of feminist economics* (pp. 72–80). Routledge.

Roemer, J. E. (2002). Equality of opportunity: A progress report, *Social Choice and Welfare, 19*, 455–471.

Roemer, J. E. (2000). *Equality of opportunity*. Harvard University Press.

Sandel, M. J. (2012). *What money can't buy: The moral limits of markets*. Farrar, Straus, & Giroux.

Sen, A. (1970). *Collective choice and social welfare*. Harvard University Press.

Sen, A. (1985). *Commodities and capabilities*. North-Holland.

Sen, A. (1999). *Development as freedom*. Knopf.

Stiglitz, J., E., & Rosengard, J. K. (2015). *Economics of the public sector* (4th ed.). W. W. Norton.

Tanzi, V. (2011). *Government versus markets: The changing economic role of the state*. Cambridge University Press.

Tversky, A., & Kahneman, D. (1974). Judgement under uncertainty: Heuristics and biases. *Science, 185*(4157), 1124–1131.

Varian, H. (2014). *Intermediate microeconomics: A modern approach* (9th ed.). W. W. Norton.

The marginal rate of substitution and marginal utility

The marginal rate of substitution between two goods, X and Y, is the maximum amount of good Y that a consumer is willing to give up in order to obtain one additional unit of good X, while keeping the level of utility constant. Formally,

$$MRS_{XY} = -\frac{\Delta y}{\Delta x} = \left|\frac{\Delta y}{\Delta x}\right|$$

where the Greek letter Δ is used to denote 'change'.

The marginal rate of substitution usually falls as we move down along an indifference curve—this is the principle of diminishing marginal rate of substitution. This is because the more of one good the consumer has, the less they value additional units of that good. If you have two biscuits and you are given one additional biscuit, that biscuit is likely to increase your utility or satisfaction by more than if you have 10 biscuits and you are given one additional biscuit (assuming you like biscuits to begin with). The eleventh biscuit will still have a positive impact on your utility, but this impact will be smaller than the impact of the third biscuit you received.

A utility function is a formula that assigns a level of utility to individual consumption bundles, where utility is the level of satisfaction that a consumer gets from a given consumption bundle. For any two goods, X and Y, utility (U) will be some function of the quantities of these two goods:

$$U = U(X,Y)$$

As the quantity of a good the individual has changes, utility will also change. Marginal utility (MU) measures the change in total utility as the quantity of the good consumed changes. The marginal rate of substitution can be expressed as the ratio of the marginal utilities of:

$$MRS_{XY} = \frac{MU_X}{MU_Y}$$

3
The evolution of the public sector

Learning objectives

By the end of this chapter, you will be able to:

3.1 Explain how the size of the public sector is measured and discuss the limitations of the measures used.
3.2 Describe how the size and composition of government spending has evolved over time.
3.3 Describe how government revenues have evolved over time.
3.4 Critically discuss the explanations offered by different theories of public sector growth for the evolution of the public sector.

Introduction

The role and size of the public sector has changed dramatically since the end of the nineteenth century. Across much of western Europe, North America, Australasia, and Japan, governments have grown significantly during this period: average government spending as a share of GDP increased from 9.8 per cent in 1890 to 47 per cent in 2022.[1] Government spending grew particularly rapidly in the aftermath of the Second World War, driven largely by increased spending on education, health, and social protection. Since the 1980s, the pace of public expenditure growth has started to slow, but this has not been consistent across countries: whereas public spending relative to GDP has continued to grow in some countries, in others it has started to fall.

What explains this evolution of the public sector? In Chapter 2, we looked at the rationale for government intervention in the economy. We saw how, from a neoclassical perspective, governments have a role to play in addressing market failures, to increase market efficiency, and in promoting a more equitable distribution of resources. These arguments provide some useful insights: understanding why governments exist should also help us understand why they have grown. However, to fully understand the evolution of the public sector, we need to think more broadly about what factors and actors shape the size of government, and how their roles may have changed over time.

We start by examining some of the commonly used measures of the size of the public sector in section 3.1. In sections 3.2 and 3.3 we paint a picture of the evolution of the public

[1] Based on data from IMF (2023)—with minor processing by Our World in Data. A similar pattern of public expenditure growth can also be seen in some Latin American countries, such as Argentina and Brazil. For the rest of the world, the patterns of public expenditure growth are more varied.

sector, by looking at how the level and composition of public expenditure and government revenues have changed over time for a selection of countries. Section 3.4 then discusses a number of theories that have been proposed to explain the growth of the public sector.

3.1 Measuring the size of the public sector

If we want to analyse the evolution of the public sector, we need an appropriate measure of its size. Ideally, we would like a measure that captures the full impact of the public sector on the economy. This would include not only the various government-provided goods and services—such as education and healthcare—but also the impact of government regulations, taxes, and transfers on economic activity. In practice, however, we are constrained by the data available.

Most measures of the public sector are therefore based on government expenditure—the sum of all government consumption, investment and transfer expenditure. This includes government spending to provide goods and services, payments to government employees, government spending on infrastructure, R&D activities, grants, subsidies, and social benefits. Most measures reported are of *general* government expenditure, which covers expenditure at all levels of government—central, state (where applicable), and local. There are two main categories of government expenditure:

- **Exhaustive expenditures** include government spending on purchasing goods and services from the private sector, including labour and machinery.
- **Transfer expenditures** include spending on transfers to individuals (e.g. unemployment benefits, sickness benefits, and pensions) and subsidies to private sector firms.

The level of government expenditure provides an **absolute measure** of the size of the public sector. Government expenditure is likely to increase from one year to the next simply as a result of the general increase in the price level in the economy. If we want to see how the size of government has changed over time, we need to adjust our measure of government expenditure for inflation, using an appropriate price index. Alternatively, we can use a **relative measure** of the public sector based on government spending as a proportion of the size of the economy, typically measured using GDP. Government spending as a share of GDP provides an intuitive way of representing the size of government relative to the size of a country's economy, and facilitates comparisons over time and across countries. However, GDP is not the only way of measuring the size of an economy. An alternative would be to use gross national product (GNP), which includes net income receipts from abroad. GDP is generally perceived to be a better measure of a country's productive potential as it measures the resources available in the economy.

Based on this relative measure, the size of the public sector will depend on three factors: the absolute level of government spending (including both exhaustive and transfer expenditures); the level of GDP; and the rate of growth of public expenditure relative to the rate of growth of GDP. Transfer expenditures are not included in calculations of GDP, but exhaustive expenditures are, so increasing exhaustive expenditures will not only increase the absolute level of government spending but also directly increase GDP. Public spending may also have an impact on GDP by either stimulating or hampering economic growth; in theory, both effects are plausible, so this is ultimately an empirical question—though one on which so far there is no consensus (see Box 3.1).

Box 3.1 Does a larger government promote or hinder economic growth?

In theory, an increase in government spending in areas such as education and health, alongside investment in infrastructure and R&D, could help boost economic growth, by increasing levels of human and physical capital, leading to improvements in productivity. However, the need to raise revenues to finance this spending, through taxes or borrowing, could potentially reduce incentives to work, save, and invest, which would have a negative impact on growth. Whether larger governments are good or bad for economic growth is ultimately an empirical question, although research in this area has produced mixed results, largely due to differences in the definitions used and countries analysed. A recent study by Bergh and Henrekson (2011) has attempted to address some of the contradictory findings, by focusing on studies of rich countries that measure the size of government using either taxes or spending as a share of GDP. Their survey of the relevant studies suggests a negative relationship between government size and economic growth: a 10 percentage point increase in government size is associated with a 0.5–1 per cent lower annual growth rate. However, Bergh and Henrekson (2011) suggest this relationship is not necessarily causal, and explore why some governments are able to sustain high taxes and above average growth.

Source: Bergh and Henrekson (2011).

When thinking about how the public sector is measured, one important question is whether government-owned corporations should be included in the measure used. Should countries where the government owns and operates public utilities, such as water, gas, and electricity, or public transport systems, be considered to have a larger public sector than countries where these services are provided by the private sector? As Hindriks and Myles (2013) argue, this should depend on how these state-owned companies are run. If they are allowed to operate as profit-maximizing firms, then there is no reason to include them in our measure of the government, because the government in this case would simply be acting as a private shareholder, allowing the firm's managers to pursue their market objectives. If we were to include them in our measure of the size of government, then we would also be compelled to include all firms where the government has a stake or is a shareholder, no matter how small. However, if the government were to use the company to pursue other objectives, such as promoting the development of a particular region, boosting regional employment, or cross-subsidizing other government-provided products or services, then the company should be included in our measure of government size.

Government spending relative to GDP is the most widely used measure of the size of the public sector. It captures the resources that the government consumes and, therefore, provides some measure of the impact the government has on the economy. Since data on government expenditure and GDP are readily available for the majority of countries, this measure is also fairly easy to calculate, making it possible to analyse how the size of the public sector has evolved over time and how it varies across countries. However, there are areas of government activity where government expenditure may be small relative to the impact these activities have on the economy. The introduction of certain laws and regulations—for example, health and safety regulations, minimum wage laws, or maximum weekly working hours regulations—are likely to have an impact on the economy that is not fully reflected in the monetary cost of designing and implementing these policies. The full economic impact of these policies would need to take into account the impact on firms' costs, and any knock-on effects on hiring decisions and employment. So while government spending as a share of GDP is a useful measure, it is unlikely to fully reflect the impact the government has on the economy.

3.2 The evolution of public expenditure

The public sector has grown dramatically since the early twentieth century and this pattern of growth has been common across countries with quite different cultural, political, and institutional backgrounds. In this section, we review historical public expenditure data for a selection of industrially developed economies. We will look at both the evolution of total government spending and how the composition of spending has changed over time for some of the main categories of expenditure.[2]

Figure 3.1 plots the evolution of public expenditure as a proportion of GDP for six developed economies from the early nineteenth century up until 2022. While there is some

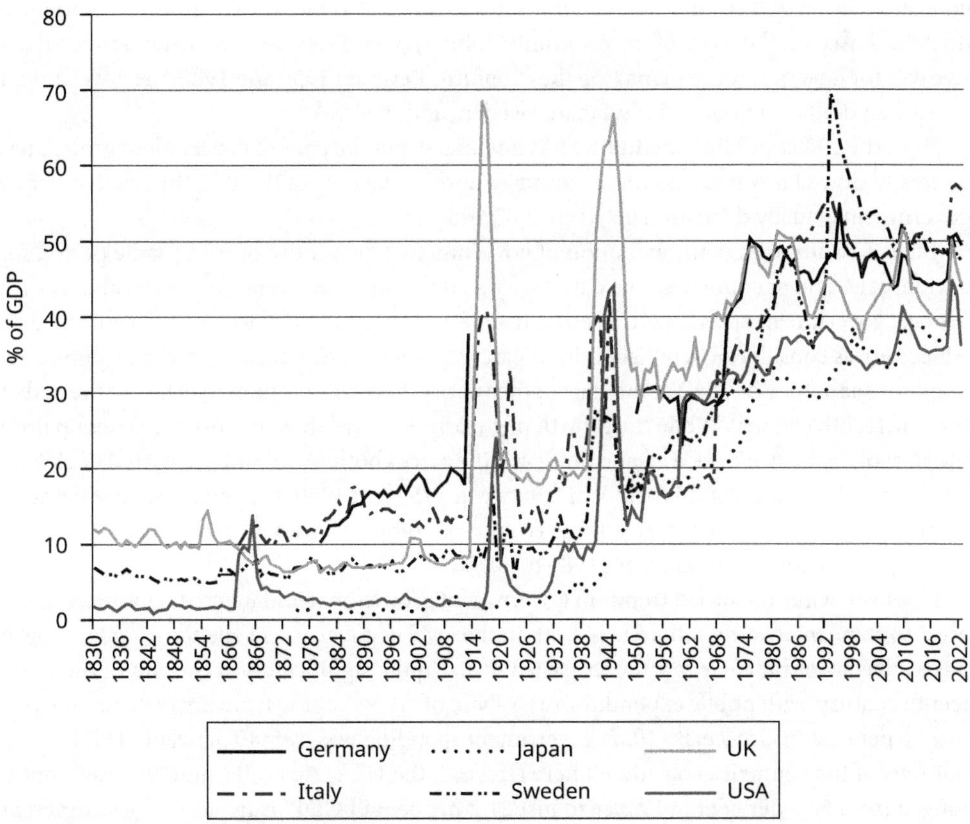

Figure 3.1 Growth of public expenditure, 1830–2022

Note: Data were not available for all years for all countries, hence the discontinuities in the lines.
Source: IMF (2023)—with minor processing by Our World in Data.

[2] Analysing historical data can be challenging, particularly when carrying out cross-country comparisons, since the way variables are defined and the corresponding data collected may change over time and may differ from one country to another. This means that some caution is needed in analysing the data presented in this section.

variation in the size of the public sector across these countries, they all saw a marked rise in spending during this period, with government expenditure increasing from around 10 per cent of GDP or less in the late nineteenth century to over 35 per cent of GDP in 2022.

We can identify four stages in the evolution of public expenditure in these countries. In the first stage, up until the start of the First World War, spending was relatively low. For the three countries for which data are available going back to 1830—the USA, the UK, and Sweden—government expenditure was mostly stagnant or, in the case of the UK, falling, up until the eve of the First World War.[3] In Germany, government spending started to increase towards the end of the nineteenth century, although it remained below 20 per cent of GDP.

In the second stage, from the start of the First World War until the end of the Second World War, government spending fluctuated significantly. Government expenditure increases sharply during the period of the two world wars in all countries, with the exception of Japan, but then falls again following the wars.

The period of sustained government growth happens in most countries following the end of the Second World War up until the start of the 1980s. This was a period of relative peace and prosperity and was marked by an increase in social spending in areas such as health and education, as we will see in more detail below. This was also the heyday of **Keynesianism**, a doctrine based on the work of the economist John Maynard Keynes, which advocated an active role for government in managing the economy. Between 1950 and 1980, the government more than doubled in size in Italy, Japan, Sweden, and the USA.

Since the 1980s, public expenditure has fluctuated, but the pace of government growth has generally slowed down across these countries and, in the case of the UK, the relative size of government actually decreased between 1980 and 2022.

Table 3.1 summarizes the evolution of government expenditure over the same period for a wider selection of countries. The data here mostly confirm the trends observed above, with average government spending increasing from 8.8 per cent in 1870 to 45.7 per cent in 2022. All countries considered here had a significantly larger government, measured by public expenditure as a share of GDP, at the start of the twenty-first century than they had at the end of the nineteenth century. While the growth of government was slow in most countries up until the start of the First World War, and quite volatile across both world wars, it started to pick up after the end of the Second World War.[4] Between 1950 and 1980, the government grew at an average rate of 127 per cent across these countries, compared with an average growth rate of just 21 per cent for the period from 1980 to 2022.

However, while the broad trends in government growth are similar across countries, there are also some interesting differences, both in the level of government spending and in how it has evolved over time. Governments varied in size quite significantly at the end of the nineteenth century, with public expenditure as a share of GDP ranging from 0.9 per cent in Japan to 23.6 per cent in Greece. By 2022, government spending was over 40 per cent of GDP in all but four of the countries considered here (Ireland, the USA, Australia, and Norway), but it ranged from 58.3 per cent in France to just 21.2 per cent of GDP in Ireland.[5] These different

[3] In the USA, we see a spike in spending from 1862 to 1865, which coincides with the American Civil War.

[4] Some caution is needed when interpreting the figures for government expenditure in the 1930s, since levels of GDP during this period would have been much lower in many countries following the Great Depression.

[5] The evolution of government expenditure in Ireland is interesting, with a general decreasing trend since the early 1980s, interrupted by a brief spike during the 2008 financial crisis.

Table 3.1 Evolution of government expenditure, 1880–2022 (% of GDP)

	Late nineteenth century	Pre- and post-First World War		Between the wars		Post-Second World War							
	1880[a]	1913	1920	1930	1938	1950	1960	1970	1980	1990	2000	2010	2022
Australia	–	2.7	7.7	5.5	4.9	12.2	21.8	25.3	33.2	36.1	35.6	37.2	38.1
Austria	11.4	–	–	19.8	–	36.4	36.3	39.5	50.0	51.5	51.9	52.5	52.8
Belgium	6.2	10.8	–	19.1	22.2	22.9	23.7	42.7	54.9	52.3	49.1	52.9	53.5
Canada	6.8	7.0	10.5	7.7	10.5	15.0	14.9	36.0	41.6	48.8	41.1	43.1	41.4
Denmark	8.8	5.4	7.2	6.9	8.5	10.0	16.4	24.4	52.7	55.4	53.7	58.5	44.9
Finland	6.9	11.6	15.3	19.8	14.1	23.9	22.5	21.9	40.1	47.9	47.9	53.9	53.0
France	13.2	10.2	–	18.6	–	24.1	22.2	20.5	46.0	49.6	51.7	56.6	58.3
Germany	10.3	37.7	–	16.3	–	27.2	22.9	39.5	48.2	44.7	45.1	47.9	49.5
Greece	23.6	17.7	–	26.0	18.9	27.1	20.0	25.2	24.2	38.0	46.4	53.0	52.5
Ireland	–	–	–	–	20.8	25.9	29.1	44.1	53.7	42.8	31.2	66.8	21.2
Italy	11.1	13.1	18.8	14.2	20.5	17.3	16.5	32.3	40.8	52.9	45.9	50.3	56.7
Japan	0.9	2.1	1.9	2.9	4.9	15.9	18.4	20.2	33.5	29.4	36.0	37.7	44.1
Netherlands	9.6	9.5	–	8.7	10.3	24.0	20.4	43.2	55.2	54.9	44.2	51.2	43.5
Norway	6.6	9.9	8.6	8.6	8.1	18.1	18.0	38.9	46.1	53.3	42.3	45.9	38.5
Portugal	6.7	7.9	12.1	7.9	9.2	9.8	14.3	15.5	32.4	38.5	41.1	51.3	44.8
Spain	8.7	11.3	12.1	10.6	–	11.7	11.0	12.3	16.3	32.8	39.2	45.6	47.1
Sweden	6.8	6.7	7.6	8.7	11.8	18.3	24.4	29.5	41.0	38.0	53.1	50.4	47.3
UK	6.2	8.2	21.0	18.7	19.5	33.2	33.1	42.0	47.6	41.1	36.8	50.6	44.3
US	2.2	1.9	7.3	3.6	7.9	13.4	28.3	32.3	34.3	37.2	33.9	39.8	36.3
Average	8.8	10.2	10.8	12.4	12.8	20.3	21.8	30.8	41.7	44.5	43.5	49.7	45.7

[a] Or closest available year; data for 1882 for Finland and 1881 for Norway.

Source: IMF (2023)—with minor processing by Our World in Data.

paths in the evolution of public expenditure highlight the important role played by local political, cultural, and institutional contexts.

It is clear from the data in Figure 3.1 and Table 3.1 that the government has grown. To help us understand what has driven this long-run growth in public expenditure, it is useful to look at how the main categories of expenditure have changed over time.[6] Figures 3.2 to 3.5 illustrate the evolution of government spending in four key areas—defence, health, education, and pensions—for the same group of six countries we looked at in Figure 3.1. These trends suggest the main driver behind the growth in government spending in the latter half of the twentieth century was increased spending on health, education, and pensions.

Spending on defence fluctuated throughout the twentieth century, but has tended to decrease in most countries (Figure 3.2). Across the whole of the OECD, government spending on defence has been falling since the 1960s, from an average of 6.5 per cent of GDP in 1960 to 2.4 per cent in 2023 (World Bank, n.d.). Spending is lowest in Ireland, at 0.2 per cent of GDP and highest in Israel, at 5.3 per cent of GDP (World Bank, n.d.).

For the other categories of expenditure—health, education, and pensions—we can see a clear upward trend across all countries, suggesting governments were taking on new responsibilities during this period (Figures 3.3 to 3.5). Government spending on health was virtually non-existent in the early 1900s, but increased dramatically in the second half of that century. It is also interesting to note that this growth happened consistently

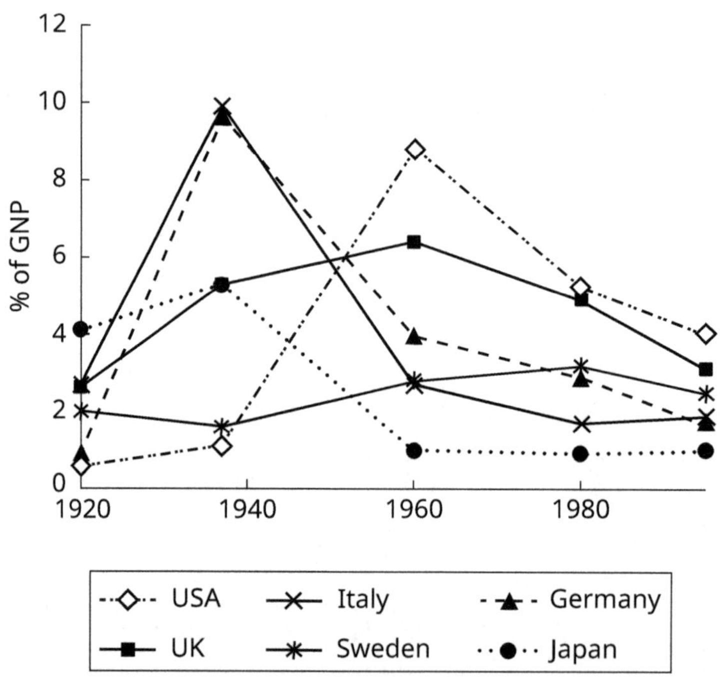

Figure 3.2 Government spending on defence, 1920–1995
Source: Tanzi and Schuknecht (2000).

[6] Some government spending decisions are made by central government, whereas others are made at the local level; in federal countries, some spending decisions are made at the state level. We look at total government spending by area of expenditure, rather than disaggregating by level of government.

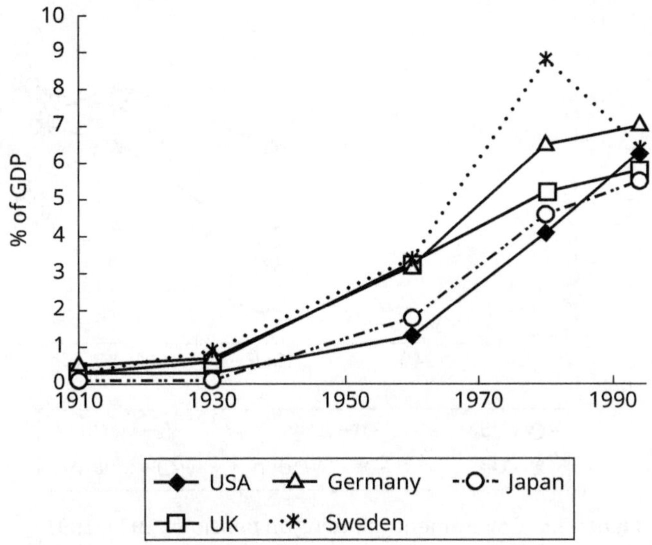

Figure 3.3 Government spending on health, 1910–1994
Source: Tanzi and Schuknecht (2000).

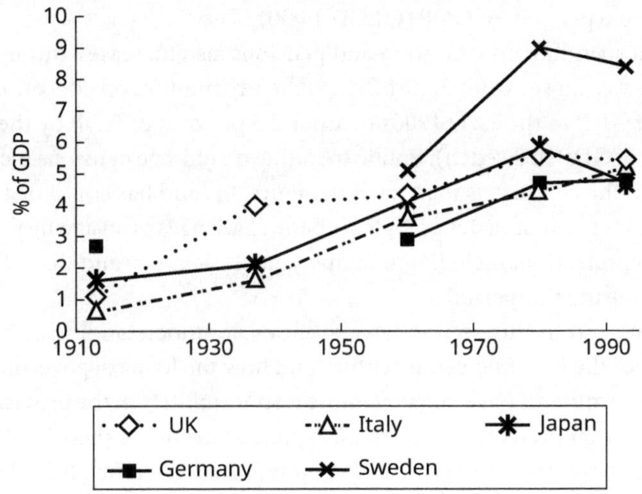

Figure 3.4 Government spending on education, 1913–1993
Source: Tanzi and Schuknecht (2001).

across countries with very different healthcare systems.[7] In the UK, with its largely publicly funded and provided healthcare system, public spending on health increased from 3.3 per cent of GDP in 1960 to 5.8 per cent of GDP in 1994.[8] In comparison, in the USA, where healthcare is largely privately funded and provided, government spending increased from 1.3 per cent to 6.3 per cent of GDP in the same period. Government spending on

[7] We discuss the different types of healthcare system in Chapter 8.
[8] The UK's National Health Service was established in 1948.

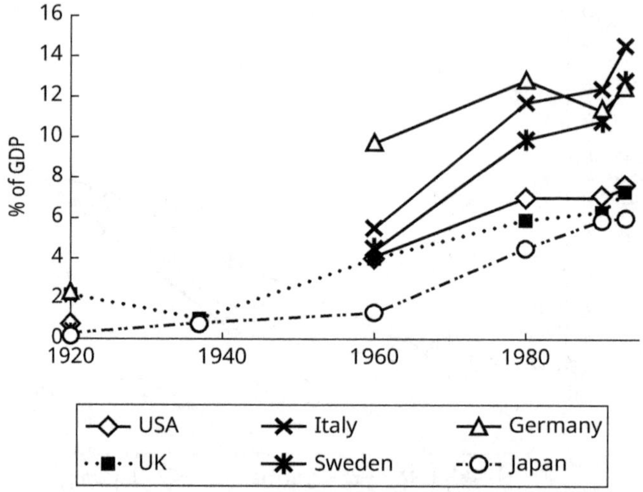

Figure 3.5 Government spending on pensions, 1920–1993
Source: Tanzi and Schuknecht (2000).

healthcare has continued to grow; in 2019, average government spending on health across the OECD was 6.6 per cent of GDP (OECD, 0000).

Government spending on education and pensions also increased throughout the twentieth century. As we can see from Figure 3.4, public expenditure on education increased from 1–2 per cent of GDP in the early 1900s to around 5 per cent of GDP by the mid-1990s (and over 8 per cent of GDP in Sweden). Public spending on old-age pensions increased sharply in the latter half of the century, as illustrated in Figure 3.5, and has continued to rise in several countries since then, as countries grapple with the challenges of an ageing population.[9] Other forms of social protection, including unemployment, sickness, and disability benefits, were also expanded during this period.

The data reviewed in this section have given us an understanding of how governments have grown since the late nineteenth century and how the focus of government has changed over time, as governments have taken on more responsibilities in the provision of healthcare, education, and social protection. Before we explore some of the theories that have been put forward to explain this long-run growth of the public sector, it is helpful to briefly look at how governments' revenue collection activities changed over this period.

3.3 The evolution of government revenues

Government expenditure needs to be paid for and there are three mechanisms that governments can use to finance their expenditures: levying taxes, borrowing, and selling off government assets. Taxation has played an important role in financing government expenditure, but the types of taxes that governments have relied on, and the amounts of tax revenues raised, have changed over time.

[9] This is a point we will return to in Chapter 11.

Figure 3.6 plots the evolution of tax revenues for the same six countries we looked at above, for the period from 1830 to 2011. Tax revenues, as a share of GDP, were low for most of these countries throughout the nineteenth century and up until the start of the First World War. Tax revenues started to rise in Italy and Germany in the second half of the nineteenth century, but even in these countries they remained below 20 per cent of GDP until the start of the twentieth century. Tax revenues rose steadily after the First World War and by the end of the twentieth century they were over 30 per cent of GDP in all of these countries, with the exception of Japan. In 2011, taxes as a share of GDP ranged from around 30 per cent in Japan and the USA to just under 50 per cent in Sweden. The evolution of tax revenues follows a similar pattern to the evolution of public expenditure we looked at above, which raises an important question: do government revenues increases to finance additional expenditure needs, or does government expenditure grow because governments have found ways to increase their revenues?[10]

The development of different tax instruments, and the growth of tax administration systems that accompanied them, certainly facilitated the expansion of tax revenues by making it easier to collect taxes. Income taxes started to emerge around 1850, but they were only more widely adopted in the early twentieth century (Besley & Persson, 2013). The value-added tax—one of the most widely used taxes on goods and services today—was only introduced in the second half of the twentieth century. Today, governments have a range of different types

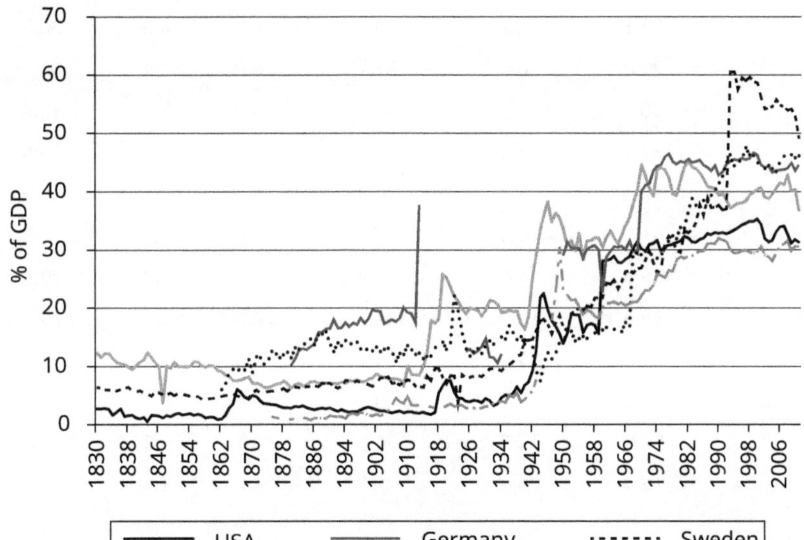

Figure 3.6 Government tax revenues, 1830–2011
Source: Mauro et al. (2013).

[10] Some researchers suggest that the growth in the availability of revenues is the main cause of the growth in government (see e.g. Holcombe 2005).

of taxes at their disposal, including taxes on individual incomes, savings, and consumption, taxes on corporate income, property taxes, land taxes, customs duties, and fuel duties. Taxes are normally separated into direct taxes, on income, wealth, and profits, and indirect taxes, on goods and services.[11]

The importance of the various types of taxes for government revenues varies across countries. Today, the majority of government tax revenues come from income taxes, social security contributions, and taxes on goods and services, which together account for 82 per cent of government tax revenues for the OECD as a whole (see Table 3.2). But the proportion of revenues raised from individual income taxes ranges from 15.2 per cent in Greece to over 50 per cent in Denmark. Indirect taxes on goods and services are an important source of government revenues across most countries, accounting for, on average, just over 30 per cent of

Table 3.2 Sources of government tax revenue, 2019 (% of total tax revenue)

	Personal income taxes	Corporate income taxes	Social security contributions	Payroll taxes	Property taxes	Taxes on goods and services	Other
Australia	42.0	17.1	0.0	4.7	9.8	26.3	0.0
Austria	22.6	6.4	34.9	6.4	1.3	27.5	1.0
Belgium	26.5	8.7	31.0	0.0	8.0	25.6	0.0
Canada	36.0	12.3	13.9	2.2	11.4	22.8	1.4
Denmark	52.1	6.7	0.1	0.6	4.3	30.3	5.9
Finland	29.0	6.0	27.9	0.0	3.4	33.7	0.1
France	20.7	4.9	33.0	4.0	8.7	27.6	1.1
Germany	27.4	5.2	37.9	0.0	2.9	26.6	0.0
Greece	15.2	5.6	30.8	0.0	7.7	39.9	0.8
Ireland	31.7	14.0	16.8	1.0	5.7	30.8	0.0
Italy	25.8	4.6	31.2	0.0	5.7	28.3	4.3
Japan	18.8	12.0	41.1	0.0	8.2	19.7	0.3
Netherlands	21.6	9.4	34.2	0.0	3.8	30.7	0.2
New Zealand	39.5	12.4	0.0	0.0	6.2	38.7	2.9
Norway	26.0	14.7	26.5	0.1	3.2	29.4	0.0
Portugal	18.4	9.0	27.8	0.0	4.1	39.8	0.8
Spain	22.7	6.0	35.3	0.0	7.1	28.9	0.0
Sweden	28.7	7.0	21.4	12.4	2.2	28.2	0.1
UK	27.6	7.0	19.7	0.4	12.4	32.8	0.0
USA	41.1	5.4	24.5	0.1	11.5	17.5	0.0
OECD average	23.5	9.6	25.9	1.3	5.5	32.6	1.5

[a] 'OECD average' represents the average across all OECD countries, not just those listed here.
Source: OECD (2025).

[11] We discuss the different types of taxes in more detail in Chapter 13.

total tax revenues across the OECD, and almost 40 per cent in New Zealand, Portugal, and Greece. Corporate income taxes play a much less significant role, ranging from 4.6 per cent in Italy to just over 17 per cent in Australia.

The role of these different sources of tax revenue has changed over time. Across the OECD, social security contributions have become increasingly important, accounting for 26 per cent of total tax revenues in 2019 on average, compared with 17.6 per cent in 1965 (OECD, 2025).[12] Value-added taxes have also grown in importance, with their average share increasing from 2 per cent of total tax revenues in 1965 to 20 per cent in 2019 (OECD, 2025).

3.4 Theories of public sector growth

We have seen that government grew considerably across many countries throughout the twentieth century. What explains this long-run growth of the public sector? In this section, we review a selection of theories that have been proposed to explain this trend. These theories differ in their focus: some focus on the demand for public sector goods and services, and how this has changed over time; others focus on the supply side and consider specific aspects of the production technology available in the public sector; yet others highlight the role played by individual actors, including voters, government bureaucrats, and politicians, in determining the level of public expenditure.[13] These theories should be able to explain not only the evolution of total government expenditure, but also the change in its composition over time.

We start by discussing three theories that focus on the role of structural factors in driving public sector growth: development models; Wagner's law; and Baumol's law. We will then focus on three public choice theories of government growth: rational choice models; budget-maximizing bureaucracy models; and the displacement effect or ratchet effect hypothesis.[14]

3.4.1 Development models

Development models of public sector growth are based on the idea that the level of public expenditure is directly tied to a country's economic development. As countries go through the process of industrialization, moving from a traditional economy to an industrial and, subsequently, post-industrial economy, the structure and needs of the economy change and this calls for different types of government intervention. There is no single development model of public sector growth, although this category of models tends to be associated with the work of Rostow (1959) and Musgrave (1969).[15]

In 'The Stages of Economic Growth' (1959), Rostow argued that countries go through five stages on the path to economic modernization. The first stage is the traditional society stage,

[12] See also Chapter 13.

[13] These theories are sometimes categorized into macro theories and micro theories. The former focus on economy-wide drivers of public sector growth, whereas the latter focus on the behaviour of the individual actors who affect the demand and supply of public sector goods and services, including voters, pressure groups, politicians, and bureaucrats.

[14] Public choice theories of government growth highlight that government is not an impartial agent existing outside the analysis, but should be part of the analysis. Such theories focus on the role of different actors (voters, interest groups, government bureaucrats, and politicians) in influencing the evolution of the public sector.

[15] It is not clear where the term 'development models' originates, though it is established in public economic textbooks, including Bailey (2002) and Hindriks and Myles (2013).

which is characterized by subsistence farming or a hunter-gatherer community. This is followed by the preconditions for take-off, take-off, the drive to maturity, and the final stage, the age of high mass consumption. In each stage, the needs of the economy are different, necessitating different types of government expenditure. In the early stages, during the preconditions for take-off and take-off, industry starts to develop and there is an increase in urbanization, as more people move to towns and cities. There is therefore a need for government expenditure on infrastructure, investing in road and transport networks, water supply, and sanitation, to support urban development. As the economy matures, the focus of government expenditure shifts towards investments in human capital (health and education) and improving quality of life, by tackling externalities associated with growing urbanization, such as crime and pollution.

Rostow's model focused on explaining economic growth, rather than on explaining the evolution of government expenditure. However, he explicitly acknowledged the important role that government has to play as part of this process, particularly in the early stages of development, creating the conditions in which economic activity can flourish by investing in social overhead capital, adopting appropriate trade policies, and promoting the diffusion of new production technologies. Increased urbanization during the drive to maturity stage puts pressure on governments to adopt measures to support social and economic security.

Musgrave (1969) proposed a similar relationship between public expenditure and economic development, although unlike Rostow, his work focused directly on explaining the patterns of public expenditure and taxation. Based on an analysis of data from a number of countries with different income levels, Musgrave suggested that the observed long-run relationship between the relative size of government and GDP per capita could be explained by the different needs and challenges that countries face at different stages of development.

Development models are useful as descriptions of how economies and governments have evolved. They highlight the role of structural factors—including demographic, social, and industrial factors—in driving the growth of public expenditure. However, they ignore the role played by actors such as voters, politicians, and bureaucrats in influencing the evolution of government expenditure. The differences in the size of the public sector across countries with similar income levels also suggest that the public sector does not necessarily grow in a linear or prescribed manner as an economy develops, particularly in the later stages of development, limiting the applicability of these models.

3.4.2 Wagner's law of increasing state activity

Wagner's law is named after the nineteenth-century German social scientist Adolph Wagner. Based on his observation of public sector expenditure in the USA, Japan, and several European countries, Wagner concluded that, as an economy develops, there is a tendency for the government to grow, both in absolute terms and relative to the size of the economy. His theory positing this positive relationship between economic development and the size of the public sector became known as Wagner's law.

According to Wagner, there are three main reasons driving increased government expenditure:

1. As the economy grows and society becomes more complex, there is an increased need for governments to enforce law and order, including enforcing contracts and providing public protection.

2. As real incomes increase, demand for culture and welfare-related goods and services with a high income elasticity of demand[16] also increases. These include goods such as education, which are typically provided more efficiently by the public sector.
3. Wagner argued that economic development and changes in technology require government intervention to restrain natural monopolies and increase economic efficiency.

A large number of empirical studies have been carried out to test Wagner's law. While early studies generally found evidence in support of this hypothesis, the results of more recent studies have been mixed (see Box 3.2). One of the big challenges these empirical studies face is establishing causality: while the evidence may support a positive relationship between the relative size of the public sector and income or GDP per capita, it is difficult to determine empirically whether this is because increases in income lead to increases in government expenditure (as Wagner's law suggests) or because increases in government expenditure lead to increases in income (as Keynesian economists would argue). Wagner's theory has also been criticized due to its focus solely on the demand for the goods and services provided by the public sector, neglecting the supply side and the choices of voters, politicians, and bureaucrats involved in the political process (Hindriks & Myles, 2013).

Box 3.2 Does the evidence support Wagner's law?

Empirical studies carried out up until the early 1990s mostly found strong evidence in support of Wagner's law for a wide range of countries (Gemmell, 1993). However, Durevall and Henrekson (2011) reviewed roughly 40 studies carried out since then and found that about 35 per cent of these studies failed to find any evidence to support Wagner's law. Of the remaining studies, only 35 per cent found unqualified support for Wagner's law, while the remainder found evidence supporting this hypothesis, but only for particular types of expenditure, or if additional variables were included in the model.

Durevall and Henrekson (2011) carried out their own assessment of Wagner's law for the UK and Sweden, using data going back to the beginning of industrialization in the nineteenth century. They found that the evidence was only consistent with Wagner's law during two periods, between 1860 and 1913, and between 1920 and 1975. Wagner's law did not fit the data during the initial industrialization stage in the early nineteenth century or during the period since the mid-1970s, when the relative size of the public sector did not change much or even decreased, even as the economy was growing. Their work suggests that changes in the age structure of the population, particularly changes in the dependency ratio,[17] can explain why Wagner's law does not hold in the period after the mid-1980s. These findings highlight the importance of demographic change for understanding the evolution of public sector growth.[18]

[16] The income elasticity of demand measures how demand for a good changes as income changes. Goods with a high income elasticity of demand are those for which the percentage change in the quantity demanded is greater than the percentage change in income—for example, if the quantity of the good demanded increases by 10 per cent in response to a 5 per cent increase in income.

[17] The dependency ratio is a measure of the number of people not in the labour force (i.e. children and people over the retirement age) as a proportion of the working-age population.

[18] This is something we will explore in more detail in Chapter 11, where we look at ageing and pensions. Shelton (2007) similarly found that both demographic change and social policy play a role in explaining the relative size of government.

3.4.3 Baumol's law

According to **Baumol's law**, the growth of government is determined by the production technology available in the public sector and is, to some extent, inevitable. This theory is based on the work of the economist William Baumol and is also known as Baumol's cost disease or the relative price effect, since government growth is believed to be driven by the relative rise in the price of the goods and services provided by the public sector.

The theory was initially developed to explain why wages had risen in the arts sector over time, in spite of low or no gains in productivity in this sector. However, the model can be applied to any sector that relies on labour-intensive technology. The underlying assumption is that the technology available in the public sector is more labour-intensive than the technology available in the private sector and, therefore, there is limited scope for productivity improvements in the public sector.[19] If we think of many of the services typically provided by the government, such as healthcare and education, these do tend to fit this picture of being relatively labour-intensive. While there is some scope for technological developments to boost productivity in these sectors, a minimum number of doctors and nurses, or teachers, is still likely to be required to deliver these services.

So why do these differences in technology between sectors matter? Technological developments lead to increases in productivity in the private sector and this causes wages to rise in the private sector, as labour is assumed to be paid the value of its marginal product, and a worker's marginal product depends on how productive they are. If labour markets are competitive, so that the public and private sectors are competing to hire the same workers, then wage increases in the private sector will feed through into the public sector. However, because the technology in the public sector is more labour-intensive, there is little scope for substituting labour for capital in the public sector. So the cost of labour increases in the public sector, leading to an increase in public sector expenditure, even if the level of output being produced is unchanged.

Baumol's law essentially states that the increase in the *relative* size of the public sector is inevitable, at least as long as the goods and services provided by the public sector continue to rely on more labour-intensive technology. Empirical studies have found some evidence that suggests that Baumol's cost disease has played a role in driving the growth of the public sector in several countries, including the USA (Semat et al., 2015), Austria (Neck & Schneider, 1988), and Sweden (Henrekson, 1988).

However, this theory is based on some fairly strong assumptions. It could be argued to underestimate the potential for productivity improvements in the public sector. While some services provided by the public sector are relatively labour-intensive, technological developments still have the potential to increase productivity in these areas, as evidenced by recent developments in artificial intelligence (AI) and the use of these technologies to analyse X-rays and scans. Other services typically provided by the public sector are in fact relatively capital-intensive today, such as the military, which invests a lot of money in R&D to increase productivity (Mueller, 2003). In addition to this, the public and private sectors may in fact not be competing over the same workers, particularly during periods of high unemployment, and there is evidence to suggest that wages might not be equalized across sectors (see Box 3.3). Some government departments may also have monopsony power,[20] which can be used to drive down costs.

[19] Increases in productivity are assumed to be driven by technological developments and these are assumed to affect the capital or machinery available, rather than workers.

[20] Monopsony power refers to situations where a buyer faces little competition for a particular good or input, such as labour, and can therefore influence the market price.

Box 3.3 Are workers paid the same in the public and private sectors?

Baumol's law relies on the assumption that the public and private sectors are competing for the same workers and therefore wages in the two sectors will be equalized. But is this true in practice? Comparing pay in the public and private sectors is notoriously difficult, given structural differences between the sectors and the need to control for any differences in working conditions. Pay may be lower in one sector, but greater workplace flexibility or better pensions may go some way towards compensating for the lower wages. Any comparison also needs to take into account differences in worker characteristics, such as age, education, and skills.

A study of the public sector–private sector pay gap in the UK by the Institute for Fiscal Studies (Cribb et al., 2019) found that average hourly pay in the public sector was around 10 per cent higher than in the private sector in 2018. However, once differences in age, education, and experience were taken into account, this differential fell to just 1 per cent; this is the smallest it has been since the early 2000s. As the authors noted, the study focused on average pay and pay inequality tends to be lower in the public sector: there tend to be fewer people on very low pay in the public sector in the UK and the highest public sector salaries are well below those paid in the private sector. There are also other employment benefits that should be taken into account when comparing remuneration across sectors, such as pensions. And public sector pensions in the UK tend to be more generous than those in the private sector.

Source: Cribb et al. (2019).

This theory offers at best only a partial explanation for rising public sector expenditure, since it focuses only on the cost of supplying public sector services and is entirely technology-driven. It is worth bearing in mind that Baumol was writing in the 1960s and is unlikely to have anticipated the pace of technological change we have witnessed in recent decades. As with the other theories discussed above, Baumol's theory does not consider the role played by individual choice and behaviours in driving government growth. This is a question we will turn to in the theories discussed below.

3.4.4 Rational choice models

The theories we have discussed so far have focused on the role of structural factors in driving the growth of the public sector. However, in democratic societies, governments are elected by voters and therefore their preferences and behaviour should influence the size of government. This is the basic tenet underlying the rational choice models of public sector growth: the size of government is the result of democratic choice and the public sector grows because people have a preference for larger government. Different individuals will have different preferences for the goods and services provided by the public sector, and they can express these preferences by voting for the political party or candidate offering the level of public sector goods (and associated expenditure) which is closest to their preferred level. Under **majority voting** mechanisms, the elected candidate will be the one chosen by the **median voter**.[21]

[21] This result, known as the Median Voter Theorem, is discussed in more detail in Chapter 4.

Why will the preferences of the median voter determine the outcome? With a simple majority voting rule, the candidate who is elected is the one that receives more than half of the votes. Suppose individual voters face a choice between two candidates, one offering a high level of public expenditure and one offering a low level of public expenditure. Each voter will vote for the candidate offering the level closest to their preferred level. If we line up all voters based on their preferred level of public expenditure, from lowest to highest, the median voter will be the voter in the middle of the distribution. All voters to the left of the median voter will prefer a lower level of government spending and all voters to the right will prefer a higher level of government spending (see Figure 3.7). The winning candidate will be the one offering the level of public expenditure closest to the preferences of the median voter, since this candidate will receive the vote of the median voter and of all voters either to the right or left of the median voter.

The size and composition of the public sector therefore reflect the preferences of the median voter, and factors that affect the position of the median voter—such as changes in the income distribution or in the gender composition of the electorate—will influence the evolution of the public sector. Meltzer and Richard (1978, 1981) proposed a model in which voters recognize both the costs (in terms of higher taxes) and the benefits (in terms of redistribution) of changes in government size, and vote for the candidate offering the programme that most closely aligns with their own interests.[22] Voters with incomes below the median are assumed to benefit from government redistribution and so extensions to the franchise to include more voters with incomes below the median income will lead to an increase in the size of government. Their model also implies that an increase in income inequality,[23] which increases mean income relative to the income of the median voter, will lead to an increase in the size of government.[24] Lott and Kenny (1999) analysed the impact of giving women the right to vote on the growth of government in the USA and found it led to an increase in government expenditures and revenue.

The key implication of the rational choice models is that governments grow because people have a preference for larger government. These theories assume that the only role of government is redistributive, and that all redistribution is from the rich to the poor (Mueller, 2003). The evidence on the evolution of government spending reviewed in section 3.2 certainly suggests that the redistributive role of government has become increasingly important, but overall empirical support for these theories has been mixed.[25] We cannot ignore the

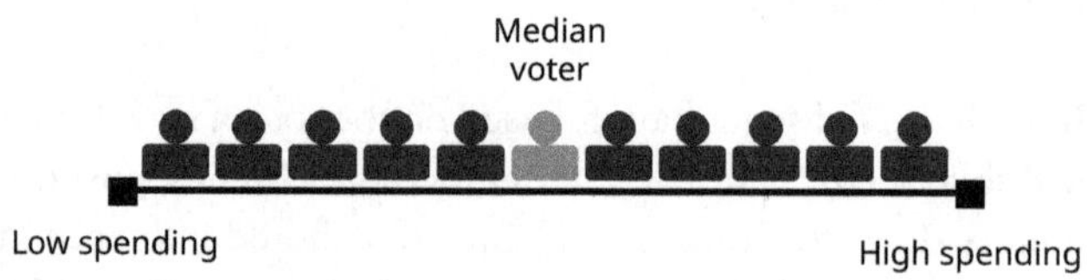

Figure 3.7 The median voter

[22] Meltzer and Richard (1978) provide a non-technical summary of the model, which is developed formally in Meltzer and Richard (1981). The model is tested using data for the USA in Meltzer and Richard (1983).

[23] If the income distribution is skewed in such a way that a large number of individuals have relatively high income, mean income will be greater than median income.

[24] In contrast, Peltzman (1980) developed a model based on voter behaviour which implies that increasing equality in the income distribution drives government growth, although his model does not rely on the median voter theorem.

[25] See Mueller (2003: ch. 21) for a review of some of the evidence.

Box 3.4 Do voters really understand the cost of providing public sector outputs?

The rational choice models assume that individual voters understand the costs and benefits of changes in government size, where the costs depend primarily on their individual tax burden. But do voters really understand how much they pay in taxes? The extensive literature on **fiscal illusion** suggests that voters may be poorly informed about how the tax system works, what their tax liabilities are, and how much they contribute to public services. The complexity of the tax system, the move towards less visible or salient taxes, **fiscal drag**, and government reliance on deficit finance can all contribute to fiscal illusion. Empirical evidence on fiscal illusion has been mixed. However, a recent study which explored fiscal illusion in the UK using a novel online experiment found that taxpayers systematically underestimated their tax liabilities and the cost of public services (Numa, 2024). These findings suggest that better-informed taxpayers are likely to prefer lower levels of taxation and public spending.

Sources: Numa (2024) and Mueller (2003).

role government plays in providing public goods or addressing externalities, for example, or the importance of other actors in the political process, such as politicians, government bureaucrats, and pressure groups.[26] Voters may also not fully understand the true costs and benefits of public sector outputs (see Box 3.4).

3.4.5 Budget-maximizing bureaucracy model

We now shift our focus from the demand side of public choice models to the supply side and introduce a model that explains the growth of government based on the behaviour of those responsible for providing public sector goods and services, the government bureaucrats. Underlying the development models, Wagner's law, and the rational choice models we have reviewed so far is the assumption of a despotic benevolent government—a government that is assumed to act in the public interest, intervening in the economy to improve efficiency or to achieve redistributive goals. The government is assumed to be both benevolent, in the sense that its sole concern is to maximize social welfare, and omniscient, in the sense that it has all the information it needs to achieve its goal. This despotic benevolent government model dominated economic analysis up until the 1960s.

Niskanen's work on bureaucracy and government (1968, 1971) marked a turning point in the public choice literature, shifting attention from the demand side of government expenditure, driven by voters and their preferences for government spending, to the mechanics of the supply of public sector goods and services. Niskanen argued that, rather than selfless public servants, the bureaucrats who run government offices are self-serving and want to maximize their power, prestige, pay, and promotion prospects, which are assumed to be a function of

[26] Some researchers, such as Aranson and Ordeshook (1981), would argue that all government expenditures involve an element of redistribution; even government investment in infrastructure involves a decision over what location to invest in, benefiting some residents to the detriment of others.

the size of their bureaus. Government bureaucrats will therefore aim to maximize the size of their budgets, which will lead to a level of government spending above what is optimal or efficient. The bureaucrats working in government are assumed to have more information on the costs and benefits of providing public sector goods and services than politicians or voters, and the opportunities for monitoring their activities are limited, allowing them to misrepresent the true costs and benefits in a way that serves their own interests.

Although Niskanen's original model focused on the behaviour of government bureaucrats, who were assumed to have all the information and power, subsequent work has built on this model, shifting the power onto politicians and the legislature. Within these models, politicians are typically assumed to be self-interested revenue-maximizers. However, they also care about re-election and therefore need to be sensitive to preferences and demands of voters. Brennan and Buchanan (1980) proposed a model that merged the legislature (Parliament or Congress) and the bureaucracy, which together exploited their monopoly power over voters to maximize the size of the public sector. In this Leviathan[27] model, the only constraints on government growth are constitutional constraints on the level of public expenditure and on revenue collection. The size of government is ultimately constrained by the maximum amount of revenues the government can raise through taxes.[28]

Testing these models empirically is difficult given the inherent difficulty in measuring the output provided by government bureaus. What would be the appropriate way of measuring the output provided by the government department of education or defence, for example? But if it is not possible to establish what the output of a particular government bureau is, it is difficult to determine whether this bureau is operating inefficiently. The models also rely on strong assumptions about the motivations—and power—of government bureaucrats, which are unlikely to be observable in practice. Studies have adopted different approaches to testing these models and there is some evidence to suggest that budget-maximizing behaviour has contributed to the growth in government.[29] Kau and Rubin (1981) found that almost all of the increase in public sector spending in the USA between 1929 and 1970 could be explained by reductions in the cost of collecting taxes. Another study for the USA by Ferris and West (1999) found evidence of government bureaucrats' ability to use their power and informational advantage to increase their salaries.

The main criticism of the budget-maximizing models is that they are static: while they may provide an explanation for why the government is larger than optimal, they do not explain the growth of government. However, Mueller (2003) argues that these models may, indirectly, offer an explanation for government growth. As the bureaucracy's ability to increase the size of its budget depends on its ability to misrepresent the true cost of providing public sector outputs and the level of output provided, which in turn is likely to depend on the size and complexity of their budget, this means that the larger the bureaucracy is, the harder it will be to monitor its activity. Although the assumption that politicians and government bureaucrats are selfless social welfare maximizers may be too strong (and there are certainly

[27] *Leviathan* is a book written by the English philosopher Thomas Hobbes in 1651, in which he argued for a strong, totalitarian state as the only way of avoiding the threat of a constant 'war of all against all'.

[28] The relationship between the tax rate and the level of tax revenue raised is captured by the Laffer curve. This relationship is assumed to have an inverted U-shape: when the tax rate is zero, no tax revenue is raised; as the tax rate increases, tax revenue initially increases; however, beyond a certain point, raising the tax rate further will lead to a decrease in tax revenue. The reasoning behind this relationship is explained more fully in Chapter 15.

[29] See Mueller (2003) for a review.

many real-world examples that suggest that they do put their own interests first), the model of budget-maximizing self-interested bureaucrat behaviour is unlikely to be suited to all areas of economic policy (Cullis & Jones, 2009).

3.4.6 The ratchet effect hypothesis and path dependence

The final model we are going to look at builds on aspects of the rational choice and budget maximization models discussed above, but it emphasizes the dynamic nature of public expenditure. The models we have looked at so far have focused on explaining government expenditure with reference to events at a particular point in time. In practice, public expenditure may exhibit **path dependence**, whereby current expenditure is not just a function of current circumstances, but also depends on previous patterns of expenditure; in other words, history matters for understanding the evolution of public expenditure.

Peacock and Wiseman (1961) originally proposed their displacement effects model based on their observation of the path of public sector expenditure in the UK during the twentieth century. In this model, the level of government expenditure is viewed as the outcome of a political equilibrium between the government and voters: the government is assumed to be a revenue or budget-maximizer and its preference is to spend money, whereas voters dislike paying taxes and their preference is to minimize their tax burden. These competing objectives are moderated by the election constraint—the desire of the government to get re-elected. For a given tolerable tax rate, tax revenues—and hence government expenditure—will increase as long as the economy is growing and incomes are rising.

During periods of significant upheaval, such as wars, depressions, or other national crises, this equilibrium is suspended and governments respond by ratcheting up expenditures; this is the displacement effect. However, once the crisis period is over, while government expenditure may fall somewhat, it will remain above the pre-crisis level. This may partly be explained by the fact that debts incurred during the crisis period need to be paid off. The crisis may also increase the tolerable tax rate, as taxpayers become accustomed to the new higher tax level and may have greater expectations about the role the government can play in improving their quality of life (the inspection effect).

Building on this work, other researchers have suggested that these ratchet effects may happen more frequently than originally proposed by Peacock and Wiseman. Bird (1971, 1972) argued that the share of government spending is also impacted by the economic cycle. Government expenditure tends to fall more slowly than GDP during recessions, so the ratio of public expenditure to GDP will rise, and the opposite is true during boom periods. For Buchanan et al. (1978), this upward ratcheting of government expenditure can be explained by the adoption of Keynesian countercyclical fiscal policies. These policies challenged the previously held norm that governments should try and maintain a balanced budget, which had helped keep government spending in check. According to Keynesian theories, increases in government spending and/or lower taxes during recessions could promote economic recovery, but the resulting government deficits should be offset by spending cuts and budget surpluses during economic booms, to ensure a balanced budget over the business cycle. In practice, however, rather than balancing the budget over the business cycle, politicians' desire to be re-elected could give rise to secular deficits.

Looking at the growth of public expenditure in the UK throughout the twentieth century (Figure 3.1), the displacement effects suggested by Peacock and Wiseman (1961) are clear.

There is a sharp increase in government spending as a share of GDP around the period of the First World War. Following the end of the war, spending falls, but it does not fall back to pre-war levels, below 10 per cent of GDP, and instead remains closer to 20 per cent of GDP until the outbreak of the Second World War. A similar pattern then arises around the Second World War. It is not surprising that the theory seems to fit the data for the UK, since these are the expenditure patterns it was originally designed to explain.

More thorough empirical tests of this theory have, however, found mixed support. An early study by Diamond (1977) did not find evidence to support the displacement effect. Durevall and Henrekson (2011) analysed the evolution of public sector spending in the UK and Sweden from the early nineteenth century until the start of the twenty-first century, and they also failed to find any consistent evidence to support a ratchet effect in either country. However, in a study of the persistence of government spending in relation to shocks in the USA over the period from 1889 to 1995, Goff (1998) did find support for a displacement effect, particularly after 1930. Hercowitz and Strawczynski (2004) looked at the impact of business cycles on government spending as a share of GDP across OECD countries between 1975 and 1998. Their findings suggest that the increase in the relative size of government during this period can be partially explained by the upward ratcheting of expenditure during economic downturns, with the spending to GDP ratio increasing during recessions and only partially reducing during economic expansions.

The ratchet effect hypothesis does highlight one important aspect of the evolution of public expenditure which has so far been overlooked and that is the role of path dependence. In practice, the government is constrained in its spending policies by past programmes which may be difficult to reform, particularly in areas such as the provision of public pensions, or unemployment and disability benefits (Tanzi, 2011).

Conclusion

We have seen how the role and size of the public sector have changed dramatically throughout the twentieth century across much of western Europe, North America, Australasia, and Japan. Government spending increased significantly during this period, driven primarily by an increase in spending in areas such as health, education, and social protection. We reviewed a number of theories that have been put forward to explain these trends. Development models, Wagner's law, and Baumol's law all focus on the role of structural factors in driving public sector growth, either on the demand side, highlighting how the structure and needs of the economy change as it develops, or on the supply side, focusing on specific aspects of the production technology available in the public sector. In contrast, rational choice models, budget-maximizing models, and the ratchet effect hypothesis highlight the role played by individual actors—voters, government bureaucrats, and politicians—in influencing the growth of government.

How well do these theories help us understand the evolution of the public sector? There is no single established theory of public sector growth which can explain the evolution of public expenditure across all countries and all time periods. The evolution of the public sector is shaped by a complex interaction of structural and behavioural factors, both on the demand and on the supply side, which the different theories we have covered in this chapter have highlighted. These theories are not mutually exclusive and different theories may apply to a particular country at different points in time.

Questions for discussion

1. Does measuring the size of the public sector using government expenditure as a proportion of GDP provide a reliable picture of the scale of government?
2. How useful are the arguments about the role of government in the economy presented in Chapter 2 for understanding the evolution of government expenditure?
3. How useful is Wagner's law of increasing state activity as an explanation for the growth of the public sector?
4. What assumptions underlie Baumol's law as an explanation for the growth of the public sector? How accurate are these assumptions?
5. According to Holcombe (2005), there is a single factor that explains the growth of government: growth in the availability of revenues. Do you agree with this view? Why or why not?

Further reading

For a discussion of the historical evolution of the public sector across a number of countries:

Tanzi, V., & Schuknecht, L. (2000). *Public spending in the 20th century: A global perspective.* Cambridge University Press.

For a discussion of some of the research on government size and economic growth:

Bergh, A., & Henrekson, M. (2011). Government size and growth: A survey and interpretation of the evidence. *Journal of Economic Surveys, 25*(5), 872–897. https://doi.org/10.1111/j.1467-6419.2011.00697.x

For a more in-depth discussion of the different theories of public sector growth:

Durevall, D., & Henrekson, M. (2011). The futile quest for a grand explanation of long-run government expenditure. *Journal of Public Economics, 95*(7–8), 708–722.

Gemmell, N. (Ed.). (1993). *The growth of the public sector: Theories and international Evidence.* Edward Elgar. Available at: https://www.elgaronline.com/edcollbook/book/9781035351350/9781035351350.xml

For a discussion of the contraction of the public sector in recent years:

Brady, D., & Lee, H. Y. (2014). The rise and fall of government spending in affluent democracies, 1971–2008. *Journal of European Social Policy, 24*(1), 56–79. https://doi.org/10.1177/0958928713511281

Bibliography

Aranson, P. H., & Ordeshook, P. C. (1981). Regulation, redistribution, and public choice. *Public Choice, 37*(1), 69–100. https://doi.org/10.1007/BF00124233

Bailey, S. J. (2002). *Public sector economics: Theory, policy and practice* (2nd ed.). Palgrave.

Baumol, W. J. (1967). Macroeconomics of unbalanced growth: The anatomy of urban crisis. *American Economic Review, 57*(3), 415–426.

Beckerman, W. (1986). How large a public sector? *Oxford Review of Economic Policy, 2*(2), 7–24.

Bergh, A., & Henrekson, M. (2011). Government size and growth: A survey and interpretation of the evidence. *Journal of Economic Surveys, 25*(5), 872–897. https://doi.org/10.1111/j.1467-6419.2011.00697.x

Besley T., & Persson T. (2013). Taxation and development. In A. Auerbach, R. Chetty, M. Feldstein, & E. Saez (Eds.), *Handbook of public economics* (Vol. 5, pp. 51–110). Elsevier.

Bird, R. M. (1971). Wagner's law of expanding state activity. *Public Finance, 26*, 1–26.

Bird, R. M. (1972). The 'displacement effect': A critical note. *FinanzArchiv/Public Finance Analysis, 30*(3), 454–463.

Brennan, G., & Buchanan, J. M. (1980). *The power to tax: Analytical foundations of a fiscal constitution*. Cambridge University Press.

Buchanan, J. M., Wagner, R. E., Meckling, W. H., & Olson, M. (1978). The political biases of Keynesian economics. In J. M. Buchanan & R. E. Wagner (Eds.), *Fiscal responsibility in constitutional democracy* (pp. 79–117). Springer. https://doi.org/10.1007/978-1-4684-7125-0_5

Cribb, J., Davenport, A., & Zaranko, B. (2019). *Public sector pay and employment: Where are we now?* Institute for Fiscal Studies briefing note BN263.

Cullis, J., & Jones, P. (2009). *Public finance and public choice: Analytical perspectives* (3rd ed.). Oxford University Press.

Diamond, J. (1977). Econometric testing of the 'displacement effect': A reconsideration. *FinanzArchiv/Public Finance Analysis, 35*(3), 387–404.

Durevall, D., & Henrekson, M. (2011). The futile quest for a grand explanation of long-run government expenditure. *Journal of Public Economics, 95*(7), 708–722. https://doi.org/10.1016/j.jpubeco.2011.02.004

Ferris, J. S., & West, E. G. (1999). Cost disease versus Leviathan explanations of rising government cost: An empirical investigation. *Public Choice, 98*(3), 307–316. https://doi.org/10.1023/A:1018358616029

Gemmell, N. (Ed.). (1993). *The growth of the public sector: Theories and international evidence*. Edward Elgar.

Goff, B. (1998). Persistence in government spending fluctuations: New evidence on the displacement effect. *Public Choice, 97*(1), 141–157. https://doi.org/10.1023/A:1004904305228

Henrekson, M. (1988). Swedish government growth: A disequilibrium analysis. In J. A. Hindriks & G. D. Myles (2013). *Intermediate public economics* (2nd ed.). MIT Press.

Hercowitz, Z., & Strawczynski, M. (2004). Cyclical ratcheting in government spending: Evidence from the OECD. *Review of Economics and Statistics, 86*(1), 353–361. https://doi.org/10.1162/003465304323023868

Holcombe, R. G. (2005). Government growth in the twenty-first century. *Public Choice, 124*(1), 95–114. https://doi.org/10.1007/s11127-005-4748-x

IMF (2023). *Government expenditure (% of GDP)* [data set]. *Public finances in modern history* [original data]. International Monetary Fund. Retrieved 13 March 2025 from https://ourworldindata.org/grapher/historical-gov-spending-gdp

Kau, J. B., & Rubin, P. H. (1981). The size of government. *Public Choice, 37*(2), 261–274. https://doi.org/10.1007/BF00138246

Lott, Jr., J. R., & Kenny, L. W. (1999). Did women's suffrage change the size and scope of government? *Journal of Political Economy, 107*(6), 1163–1198. https://doi.org/10.1086/250093

Mauro, P., Romeu, R., Binder, A., & Zaman, A. (2013). *A modern history of fiscal prudence and profligacy*. International Monetary Fund working papers, no. WP/13/5.

Meltzer, A. H., & Richard, S. F. (1978). Why government grows (and grows) in a democracy. *Public Interest, 52*, 111–118.

Meltzer, A. H., & Richard, S. F. (1981). A rational theory of the size of government. *Journal of Political Economy, 89*(5), 914–927. https://doi.org/10.1086/261013

Meltzer, A. H., & Richard, S. F. (1983). Tests of a rational theory of the size of government. *Public Choice, 41*(3), 403–418. https://doi.org/10.1007/BF00141072

Mueller, D. C. (2003). *Public choice III*. Cambridge University Press.

Musgrave, R. (1969). *Fiscal systems*. Yale University Press.

Neck, R., & Schneider, F. (1988). The growth of the public sector in Austria. In J. A. Lybeck & M. Henrekson (Eds.), *Explaining the growth of government* (pp. 231–262). North-Holland.

Niskanen, J. (1971). *Bureaucracy and representative government*. Routledge. https://doi.org/10.4324/9781315081878

Niskanen, W. A. (1968). The peculiar economics of bureaucracy. *American Economic Review, 58*(2), 293–305.

Numa, K. (2024). Fiscal illusion at the individual level. *Public Choice*. https://doi.org/10.1007/s11127-024-01187-9

OECD (0000). *Health expenditure and financing*. Organization for Economic Cooperation and Development. Data explorer. https://data-explorer.oecd.org (accessed 24 April 2026).

OECD (2025). *Global revenue statistics—Comparative tax revenues*. Organization for Economic Cooperation and Development. Data explorer. https://data-explorer.oecd.org (accessed 10 March 2025).

Peacock, A., & Wiseman, J. (1961). *The growth of public expenditure in the United Kingdom*. Princeton University Press.

Peltzman, S. (1980). The growth of government. *Journal of Law and Economics, 23*(2), 209–287. https://doi.org/10.1086/466962

Rostow, W. W. (1959). The stages of economic growth. *Economic History Review, 12*(1), 1–16. JSTOR. https://doi.org/10.2307/2591077

Semat, J., Lowery, D., Linn, S., & Berry, W. D. (2015). The cost growth of government revisited. *Business and Politics, 17*(4), 723–737. https://doi.org/10.1515/bap-2015-0009

Shelton, C. A. (2007). The size and composition of government expenditure. *Journal of Public Economics, 91*(11), 2230–2260. https://doi.org/10.1016/j.jpubeco.2007.01.003

Tanzi, V. (2011). Government versus markets: The changing economic role of the state. Cambridge University Press.

Tanzi, V., & Schuknecht, L. (2000). *Public spending in the 20th century: A global perspective*. Cambridge University Press.

World Bank (n.d.). *Military expenditure (% of GDP), OECD members*. Available at: https://data.worldbank.org/indicator/MS.MIL.XPND.GD.ZS?locations=OE

4
Public choice

Learning objectives

By the end of this chapter, you will be able to:

4.1 Explain Arrow's Impossibility Theorem and how it can be addressed.
4.2 Discuss the properties of the majority voting rule and its implications for social welfare.
4.3 Assess the usefulness of the median voter model for understanding the behaviour of politicians and political parties.
4.4 Discuss the role of special interest groups in the policymaking process.
4.5 Discuss the sources of government failure and the challenges of policymaking in the real world.

Introduction

In January 2025, the UK government announced its support for the construction of a third runway at Heathrow airport in London. This announcement came more than 10 years after plans to expand the airport were originally proposed by the Labour government in 2009. These plans had been cancelled by the Coalition government in 2010 but were revived by the Conservative government in 2016, and a vote in Parliament in 2018 saw a majority of 415–119 vote in favour of the third runway. Although this was challenged by the leaders of four London boroughs, the London mayor, and environmental campaign groups, a decision by the UK Supreme Court in 2020 allowed the plans to go ahead. While the aviation industry and other businesses welcomed this latest announcement as a necessary stimulus to the economy, environmental groups and local residents opposed the expansion due to its impact on efforts to tackle climate change and noise pollution.

This example illustrates some of the complexities of the policymaking process. While economic theory can help governments understand why particular policy problems arise and suggest solutions for addressing them, in order to understand what policies get chosen, we need to understand the political decision-making process: what drives the decisions of voters, politicians, government officials, and special interest groups, and how these political actors interact. Public choice provides a framework for analysing these non-market decisions using the analytical tools from economics, particularly the rational choice model that we reviewed in Chapter 2. In a democratic system, government decisions should reflect the views of the electorate, but these views will vary significantly. Some people may want the government to spend more on health and education, while others may prefer higher government spending on defence. Some people may be willing to pay higher taxes to finance a larger government, while others would prefer a smaller government and lower tax burden. How can the government combine the disparate preferences of the electorate and translate these into a collective choice? Will the political process deliver what the people want?

We start by analysing the problem of how best to aggregate individual preferences into a social choice in section 4.1. In section 4.2, we look at the features of one particular preference aggregation mechanism—majority voting—and its implications for social welfare. Section 4.3 extends the analysis to the context of representative democracies, where individual voters elect representatives who make decisions on their behalf. Section 4.4 explores the role of special interest groups in the policymaking process. In section 4.5, we discuss some of the barriers to effective policymaking.

4.1 The problem of preference aggregation

In markets, individuals decide what goods and services to buy based on their preferences and budgets, while firms decide what goods and services to sell, and what prices to sell them at, based on their costs of production and market conditions. Resources are allocated through the interaction of these forces of demand and supply, where market prices play an important role as a coordinating mechanism. In the public sector, however, decision-making is more complicated. Different individuals will have different preferences about what the level of government spending should be, how this spending should be allocated, and what policies should be prioritized—but ultimately a single decision will have to be made that will affect all individuals living within a given society. How can we combine these different individual preferences into a collective or social decision?

In democratic systems, voting rules provide the main mechanism for aggregating individual preferences. Examples include simple majority voting (introduced in Chapter 3), whereby an option or policy is chosen if it is selected by 50 per cent of voters plus one voter, and **unanimity voting**, which requires unanimous approval for a given alternative to be chosen. Is there an optimal mechanism for aggregating preferences? What properties should a good mechanism for aggregating preferences satisfy? Is there a single mechanism or voting rule that satisfies these properties? These are the questions we will be focusing on below.

4.1.1 Social choice and Arrow's Impossibility Theorem

Social choice theory focuses on the question of how to aggregate individual preferences into a social decision. It is closely related to public choice, although these are two distinct fields (see Box 4.1). Suppose we have a society made up of two individuals, Alfie and Leni, who together have to decide whether funding should be used to build a park or a library. Alfie prefers the park over the library, while Leni prefers the library over the park. How should this society decide which alternative to choose?

There are five properties that an ideal mechanism for aggregating individual preferences should satisfy:

- **Transitivity**: given three alternatives, X, Y, and Z, if X is preferred to Y, and Y is preferred to Z, then transitivity implies that X must be preferred to Z. The transitivity property imposes a degree of logical consistency on a preference ordering.

Box 4.1 Public choice and social choice

The fields of public choice and social choice theory both developed in the aftermath of the Second World War. They were driven by a shared interest in analysing the processes of collective decision-making and understanding how governments and other political actors make decisions, applying the analytical tools from economics, particularly the theory of rational choice. Research in social choice theory tends to be more normative and theoretical, focusing on topics such as the properties of different mechanisms for aggregating individual preferences, while public choice focuses more on a positive and empirical analysis of political processes and institutions.

The development of social choice theory is typically associated with the work of Kenneth Arrow (1963) and Kenneth May (1952) on the properties of preference aggregation mechanisms. Key contributors to the development of public choice include Duncan Black (1948a, 1948b) and his work on the properties of voting rules, James Buchanan's work (1954) on individual voting behaviour, Anthony Downs's (1957) spatial theory of voting, and Gordon Tullock's (1959) analysis of voting institutions. Buchanan was subsequently awarded the Nobel Prize in Economics for his work in the field of public choice.

The public choice approach highlights the importance of thinking about the interests and motivations of voters, politicians, bureaucrats, and other political actors. The assumption underlying this framework—based, as it is, on the theory of rational choice—is that these actors are self-interested utility-maximizers. The main motivation of politicians is not to promote the public interest, but to secure political power and, to do so, they must maximize the votes they receive. Government bureaucrats are driven not by public service, but by a desire to maximize the size of their bureaus, pay, and prestige. Voters will weigh up their individual costs and benefits before deciding whether to vote or who to vote for. In assuming that individual behaviour is guided primarily by rational self-interest, the public choice approach leaves little room for public service or intrinsic motivations.

Sources: Coyle (2020) and Mueller (2015, 2003).

- **Pareto principle**: if at least one individual strictly prefers option X over option Y, and no individual strictly prefers option Y to option X, then society should prefer option X to option Y.
- **Unrestricted domain**: the social choice process must work for any set of individual preferences and any set of alternatives. A voting rule that states 'X should be chosen over Y if a majority vote for X; and Y should be chosen if a majority votes for Y' does not satisfy universal domain because it does not consider a situation in which neither X nor Y receives a majority of votes.
- **Non-dictatorship**: the social decision should not be determined by the preferences of a single individual. This ensures a minimum level of fairness in weighing up individual preferences, so no single individual has the ability to dictate the outcome.
- **Independence of irrelevant alternatives**: the social choice between any two alternatives, X and Y, should only depend on the individual rankings of X and Y, and should not be affected by the introduction of a separate alternative Z. If a group prefers a park over a library, introducing a third option, say a leisure centre, should not lead the group now to prefer the library over the park.

These seem to be reasonable requirements for a mechanism for aggregating individual preferences. However, as the American economist Kenneth Arrow (1963) demonstrated, in fact there is no collective decision-making process that satisfies all of these properties in all contexts. This is one of the key results in social choice theory and is known as **Arrow's Impossibility Theorem**.

We are not going to go into the details of the proof of Arrow's Impossibility Theorem here,[1] but a few examples can help illustrate the challenge of finding a preference aggregation mechanism that satisfies all of these properties. Unanimity voting violates the unrestricted domain requirement, since this property requires the voting rule to work for any set of preferences, including those where there is no unanimously preferred option. Voting rules that are based on the ranking of alternatives, such as the **Borda count method** and **plurality voting** (see Box 4.3), violate the requirement for independence of irrelevant alternatives. Under these types of voting rules, individuals rank the alternatives and a score is assigned to each alternative; these scores are then added together and the alternative with the highest or lowest score is chosen. Here, the introduction of new alternatives may affect the aggregate ranking of two alternatives, say X and Y, even if the individual rankings of these two alternatives have not changed.[2]

One of the most widely used voting rules, the simple majority voting rule, is susceptible to the problem of cyclical voting in contexts where individuals need to choose between three alternatives, thus violating the transitivity requirement. Suppose there are three individuals, Ana, Ben, and Chris, who have to choose between three options, X, Y, and Z. These could be options of where to go for dinner, or whether the local council should invest in a library, a leisure centre, or a park. Ana prefers option X over Y, and Y over Z; Ben prefers option Z over X, and X over Y; and Chris prefers option Y over Z, and Z over X. These rankings are summarized in Table 4.1 below, in order of preference, with 1 representing the most preferred option.

What option should they choose? If they decide to vote on their preferred outcome using a simple majority voting rule to guide their collective decision, then in a choice between X and Y, X would be chosen, since Ana and Ben both prefer X over Y. In a choice between Y and Z, Y would be chosen, since Ana and Chris both prefer Y over Z. To satisfy the property of transitivity, X should be preferred over Z, since X is preferred to Y by a majority, and Y is preferred to Z by a majority. However, in a choice between Z and X, under majority voting, Z would be chosen, since Ben and Chris both prefer Z over X. This problem is known as the **Condorcet paradox**, named after the eighteenth-century Marquis de Condorcet. It demonstrates how, when there are more than two alternatives, majority voting can lead to intransitive **social preferences**. This problem could be avoided by allowing one individual to

Table 4.1 Individual rankings of alternatives

	X	Y	Z
Ana	1	2	3
Ben	2	3	1
Chris	3	1	2

[1] This proof is somewhat technical. Interested readers can consult Vickrey (1960) or Mueller (2003) for a summary of the logic of the proof.

[2] See Cullis and Jones (2009: 104) for an example that illustrates this point.

dictate the outcome; however, this would violate the non-dictatorship requirement. Essentially, there is no preference aggregation mechanism that will satisfy all five properties listed above and deliver a complete and coherent ranking of alternatives.

This example also highlights how, if pairs of alternatives are going to be voted on sequentially, then the order in which alternatives are voted on can affect the result. Looking at the rankings in Table 4.1, if the first vote is between X and Y, and the second vote is between X and Z, then Z will be chosen by majority voting. However, if instead the first vote is between Y and Z, followed by a vote between X and Y, then X will be chosen. So under majority voting, the ability to set the agenda and determine the order in which the alternatives are voted on can influence the outcome.

If the individuals know that the alternatives are going to be voted on following a particular sequence, they may also have an incentive to vote strategically. Suppose that, in this example, the voters know that they will first be asked to vote on a choice between Y and Z, followed by a vote on the choice between the alternative chosen in this first-stage vote and the remaining alternative, X. If the individuals vote based on their true preferences, then the chosen alternative following this sequential voting will be X. Knowing this, Chris would have an incentive to behave strategically and vote for Z in the initial choice between Y and Z, in the hope that the second-stage vote will be between Z and X, and that his preferred choice Z will then be chosen. This illustrates how, under majority voting, individuals will not always have an incentive to vote truthfully. However, this does rely on individual voters having all the necessary information about the sequence of votes and the preferences of other voters.

4.1.2 Overcoming the Impossibility Theorem: single-peaked preferences

Research into addressing the Impossibility Theorem has focused on the implications of relaxing some of the properties that we would like an ideal mechanism for aggregating individuals preferences to satisfy. Particular attention has focused on relaxing the unrestricted domain criterion, which requires that the social choice process must work for any set of individual preferences and any set of alternatives.

Consider the two sets of preferences illustrated in scenario 1 and scenario 2 in Table 4.2. Ana and Ben's rankings of the three alternatives, X, Y, and Z, are the same in both scenarios, but Chris's ranking between X and Y has changed. In scenario 1, Chris's most preferred alternative is Z and his least preferred alternative is X, with Y ranked in the middle; whereas in scenario 2, his least preferred alternative is now Y, with X ranked in the middle. Why does this matter?

Table 4.2 Single-peaked and multiple-peaked preferences

	Scenario 1				Scenario 2		
	X	Y	Z		X	Y	Z
Ana	1	2	3	Ana	1	2	3
Ben	3	1	2	Ben	3	1	2
Chris	3	2	1	Chris	2	3	1

In scenario 2, applying the majority voting rule will violate the principle of transitivity:

1. Choice between X and Y: $X \succ Y$ by a majority[3]
2. Choice between Y and Z: $Y \succ Z$ by a majority
3. Choice between Z and X: $Z \succ X$ by a majority

In scenario 1:

1. Choice between X and Y: $Y \succ X$ by a majority
2. Choice between Y and Z: $Y \succ Z$ by a majority
3. Choice between Z and X: $Z \succ X$ by a majority

In scenario 1, option Y is preferred to option Z, option Z is preferred to X, and Y is preferred to X, so the social ranking satisfies the principle of transitivity. However, in scenario 2, we run into the problem of cyclical voting, as X is preferred to Y by a majority, Y is preferred to Z by a majority, but Z is also preferred to X by a majority. To understand how we might avoid the problem of cyclical voting, it is helpful to think about what distinguishes the preference orderings in these two cases.

The preferences illustrated in scenario 1 are an example of what are known as **single-peaked preferences**, whereas scenario 2 illustrates **multiple-peaked preferences**. A 'peak', in this context, refers to a local maximum, an option that is preferred to all other options in its immediate proximity. Suppose we were to organize the set of alternatives that individuals are voting on along a line. If an individual has a most preferred option and any alternative that is further away from this most preferred option is preferred less, then these preferences are single-peaked. With multiple-peaked preferences, as the name suggests, the preference relation can have multiple peaks, which means that the individual does not consistently rank the alternatives lower as we move away from the most preferred alternative.

This distinction is perhaps more easily understood with an illustration. Figure 4.1 depicts the preference orderings from Table 4.2, where the options that the individuals are voting on are listed along the horizontal axis, while the vertical axis shows the respective rankings. Panel (a) illustrates the preference orderings from scenario 1, where Ana, Ben, and Chris all have single-peaked preferences. For Ana, alternative X is the most preferred outcome; Y is ranked below X, and Z is ranked below Y. For Chris, the ranking is reversed, with alternative Z being the most preferred. For Ben, Y is the most preferred alternative, while X and Z are both ranked below it. Panel (b) illustrates the preference orderings from scenario 2. Ana and Ben's rankings of the three alternatives have not changed and their preferences still have a single peak. However Chris's preferences are now V-shaped and have two peaks: both options X and Z are preferred to option Y.

If we can rule out multiple-peaked preferences, we can overcome the problem of cyclical voting and majority voting will lead to an equilibrium outcome.[4] But how reasonable is it to rule out multiple-peaked preferences? Suppose the alternatives that the individuals are voting on involve levels of local government expenditure and these are ordered such that X represents a high level of spending, Y represents an intermediate level of spending, and Z

[3] The symbol $\succ$ means one option is strictly preferred to another. In this case, X is strictly preferred to Y.

[4] The importance of single-peaked preferences for ensuring a social ordering of preferences that does not violate transitivity was first highlighted by Duncan Black (1948a).

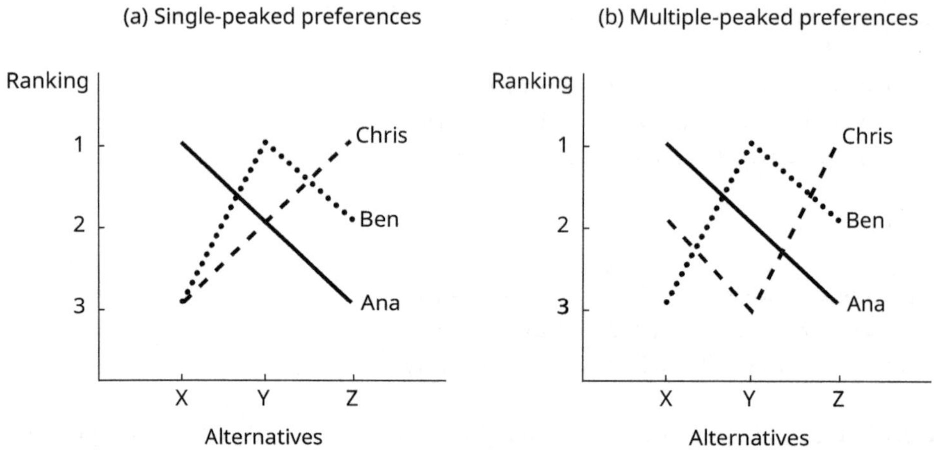

Figure 4.1 Single-peaked preferences and multiple-peaked preferences

represents a low level of spending. In this case, the preferences illustrated in scenario 1 would make sense. Ana's most preferred outcome would be X, a high level of spending; followed by Y, a medium level of spending; and her least preferred outcome would be Z, a low level of spending. Similarly, Chris's most preferred outcome would be option Z, a low level of spending, and his least preferred outcome would be option X, a high level of spending. Ben's most preferred outcome would be an intermediate level of spending (option Y), followed by a low level of spending (option Z), and his least preferred outcome would be a high level of spending (option X). These three sets of preferences all seem to be logical and coherent.

Now compare this with the preferences illustrated in scenario 2, and in particular Chris's preferences: his most preferred outcome is Z, a low level of government spending; but his second most preferred outcome is X, a high level of spending, rather than an intermediate level of spending. This seems illogical. While we can conceive of these 'all or nothing' preferences, and there are likely to be individuals with such preferences, we would expect most people's preferences over an issue like the level of government spending to follow those illustrated in scenario 1 and to be single-peaked.

However, there are situations in which it might not make sense to expect individuals to have single-peaked preferences. Suppose the alternatives being voted on involved discrete choices—for example, whether the local council should invest in a new library, a playground, or a leisure centre. There is no logical order in which to present these alternatives and it would seem perfectly plausible for individual preferences over these alternatives to be multiple-peaked. Where the alternatives being voted on involve the quality of a good, multiple-peaked preferences may also be logical. If the options that individuals are faced with are between a very nice playground (which would involve a significant investment from the council), a low-quality playground, and no playground, preferring either a very nice playground or no playground over a low-quality playground would not seem unreasonable.

So we can avoid the problem of cyclical voting and go some way towards overcoming Arrow's Impossibility Theorem if individual preferences follow a specific pattern and are single-peaked. While this requirement may be plausible in some circumstances, in practice we cannot completely rule out multiple-peaked preferences. Another important practical question we have not considered in our analysis of voting so far is *why* individuals vote.

In the context of collective decision-making, voting provides a mechanism for individuals to express their preferences, but is voting a rational decision? While low voter turnout is a growing concern in many countries, research suggests that perhaps the key paradox lies in understanding why people vote at all (see Box 4.2).

Box 4.2 The paradox of voting

In many countries across the world today, low voter turnout at elections is becoming a growing concern. In Ireland, Italy, Japan, Canada, and Austria, just over half of people of voting age turned up to vote, compared with 80 per cent of the population of voting age in Sweden (see Figure 4.2).

To understand why voter turnout is low, we need to understand why people vote. In some countries—including Argentina, Australia, and Belgium—voting is compulsory, and sanctions range from being required to provide an explanation for not voting, to fines or even prison sentences. However, in the vast majority of countries, voting is optional. Voting involves a cost: there's the cost of travelling to the polling station, the opportunity cost of the time spent going to vote, and the cost of researching the different candidates and their policies and deciding whom to vote for. A rational, utility-maximizing individual should only vote if the expected benefits of voting are greater than the costs. The benefits include the value to the individual of the policies that their preferred candidate would implement, and the probability that their vote is decisive and will influence the outcome of the election. The latter will depend on the size of the electorate and how close the election is. Downs (1957) argued that it is not rational for people to vote, as the costs of voting will generally outweigh the expected

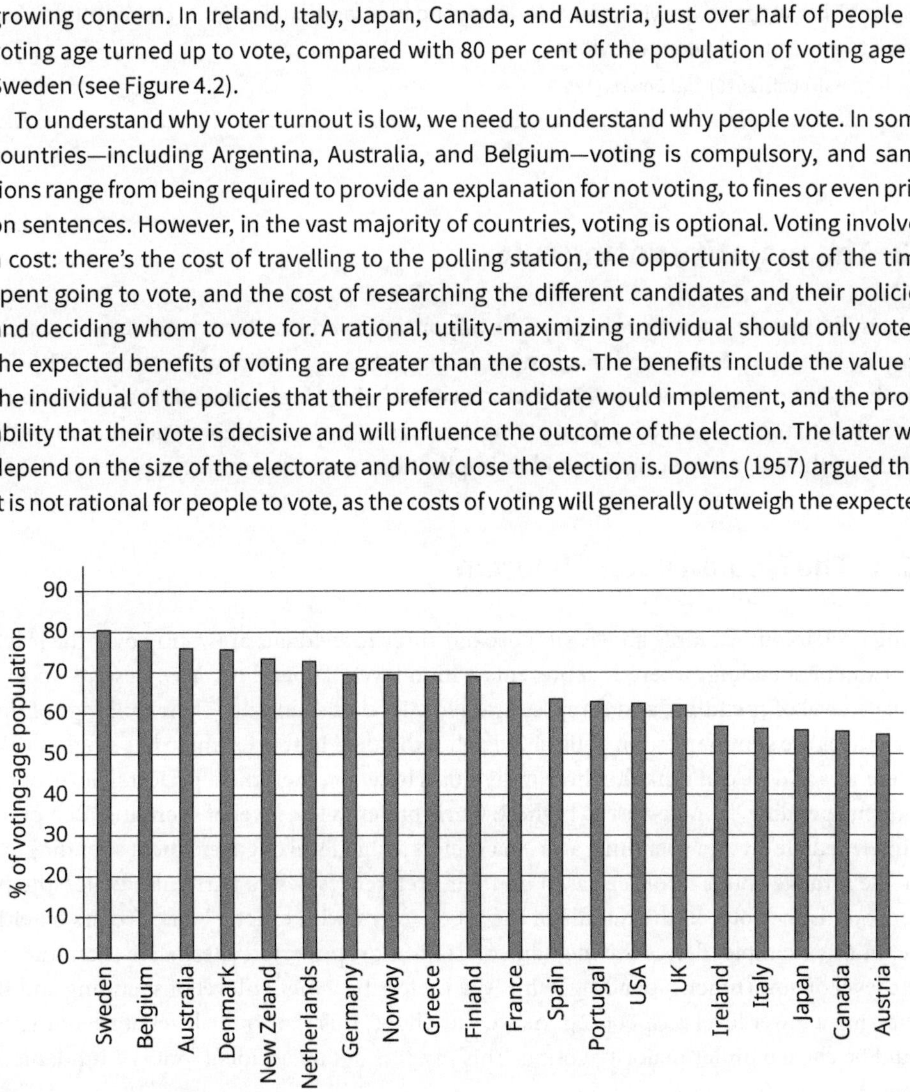

Figure 4.2 Voter turnout in a selection of countries, 2023[a]

[a] Or the closest available year.

Source: Voter turnout data from V-Dem (2024)—processed by Our World in Data.

benefits because the likelihood of any one individual's vote being decisive is very low. Many people vote, even though the expected utility of voting is likely to be negative—this is the **paradox of voting**.

So perhaps the question is not why is voter turnout so low, but rather why do people vote at all? Alternative models of voting behaviour suggest we should allow for non-selfish motivations and for the fact that people may also derive some utility from the act of voting. Voting can also be viewed as a relatively low-cost way for individuals to express their preferences (the expressive voter hypothesis). Bali et al. (2020) analysed the role of different psychological motives for voting, including selfishness, duty, altruism, belonging, and social approval. They found that altruism and duty were the most important reported motives for turning out to vote. This suggests we will need to look beyond the traditional rational choice model if we want to understand voter behaviour.[5]

Sources: Bali et al. (2020) and Downs (1957).

4.2 The majority voting rule

The simple majority voting rule plays an important role in collective choice processes in many democracies. Is it a good mechanism for aggregating individual preferences? We have already seen how, unless we restrict preferences to being single-peaked, majority voting is susceptible to the problem of cyclical voting. In this section, we review some other important features of the majority voting rule and its implications for social welfare.

4.2.1 The Median Voter Theorem

Going back to our example above, suppose our three individuals are voting over the level of government spending, where X represents a high level of spending, Y represents an intermediate level of spending, and Z represents a low level of spending. Their rankings of these alternatives are summarized in Table 4.3. Each individual in this example has single-peaked preferences and we can rank the three individuals based on their most preferred level of government spending, from lowest to highest: Chris prefers a low level of spending, Ben prefers an intermediate level of spending, and Ana prefers a high level of government spending.

If we arrange voters in order based on their preferences over a particular issue,[6] the median voter is the voter in the middle of the set of voters, with exactly half of voters on either side. In this example, Ben is the median voter: his most preferred alternative is an intermediate level of government spending, with Ana preferring a higher level of spending and Ben preferring a lower level of spending. As we saw above, this is also the level of spending that would be chosen under majority voting. This result is not an accident, but is a fundamental

[5] The rational voter hypothesis is just one of the models that have been proposed to explain voter behaviour. For a discussion of some of the alternatives and the empirical evidence, see Mueller (2003).

[6] For example, this could be the level of government spending or taxation, or we could rank voters based on where their preferences lie on the political spectrum, from the most left-wing to the most right-wing.

Table 4.3 Individual preferences over the level of government spending

	Level of government spending		
	X—high	Y—intermediate	Z—low
Ana	1	2	3
Ben	3	1	2
Chris	3	2	1

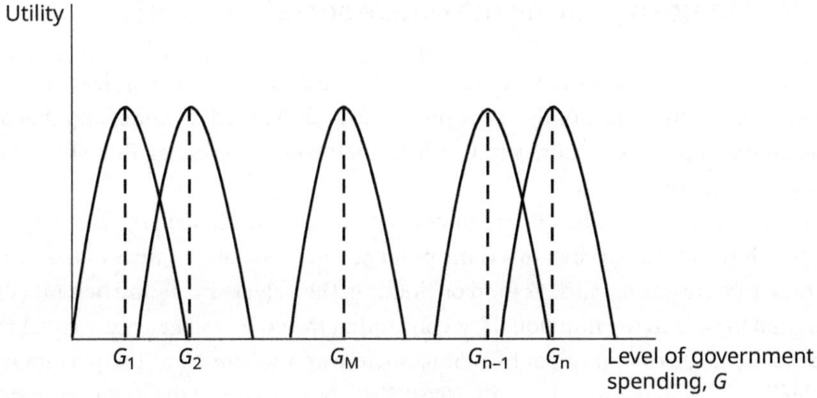

Figure 4.3 Government spending and the median voter

feature of the majority voting rule and is known as the **Median Voter Theorem**. According to this theorem, under majority voting, the preferences of the median voter determine the outcome—the chosen outcome will be the one preferred by the median voter.[7]

This result holds for any number of voters. Suppose we have n voters with single-peaked preferences, as illustrated in Figure 4.3. Each point along the horizontal axis, $G_1, G_2, \ldots, G_n$, represents that voter's most preferred level of government spending, organized from lowest to highest. The median voter is the voter in the middle and their preferred level of government spending is G_M. This means that exactly half of voters would prefer a level of spending below G_M and half would prefer a level of spending above G_M. This level, G_M, is also the level that would be chosen by majority voting. To see why, suppose voters face a choice between G_M and any level of spending below G_M: the median voter and all voters who prefer a higher level of government spending will vote for G_M, and therefore G_M will be the level of spending voted on by the majority. Now suppose voters face a choice between G_M and any level of spending above G_M: the median voter will again vote for G_M, and all voters who prefer a lower level of spending will also vote for G_M. Therefore G_M will again be the level of spending chosen by the majority.

The Median Voter Theorem holds both in the case of **direct democracy** and in the case of **representative democracy**, which we discuss in section 4.3 below. This result highlights

[7] If there is an even number of voters, there is no median voter. In this case, there will be a tie in voting between the two voters in the middle.

the power of the median voter, and the fact that majority voting is less sensitive to strategic behaviour by voters. This theorem implies that the best strategy for each individual is to vote honestly, since no individual will benefit by misrepresenting their preferences. The only way for any voter to the left of the median voter to shift the final outcome would be to choose a quantity to the right of the median voter, but this will be higher than their preferred level of government spending, and would shift the equilibrium outcome further away from their preferred outcome; and similarly for any individual to the right of the median voter. Therefore, the best strategy for each voter is to vote in accordance with their true preferences.

4.2.2 Will majority voting maximize social welfare?

We have seen that, if preferences are single-peaked, majority voting will lead to an equilibrium outcome which corresponds to the preferences of the median voter, and that all voters will have an incentive to vote honestly, based on their true preferences. But will this majority voting equilibrium be efficient?

As we saw in Chapter 2, efficiency requires that the marginal benefit of providing a good or service equals the marginal cost; this is the point at which social welfare is maximized. In the case of pure **private goods**, such as food or clothing, the **private marginal benefit (PMB)** (or the marginal benefit to the individual) of consuming the good will generally equal the social marginal benefit (or the marginal benefit to society as a whole), and the **private marginal cost (PMC)** will equal the social marginal cost.[8] However, many of the goods provided by the government—such as defence, or physical infrastructure such as roads and footpaths—have the characteristics of public goods; in particular, they are non-rival in consumption. A good is non-rival if consumption of the good by one person does not reduce the amount available for others to consume.[9] Whatever quantity of the good is supplied can be consumed equally by all individuals. As we discuss in more detail in Chapter 6, this means that to determine the social marginal benefit of providing a given quantity of these goods, we need to sum together the individual private marginal benefits. Some individuals will derive a greater benefit from the good than others and the social marginal benefit should reflect this—that is, it should reflect the total aggregate benefit that all individuals derive from the good.

Majority voting will not necessarily lead to this socially optimal outcome because the median voter outcome does not take into account the intensity of individual preferences for the good. Suppose the value that the median voter places on the publicly provided good is given by MB_{median}. With n voters, the level of the good that will be provided will be $n \times MB_{median}$. Will this equal the social marginal benefit? This would require

$$n \times MB_{median} = \sum MB_i$$

where the term on the right represents the sum of the marginal benefits for all voters. Rearranging this expression, we can see that this is equivalent to

$$MB_{median} = \frac{1}{n}\sum MB_i = MB_{mean}$$

[8] Assuming there are no externalities (see Chapter 2).

[9] The concept of public goods and their properties were introduced in Chapter 2 and are discussed in more detail in Chapter 6. Whether a good is rival in consumption will often depend on how many people are already consuming it—for example, an extra car on a busy road reduces the amount of space available for other drivers, while an extra car on a fairly empty road does not.

So the median voter outcome will only be efficient if the preferences of the median voter equal average preferences. This requires that the distribution of preferences be symmetric and that there is no difference in the intensity of preferences on either side of the median voter.

To illustrate this point, suppose a community of 1,001 individuals is deciding whether to build a new park.[10] The total cost of the park is £50,050, which would be financed by levying a uniform £50 tax on each voter. Just under half of the voters—500 voters—would value the park very highly and would be willing to pay up to £120 each for the park to be built. However, the remaining 501 voters do not want a park and would not be willing to pay anything for it. The social marginal benefit of building the park equals $(500 \times 120) + (501 \times 0) = 60{,}000$. This is greater than the social marginal cost of building the park, which is £50,050, therefore the efficient outcome is for the park to be built. However, if the individuals vote on the proposal to build the park financed by a £50 tax paid by each voter, the majority voting outcome will be for the park not to be built, because the median voter will not be willing to pay £50 to build the park.

So the majority voting equilibrium will not necessarily be efficient because the median voter outcome does not reflect the intensity of individual preferences or how strongly individuals feel about particular alternatives. More generally, majority voting will only lead to an efficient outcome if this aligns with the preferences of the median voter, and there is no reason why this should be the case. Each individual's most preferred level of public expenditure or publicly provided goods will depend on the benefits they derive from these goods and the cost of providing them, which, in turn, will depend on their preferences, the tax price of the goods, and their income.

Another potential source of inefficiency under majority voting arises as a result of agenda setting. As discussed above, when individual preferences are such that majority voting leads to cyclical voting, the ability to set the agenda and determine the order in which the alternatives are voted on can influence the outcome. Agenda setting can therefore distort the outcome of majority voting, resulting in an outcome that does not maximize social welfare.

One voting rule that will guarantee a Pareto improvement is the unanimity voting rule. Because all individuals have to agree, this voting rule ensures that only alternatives that will make at least some people better off and no one worse off will be voted on. However, getting everyone to agree is itself costly. Buchanan and Tullock (1965) highlighted the importance of considering the different types of costs associated with voting rules. These costs can be divided into two main components:[11] the external costs created by the winning majority, which reflect the fact that the minority will now be subjected to the decisions of the majority, which will probably have a negative impact on their welfare; and the decision-making costs, which are the costs required to reach an agreement. The external costs decrease with the number of people required to reach an agreement under a particular voting rule, whereas the decision-making costs increase. A unanimity voting rule will require the support of all individuals, so the external costs will be zero, but the decision-making costs—the cost of achieving a consensus—will be very high. Getting everyone to agree on a particular alternative will involve costly negotiation processes, possibly slower implementation of policies, and perhaps side-payments or other forms of corruption. A majority voting rule, on the other hand, will involve lower decision-making costs, but higher external costs. Box 4.3 summarizes some other alternatives to the majority voting rule.

[10] This illustration is based on an example provided by Gruber (2013).
[11] Buchanan and Tullock (1965), as summarized by Cullis and Jones (2009).

Box 4.3 Alternatives to majority voting

We have already looked at one alternative to majority voting—the unanimity voting rule. This is the only rule that will guarantee a Pareto improvement because, in order to achieve unanimity, no individual can be made worse off by the policy in question, otherwise they would not vote for it. However, the costs of achieving a consensus are likely to be very high, making this rule impracticable in many situations.

The **Borda count method** involves assigning each candidate or alternative being voted on a number of points based on their ranking. So, if there are n alternatives, then each voter's first choice is awarded n points, the second choice receives $n-1$, and so on. The alternative with the greatest number of points is the one that is chosen. Under **plurality voting**, a score is given to each alternative based on an individual's ranking of the alternatives, so their first choice is given a score of 1, their second choice is given a score of 2, etc. Here the option with the lowest number of points is chosen.

Point voting follows a similar principle, but here voters have a fixed number of points to distribute across the alternatives. For example, they may have 10 points to spread across three alternatives. A voter could then award, say, 5 points to their most preferred option, 3 to their next preferred, and 2 points to the final option. The option with the largest number of points is selected. As point voting allows the intensity of voter preferences to be taken into account, it could be argued to better represent voter preferences. However, this is based on the assumption that voters are truthfully revealing their preferences. One of the drawbacks of point voting is that the outcome is more susceptible to being influenced by strategic behaviour. For example, if a voter believes their most preferred option is unlikely to win, they have an incentive to change their point allocation to ensure their second most preferred option wins.

Source: Mueller (2003).

4.3 The role of politicians

So far we have focused on the problems that arise in the context of direct democracy, where individuals vote directly on their preferred policy alternatives—for example, through referenda and initiatives.[12] In practice, most policymaking takes place in the context of representative democracies, where individual voters elect representatives—for example, members of Parliament or local councillors—who make decisions on their behalf, without consulting them on each individual issue. What can public choice theory tell us about how these elected representatives are likely to behave?

Politicians and political parties select what policies to offer the electorate, and public choice theory can help us understand what types of policies are more likely to be offered. The key result here is based on the work of Anthony Downs (1957), who developed a spatial model

[12] For example, the UK held a referendum on its membership of the EU in 2016, and before that the country held a referendum on proposed changes to the parliamentary voting system, in 2011. Referenda in other countries have covered proposed changes to the constitution, whether to adopt the single currency (euro), and whether to legalize abortion. Referenda are not necessarily binding, so the government may not be required to implement whatever alternative the majority of voters have selected.

of voting to explain the dynamics of competition between political parties.[13] Politicians are assumed to be self-interested and to care primarily about securing political power. In a democratic system, to secure political power, politicians need to maximize the number of votes they receive. Downs demonstrated that, in this framework, the preferences of the median voter will play a crucial role in determining the outcome: vote-maximizing politicians will select the policies that are preferred by the median voter. In a two-party system, the candidates or parties will therefore tend to gravitate towards the centre in their policy offerings.

Suppose that voter preferences can be arranged along a single dimension—say, the level of government spending, G—which can be represented along a straight line, as depicted in Figure 4.4. The level of government spending ranges from low, G_L, to high, G_H, and voters are assumed to be evenly distributed along this line, depending on their preferred level of government spending. Preferences are single-peaked, so that each voter has a single most preferred outcome. Voters will vote for the candidate that most closely represents their views and a simple majority voting rule will decide the outcome. In Figure 4.4, G_M represents the level of spending preferred by the median voter.

If there are two political parties, A and B, and each party wants to maximize the number of votes it receives, what is the optimal or vote-maximizing position for each party to take? This will depend on the choice made by the other party. Suppose that initially party A favours a low level of government spending and party B favours a high level of government spending, such that their initial position is as shown in panel (a) of Figure 4.4. Because voters will vote for the party that is closest to their own views (i.e. the party that is closest to the voter along the line), each party will attract half of the voters. However, this is not a stable outcome, since each party has an incentive to shift its positioning slightly in order to win over some of

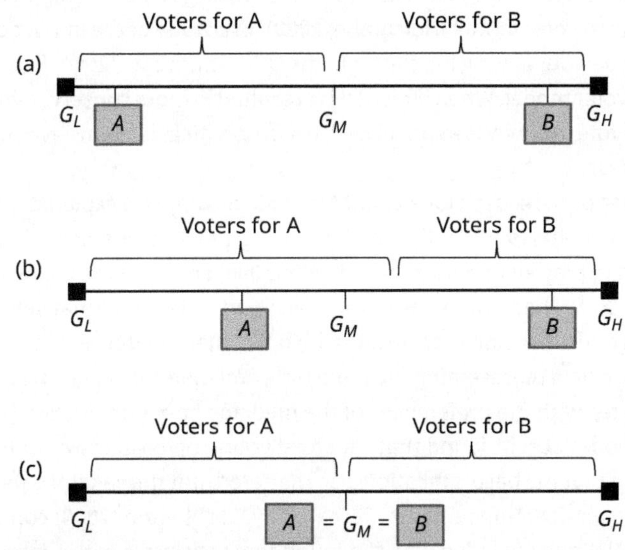

Figure 4.4 The Hotelling model of spatial competition applied to voters

[13] This model was based on a model of the location decisions of retailers developed by Harrold Hotelling in 1929. Hotelling's work looked at the optimal location decision of two ice-cream sellers along a beach, given an even distribution of consumers along the beach.

the other party's voters. If party A were to advocate for a slightly higher level of government spending, moving its position as shown in panel (b), it would continue to appeal to voters who prefer a low level of spending, but it would now also attract some of the voters who were previously voting for party B, since the party would now be closer to these voters along the line. Party A would then attract the majority of voters.

But party B has the same incentive to shift its position slightly, advocating for a slightly lower level of spending in order to attract more voters. Each party has an incentive to continue to modify its position, moving closer towards the centre, in order to attract voters from the rival party and increase its vote share. The only equilibrium is where both parties have positioned themselves in the middle of the distribution, settling on the preferred option of the median voter, G_M, as shown in panel (c). This is the key result: vote-maximizing politicians will choose the alternative preferred by the median voter.

The median voter model helps to explain the increase in consensus politics in two-party systems and why politicians and political parties will tend to move towards the centre to maximize their vote share. Are the predictions of the model supported by the evidence? Several empirical tests of the median voter model have been carried out and the evidence to date has been mixed: while voter preferences do seem to matter, factors such as political affiliation and personal ideology also influence the voting behaviour of elected representatives (see Box 4.4).

Box 4.4 The median voter model in practice

Tests of the median voter model have tended to focus on analysing the impact of voter preferences on the voting behaviour of legislators. There is a large body of empirical evidence supporting the median voter model (Holcombe, 1989). In a study of the impact of redistricting[14] on the voting behaviour among legislators in the USA, Stratmann (2000) finds strong support for the median voter model. When redistricting resulted in more conservative districts, politicians started to vote more conservatively, even if the politicians themselves had not changed during this process.

However, voter preferences alone cannot provide a complete explanation of what drives legislators' voting behaviour. Political affiliation and personal ideology, in particular, have also been found to play an important role. Levitt (1996) analysed the voting behaviour of US senators where states had one senator from each party. He found that senators voted very differently from one other, and more in line with how other senators in their own party voted, even though they were representing the same state and therefore would be expected to want to align their votes with the preferences of the median voter in their state (according to the median voter model). Levitt found that senators' voting behaviour was influenced by voter preferences, and that the party affiliation also mattered, but the senator's personal ideology was the main driver of voting patterns. Research by Washington (2008) confirms the important role played by personal ideology: she found that legislators with a larger proportion of children who are daughters were more likely to vote in favour of issues that primarily affect women, such as reproductive rights and women's safety.

[14] Redistricting refers to the practice of redrawing electoral district boundaries. In the USA, this process is carried out every 10 years in response to the census results, to reflect changes in the population.

The median voter model provides a useful framework for understanding the behaviour of politicians and political parties. However, it relies on some fairly strong assumptions:

- **Individuals vote along a single dimension**: the median voter model assumes that individuals base their votes on a single issue and that individuals have preferences that are single-peaked. In practice, many issues are multidimensional and politicians and political parties will campaign on a bundle of issues. If voter preferences on these different issues are highly correlated—so that, for example, voters who prefer a high level of spending on health and education also support higher taxes and more redistribution—then this should not be a problem. But if voter preferences vary significantly across the different issues, then the median voter is harder to define and identify, making it more difficult for politicians to target their policies at the median voter.
- **There are only two candidates or parties**: the model assumes there are only two candidates. With three or more candidates, the equilibrium outcome will no longer be for the candidates to select their policies to appeal to the median voter (Palfrey, 1984). Suppose there are three candidates who are all proposing a level of government spending that matches the preferences of the median voter. Now, each candidate will have an incentive to deviate slightly from this outcome, offering a slightly higher or lower level of government spending, in order to increase their share of the vote.
- **It ignores participation in the political process**: voting imposes a cost on individuals, in terms of time and money, and this cost can affect voter turnout. Voters with preferences close to the median voter may be less likely to vote as they may feel their vote will have less of an impact, whereas voters with more extreme views may be more likely to vote. These variations in voter turnout are likely to influence the electoral outcome.
- **It ignores the role of ideology**: the median voter model assumes that politicians are driven primarily by a desire to maximize votes, but personal ideology also plays an important role in influencing politicians' voting behaviour. Rather than assuming that voter preferences drive party platforms, it is possible that politicians devise their own platforms and then persuade voters that these are the issues they should care about (Cullis & Jones, 2009). Research suggests that the polarization of political candidates and other elites can lead to the polarization of voters' ideological views (Druckman et al., 2013). Standing as a political candidate is expensive and taking an extreme position on certain issues may help candidates attract more campaign funding.

The median voter model cannot explain the increasing political polarization and the widening gap between the 'left' and the 'right' that we see in many democracies today. To explain these trends, we need to rely on different models. Jones et al. (2022) propose a model of voter choice that examines three potential mechanisms that may contribute to political polarization: a relative cost of voting that may discourage voters who are indifferent between the two main candidates; ideologically driven third-party candidates who attract extreme voters; and a bimodal distribution of voter ideology. They find that, given these conditions, it may be rational for the major-party candidates to seek to reinforce polarization, rather than moving towards the centre, potentially becoming even more polarized than their electorate. Crucially, in their model, political polarization is not the result of politicians' commitment to a particular ideology, but rather follows from their desire to win and secure political power.

So where does all this leave the median voter model? This model is a useful tool for understanding the behaviour of politicians and political parties, and it works very well in some circumstances. The model also sheds some light on why politicians might not implement policies that maximize social welfare or the public interest, as they may be more concerned with re-election and therefore focus on the popularity of particular policies among voters. Long-term investment projects, where the benefits of the project will be experienced a long time in the future, may thus be neglected in favour of projects with more immediate payoffs which will be more appealing to voters today. The fact that the median voter model cannot explain all patterns of behaviour should not invalidate it, but it is important to be aware of its limitations and the circumstances in which it is more likely to be applicable.

Our discussion in this section has focused on political decision-making in representative democracies. Historically, however, democratic governments account for a very small fraction of all governments. As of 2024, just over half of all countries in the world were classed as autocracies[15] (V-Dem, 2025). Public choice can provide some useful insights for understanding political behaviour in autocratic regimes. Although going into this subject in detail falls outside of the scope of this chapter, Box 4.5 provides an overview of some of the contributions of public choice theory in this space.

Box 4.5 Decision-making in autocracies

Autocratic regimes are centred around a single individual, normally a dictator or absolute ruler. However, to understand how these regimes develop and survive over time, we need to understand not only the preferences and actions of these autocratic rulers, but also the behaviour of the bureaucracies that help them sustain their power and the mechanisms that enable these regimes to effectively control or supress their citizens.

Most early work in public choice theory focused on the analysis of democratic governments, but interest in studying autocratic regimes has grown since the 1990s. This work has aimed to explore questions such as how dictatorships originate, what the goals of dictators are, and what conditions are required to ensure the continued survival of these regimes. In his book *Autocracy*, Tullock (1987) was one of the first to highlight the need for public choice scholars to understand governments that were not democratically elected and he identified one of the main challenges facing autocratic rulers: how to ensure their survival in office. Olson (1993, 2000) analysed the origins of dictatorships.[16] He viewed dictators as wealth-maximizers whose goal is to transfer the wealth created by those they rule over to themselves. However, even autocratic regimes have an incentive to care about what proportion of the population's resources they take, as the more they take, the weaker the incentive individuals will have to produce, leaving less wealth for the ruler to appropriate. This, in Olson's view, meant that dictators would have an incentive to exercise their power in a way that aligned at least in part with the wider interests of society.

[15] Autocracy refers to a system of government in which power is concentrated in a single person; these include dictatorships, absolute monarchies, and elective monarchies (e.g. the Vatican City).

[16] Olson used his famous metaphor of roving and stationary bandits to analyse the evolution of autocratic regimes. Autocratic leaders who want their regime to survive have an incentive to behave like stationary bandits, limiting the share of their citizens' resources that they take. However, if they fear they will soon be overthrown, they are more likely to behave like roving bandits, taxing their citizens more heavily and appropriating a larger share of their resources.

More recent work has focused on how the nature of autocratic regimes has changed. Guriev and Treisman (2020) highlight how contemporary autocracies differ from the classic dictatorships of the twentieth century. Whereas rulers such as Hitler, Stalin, Pinochet, and Idi Amin all relied on violence and brutality to intimidate potential opponents and secure their power, today, faced with a world of (mostly) open borders and international media, a new type of autocracy has emerged.[17] These autocratic regimes are not completely non-violent, but repression is often less overt—for example, dissidents are more likely to be prosecuted on charges such as **tax evasion** or fraud than on political charges. Propaganda and censorship are key for explaining the survival of most modern dictatorships, where leaders manipulate public opinion with the aid of censored or co-opted media, basing their legitimacy more on popularity than fear.

4.4 The role of special interest groups

Special interest groups or **pressure groups** are groups of individuals or organizations that share a common interest or goals and who work together to attempt to influence public policy in their favour. These shared goals might involve advancing the interests of particular groups in society, such as farmers or the insurance industry, but they can also involve promoting the broader public interest—for example, by campaigning to reduce air pollution. Examples of special interest groups include environmental groups, animal rights groups, professional associations (e.g. for doctors, nurses, and accountants), industrial and trade associations, labour unions, and farmer associations.

Special interest groups influence public policy by lobbying policymakers. Lobbying, introduced in Chapter 1, refers to the process whereby individuals or groups attempt to persuade policymakers to support a particular policy or campaign. This can involve running public relations or media campaigns, providing corporate hospitality, or funding research by think-tanks. Individuals can also lobby policymakers, for example by sending emails or letters to their MPs, or by organizing petitions. Special interest groups have a range of resources they can draw on to influence government decisions—not just financial resources, but also knowledge, expertise, legitimacy, and political support. Although we might expect larger special interest groups to be more effective in influencing public policy, research suggests that in fact this might not be the case (see Box 4.6).

Lobbying often has a negative connotation, but it can play an important role in the political process and have a positive impact on social welfare. One of the challenges that policymakers face in designing effective policies is a lack of information, as we discuss below. Because special interest groups typically have a strong interest in a particular issue, they are more likely to be well informed about the issue and to be well placed to advise policymakers on it. Lobbying can therefore be seen as a way of conveying information about specific issues and how strongly voters feel about them, which can support the policymaking process. Special interest groups can also support voters, by reducing the cost to voters of acquiring information and monitoring the actions of politicians and government agencies.

[17] The authors do acknowledge that some more violent autocratic regimes still remain.

Box 4.6 The challenge of collective action: pressure group size and influence

Special interest groups can be large or small—what unites them is having a shared interest or goal. But having a shared goal means that advancing this goal has the properties of a public good for the group, which creates an incentive for individuals in the group to free ride. If the rail workers' union manages to secure higher wages or better working conditions, these will benefit all rail workers, not only those who are members of the union.[18] This is one of the key insights from Mancur Olson's work, *The Logic of Collective Action* (1965), in which he analysed the conditions required for collective action to succeed when there are many individuals involved. He argued that it is easier to form an effective special interest group when the number of potential members is small. For larger special interest groups to be effective, additional mechanisms need to be in place to incentivize individuals to contribute, and to limit the risk of free riding. The large subsidies paid to farmers in developed countries, where the farming sector is relatively small, compared to the small or negative subsidies paid to farmers in developing countries with typically larger agricultural sectors, would seem to support this theory. Van Bastelaer (1998) analysed the effective subsidies paid to farmers in a number of countries and found that these ranged from 26.9 per cent in Ghana to 85.9 per cent in Switzerland. Other experimental evidence on the free rider problem lends further support to Olson's hypothesis.[19]

While lobbying by special interest groups can lead to policies that enhance social welfare, it can also be perceived as a wasteful use of resources. Lobbying is a form of **rent-seeking**, whereby individuals or organizations use resources to advance their own goals and gain economic benefits, rather than investing these resources in productive economic activities. Lobbying can therefore have a negative impact on economic growth: research suggests that countries with more interest groups tend to grow more slowly, accumulate less capital, and have lower productivity growth (Coates et al., 2011). Estimating the total cost of lobbying is difficult in practice, but figures suggest this is likely to be high. According to figures from the Corporate Europe Observatory, in 2024, the 162 largest corporations and trade associations[20] spent €343 million on lobbying EU legislators and officials (Corporate Europe Observatory, 2025). This cost is ultimately paid by consumers in the form of higher prices.

There is also a risk that special interest groups might exert undue influence on the political process, resulting in **policy capture** and an erosion of trust in government. Lobbies have their own interests, so the information they provide may not be complete or impartial, and they will typically provide rewards or incentives to politicians who advance their causes by contributing to their campaigns or encouraging people to vote for particular parties. Policy capture arises when public policy decisions consistently target particular interests rather than the public interest. Research has found, for example, that lobbying by businesses in the

[18] The concepts of public goods and free riding were introduced in Chapter 2 and are discussed in more detail in Chapter 6.

[19] See, for example, Mueller (2003: ch. 2) for a review.

[20] Only organizations spending over €1 million annually on EU lobbying are required to declare their lobbying budgets in the EU's Transparency Register.

fossil fuel sector, including coal, automotive, and other heavy industry, has played a major role in blocking action by governments globally to implement regulations designed to combat climate change (OECD, 2021). These practices can exacerbate inequalities and erode trust in government. According to the OECD Trust Survey (2022), almost half of people (47.8 per cent) across 22 OECD countries believe that an elected or appointed political official would grant a political favour in exchange for the offer of a well-paid private sector job.

What can governments do to mitigate the risks of harmful lobbying? Policymakers and government officials should work to engage with a broad range of stakeholders to minimize the risk of policy capture and create an inclusive and fair policymaking process, as well as promoting integrity and transparency in lobbying activities and political financing. Competition authorities, regulatory agencies, and audit institutions have an important role to play in promoting accountability, but these organizations are also prime targets for undue influence, so it is important that they are properly monitored.[21] The EU has developed a Transparency Register, a database which lists 'interest representatives' who carry out activities which aim to influence EU policy. This register is designed to make public information on which interests are being represented at the EU level and by whom, and what resources are being devoted to these activities—namely, through financial support, donations, and sponsorship. However, in spite of this and other initiatives, transparency remains limited. Only 17 out of 32 OECD countries for which data are available provide transparency through a publicly available lobbying register (OECD, 2022).

4.5 Government failure

We have seen how the influence of special interest groups can distort the policymaking process and how governments may be driven more by a desire to maximize votes rather than a concern for promoting the public interest. These are examples of sources of government failure, a concept introduced in Chapter 1. As we saw in Chapter 2, market failures arise when private markets fail to achieve an efficient allocation of resources, and addressing these market failures provides one of the leading arguments for government intervention. But government intervention will not always improve on the market outcome and in some cases may end up increasing inefficiency. Government actions may also contribute to exacerbating inequalities—for example, by rewarding special interest groups, or giving contracts, money, or power to individuals and organizations without merit.

There are two main sources of government failure: a lack of information and expertise; and problems that arise as a result of the incentives and motivations of policymakers. We discuss each of these in turn below.

4.5.1 Lack of information and expertise

Problems of incomplete and asymmetric information are one of the leading causes of market failure, but governments are not immune to these problems. To plan, design, and implement policies effectively, policymakers require vast amounts of information, which are not always

[21] See OECD (2017) for a more detailed discussion of these strategies.

available in practice. To provide the socially optimal level of goods and services, governments need information on the marginal benefits that individuals derive from them, which can be difficult to obtain, particularly when individuals might not have the incentive to truthfully reveal their preferences.[22] Governments are also unlikely to have all the information they need to determine the right level at which to set taxes, in order to tackle externalities such as environmental pollution, or to be able to effectively identify the households that need financial support, in order to ensure this support is provided to all households that need it, and only those that need it.[23]

Governments cannot control how individuals will respond to a policy, but failure to take these responses into account when designing policies means that they may end up being ineffective or even counterproductive. Good policymaking will generally try to anticipate and, where possible, estimate the size of these behavioural responses. Estimates of the elasticity of demand[24] for a particular good—say, sugary drinks—can be used to assess the likely impact of a tax on sugary drinks, or tax revenue elasticities can help assess the likely impact of changes in taxes on government revenues, taking into account how supply and demand are expected to change in response to the tax change.

However, as we discuss in Chapter 5, it is not always possible to predict how individuals will respond to a policy or to quantify these behavioural responses. Sometimes people will respond to policies in ways that had not been anticipated. A study of the UK government's pension automatic enrolment policy[25] found that, while individuals did increase their pension savings as a result of the policy, levels of unsecured debt, including personal loans and overdrafts, also increased (Beshears et al., 2024). Following the introduction of an EU regulation banning retailers from imposing credit card surcharges, which came into force in 2018, many retailers introduced administrative charges that were often higher than the previous surcharge (Coyle, 2020). Anticipating the effects of public policies is challenging, and it is unlikely that governments will ever be able to fully anticipate *all* effects, but research can help to address some of these gaps. Behavioural economics can generate better predictions about the effects of public policies by incorporating a more nuanced understanding of individual behaviour. Work in this area has already led to a better understanding of the impact of economic incentives such as retirement saving subsidies and income tax policies on individual behaviour (Chetty, 2015; Chetty et al., 2014).

Policymaking is generally a slow process, which involves consultations and negotiations, and the ability of public policies to respond to new information—for example, as a result of technological developments or changes in **social norms**—is more limited than that of markets. For example, although private e-scooters have been on the market in the UK since around 2015—and their use really took off during the Covid-19 pandemic—as of 2025 it was still illegal to use a privately owned e-scooter on public roads, footpaths, and cycle lanes.[26]

[22] This is a problem we discuss in Chapter 6, in the context of the provision of public goods.

[23] We return to some of these questions later in the book.

[24] The elasticity of demand measures the sensitivity of the quantity demanded of a good to a change in its price.

[25] This policy was designed to encourage individuals to save for their retirement by making it compulsory for employers to enrol their employees into a pension. Rather than having to decide how much to save into a pension each month (and whether to save at all), pension payments are deducted automatically from individual salaries, although employees have the choice to opt out of this. We discuss this policy in more detail in chapter 11.

[26] This contrasts with many other European countries, where both privately owned and rented e-scooters are widely used. In the UK, a small number of government-regulated e-scooter rental trials were due to run until 2026, and the outcome of these trials will inform the government's decision-making on the use of e-scooters.

In some cases, the problem is not so much that policymakers lack information, but that they lack the relevant knowledge and practical experience, which can lead to significant cost overruns and delays, particularly in the context of delivering large infrastructure projects. The Sydney Opera House, which was due to open in 1963 at an initial projected cost of AU$7, opened 10 years later and the total cost came to AU$102 million, more than 14 times the original estimate (Coyle, 2020; Flyvbjerg, 2014). It is important that public officials have the necessary knowledge and skills to draw up realistic cost estimates, manage large-scale projects, negotiate contracts, and monitor the work being carried out. However, in practice, budget cuts to government departments in many countries mean that governments no longer have this store of expertise.

4.5.2 Individual incentives and motivation

Another important source of government failure is related to the incentives and motivations of policymakers, including politicians, government officials, and regulators. One of the key features that is supposed to distinguish the government as an institution from markets is its motivation: whereas private markets are assumed to care only or mainly about maximizing profits, governments are assumed to be driven by a desire to act in the public interest and to maximize social welfare. In practice, governments are made up of individuals who will have their own interests and motivations, and these might not always align with promoting social welfare.

Governments do not have the power or ability to singlehandedly implement their policies. They need to rely on other agents (individuals or organizations) to carry out their policies, and these agents may not share the same goals or objectives as the government. This gives rise to principal–agent problems, where a principal tasks an agent to carry out an action on its behalf. The principal could be a politician relying on an agent—a government official or bureaucrat[27]—to implement a particular policy. If the principal cannot fully observe or monitor the actions of the agent, and if the interests of the two differ, this may result in ineffective policies.

Niskanen's work on bureaucracy and government (1968), discussed in Chapter 3, highlights how government bureaucrats might not be selfless public servants, but instead may be motivated more by a desire to enhance their power, pay, and prestige. This will result in a level of government spending above what is optimal or efficient, as government bureaucrats strive to maximize the size of their government budgets, using their knowledge and expertise to extract larger budgets from less informed politicians. Niskanen's view may seem extreme—it is unlikely that all employees working across different levels of government will share the same self-interested motivations. Many people work in government because they genuinely care about improving societal well-being and promoting the public interest. However, this perspective highlights the general problem of the potential misalignment between the incentives and motivations of politicians and those who are entrusted with implementing policies, and the impact this may have.

[27] The term 'bureaucracy' is generally used to refer to those responsible for implementing government policy and serving the government. It includes civil servants working in different government departments, but also teachers in state schools and doctors and nurses in the public health system.

But it is not just government bureaucrats who may be driven by their own self-interest. Politicians may be more concerned about re-election, or securing lucrative positions in the private sector once their term in office is over, than about increasing social welfare. This can lead to policy myopia, introduced in Chapter 1, where government policy interventions prioritize short-term gains over longer-term solutions, and may leave politicians more vulnerable to lobbying and corruption. Personal ideology and beliefs may also play a role in driving policies, as we saw above.

This may leave government officials and politicians susceptible to **regulatory capture**. In its narrow sense, regulatory capture refers to situations where a regulatory agency (or those who work there) gradually comes to identify itself with the interests of the firm or sector that it is responsible for regulating, and may therefore focus on advancing these interests rather than acting in the best interests of consumers and society. A broader understanding of regulatory capture includes the possibility of capture by special interest groups as well. The term 'regulatory capture' is derived from the work of George Stigler (1971) and his analysis of regulations and who benefits from them. He argued that industries would try to use political influence to limit competition and earn monopoly rents. The extent of direct lobbying of governments by industry groups and firms provides evidence of the importance of regulatory capture, since the monopoly rents that firms earn must be greater than the cost of lobbying to firms (Coyle, 2020). While it is difficult to estimate the total cost of lobbying, as we saw above, the evidence suggests it is likely to be significant.

It is not uncommon for politicians or people working for regulators to get jobs in the sectors they were previously responsible for regulating, or for people who work in particular businesses to subsequently start working for the regulatory bodies. This can have benefits—for example, someone who previously worked for a water company and then goes on to work for the water regulator will have a good understanding of how the industry works. However, there is also the risk that advancing personal financial interests may take the place of promoting the public interest. This will have implications for inequality, particularly if some groups (especially those on higher incomes) are more likely to have their voices heard.

Policymakers are human and they will no doubt be driven, at least in part, by their own self-interest. But this does not mean that they cannot also be motivated by a desire to promote the public interest. By assuming all politicians and government officials are purely self-interested, there is a risk this may become a self-fulfilling prophecy, driving out a concern for public service and other intrinsic motivations among policymakers (Coyle, 2020).

Conclusion

If we want to understand public policy and the role of government in the economy, it is not enough to focus on the economic theories and models of how markets work (or not). We also need to look at how decisions about policies are made. This chapter has focused on the problem of collective choice—the difficulty in aggregating individual preferences—and how, in representative democracies, governments act on behalf of their citizens. We have seen how, just as markets can fail, government interventions may also fail to maximize social welfare. This chapter has highlighted that there is often a cost to correcting market failures. The government is not an omniscient, benevolent social planner, and its ability to act is constrained by the information and expertise it has available. The government is also not a single entity; it is made up of different individuals working across different departments and organizations, each with their own interests and motivations.

This is not to say that government intervention cannot improve on market outcomes; rather, the point is to highlight the challenges that governments face in designing and implementing policies to tackle societal problems. Policymaking is an inherently complex and messy process. Government intervention is not a panacea, and the need or desirability for government intervention should be weighed against the impact of that intervention, acknowledging the limitations governments face. It is also important to keep in mind that the government and the market are not the only institutions. Other institutions, including the family, communities, and voluntary organizations, also have a role to play in offering collective solutions to market failures.[28]

Questions for discussion

1. Why do people vote? Is this a rational decision?
2. 'Unanimity voting is the only voting rule that can guarantee Pareto improvements; it is therefore superior to the simply majority voting rule.' Do you agree with this statement? Why or why not?
3. Will majority voting maximize social welfare?
4. Will vote-maximizing politicians always select the outcome that is preferred by the median voter?
5. Why might government intervention fail to increase social welfare? Does this mean governments should refrain from intervening in the market?

Further reading

For a more detailed discussion of the field of public choice, and the application of public choice theory to a developing country context:

Kimenyi, M. S., & Mbaku, J. M. (2019). *Institutions and collective choice in developing countries: Applications of the theory of public choice*. Routledge.

McNutt, P. (2002). *The economics of public choice*. Edward Elgar.

Mueller, D. C. (2003). *Public choice III*. Cambridge University Press.

Classical texts on the theory of public choice include:

Arrow, K. J. (1963). *Social choice and individual values* (2nd ed.). Yale University Press.

Black, D. (1948a). The decisions of a committee voting a special majority. *Econometrica*, *16*, 245–261.

Black, D. (1948b). On the rationale of group decision-making. *Journal of Political Economy*, *56*(1), 23–34.

Buchanan, J. M. (1954). Individual choice in voting and the market. *Journal of Political Economy*, *62*(4), 334–343.

Buchanan, J. M., & Tullock, G. (1962). *The calculus of consent*. University of Michigan Press.

Downs, A. (1957). *An economic theory of democracy*. Harper & Row.

[28] See, for example, Coyle (2020) for a discussion.

May, K. O. (1952). A set of independent, necessary and sufficient conditions for simple majority decision. *Econometrica, 20*, October, 680–684.

Tullock, G. (1959). Some problems of majority voting. *Journal of Political Economy, 67*, December, 571–579.

On individual voting behaviour:

Aldrich, J. H. (1997). When is it rational to vote? In D. C. Mueller (Ed.), *Perspectives on public choice: A handbook* (pp. 373–390). Cambridge University Press.

Congleton, R. D. (2001). Rational ignorance, rational voter expectations, and public policy: A discrete informational foundation for fiscal illusion. *Public Choice, 107*(1), 35–64. https://doi.org/10.1023/A:1010337412291

Feddersen, T. J. (2004). Rational choice theory and the paradox of not voting. *Journal of Economic Perspectives, 18*(1), 99–112.

Geys, B. (2006). 'Rational' theories of voter turnout: A review. *Political Studies Review, 4*(1), 16–35.

Hudson, J., & Jones, P. R. (1994). The importance of the 'ethical voter': An estimate of 'altruism'. *European Journal of Political Economy, 10*(3), 499–509.

Kaniovski, S. (2018). Why do voters vote? In R. D. Congleton, B. N. Grofman, & S. Voigt (Eds.), *The Oxford handbook of public choice* (Vol. 1, pp. 310–332). Oxford University Press.

Some selected empirical studies of the median voter model:

Brunner, E. J., & Ross, S. L. (2010). Is the median voter decisive? Evidence from referenda voting patterns. *Journal of Public Economics, 94*(11–12), 898–910.

Holcombe, R. G. (1989). The median voter model in public choice theory. *Public Choice, 61*(2), 115–125.

Scervini, F. (2012). Empirics of the median voter: Democracy, redistribution and the role of the middle class. *Journal of Economic Inequality, 10*, 529–550.

Stratmann, T. (2000). Congressional voting over legislative careers: Shifting positions and changing constraints. *American Political Science Review, 94*(3), 665–676.

On autocratic regimes:

McGuire, M. C., & Olson, M. (1996). The economics of autocracy and majority rule: The invisible hand and the use of force. *Journal of Economic Literature, 34*(1), 72–96.

Mueller, D. C. (2003). *Public choice III*. Cambridge University Press. Chapter 18 provides a very good overview of public choice research on non-democratic governments.

Olson, M. (1993). Dictatorship, democracy, and development. *American Political Science Review, 87*(3), 567–576.

Olson, M. (2000). *Power and prosperity: Outgrowing communist and capitalist dictatorships*. Basic Books.

Tullock, G. (1987). *Autocracy*. Kluwer Academic.

Wintrobe, R. (1990). The tinpot and the totalitarian: An economic theory of dictatorship. *American Political Science Review, 84*(3), 849–872.

On the role and dynamics of special interest groups:

Becker, G. S. (1983). A theory of competition among pressure groups for political influence. *Quarterly Journal of Economics, 98*(3), 371–400.

Dür, A. (2013). Interest groups in the European Union: How powerful are they? In J. Beyers, R. Eising, & W. Maloney (Eds.), *Interest group politics in Europe* (pp. 110–128). Routledge.

Krueger, A. O. (2008). The political economy of the rent-seeking society. In R. D. Congleton, A. L. Hillman, & K. A. Konrad (Eds.), *40 years of research on rent seeking* (Vol. 2, pp. 151–163). Springer.

Olson, Mancur (1965). *The logic of collective action: Public goods and the theory of groups*. Harvard University Press.

For an alternative perspective, building on ideas in complexity to develop more effective policy:

Kupers, R., & Colander, D. (2014). *Complexity and the art of public policy: Solving society's problems from the bottom up*. Princeton University Press.

Bibliography

Arrow, K. J. (1963). *Social choice and individual values* (2nd ed.). Yale University Press.

Bali, V. A., Robison, L. J., & Winder, R. (2020). What motivates people to vote? The role of selfishness, duty, and social motives when voting. *Sage Open*, *10*(4). https://doi.org/10.1177/2158244020950376

Beshears, J., Blakstad, M., Choi, J. J., Firth, C., Gathergood, J., Laibson, D., Notley, R., Sheth, J., Sandbrook, W., & Stewart, N. (2024). *Does pension automatic enrollment increase debt? Evidence from a large-scale natural experiment*. National Bureau of Economic Research (no. w32100).

Black, D. (1948a). The decisions of a committee voting a special majority. *Econometrica*, *16*, 245–261.

Black, D. (1948b). On the rationale of group decision-making. *Journal of Political Economy*, *56*(1), 23–34.

Buchanan, J. M. (1954). Individual choice in voting and the market. *Journal of Political Economy*, *62*(4), 334–343.

Buchanan, J. M., & Tullock, G. (1965). *The calculus of consent*. University of Michigan Press.

Chetty, R. (2015). Behavioral economics and public policy: A pragmatic perspective. *American Economic Review*, *105*(5), 1–33.

Chetty, R., Friedman, J. N., Leth-Petersen, S., Nielsen, T. H., & Olsen, T. (2014). Active vs. passive decisions and crowd-out in retirement savings accounts: Evidence from Denmark. *Quarterly Journal of Economics*, *129*(3), 1141–1219.

Coates, D., Heckelman, J. C., & Wilson, B. (2011). Special-interest groups and growth. *Public Choice*, *147*, 439–457.

Congleton, R. D. (2015). The logic of collective action and beyond. *Public Choice*, *164*, 217–234.

Corporate Europe Observatory (2025). *The EU's lobby league table: Tech, banking, energy, chemicals dominate* (published 24 February). Available at: https://corporateeurope.org/sites/default/files/2025-02/EU%20Lobby%20League%20briefing%2024.2.2025.pdf

Coyle, D. (2020). *Markets, state and people: Economics for public policy*. Princeton University Press.

Cullis, J., & Jones, P. (2009). *Public finance and public choice: Analytical perspectives* (3rd ed.). Oxford University Press.

Downs, A. (1957). *An economic theory of democracy*. Harper & Row.

Druckman, J. N., Peterson, E., & Slothuus, R. (2013). How elite partisan polarization affects public opinion formation. *American Political Science Review*, *107*(1), 57–79.

Flyvbjerg, B. (2014). What you should know about megaprojects and why. *Project Management Journal*, *45*(2), 6–19.

Furton, G., & Martin, A. (2019). Beyond market failure and government failure. *Public Choice*, *178*(1), 197–216.

Gruber, J. (2013). *Public finance and public policy* (4th ed.). Worth Publishers.

Guriev, S., & Treisman, D. (2020). A theory of informational autocracy. *Journal of Public Economics*, *186*, 104158.

Hallsworth, M. (2011). Policy-making in the real world. *Political Insight*, *2*(1), 10–12. https://doi.org/10.1111/j.2041-9066.2011.00051.x

Holcombe, R. G. (1989). The median voter model in public choice theory. *Public Choice*, *61*(2), 115–125.

Hindriks, J., & Myles, G. (2013). *Intermediate public economics* (2nd ed.). MIT Press.

Jones, M. I., Sirianni, A. D., & Fu, F. (2022). Polarization, abstention, and the median voter theorem. *Humanities and Social Sciences Communications*, *9*(1), 1–12.

Levitt, S. D. (1996). How do senators vote? Disentangling the role of voter preferences, party affiliation, and senator ideology. *American Economic Review*, *86*(3), 425–441.

May, K. O. (1952). A set of independent, necessary and sufficient conditions for simple majority decision. *Econometrica*, 20, October, 680–684.

McGuire, M. C., & Olson, M. (1996). The economics of autocracy and majority rule: The invisible hand and the use of force. *Journal of Economic Literature*, *34*(1), 72–96.

Mueller, D. C. (2003). *Public choice III*. Cambridge University Press.

Mueller, D. C. (2015). Public choice, social choice, and political economy. *Public Choice*, *163*(3), 379–87. https://doi.org/10.1007/s11127-015-0244-0

Niskanen, W. A. (1968). The peculiar economics of bureaucracy. *American Economic Review*, *58*(2), 293–305.

OECD (2017). *Preventing policy capture: Integrity in public decision making*. Organization for Economic Cooperation and Development. Public governance reviews. Available at: https://doi.org/10.1787/9789264065239-en

OECD (2021). *Lobbying in the 21st century: Transparency, integrity and access*. Organization for Economic Cooperation and Development. Available at: https://doi.org/10.1787/c6d8eff8-en

OECD (2022a). *Public integrity indicators* [data base]. Organization for Economic Cooperation and Development. Available at: https://oecd-public-integrity-indicators.org (analysis available at: https://www.oecd.org/en/topics/sub-issues/lobbying.html)

OECD (2022b). *Trust survey*. Organization for Economic Cooperation and Development. Available at: https://www.oecd.org/en/topics/sub-issues/lobbying.html

Olson, M. (1965). *The logic of collective action: Public goods and the theory of groups*. Harvard University Press.

Olson, M. (1993). Dictatorship, democracy, and development. *American Political Science Review*, *87*(3), 567–576.

Olson, M. (2000) *Power and prosperity: Outgrowing communist and capitalist dictatorships*. Basic Books.

Palfrey, T. R. (1984). Spatial equilibrium with entry. *Review of Economic Studies*, *51*(1), 139–156.

Stigler, G. (1971). The economic theory of regulation. *Bell Journal of Economics*, *2*(1), 3–21.

Stratmann, T. (2000). Congressional voting over legislative careers: Shifting positions and changing constraints. *American Political Science Review*, *94*(3), 665–676.

Tullock, G. (1959). Some problems of majority voting. *Journal of Political Economy*, *67*, December, 571–579.

Tullock, G. (1987). *Autocracy*. Kluwer Academic.

Van Bastelaer, T. (1998). The political economy of food pricing: An extended empirical test of the interest group approach. *Public Choice*, *96*(1), 43–60.

V-Dem (2024). *Voter turnout of voting-age population* [data set]. *V-Dem country-year (full + others) v14* [original data]. V-Dem Institute. Retrieved 16 August 2024 from https://ourworldindata.org/grapher/voter-turnout-of-voting-age-population

V-Dem (2025). *Closed autocracies* [data set]. *Democracy report v15* [original data]. V-Dem Institute. Available at: https://ourworldindata.org/grapher/democracies-autocracies-amb-row

Vickrey, W. (1960). Utility, strategy, and social decision rules. *Quarterly Journal of Economics*, *74*(4), 507–535.

Washington, E. L. (2008). Female socialization: How daughters affect their legislator fathers' voting on women's issues. *American Economic Review*, *98*(1), 311–332.

5
Tools for policy evaluation

Learning objectives

By the end of this chapter, you will be able to:

- 5.1 Explain the difference between private and social cost–benefit analysis (CBA) and the decision rules that are used to carry out a CBA.
- 5.2 Discuss the theoretical foundations underlying CBA.
- 5.3 Discuss the steps involved in carrying out a CBA and the associated challenges.
- 5.4 Assess the limitations of CBA as a tool for evaluating public policies.
- 5.5 Discuss alternative tools for evaluating public policies and when they might be more appropriate than CBA.

Introduction

Governments intervene in a wide range of areas, but the resources available to them—and to society—are limited. Governments must choose among competing projects and policy proposals, selecting those that will have the greatest impact on social welfare. If a government has a budget to be allocated to improving infrastructure, should this be invested in renovating the road network or in building more cycle paths? How can the government determine whether investing in a green energy project will deliver value for money and increase social welfare? To answer these types of questions, governments need tools to evaluate and compare the impacts of different policies and projects.

One of the most widely used tools is cost–benefit analysis (CBA). CBA provides a framework for systematically weighing up the costs and benefits of a policy or project in order to decide whether it should be implemented.[1] This tool has a wide range of applications in areas including transport, health, and environmental protection. In the UK, CBA is required by the Treasury for all major government spending proposals. For the EU, CBA is an important decision-making tool for allocating funds to regional development projects.

In fact, we all employ some form of CBA in our day-to-day lives. We often consider the costs and benefits of alternative actions before making a decision, from the more mundane—for example, should we walk or take the bus—to significant life decisions—for example, should we go to university or go straight into the job market. However, the CBA used by governments is fundamentally different from the type of CBA individuals and private firms use. We start by reviewing these differences, alongside the CBA decision rules, in section 5.1. In section 5.2, we discuss the theoretical foundations of CBA. Section 5.3 explores the main

[1] In this chapter, we will mainly refer to the use of CBA in the context of policies and projects, and we will use these terms interchangeably. However, CBA can be applied more generally to policies, projects, programmes, regulations, and other government interventions.

steps involved in carrying out a CBA and the difficulties that may arise. Section 5.4 discusses the main limitations of CBA and Section 5.5 introduces some of the alternative tools for policy evaluation available to governments.

5.1 What is cost–benefit analysis?

Cost–benefit analysis (CBA) involves systematically identifying the costs and benefits associated with a policy or project and placing a monetary value on these costs and benefits in order to derive a measure of the policy or project's overall net benefit. It is a tool that can be used to assess whether a particular policy will deliver value for money and should be implemented, but it can also be used for comparing alternative policies or projects to determine which ones should be adopted. While individuals and firms often use some form of CBA to guide their decisions, there is an important difference between this and the type of CBA that governments use. We start by reviewing the difference between private and social CBA, and then look at the decision rules used in CBA.

5.1.1 Private versus social cost–benefit analysis

To illustrate the difference between private and social CBA, let us consider some examples.

- A prospective student deciding whether to go to university will probably think about how getting a degree might affect their career opportunities and future income, as well as the opportunities this may offer in terms of meeting new people and developing friendships. These benefits will be balanced against the cost of tuition fees and accommodation, the challenges or pressures of living away from home, and perhaps also the income that they could have earned had they chosen to go into work full-time instead.[2]
- A business owner considering whether to invest in a new machine that will help speed up production will want to think about how much the machine will cost (both the initial investment and maintenance costs), what the costs or savings in terms of other inputs will be—will the machine require workers to have different skills; will it be more energy efficient and reduce the need for other inputs?—and how much additional output per day will be produced. These costs and benefits will need to be expressed in monetary terms so that the business owner can then determine the overall profitability of investing in the new machine.

These are examples of **private CBA**, where individuals or firms weigh up their own private costs and benefits before making a decision. Whereas individuals will mainly be concerned about the impact on their personal finances and well-being, and firms are primarily concerned with the profitability of a particular project, governments will typically be concerned

[2] This is an example of an opportunity cost, an important element when carrying out a CBA. We discuss opportunity costs in section 5.2.

about how the policy or project affects social welfare. **Social CBA** will therefore take into account the wider social costs and benefits, as well as the private costs and benefits.[3] This type of CBA has a long history; see Box 5.1 for a brief overview.

Suppose the government is considering whether to invest in the development of a new high-speed rail link. When evaluating the project, it will want to consider the private costs, such as the cost of raw materials and labour, the cost of any land it needs to buy, along with the private benefits, such as the expected revenue that will be generated from ticket sales. However, the government will also need to consider wider costs and benefits, including the environmental impact of the new rail line (e.g. any loss of natural habitats), the impact in terms of sound pollution for residents along the route of the proposed new rail line, and the potential benefits in terms of travel time saved for the users of the new line and reduction in emissions if the new line encourages some individuals to take the train instead of driving. This is the key difference between private and social CBA: unlike a private firm, which is concerned primarily with profitability, when carrying out a CBA the government is concerned about the wider social impact of a project.[4]

Box 5.1 From its origin to current use: how social CBA has been used to evaluate transport projects over time

There is some debate around the origins of CBA, although it is often credited to the French civil engineer and economist Jules Dupuit. In an article written in 1848, he proposed a method for calculating the social profitability of transport projects, such as the construction of a road or bridge, which was based on individuals' willingness to pay as a measure of the utility they would derive from using the road or bridge.[5] On a more practical level, the US Flood Control Act, introduced in 1936, established the principle of comparing costs and benefits when evaluating public investment decisions and thus paved the way for the use of CBA in various areas of government planning and budgeting from the 1950s and 1960s. It was also at this time that academic interest in the mechanics of CBA began to develop.

CBA has been used in a wide range of areas, but it has proved to be a particularly useful tool for assessing transport projects. One early example of the application of CBA in this context was a study by Foster and Beesley (1963), which estimated the expected gains and losses from building the Victoria underground line in London. Alongside measures of the initial capital invested, the operating costs, and the revenues generated from ticket sales, the study also considered the broader social costs and benefits of the project, including time savings, the benefits to drivers and bus operators from the reduction in traffic congestion, and the value of increased comfort and convenience. The results of the study gave an indication of the magnitude and distribution of the net benefits of the project. However, some costs and benefits—for example, the reduction in accidents or increased noise—had to be excluded from the analysis as there was no clear way to measure them.

[3] Throughout this chapter we will refer simply to CBA, rather than social CBA.

[4] Social CBA is based on the assumption that governments want to maximize social welfare. In practice, politicians and government bureaucrats may be motivated more by political or personal factors than by welfare economics, as we saw in Chapter 4.

[5] Some have argued that the earliest example of applied CBA dates back to 1768 in Scotland and that several applied CBA studies were subsequently carried out in India in the mid-nineteenth century (Pingle, 1978).

Today, the Department for Transport in the UK is required to carry out a CBA of all major transport-related projects. One such project was the high-speed railways network connecting London with the Midlands and north of England, known as HS2, which was proposed in 2009. The main aim of the project was to enhance rail capacity, creating a world-class high-speed rail network, and promoting connectivity between the major urban areas in Britain. The CBA that was carried out for the appraisal of HS2 estimated a benefit–cost ratio (see below) for the project of 2.3: each £1 invested in the project would generated a benefit worth £2.30 (Department for Transport, 2013: table 15). This estimate included the wider economic impacts of the network. Many impacts of the project involved costs and benefits that are difficult to quantify, such as travel time savings, reductions in carbon emissions, and impacts on protected wildlife sites, threatening important natural habitats. Finding appropriate ways to value these non-monetary costs and benefits is an ongoing challenge in applied CBA, as we discuss in section 5.3. In spite of various environmental concerns raised in relation to the project, construction began in 2020.

Another important difference between private and social CBA involves how the costs and benefits are valued. Firms will typically rely on market prices to evaluate their costs of production and the benefits or revenue they get from selling their output. However, as we will see below, market prices are not available for many of the benefits that factor in social CBA applications. How should we place a monetary value on time saved or natural resources, for example? In other cases, market prices may exist, but these will be distorted by market failures, so that these market prices no longer represent the true social costs or benefits. We will explore how these challenges are addressed in section 5.3, but first we are going to look into the mechanics of CBA, and the theory that underpins it, in a bit more detail.

5.1.2 Criteria for selecting projects

Carrying out a CBA involves a comparison of costs and benefits. As some of these costs and benefits will be experienced in the future, we need a mechanism for making these future costs and benefits comparable to costs and benefits experienced today. In general, £1 today is worth more than £1 received in the future. For individuals, impatience and uncertainty mean that most people would prefer to have £1 today rather than at some point in the future—in other words, most people have a positive **rate of time preference**. For producers, £1 invested today can produce more than £1 invested in a year's time. This is the **rate of capital productivity**, or the value of the additional goods which could be produced in a year's time, if £1 is invested in producing them today.

We therefore need to discount future costs and benefits to make them comparable to costs and benefits today. The **discount factor** is given by $\frac{1}{1+r}$, where r is the rate of interest or the **discount rate**. This captures the fact that a pound received next year is worth $(1+r)$ times less than a pound received today, because that pound could earn interest of r per cent if it were received today and invested. The further into the future we go, the lower the discount factor: for example, the discount factor for payments received two years from now is $1/(1+r)^2$, and for payments received three years from now it is $1/(1+r)^3$. In general, for a payment received T years from now, the discount factor is $1/(1+r)^T$.

To see why this makes payments received at different points in time comparable, it is helpful to look at an example. How much would £100 received in a year's time be worth to you today? To calculate the **present value** of £100 received in a year's time, we multiply this by the discount factor. Suppose the interest rate is 10 per cent, then the discount factor will be $1/(1+0.10)=0.91$, and the value today of £100 received in a year's time will be $£100/1.1=£90.91$. This means you would be indifferent between receiving £90.91 today or £100 in a year's time. Why? Because if you received £90.91 today and put it in the bank earning 10 per cent interest, you would have £100 a year from now.[6]

Discounting future costs and benefits plays a central role in the decision rule for carrying out a CBA. This decision rule can be expressed in three alternative ways: the net present value (NPV), the benefit–cost ratio (BCR), and the internal rate of return (IRR).[7]

The **net present value (NPV)** equals the discounted sum of the net benefits—or benefits minus costs—over the relevant time horizon of the project or policy. Suppose the impacts of a project or policy are expected to span T years, then the NPV is given by:

$$NPV=(B_0-C_0)+\frac{B_1-C_1}{(1+r)}+\frac{B_2-C_2}{(1+r)^2}+\frac{B_3-C_3}{(1+r)^3}+\ldots+\frac{B_T-C_T}{(1+r)^T}$$

where B_t are the benefits and C_t are the costs in year t. This is equivalent to:[8]

$$NPV=\sum_{t=0}^{T}\frac{B_t-C_t}{(1+r)^t}$$

Projects with a positive NPV should be undertaken, whereas those with a negative NPV should not. Projects can also be ranked according to their NPV. If the government has a fixed budget and can choose various projects from a selection of feasible projects (i.e. where $NPV>0$), the projects should be selected in order based on their NPV.

Table 5.1 provides an example to illustrate how the NPV can be calculated for a private investment project. Suppose a firm has to decide whether to invest in a new piece of machinery

Table 5.1 Example NPV for a private investment project

Year	Annual benefits	Annual costs	Net profits	Discount factor	Net discounted profits (NPV)
1	0	5,000	−5,000	1.000	−5,000
2	2,000	500	1,500	0.909	1,364
3	2,000	500	1,500	0.826	1,240
4	2,000	500	1,500	0.751	1,127
5	2,000	500	1,500	0.683	1,025
6	2,000	500	1,500	0.621	931
Total	10,000	7,500	2,500		686

[6] To check this, note that depositing £90.91 in the bank with an interest rate of 10 per cent would earn you £9.091 in interest, giving you a total of £100: $£90.91(1+0.10)=£100$.

[7] These three ways of expressing the CBA decision rule are broadly equivalent, although as we will see below, they can lead to different rankings when comparing policies or projects. See Cohn (2003) for a more detailed discussion of these alternatives.

[8] This formula is sometimes written with an initial cost, C_0, in time period 0 (the current year) and no benefits.

which will increase productivity (and hence revenues), but will become obsolete after six years. Assume the discount rate is 10 per cent and the project involves:

- an upfront cost of £5,000 to buy the new machinery;
- annual maintenance costs of £500;
- annual revenues of £1,500 after the first year of the project.

The overall net present value of the project is £686, so the project is profitable. However, as we can see from the table, there is a significant difference between the total net discounted profits and the total net profits, at £2,500.

The choice of discount rate is crucial and will determine which projects are adopted and which are not. Most projects typically involve a large upfront initial cost, with maintenance and operational costs spread over the medium to long term, whereas the benefits are typically spread over the duration of the project. A higher value of the discount rate r (or, equivalently, a lower discount factor) will favour projects where the benefits are more immediate or the bulk of the costs are experienced further into the future. A lower value of r (and a higher discount factor) will tend to favour projects where the benefits are experienced further into the future. This has important implications, particularly in the context of projects with environmental impacts, as we will see in section 5.3.3.

The NPV is one way of expressing the decision rule that can be used to evaluate and compare projects. An alternative is the **benefit–cost ratio (BCR)**, which measures the ratio of the discounted benefits and costs. This rule is intuitively appealing, as it measures returns per unit of costs. If aggregated discounted benefits outweigh aggregated discounted costs, then the BCR will be greater than 1 and the project is viable. Formally this is given by:[9]

$$BCR = \frac{\sum_{t=0}^{T} B_t / (1+r)^t}{\sum_{t=0}^{T} C_t / (1+r)^t}$$

The BCR rule can also be applied to selecting one or more projects from a series of feasible projects (i.e. where $BCR > 1$). In this case, the projects with the highest BCR should be selected first. However, while the BCR rule is similar to the NPV rule, the two rules will not necessarily provide the same ranking when comparing multiple projects. Choosing the project that maximizes net benefits (or NPV) is not the same as choosing the project that maximizes the BCR, since the benefits and costs of a project may be relatively small, but the costs may be proportionately smaller than the benefits, resulting in a high BCR, but a low NPV. Table 5.2 provides an example to illustrate this point, borrowed from Cohn (2003). The table shows the discounted sum of benefits and costs, as well as the NPV and BCR, for five different projects. If the NPV rule is applied, the project selected will be project A, since it has the highest NPV. However, according to the BCR rule, the project which should be selected is E.

The BCR rule can also lead to wrong decisions when choosing among various projects because of inconsistencies in the manner in which maintenance costs are accounted for. In some projects, maintenance costs may be included in the denominator of the BCR rule, but

[9] This formula is equivalent to $BCR = \frac{\sum_{t=0}^{T} B_t (1+r)^{-t}}{\sum_{t=0}^{T} C_t (1+r)^{-t}}$.

Table 5.2 Project ranking according to the NPV and BCR

Project	Discounted sum of benefits (B)	Discounted sum of costs (C)	NPV	BCR
A	1,200	1,000	200	1.20
B	999	800	199	1.25
C	720	600	120	1.20
D	250	200	50	1.25
E	260	200	60	1.30

Source: Cohn (2003: 543).

in other projects these costs may be subtracted from the gross benefits in the numerator *B* (McKean, cited in Cohn, 2003).

The **internal rate of return (IRR)** is the value of the discount rate, *r*, which ensures that the discounted benefits equal the discounted costs. Formally, the IRR is the value of r^* such that:

$$NPV = \sum_{t=0}^{T} \frac{B_t - C_t}{(1+r)^t} = 0$$

If the IRR of a project is greater than the baseline or market interest rate, then the project is profitable and should be considered. The IRR allows for a direct comparison with market interest rates and may be the preferred decision criteria when an appropriate discount rate for calculating the NPV cannot be determined. When selecting from a list of feasible projects (i.e. where the IRR is greater than the appropriate discount rate), the project with the highest IRR should be selected. However, as with the BCR rule, when it comes to ranking projects, the IRR rule may not lead to the same ranking as the NPV rule.

There are some limitations with using the IRR. First, there may not always be a unique solution for the internal rate of return, particularly when the flow of net benefits fluctuates between positive and negative values. Secondly, in the case of mutually exclusive projects, the IRR may provide recommendations that are inconsistent with the NPV rule. A high IRR for one project only demonstrates that the project is more profitable than another project with a lower IRR, but both projects may be desirable and feasible (provided the IRR is above the appropriate discount rate).

All three rules—the NPV, BCR, and IRR—can be used to assess the viability of individual projects and, in general, they should all lead to the same outcome if there is no budget constraint. That is, all projects where $NPV > 0$ should also satisfy $BCR > 1$ and an IRR which exceeds the appropriate discount rate. However, complications arise when there are multiple projects to choose from and a fixed budget, so not all feasible projects can be selected. Here the three decision rules can give inconsistent rankings. In general, the NPV rule is preferred here because of its normative foundations, which we discuss in section 5.2.

5.2 Theoretical foundations of cost–benefit analysis

What makes CBA a good tool for evaluating public policies? Basing a decision on whether the benefits outweigh the costs is, of course, intuitively appealing. As we will see below, CBA is also related to the efficiency criteria that we introduced in Chapter 2.

5.2.1 CBA and potential Pareto improvements

What does it mean to say that a policy has a net present value (NPV) of £50,000? It does not imply that everyone will be made better off as a result of the policy. Some people will gain from the policy whereas others will lose out, but overall the net gain will be positive, so the benefits to those who gain from the policy will outweigh the losses. In this sense, the NPV formula is essentially applying the Kaldor–Hicks efficiency criterion that we introduced in Chapter 2. According to this criterion, if the gainers from a policy could potentially compensate the losers from the same policy and still be better off, then the policy will lead to an increase in social welfare and should be implemented. The Kaldor–Hicks efficiency criterion is also known as the **potential Pareto improvement (PPI)** criterion. As we saw in Chapter 2, an allocation is Pareto efficient if there is no way to make at least one individual better off without making anyone else worse off. A Pareto improvement, then, implies a change that would make at least one person better off without making anyone else worse off. The Kaldor–Hicks criterion focuses on *potential* rather than actual Pareto improvements.

The PPI criterion provides the welfare economics foundation of modern CBA. Crucially, it does not require any *actual* compensation and, in most cases, the losers are still worse off as a result of the policy or project. This is one the criticisms of both the PPI criterion and CBA. However, governments will implement multiple policies and different policies will affect different groups in society. Provided these policies are neutrally designed—rather than being designed to consistently favour a particular group—and provided each policy increases total welfare, then most people should benefit overall. Not having a requirement to pay actual compensation also has its advantages, as it simplifies the implementation of policies and avoids preference revelation problems, which arise when individuals lack the incentive to truthfully reveal their preferences.[10] However, is it fair to assume that most policies are neutrally designed, or do they tend to favour particular groups or regions?

Another criticism of the PPI criterion—and of CBA—is based on the fact that measuring gains and losses in monetary terms will not necessarily accurately capture changes in utility and social welfare. Suppose there is a proposal to build a new road and the benefits of this

[10] We discuss preference revelation problems in more detail in Chapter 6. In essence, this refers to the problem that governments face in eliciting individuals to truthfully reveal their preferences for a particular good or service, particularly in situations where individuals may benefit from not being completely truthful. For example, if the government were to offer compensation to people affected by the pollution generated by a new road and asked people to come forward to say how badly they were affected in order to determine the value of the compensation, then people would have a clear incentive to overstate how badly they had been affected.

project to group A are estimated at £200,000, while the costs to group B, who live alongside the new road, are estimated at £150,000. Given these costs and benefits, the NPV of building the new road is £50,000 and the project should go ahead. However, a change in money resources is not the same as a change in welfare or utility. If group A has a higher income than group B, then, given a diminishing marginal utility of income,[11] the actual utility value of the losses to group B, whose members have a lower income, may outweigh the utility value of the gains to group A, whose members are wealthier. So applying the PPI criterion could actually lead to the adoption of a policy that would result in a reduction in total welfare. One way of dealing with this problem is to use distributional weights in the calculations—for example, giving a greater weight to the monetary losses or gains to those on lower incomes relative to those on higher incomes. The challenge then is to determine the value of the weights to be used in practice—are the gains or losses to those on lower incomes worth twice as much as those on higher incomes, or 10 times as much?

It has also been argued that the PPI criterion may not always provide a clear decision rule: in some circumstances, both carrying out a project and cancelling a project can satisfy the PPI criterion. This problem is known as the Scitovsky paradox. The paradox arises when the gainers from the change from a given initial allocation X to an allocation Y could compensate the losers for making the change; but the losers could then also compensate the gainers for going back to the original position (see Box 5.2). Research suggests that the circumstances in which this is likely to be the case in practice are limited (Just et al., 2012).

Box 5.2 The Scitovsky paradox

Suppose a proposed project involves the construction of a new road. Figure 5.1 illustrates two utility possibility frontiers[12]: UPF_0 represents the utility possibility frontier if the new road is not built, and UPF_1 represents the utility possibility frontier if the road is built. Point C represents the outcome if the road is not built and E represents the outcome if the road is built. Clearly E is not a Pareto improvement on C, since it lies within utility possibility frontier UPF_0. However, if the road were built, it would be possible to transfer income from group B to group A, leading to point D rather than E, and D is a Pareto improvement on C; so building the road is a potential Pareto improvement over the situation with no new road. But if the road is not built, an income transfer from group A to group B would lead to point F, which is Pareto preferred to point E; so not building the road is also a PPI over building the road.

This problem arises because the change in technology—that is, the construction of the new road—has resulted in utility possibility frontiers that cross. More generally, the Scitovsky paradox may also arise if one of the goods in question is an inferior good—that is, a good for which demand decreases as income increases. However, research suggests that for most real-world applications of CBA, this paradox is unlikely to be a significant problem,

[11] The marginal utility of income captures the increase in utility from increasing income by one unit. In general, the marginal utility of income is assumed to fall as income rises: an extra £10 will have a larger impact on utility for an individual with an income of £10,000 than for an individual with an income of £100,000.

[12] As we saw in Chapter 2, the utility possibility frontier (UPF) illustrates the maximum levels of utility that individuals in an economy can achieve given the resources and technology available.

as technological change tends to happen incrementally and projects and policies may be scaled up or down, and therefore alternatives are rarely represented by two distinct UPFs (Just et al., 2012).

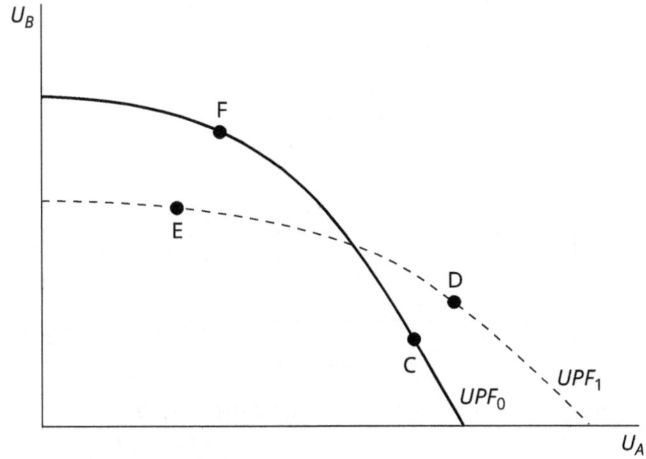

Figure 5.1 The Scitovsky paradox

5.2.2 Willingness to pay and consumer surplus

To carry out a CBA we need to measure both benefits and costs. How can we measure the benefits to individuals of a policy or project? In Chapter 2 we introduced the concept of individuals' willingness to pay (WTP), which captures the maximum amount that individuals would be willing to spend to enjoy the benefits of consuming a good. We can use this same concept of WTP to capture the benefits to individuals of a policy or project.[13] As we saw in Chapter 2, we can measure the aggregate WTP of all individuals using consumer surplus, which is given by the area under the compensated demand curve and above the price that individuals have to pay.[14]

Suppose the government introduces a policy that leads to a fall in electricity prices from P_0 to P_1 and, as a result, energy demand increases from Q_0 to Q_1, as illustrated in Figure 5.2. The gain to consumers from the lower price is given by the shaded area in the figure, which measures the change in consumer surplus following the price fall. Note that here we are interested in the *change* in consumer surplus as a result of the policy, rather than the total consumer surplus. Total consumer surplus is given by the entire area below the demand curve and above price P_1. However, the unshaded triangle above area A in the figure was the surplus that consumers already enjoyed before the introduction of the policy and therefore should not be

[13] If the impact of the policy or project on individual well-being is negative, the concept of willingness to accept (WTA) is sometimes used to refer to the minimum amount that the individual would need to receive to bear the impact of the policy.

[14] Recall from Chapter 2 (Box 2.3) that the compensated demand curve measures how demand for a good changes as the price changes, assuming that money is given or taken away from the individual to ensure their utility from buying the good is unchanged, so individual utility is constant along the compensated demand curve.

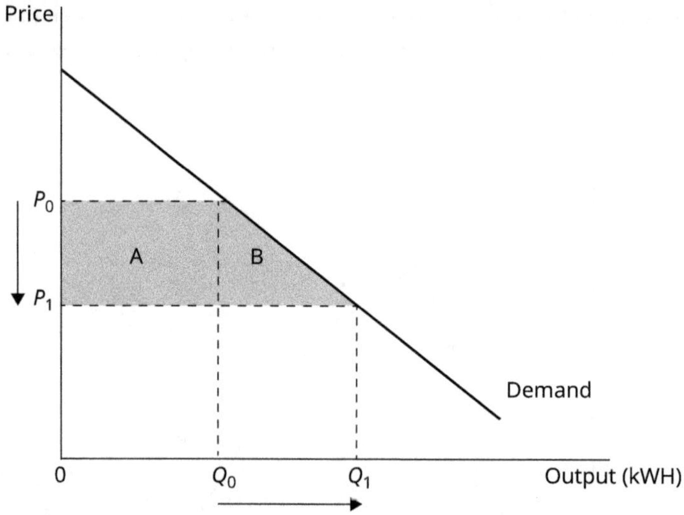

Figure 5.2 Evaluating benefits: consumer surplus

included in the evaluation of the benefits to individuals of the policy. The change in consumer surplus includes both the benefit to existing consumers from the lower price (area A) and the benefit to new consumers who can now afford more electricity at the new lower price (area B). For example, if the price per kWH (measured in pence) fell from $P_0 = 17.2$ to $P_1 = 15$, and the quantity increased from $Q_0 = 500{,}000$ to $Q_1 = 550{,}000$, then the change in consumer surplus would be £11,550.[15] This provides a measure of the benefit to individuals from the policy.

Strictly speaking, consumer surplus provides a measure of aggregate WTP if it is measured as the area under the *compensated* demand curve. In practice, the demand curve that economists typically work with is the ordinary or uncompensated demand curve.[16] However, the difference between the compensated and uncompensated demand curves is likely to be small in the case of goods that individuals spend only a small proportion of their income on, so the area under the ordinary demand curve will provide a good approximation for the exact consumer surplus in these cases.

There are other limitations with using WTP as a measure of the benefits of a policy. An individual's willingness to pay for the impact of a particular policy will depend on their income: those with higher incomes will typically have a higher WTP. Aggregate WTP will therefore depend on the distribution of income in society, and if the distribution of income changes, then the sum of individual WTP is likely to change as well, which will affect the calculation of the benefits of the policy. There is also the question of whose WTP should be considered when calculating the net benefits of a policy, a question that we return to below.

[15] This is the value of the shaded area, calculated as: $(17.2-15)500{,}000+\frac{1}{2}(17.2-15)50{,}000 = 1{,}155{,}000$ measured in pence, which equals £11,550.

[16] This is sometimes referred to as the Marshallian demand curve and includes both the income and substitution effects of a price change (see Box 2.3 in Chapter 2).

5.3 Applying cost–benefit analysis

There are four key questions that we need to consider when carrying out a CBA:

1. Which costs and benefits should be included?
2. How can these costs and benefits be valued?
3. How should future costs and benefits be discounted?
4. How can we accommodate risk and uncertainty in our calculations?

We discuss each of these questions in turn below.

5.3.1 Identifying costs and benefits

The first step in carrying out a CBA involves identifying all relevant costs and benefits. What is considered relevant will depend on the scope of the analysis. Is this local, national, or global? Whose costs and benefits should be considered? What is the appropriate time horizon for evaluating the policy? There is no definitive answer to these questions. It will depend on context.

Let us consider an example to illustrate the difficulties involved in identifying the relevant costs and benefits. Suppose the government is considering investing in the construction of a wind farm. You work as a government adviser and have been asked to carry out a CBA of the project. What costs and benefits should you include in your analysis?

It can be useful to start by thinking about which groups are likely to be affected by the project, to determine whose costs and benefits should be included.[17] These will include local residents, workers employed to build and maintain the wind turbines, consumers who buy the electricity generated by the wind farm, and visitors to the area. Should future generations, who may benefit if construction of the wind farm results in lower carbon emissions, also be included? Setting a time horizon for the assessment can help narrow down the scope. In general, the appropriate time horizon will depend on when we expect the costs and benefits to arise. The majority of costs will typically fall at the start of the project, but the flow of benefits will likely span several years. In this example, it would seem reasonable to base this on the projected lifespan of the wind turbines, which is generally between 20 and 25 years.

We know that we need to consider both social and private costs and benefits. Private costs would include the costs of the materials required to build the wind turbines and the cost of hiring workers; social costs would include the visual impact of the turbines and any negative impacts on wildlife. Private benefits would include the revenues from the sale of the electricity generated, whereas social benefits would include environmental benefits from lower carbon emissions. How can we be sure we have identified *all* relevant private and social costs and benefits? This is challenging in practice and it is helpful to have a taxonomy or framework to categorize the various cost and benefits of a project.[18]

There are different ways of classifying costs and benefits, as summarized for this example in Table 5.3. Direct costs and benefits refer to the more immediate impacts of a policy or project—for example, building a wind farm will create jobs and increase the supply of electricity. Indirect costs and benefits refer to secondary effects, which in this case might include

[17] This is sometimes referred to the issue of standing. See, for example, Whittington and MacRae (1986).
[18] There are different ways one can classify costs and benefits. See, for example, Cullis and Jones (2009).

Table 5.3 Classifying the costs and benefits of a wind farm

		Costs	Benefits
Direct			
	Tangible	Cost of raw materials to build turbines	Energy generated
	Intangible	Scenic costs	Impact of reduced carbon emissions
Indirect			
	Tangible		
	Intangible	Impact on local wildlife	Improved health outcomes due to reduced emissions

impacts on local wildlife.[19] We can also categorize costs and benefits based on whether they can be measured in the market. Tangible costs and benefits are ones for which market prices exist—for example, the raw materials needed to build the wind turbines. Intangible costs and benefits are ones for which market prices are not immediately available—for example, the impact on local wildlife. We will explore the challenges involved in valuing intangible costs and benefits in section 5.3.2 below, but it is worth acknowledging that we cannot always anticipate all impacts of a policy (see Box 5.3).

Box 5.3 Can we ever capture all costs and benefits?

Some would argue that, no matter how hard you try, there will always be outcomes that you had not anticipated. In *Aftermath: The Unintended Consequences of Public Policies* (2014), Thomas Hall argues that 'Policies created for one set of purposes almost always create an additional set of results that were not part of the original plan.' He examines four instances of significant unintended consequences of major public policies: the introduction of federal income tax, cigarette taxes, minimum wage laws, and alcohol prohibition. Each policy was introduced as a positive measure, but each had harmful side-effects. For example, cigarette taxes led to a rise in the underground market for cigarettes, while alcohol prohibition led to a rise in criminal activity. Sometimes these consequences can be so serious that the policy itself may be deemed a failure.

Each of these cases is an example of what has become known as the 'cobra effect'. This effect takes its name from a famous anecdote which describes a scheme purportedly employed by the British colonial rulers in India to control the population of venomous cobras that plagued the city of Delhi. The scheme involved paying a bounty for each dead cobra that was handed in. Initially, the scheme appeared to be successful, with many dead cobras being handed in and the population of cobras in the city seeming to decline. However, the number of cobras being handed in each month tended to rise rather than falling. It turns out that the bounty being offered provided an incentive for some of the more entrepreneurial citizens to start breeding cobras in order to kill them and hand them in.

[19] The distinction between direct and indirect costs and benefits is not always clear-cut and there is an inevitable element of subjectivity in some of these categorizations.

5.3.2 Valuing costs and benefits

Once we have identified the relevant costs and benefits, we need to assign them a monetary value so they can be incorporated into the NPV formula. Measuring costs is typically more straightforward than measuring benefits, since benefits will often involve impacts on health, life, or the environment, which are more difficult to place a monetary value on.

We can measure the benefits of a policy using WTP, as we saw in section 5.2. When estimating costs, we are interested in the **opportunity costs** of the resources used to implement the policy. The opportunity cost of a resource measures the value of the next best alternative use of that resource. For example, building a wind farm will require the use of steel, concrete, construction machinery, land, and labour which could be used to produce other goods of value to society. The opportunity cost of using these inputs to build the wind farm is their value in their best alternative use.

When markets exist and work well, we can use market prices to capture social costs and benefits. In practice, however, market prices may be distorted as a result of market failures such as externalities or imperfect competition, and will therefore no longer reflect the true social costs and benefits. For example, the market wage rate when there is involuntary unemployment will tend to overestimate the true opportunity cost of labour. Suppose an employer is hiring workers at a wage of £60 an hour. If someone who was previously unemployed gets hired, the value of their time may be less than the £60 per hour they are now getting paid—the value of their time is the value of the output lost if they accept the job. If they previously used their time carrying out odd jobs and this was valued at £20 per hour, then this would be the correct estimate of the opportunity cost of their time. Similarly, if production of a good involves negative externalities, then the market price will overestimate the true opportunity cost. A laptop computer may be priced at £450, but if production generates pollution which is valued at £100 per laptop, then the true marginal value of the laptop is £350.

In some cases, market prices may not even exist for the costs and benefits we want to include in our calculations—for example, where benefits concern time or lives saved, environmental benefits, or cultural and amenity values of assets such as a historic site or park. When market prices do not reflect the true social costs and benefits, or no market prices exist, we need to rely on **shadow prices**. Shadow prices do not exist in the market; they are estimates of the value of the true social costs and benefits. Shadow prices play a very important role in CBA, but estimating them is challenging. There are two main approaches: revealed preference methods and stated preference methods.

Revealed preference methods

Revealed preference methods rely on using information about individual behaviour and the choices individuals make to infer a value for the good or resource being measured. Examples of revealed preference methods include the following:

- **Market-based measures, such as wages**: in a perfectly competitive labour market where individuals are free to choose how many hours they want to work, the wage rate captures the value of time spent at work and the value of an individual's leisure time. This is because in the competitive model, individuals choose to work up to the point where the value of their leisure time equals the wage rate (or equivalently, where the marginal utility of leisure equals the wage rate). Wages can thus be used to estimate the value of time saved by specific projects or policies (see Box 5.4). Wages can also be used to place a value on human life (see Box 5.5).

Wage-based measures do have their limitations. This method assumes there are no labour market imperfections and that individuals are free to choose how many hours they want to work, whereas in reality most people do not have full control over the number of hours they work. It also disregards the non-monetary benefits that may be associated with work—I may accept a slightly lower wage for a job which offers more flexibility, better working conditions or other benefits, such as private health insurance.

- **Travel cost approach**: this method involves valuing amenities based on the distance people are willing to travel to enjoy them. For example, we can estimate the value individuals place on a national park based on how much it costs them to travel there, including the cost of train tickets or fuel, and the value of the time it takes them to travel there. If market wages are used to value time costs, then we run into the same problems discussed above. This approach also ignores the fact that some people may value the existence of a natural or historic site even though they might not actually visit it. Individuals may derive utility simply from knowing there are green spaces available in their city or region, even if they do not actually visit them.
- **Hedonic pricing**: this method is used to value certain amenities based on the implicit prices revealed by the market. For example, a house can be viewed as a bundle of attributes, including the number of bedrooms and bathrooms, whether it has a garden, its location, etc. The price of the house is a reflection of the combined value of all of these attributes. Regression techniques[20] can be used to estimate the value of each characteristic based on information on house prices. We can estimate the value of noise (or the lack of it), by comparing the value of homes in busier and noisier locations with those in quieter locations. In practice, not all differences in attributes between houses are observable and it can be difficult to disentangle the value of all of the separate attributes. For example, it may be difficult to separate the impact of noise pollution on house values from that of visual pollution.
- **Government revealed preference**: in some contexts, it is possible to infer values implicit in certain government decisions and policies. This approach has been used to derive estimates of the value of a human life. A study by Morrall (2003) analysed information from 76 regulations from various government agencies in the USA, ranging from food labelling regulations to regulations around the use of seatbelts in cars and exposure to asbestos. Government health and safety regulations imply costs, but they also help save lives. This information can be used to estimate the implicit cost per life saved. These estimates vary significantly depending on the regulation analysed, as Table 5.4 illustrates. If a relatively inexpensive policy is effective in saving lives, should we infer that human lives are not worth that much?

[20] **Regression analysis** is a statistical method used to establish the strength and nature of the relationship between variables, for example, between house prices and house characteristics.

Table 5.4 Value of a human life implied by various government regulations (USA)

Regulation	Year	Opportunity cost per statistical life saved ($ million, 2002 prices)
Childproof lighters	1993	0.1
Food labelling regulations	1993	0.4
Floor emergency lighting	1984	1.2
Children's sleepwear flammability	1973	2.2
Rear/up-shoulder seatbelts in cars	1989	4.4
Asbestos ban	1989	78
Drinking water (phase II)	1992	19,000

Source: Morrall (2003), table 2 (abridged).

Stated preference methods

Stated preference methods rely on asking individuals directly how much they value a particular good or resource using surveys or questionnaires. One of the leading approaches is **contingent valuation**, where individuals are asked to state their willingness to pay (or willingness to accept compensation) for a hypothetical change in the level of provision of a good or service. The development of contingent valuation methods was boosted by the Exxon Valdez oil spill in Alaska in 1989. Following this disaster, the US National Oceanic and Atmospheric Administration established a commission of eminent economists to propose how best to value the intangible environmental impacts of the disaster.[21] Their report, published in 1993, advocated using contingent valuation methods, but noted the limitations of this approach and included proposals on how to address some of these.

There are several problems with contingent valuation methods.[22] Because individuals are faced with hypothetical questions, their answers may be biased and WTP values are likely to be overestimated. The answers given are also very sensitive to how the questions are worded and presented, a problem known as framing bias. Whether questions are asked in isolation or as part of a set of questions affects individual responses, as does the order in which questions are asked. A study by Samples and Hollyer (1990) asked individuals how much they would be willing to pay to protect seals and whales. Some respondents were asked how much they would pay to protect seals first, followed by whales, and other respondents were asked the questions in the reverse order. The value given for protecting seals tended to be lower if this question was asked after asking individuals how much they were willing to pay to protect whales. People also tend to give similar WTP values for a good assessed on its own and as part of a larger package—a problem known as the embedding effect. For example, Desvousges et al. (1993) found that individuals had roughly similar WTP values when faced with a problem that involved killing 2,000, 20,000, and 200,000 birds. Since the number of birds saved in the first case is significantly higher, individuals should, in theory, be willing to pay more for this outcome.

Because of these limitations, some economists are sceptical about the usefulness of contingent valuation methods. However, these methods are still widely used, particularly for valuing environmental impacts where there are few or no alternative valuation methods available.

[21] This commission was chaired by two Nobel laureates in economics, Kenneth Arrow and Robert Solow.
[22] See, for example, Hausman (2012) for a critique of this approach.

There has been extensive research into how to mitigate the limitations of these methods—for example, by adopting more structured questionnaires or choice experiments.[23]

As the discussion above has highlighted, researchers have devised various creative ways to overcome the challenges of valuing intangible costs and benefits. While none of these approaches is perfect, if we want to carry out a CBA, we need to place a monetary value on all relevant costs and benefits. Boxes 5.4 and 5.5 discuss how these various methods have been employed to place a monetary value on two key intangibles: time saved and human lives.

Box 5.4 Valuing time

Many public sector projects include time savings as part of their benefits. Most transport projects—whether it is the construction of a new road, expanding an airport, or building a new rail link—will have an impact on how long it takes consumers and producers to travel to their destinations. How should we value the benefits of these time savings? For producers, the answer is fairly straightforward: the benefits to producers will lead to a reduction in the cost of supplying goods. For consumers, the answer is a bit more complicated.

There are three main approaches to valuing time saved for consumers:

1. **Using wages**: as we saw above, in a perfectly competitive labour market where individuals are free to choose how many hours they want to work, the wage rate captures the value of an individual's time. If a new rail link reduces travel time by 30 minutes and the average hourly wage is £15 an hour, then the value of those 30 minutes saved for each individual is £7.50. We can then calculate aggregate benefits by multiplying this value by the estimated number of passengers. The main problems with this approach are that it assumes individuals have the flexibility to choose the number of hours they work and it ignores any non-monetary benefits individuals may derived from their work.
2. **Hedonic pricing**: we can use information on other choices that individuals make to try and infer the value that they place on time. For example, we could use information on differences in house prices for houses at different distances from the city centre, where most jobs are typically located, to see how much more people will pay to live in a house that is closer to where they work. The problem here is that it can be difficult to isolate the impact of proximity to work from all the other attributes individuals may value in their home. Any characteristics that are observable, such as the number of rooms or whether the house has a garden, can be controlled for in this approach. The challenge involves characteristics that are not directly observable, such as how well maintained the house is or the quality or safety of the neighbourhood. The rise in home working and flexible working raises further challenges for this approach.
3. **Contingent valuation**: one of the difficulties with revealed preference approaches is that, to arrive at reliable estimates, they require a lot of information about the context in which people make decisions (e.g. how important is the quality of local schools to an individual when buying their home?). This has led to an increase in the use of

[23] See, for example, Johnston et al. (2017).

stated preference methods, such as surveys, to estimate the value of time. If you want to know how much people value time saved, why not just asked them how much they would be willing to pay to save 30 minutes on their journey time? Notwithstanding the limitations with this approach discussed above, a lot of work has been invested in developing surveys that minimize the biases that arise as a result of people not treating these hypothetical questions in the same way as they would a real-world decision.

Many empirical studies have tried to estimate the value of time using these different methods. Small (2012) reviews a selection of these studies and finds that the value of time for commute trips is, on average, around half of the gross wage rate. However, values vary significantly depending on the purpose of the trip (e.g. whether it for business or leisure), the time of day travelled and how time is spent (e.g. walking or waiting time on public transport is valued more highly than time spent waiting in vehicles), as well as the method used to estimate the value of time. The value of time rises with income, but this increase is less than proportional, so someone with an annual income of £50,000 will place a higher monetary value on an hour of their time than someone with an income of £25,000, but this value will be less than double.

Box 5.5 Valuing life

In many cases, the benefits of a policy will involve the preservation of human lives. How can we place a monetary value on lives saved? This is a complex ethical issue. Some may argue that human life is priceless and that trying to place a monetary value on it is immoral. Others would argue that governments have limited budgets and cannot spend an infinite amount on saving lives. Moreover, people make decisions every day that reflect the value they place on their life and health—for example, in deciding whether to smoke or drink, or how often to exercise. Since a value is already placed on human life implicitly, is it not preferable to make this value explicit?

The **value of a statistical life (VSL)** is a measure of how much individuals are willing to pay to reduce the risk of death. There are three main approaches that are used to estimate the value of a human life:

1. **Wage-based measures**: under this approach, the value of a human life equals the present discounted value of lifetime earnings. This approach essentially reduces an individual's life to work and implies that life only matters if we can be 'productive' in the narrow economic sense. It does not consider the value of work produced outside of formal employment, such as caring for children or other relatives. This approach also implies that older people's lives will be valued less because they have fewer years of life remaining. Should the value of a human life depend on age?
2. **Contingent valuation**: asking individuals what they believe their lives are worth is problematic for many reasons. The alternative is to ask people how much they would be willing to pay for an increase or decrease in the probability of death in hypothetical scenarios. For example, how much less would people pay to live in a house in an area with pollution that will reduce their life expectancy by one year? Estimates of the

(Continued)

value of a human life based on contingent valuation methods vary significantly, from \$1 million to \$28 million per life saved.[24] There are questions about the reliability of this approach, given the limitations of contingent valuation methods discussed above.

3. Revealed preference: this method infers the value of a human life based on choices that individuals make that involve a change in the probability of death. These values can be based on price–risk trade-offs—for example, how much individuals are willing to pay for products that will reduce their probability of death, such as cycle helmets or carbon monoxide alarms. They can also be based on wage—risk trade-offs, which capture how much more individuals need to be paid to accept a riskier job with a higher probability of death. Revealed preference methods can also be applied to government policies and regulations, as we saw above.

Price–risk or wage–risk trade-offs are captured using hedonic price or wage models which aim to control for other characteristics of products or jobs that individuals may value (e.g. working conditions or other job benefits). This approach assumes individuals are well informed about the risks they face, but does a hazardous waste disposal professional, for example, really know what the increased risk of death from their job is? How good are people at evaluating these risks?[25] It also ignores differences in individual risk preferences. Different people have different tastes, which will lead to different estimates of the value of a human life using revealed preference methods. Are people who take riskier jobs with a higher probability of death representative?

As Table 5.5 shows, estimates of the value of a human life using labour market data vary significantly. There have been a large number of studies for the USA, with the majority finding

Table 5.5 Value of a statistical life based on labour market data

Country	Value of a statistical life (\$ million, 2000 prices)
Australia	3.9–19.1
Canada	2.2–21.7
Hong Kong	1.7
India	1.0–4.1
Japan	9.7
South Korea	0.8
Taiwan	0.2–0.9
UK	4.2–11.5
USA	0.7–20.8

Source: Viscusi and Aldy (2003), tables 2 and 4.

[24] See Viscusi (1993), table 2. Values updated to 2012 dollars.

[25] Research suggests that, in general, people have difficulties evaluating risks and tend to overstate very small risks and understate larger risks (Robinson et al., 2011).

a VSL between $4 million and $9 million, although lower estimates can be below $1 million (in 2000 dollars). Estimates vary both within and across countries and seem to imply a higher VSL in higher-income countries. How can policymakers reconcile this broad range of VSL estimates? Should the value of a human life depend on income? Are estimates taken from a labour market context relevant for analysing health or environmental policies?

5.3.3 Valuing the future

Because some of the impacts of a policy or project will be experienced in the future, we need to discount future costs and benefits to make them comparable to costs and benefits experienced today. What discount rate should the government use? Should this discount rate be constant or vary over time?

The appropriate discount rate for a firm is the opportunity cost of the money the firm is using; if the firm could invest the money and earn 5 per cent interest, then this would be the appropriate discount rate.[26] The appropriate discount rate for government policies and projects will generally be lower than the market interest rate to reflect the interests of different generations—including future generations who otherwise would not have a voice in the policy process—and because they typically involve longer time horizons and therefore greater uncertainty.

The discount rate used by the government is the **social discount rate**. It is important to choose the appropriate social discount rate, particularly for long-lived policies and projects, such as environmental policies. The importance of selecting an appropriate discount rate was highlighted by the debate around the Stern Review on *The Economics of Climate Change* (2007). This report called for immediate and sharp reductions in greenhouse-gas emissions to combat the impacts of climate change. However, these findings were challenged by several economists who argued that they were entirely dependent on the value of the social discount rate chosen, which they argued was far too low.[27] Many projects will have costs that are experienced in the present, while the benefits tend to be spread over future years. A higher discount rate will favour projects where the benefits are more immediate, whereas a lower discount rate will favour projects where the benefits are experienced further into the future. To illustrate, the present value of £100 received 50 years from now is roughly £37 if the discount rate is 2 per cent, just under £9 if the discount rate is 5 per cent, and less than £1 if the discount rate is 10 per cent.

There are two methods for determining the social discount rate, which are related to the two arguments for discounting the future we discussed in section 5.1. The first argument was based on the fact that most individuals would favour consumption today over consumption in the future. The social discount rate will determine how much investment will be carried out in the present, and therefore how much current consumption must be sacrificed for the sake of future consumption. In this sense, the social discount rate should reflect the **social time preference rate**, or the value that society attaches to present consumption relative to

[26] If the firm pays taxes on interest earned, this should be taken into account and the net return calculated.

[27] The Stern Review argued for a social discount rate of 1.4 per cent, whereas the economist William Nordhaus, for example, recommended a higher rate of around 4 per cent (Nordhaus, 2007). See Cole (2008) for an overview of the debate.

future consumption. The social time preference method builds on the work of Frank Ramsey. The Ramsey rule for the social discount rate is given by:

$$r_t = \delta + \eta \times g_t$$

where δ is the pure social time preference rate (which reflects the degree of impatience), η is the elasticity of the marginal utility of consumption with respect to changes in consumption,[28] and g_t measures the growth rate of consumption per capita in time t. According to this formula, the social discount rate depends on consumption growth, the increase in utility this growth in consumption will generate, and the value society places on the well-being of future generations.

The second argument for discounting the future is based on the fact that public sector projects divert resources from the private to the public sector, and therefore the social discount rate should reflect the opportunity cost of capital in the private sector. This is the idea encapsulated in the **social opportunity cost of capital**. In this view, the social discount rate is based on a weighted combination of the rate of return on investment and the opportunity cost of forgone consumption.[29]

Alongside the theoretical question of what method should be used to calculate the social discount rate, there is the practical challenge of estimating this rate, particularly given the presence of market imperfections. Both the UK and the EU recommend an approach based on the social time preference method. The UK government currently uses a discount rate of 3.5 per cent for the majority of public sector projects, although a lower rate is recommended for certain projects. For the EU, the European Commission acknowledges different member states may want to estimate their own social discount rate but, in the absence of national estimates, recommends a rate of 3 per cent (see Box 5.6).

Another important question to consider is whether the discount rate should be constant over time. The NPV formula introduced in section 5.1 uses standard exponential discounting with a constant discount rate. This implies, assuming a discount rate of 10 per cent, that individuals are indifferent between having £100 today, £110 in one year, or £121 in two years. However, research suggests that, when it comes to time, our preferences are dynamically inconsistent. In other words, there is a conflict between what we think we will want in the future today, and what we actually want when that future comes around. For example, we might decide today that we need to start saving more and we plan to start doing this in a year's time, but in a year's time, we will probably prefer to postpone that decision for another year. A constant discount rate does not allow for this, since it implies that the way we discount the future does not depend on whether that future is tomorrow or ten years from now. This type of preference suggests that discount rates that fall over time might be more appropriate, with a relatively high discount rate over short horizons to reflect a higher degree of impatience, and a lower discount rate as we move into the more distant future.[30]

The standard approach to discounting the future assumes a discount rate that is not only constant over time, but also constant across costs and benefits, regardless of the original 'units' in which these costs and benefits arise. But is there a difference between saving 100

[28] The marginal utility of consumption measures the change in utility as consumption increases by one unit. The elasticity of the marginal utility of consumption measures how quickly utility changes as consumption increases over time.

[29] This method is based on the work of Arnold Harberger, as stated in Boardman et al. (2018).

[30] See Ainslie (1992) for a review of the evidence. See also Ainslie (1991).

Box 5.6 Discounting future costs and benefits in practice

The UK government's Green Book (2024), published by HM Treasury, sets out the framework for assessing major public investment projects, based on an analysis of costs and benefits. Future costs and benefits are converted to present values using a standard discount rate of 3.5 per cent per annum, and this rate has been used in the UK since 2003. A reduced rate of 1.5 per cent is applied to policies that have an impact on health or life outcomes to ensure that any benefits pertaining to future health and life are not discounted by as much as other future benefits. The government recognizes that the usual discounting techniques may not be appropriate for projects which have impacts spanning far into the future, such as projects to mitigate climate change. For time horizons over 30 years, a declining discount rate is recommended to allow for future uncertainty: 3 per cent for periods between 31 and 75 years, and 2.5 per cent for 76 to 125 years. For cases where the effects are very long term and involve substantial wealth transfers between generations, the government recommends a long-term discount rate of 2 per cent for periods between 126 and 200 years, 1.5 per cent for 201 to 300 years, and 1 per cent for periods over 300 years.

For the EU, in the absence of national estimates, the European Commission (EC) recommends countries use a rate of 3 per cent, but acknowledges that different member states may want to assess their own social discount rate. The EC guidance recommends adopting the social time preference method and allowing for a declining social discount rate for projects with very long-term impacts. A study by Catalano and Chiara (2022) provides estimates of the social discount rate for a selection of countries, ranging from 8.13 per cent in Estonia to 0.80 per cent for Italy, with an average rate across the EU of 3.6 per cent.

Sources: European Commission (2021) and HM Treasury (2024).

lives today and saving 100 lives in a year's time? Parsonage and Neuburger (1992) argue that when it comes to non-monetary health benefits in particular, these should not be discounted at the same rate as costs and benefits expressed in monetary terms, and the appropriate discount rate should be zero or close to zero.[31]

There is no consensus over what the social discount rate should be, and some would go as far as to argue that no discount rate should be used, particularly when evaluating projects which have a significant impact on the environment. Given how sensitive CBA calculations are to the choice of discount rate, it is always advisable to carry out a **sensitivity analysis**, as we discuss in section 5.3.4 below.

5.3.4 Dealing with risk and uncertainty

When drawing up the list of costs and benefits for our CBA, it is unlikely that we will know exactly what all these costs and benefits are, and this problem becomes more severe the further into the future the impacts of our project extend. Going back to our wind farm example,

[31] See also Goodin (1982) for an assessment of the arguments for discounting and whether the discount rate should be the same for all goods and all periods.

one of the benefits of the project is the energy generated, but in order to quantify this benefit we need to know how much electricity will be generated and what electricity prices will be over the lifespan of the wind farm, which could be 20–30 years. While we can derive predictions of these values, we are unlikely to know them with certainty, so we need to think about how to handle this uncertainty within our CBA.

Although the concepts of risk and uncertainty are often used interchangeably, in economics there is a subtle yet important different between them. The concept of risk refers to situations in which we might not know exactly what will happen, but we can determine the probability or likelihood of different outcomes. For example, we might be able to say there is a 60 per cent probability that the wind farm will generate 15,000 kWH or more of electricity per day, and a 40 per cent probability that it will generate less than this. In contrast, uncertainty refers to situations in which we cannot assign these probabilities and, in fact, we might not even know what all the possible outcomes are.[32] In this section, we will focus on risk.

One approach to dealing with risk is to use a higher discount rate to reflect the degree of risk aversion. If, in general, governments and society dislike risk, then a lower *certain* value may provide a higher level of utility or well-being than a higher **expected value**. Applying a higher discount rate will achieve this. Suppose the net benefits of a project spanning five years are valued at £50,000. At a discount rate of 5 per cent, the NPV today is just over £39,000, whereas if the discount rate is 10 per cent, the NPV of the same project is just over £31,000. A higher discount rate has the effect of making the project seem less attractive, which is what you want if the outcomes are risky. However, a higher discount rate will also make the NPV of any future costs associated with a risky project seem lower, which could potentially make a risky project more attractive. Using a higher discount rate confounds the evaluation of income at different points in time with the evaluation of risk.[33]

In some situations, we can incorporate risk into our CBA by working with expected values. The expected value takes into account all possible outcomes and their associated probabilities. For example, if there is a 60 per cent chance that the wind farm will generate £25,000 worth of electricity and a 40 per cent chance it will generate £5,000 worth of electricity, then the expected value is $EV = 0.6(25{,}000) + 0.4(5{,}000) = 17{,}000$. We can then incorporate this into our NPV calculations. By doing this, we are effectively treating these expected values as if they were certain amounts.

Treating expected values as if they were certain amounts implies preferences that are risk neutral.[34] To allow for some degree of risk aversion,[35] we should instead convert net benefits into **certainty equivalent values**. The certainty equivalent value is the amount that, if received with certainty, would leave us indifferent between that certain amount and taking the risk. Suppose a risky project involves a net benefit of either £200 or £0, with equal probability. The expected value of this project is £100. If we are indifferent between this risky project and accepting a project with a certain net benefit of £80, then £80 is the certainty equivalent of the risky project. We can then calculate the NPV of the certainty equivalent values. Risky projects

[32] This is sometimes referred to as Knightian uncertainty, after the economist who first highlighted this distinction, Frank Knight (1885–1972).

[33] See, for example, Stiglitz and Rosengard (2015).

[34] An individual's risk preferences are risk neutral if they would be indifferent between receiving a certain amount and a lottery with the same expected value—for example, if you are indifferent between receiving £50 for sure and a lottery with an expected payoff of £50, then your preferences are risk neutral.

[35] An individual is risk averse if they would prefer a certain amount over a lottery with the same expected value.

should earn a higher return (or risk premium) than safe projects with the same certainty equivalent, to compensate for the higher level of risk.

Given the uncertainty around future costs and benefits, and the challenges in selecting an appropriate social discount rate discussed above, all CBA should include a sensitivity analysis. A sensitivity analysis provides a means of checking how robust the estimates of net benefits are to changes in the underlying assumptions.[36] This could involve estimating the NPV of a project or policy using different values for the discount rate or different certainty equivalents. This will provide the policymaker with a more complete picture of what the potential net gains from implementing the project or policy are.

5.4 Criticisms of cost–benefit analysis

The discussion above has highlighted some of the challenges involved in carrying out a CBA, as well as how these can be addressed. Some would argue, however, that these solutions are not satisfactory and that CBA is not the right tool to use in all contexts. In this section, we review the main criticisms of CBA.[37]

- **It assumes everything can be monetized**: the nature of costs and benefits varies, but CBA relies on measuring all costs and benefits using the same unit—money. While costs are often easily expressed in monetary terms, the same is not true for benefits, which often involve impacts on health, life, or the environment. We discussed above some of the approaches economists have used to monetize intangible costs and benefits, but given the limitations with these approaches, how meaningful are the estimates they produce? Valuations of environmental resources are particularly problematic, as they depend on estimates given by individuals and therefore assume the natural environment has no value beyond that placed on it by human beings. Ackerman (2008) provides an example to illustrate the nonsensical nature of some of these artificial valuations: according to some US estimates, Americans would be willing to pay $18 billion to protect the humpback whale; so if a billionaire offered to pay $36 billion to hunt and kill all humpback whales, should this be accepted?
- **Inadequate handling of distributional issues**: all policies and projects typically involve gainers and losers. The standard CBA approach assumes that costs and benefits have the same impact regardless of who bears the costs or reaps the benefits. As long as the benefits outweigh the costs, then the project satisfies the potential Pareto improvement criterion and should go ahead. But no *actual* compensation needs to happen: in reality, the losers are still left worse off as a result of the policy or project. For society, who is negatively affected matters. A project that would entail low-income households losing £100 and high-income households gaining £200 will not be viewed in the same way as a project that would entail high-income households losing £100 and low-income households gaining £200. These concerns can be addressed by incorporating distributional weights into the analysis. If £1 is worth more, in terms of welfare, to someone on a lower income than to someone on a higher income, then appropriate weights can be attached

[36] See, for example, Boardman et al. (2018) for a discussion of the different approaches to carrying out a sensitivity analysis.

[37] See Ackerman (2008) for a more detailed discussion of these arguments.

to the costs and benefits to reflect this. However, the challenge then lies in determining the appropriate weights and what the relevant income cut-offs should be.

- **Inadequate handling of uncertainty**: while CBA can accommodate risk, it is not suited to handling uncertainty. Yet many of the important policy problems we face today, particularly those related to the environment, involve genuine uncertainty. We are unlikely to know the full range of impacts that global warming will have on the environment, our societies, and our economies. We do not know by how much sea levels will rise as a result of global warming, or what impacts the destruction of the Amazon rainforest will have on biodiversity. However, CBA requires precise values to be entered into our NPV or BCR formulas, and this risks obscuring the complexity of what we are trying to capture.
- **Poor choice of discount rate distorts the future**: as we saw above, there are both conceptual and practical challenges involved in determining the appropriate discount rate for public sector projects, and the choice of discount rate can have serious implications for policy, as illustrated by the debate around the Stern Review on *The Economics of Climate Change* (2007). In some cases, it is not even clear whether we should be discounting the future at all, particularly when we are dealing with intangible benefits. For example, what is the difference between saving 100 lives today and saving 100 lives five years from now, or 50 years from now? There are also questions about how we should compare the impacts affecting different generations, especially whether the benefits and costs experienced by future generations should be given the same weight as those experienced by current generations. After all, these future generations do not have a say in the policy process today.
- **Tendency to overestimate costs**: certain costs tend to be overestimated in CBA calculations, particularly those associated with new regulations. Cost estimates here tend to disregard the potential for innovation that arises as a result of regulation, as new regulations encourage individuals and businesses to find new ways of doing things to minimize their impact. These innovations are difficult to predict and, of course, will not apply to all costs. However, the fact that they are often disregarded means that some projects which could potentially have significant benefits in the distant future may not go ahead due to overinflated costs. This problem will be exacerbated if the wrong discount rate has been applied to these benefits.
- **Susceptible to biases**: CBA appears to be an objective, transparent, and impartial tool, where costs and benefits are compared to calculate the net benefit of a policy or project. In practice, however, this is not always the case, and CBA is seldom applied by individuals who are perfectly informed, rational, and unbiased. Policymakers may have an incentive to underestimate costs or inflate benefits to make particular projects more attractive. CBA is susceptible to biases at the level of the alternatives selected for assessment. For example, in order to deal with the problem of traffic congestion on a busy road, the government may apply CBA to compare a project that involves expanding the existing road with a project that involves building a new road, and the project with the highest NPV should be selected. However, the choice between just these two projects ignores other approaches that could have been used to tackle congestion and which may be preferable, such as investing in public transport or expanding the cycle network. The projects chosen for comparison will influence which project is ultimately selected,

and these projects are chosen by a person or committee, which is likely to have its own interests and objectives. CBA is also susceptible to biases in the interpretation of the data available. A lot of the evidence used in CBA applications is technical and complex, and the complexity of the information means that it can more easily be misconstrued, intentionally or unintentionally.

In spite of these limitations, CBA has its advantages. By requiring policymakers to clearly lay out the options being considered and their associated costs and benefits, it increases the transparency of policy decision-making, allowing questions to be asked and criticisms to be made. However, it may not be the right tool for all contexts. The next section reviews some of the alternatives available.

5.5 Alternative tools for policy evaluation

Although CBA is the most widely used tool for evaluating public policies, there are other tools which avoid some of the limitations of CBA that we have just discussed. In this section we briefly review three of these: cost-effectiveness analysis, multi-criteria analysis, and the precautionary principle.

5.5.1 Cost-effectiveness analysis

One of the key limitations of CBA is the need to convert all costs and benefits into monetary values, which can be particularly problematic when the benefits concern saving lives, protecting species from extinction, or preserving natural resources. **Cost-effectiveness analysis (CEA)** avoids this challenge by focusing only on the costs of particular projects or policies, which, as we have seen, tend to be easier to monetize. Once the policy or project goals have been set, CEA provides a framework for identifying the most cost-effective way of achieving these goals and therefore provides a mechanism to help prioritize the allocation of resources. CEA is widely used in the context of healthcare and environmental policies. For example, the UK government has set the goal of becoming a 'net zero' emitter by 2050. CEA can be used to calculate the costs of alternative projects and help identify the most cost-effective way of achieving this goal, without the need to quantify and value the expected environmental and health benefits. Since most costs arise at the start of a project, whereas benefits tend to span further into the future, the choice of selecting an appropriate social discount rate is often less problematic in CEA than in CBA. However, CEA does have its limitations—in particular, it still requires all costs to be expressed in monetary terms and therefore is not immune to the difficulties of estimating shadow prices for certain inputs.

5.5.2 Cost–utility analysis

Cost–utility analysis (CUA) is a particular type of cost-effectiveness analysis that is often used in healthcare to assess which drugs, medical interventions, and devices should be provided. In

CUA, health effects are measured using **quality-adjusted life years (QALYs)**, which combine both the quantity and quality of life gained as a result of a particular health intervention.

5.5.3 Multi-criteria analysis

Multi-criteria analysis (MCA) acknowledges the multidimensional nature of many of the environmental and health impacts that often arise in public policies and public sector projects. Rather than attempting to reduce everything to a single number, MCA allows decision-makers to incorporate a range of criteria in evaluating projects or policies, including environmental, social, technical, and economic criteria. There are various approaches to MCA, which differ in their level of computational complexity and data and time requirements. The exact number of criteria can vary, but these should be clearly specified. A project may look positive based on some criteria but not others, and multi-criteria analysis will make this transparent. The challenge is then how to weigh up the different criteria against one another. For example, in comparing two transportation projects, one may have a lower environmental impact but a higher financial cost, whereas the other project may imply a higher cost to the environment but a lower financial cost. If financial costs are measured in monetary terms and environmental costs are measured by wildlife and habitat loss, how should the projects be compared? This will depend on the relative weights assigned to the different criteria used in the analysis. Flexibility around the choice of what criteria should be included and what weight should be given to each is one of the key advantages of MCA, but it also means this method is susceptible to biases, as there is scope for decision-makers to give greater weight to certain criteria—for example, to further their own agendas.

5.5.4 The precautionary principle

One of the criticisms of CBA discussed above is its inability to handle uncertainty. The precautionary principle is a policy evaluation tool that can be applied in situations of genuine uncertainty, where we do not know the probabilities of different outcomes (or know very little about these probabilities), or perhaps we do not even know what all the possible outcomes are. The precautionary principle argues that instead of focusing on averages—as in the standard approach to risk based on expected values—we should focus on the extreme outcomes, in a range of credible forecasts. For example, in the case of regulation of exposure to toxic chemicals, where the full impacts of different levels of exposure are not known, applying the precautionary principle would involve identifying the best- and worst-case scenarios (based on sound evidence) and using this as a guide to policy. Analysis of the extreme outcomes does not need to be carried out using the same units—for example, some outcomes may focus on economic cost while others focus on health or environmental costs.

The precautionary principle encapsulates the idea of 'better safe than sorry', which is especially relevant in situations involving potentially catastrophic and irreversible events, such as climate change. The precautionary principle has been applied in a wide range of areas, including health, environmental regulation, and emerging technologies, and it is a core principle in

[38] Article 191(2) of the Treaty on the Functioning of the EU3 requires EU institutions to ensure that EU environmental policy is based on the precautionary principle.

EU environmental law, having been formally adopted in the Maastricht Treaty in 1992.[38] A common criticism of the precautionary principle is that it is poorly defined and it can be difficult to reach agreement on how to apply the principle because of differences in how individuals and decision-makers understand and perceive risk. It has also been suggested that applying the principle requires potentially very expensive responses to relatively small fears about irreversible damages. However, this criticism misunderstands the nature of this approach, since it does involve weighing up alternatives. It is not true that the precautionary principle would necessarily advocate adopting a project that would, at best, save a very small number of lives but at worst imply huge economic costs.

This discussion of some of the alternatives to CBA suggests that there may not be a single perfect tool for evaluating all public policies and projects. Each tool has its advantages and limitations, and different tools may be appropriate in different contexts. These policy evaluation tools are also not mutually exclusive and decision-makers may use a combination of tools.

Conclusion

Government resources are limited and therefore governments often need to choose among competing policies and projects, selecting those that will maximize social welfare. In order to make these choices, they need tools to evaluate and compare policies and projects. Cost–benefit analysis is one of the most widely used tools for policy evaluation, providing a framework for weighing up the costs and benefits of a project to determine whether it should be carried out.

To carry out a CBA, we need to be able to identify all relevant costs and benefits and assign them a monetary value. But many public sector projects involve benefits that are not easily converted into monetary values—such as natural resources, time, or lives saved. One of the greatest advantages of CBA is perhaps also its greatest weakness—its ability to convert complex assessments of projects or policies into a single number. There are other challenges involved, for example, in comparing costs and benefits occurring at different points in time, in ensuring the distribution of costs and benefits does not consistently disadvantage certain groups in society, in handling the uncertainty surrounding costs and benefits, and in preventing the misuse of CBA to further personal or political goals.

So what does all this mean for CBA? Should we abandon this approach? There are alternative tools that governments can use to evaluate policies, including multi-criteria analysis, cost-effectiveness analysis, and the precautionary principle. These tools overcome some of the limitations of CBA, but they involve challenges of their own. There is no single perfect tool for policy evaluation. Different tools may be appropriate in different contexts, depending on the nature of the projects being assessed, and part of the skill in evaluating projects involves knowing which approach is most appropriate in each case.

Questions for discussion

1. What is the difference between private and social CBA? Why is this distinction important?

2. Should the social discount rate be zero? What are the implications of a zero discount rate for current and future generations?
3. Can time and life be valued in monetary terms? Should they be valued in monetary terms?
4. What policy evaluation tool (CBA, multi-criteria analysis, cost-effectiveness analysis, or the precautionary principle) would be the most appropriate for evaluating the following projects and why:
    a. construction of a new airport;
    b. construction of a wind farm;
    c. building a prison;
    d. introducing a new cancer screening test.
5. 'The main advantage of CBA is that it can reduce a complex problem to a single number, facilitating decision-making among policymakers. This makes CBA inherently superior to alternatives, such as multi-criteria analysis, which make comparisons across projects impossible.' Do you agree with this statement? Why or why not?

Further reading

For a more in-depth discussion of cost–benefit analysis:

Adler, M. D., & Posner, E. A. (1999). Rethinking cost–benefit analysis. *Yale Law Journal, 109*, 165.

Boardman, A. E., Greenberg, D. H., Vining, A. R., & Weimer, D. L. (2018). *Cost–benefit analysis: Concepts and practice* (5th ed.). Cambridge University Press.

Cohn, E. (2003). Benefit–cost analysis: A pedagogical note. *Public Finance Review, 31*(5), 534–549.

OECD (2018). *Cost–benefit analysis and the environment: Further developments and policy use*. Organization for Economic Cooperation and Development.

Robinson, L. A., Loomis, J. B., & Hammitt, J. K. (2011). *Behavioral economics, distribution, and benefit-cost analysis*. Report prepared for the annual meeting of the American Economic Association.

Sunstein, C. R. (2018). *The cost–benefit revolution*. MIT Press.

On approaches to valuing costs and benefits:

Arrow, K., Cropper, M., Eads, G., Hahn, R., Lave, L., Noll, R., Portney, P., Russel M., Schmalensee, R., Smith, V., & Stavins, R. (1996). Is there a role for cost–benefit analysis in environmental, health and safety regulation? *Science*, April, 222–223.

Cropper, M. L., & Oates, W. E. (1992). Environmental economics: A survey. *Journal of Economic Literature, 30*(2), 675–740.

Cullis, J. G., & Jones, P. R. (1996). 'What a difference a day makes . . .': Concern about a new approach to valuing a life. *Journal of Public Economics, 61*(3), 455–457.

Diamond, P. A., & Hausman, J. A. (1994). Contingent valuation: Is some number better than no number? *Journal of Economic Perspectives, 8*(4), 45–64.

Dorman, P. (1996). *Markets and mortality: Economics, dangerous work, and the value of human life*. Cambridge: Cambridge University Press.

Fujiwara, D., & Campbell, R. (2011). *Valuation techniques for social cost–benefit analysis: Stated preference, revealed preference and subjective well-being approaches—A discussion of the current issues*. HM Treasury.

Hausman, J. (2012). Contingent valuation: From dubious to hopeless. *Journal of Economic Perspectives*, *26*(4): 43–56. https://doi.org/10.1257/jep.26.4.43

Johnston, R. J., Boyle, K. J., Adamowicz, W. (Vic), Bennett, J., Brouwer, R., Cameron, T. A., Hanemann, W. M., Hanley, N., Ryan, M., Scarpa, R., Tourangeau, R., & Vossler, C. A. (2017). Contemporary guidance for stated preference studies. *Journal of the Association of Environmental and Resource Economists*, *4*(2), 319–405. https://doi.org/10.1086/691697

List, J. A., Sinha, P., & Taylor, M. H. (2006). Using choice experiments to value non-market goods and services: Evidence from field experiments. *BE Journal of Economic Analysis and Policy*, *6*(2).

Louviere, J., Hensher, D., Swait, J., & Adamowicz, W. (2000). *Stated choice methods: Analysis and applications*. Cambridge University Press.

Mendelsohn, R. (2019). An examination of recent revealed preference valuation methods and results. *Review of Environmental Economics and Policy*, *13*(2), 267–282.

On approaches to discounting the future:

Arrow, K. J., Cropper, M., Gollier, C., Groom, B., Heal, G. M., Newell, R. G., . . . & Weitzman, M. (2013). *How should benefits and costs be discounted in an intergenerational context? The views of an expert panel*. 19 December. Resources for the Future discussion paper (12–53).

Cairns, J., & Van der Pol, M. (2000). Valuing future private and social benefits: The discounted utility model versus hyperbolic discounting models. *Journal of Economic Psychology*, *21*(2), 191–205.

Gollier, C. (2013). *Pricing the planet's future: The economics of discounting in an uncertain world*. Princeton University Press.

Gollier, C., & Weitzman, M. (2010). How should the distant future be discounted when discount rates are uncertain? *Economics Letters*, *145*, 812–829.

Goodin, R. E. (1982). Discounting discounting. *Journal of Public Policy*, *2*(1), 53–71.

Moore, M. A., Boardman, A. E., Vining, A. R., Weimer, D. L., & Greenberg, D. H. (2004). 'Just give me a number!' Practical values for the social discount rate. *Journal of Policy Analysis and Management*, *23*(4), 789–812. https://doi.org/10.1002/pam.20047

For a critique of CBA:

Ackerman, F. (2008). *Critique of cost–benefit analysis, and alternative approaches to decision-making*. A report to Friends of the Earth England, Wales and Northern Ireland.

Cole, D. H. (2008). The Stern review and its critics: Implications for the theory and practice of benefit–cost analysis. *Natural Resources Journal*, *48*(1), 53–90.

Nyborg, K. (2012). *The ethics and politics of environmental cost–benefit analysis*. Taylor & Francis.

Turner, R. K. (2007). Limits to CBA in UK and European environmental policy: Retrospects and future prospects. *Environmental and Resource Economics*, *37*, 253–269.

On alternative approaches to policy evaluation and policy assessment more broadly:

Adler, M., & Fleurbaey, M. (2016). *The Oxford handbook of well-being and public policy*. Oxford University Press.

Dodgson, J. S., Spackman, M., Pearman, A., & Phillips, L. D. (2009). *Multi-criteria analysis: A manual*. Department for Communities and Local Government.

Riegg Cellini, S., & Edwin Kee, J. (2015). Cost-effectiveness and cost–benefit analysis. In S. Cellini & J. E. Kee (Eds.), *Handbook of practical program evaluation* (pp. 636–672). Wiley.

For some examples of applications of CBA:

European Commission (2021). *Economic appraisal vademecum 2021–2027: General principles and sector applications*.

Frayman, D., Krekel, C., Layard, R., MacLennan, S., & Parkes, I. (2024). *Value for money*. London School of Economics, Centre for Economic Performance report.

Bibliography

Ackerman, F. (2008). *Critique of cost–benefit analysis, and alternative approaches to decision-making*. A report to Friends of the Earth England, Wales and Northern Ireland.

Ainslie, G. (1991). Derivation of 'rational' economic behavior from hyperbolic discount curves. *American Economic Review, 81*(2), 334–340.

Ainslie, G. (1992). *Picoeconomics: The strategic interaction of successive motivational states within the person*. Cambridge University Press.

Ashenfelter, O. (2006). Measuring the value of a statistical life: Problems and prospects. *The Economic Journal, 116*(510), C10–C23.

Boardman, A. E., Greenberg, D. H., Vining, A. R., & Weimer, D. L. (2018). *Cost–benefit analysis: Concepts and practice* (5th ed.). Cambridge University Press.

Catalano, G. & Chiara, P. (2022). *Estimations of SDRs in selected countries*. Centre for Industrial Studies working papers, no. N01/2022.

Cohn, E. (2003). Benefit–cost analysis: A pedagogical note. *Public Finance Review, 31*(5), 534–549.

Cole, D. H. (2008). The Stern review and its critics: Implications for the theory and practice of benefit–cost analysis. *Natural Resources Journal, 48*(1), 53–90.

Cullis, J., & Jones, P. (2009). *Public finance and public choice: Analytical perspectives* (3rd ed.). Oxford University Press.

Department for Transport (2013). *The economic case for HS2*. Available at: https://assets.publishing.service.gov.uk/media/5a7ed959e5274a2e8ab48972/S_A_1_Economic_case_0.pdf

Desvousges, W. H., et al. (1993). Measuring natural resource damages with contingent valuation: Tests of validity and reliability. In J. Hausman (Ed.) *Contingent valuation: A critical assessment* (pp. 91–164). North Holland Press.

Diamond, P. A., & Hausman, J. A. (1994). Contingent valuation: Is some number better than no number? *Journal of Economic Perspectives, 8*(4), 45–64.

European Commission (2021). *Economic appraisal vademecum 2021–2027: General principles and sector applications*.

Foster, C. D., & Beesley, M. E. (1963). Estimating the social benefits of constructing an underground railway in London. *Journal of the Royal Statistical Society*, Series A, *126*, 46–58.

Goodin, R. E. (1982). Discounting discounting. *Journal of Public Policy, 2*(1), 53–71.

Hall, Thomas E. (2014). *Aftermath: The unintended consequences of public policies*, Cato Institute.

Hausman, J. (2012). Contingent valuation: From dubious to hopeless. *Journal of Economic Perspectives, 26*(4), 43–56. https://doi.org/10.1257/jep.26.4.43

HM Treasury (2024). *The Green Book 2022: Appraisal and evaluation in central government*. Updated 16 May 2024.

Johnston, R. J., Boyle, K. J., Adamowicz, W. (Vic), Bennett, J., Brouwer, R., Cameron, T. A., Hanemann, W. M., Hanley, N., Ryan, M., Scarpa, R., Tourangeau, R., & Vossler, C. A. (2017). Contemporary guidance for stated preference studies. *Journal of the Association of Environmental and Resource Economists, 4*(2), 319–405. https://doi.org/10.1086/691697

Just, R. E., Schmitz, A., & Zerbe, R. O. (2012). Scitovsky reversals and practical benefit–cost analysis. *Journal of Benefit–Cost Analysis, 3*(2). https://doi.org/10.1515/2152-2812.1109

Kniesner, T. J., & Viscusi, W. K. (2019). The value of a statistical life. Forthcoming in *Oxford research encyclopedia of economics and finance*. Vanderbilt law research papers, no. 19–15.

Morrall III, J. F. (2003). Saving lives: A review of the record. *Journal of Risk and Uncertainty, 27*(3), 221–237.

Nordhaus, W. D. (2007). A review of the Stern Review on the Economics of Climate Change. *Journal of Economic Literature, 45*(3), 686–702. https://doi.org/10.1257/jel.45.3.686

Parsonage, M., & Neuburger, H. (1992). Discounting and health benefits. *Health Economics, 1*(1), 71–76.

Pingle, G. (1978). The early development of cost–benefit analysis. *Journal of Agricultural Economics, 29*, 63–71. https://doi.org/10.1111/j.1477-9552.1978.tb02399.x

Robinson, L. A., Loomis, J. B., & Hammitt, J. K. (2011). *Behavioral economics, distribution, and benefit–cost analysis*. Report prepared for the annual meeting of the American Economic Association.

Samples, Karl C., & Hollyer, J. R. (1990). Contingent valuation of wildlife resources in the presence of substitutes and complements. In R. L. Johnson & G. V. Johnson (Eds.), *Economic valuation of natural resources: Issues, theory and applications* (pp. 177–192). Westview Press.

Small, K. A. (2012). Valuation of travel time. *Economics of Transportation, 1*(1–2), 2–14.

Stern, N. (2007). *The economics of climate change: The Stern review*. Cambridge University Press.

Stiglitz, J. E., & Rosengard, J. K. (2015). Economics of the public sector (4th ed.). W. W. Norton.

Viscusi, W. K. (1993). The value of risks to life and health. *Journal of Economic Literature, 31*(4), 1912–1946.

Viscusi, W. K., & Aldy, J. E. (2003). The value of a statistical life: A critical review of market estimates throughout the world. *Journal of Risk and Uncertainty, 27*(1), 5–76.

Whittington, D., & MacRae Jr., D. (1986). The issue of standing in cost–benefit analysis. *Journal of Policy Analysis and Management, 5*(4), 665–682. https://doi.org/10.1002/pam.4050050401

PART II

AREAS OF GOVERNMENT EXPENDITURE

6
Public goods

Learning objectives

By the end of this chapter, you will be able to:

- 6.1 Explain the difference between public goods and private goods.
- 6.2 Explain how the socially optimal level of provision of public goods is determined.
- 6.3 Discuss whether private markets can provide the efficient level of public goods and the circumstances in which private provision is likely to work.
- 6.4 Discuss the challenges that governments face in providing the efficient level of public goods.

Introduction

Communities across the world are increasingly at risk from flooding. Building and maintaining flood defences, such as sea walls, culverts, or levees, involves a significant cost, but once these flood defences are in place, everyone living in at-risk areas will benefit from the additional flood protection provided. If contributions are made on a voluntary basis, individuals have an incentive not to contribute, because they know they cannot be prevented from benefiting from the flood defences once these have been built—in other words, they have an incentive to free ride. The problem is that if everyone thinks like this, no one will contribute and the flood defences will not be built.

Flood defences are an example of a public good: once these defences are in place, everyone in the area benefits from the same level of protection, no one can be excluded from the benefits of flood protection, and the benefits enjoyed by any one person do not reduce the level of protection available to others. A significant number of public policy issues involve the provision of public goods, including the protection of the environment, tackling poverty, and funding basic research. Because individuals cannot be prevented from enjoying the benefits of a public good, private markets will tend to undersupply these goods, which provides an argument for government intervention. Can markets overcome the free rider problem and provide the efficient level of public goods? What are the challenges to government provision of public goods?

These are the questions we will be focusing on in this chapter. We start by reviewing the definition of public goods and how they differ from private goods in section 6.1. We then explore the conditions required for the optimal or Pareto-efficient level of public goods in section 6.2. In section 6.3, we discuss why markets will typically fail to provide the optimal level of public goods and the circumstances under which private provision of public goods is more likely to succeed. Section 6.4 discusses the role of government in the provision of public goods and the challenges governments face in determining the optimal level of provision.

6.1 What are public goods?

Pure public goods are goods that exhibit the following two characteristics: they are non-excludable, which means that it is impossible (or extremely costly) to prevent any one individual from consuming the good; and they are non-rival in consumption, which means that consumption of the good by one person does not reduce the amount of the good that is available for others to consume. Non-rivalry means that the marginal cost of providing the good to an additional individual is effectively zero.[1] An example of a pure public good is streetlighting. A person walking down the street can benefit from the light provided and this does not reduce the amount of light that is available for others to enjoy, so streetlighting is non-rival in consumption. Once the streetlights have been put in place, it will be virtually impossible to prevent someone from benefiting from the light they provide, and therefore street lighting is non-excludable. Other examples of pure public goods are national defence, lighthouses, and fireworks displays (see Box 6.1).

Full non-rivalry and non-excludability are very strict requirements and there are few examples of goods that satisfy both these conditions. In practice, many goods exhibit these characteristics to some degree—these are known as **impure public goods**, goods that are rival but non-excludable, or non-rival and excludable.

As we saw in Chapter 2, there are two types of impure public goods: common-pool resources and club goods. Common-pool resources are rival but non-excludable—for example,

Box 6.1 Is information a public good?

The typical examples of public goods provided in most textbooks tend to involve more tangible goods, such as national defence, lighthouses, streetlights, or fireworks. But there are also examples of less tangible public goods, such as information. Why might information be considered a public good? It is certainly non-rival: my consumption of information—say, about recent political events, or the London to Bristol train timetable—does not reduce the amount of information that is available for others to consume. But is information non-excludable? It was perhaps easier in the past to prevent people from having access to information. Before the advent of the internet, to access the news, you would have had to buy a printed newspaper or magazine, whereas nowadays many provide a lot of their content online free of charge. Of course, newspapers are not the only providers of information: there are radio and television stations, podcasts and blogs, and other providers of online content. While restricting access to information in the digital age is still possible—and some providers do charge users to access their content—it has arguably become harder. And once one individual has access to information, it is virtually impossible to prevent them from sharing it. Ultimately, whether information can be considered a pure public good depends on how we define it—in other words, whether we are referring to individual facts or specific news items—and who is providing it.

[1] The marginal cost of providing the good to an additional individual is not the same as the marginal cost of producing an additional unit of the good. The marginal cost of production will be positive, but once the public good is produced, providing it to an additional individual does not imply any additional cost. In contrast, with private goods, the marginal cost of production and the marginal cost of providing the good to an additional individual are the same.

fish stocks in the ocean: one additional boat fishing in an area where fish stocks are heavily depleted will have a significant impact on the amount of fish available to other fishing vessels, but it would be very difficult or extremely costly to prevent a boat from fishing in the ocean. Club goods are non-rival but excludable—for example, online movie streaming: if one person is watching a film on an online streaming service, this does not mean that other people cannot also watch the same film, but it is possible to exclude people from accessing this film by requiring them to pay for it.

Private goods are goods that are both rival and excludable, such as an apple: if you eat an apple, that apple is not available for anyone else to eat (hence it is rival); and it is perfectly possible to prevent someone from eating an apple by not selling it to them (hence it is excludable). Table 6.1 summarizes these different types of goods.

In practice, the boundaries between these different types of goods are not always clear-cut. Whether a good is rivalrous in consumption will often depend on how many people are already consuming it—for example, an extra pedestrian on a busy footpath reduces the amount of space available for others to enjoy in a way that an extra pedestrian on a fairly empty footpath does not. These boundaries can also change over time, particularly as a result of changes in technology. Whether a good is excludable or not depends on the technology available, and technological advances can make goods that were previously non-excludable excludable: roads can be made excludable by introducing toll systems,[2] and television and radio broadcasts can be made excludable by requiring users to pay subscription fees to access them. It therefore makes more sense to think of types of goods as varying along a spectrum, depending on their degree of rivalry (measured by the marginal cost of adding an additional user) and how easy it is to exclude individuals from consuming them. This is depicted in Figure 6.1.

Public goods can also be defined based on the areas over which they are available. **Local public goods** are goods that are available only within a limited geographical area, such as a city park, whereas national or global public goods are available on a much wider scale—for example, climate change mitigation actions. There are also examples of public goods provided within the family, such as childcare.

Public goods are effectively goods that create positive externalities. As we saw in Chapter 2, a positive externality arises when the action of an individual imposes a benefit on other individuals who are not directly involved in the action. If an individual decides to invest in streetlights outside their home, any person walking past their house will be able to benefit from these streetlights. Or if a group of people decide to clear litter from a local park, all individuals who visit the park will benefit from the cleaner environment. The non-rival nature of public goods implies social benefits that are greater than private benefits, which is the defining feature of a positive externality.

Table 6.1 Types of goods

	Excludable	Non-excludable
Rival	Private good (e.g. apples)	Common-pool resources (e.g. ocean fish stocks)
Non-rival	Club goods (e.g. online streaming platforms)	Pure public good (e.g. streetlights)

[2] Although toll systems have been around for some time, technological advances have made them easier to implement.

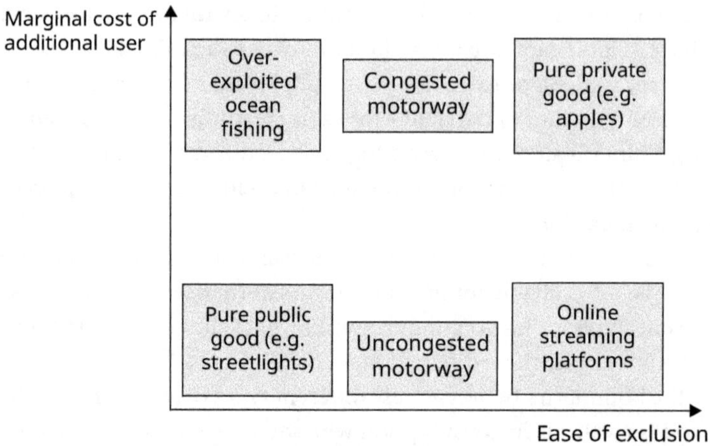

Figure 6.1 Types of goods by ease of exclusion and marginal cost of use

One very important distinction to keep in mind is that public goods are not the same thing as publicly provided goods. Publicly provided goods are goods that are provided by the government—these may include public goods, but will also include a number of other goods, such as education and healthcare, which are not public goods. It is possible to exclude an individual from accessing a school or hospital, and providing education or healthcare to one individual, through a teacher or doctor, reduces the amount of education or healthcare that is available for others—a doctor cannot treat multiple patients at the same time, and there is a limit to how many students a teacher can support at a given time.

6.2 Optimal provision of public goods

What is the optimal level of provision of public goods? Before answering this question, it is helpful to revisit the conditions for the optimal provision of private goods that we looked at in Chapter 2. Suppose we have two individuals, Alfie and Leni, who are deciding what quantities of two private goods—biscuits and cheese.—to consume. For simplicity, we will assume that cheese is our **numeraire good** and each piece of cheese costs £1.[3]

Panels (a) and (b) in Figure 6.2 illustrate Alfie and Leni's individual demand curves for biscuits, which reflect their willingness to pay for biscuits. At a price of P_1, Alfie demands the quantity of biscuits Q_1, whereas Leni demands the quantity of biscuits Q_2. The aggregate or market demand for biscuits is illustrated in panel (c). This is derived by summing the individual demand curves *horizontally*: for each possible price, we add together the quantity of biscuits that Alfie demands and the quantity that Leni demands to determine the total quantity of biscuits demanded in the market. For example, at a price of P_1, the total quantity of biscuits

[3] A numeraire good is a good that is used as a basis for valuing all other goods and whose price is set equal to 1. This simplification is possible because, in general equilibrium, it is only relative prices that matter. For example, if the price of a biscuit is £4 and the price of cheese is £2, the relative price ratio is $p_B / p_C = 4/2 = 2$. If we set cheese to be our numeraire good and divide both prices by the price of cheese, the price of a biscuit is now £2 and the price of cheese is £1, and the relative price ratio remains 2.

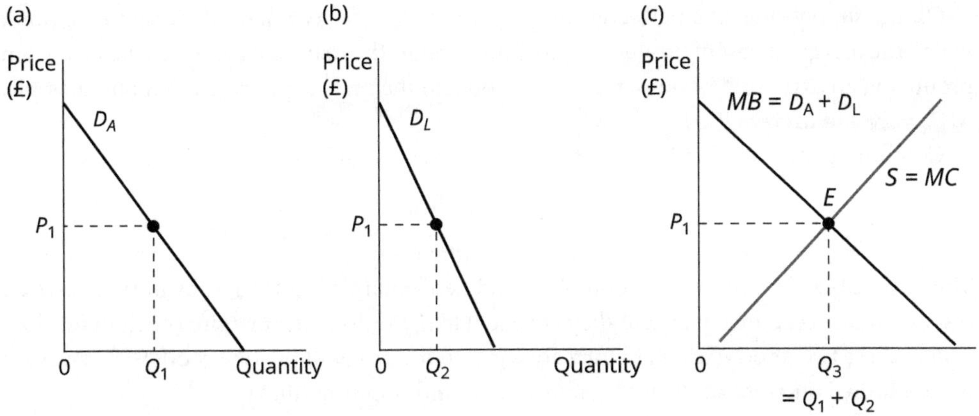

Figure 6.2 Optimal provision of private goods

demanded equals the sum of Alfie's demand at that price and Leni's demand at that price, which is given by $Q_3 = Q_1 + Q_2$. Because private goods are rival in consumption, if more of the good is demanded, more needs to be produced. The aggregate demand curve represents Alfie and Leni's marginal benefit from biscuit consumption (*MB*).

In a perfectly competitive market, the supply curve for biscuits is determined by firms' marginal cost of production (*MC*), or the cost of producing an additional biscuit. The market equilibrium is given by the point at which the demand and supply curves intersect, where marginal benefit equals marginal cost—this is shown by point E in the figure, where the equilibrium price is P_1 and the equilibrium quantity is Q_3. This outcome is efficient as it maximizes total welfare, or the sum of consumer and producer surplus.[4]

We can represent this equilibrium result mathematically. As we saw in Chapter 2, for any two goods, each individual's optimal choice—or the quantities of the two goods that will maximize their utility, given their income and the prices of the goods—is determined by the point at which their budget constraint is tangent to their highest possible indifference curve. This tangency condition implies that the slope of the indifference curve and the slope of the budget constraint are equal at this point. The slope of an indifference curve is given by the marginal rate of substitution between the goods, which tells us the rate at which the individual is willing to exchange one good for the other while holding their utility constant; the marginal rate of substitution is equal to the ratio of the marginal utilities of the two goods. The slope of the budget line is given by the ratio of the prices of the goods. Therefore, if Alfie and Leni are both maximizing their utility, their demand for the two goods, biscuits and cheese, must satisfy the following efficiency condition:

$$\frac{MU_B^A}{MU_C^A} = MRS_{BC}^A = MRS_{BC}^L = \frac{MU_B^L}{MU_C^L} = \frac{P_B}{P_C}$$

where MU_B^A and MU_C^A represent Alfie's marginal utility of biscuits and cheese, respectively, and MRS_{BC}^A represents Alfie's marginal rate of substitution between the two goods (and similarly for Leni). So the optimal level of consumption of the two goods is given by the point where the ratio of their marginal utilities equals the price ratio.

[4] See Chapter 2 for a discussion of these concepts.

On the supply side, in a perfectly competitive market, firms will produce up to the point where the marginal cost of production, MC, just equals the marginal benefit to the firm from producing an extra unit of output, which is equal to the market price, P. So in our example, $MC_B = P_B$ and $MC_C = P_C$.

Combining these demand and supply conditions, in equilibrium we therefore have:[5]

$$MRS_{BC} = \frac{MC_B}{MC_C}$$

This tells us that, in equilibrium, both Alfie and Leni's marginal rates of substitution between biscuits and cheese are equal, and they are equal to the ratio of the marginal costs of production of these two goods (which in turn are equal to the prices of the two goods).[6] Because we have assumed the price of cheese equals £1, this condition simplifies to:

$$MRS_{BC} = MC_B$$

The marginal rate of substitution tells us how many pieces of cheese these individuals are willing to give up in exchange for an extra biscuit. It therefore captures the value that each individual places on an additional biscuit (relative to cheese). In equilibrium, the marginal value or benefit of consuming one extra unit of the good for each individual just equals the marginal cost of producing it, so the equilibrium outcome is efficient.

With private goods, individuals face the same prices, but the individual quantities demanded can vary. Public goods, however, are non-rival in consumption, which means that whatever quantity is produced is consumed equally by all individuals. This has implications for how we derive the aggregate demand for public goods and, therefore, how we determine the optimal level of public goods.

Suppose that Alfie and Leni are now choosing between a public good, such as streetlights, S, and a private good, cheese, C, and that once again cheese is our numeraire good, so its price is £1 per unit. Panel (a) in Figure 6.3 shows Alfie and Leni's individual demand curves for streetlights, or how much they are willing to pay for each additional streetlight. They have

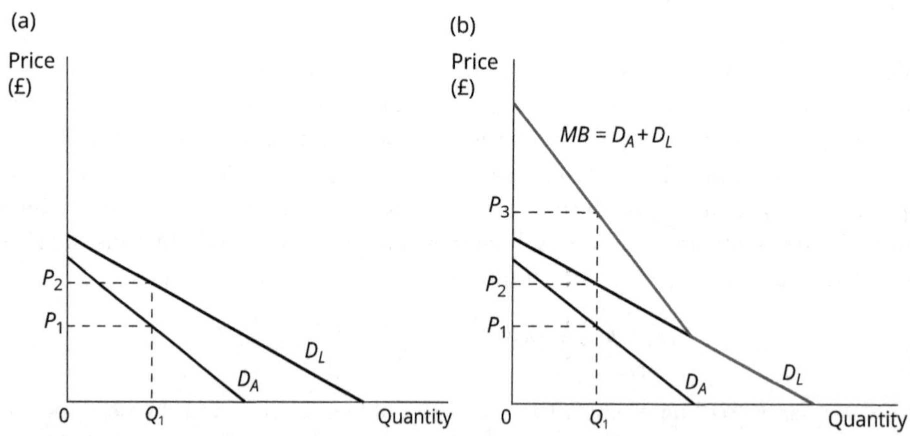

Figure 6.3 Deriving the aggregate demand for public goods

[5] Because Alfie and Leni's marginal rates of substitution are equal at this point, we have removed the superscript that indicates the individual.

[6] As we saw in Chapter 2, the ratio of the marginal costs is equivalent to the marginal rate of transformation, which measures the opportunity cost of producing one good in terms of the other.

different tastes, which are reflected in the different demands: Alfie is willing to pay only P_1 for quantity Q_1 of streetlights, whereas Leni is willing to pay the higher price P_2 for the same quantity of streetlights.[7]

Because whatever quantity of streetlights is provided must be consumed equally by both individuals, to work out the aggregate demand for streetlights we need to combine Alfie's willingness to pay for each quantity of streetlights and Leni's willingness to pay for the same quantity of streetlights. This means that rather than summing the individual demand curves horizontally, as we did in the case of private goods, we need to sum them *vertically*: this tells us the total willingness to pay for each additional streetlight. The aggregate demand for streetlights is illustrated in panel (b) in Figure 6.3. For example, for the quantity of streetlights Q_1, Alfie and Leni together are willing to pay $P_3 = P_1 + P_2$. This captures the total marginal benefit (MB) from the provision of streetlights.

As in the case of private goods, the supply curve for the public good just equals the marginal cost of production. The market equilibrium is given by the point where the aggregate demand curve and the supply curve intersect, illustrated by point E in Figure 6.4. The equilibrium level of the public good is Q^* and the price is P^*. This equilibrium output level is efficient because, at this point, the total marginal benefit from producing an additional unit of the public good, captured by the aggregate demand curve, equals the marginal cost of producing it.

We can also demonstrate this result formally. The value of one additional streetlight for Alfie is given by his marginal rate of substitution, or how many units of the private good he would be willing to give up for one additional streetlight, and similarly for Leni. So the total value of one additional streetlight equals the sum of these individual marginal rates of substitution—this provides a measure of the total marginal benefit of one additional streetlight. In equilibrium, this total marginal benefit equals the marginal cost of producing one extra streetlight:

$$MRS^A_{SC} + MRS^L_{SC} = MC$$

where MRS^A_{SC} and MRS^L_{SC} represent Alfie and Leni's marginal rates of substitution between the public good, streetlights, and the private good, cheese, and MC is the marginal cost of

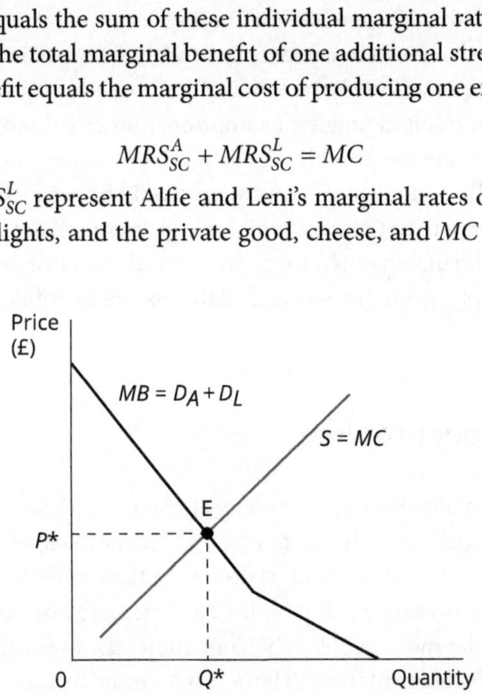

Figure 6.4 Optimal provision of public goods

[7] Note that here the willingness to pay refers to each individual's willingness to pay for *one additional unit* of the public good, or one additional streetlight—that is, it is a measure of their marginal willingness to pay. For example, if $Q_1 = 3$, the demand curve would represent the individual willingness to pay for the third streetlight.

producing the public good. This is the efficiency condition for the provision of public goods. It is known as the Samuelson condition, after the economist Paul Samuelson (1954). The marginal rate of substitution measures the marginal benefit of one more unit of the public good, so efficiency is maximized when the total marginal benefit (i.e. the sum of individual marginal benefits) just equals the marginal cost of producing one extra unit.

Unlike in the case of private goods, where efficiency is maximized when the individual marginal rates of substitution equal marginal cost, with public goods total welfare is maximized when the *sum* of the individual marginal rates of substitution equals the marginal cost of producing the public good.[8] Because one extra unit of the public good will be consumed by all individuals, it will have an impact on the utility of all individuals, so the total benefit of this unit is given by the sum of the individual marginal benefits. In contrast, with private goods, an additional unit can only be consumed by one individual, so efficiency is maximized when it does not matter which individual consumes this extra unit because all individual marginal benefits are equal to one another.

6.3 Will markets provide the optimal level of public goods?

We have seen how, to maximize total welfare, public goods should be produced up to the point where the marginal cost of production equals the sum of the marginal rates of substitution for all individuals, which measures the marginal benefit of providing the goods. Will private markets provide this efficient level of public goods?

There are two sources of inefficiency associated with the provision of public goods, which are related to each of their two key characteristics. Because public goods are non-rival, charging a price for them can result in underconsumption: the price discourages some individuals who would like to consume the good from consuming it, even though the marginal cost of providing the good to these additional consumers would be zero. This outcome is inefficient because the marginal benefit to these individuals is greater than the marginal cost. An example is charging tolls on an uncongested road. The second source of inefficiency arises because of the risk of undersupply given the non-excludable nature of public goods. We focus on this second problem below.

6.3.1 The free rider problem

Suppose a group of residents share access to a local open green space which has become overgrown and filled with litter. They decide to hire a gardener to clean up the space so they can all enjoy it. They carry out a survey of all residents in their neighbourhood to find out who would like to contribute towards paying for the gardener and how much they would each be willing to contribute. The more people who contribute, the lower the cost to each resident. However, if a resident decides not to contribute, they cannot be prevented from accessing the green space. Each resident therefore has a strong incentive not to contribute, since they will still be able to enjoy the benefits of the green space.

[8] The general rule for any number of individuals, n, is given by: $\sum_{i=1}^{n} MRS_i = MC$.

As the above example illustrates, if individuals cannot be excluded from consuming the good, they have an incentive to understate their true valuation of the good, or even say they do not value it at all, so that they can enjoy the benefits without paying for the good, or by paying less—in other words, individuals have an incentive to free ride. This problem can be particularly severe when there are a large number of potential contributors, so each individual believes their contribution is small relative to the total and is therefore less likely to have an impact. The problem is that if everyone thinks like this, then no one will contribute to the cost of the good and the good will not be provided.[9] This is the free rider problem: if every potential consumer of a public good understates his or her true valuation in the hope of enjoying the good more cheaply or even for free, then the public good will be underprovided.

The free rider problem leads to market failure because total welfare is not maximized. This is illustrated in Figure 6.5. The cost of providing the public good, given by the supply curve $S = MC$, is greater than each individual's willingness to pay for the good, as captured by their respective demand curves, D_A and D_L. Neither individual values the good highly enough to be willing to pay for it, so the good will not be produced. However, this outcome is inefficient, since if we consider the total willingness to pay for the good, captured by the aggregate demand curve MB, this exceeds the marginal cost of producing it, at least up to the output level Q_G^*; this is the optimal level of provision of the public good. But this optimal level will be produced only if both individuals truthfully reveal their willingness to pay for the public good.

The difficulty is that free riding is often a rational strategy for each individual. We can use the tools of **game theory** to explain why this is the case. Suppose an individual is deciding whether to contribute towards a public good, where the cost is shared among a large number of people. Each individual contribution is £5, and if the public good is provided, each individual benefits to the value of £10 from consuming the public good. The public good will be provided as long as a sufficient number of people contribute towards it. If everyone contributes, the public good is provided and everyone enjoys a net benefit of £5, which is equal to their individual benefit (£10) minus the cost of their contribution (£5). If no one contributes, the public good is not provided and each individual's net benefit is £0. If just one individual

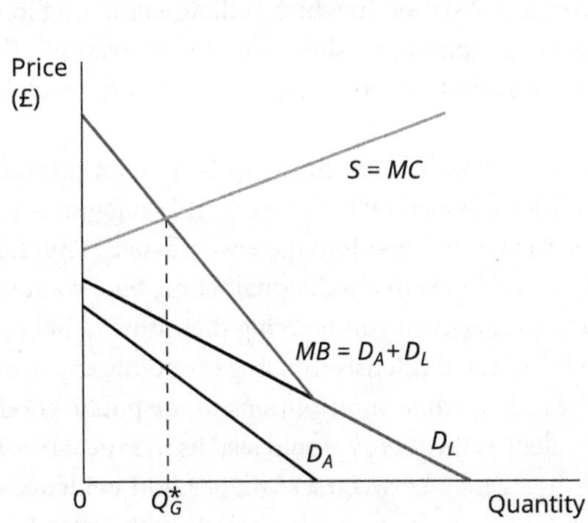

Figure 6.5 Market failure in the provision of public goods

[9] Even if just a large enough proportion of people think like this, the good will be seriously underprovided.

Table 6.2 Hypothetical payoff matrix for public goods

	Others contribute (public good provided)	Others free ride (public good not provided)
Individual contributes	**£5**, £5	**−£5**, £0
Individual free rides	**£10**, £5	**£0**, £0

free rides, the public good will still be provided, and the free rider enjoys a net benefit of £10 (since they did not have to pay the £5 contribution), whereas everyone else has a net benefit of £5. If only one person contributes and everyone else free rides, the public good will not be provided and the individual contributor makes a loss of £5. These payoffs are illustrated in Table 6.2, where the payoffs for the individual contributor appear first in each cell, highlighted in bold.

What should a rational individual do? Assuming the individual does not know what everyone else is going to do, they should base their decision on their expected payoffs. If they choose to contribute to the public good, they will either gain £5 (if everyone else contributes) or lose £5 (if everyone else free rides). If they decide to free ride, they will gain either £10 (if everyone else contributes) or £0 (if everyone else also free rides). Free riding is the rational strategy for the individual because it always leads to a higher payoff: if everyone else contributes, by free riding the individual earns a payoff of £10 rather than £5; if everyone else free rides, the individual earns a payoff of £0 instead of making a loss of £5. Free riding is an example of a **dominant strategy**: a strategy that is optimal, in the sense of leading to a higher payoff, regardless of what everyone else does.

Each individual in this game, when faced with this decision, has an incentive to free ride and not to contribute to the public good. The equilibrium outcome, therefore, is where everyone free rides and the public good is not provided, even though everyone would be made better off by contributing and receiving a net benefit of £5. This is an example of what is known as the **prisoner's dilemma**: a situation in which individuals acting in their own self-interest lead to an outcome that is not optimal for the group. In our example, the group would clearly be better off if everyone contributed to the public good, but for each individual it is rational to free ride.

Economic theory tells us that, because individuals have an incentive to free ride, public goods are likely to be underprovided by the market. This suggests a role for government intervention in the provision of public goods to increase efficiency. But how pervasive is the free rider problem in practice? We know that individuals contribute voluntarily to public goods—for example, by donating to charity or volunteering their time to help others. The predictions of the theory have also been tested extensively using economic experiments. The results from these experiments suggest that, while contributions to the public good are far from optimal, free riding is not as prevalent as the theory would lead us to expect (see Box 6.2).

What explains this divergence between the theory and evidence on free riding? Some have argued that the evidence merely shows that people make mistakes and participants may misunderstand the instructions in the experiments. However, other research suggests that the assumption of self-interested utility-maximizing behaviour that underlies the free rider problem may not be entirely accurate. In reality, the motives that drive individual behaviour are complex, and may include altruistic motives, a concern for fairness, wanting to comply

Box 6.2 Do people free ride as much as the theory suggests?

Experiments to test the free rider hypothesis go back several decades and have been carried out by economists, psychologists, and sociologists. The typical set-up for an economics experiment involves gathering a group of participants[10] who are each given a number of tokens which represents their income, and they can allocate these tokens to a private good or a public good. The private good has a higher private benefit, whereas the public good has a higher social benefit. The return on the investment in the public good will depend on what the other participants do. Typically, contributions to the public good are doubled by the person running the experiment, and then divided up equally among all participants. For example, if there are 10 participants and the total contribution to the public good is 10 tokens, this is then doubled and every participant receives two tokens. The total payoff to participants is the sum of the benefits from consuming the private good and from consuming the public good (if the public good is provided). If all participants contribute to the public good, their payoff is maximized. However, each individual has an incentive not to contribute to the public good and to spend all their tokens on the private good in the hope that other participants will fund the public good.

Different variations of the public goods experiment have been tested, using groups of various sizes, with different types of participants, repeating the experiment to see whether participants learn or change their strategies over time, and allowing participants to communicate with one another. Marwell and Ames (1981) carried out a number of early public goods experiments, exploring the impact of differences in the payoffs, group size, level of experience, and whether individuals received feedback on the intentions of other participants. They found that individual contributions to the public good across these experiments ranged from 40 to 60 per cent of resources, on average. One clear exception was their experiment involving economics graduate students, where the average contribution to the public good was only 20 per cent of resources. A study by Isaac and Walker (1988) analysed the relationship between variations in group size and free riding behaviour in voluntary contributions to public goods. They found that contributions tended to fall as the group size increased, but this only occurred when there was also a decrease in the marginal return from the public good, and was not purely due an increase in the group size.

Ledyard (1995) reviewed several of these early public goods experiments and found that average contributions to the public good in experiments where free riding was the individually rational strategy ranged from 30 to 70 per cent.[11] The willingness to contribute to the public good tended to fall if experiments were repeated, suggesting that participants learn and change their strategies over time. Allowing participants to communicate with one another—particularly in face-to-face communication—led to an increase in contributions.

More recent research exploring the reasons for cooperation in public goods experiments has focused on the idea that there are different types of individuals, with different social preferences and different beliefs about their peers.[12] Many participants in these experiments appear to be 'conditional cooperators' whose contribution to the public goods is tied to

(*Continued*)

[10] These are often, though not always, college or university students.
[11] In instances where the game was not repeated or in the early rounds of repeated games.
[12] See Chaudhuri (2011) for a comprehensive review of these studies.

their beliefs about the average group contribution. These conditional cooperators can sustain high levels of contributions to the public good by resorting to monetary punishments of free riders, as well as less punitive mechanisms such as expressions of disapproval or giving advice (Chaudhuri, 2011).

Some have argued that experimental settings do not provide a realistic context for assessing people's real-world responses, but evidence from real-world settings also suggests that free riding is not as pervasive as the theory would have us believe. For example, a study by Kingma (1989) analysed contributions to a specific public good—the operation of public radio stations in the USA. He looked at data on voluntary member contributions to public radio stations and found that about half of the individuals in the sample contributed a positive amount.

Overall, the evidence suggests that, while some individuals do free ride, not everyone does, and voluntary contributions to public goods are often positive. The key question, then, is: *why* do people contribute to public goods, even though it may not be rational to do so? This has been the focus of a lot of the recent research in this area. Understanding why people behave in this way can inform the design of better institutions that can help support cooperation in the provision of public goods.

with social norms, or wanting to protect their reputation. People may cooperate in the provision of public goods not because they are misguided, but because they have a preference for cooperative behaviour.[13]

While the results from economic experiments provide useful insights, they also have their limitations. Scenarios played out in a laboratory are not the same as lived experiences, and participants may respond differently in the experiments, where the stakes are lower, than they would in real life. The participants in economic experiments are often students, and their responses may not be representative of how the general population would behave in the same situations.

6.3.2 Private provision of public goods

The evidence discussed in the previous section suggests that the free rider problem may not be as pervasive as the theory would imply, opening up the possibility for market provision of public goods. In fact, lighthouses— one of the classic examples of a public good—were for a long time privately provided in Britain (see Box 6.3). Other examples of public goods that are privately provided include charity donations, public goods within the family, and intergenerational altruism.

So, when is the market likely to be able to provide public goods? Four factors contribute to the successful market provision of public goods: when there is scope to provide complementary goods; when there are differences in individual demands for the public good; when individuals have altruistic preferences; and when individuals care about social norms. We discuss each of these in turn below.

[13] See Andreoni (1995a) for a discussion of the reasons behind cooperative behaviour in public goods experiments.

Box 6.3 Private provision of lighthouses

Lighthouses have long been considered a classic example of a pure public good. They are non-rival, as the fact that one ship benefits from the light provided does not reduce the amount available for other ships, and they are also non-excludable, as it would be extremely difficult to prevent passing ships from benefiting from the light of a lighthouse. The nineteenth-century philosopher and political economist John Stuart Mill was one of the first to argue that lighthouses should be provided by the government because 'it is impossible that the ships at sea which are benefitted by a lighthouse, should be made to pay a toll on the occasion of its use, no one would build lighthouses from motives of personal interest, unless indemnified and rewarded from a compulsory levy made by the state' (quoted in Coase, 1974: 357).

However, up until 1842, lighthouses in Britain were financed and built by private individuals who then levied a toll on the shipowners when they came into the ports. These tolls varied with the lighthouse and the ship size, and ships were required to pay a toll for each lighthouse they had passed on their journey. The British government bought all private lighthouses in the mid-nineteenth century and took them into public ownership. It was argued that this would lead to lower prices, although in practice this appears not to have happened (Coase, 1974). Under government ownership, the British lighthouse service was financed from a General Lighthouse Fund, whose income came from light dues paid by commercial vessels that stopped at ports in the British Isles—a system that is still in place today. The General Lighthouse Fund is under the stewardship of the Department of Transport, which sets the rates of the light dues paid by shipowners.

Sources: Coase (1974), Coyle (2020), and Trinity House (2016).

Providing complementary goods

While private firms cannot exclude individuals from consuming a pure public good, they may be able to provide an *excludable* good which is complementary to the non-excludable public good. The proceeds from selling the excludable good can then be used to finance the provision of the non-excludable public good. The case of lighthouses discussed in Box 6.3 provides one example. As a further example, consider a business that is responsible for maintaining a stretch of beach. While restricting access to the beach is in theory possible, it would be very costly, so the beach can be considered a non-excludable good. Provided the beach is not overcrowded, it is also non-rival. Maintaining the cleanliness of the beach involves a cost, but it would be difficult to charge individuals to access the beach, given the potential to free ride. As an alternative, the business owner could rent out sun loungers and use these revenues to pay for keeping the beach clean and tidy. So, coupling public and private goods provides a useful mechanism for firms to finance the provision of public goods.

Differences in demand for the public good

Private provision of pure public goods is more likely to succeed when individuals have different demands for the public good, particularly where some individuals have a very high demand for the good. As we have seen, each individual's willingness to contribute to the public good will depend on the utility they derive from consuming it minus the cost of their contribution. If an individual derives a high level of utility from consuming the good and/or if they have a high level of income, their willingness to pay will be higher and more of the good is likely to be provided. This may explain why people donate to charity or political campaigns. However, while a strong preference for a particular public good or higher incomes will help mitigate the free rider problem, it might not eliminate it completely. If, when deciding how much of the public good to consume, each individual only takes into account their own personal benefit or utility from consuming the good and not the benefits to other individuals, then the public good is still likely to be underprovided. But individuals might care about more than just their private level of consumption of public goods, as we discuss next.

Altruism and warm glow

The standard model of public goods, discussed in section 6.2, assumes that individuals are rational self-interested utility-maximizers who care only about their own consumption of public and private goods. In practice, evidence suggests that individuals care about the well-being of others and often engage in altruistic behaviour. Altruism can help explain why people contribute to public goods—for example, by donating to charity or volunteering, giving up their time to help others. Altruism need not imply self-sacrifice—that is, an individual does not have to suffer some loss as a result of carrying out an altruistic action—and it does not have to be the only motive driving individual behaviour: actions may be driven by a combination of motives, some of which may be altruistic and some self-interested.

Pure altruism is defined as a preference for the well-being of others: my utility or well-being increases if the well-being of others is increased. Impure altruism, in contrast, allows for individuals also to derive a private benefit from the act of giving itself. In the context of public goods, such as charitable giving, pure altruism implies that individuals only derive utility from their consumption of private goods and the total quantity of the public good provided, whereas impure altruism implies that individuals also care about how much they contribute to the public good. This is the basis of the warm glow model originally proposed by Andreoni (1989, 1990).[14]

The warm glow model can help us understand the evidence on individual contributions to public goods, both in experimental settings and in the real world, but the mechanisms that underlie warm glow behaviour are still not fully understood. People might care about their contributions to the public good because they experience positive emotions, such as pride, when they feel their contribution meets certain standards, or because they experience negative emotions, like guilt or shame, if they feel they have fallen below these standards. Individuals might contribute to public goods because they care about how other people perceive them, especially in small communities where people are more likely to know one another and may feel a degree of social responsibility. Understanding the reasons behind warm glow behaviour matters for policy: if introducing economic incentives to contribute to public goods—for example, by subsidizing contributions—means that people experience less pride when making contributions, then a policy of subsidizing private contributions to a public good may actually end up reducing the level of private contributions.[15]

[14] Warm glow refers to the pleasurable feeling individuals get from the act of giving. It is a private benefit that is experienced by the individual making the contribution. In the warm glow model, individual utility depends on an individual's contribution to the public good, along with their consumption of the private good and the total level of the public good provided.

[15] We return to this point in section 6.4.2, where we discuss the problem of government crowding out private contributions to public goods.

Social norms

The discussion above highlighted how individual behaviour may be driven by motives other than rational self-interest, which can help explain why people contribute to public goods. A desire to comply with social norms can also help explain voluntary contributions to public goods, particularly if individuals care about how others perceive their actions and decisions. Social norms are the often-unwritten rules that guide the standards of what is considered acceptable behaviour in a particular society.[16] Failure to comply with social norms can lead to feelings of guilt or shame. Examples of social norms include telling the truth and keeping promises. There may be an accepted social norm that littering is wrong, which will help discourage people from littering, thereby contributing to the public good of clean streets. More generally, truthfully revealing one's demand for a public good, and contributing accordingly, can be a powerful social norm and support voluntary contributions to public goods. People value fairness and this can play an important role in guiding individual behaviour. Contributions to public goods may also be guided by a desire to establish a norm of **reciprocity**. Reciprocity refers to the propensity to respond in kind—for example, by rewarding generosity and punishing opportunistic behaviour—and this can help promote future cooperation.

To sum up, there are several factors that enable markets to overcome the free rider problem and support private provision of public goods. However, these factors alone will not guarantee that the socially optimal level of public goods is provided, suggesting there is still a role for government intervention to increase efficiency. These factors are also likely to be more effective in the context of local public goods and may not work as well with global public goods. Social norms may help ensure the park and streets in your neighbourhood are kept clean and tidy, but may be less effective in tackling global problems such as reducing the amount of plastic waste in the oceans.

6.4 Government provision of public goods

As we have seen, the private sector will generally fail to provide the efficient or socially optimal level of public goods. Can government intervention improve on the market outcome? The government does not face the same constraints as private firms—in particular, it does not need to rely on charging a price to finance the provision of a public good. If the government knows individual demands for the public good, it can determine the efficient level of provision—using the Samuelson condition we discussed in section 6.2—and finance this through general taxation.

In practice, there are two key challenges that affect the government's ability to provide the efficient level of public goods. First, the government is unlikely to have the necessary information on individual demands for the public good and, as we have seen, individuals have an incentive to understate their true preferences or valuation of the public good, particularly if this will affect how much they are required to contribute towards it. Is there an allocation mechanism that can be used to elicit individual preferences and ensure the efficient level of

[16] See Ostrom (2000) for a discussion of the development of social norms and the role they play in supporting cooperative behaviour.

the public good is provided? The second challenge involves the impact that government intervention may have on the level of private contributions towards the public good—in other words, the risk that government provision may **crowd out** private sector provision. We discuss each of these issues in turn below.[17]

6.4.1 Alternatives to the market allocation mechanism

We have seen how market provision of public goods is susceptible to the free rider problem. Here we consider three alternative allocation mechanisms: personalized prices, voting, and preference revelation mechanisms.

Personalized prices

One approach to the problem of providing the efficient level of public goods is based on personalized prices, where each individual faces a different price depending on their own willingness to pay for the public good. With private goods, in a competitive market, all individuals face the same prices, but they can adjust the quantities of the goods they consume. Therefore efficiency is achieved by adjusting individual consumption so that each individual chooses the quantity of the good that ensures their marginal benefit from consumption equals the market price. With pure public goods, however, individuals cannot adjust their level of consumption of the good, since everyone must consume the same quantity. Instead, we should adjust the price that each individual pays for the public good to match their own marginal benefit or willingness to pay for the good. An individual who places a low value on the public good will therefore face a low price, whereas an individual who places a high value on the public good will face a high price. These personalized prices are known as **Lindahl prices.**[18]

How would such a mechanism work? First, the government would announce a set of tax prices for the public good, which represent the share of the cost of providing the good that each individual must bear. For example, in a society with just two individuals, the government might announce that each will pay for half of the cost of providing the public good. Each individual then states what quantity of the public good they would demand given those tax prices. If these quantities are equal, then this is the level of the public good that is provided. However, if the quantities stated by the two individuals differ, then the government will announce a new set of tax prices and individuals again state the quantity they wish to consume at those prices. This process is repeated until a set of tax prices is announced such that at those prices both individuals want to consume the same quantity of the public good. This point is the **Lindahl equilibrium**. The Lindahl equilibrium is therefore a set of tax prices which add up to the marginal cost of producing the good, such that at those prices everyone demands the same quantity of the public good.

If individuals truthfully reveal their demands or willingness to pay for the public good, then the Lindahl equilibrium is efficient. Suppose that, in equilibrium, our two individuals, Alfie and Leni, have to pay prices p_G^A and p_G^L, respectively, to supply quantity G of the public good.

[17] In addition to these two challenges, we also need to consider the implications of how the provision of the public good is financed. If the public good is paid for from tax revenues, this will also have an impact on efficiency, as most taxes used by the government are distortionary. We discuss this in more detail in Chapter 13.

[18] Named after the Swedish economist, Erik Lindahl, who originally proposed this approach in an article published in 1919.

Alfie's total contribution to the public good is then $p_G^A G$ and Leni's total contribution is $p_G^L G$.[19] To maximize their utility, each individual's choice must satisfy the condition that their marginal rate of substitution between the public good, G, and the private good, X, equals the price ratio. Assuming the price of the private good is 1, this implies $MRS_{GX}^A = p_G^A$ for Alfie and $MRS_{GX}^L = p_G^L$ for Leni.[20] Aggregating across both individuals, we have:

$$MRS_{GX}^A + MRS_{GX}^L = p_G^A + p_G^L$$

So, the sum of the marginal rates of substitution equals the marginal cost of providing the public good, which is the Samuelson condition we derived above. This demonstrates that the Lindhal equilibrium is Pareto efficient.

While the Lindahl pricing mechanism may work if we have a small number of individuals, it is difficult to see how it could be implemented across a larger group. Repeatedly announcing and adjusting individual prices until an equilibrium is reached would be very challenging in practice, even with a relatively small group of 50 people, let alone the population of a city or country.

This mechanism also fails to provide the incentive for individuals to truthfully reveal their valuation of the public good. This is the preference revelation problem: because the tax price that each individual faces is directly tied to their stated willingness to pay for the good, individuals have an incentive to understate their true preferences or true valuation of the good to reduce the cost they face. As with the private provision of public goods discussed above, there is an incentive for individuals to free ride.

It is also possible that individuals might not know their true preferences for the public good. Whereas most of us could easily say how much we value and would be willing to pay for a cup of coffee, a new pair of shoes or a laptop, a car, or even a house, how many people could accurately say how much they value a good like national defence or basic research? What tax price would you be willing to pay for an improvement in air quality?

Voting

An alternative approach is to collect information on individual preferences for public goods through the political process, and this is how the level of expenditure on public goods is often determined in practice. Individuals do not vote on quantities of specific public goods, but rather elect representatives who promise to deliver a particular bundle of public goods and taxes.

Allocation through voting will help tackle the preference revelation problem, since individuals have no incentive to misrepresent their true preferences. As we saw in Chapter 4, under majority voting, the preferences of the median voter will determine the outcome. Suppose that $G_1, G_2, \ldots, G_n$ represent each voter's most preferred bundle of public goods spending and taxes, and these bundles are organized along a line from lowest to highest, where G_1 represents voter 1's most preferred bundle (for low spending and low taxes) and G_n represents the nth voter's most preferred bundle (for high spending and high taxes). The median voter is the voter in the middle and their preferred level of government spending and taxes is G_M. This means that exactly half of voters would prefer a level of spending below G_M and half would

[19] Suppose the level of the public good, G, is 10 streetlights. The cost of providing one streetlight is £75, and Alfie faces a price of £25 per streetlight and Leni faces a price of £50 per streetlight. Alfie will contribute a total of £250 towards the provision of 10 streetlights and Leni will contribute £500.

[20] See section 6.2 above for a quick review, or Chapter 2 for a more detailed explanation, of the condition for utility maximization.

prefer a level of spending above G_M. Anyone to the left of the median voter (with a preference for lower public goods expenditures and lower taxes) can only affect the final outcome if they vote for a quantity to the right of the median voter, which would shift the outcome even further from their preferred position; similarly, anyone to the right of the median voter (with a preference for higher public goods expenditures and higher taxes) can only affect the final outcome if they vote for a quantity to the left of the median voter, which would again shift the outcome even further from their preferred position. Therefore, under majority voting, no one has an incentive to misrepresent their preferences, so sincere voting is always the best strategy.

However, majority voting will not, in general, lead to the efficient level of public good provision. The level of the public good provided will be that which is preferred by the median voter and this will only be equal to the efficient level of the public good if the marginal rate of substitution of the median voter equals the average marginal rate of substitution of all voters.[21] The majority voting outcome only considers the preferences of the median voter. If the preferences for the public good of other voters change, we would expect this to affect the efficient level of the public good. However, this will not change the level actually provided under majority voting, unless it changes the position of the median voter.

Preference revelation mechanisms

The limitations with the Lindahl equilibrium, particularly the preference revelation problem, have led economists to devise other, typically more complex schemes to encourage individuals to truthfully reveal their demands for the public good.

As we saw above, in the Lindahl mechanism, individual contributions to the public good are tied to their stated willingness to pay for the good and therefore individuals have an incentive to understate their true valuation of the good to reduce the cost of their contribution. Even if there is no link between individual contributions and their stated valuations—for example, if everyone faces a fixed charge for the public good—individuals may still have an incentive to over- or understate their true valuation. If individuals have a strong preference for a particular good, such as a local park, to be provided, they may overstate their true valuation in the hope of swaying the government's decision.

Mechanism design involves the search for allocation mechanisms that provide incentives for individuals to reveal their true preferences for the public good. Although these preference revelation mechanisms have been shown to be effective in encouraging truthful behaviour in theory, they are often quite complicated and costly to administer in practice, particularly when the number of individuals covered is large (see Box 6.4).[22]

However, it might not be necessary to devise complex and costly preference revelation mechanisms to determine how much individuals value public goods. As we saw in Chapter 5, we may be able to infer these values based on information on individual behaviour and the choices that people make using revealed preference methods.[23] Examples included valuing amenities, such as a national park, based on the distance people are willing to travel to enjoy them and the cost incurred (both the monetary and time cost), or using hedonic pricing methods, which involve valuing amenities based on the implicit prices revealed by the market. For example, a house can be viewed as a bundle of characteristics, including

[21] See Chapter 4, section 4.2.2, for an explanation of this argument.

[22] The details of these mechanisms are fairly complex. Interested readers are advised to consult the items suggested in the Further Reading at the end of this chapter.

[23] See section 5.3.2 in Chapter 5 for a more detailed discussion of revealed preference methods.

Box 6.4 The Clarke tax

One solution to the preference revelation problem is the Clarke tax (Clarke, 1971). The intuition behind this mechanism involves making each individual feel as if their behaviour is critical to the provision of the public good, in order to discourage them from either under- or overstating their valuation of the public good. Each individual is treated as a possible 'pivotal agent'—where their reported valuation could change the collective decision from provision to non-provision of the public good, or vice versa. The tax is designed to ensure the pivotal agent faces the full social cost of their decision: if the choice of the pivotal agent means the public good is not provided, then the tax they face equals the social cost to the other individuals (i.e. the sum of the net values that all other individuals placed on the public good); if the choice of the pivotal agent means the public good is provided, then the tax they face equals the absolute value of the sum of the net values of the good to all other individuals. Essentially, the tax paid by the pivotal agent equals the value of the loss to others from the decision. The Clarke tax is designed to make truthful revelation the dominant strategy for each individual.

the number of bedrooms, whether it has a garden, its location, etc., and the price of the house reflects the combined value of all of these attributes. Regression techniques can be used to estimate the value of each characteristic using information on house prices. This method can be used to infer how much people value certain amenities, such as the lack of noise, by comparing the value of homes in busier and noisier locations with those in quieter locations.

The design of preference revelation mechanisms also rests on the assumption that individuals will behave in a rational and strategic manner. As the discussion in section 6.3.2 highlighted, individuals do not always behave in this way, particularly in the context of the provision of public goods, and individual behaviour may be influenced by altruism, social norms, or a concern for fairness.

6.4.2 Does public provision crowd out private provision?

As we saw in section 6.3, there are situations where markets will provide public goods, even if they may not provide the efficient level. What impact will government provision of public goods have on the level of private provision in these cases?

In some situations, government provision of public goods may 'crowd out' private provision: as the government intervenes to provide a public good, the market may respond by reducing the amount of the public good it provides, so the total amount of the public good provided is either unchanged or not significantly increased. As an example, suppose that initially, prior to government intervention, Alfie and Leni each contribute £200 to fund the provision of 10 streetlights in their local area, at a total cost of £400. The government wants to increase the provision of streetlights and therefore decides to tax Alfie and Leni £100 each and use this revenue to fund an additional 5 streetlights. As a result of the tax, Alfie and Leni now have £100 less to spend, but the government is now providing 5 streetlights. Alfie and Leni might therefore choose to reduce their own private spending on streetlights by £100 each, so that their total individual spend on streetlights is unchanged (£100 in voluntary contributions, plus £100 in tax) and the same total of 10 streetlights is provided.

This simple example illustrates the essence of the crowding-out problem.[24] It is an example of full crowding out, where individuals see their own private contributions and government contributions as perfect substitutes, so government spending replaces private spending on a one-for-one basis. In practice, research suggests that while government provision may crowd out private provision to some degree, this is far from complete or one-for-one crowding out, where one additional pound of government spending towards the public good reduces private contributions by exactly one pound (see Box 6.5).

Box 6.5 How extensive is crowding out in practice?

There is an extensive empirical literature testing the crowding-out hypothesis. The evidence to date has been mixed, and results vary depending on the context analysed and the methods used. For example, a couple of early studies looked at the funding of public radio stations in the USA and found that government spending crowds out private contributions by between 12 and 19 per cent (Kingma, 1989; Kingma & McClelland, 1995). However, a subsequent study by Manzoor and Straub (2005) using the same methodology and updated data on contributions to public radio failed to find evidence of a significant crowding-out effect.

Andreoni and Payne (2003) explored the question of whether government grants to private charities crowd out private contributions and found that private contributions to charities did indeed fall when they received a government grant. Their results implied that a $1,000 increase in government grants reduced fundraising in the arts sector by $265 and in the social services sector by $54. Grants decreased fundraising by about 52 per cent for arts organizations and 32 per cent for social service organizations. Part of this effect may reflect classic crowding out, whereby donors reduce their donations to charities as they feel they are already donating through taxes. However, it may also reflect the fact that fundraising is costly and charities may respond to a grant by substituting their efforts away from fundraising activities and towards other charitable activities. Andreoni and Payne (2011) explored this question using a panel of over 8,000 charities in the USA. They found that overall crowding out was significant, at about 75 per cent, but that it was primarily driven by reduced fundraising: classic crowding out accounted for between 30 per cent of all crowding out and a slight crowding-in effect, whereas fundraising crowding out accounted for between 70 per cent and over 100 per cent of total crowding out.

In a study of the impact of government grants on charities' incomes in the UK, Andreoni et al. (2014) found no evidence that receiving a grant crowds out other funding sources overall, although the effect of funding varied with the size of the charity. For some smaller charities, they actually found evidence of crowding in, where each £1 of grant income increased the charity's income by more than £1.

De Wit and Bekkers (2017) carried out a comprehensive review of 70 studies of the crowding-out hypothesis in the context of charitable donations. About two-thirds of

[24] For a fuller exposition of the model of crowding out, see, for example, Bergstrom et al. (1986) in the Further Reading at the end of the chapter.

the studies reviewed found evidence of crowding out, while one-third found evidence of crowding in. The magnitude of these effects depended heavily on the type of research method used: in experiments, a \$1 increase in government support was associated with an average \$0.64 decrease in private donations, whereas non-experimental evidence found an average increase in private donations of \$0.06. There was some variation in impacts across countries, although the majority of the studies reviewed came from Western countries. These findings not only matter for our understanding of crowding out in the real world, but also have implications for how governments structure their support to charitable organizations.

The extent to which government provision of public goods crowds out private provision is likely to depend on the specific public good in question and the preferences and motivations of the individuals in providing the good. If individuals only care about the total amount of the public good that is provided and not their own contributions—so there is no role for warm glow giving—and if there are no strong social norms that encourage voluntary donations, then government provision of the public good will be more likely to crowd out private provision. However, government intervention may force individuals who would otherwise not have contributed to the public good to become contributors, thereby increasing total contributions and the level of the public good that is provided.

It is clear that governments face similar problems to those affecting private providers when it comes to supplying the efficient level of public goods. It is not easy for the government to estimate individual demands for public goods. If the government could observe individual preferences, it could charge each individual a tax price based on their marginal benefit, and provide the efficient level of the public good. However, in general, individual preferences are not directly observable and individuals may have an incentive to misrepresent their true preferences in the hope of free riding on other people's contributions. While voting mechanisms ensure individuals will honestly reveal their preferences, they do not guarantee an efficient outcome. There is a further risk that government intervention may crowd out private contributions to public goods, although the evidence on the magnitude of these effects is inconclusive.

Conclusion

Many goods on which our societies rely have the characteristics of public goods, from streetlights and flood defences to national defence and clean air. Public goods are non-rival, so consumption by one person does not reduce the amount available for others to consume. They are also non-excludable, and because people cannot be excluded from enjoying the benefits of a public good, they have an incentive to understate how much they value the good in the hope of paying less for it or even consuming it for free. As a result of this free rider problem, private markets will typically not provide the efficient level of public goods and there is an argument for government intervention to improve efficiency.

As we have seen in this chapter, the evidence on free riding suggests it is not as pervasive as the theory implies, and there are many examples where individuals make private contributions to public goods, such as by donating to charity or volunteering for a neighbourhood watch group. People might be driven by altruistic motives or the desire to comply with social norms, or they might care about their own contributions to public goods. If businesses are able to charge for complementary products, this may also help mitigate the free rider problem. However, if left to the market, the provision of public goods is likely to fall short of the Pareto-efficient level. Whether the government can improve on the private market outcome will depend on its ability to estimate individuals' true demands for the public good. If public goods are funded through distortionary taxes, this will lead to further inefficiency and may offset any efficiency gains from government provision.

So what is the best mechanism for groups to overcome the free rider problem and ensure the optimal quantity of public goods is provided? This is likely to depend on context and the nature of the public good in question: some public goods may more easily be provided through voluntary agreements between individuals at the local or community level, whereas other more global public goods, such as climate change mitigation actions, are likely to require government intervention.

Questions for discussion

1. Can the following be considered examples of public goods? Why or why not?
   a. Wikipedia
   b. Public health
   c. Education
   d. A radio programme
   e. Donations to an international environmental charity
2. Discuss the role of technological developments in turning a public good into a private good.
3. How is the efficient level of public goods determined? How does this differ from private goods?
4. To what extent does the free rider problem affect the ability of private markets to provide the efficient level of public goods?
5. Can governments ensure the efficient level of public goods is provided?

Further reading

The seminal paper on the optimal provision of public goods is:

Samuelson, P. A. (1954). The pure theory of public expenditure. *Review of Economics and Statistics, 36*, 387–389.

For a review of the empirical evidence on free riding in public goods experiments:

Chaudhuri, A. (2011). Sustaining cooperation in laboratory public goods experiments: A selective survey of the literature. *Experimental Economics, 14*(1), 47–83.

Ledyard, J. O. (1995). Public goods: A survey of experimental research. In J. H. Kagel and A. E. Roth (Eds.), *The handbook of experimental economics* (pp. 111–194). Princeton University Press.

Marwell, G., & Ames, R. E. (1981). Economists free ride, does anyone else? Experiments on the provision of public goods, IV. *Journal of Public Economics, 15*(3), 295–310.

On the role of altruism and social norms in encouraging voluntary contributions to public goods:

Andreoni, J. (1990). Impure altruism and donations to public goods: A theory of warm-glow giving. *Economic Journal, 100*(401), 464–477.

Andreoni, J. (1995a). Cooperation in public-goods experiments: Kindness or confusion? *American Economic Review, 85*(4), 891–904.

Crumpler, H., & Grossman, P. J. (2008). An experimental test of warm glow giving. *Journal of Public Economics, 92*(5–6), 1011–1021.

Fehr, E., & Fischbacher, U. (2004). Social norms and human cooperation. *Trends in Cognitive Sciences, 8*(4), 185–190.

Ostrom, E. (2000). Collective action and the evolution of social norms. *Journal of Economic Perspectives, 14*(3), 137–158.

For a more in-depth accessible discussion of the Lindahl pricing mechanism and mechanism design:

Hindriks, J., & Myles, G. (2013). *Intermediate public economics* (2nd ed.). MIT Press. See chapter 6 on public goods.

The classical model of crowding out is discussed in:

Bergstrom, T. C., Blume, L., & Varian, H. (1986). On the private provision of public goods. *Journal of Public Economics, 29*, 25–49.

For a discussion of some of the evidence of crowding out:

Andreoni, J., & Payne, A. (2011). Is crowding out due entirely to fundraising? Evidence from a panel of charities. *Journal of Public Economics, 95*(5–6), 334–343.

Andreoni, J., Payne, A., & Smith, S. (2014). Do grants to charities crowd out other income? Evidence from the UK. *Journal of Public Economics, 114*, 75–86.

De Wit, A., & Bekkers, R. (2017). Government support and charitable donations: A meta-analysis of the crowding-out hypothesis. *Journal of Public Administration Research and Theory, 27*(2), 301–319.

For a discussion of the challenges posed by global public goods:

Bechtel, M. M., Genovese, F., & Scheve, K. F. (2019). Interests, norms and support for the provision of global public goods: The case of climate co-operation. *British Journal of Political Science, 49*(4), 1333–1355.

Buchholz, W., & Sandler, T. (2021). Global public goods: A survey. *Journal of Economic Literature, 59*(2), 488–545.

Nordhaus, W. D. (2010). *Some foundational and transformative grand challenges for the social and behavioral sciences: The problem of global public goods.* American Economic Association, Ten Years and Beyond: Economists Answer NSF's Call for Long-Term Research Agendas. Available at: http://dx.doi.org/10.2139/ssrn.1889357

Stiglitz, J. E. (1999). Knowledge as a global public good. In I. Kaul, I. Grunberg, & M. Stern (Eds.), *Global public goods: International cooperation in the 21st century* (pp. 308–325). Oxford University Press.

Bibliography

Andreoni, J. (1989). Giving with impure altruism: Applications to charity and Ricardian equivalence. *Journal of Political Economy, 97*(6), 1447–1458.

Andreoni, J. (1990). Impure altruism and donations to public goods: A theory of warm-glow giving. *Economic Journal, 100*(401), 464–477.

Andreoni, J. (1995a). Cooperation in public-goods experiments: Kindness or confusion? *American Economic Review, 85*(4), 891–904.

Andreoni, J. (1995b). Warm-glow versus cold-prickle: The effects of positive and negative framing on cooperation in experiments. *Quarterly Journal of Economics, 110*(1), 1–21.

Andreoni, J., & Payne, A. A. (2003). Do government grants to private charities crowd out giving or fund-raising? *American Economic Review, 93*(3), 792–812.

Andreoni, J., & Payne, A. (2011). Is crowding out due entirely to fundraising? Evidence from a panel of charities. *Journal of Public Economics, 95*(5–6), 334–343.

Andreoni, J., Payne, A., & Smith, S. (2014). Do grants to charities crowd out other income? Evidence from the UK. *Journal of Public Economics, 114*, 75–86.

Bergstrom, T. C., Blume, L., & Varian, H. (1986). On the private provision of public goods. *Journal of Public Economics, 29*, 25–49.

Bernheim, B. D., & Rangel, A. (2005). *Behavioral public economics: Welfare and policy analysis with non-standard decision-makers*. NBER working papers, no. 11518.

Chaudhuri, A. (2011). Sustaining cooperation in laboratory public goods experiments: A selective survey of the literature. *Experimental Economics, 14*(1), 47–83.

Clarke, E. H. (1971). Multipart pricing of public goods. *Public Choice, 11*, 17–33.

Coase, R. H. (1974). The lighthouse in economics. *Journal of Law and Economics, 17*(2), 357–376.

Coyle, D. (2020). *Markets, state and people: Economics for public policy*. Princeton University Press.

Cullis, J., & Jones, P. (2009). *Public finance and public choice: Analytical perspectives* (3rd ed.). Oxford University Press.

De Wit, A., & Bekkers, R. (2017). Government support and charitable donations: A meta-analysis of the crowding-out hypothesis. *Journal of Public Administration Research and Theory, 27*(2), 301–319.

Fehr, E., & Fischbacher, U. (2004). Social norms and human cooperation. *Trends in Cognitive Sciences, 8*(4), 185–190.

Isaac, R. M., & Walker, J. M. (1988). Group size effects in public goods provision: The voluntary contributions mechanism. *Quarterly Journal of Economics, 103*(1), 179–199.

Kingma, B. R. (1989). An accurate measurement of the crowd-out effect, income effect, and price effect for charitable contributions. *Journal of Political Economy, 97*(5), 1197–1207.

Kingma, B. R., & McClelland, R. (1995). Public radio stations are really, really not public goods: Charitable contributions and impure altruism. *Annals of Public and Cooperative Economics, 66*(1), 65–76.

Ledyard, J. O. (1995). Public goods: A survey of experimental research. In J. H. Kagel & A. E. Roth (Eds.), *The handbook of experimental economics* (pp. 111–194). Princeton University Press.

Manzoor, S. H., & Straub, J. D. (2005). The robustness of Kingma's crowd-out estimate: Evidence from new data on contributions to public radio. *Public Choice, 123*(3), 463–476.

Marwell, G., & Ames, R. E. (1981). Economists free ride, does anyone else? Experiments on the provision of public goods, IV. *Journal of Public Economics, 15*(3), 295–310.

Ostrom, E. (2000). Collective action and the evolution of social norms. *Journal of Economic Perspectives, 14*(3), 137–158. https://doi.org/10.1257/jep.14.3.137

Samuelson, P. A. (1954). The pure theory of public expenditure. *Review of Economics and Statistics, 36*: 387–389.

Trinity House (2016). *How is the lighthouse service funded?* Available at: https://www.trinityhouse.co.uk/about-us/trinity-house-faq/how-is-the-lighthouse-service-funded

This appendix describes the mathematics behind the provision of public goods and provides a formal illustration of the free rider problem.

Suppose we have a simple society with two individuals, Alfie and Leni. They each have an income of £150 which they allocate to consuming a private good, X, and a public good, G. The prices of the private good and the public good are both £1 per unit: $P_X = 1$ and $P_G = 1$. Each individual's utility function is given by, for individual i:

$$U(X_i, G) = 2\log X_i + \log G$$

where each individual consumes the total amount of the public good provided, which is given by:

$$G = G_A + G_L$$

Individual utility is maximized subject to the budget constraint:

$$P_x \cdot X_i + P_G \cdot G_i = 150$$

Given the prices of both goods are equal to £1 per unit, this simplifies to:

$$X_i + G_i = 150$$

Private provision

Each individual's utility will depend on their contribution to the public good, as well the other individual's contribution, so their utility-maximizing choice will be a function of the level of the public good chosen by the other individual. An equilibrium will exist if there is a set of mutually compatible utility-maximizing strategies for both individuals.

To maximize his utility, Alfie solves the following problem:

$$Max\, U_A = 2\log(150 - G_A) + \log(G_A + G_L)$$

From our discussion in section 6.2 (and Chapter 2), individual utility is maximized at the point where the individual's marginal rate of substitution equals the price ratio:

$$MRS^i_{GX} = \frac{P_G}{P_X}$$

The marginal rate of substitution equals the ratio of the marginal utilities of the two goods, which we can derive by differentiating the utility function with respect to each good:

$$MRS_{GX} = \frac{MU_G}{MU_X}$$

So, for Alfie:

$$MRS^A_{GX} = \frac{150 - G_A}{2(G_A + G_L)}$$

The price ratio is $\frac{P_G}{P_X} = 1$.

Applying the utility maximization condition we have:

$$MRS^A_{GX} = \frac{150 - G_A}{2(G_A + G_L)} = 1$$

Solving this for Alfie's demand for the public good, G_A, we have:

$$\frac{150-G_A}{2(G_A+G_L)}=1 \Leftrightarrow 150-G_A=2(G_A+G_L)$$

$$\Leftrightarrow 150-2G_L=2G_A+G_A \Leftrightarrow 150-2G_L=3G_A$$

$$\Leftrightarrow \frac{150-2G_L}{3}=G_A$$

which is equivalent to:

$$G_A=\frac{150-2G_L}{3}$$

This represents Alfie's individual demand or willingness to pay for the public good, which, as we can see, is a function of Leni's demand for the public good, G_L. This is the quantity that Alfie would be willing to contribute to the public good.

Since Leni has the same preferences and income and faces the same prices as Alfie, her demand or willingness to pay for the public good is given by the analogous expression:

$$G_L=\frac{150-2G_A}{3}$$

These two equations illustrate the essence of the free rider problem, since each individual's demand or willingness to pay for the public good falls as the other individual's willingness to pay increases.[25]

We can solve these two equations simultaneously to determine the individual quantities, G_A and G_L, in equilibrium. Substituting Leni's demand, G_L, into the equation for Alfie's demand:

$$G_A=\frac{150-2\left(\frac{150-2G_A}{3}\right)}{3}$$

Solving this for G_A we get:

$$G_A=30$$

Substituting this into Leni's demand for the public good:

$$G_L=\frac{150-2(30)}{3}=30$$

With Alfie and Leni each contributing 30 to the public good, the total quantity of the public good that would be provided is 60.

How does this compare with the socially optimal level of the public good?

Socially optimal provision of the public good

As we saw in the chapter, the Samuelson condition tells us that the socially optimal level of the public good is determined by setting the sum of the marginal rates of substitution equal to the price ratio. From our analysis above, Alfie and Leni's marginal rates of substitution are given by:

$$MRS_{GX}^{A}=\frac{150-G_A}{2(G_A+G_L)}$$

[25] To see this, as an exercise, try plotting each individual's demand for the public good as a function of the other individual's demand.

and

$$MRS_{GX}^{L} = \frac{150 - G_L}{2(G_A + G_L)}$$

The price ratio is $\frac{P_G}{P_X} = 1$.

Applying the Samuelson condition:

$$MRS_{GX}^{A} + MRS_{GX}^{L} = 1 \Leftrightarrow \frac{150 - G_A}{2(G_A + G_L)} + \frac{150 - G_L}{2(G_A + G_L)} = 1$$

Given that $G = G_A + G_L$, this simplifies to:

$$\frac{300 - G}{2G} = 1 \Leftrightarrow G = 100$$

So, the socially optimal or efficient level of the public good is 100, which is greater than the level that would be privately provided.

Different incomes

Suppose that instead of both individuals having the same level of income, Alfie's income is £100 and Leni's income is £200. How will this affect each individual's contribution to the public good?

Alfie's utility maximization problem is now given by:

$$Max\, U_A = 2\log(100 - G_A) + \log(G_A + G_L)$$

So Alfie's demand for the public good will be:

$$G_A = \frac{100 - 2G_L}{3}$$

Leni's utility maximization problem is now given by:

$$Max\, U_L = 2\log(200 - G_A) + \log(G_A + G_L)$$

So Leni's demand for the public good will be:

$$G_L = \frac{200 - 2G_A}{3}$$

If we solve these two equations simultaneously, we find that $G_A = -20$ and $G_L = 80$. Individuals cannot provide a negative quantity of the public good, which means that in this case Alfie's contribution to the public good is zero while Leni contributes 80, so the total quantity of the public good supplied is now 80. This illustrates how, if one individual has a higher income, this will lead to an outcome that is closer to the socially optimal level of the public good.

7
Public ownership, privatization, and regulation

Learning objectives

By the end of this chapter, you will be able to:

7.1 Explain the concepts of public ownership, nationalization, and privatization.
7.2 Discuss the economic efficiency, equity, and political arguments for nationalizing a business or industry.
7.3 Discuss the economic and political arguments for privatizing a business or industry.
7.4 Assess the advantages and disadvantages of contracting out production of goods and services to the private sector.
7.5 Discuss the need for regulation of private companies and the challenges of effective regulation.
7.6 Discuss whether ownership matters for economic performance.

Introduction

If we were to travel back to England in the 1970s, utilities such as gas, electricity, and water were being provided by state-owned regional gas and electricity boards and water authorities. The state was responsible for telecommunications, through the state-owned British Telecom. If you wanted to travel by train, you would buy your ticket from the state-owned British Rail, and if you wanted a trip abroad, you would probably book your flight with the government-run British Airways. Fast-forward to the present day and you have around 20 different private sector providers for gas and electricity, each offering different prices for the same basic commodity—energy. For water, another essential resource, you only have one option, which depends on where you live, but these regional water companies are no longer state-owned. If you want to travel by train, your choice of provider again is limited, but the majority are privately run for-profit companies.[1] More choice is available if you are looking to fly somewhere—not only is British Airways now outside of direct government control, but there are many different private airlines that you can choose from.

Since the 1980s, we have witnessed a dramatic shift in ownership from the public to the private sector, and this rolling back of the state from various areas of production was not unique to the UK, but was a common trend across most of the world. During the 1990s alone, $1 trillion worth of state-owned enterprises were transferred from the public to the private sector across the world (OECD, 2002). The role of the state has changed from being

[1] This is set to change under the Labour government's Passenger Railway Services (Public Ownership) Act 2024, which will gradually bring all passenger services back into public ownership.

a key producer of goods and services, with direct control over the means of production, to becoming a regulator of private sector firms. However, differences in ownership across countries remain, with some governments retaining control over utilities, public transport, and even banking. The 2008 financial crisis and, more recently, the Covid-19 pandemic have led to a resurgence of interest in nationalization, whereby the government takes over a private company. Why are some goods and services provided by the market while others are provided by the state? What impact does this have on the economy and on society?

We will start by analysing the distinction between public and private ownership in section 7.1. We then discuss the main arguments for public ownership or nationalization in section 7.2. In section 7.3, we explore the arguments for privatization, and in section 7.4, we discuss the arguments for and challenges involved in the private provision of publicly funded goods and services, or contracting out. Section 7.5 focuses on the role of government in regulating private companies and the challenges of effective regulation. Section 7.6 discusses some of the evidence on the impact of ownership (public or private) on economic performance.

7.1 Public or private ownership: a classification system

The distinction between public (or state) and private ownership is more complex than it may at first appear. Public ownership is a broad concept that refers to situations in which the government owns a business or industry; this can be at the national, regional, or local government level. **Nationalization** refers to the process by which the government takes control of a private company or industry, although the terms 'nationalization' and 'public ownership' are often used interchangeably.[2] For example, in the UK in the 1970s, the government ran the national telephone company (British Telecom), the main airline (British Airways), and the gas supply network (British Gas). As well as nationalized industries, other forms of public ownership include state-owned enterprises and municipally owned services.

Privatization is usually associated with the transfer of assets from the state to the private sector—a process known as **denationalization**. This is what occurred in the UK in the 1980s and 1990s, when the government sold many state-owned companies such as British Telecom, British Airways, and British Gas to the private sector. However, the concept of privatization is much broader and refers to a collection of policies designed to strengthen the market and reduce the role of the public sector, which include **deregulation** and **market testing**. Deregulation involves the reduction or removal of barriers to entry into markets, as illustrated by the deregulation of banking in the UK in the 1980s, which allowed building societies to offer banking services to customers. Market testing involves the creation of external markets to provide goods and services that were previously provided by the government. This is achieved through **competitive contracting** or tendering, where private contractors bid to provide certain goods or services such as street cleaning, rubbish collection, catering and cleaning services, and security.[3] If an external contractor wins the contract put out to tender, then the service is **contracted out** (or outsourced). In-house providers may also bid, and if

[2] If this process of taking back control from the private sector happens at the local or municipal level, it is known as **remunicipalization**.

[3] In some cases, governments may approach a specific private company to deliver a service, such as residential care for the elderly, rather than requiring various companies to put in rival bids to deliver this service; this is referred to as non-competitive strategic contracting.

their bid wins, then the service is **contracted in.** **Franchising** is another way in which governments can encourage private firms to provide public services, but here provision generates its own revenue through user fees (e.g. rail passenger services), whereas with contracting out, the service is still mainly funded by the government.

The above discussion highlights the importance of drawing a distinction between government finance and government production of goods and services.[4] There may be an argument for certain goods to be *financed* by the government—as in the case of public goods that we discussed in Chapter 6—but this does not necessarily mean they should be *produced* by the government. Table 7.1 summarizes the different ways in which finance and production can be shared between the public and the private sector. For example, in many countries, defence, education, and healthcare are both funded and provided by the state,[5] whereas telecommunications and, in some countries, utilities are privately funded and provided. Some services, such as rubbish collection, are funded by the state, but privately provided; whereas other services, such as public broadcasting services in the UK, are mainly privately funded through licence fees but publicly provided.

This table presents only a broad classification system and the examples provided are mainly UK-based, but it does highlight how there is not a simple state versus private ownership distinction. Moreover, even in countries where healthcare and education are funded and provided by the state, private providers may also play a role, and there are areas where the finance of production may be mainly private—for example, through licence fees—but may also receive some public funding.

In some cases, the private sector is involved in both financing and providing infrastructure and services for the public sector in return for annual rental payments, which further blurs the distinction between the categories illustrated above. These **public–private partnerships (PPPs)** were popular in the late twentieth century and have been used by countries across the world, partly in response to concerns around public sector debt. However, the popularity of PPPs started to decline following the 2008 financial crisis, as the cost of private finance increased (see Box 7.1).

Table 7.1 Taxonomy of provision

		Production	
		Private	**Public**
Finance	**Private**	Telecommunications Energy (gas, electricity) Water	BBC TV and Radio (UK)
	Public	Rubbish collection Cleaning and catering services in hospitals	Defence Education Healthcare

[4] This chapter will focus mainly on the role of government in the finance and production of goods and services. The government also plays an important organizing role, as in the case of many types of regulation, such as mandatory insurance and automatic enrolment into pension saving (a topic we return to in Chapter 11).

[5] We discuss the role of the government in healthcare and education, and how this varies across countries, in Chapters 8 and 9.

Box 7.1 The rise and fall of public–private partnerships

Public–private partnerships (PPPs) are a form of long-term agreement between the government and the private sector, where the private sector is contracted to fund, design, and deliver public sector services or infrastructure, in return for regular repayments from the government. PPPs have been used throughout the world, primarily to fund large public sector infrastructure projects, such as roads and bridges, schools, hospitals, and prisons. In the UK, the Private Finance Initiative (PFI) was a particular type of PPP, introduced by the Conservative government in 1992. It was subsequently reformed by the Labour government, but continued to be used as a source of finance for public sector projects. In 2016, the UK had around 700 PFI projects, with annual charges amounting to £10.3 billion in 2016/17, and the National Audit Office estimated that even if no new deals were signed, future charges would need to be made until the 2040s and would amount to £199 billion (NAO, 2018).

Perceived benefits of PPPs include cost savings, the transfer of risks from the public to the private sector, and the scope for the public sector to benefit from the expertise and innovation of the private sector and increased investment. The empirical evidence on the benefits of PPPs is limited and, while this sort of private finance can increase the spending power of government departments in the short term, it does imply a significant long-term financial commitment. Critics have pointed out that the cost of borrowing under PPPs is higher than in the public sector, and the long-term nature of contracts implies a significant burden on future taxpayers. A study by the National Audit Office in the UK concluded that the PFI was in fact more expensive and less efficient in supporting public infrastructure and service than public finance (UK Parliament, 2011).

The public versus private ownership distinction is further complicated by the existence of different organizational forms. For instance, there are **quasi-government agencies**,[6] which are public bodies set up by the government but which operate at arm's length from government departments; examples in the UK include the Care Quality Commission and the Office for Budget Responsibility. There are also public corporations, such as the BBC and the Civil Aviation Authority which, although controlled by the government, cover part or all of their costs from the sale of goods and services in the market and retain substantial operating independence. Governments may own equity in private companies, and there are a host of not-for-profit organizations such as charities and trusts which, although not under direct government control, are not driven by the same profit-maximizing motives as most private firms. There are also different types of private ownership and not all private firms are profit-maximizing: there are non-profit firms that reinvest all their profits back into the services they provide and the community; there are commercial firms owned by their employees or members (e.g. John Lewis or the Nationwide Building Society in the UK); and there are firms owned by a trust set up to protect certain values (e.g. the *Guardian* newspaper).

As the discussion above illustrates, there is no simple state versus private ownership distinction and it is important to keep this in mind when assessing the various arguments for and against government ownership. An argument may provide a justification for government

[6] These are sometimes referred to as non-departmental public bodies in the UK, or NDPBs.

involvement in the provision of a good or service, but this does not mean the government should necessarily be responsible for producing it.[7] We start by focusing on the arguments for government production in the next section, before turning to the arguments for private sector production in section 7.3.

7.2 Rationale for nationalization

In most of western and eastern Europe, the heyday of nationalization came after the end of the Second World War, when key industries, mines, banks, and insurance companies were transferred from the private sector to the state. In the UK, the election of a Labour government led to a widespread programme of nationalizations, with the state taking over control of major industries, including coal, iron and steel, gas and electricity, and railways through various Acts of Parliament. In some sectors (e.g. aviation), nationalization programmes had already been initiated by the previous Conservative government, highlighting that the nationalization programme was not purely a political or ideological decision. Nationalization of key industries in African and Asian countries came with the end of colonialism in the 1950s and 1960s. At the start of the 1980s, state-owned enterprises accounted for roughly 6 per cent of GDP in advanced economies and 15 per cent in low-income countries; by 1999, these proportions had fallen to 4 per cent and 2.5 per cent, respectively (Sheshinski & López-Calva, 2003).

In most European countries, political, economic, and social pressures at the time played a significant role in driving this mass programme of nationalizations. The need to rebuild economies and the infrastructure that had been destroyed by the war, the strategic importance of industries such as coal, steel, and transport as engines of growth, the importance of defence industries for national security—all contributed to provide support for the state taking a more active role in the running of these sectors. It was also felt that it was 'wrong' for private firms to enjoy excessive profits during such a period of national crisis. Although recent decades have seen a shift towards privatization, state-owned firms still play an important role in the world today and many have expanded from their domestic markets and taken on a global role.[8]

In this section, we review the main economic and political arguments for nationalization. Within our economic arguments, we consider both economic efficiency and equity or public interest arguments.

7.2.1 Efficiency arguments for nationalization

There are three reasons why public production may be justified to increase economic efficiency: in cases of natural monopoly; if there are significant externalities or public goods; or if there are problems of imperfect or asymmetric information.[9]

Natural monopoly

The main economic argument for public production is based on situations where firms have monopoly power, particularly natural monopolies. Natural monopolies arise when

[7] Public production also does not entail that the good or service will be provided for free.

[8] See, for example, IMF (2020: ch. 3) on the growth of state-owned enterprises in the last decade.

[9] See Chapter 2 for a review of these concepts.

economies of scale are so significant that a single firm may be able to produce the entire output of a market at a cost below the cost if there were several firms operating in the market. This is a common feature of many public utilities, such as water, gas, and electricity, where the fixed costs associated with establishing the network of pipes or cables is high, but the marginal cost of supplying water, gas, or electricity to one additional household is relatively low, and therefore it would be inefficient to have multiple suppliers setting up parallel distribution networks alongside each other.

The natural monopoly scenario is illustrated in Figure 7.1.[10] The significant economies of scale imply an average cost curve that is declining over a large output range. Marginal costs are assumed to be constant for simplicity, and as long as marginal costs are below average costs, the average cost curve will be decreasing. As the monopolist is the sole producer in the market, it faces a downward-sloping demand curve, and its **marginal revenue** curve will also be downward sloping and will lie below the demand curve. Any firm wishing to maximize profits will produce at the output level where marginal revenue equals marginal cost—given by Q_M in the figure. The corresponding profit-maximizing price is P_M and the profits earned by the monopolist are given by the shaded area in the figure.

Although this price and output level maximize the firm's profits, they do not maximize total welfare, since at the profit-maximizing output level Q_M, marginal benefit (as measured by the demand curve) is above marginal cost. This outcome is therefore allocatively inefficient. The efficient level of output is Q_C, where the marginal cost equals marginal benefit. The efficiency cost or **deadweight loss (DWL)** associated with the monopoly is given by the triangle ABC.

The monopolist's profit-maximizing price and output levels also have implications for equity, particularly if the good in question is an essential commodity, such as water or energy, as many consumers may be unable to afford this basic commodity at the high prices charged

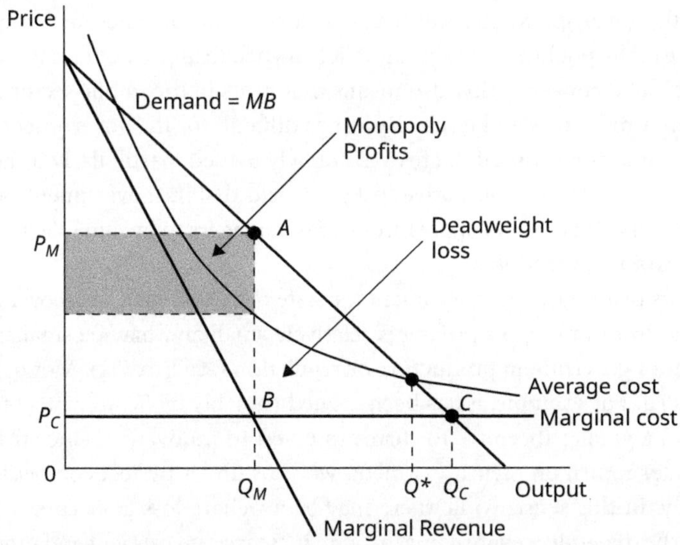

Figure 7.1 Natural monopoly and inefficiency

[10] See the appendix at the end of this chapter for a review of profit maximization for a monopolist and how to determine the efficiency loss from monopoly.

by the monopolist. There is also the potential for firms to abuse their monopoly position, particularly where demand is more price inelastic, as it typically is with essential commodities such as water or energy.

The traditional policy prescription to achieve allocative efficiency involves promoting competition in the market. However, in cases of natural monopoly, competition may be neither feasible—given the structure of the industry and the presence of significant fixed or sunk costs—nor desirable. By breaking up the market and requiring, say, two firms to provide the total level of output, each firm would inevitably be producing on a higher point of its average cost curve and therefore the costs of production would not be minimized.

So assuming it is beneficial for the firm to retain its monopoly power to minimize the costs of production, what can the government do to increase total welfare? At the allocatively efficient output level, Q_C, the firm would be making a loss, because the price P_C at which it would sell each unit of output is less than the average cost of producing that output. Therefore, if the government wanted to encourage a private firm to produce the efficient output level, it would need to subsidize production to cover the firm's losses. However, the firm would have an incentive to overstate its true costs of production to increase the level of the subsidy it received. Alternatively, the government could encourage the firm to produce at Q^*, where marginal benefit equals the average cost of production—this is the zero-profit or break-even level of output. This would maximize output without the firm producing at a loss. The government would still need to provide the right incentives to encourage the firm to produce at this output level.

Faced with limited information about the firm's costs of production, which would enable it to set the appropriate level of subsidies, the government may instead opt to take over production of the good or service. The government-run firm could then produce either the break-even output level Q^* or the efficient output level Q_C. The latter would still require some subsidy from the government, to cover the firm's losses, but subsidies may be easier to monitor and enforce in the public sector, since publicly owned firms do not face the same pressures to maximize profits. However, this also means that firms in the public sector have less of an incentive to minimize costs and it may be just as difficult for the government to get reliable information on marginal costs if the firm is publicly owned, particularly if the industry is a monopoly, as there will be no alternative cost yardsticks that the government can use to assess true marginal costs. This creates opportunities for managers to become slack and inefficient, a problem we explore in section 7.3.

Some authors believe that this argument for state ownership has been overstated and that the welfare loss from monopoly pricing is relatively small and may be smaller than the loss in efficiency from government production or regulation (see Box 7.2). Monopoly power can also be beneficial. For example, it has been argued (notably by Schumpeter) that monopoly power provides a greater incentive for firms to invest in innovation, since firms can expect to make a greater return on their investment, whereas under perfect competition profits are competed away. In this sense, while there may be a welfare loss associated with monopoly, there may also be dynamic welfare gains through increased investment and innovation. However, if the monopolist's position is secure and the barriers facing other potential entrants into the market are significant, then the lack of any actual or potential competition may mean that the firm's managers become lax and have less incentive to minimize costs or to invest in

Box 7.2 How large is the welfare loss from monopoly power?

One of the earliest studies which estimated the deadweight loss of natural monopoly was carried out by Arnold Harberger in 1954. Harberger studied the impact on consumer welfare from monopoly pricing in US manufacturing in the late 1920s and arrived at an estimate of a welfare loss of $225 million (in 1954 prices), which was equivalent to less than one-tenth of a percentage point of national income. Although limitations have been identified in his study, subsequent research also suggests the direct welfare impact of monopoly pricing is relatively small. A study by Cowling and Mueller (1978) estimates a welfare loss of approximately 4 per cent for both the USA and the UK. Peterson and Connor (1995) focus on US food manufacturing and arrive at an estimate of 0.16 per cent. Gisser (1986) focuses on US manufacturing and arrives at an even smaller estimate of 0.11 per cent. However, these estimates are based solely on the direct welfare cost of monopoly pricing, as captured by the deadweight loss triangle in Figure 7.1. Once rent-seeking behaviour to help secure the monopolist's position is taken into account, these estimates increase to 5–13 per cent, suggesting the welfare cost of monopoly power can be substantial.

innovation.[11] As we will see below, there is still some debate as to whether the public or the private sector is more likely to invest in innovation, particularly with high-risk projects.

It has been suggested that state-owned companies may play a useful role as a source of competition for private monopolies or oligopolies. For example, Allais (1948) argued for nationalizing a few firms in each industry to make it easier to compare public and private ownership. However, having a state-owned firm in the market might deter other firms from entering, particularly if the state-owned firm is subsidized.

Externalities and public goods

As we saw in Chapter 2, externalities arise when an action by a producer affects other economic agents and this effect is not reflected in the market price, creating a gap between private and social costs and benefits. Examples include when production generates pollution (negative externality) or when there are substantial spillovers associated with R&D activities (positive externality).

In areas where there are significant externalities, public production allows social costs and benefits to be incorporated directly into decision-making. The usual economic response to dealing with externalities is to impose taxes on activities generating negative externalities (e.g. highly polluting activities) and to provide subsidies for activities generating positive externalities (e.g. R&D expenditures). However, if the industry in question is government-owned, then these external costs and benefits can be incorporated directly into production decisions, helping to mitigate any asymmetries in information between the government and the owners or managers of the firm. Under private ownership, the firm's managers may face an incentive

[11] This problem would affect not only natural monopolies, but also other areas where firms benefit from monopoly power—for example, due to high sunk costs that act as barriers to entry (e.g. R&D expenditure in the pharmaceutical industry).

to underreport any negative costs or overreport benefits, in order to reduce the amount of tax paid or to maximize the level of subsidies received.

We discussed the role of government in the provision of public goods in Chapter 6. The government need not be responsible for *producing* all public goods; however, in some cases government production may be desirable. For example, public ownership of certain industries, such as steel or aerospace, may be justified on the grounds that these sectors play a vital role in providing national security, a public good.[12]

Imperfect and asymmetric information

Public production may help address problems of imperfect or asymmetric information—for example, if there are moral hazard problems associated with private production. Moral hazard problems arise when one party or agent in a transaction increases their exposure to risk when they know some other party will bear the cost; there is an incentive to change behaviour when the costs of risk-taking behaviour are borne by others.[13] This is sometimes provided as an additional justification for government provision of defence services, since private armies may face an incentive to 'create' work for themselves if faced with the threat of unemployment, although historically state-owned armies seem to be responsible for the majority of conflicts (Cullis & Jones, 2009). Moral hazard problems can also arise in other areas, such as the private provision of work capability assessments which determine people's eligibility for certain welfare benefits (e.g. employment and support allowances in the UK). Private contractors may have an incentive to increase the number of individuals they assess as fit for work, as this will signal to the government that they are offering value for money.

Problems of imperfect information may also contribute to significant **transaction costs**, providing a further argument for government production. Transaction costs are the costs associated with organizing and running a market, including search costs, the costs of drawing up and enforcing contracts, and some administrative costs (e.g. costs of administering different provision schemes). If transaction costs are sufficiently high, it may be more efficient for a good to be provided by the government. For example, proponents of privatizing the provision of education have suggested that equity or equal access goals could be achieved through a voucher system, but evidence suggests the costs of administering such schemes can be significant.[14] Similarly, it has been argued that the privatized structure of rail services in the UK has led to significant transaction costs of contracting between different companies, namely the various train operating companies and the company managing the railway network.

7.2.2 Equity and public interest arguments

Alongside the efficiency arguments we have just discussed, there are wider equity or public interest arguments which may justify government production of certain goods and services.

[12] An argument for government production of national defence equipment can also be based on the presence of significant transaction costs. See, for example, Cullis and Jones (2009: ch. 5).

[13] See Chapter 2 for a review of this concept.

[14] Kent County Council in the UK ran a trial education vouchers scheme in 1990 and found the administrative costs of the scheme were substantial (Cullis & Jones, 2009).

Guaranteeing universal access

The actions of private profit-maximizing firms might not reflect the broader public interest, particularly in areas where there might be a conflict between the economic viability of production and other goals, such as the desire to guarantee universal access. For example, the government might want to ensure that everyone has access to postal services, high-speed reliable internet, or public transport, for the same price, regardless of where they live, but the cost of providing these services will vary between urban and more remote rural areas. There is a danger that private firms will charge higher prices to deliver services in more remote areas, to reflect the higher cost of provision. However, state ownership is not the only way of ensuring universal access and provision; these are often enshrined in the objectives of government bodies that are responsible for regulating a particular industry. For example, one of the conditions at the time of the privatization of Royal Mail in the UK was that the company should provide a universal postal service, delivering and collecting mail six days a week and offering a 'one price goes anywhere' postal service, and this is monitored by the sector regulator.

Ensuring quality

Public production may help ensure quality. This is likely to be particularly important in areas such as social care and the prison sector, where quality metrics may be hard to define. Private firms, driven by the goal of maximizing profits, may face competitive pressures to reduce costs, sacrificing quality in the process.

Achieving wider policy objectives

State ownership of particular industries may enable the government to achieve wider policy objectives—for example, promoting employment, regional development, or the development of a green economy. Whereas private firms will base their employment and location decisions on whether they minimize costs or maximize profits, a state-owned firm may be located in a particular area in order to foster the economic regeneration of the region. Achieving full employment was one of the goals set for the newly nationalized industries in the UK in the post-war period, and the pursuit of these objectives by firms under government control may help secure political support for those in power. State-owned firms may also be better placed to more rapidly implement renewable energy policies to tackle the climate crisis. However, the objectives of managers of publicly owned companies might not always be clear and may sometimes conflict with one another—for example, there may be a trade-off between promoting employment and reducing costs—which can lead to inefficiencies and wasted resources.

Although there are strong equity and public interest arguments for government production of some goods and services, there is a risk that these arguments could be used as a case for blanket subsidies to state-owned firms, which might end up financing inefficient production methods or wasteful management practices. The possible conflict between different objectives for state-owned firms and lack of clarity over which objectives should be prioritized may also lead to inefficiency.

7.2.3 Political arguments for nationalization

Government control over the production of certain goods and services can also help achieve certain political objectives. Governments may wish to retain control over the 'commanding heights' of the economy—sectors which are deemed to be of strategic importance for economic growth and the stability of the country. This was an important objective behind the nationalizations that took place in many western European countries in the period following the end of the Second World War, when the need for reconstruction and to promote economic growth helped justify the state taking control over strategic industries such as coal, steel, and transport. More recently, the rapid economic development of China, where state-owned firms play an important role in the domestic economy, has highlighted the potential for state-owned enterprises to act as engines of growth.[15]

Certain sectors of the economy may also be deemed important for national security. As a public good, government provision of national security may be justified on efficiency grounds, as discussed above. However, this does not entail that governments should take responsibility for *producing* these goods; merely that they should take steps to ensure the socially optimal level of these goods is provided. This may, for example, involve the government taking a role in financing provision of these goods through general taxation, but leaving production itself to the private sector. In fact, many of the industries that play an important role in defence are now under private ownership, such as Lockheed Martin, one of the world's largest defence contractors, and Airbus.[16] The last few decades have also seen an increase in the role of private military contractors throughout the world.[17] However, privatization and foreign ownership leave a country exposed to potentially damaging foreign political interference in the supply of weapons and other defence equipment, and the government may still need to step in to guarantee an adequate level of provision. This was clearly illustrated by the failure of private security services company G4S to supply sufficient security guards to police the London 2012 Olympics, forcing the military to step in to make up for the shortfall. If the government should retain some control over production in strategically important sectors, what sectors should be considered strategically important? Why steel and shipbuilding, and not water or banking? (See Box 7.3.)

Ideology has also played an important role in driving nationalization programmes. Traditionally, more left-leaning political parties see ownership of the means of production as vital for preventing the exploitation of workers. An extreme example of this was provided by the command economy instituted by Stalin in the Soviet Union in the 1920s. However, political ideology has played a role in other contexts as well. In the UK, in the post-war years, the Labour Party saw control over the means of production and distribution as an important source of economic and political power. Portugal also witnessed an extensive programme of nationalizations following the Carnation Revolution of 1974, covering sectors including steel, cement, shipbuilding, banking, and insurance. Protection for this programme of nationalization was enshrined in the Portuguese Constitution of 1976, although this has subsequently been revised. In recent years, the prevailing political and economic ideologies have shifted towards advocating less state interference.

Having reviewed the main arguments for public provision of goods and services, we now consider some of the drawbacks by focusing on the rationale for privatization.

[15] Other emerging economies, such as Brazil, India, and Egypt, have been less successful in this respect, which has led to moves to privatize some of the larger state-owned firms in these countries.

[16] Foreign ownership in defence is also fairly common. In the UK, for example, the proportion of overseas suppliers was around 19 per cent in 2021 (UK Parliament, 2021).

[17] For a comprehensive review, see Singer (2007).

Box 7.3 A case for state-run banks?

Banks and other financial institutions are often seen as the epitome of the capitalist market system. However, the financial crisis of 2008 shone a spotlight on the fragilities of the Western financial system. In the UK, this led to the nationalization of the Northern Rock bank and a government bailout of the Royal Bank of Scotland that resulted in the government owning 84 per cent of the bank. These interventions were intended as temporary measures, driven by the need to stabilize the UK banking system and help restore market confidence. But given the importance of the banking system in the modern economy, why shouldn't there be a government-owned bank?

This is not unheard of in other countries. In Germany and Portugal,[18] public banks held just under 40 per cent of banking system assets in 2016; in China and India, this figure was over 60 per cent (IMF, 2020: 48). Commercial banks do not have the characteristics of a natural monopoly, although they can benefit from other sources of market power. This can lead to banks becoming 'too big to fail', leading to a moral hazard problem whereby banks may increase their exposure to risk, safe in the knowledge that the government will bail them out if necessary. In contrast, state-owned banks may lack the incentives to increase efficiency or foster innovation, and may be subject to potentially damaging political interference.

7.3 Rationale for privatization

Starting in the 1980s, a wave of privatizations swept across western and eastern Europe. In the UK alone, between 1977 and 1999, over £70 billion worth of assets were transferred from the state to the private sector (Parker, 2004). Globally, close to $1 trillion worth of state-owned enterprises were transferred to the private sector in the 1980s and 1990s (OECD, 2002). A combination of economic, social, political, and technological factors helped drive this wave of privatizations.

As we saw in section 7.1, privatization is a broad concept which encompasses a series of market liberalization policies designed to roll back the state and strengthen the role of the market. In this section, we are going to focus specifically on the arguments for denationalization, or the transfer of assets from the state to the private sector. This transfer of assets can take different forms (see Box 7.4). Below we review the main economic and political reasons for privatization.

7.3.1 Economic arguments for privatization

We are going to focus on four economic arguments for privatization: reducing X-inefficiency; tackling problems of asymmetric information; raising revenues for the government; and boosting investment and innovation.

Reducing X-inefficiency

As we saw above, the allocative inefficiency associated with private monopolies provides one of the leading arguments for nationalization. There is another source of inefficiency often

[18] The state-owned Caixa Geral de Depósitos is the second largest bank in Portugal.

Box 7.4 Privatization in practice: the case of the UK

The privatization programme in the UK started at the end of the 1970s, but really took off in the 1980s. Table 7.2 illustrates just how extensive this programme was at the time. This has been followed more recently by further privatizations, such as the sale of the Royal Mail postal service in 2013 and the sale of portions of student loan debt.

Table 7.2 Overview of major UK privatizations of the 1980s and 1990s

Year	Company
1979	British Petroleum
1981	British Aerospace, Cable & Wireless
1982	Britoil, Amersham International
1983	Associated British Port Holdings
1984	British Telecom, Jaguar
1986	British Gas
1987	British Airways, BAA, Rolls-Royce
1988	British Steel
1989	Regional water authorities in England and Wales
1990	Regional electricity companies
1994	British Coal
1996	British Rail

Note: Some of these were initially partial privatizations. For example, the privatization of British Petroleum involved selling the government's shareholding in the company, which happened in three stages (1979, 1983, and 1987). The privatization of Cable & Wireless started in 1981, with the government selling half of its shareholding, but it was not completed until several years later.

Source: Parker (2004).

The transfer of assets from the state to private sector can take different forms. In some cases, it involved the sale of entire industries (e.g. British Gas),[19] whereas in others it involved the sale of government shareholdings in publicly owned companies (e.g. British Petroleum). The government also sold other publicly held assets, such as council housing and land.

Each privatization in the UK involved an Act of Parliament, which specified the intention to privatize and established an industry regulator or watchdog. Before privatizing an industry, the government had two key issues to consider: what the structure of the industry should be following privatization, particularly whether the state-owned monopolies should be converted into privately owned monopolies or if these should be broken up; and how the assets should be sold, namely whether these should be sold to the highest bidder, sold at a fixed price, or given away at a zero price. Offering shares to the highest bidder would ensure the government maximized the revenue being raised, but this process is more inequitable, since

[19] In general, the sale of entire companies may take the form of a trade sale, where the company is sold directly to another firm or a consortium of firms; it may involve a management or employee buyout; or it may involve the public issue of shares.

people with fewer resources will be unable to buy shares. To encourage competition, the government would need either to break up the firm before selling it or take active steps following the sale to promote competition. This could make the firm less attractive to potential investors and, if the industry is a natural monopoly, reduce efficiency by sacrificing the benefits of economies of scale. However, by turning a state-owned monopoly into a privately run monopoly, allocative efficiency will be lost.

With many of the early privatizations (e.g. British Telecom and British Gas), the firms retained their monopoly after privatization, so the government did not fully exploit the potential to increase efficiency in the sectors. Only one company (Mercury) was granted a licence to operate in telecommunications alongside British Telecom until 1991. Electricity and water were restructured at the time of privatization to create regional suppliers, and a separate generation company was set up in the case of electricity. Rail passenger services were franchised out, with limited scope for competition once a franchise was awarded.

Regarding how the assets were sold, the UK government mainly used a fixed-price auction and priority was given to smaller bids and employees, since one of the goals of early privatizations had been to encourage wider share ownership. However, many shareholders did not hold on to their shares for long and therefore privatization did not lead to widespread share ownership. The government initially held a 'golden share', or sizeable shareholding, in several of the privatized companies, but the majority of these shares have subsequently been sold.

associated with monopoly power which arises because firms face less pressure to minimize their costs—this is known as **X-inefficiency**. X-inefficiency refers to situations where a firm's costs of production are higher than necessary. This can be due to several factors, including a lack of direct competition, inefficient production processes, and poor internal organization and management practices. State-owned companies are arguably more inefficient in this sense.[20] These firms are typically not driven by the need to maximize profits and they face a soft budget constraint, which means that they can make losses and do not face a real threat of bankruptcy since they are funded by the state.[21] Managers of state-owned firms therefore face lower incentives to minimize costs or maximize productivity. So while promoting allocative efficiency provides a key argument for nationalization, reducing X-inefficiency provides a leading argument for privatization.

The problem of X-inefficiency is illustrated in Figure 7.2. The state-owned monopoly aiming to reduce allocative inefficiency would adopt marginal cost pricing and produce output level Q_G and sell it at price P_G. If privatization led to significant improvements in productivity, marginal costs would be reduced to M_C' and the private monopoly would produce the higher level of output Q_M and sell it at price P_M. While in this scenario output is higher and the price is lower than what would prevail under state ownership, the outcome would still be allocatively inefficient since at the output level Q_M marginal benefit exceeds marginal cost.

[20] We discuss the evidence on the inefficiency of public ownership in section 7.6, which paints a more mixed picture.

[21] Although this was true for the majority of firms that were nationalized in the post-war period, state-owned enterprises today have a variety of goals, which may include maximizing returns, and they may be expected to compete with private enterprises (OECD, 2024).

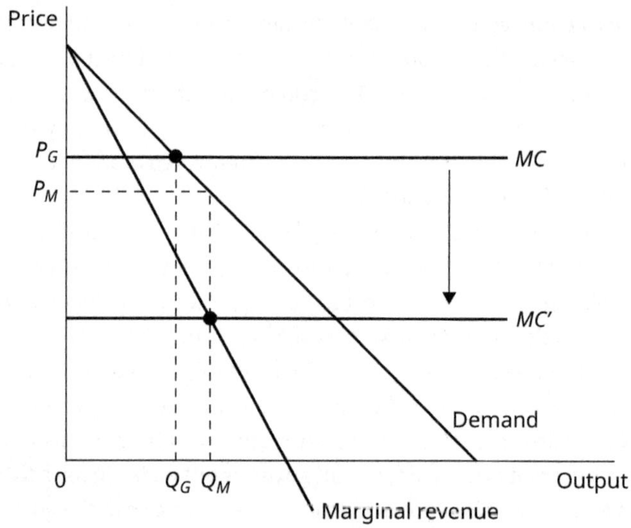

Figure 7.2 X-inefficiency of a monopoly under government ownership

In practice, the incentives to minimize costs may not be significantly stronger for a private monopoly, particularly if the firm does not face the threat of real or potential competition. Changing ownership from the state to the private sector will not in itself make an industry more competitive or efficient, and a lot hinges on the structure of the market and whether there is scope for competition (and whether promoting competition is desirable). If, following privatization, the structure of the market is unchanged and the private firm still benefits from monopoly power, then problems of X-inefficiency may persist. Addressing problems of X-inefficiency where firms have monopoly power—either in the public or private sector—involves setting the right incentives for managers to work to minimize costs.

However, in the private sector, capital markets may provide additional pressures to encourage efficiency. Private firms are subject to the threat of takeovers and bankruptcy, which may lead to managers ultimately losing their jobs, and should provide an incentive for these managers to minimize costs. But private capital markets are imperfect. The presence of transaction costs in trading shares means that a takeover bid is only likely if the bid price of the underperforming firms is sufficiently low, compared to potential profits, and the threat of bankruptcy may not always be credible—while some companies do indeed go bankrupt, the government is unlikely to allow important firms to fail, as illustrated in the UK by the case of the Northern Rock bank, which was nationalized during the financial crisis in 2008.

There are other reasons why costs may be higher in state-owned firms. These firms may face constraints on hiring and firing workers or excessively bureaucratic procurement procedures, which lead to increased costs. The managers of state-owned firms, rather than being selfless public workers driven by a desire to maximize social welfare, may instead have their own interests and care about their power, prestige, and promotion, as in Niskanen's model of budget-maximizing bureaucrats that we discussed in Chapter 3. In this model, government bureaucrats have monopoly over the provision of certain goods or services and their pay depends on the total measurable output of their department. The goal of the bureaucrat then becomes one of maximizing the size of their department and budget, rather than providing the efficient level of output. This is potentially exacerbated by problems of asymmetric information between the bureaucrat or manager of the state-owned firm and the government, which make it difficult for the government to enforce efficiency requirements, since they have less information about the costs of production. But how different are the motivations of managers of state-owned firms likely to be, compared to managers of privately run firms?

Asymmetric information and agency problems

This budget-maximizing behaviour is an example of the principal–agent problem that we introduced in Chapter 2. Agency problems arise when a principal delegates a task to an agent, but cannot observe the agent's actions, and therefore cannot ensure that the principal's objectives are maximized. In this case, the government (principal) wants to ensure the managers (agents) of state-owned firms work to minimize costs and maximize social welfare, but the managers may have different objectives. The severity of agency problems will depend on how easy it is to define and measure the goals of the principal and put in place an incentive mechanism that encourages the agent to work towards these goals.

Agency problems affect the private sector as well as the public sector, but have been argued to be more prevalent in the public sector.[22] In the public sector, the chain of principal–agent relationships is often more complex, and the managers of state-owned companies may be set multiple goals—for example, to reduce costs, but also to promote employment, guarantee access, or achieve environmental targets. These goals might not be mutually consistent and it might not be clear which ones should be prioritized. Having multiple goals will also make it more difficult to measure performance, particularly if some of the goals conflict. In the private sector, the career structure, job insecurity, and performance-related pay can help mitigate the principal–agent problem.

In practice, performance-related targets are used in both the public and the private sectors, and evidence suggests that factors such as staff training, good communication, and cooperative decision-making all play an important role in mitigating the principal–agent problem—and these are available in both the public and private sectors. It could also be argued that public sector employees may in fact be more likely to share in the goals of their principal. Individuals working in the public sector might care not only about their pay, but also about the value of the work they are doing and how this impacts on society.

Raising revenues

Privatization can also be a means of raising revenue for the government, helping to improve public sector finances by reducing deficits and debt. This was an important objective of the early privatizations in the Netherlands and the UK, as well as in Italy and Spain in the 1990s. As Figure 7.3 shows, the proceeds from privatization continued to grow throughout the 1990s and 2000s across the world, reaching a record level of \$319.9 billion in 2015.[23]

As well as reducing public sector borrowing, the windfall gains from privatization can be used to fund investment in other areas of the economy. Privatization also reduces the risk for

[22] In the private sector, agency problems arise where there is a separation between ownership and control of a company, where shareholders (principal) may want the managers (agents) of the company to pursue certain goals which may conflict with the priorities of the managers.

[23] These figures include partial privatizations, involving the sale of partial stakes in publicly owned companies, as well as the transfer of shares, loans, and other forms of financial assistance provided to private sector banks following the financial crisis of 2008 back to the private sector.

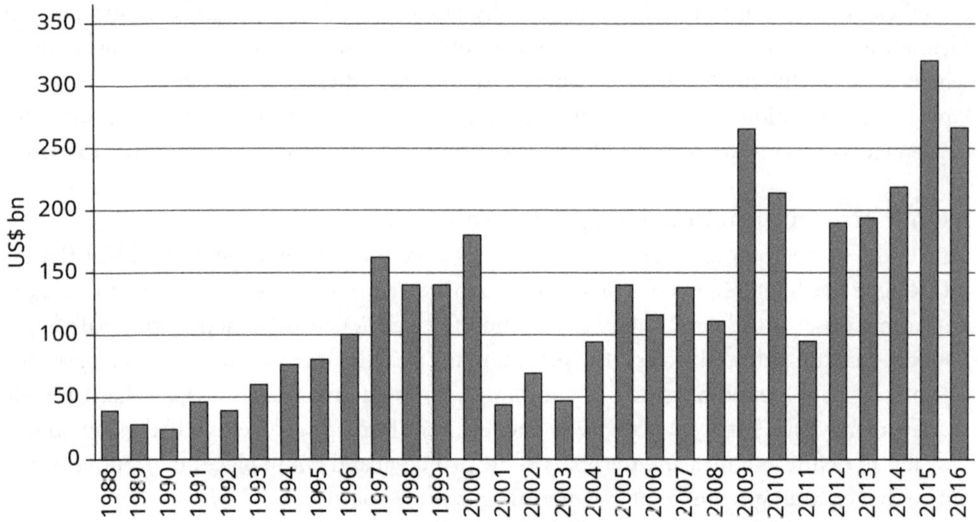

Figure 7.3 Worldwide revenues from privatization, 1988–2016
Source: Privatization Barometer (2017), table 1.

governments, which are no longer liable for sustaining loss-making companies, and can help promote the growth of domestic stock markets. The level of revenues raised through privatization will depend on how the assets are transferred to the private sector. For example, in the UK, the revenues from some of the early privatizations of the 1980s were not maximized, as the firms were deliberately undervalued, in part to help ensure the success of the privatization programme and garner political support.

While selling state-owned assets may improve public finances at the time the assets are sold, this is a one-off gain and should be balanced against the potential profit stream over the long term if the state retains ownership of the asset, since any profits previously made by these firms will now go to private shareholders and not the government.[24] Privatization essentially converts a future revenue stream for the government into a present one-off cash sum. In several countries, subsidies continue to be paid by the government to the privatized industries—for example, in the case of train services and the nuclear industry in the UK. Raising revenues by selling bonds will generally involve lower transaction costs, although some governments may be constrained in their ability to sell bonds, particularly if government borrowing is already high (Vickers & Yarrow, 1991).

Boosting investment and innovation

Constraints on public expenditure and borrowing often meant that nationalized industries were starved of investment, and this lack of investment may have contributed to inefficiency. This was particularly true in the case of British Telecom, British Rail, and the nationalized

[24] The importance of taking into account government assets when assessing the health of public finances is reflected in the International Monetary Fund's public sector balance sheet approach, which is discussed in Chapter 16. See, for example, IMF (2018).

Box 7.5 The role of the government in supporting innovation

The evidence on the relationship between firm ownership and innovation does not provide a definitive answer on whether public or private ownership is more likely to support innovation (Belloc, 2014; Sterlacchini, 2012). However, there is clear evidence that historically the state has played an important role in driving technological breakthroughs.

Mazzucato (2013, 2018) has done extensive research on the extent of innovation in the public and private sectors and has found that private firms are often reluctant to invest until they can see a clear business opportunity. Investing in R&D is often a very costly activity, with little guarantee of a return on the investment, and government money has helped fund larger and more risky technological developments. For example, the origins of the internet date back to research commissioned by the US government to build a computer-based communications network, the Advanced Research Projects Agency Network (ARPANET), which was funded by the US Defense Department in the late 1960s and started off as a military communications network. Many of the other technologies we benefit from today, including the Global Positioning System (GPS) and touch-screen technology, also started off as public sector investments. Clò et al. (2020) explore the role of state-ownership in supporting innovation in the telecommunications sector across 91 countries and also find that firms under public control are active players in technological creation in this sector.

water companies in England. Firms in the private sector typically have easier access to financial markets and can more easily borrow to fund investment to boost productivity.

Privatization was also seen as a way of promoting innovation. The lack of market incentives, constraints on investment, and the risk of political capture reduce the incentives for innovation of firms in the public sector. For private sector firms, on the other hand, competitive market pressures and the desire to maximize profits arguably provide a stronger incentive for these firms to invest in R&D and to strive to develop new products and production processes. However, the uncertainty of returns to investment in R&D and the positive externalities associated with knowledge spillovers may constrain private firms' R&D activities, particularly where these involve large and risky projects.[25] There are, of course, many examples of highly innovative firms operating in the private sector. However, historically the state has also played a key role in funding innovations, particularly where these have involved large high-risk technological developments (see Box 7.5).

7.3.2 Political arguments for privatization

Political objectives played an important role in the privatization programme of the 1980s and 1990s. Privatization was seen as a way to reduce potentially damaging government

[25] There are several ways in which governments can support R&D investment—for example, by providing subsidies or establishing collaborations between public universities and firms. Mazzucato (2013, 2016), however, argues that the role of the government goes beyond correcting market failures, since it can support technological breakthroughs, creating entirely new markets.

interference in the economy. With state-owned companies, politicians may try to influence the managers of these companies to gain political support, allowing their decisions to be guided by voter preferences rather than what makes sound economic sense. For example, they may have an incentive to keep inefficient or loss-making plants open in certain areas to boost their electoral support.

However, the process of privatization also provided a means to garner political support, where those who benefited from the sale of state-owned companies were more likely to become political supporters of the parties in power, and it is itself susceptible to corruption, as illustrated by several cases of privatization in the former Soviet Union. Following privatization, if firms are monitored by government-backed regulatory bodies, there is a risk that this political interference will continue, leading to regulatory capture.[26] The privatization programme was also seen as a way to reduce the political and economic power of trade unions in some countries, such as the UK.

Just as ideology played a role in driving the earlier wave of nationalizations, the massive privatization programme of the 1980s and 1990s was often viewed as representing the triumph of free market ideology, which sees state intervention as largely a hindrance to private entrepreneurship. The period saw a shift from a more paternalistic view of the state to a focus on individual liberties and an assumption of the primacy of the market.

In several countries, including the UK, privatization was seen as an opportunity to promote popular capitalism by encouraging company employees and the wider population to become shareholders of the newly privatized companies, fostering the emergence of what became known as a shareholder democracy. However, there is little evidence to suggest that privatization led to a significant increase in individual shareholding, at least in the UK. The proportion of UK quoted shares held by individuals had been falling since the 1960s: from a high of 54 per cent in 1963, it fell to 28 per cent in 1981 and by the end of the 1990s stood at just over 15 per cent (ONS, 2020). During this period, share ownership became more heavily concentrated among institutional shareholders, such as insurance companies and pensions funds, as well foreign interests—including foreign governments.

In this section, we have reviewed a number of arguments for privatization. Considering these alongside the arguments for nationalization discussed above, there does not appear to be a clear case in favour of either state or private ownership; instead, this is likely to depend on context. Both nationalization and privatization happen in specific political, social, technological, and institutional contexts, and changes in these contexts may mean that the original rationale for state ownership or privatization no longer applies. Changes in technology, in particular, have facilitated changes in market structures, changing the nature of some industries and creating more room for competition, as illustrated by telecommunications technology with the rise in use of mobile phones, or the expansion of the non-rail transport sector.

7.4 Private provision of publicly funded services

We have reviewed the arguments for privatizing both the finance and production of goods and services. In some cases, there may be an argument for continued government involvement in funding a particular good or service but allowing it to be produced by the private sector. This is achieved through market testing or competitive contracting

[26] The concept of regulatory capture was introduced in Chapter 4, and we return to it in section 7.5.

(or tendering), where firms bid for contracts to deliver goods and services put out to tender by the government.[27] Competitive contracting is therefore sometimes referred to as the 'make or buy decision'. This contrasts with other mechanisms through which the private sector may deliver public services, such as franchising, since under competitive contracting the government is still responsible for paying for the good or service.

Competitive contracting is a form of partial privatization, since it does not involve the sale of assets to the private sector and ultimate responsibility for providing the good or service still lies with the government. The government retains responsibility for specifying what is required and contracts are normally specified for a limited period, after which a new tendering process is opened up. Market testing is a means of encouraging competition between providers, rather than a means of securing private sector production, since public sector providers such as local authorities are also typically allowed to bid for contracts. If the public sector provider wins the contract, the service is contracted in rather than contracted out. Provision is more likely to be contracted in where the potential for profits is low.

Competitive contracting is not new. For example, in the UK, the Conservative government of the 1980s and 1990s made competitive contracting compulsory for a variety of local government services. Although it is no longer compulsory, competitive contracting continues to be actively encouraged in the UK and many other countries across the world. Competitive tendering is one aspect of **public procurement**, where the government is involved in buying goods and services from the private sector. This is big business, as Figure 7.4 shows. In the Netherlands, for example, just under 45 per cent of total government expenditure is channelled through the private sector.

Governments buy all sorts of goods and services from the private sector: from office furniture and computers to defence equipment, pharmaceutical products, communications systems, nuclear power stations, buildings (e.g. schools, hospitals, roads, and bridges), and

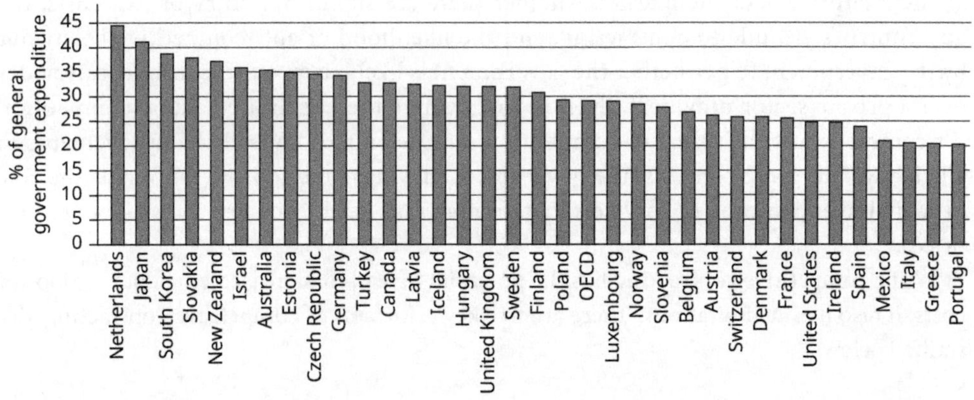

Figure 7.4 Government procurement spending as a share of government spending, 2015
Note: Data include spending on large infrastructure projects and **outsourcing** of other goods and services provided and used by the government.
Source: OECD (2017).

[27] The coverage in this section is necessarily brief. See suggestions for further reading at the end of the chapter.

services such as catering, cleaning, security, accountancy, and financial and legal services. When should these activities be undertaken 'in-house' by the government or government producers and when should they be outsourced to the private sector?

7.4.1 Rationale for and limitations of competitive contracting

As we saw in section 7.2, government involvement in the production of goods and services can increase efficiency—for example, if a sector is characterized by strong economies of scale, if there are substantial problems of imperfect and asymmetric information, if production involves significant externalities, or if the goods in question have the characteristics of public goods. However, when goods and services are produced in-house by the government—and the government is the only or main supplier—we effectively have a state-owned monopoly, which may lack the incentives to promote efficiency and minimize costs. In the absence of competition, there are also no alternative cost yardsticks or sources of information with which to assess the efficiency of public sector producers.

Competitive contracting introduces *ex ante* competition—that is, competition to *deliver* a good or service. By opening up production to private sector firms, competitive contracting fosters competition and should lead to increased efficiency and lower costs, and therefore lower public expenditure. Firms in the private sector generally face greater pressure to reduce costs and are arguably better managed, more efficient, more innovative, and more responsive to consumer demands. There is also scope for private firms to benefit from scale effects, since one firm can provide the same good or service to multiple government departments or local authorities.

The degree of competition—and hence the scope for increased efficiency and lower costs—will depend on the number of bidders for the government contracts, which in turn will depend on the potential for profits. The scope for profits will depend on factors such as the relative size of the market, whether there are significant entry or exit costs, the government's attitude to contracting, and the likelihood of anti-competitive behaviour by the government (e.g. whether the government is likely to favour the in-house provider over a private sector provider). Even in cases where there is limited actual competition for contracts, just the threat of competition may be enough to lead to improvements in efficiency.[28] In some contexts, the government may have monopsony power, as the sole or main buyer of a good or service, and therefore may be able to apply pressure to reduce prices.[29]

While competitive contracting has the potential to lead to increased efficiency and lower costs, it also has its limitations. There are five key criticisms of competitive contracting, described below.

[28] This is a point highlighted by the theory of contestable markets (Baumol et al., 1982). Contestable markets are markets where firms face no or very low entry and exit costs, and the threat of entry alone is enough to ensure incumbent firms behave in a competitive manner. Therefore, a market with a single firm or a small number of firms may resemble a perfectly competitive market.

[29] Examples include countries with publicly funded and provided healthcare and education, where the government is a major buyer of labour (e.g. teachers, doctors, and nurses) and other inputs such as medical equipment and medicines.

Poor quality and unreliable service

Firms competing to be awarded government contracts are under pressure to offer lower costs to undercut their rivals. However, in efforts to reduce costs, it is important to distinguish genuine waste from necessary expenditures. Non-price criteria such as quality, technical specifications, and wider policy objectives play an important role in the delivery of many publicly provided goods and services, but these criteria can be difficult to specify in a contract, and therefore cost reductions may come at the expense of these non-price criteria, leading to lower-quality products or services. If firms significantly underestimate the cost of delivering a service, this may result in gaps in provision; in extreme cases, there is a risk of private contractors failing due to bankruptcy.[30] Cost savings are often short-lived and there is a tendency for cost escalation over the course of a project. Low bids by private sector firms may push public sector providers out of the market, leaving the public sector dependent on a private monopoly in the future.

Cost savings may also imply lower pay and worse working conditions (longer hours, less holiday time, reduced pension benefits), which can exacerbate existing inequalities in society. Reducing costs by lowering wages or firing workers may result in increased costs to the state in the form of higher welfare payments, although these may be partially offset by higher tax revenues from profits generated (Bailey, 2002).

Lack of competition

This may arise both before and after a contract has been awarded. At the bidding stage, larger projects may need to be carried out by larger firms, so the sector may be more monopolistic than competitive to begin with, and there is also scope for collusion between contractors to raise prices. Once a contract has been awarded, firms have little incentive not to exploit their monopoly power, which may lead to higher costs and inefficiency, although regular re-contracting means that the contractor, service level, and costs can be reviewed. Whether these higher costs can be passed on to the government depends on the detail of the contract, but the government may be reluctant to risk the service not being provided by refusing to cover the costs. There is also scope for anti-competitive behaviour by the government, particularly where it has monopsony power.

Hidden costs

Contracting out is not costless. There are costs involved in drawing up, negotiating, monitoring, and enforcing contracts, as well as costs associated with organizing and assessing bids. Contracting out the provision of goods and services to the private sector can also reduce the knowledge and expertise of government departments, making their monitoring and enforcing role more challenging—how can a government department monitor the delivery of a large infrastructure project, such as a new motorway, if it no longer has engineers with the

[30] For example, in the UK, the private security services company G4S was unable to supply sufficient security guards to police the London 2012 Olympics and the government had to bring in army reinforcements to provide security for the event. In 2018, the large outsourcing company Carillion collapsed; at the time, the company was responsible for delivering over 400 public sector projects, including schools and hospital, as well as being responsible for the maintenance and cleaning of 40 prisons.

expert knowledge of what is required to build a motorway? Over time, governments may learn how to better specify and enforce contracts, although retaining some technical expertise is vital.

Loss of public sector accountability

There is a risk that if the goods and services are being delivered by private firms, then the public sector can no longer be held responsible for any problems that arise in the delivery of those goods and services. However, this argument ignores the fact that the public sector is still accountable for providing the good or service, even if the delivery itself has been delegated to the private sector. If a local authority has outsourced rubbish collection to private firms, customer complaints about rubbish not being collected are still directed to the local authority rather than the private firm.

Scope for bribery and corruption

Private sector firms may lobby government officials to increase their chances of being awarded a particular contract, and the fact that non-price criteria are harder to specify in contracts may open the door to discretionary behaviour, such as favouritism and corruption, by government officials. This entails a wasteful use of resources and may also affect the quality and cost of the goods and services being delivered. Problems with the delivery of personal protective equipment (PPE)[31] to healthcare professionals in the UK during the Covid-19 pandemic highlighted the dangers of awarding government contracts to private providers without proper scrutiny.

Given these limitations of contracting out, how significant are the potential cost savings? Box 7.6 discusses some of the empirical evidence. While early studies showed potentially large reductions in costs from contracting out, more recent evidence suggests these have been falling over time.

Box 7.6 How large are the cost savings from contracting out?

Many empirical studies have attempted to gauge the magnitude of the cost savings from contracting out. The findings in earlier studies suggest that savings of around 20 per cent are possible, at both the local and central government levels, but these savings are largely independent of whether the contracts are awarded to private contractors or in-house providers.[32] There is, however, a lot of variation in savings across sectors, with estimated cost savings of around 20–5 per cent for refuse collection in most countries, higher savings for office cleaning, but lower savings for leisure activities and childcare

[31] During the Covid-19 pandemic, the UK government bypassed the normal competitive tendering processes to secure supplies of PPE, which resulted in several contracts being awarded to companies with little or no experience in providing PPE. A recent government report estimated that failed contracts and defective PPE cost the taxpayer £1.4 billion (HM Treasury, 2025).

[32] See, for example, Bailey (2002), Domberger and Jensen (1997), and Parker (1990) for an overview of some of the early evidence. Domberger and Jensen (1997) review the international evidence and find savings in the order of 20 per cent are achievable, without sacrificing quality, across various sectors, including refuse collection, cleaning, and hospital domestic services. Parker (1990) also reviewed a range of international studies and founds savings of 20 per cent (sometimes significantly more), covering areas such as refuse collection, fire services, office cleaning, NHS catering and domestic services, and street paving.

(Bailey, 2002; Parker, 1990). Some research has also suggested that cost savings are significantly lower, at around 6–7 per cent, once tendering and contract costs are taken into account (Bailey, 2002). More recent studies suggest that cost savings have been falling over time and tend to vary across sectors and countries: savings are larger in technical as opposed to social services, and the economic effects are significantly greater in Anglo-Saxon countries (Petersen et al., 2018). It is difficult to determine whether cost savings come at the expense of quality, as few studies assess this in a comprehensive way (Petersen et al., 2018). Quality can be difficult to measure in practice, involving inevitable value judgements (how would you measure the quality of a cleaning service?), and it was often not being measured systematically before the introduction of contracting, making direct comparisons difficult.

There is also a question about whether cost savings represent genuine gains in efficiency or whether they are better classed as wealth transfers: if the lower costs are achieved through lower salaries and worse working conditions, then the managers and shareholders of the private firms are benefiting at the expense of their workers. The restricted nature of many of the early studies, which focused on a single service and country or local authority, suggest it is risky to generalize from these findings (Boyne, 1998).

7.4.2 What services should be subject to competitive contracting?

Some authors would argue that the vast majority of public services can and should be contracted out to the private sector: provided the government knows exactly what it wants, it can draw up a contract that specifies this and leave production to the private sector in order to benefit from lower costs and improved efficiency.[33] In general, if transaction costs are low, then buying the good or service from the private sector rather than providing it directly may be preferable.[34] Transaction costs are likely to be low in sectors where:

- the characteristics (including quality) of the good or service to be provided can be easily specified in a contract, so performance can be easily monitored and problems of bounded rationality are limited;[35]
- there are a number of alternative service providers, so there is limited scope for contractors to exploit the government through opportunistic behaviour and the risks if the provider goes bankrupt or otherwise fails to deliver are lower;
- production does not rely on unique or specific equipment or assets, so the government is not tied to a particular provider.

Examples include cleaning services, refuse collection, and vehicle maintenance.

[33] See, for example, Shleifer (1998).

[34] Transaction costs include the cost of searching for suitable suppliers, dealing with lack of performance or failure to deliver (legal costs), monitoring costs, loss of knowledge, and the increased scope for corruption (i.e. favouritism in the award of contracts).

[35] We discuss problems of bounded rationality in general in Chapter 2.

Where problems of bounded rationality are more prevalent, where non-price criteria are important but more difficult to specify and monitor,[36] and where failure of the contractor to deliver would lead to large potential losses, direct production by the government may be preferable. Examples include the provision of defence equipment, as well as social care and prison services. Non-price criteria such as quality, which can be difficult to measure, play an important role in social care or prison services (see Box 7.7). Here incentives to reduce costs may impact on non-contractable quality, and monitoring and enforcement costs are likely to be high. Non-competitive contracting may provide an alternative because it limits the incentives to reduce costs by sacrificing quality, since there is no pressure to offer the lowest costs in order to be awarded the contract.

If individuals buy the good or service directly and there is enough competition between providers to ensure consumers have some degree of choice, then the impact of incentives to

Box 7.7 Should prison services be provided by the government or contracted out to the private sector?

Most people would consider the administration of criminal justice to be one of the core responsibilities of the government and that the government alone should be responsible for providing this. However, several countries rely on private firms to build and run prisons, including Australia, Brazil, and the USA. In the UK, privately run prisons were introduced in the 1990s and, as of 2020, 13 out of the 117 prisons in England and Wales were privately managed, with 18 per cent of the prison population held in privately run prisons (Prison Reform Trust, 2021).

The main argument for privatizing the provision of prison services is based on the potential for cost reductions and increased efficiency, particularly in the context of rising incarceration rates. Private firms typically have easier access to the finance required to build new facilities and their greater incentives to reduce costs can lead to more innovation. Privatization may also improve the performance of public sector prisons, since they now face the threat of competition. However, incentives to reduce costs may encourage private providers to cut back on essential services such as staff training, healthcare, and cleaning, which could make prisons more dangerous.[37] Having privately run prisons may also create a perverse incentive to maintain—or increase—incarceration rates. Difficulties in determining the full contracting costs and in measuring quality make it difficult to assess the cost effectiveness of private prisons, and the empirical evidence on the cost savings of private prisons is mixed (Kish & Lipton, 2013).

Private provision does not have to be for profit though. In the Netherlands, for example, private providers have long played an important role in providing prisons services, but these are non-profit organizations. Even when prison services are contracted out to profit-maximizing firms, suitable incentives can be incorporated into contracts. For example, in Australia and New Zealand, contracts with private prisons include incentives to reduce recidivism rates by offering bonuses if certain targets are achieved (Eisen, 2019).

[36] Governments may also care about achieving wider social objectives (e.g. encouraging people to be more physically active), which can also be difficult to fully specify in a contract.

[37] In 2019, in the UK, His Majesty's Prison and Probation Service took over the management of HMP Birmingham from the private company G4S, ending the contract seven years early, due to concerns over safety and security.

reduce costs on non-contractible quality may be less severe. Consumers can change providers if they are dissatisfied with the service provided, and if firms want to keep business, they have an incentive to establish a reputation for offering good value for money. However, problems of imperfect information or bounded rationality may limit the extent of genuine choice.

In sum, competitive tendering will not automatically lead to lower costs—markets need to be genuinely competitive or contestable—and lower costs may involve sacrificing quality and other non-contractible characteristics. Whether contracting out is the best option will depend on the nature of the good or service, namely how well the requirements can be specified in the contract and how easy contracts are to monitor and enforce.

7.5 Regulating private companies

The privatization programme of the 1980s and 1990s may have addressed some of the problems afflicting the former state-owned monopolies, but it also created new challenges of its own: would the newly formed private companies work in the best interests of consumers and society? What controls should be put in place to protect consumers? How would these mechanisms affect firms' incentives to promote efficiency and reduce costs? In this section, we review the need for regulating privatized companies, the main forms of regulation, and some of the key challenges involved in designing effective regulations.

7.5.1 The rationale for regulation

Regulation refers to the use of rules, incentives, and penalties by the government to control and modify the behaviour of firms and individuals. Examples include limits on environmental pollution, and health and safety regulations. Although the overall regulatory framework is determined by the government, individual regulatory agencies are usually formally independent of the government and politicians, providing some degree of political impartiality.

In the UK, there are over 90 regulatory bodies, with a total annual expenditure over £4 billion (NAO, 2017). They cover a wide range of areas, including utilities, education, transport, communications, financial services, and healthcare. Table 7.3 lists a selection of UK economic regulators. Other key regulatory authorities include the Financial Conduct Authority (FCA), the Food Standards Agency (FSA), the Health and Safety Executive (HSE), and the Office for Standards in Education, Children's Services and Skills (Ofsted).

The primary purpose of regulation is to overcome various forms of market failure—whether this is due to imperfect competition, externalities, or asymmetric information—as well as to promote equity and the public interest. The arguments for regulation are summarized below.

Preventing abuses of market power

Transferring ownership of production from the state to the private sector does not, by itself, change the market environment and therefore does not mean that the private sector firm(s) will automatically be more efficient and innovative. This is especially true in the case of natural monopolies, such as water and energy companies. Here, the features of the production technology available limit the scope for beneficial competition and in many cases

Table 7.3 Selected regulatory bodies in the UK

Regulator	Remit	Expenditure 2016/17 (£m)
Office of Gas and Electricity Markets (Ofgem)	Regulates the gas and electricity markets. Protects the interests of consumers, including ensuring security of supply and reducing environmental impacts.	86.6
Water Services Regulation Authority (Ofwat)	Regulates the water and sewerage sector in England and Wales. Protects the interests of consumers, ensuring water companies are efficiently run and can meet current and future demand.	22.1
Office of Communications (Ofcom)	Regulates electronic communications services, including TV and radio, telephone (fixed and mobile), and postal services. Promotes competition between providers and quality of services, and protects consumers from harmful or offensive content.	138.9
Office of Road and Rail (ORR)	Regulates the rail and road network in Britain. Promotes competition and protects consumer interests, working to improve the passenger experience.	31.0
Civil Aviation Authority (CAA)	Regulates, directly and indirectly, all aspects of civil aviation in the UK, including airports and traffic control. Focuses on ensuring choice, safety, value for money, and fair treatment for consumers. Promotes improvements in airlines' and airports' environmental performance.	130.9

Source: NAO (2017).

privatization essentially transformed state-owned monopolies into privately owned monopolies.[38] The role of the regulator then is to intervene to protect consumers and prevent firms from exploiting their monopoly power by charging excessively high prices or cutting back on quality. In other areas, competition may be desirable but not feasible, and here the role of the regulator may be to promote competition. Over time, technological changes may open up new possibilities for competition—for example, mobile phone services increased competition in the telecommunications market—reducing the need for regulation.

Preventing market instability

Regulators have a role to play in ensuring the stability of supply, particularly in vital sectors such as energy and water supply. Failure to meet the demand for these services has a serious impact on economic, social, and physical well-being. Regulation has an equally important role to play in the banking and financial services sectors, to prevent or mitigate the impact of potential large-scale bankruptcies or financial mismanagement.

[38] The privatization of water and sewerage services in England is one example of this.

Addressing externalities

The presence of externalities provides a further rationale for regulation, to encourage firms to take into account the social costs and benefits of their actions. For example, the regulator might set rules on how water companies treat wastewater to reduce pollution in rivers, an example of a negative externality. The supply of utilities such as gas, electricity, and water, and the provision of train services, requires access to a shared distribution network (e.g. railway tracks, water pipes, or electricity cables). If the network is controlled by a monopolist, the regulator may need to regulate the prices charged to distribution firms.

Mitigating problem of asymmetric information and bounded rationality

Firms generally have more information about the products or services they provide than consumers, and they may not always have an incentive to accurately disclose all of this information. In other cases, the information provided to consumers can be quite technical and complex—for example, information on different energy tariffs, financial services, or medications. Individuals are also prone to problems of bounded rationality and have a limited ability to collect and process all relevant information, as we saw in Chapter 2. Regulators have a role to play in establishing information requirements, setting minimum standards for what information should be provided to consumers, and monitoring its accuracy.

Promoting equity and the public interest

As we saw in section 7.2, the actions of private profit-maximizing firms might not reflect the broader public interest. For example, private firms do not always have an incentive to provide a universal service, particularly where the costs of providing the service varies significantly across locations. Private firms may opt to charge different prices based on costs (with implications for equity) or may choose not to provide the service where it is not profitable to do so. This could potentially leave more remote areas without access to services such as fast and reliable internet, public transport, and postal services. Regulators can ensure that universal access is protected.[39]

7.5.2 Different forms of regulation

There are a variety of forms of regulation, including price and quality regulation, as well as lighter-touch forms of regulation, such as guidance and codes of practice.

Price regulation

Price regulation involves setting price limits on goods and services. There are two main forms of price regulation:

- **Rate of return regulation**: this type of regulation involves restricting the profits a firm can earn to a given proportion of their capital. The main advantage of this form of regulation is its perceived fairness in preventing consumers from being exploited by firms with monopoly power. However, it does not provide incentives for firms to reduce costs,

[39] In the UK, one of the duties of the communications regulator, Ofcom, is to ensure that Royal Mail provides a universal postal service, delivering and collecting mail six days a week and offering a 'one price goes anywhere' postal service.

since the profits a firm can earn are limited. It can also lead to a bias towards more capital-intensive production methods. Firms have an incentive to expand their capital base in order to increase their absolute profits, but this may not result in the most efficient combination of inputs, resulting in X-inefficiency. This form of regulation was primarily used in the USA to regulate utility companies, but has gradually been replaced by other forms of regulation, such as price caps.

- **Price controls**: this form of regulation involves setting a maximum price that firms can charge, or a price cap. In industries with multiple tariffs, an average of a basket of prices is regulated, rather than regulating every single price, which would be too costly and complex to administer. Firms therefore retain some flexibility over setting individual prices. Unlike rate of return regulation, price controls do provide incentives for firms to reduce costs and do not bias production towards more capital-intensive methods. Price controls are also generally easier to administer. However, firms have little incentive to reduce prices beyond the level of the price cap and, depending on the form of price cap adopted and how long it is in place for, it may generate considerable uncertainty (see Box 7.8).

Regulators also make use of yardstick competition. This is not a formal type of regulation but provides a way for regulators to mitigate problems of imperfect information, where firms will have more information about their costs of production, but have little incentive to disclose these fully to the regulator. In sectors where there are rival firms providing the same good or service (e.g. in the case of the regional water companies in England and Wales), the regulator can collect information from the various firms and use this to inform the level of the price cap.

Box 7.8 Regulation in practice

The main form of price regulation used in the UK is the 'RPI minus *X*' (or RPI – *X*)[40] form originally proposed by Stephen Littlechild for the regulation of British Telecom in the early 1980s. Under this approach, the firm's prices cannot increase by more than the value of RPI – *X*, where RPI is a measure of inflation and *X* represents potential efficiency gains (e.g. from technological advances or improvements in managerial efficiency). The value of *X* is set by the regulator, normally for a period of four to five years, and it is based on the best information the regulator has about the efficient cost of providing the regulated product or service. *X* can be set to zero or it can be negative, in cases where the regulator recognizes the need for prices to rise to finance investment in the industry. The regulated firm has an incentive to increase efficiency and reduce costs—any increase in efficiency beyond *X* will translate into higher profits for the firm until the new price cap is set. However, the choice of the length of the regulatory period can create problems: if it is too short, this may lead to short-termism by the regulated firm; if it is set too long, then the firm may make excessive profits for a prolonged period of time, potentially damaging consumer trust in the regulator. It is also a forward-looking mechanism, where the regulator needs to predict the rate of technological advances and associated potential cost reductions, which can be challenging.

[40] RPI is the Retail Prices Index.

Quality regulation

Regulators can also regulate quality standards, particularly in areas where pressure to reduce costs may lead firms to skimp on quality. It is often difficult to find a single suitable measure of quality and the indicators used vary across sectors. Examples include standards for the quality of drinking water, standards for response times for dealing with faults, and the level of compensation to be provided to consumers if firms fail to meet these standards.

7.5.3 Challenges of effective regulation

Regulators are expected to protect consumers from potential abuses of market power; to promote competition, efficiency, and innovation; to minimize the burden of regulations on firms; to ensure health and safety and environmental standards are adhered to; and to achieve any other policy objectives set by the government. In practice, it can be difficult for regulators to achieve all of these objectives, particularly where some may conflict. Some of the challenges regulators face when it comes to designing and enforcing effective regulations include the following:

- **Problems of imperfect or asymmetric information**: regulatory bodies are constrained by problems of asymmetric information, as they often need to rely on firms for information about costs, market demand, and the impact of their activities. Firms, however, may have an incentive to misreport this information to minimize the impact of the regulations on their activities.
- **Potential to promote inefficiency**: regulations create distortions in the market. Profit-maximizing firms should take existing regulations into account when devising their production plans, and this may result in inefficiencies—for example, the use of suboptimal input combinations. Poorly designed regulations may also reduce incentives to innovate and stifle technological development.
- **Regulation is costly**: these costs include both the direct costs involved in designing and enforcing regulations and the costs to individuals and businesses of complying with them. In the UK, for instance, the estimated running costs of the 90 regulatory bodies in operation is over £4 billion (NAO, 2017). Regulatory officials may also have an incentive to expand the regulatory regime beyond the efficient or required level, increasing costs further.
- **Risk of regulatory capture**: regulatory capture arises when the regulatory agency (or those who work there) gradually comes to identify itself with the interests of the firm that it regulates, making it vulnerable to bribery and lobbying by the firm's managers. The regulator may then stop acting in the best interests of consumers and society, and instead work to advance the interests of the industry it is supposed to regulate.
- **Potential lack of impartiality**: while regulatory bodies are formally independent of governments, in practice they may not be completely free from governmental interference. Decisions made by regulators have political consequences and regulators rely on governments for their own survival.

One of the aims of privatization was to reduce government interference in the economy. However, the potential for market failure and the desire to achieve wider economic and social objectives suggests that governments still have an important role to play in regulating the activities of private firms. Regulation itself is subject to its own failures and imperfections, and these need to be balanced against the risk of market failures and government failures.

7.6 How inefficient is the public sector?

As the discussion above has highlighted, there are sources of inefficiency under both public and private ownership. Therefore assessing whether the public sector is inherently less efficient than the private sector is ultimately an empirical question. To assess the relative performance of the public and private sectors, empirical studies can either analyse the performance of a particular firm or industry before and after privatization, or they can compare the performance of similar industries at a given point in time. There are practical challenges with both these approaches.

First, we need to decide on the appropriate indicators to measure and compare performance, given that firms in the public sector may pursue multiple objectives, not just profit maximization. We should consider a wider range of indicators, including measures of labour productivity, levels of employment, and exports. Some of these indicators will be easier to measure than others. For example, if we want to compare the efficiency of public and privately provided education, we need to think about how we measure inputs (should this be the number of teachers, facilities, or the use of technology?) and outputs (is academic performance a reliable indicator?) to arrive at reliable estimates of productivity. We also need to control for any other factors which may affect our results. If we are comparing the performance of an industry before and after privatization, we need to control for any increase in investment following privatization. The transfer of ownership from the public to the private sector (or vice versa) may also lead to the pursuit of different objectives and this should be taken into account.

In spite of these challenges, several studies have estimated the impact of ownership on performance and efficiency. These studies range from case studies focusing on individual firms in specific countries to studies covering a large number of firms within and across countries. Megginson and Netter (2001) and Sheshinski and López-Calva (2003) review some of the empirical studies comparing public and private ownership and conclude that state-owned firms tend to be less profitable, less productive, and less efficient than privately owned firms, even after controlling for size, market share, and other relevant factors. Perhaps the finding that privatization tends to increase profitability is not surprising, given that profit maximization is not usually an explicit goal pursued by state-owned firms. Mueller (2003) reviewed the findings from 71 studies comparing the provision of similar services by public and private sector firms in a range of areas including airlines, banking, bus and rail services, cleaning, energy, housing, and refuse collection. He found that in only five cases were public firms more efficient than their private sector counterparts. In 10 of the studies, no significant differences between public and private sector provision were found, whereas in the remaining 56 studies, publicly owned firms were found to be significantly less efficient than private sector firms providing the same good or service.

Other studies, however, have found less conclusive evidence in support of private ownership. Hall (2014) reviews a number of studies analysing the impact of the privatization of various public services, covering sectors such as water and waste management, electricity, telecommunications, and rail and bus services, and he concludes that there are no significant differences in terms of efficiency between public and privately owned public services companies. Firms that are performing well are more likely to be privatized, and if this is not taken into account in the empirical studies, the results are likely to be biased in favour of privatization. Knyazeva et al. (2013) do take this into account and compare the performance of all companies in western and eastern Europe that were privatized between the mid-1980s and 2009. They found that, after controlling for the fact that governments are more likely to privatize better-performing firms, privatized firms in fact tend to perform worse than firms that remain in the public sector, particularly in the short run. They attribute this in part to the costly adjustment that firms need to go through following privatization. They also highlight the importance of a strong property rights and contracting rights regime in order to allow the newly privatized firms to prosper.

The improved performance of privatized firms found in some studies may also reflect the impact of broader developments in technology, rather than the impact of a change in ownership. A project comparing the long-term trends in productivity before and after privatization for a selection of countries between 1970 and 2004 found that fluctuations in productivity over time could be largely attributed to changes in technology, such as the development of digital and wireless telecommunications (PIQUE, 2009).

The existing empirical evidence therefore does not seem to suggest that the private sector is inherently more efficient. Whether public or private ownership is to be preferred is likely to depend on the sector—there is no one-size-fits-all policy. Privatization may work for some goods and services, such as telecommunications, but it may not work as effectively for others, such as welfare or prisons.[41] Some would argue that the ownership of production—public or private—is largely irrelevant and what matters is the incentive structure that is created (Rees, 1985). As we have seen, principal–agent problems affect both the public and the private sectors, and many of the tools for overcoming these problems are available to governments and private firms alike.

The indicators considered in many studies are often limited. Governments—and society—may care about objectives other than maximizing efficiency and profits, such as promoting a greener, more sustainable economy, reducing inequality, or promoting innovation. Are public or privately owned firms best placed to achieve these goals? (See Box 7.9.)

Box 7.9 Should railways be run by the public or the private sector?

Britain's privately run railways have long been the subject of complaints because of high ticket prices and services plagued by delays and overcrowding. Are these problems due to the fact that most service providers are privately owned? How does the UK system compare with some of its European counterparts?

Rail in the UK was privatized by the Conservative government in 1993, which separated responsibility for maintaining the rail infrastructure, including tracks, signalling, and stations, from responsibility for providing train services. The former was initially awarded to the privately run Railtrack, while private companies competed for franchises to provide train

(Continued)

[41] See, for example, Blank (2000) for a discussion of the private provision of social services, and Hart et al. (1997) on the role of the private provision of prison services.

services. Following the collapse of Railtrack in 2002, responsibility for the network infrastructure was handed over to a not-for-profit company, Network Rail.[42]

Table 7.4 compares the performance of the UK rail system with the mainly publicly owned and managed railway systems in place in Germany, France, and Italy. Out of all four countries considered here, the UK has the smallest but also the busiest network, and it has seen the largest increase in passenger numbers. The UK system scores highly on punctuality, but it has also seen the largest increase in fare prices. Even though train operating companies in the UK are privatized, the government still provides subsidies, estimated at €5.1 billion in 2009. Subsidies to the state-owned operator in Italy are higher, but the system there performs better in terms of punctuality and has seen lower fare increases over the same period. The German system seems to be the worst performing of the four during this period, with the lowest punctuality score and a sizeable—albeit decreasing—government subsidy.

Table 7.4 Performance indicators of different national rail systems

	France	Germany	Italy	UK
Real increase in cost of rail travel (2000–2011) (%)	10	16	25	34
Punctuality (2011) (%)	90.8	80	93.3	91.5
Government subsidy (2009) (€bn)	10.9	13.5	8.1	5.1
Change in public subsidy (2000–2008) (%)	+48	−20	+28	−23
Passenger km growth (1995–2008) (%)	8	19	10	71

Source: European Commission (2013).

Conclusion

In this chapter, we have discussed the main arguments for nationalization, including primarily economic arguments based around natural monopoly and transaction costs, as well as broader public interest and political arguments. We have also explored some of the leading arguments against nationalization—or in favour of privatization. The main aim of privatization is to promote competition and efficiency, but privatization alone will not ensure this, particularly if the industry in question is a monopoly. Selling a state-owned monopoly to the private sector will not, by itself, lead to more competition, and regulation of private sector firms by the government has an important role to play. Regulation itself is subject to its own failures and imperfections, and these need to be balanced against the risk of market failures and government failures.

One of the leading arguments against public ownership is based on the purported inefficiency of the public sector, but neither the theory nor the available empirical evidence

[42] Under current government plans, all passenger services will gradually be brought back into public ownership, and a new state-owned company, Great British Railways, is set to operate most rail infrastructure and passenger rail services in England.

appears to provide overwhelming support for either nationalization or privatization, which raises the question: does ownership matter? Focusing on the public versus private ownership distinction also risks oversimplifying the issue. As we have seen, there are many different forms of private ownership and there is also no simple public versus private dichotomy.

Questions for discussion

1. Should production in the following sectors be public or private?
   a. Prisons
   b. Air traffic control
   c. Pharmaceutical industry
   d. Social care
2. Are agency problems more pervasive in the public sector or in the private sector? Provide some examples to illustrate your answer.
3. Why do many countries have a state-owned police force but also private sector security firms?
4. Why do governments contract out the provision of military equipment, such as tanks and machinery, but not the manning of military ships and planes?
5. Who gains and who loses from privatization?
6. Allais (1948) argued for nationalizing a few firms in each industry to make it easier to compare public and private ownership. Do you agree with this proposal? Why or why not?

Further reading

For a discussion of the impacts of privatization across countries:

Estrin, S., & Pelletier, A. (2018). Privatization in developing countries: What are the lessons of recent experience? *World Bank Research Observer*, *33*(1), 65–102.

OECD (2009). *Privatisation in the 21st century: Recent experiences of OECD countries, Report on Good Practices*. Organization for Economic Cooperation and Development. January.

OECD (2003). *Privatising state-owned enterprises: An overview of policies and practices in OECD countries*. Organization for Economic Cooperation and Development.

Parker, D. (2004). *The UK's privatisation experiment: The passage of time permits a sober assessment*. Available at: http://dx.doi.org/10.2139/ssrn.514224

On competitive contracting:

Albalate, D., Bel, G., Gradus, R., & Reeves, E. (2021). Re-municipalization of local public services: Incidence, causes and prospects. *International Review of Administrative Sciences*, *87*(3), 419–424.

Bailey, S. J. (2002). *Public sector economics: Theory, policy and practice* (2nd ed.). Palgrave. Provides a discussion of the history of market testing in the UK.

Blank, R. M. (2000). When can public policy makers rely on private markets? The effective provision of social services. *Economic Journal*, *110*(462), C34–C49.

Domberger, S., & Jensen, P. (1997). Contracting out by the public sector: Theory, evidence, prospects. *Oxford Review of Economic Policy*, *13*(4), 67–78.

Hart, O., Shleifer, A., & Vishny, R. W. (1997). The proper scope of government: Theory and an application to prisons. *Quarterly Journal of Economics, 112*(4), 1127–1161.

Petersen, O. H., Hjelmar, U., & Vrangbæk, K. (2018). Is contracting out of public services still the great panacea? A systematic review of studies on economic and quality effects from 2000 to 2014. *Social Policy and Administration, 52*(1), 130–157.

Tisdell, C. A., & Hartley, K. (2008). *Microeconomic policy: A new perspective.* Edward Elgar. See in particular chapter 15 on the contract state.

On the role of government in supporting innovation:

Mazzucato, Mariana (2013). *The entrepreneurial state: Debunking public versus private sector myths.* Anthem Press.

Mazzucato M. (2016). From market fixing to market-creating: A new framework for innovation policy. *Industry and Innovation, 23*(2), 140–156.

Mazzucato, M. (2018). *Mission-oriented research and innovation in the European Union: A problem-solving approach to fuel innovation-led growth.* European Commission, Directorate-General for Research and Innovation.

On the challenges of effective regulation:

Dal Bó, E. (2006). Regulatory capture: A review. *Oxford Review of Economic Policy, 22*(2), 203–225.

Decker, C. (2014). *Modern economic regulation: An introduction to theory and practice.* Cambridge University Press.

Helm, D. (2013). British infrastructure policy and the gradual return of the state. *Oxford Review of Economic Policy, 29*(2), 287–306.

Helm, D. (2020). Thirty years after water privatization—is the English model the envy of the world? *Oxford Review of Economic Policy, 36*(1), 69–85.

Stigler, G. (1971). The economic theory of regulation. *Bell Journal of Economics, 2*(1), 3–21.

For a review of the evidence comparing public and private sector performance:

Hall, D. 2014. *Public and private sector efficiency.* Public Services International Research Unit, University of Greenwich. Available at: http://www.psiru.org/sites/default/files/2014-07-EWGHT-efficiency.pdf

Knyazeva, A., Knyazeva, D., & Stiglitz, J. E. (2013). Ownership change, institutional development and performance. *Journal of Banking and Finance, 37*(7), 2605–2627.

Megginson, W. L., & Netter, J. M. (2001). From state to market: A survey of empirical studies on privatization. *Journal of Economic Literature, 39*(2), 321–389.

Musacchio, A., & Lazzarini, S. G. (2018). State-owned enterprises as multinationals: Theory and research directions. In A. Cuervo-Cazurra (Ed.), *State-owned multinationals: Governments in global business* (pp. 255–276). Palgrave Macmillan.

Sheshinski, E., & López-Calva, L. F. (2003). Privatization and its benefits: Theory and evidence. *CESifo Economic Studies, 49*(3), 429–459.

On the resurgence of state ownership and expansion of state-owned enterprises:

IMF (2020). *Fiscal monitor.* International Monetary Fund. April. Available at: https://www.imf.org/en/Publications/FM/Issues/2020/04/06/fiscal-monitor-april-2020. See, in particular, chapter 3 on state-owned enterprises.

Megginson, W. L. (2017). Privatization, state capitalism, and state ownership of business in the 21st century. *Foundations and Trends® in Finance, 11*(1–2), 1–153.

OECD (2024). *Ownership and governance of state-owned enterprises 2024.* Organization for Economic Cooperation and Development. Available at: https://doi.org/10.1787/395c9956-en

Bibliography

Allais, M. (1948). Le problème de la planification dans une économie collectiviste. *Kyklos*, *2*(1), 48–71.

Bailey, S. J. (2002). *Public sector economics: Theory, policy and practice* (2nd ed.). Palgrave.

Baumol, W., Panzar, J., & Willig, R. (1982). *Contestable markets and the theory of industry structure*. Harcourt Brace Jovanovich.

Belloc, F. (2014). Innovation in state-owned enterprises: Reconsidering the conventional wisdom. *Journal of Economic Issues*, *48*(3), 821–848.

Blank, R. M. (2000). When can public policy makers rely on private markets? The effective provision of social services. *Economic Journal*, *110*(462), C34–C49.

Boardman, A. E., & Vining, A. R. (1989). Ownership and performance in competitive environments: A comparison of the performance of private, mixed and state-owned enterprises, *Journal of Law and Economics*, *32*(1), 1–33.

Boyne, G. A. (1998). Competitive tendering in local government: A review of theory and evidence. *Public Administration*, *76*(4), 695–712.

Clò, S., Florio, M., & Rentocchini, F. (2020). Firm ownership, quality of government and innovation: Evidence from patenting in the telecommunication industry. *Research Policy*, *49*(5), art. 103960.

Cowling, K. G., & Mueller, D. C. (1978). The social costs of monopoly power. *Economic Journal*, 88, 727–748.

Cullis, J., & Jones, P. (2009). *Public finance and public choice: Analytical perspectives* (3rd ed.). Oxford University Press.

Domberger, S., & Jensen, P. (1997). Contracting out by the public sector: Theory, evidence, prospects. *Oxford Review of Economic Policy*, *13*(4), 67–78.

Dunsire, A., Hartley, K., & Parker, D. (1991). Organisational status and performance: Summary of findings, *Public Administration*, *69*(1), 21–40.

Eisen, L. (2019). *The private prison experiment: Is there any positive in for-profit imprisonment?* Pulitzer Center. 25 February.

European Commission (2013). *Commission staff working document: Impact assessment*. Available at: https://ec.europa.eu/archives/commission_2010-2014/kallas/headlines/news/2013/01/doc/swd(2013)-10-part3.pdf

Gisser, M. (1986). Price leadership and welfare losses in US manufacturing. *American Economic Review*, 76, 756–767.

Hall, D. 2014. *Public and private sector efficiency*. Public Services International Research Unit, University of Greenwich. Available at: http://www.psiru.org/sites/default/files/2014-07-EWGHT-efficiency.pdf

Harberger, A. C. (1954). Monopoly and resource allocation. *American Economic Review*, *44*(2), 77–87.

Hart, O., Shleifer, A., & Vishny, R. W. (1997). The proper scope of government: Theory and an application to prisons. *Quarterly Journal of Economics*, *112*(4), 1127–1161.

HM Treasury (2025). *Failed Covid contracts cost British taxpayer £1.4 billion* (press release, 2 June). Available at: https://www.gov.uk/government/news/failed-covid-contracts-cost-british-taxpayer-14-billion.

IMF (2018). *Fiscal monitor*. International Monetary Fund. October. Available at: https://www.imf.org/en/Publications/FM/Issues/2018/10/04/fiscal-monitor-october-2018

IMF (2020). *Fiscal monitor.* International Monetary Fund. April. Available at: https://www.imf.org/en/Publications/FM/Issues/2020/04/06/fiscal-monitor-april-2020

Jackson, P., & Price, C. M. (Eds.). (1994). *Privatisation and regulation: A review of the issues.* Longman.

Jensen, P. H., & Stonecash, R. E. (2005). Incentives and the efficiency of public sector-outsourcing contracts. *Journal of Economic Surveys, 19*(5), 767–787.

Kish, R. J., & Lipton, A. F. (2013). Do private prisons really offer savings compared with their public counterparts? *Economic Affairs, 33*(1), 93–107.

Knyazeva, A., Knyazeva, D., & Stiglitz, J. E. (2013). Ownership change, institutional development and performance. *Journal of Banking and Finance, 37*(7), 2605–2627.

Martin, S., & Parker, D. (1997). *The impact of privatisation.* Routledge.

Mazzucato, M. (2013). *The entrepreneurial state: Debunking public versus private sector myths.* Anthem Press.

Mazzucato, M. (2016). From market fixing to market-creating: A new framework for innovation policy. *Industry and Innovation, 23*(2), 140–156.

Mazzucato, M. (2018). *Mission-oriented research and innovation in the European Union: A problem-solving approach to fuel innovation-led growth.* European Commission, Directorate-General for Research and Innovation.

Megginson, W. L. (2017). Privatization, state capitalism, and state ownership of business in the 21st century. *Foundations and Trends® in Finance, 11*(1–2), 1–153.

Megginson, W. L., & Netter, J. M. (2001). From state to market: A survey of empirical studies on privatization. *Journal of Economic Literature, 39*(2), 321–389.

Mueller, D. C. (2003). *Public choice III.* Cambridge University Press.

NAO (2017). A short guide to regulation. National Audit Office. https://www.nao.org.uk/overviews/a-short-guide-to-regulation-2/

NAO (2018). *PFI and PF2.* Report by the Comptroller and Auditor General. National Audit Office/HM Treasury. Available at: https://www.nao.org.uk/reports/pfi-and-pf2/

OECD (2002). *OECD in figures 2002: Statistics on the member countries.* OECD Observer 2002/Supplement 1. Organization for Economic Cooperation and Development.

OECD (2003). *Privatising state-owned enterprises: An overview of policies and practices in OECD countries.* Organization for Economic Cooperation and Development.

OECD (2017). Public procurement. In *Government at a glance 2017* (chapter 9). Organization for Economic Cooperation and Development. Available at: http://dx.doi.org/10.1787/888933533131

OECD (2024). *Ownership and governance of state-owned enterprises 2024.* Organization for Economic Cooperation and Development. Available at: https://doi.org/10.1787/395c9956-en

ONS (2020). Ownership of UK quoted shares: 2018. Office for National Statistics. Available at: https://www.ons.gov.uk/economy/investmentspensionsandtrusts/bulletins/ownershipofukquotedshares/2018.

Parker, D. (1990). The 1988 Local Government Act and compulsory competitive tendering. *Urban Studies, 27*(5), 653–667.

Parker, D. (2004). *The UK's privatisation experiment: The passage of time permits a sober assessment.* CESifo working papers, no. 1126.

Petersen, O. H., Hjelmar, U., & Vrangbæk, K. (2018). Is contracting out of public services still the great panacea? A systematic review of studies on economic and quality effects from 2000 to 2014. *Social Policy and Administration, 52*(1), 130–157.

Peterson, E. B., and Connor, J. M. (1995). A comparison of oligopoly welfare loss estimates for US food manufacturing. *American Journal of Agricultural Economics*, *77*, 300–308.

PIQUE (2009). *Privatisation of public services and the impact on quality, employment and productivity (PIQUE): Summary report*. Available at: https://repository.mdx.ac.uk/download/58ef7e2befdb11d27bd0dac0b8f7d99324d7494a90f64a1a6546d258ba057985/778940/R1294.pdf

Prison Reform Trust (2021). *Bromley Briefings prison factfile: Winter 2021*. https://prisonreformtrust.org.uk/wp-content/uploads/2022/01/Bromley_Briefings_winter_2021.pdf

Privatization Barometer (2017). *Privatization Barometer report 2015/16*. Available at: https://assets.kpmg/content/dam/kpmg/it/pdf/2017/01/ThePBReport2015-2016.pdf

Rees, R. (1985). The theory of principal and agent. *Bulletin of Economic Research*, *37*(1 and 2), 3–26 and 75–97. https://doi.org/10.1111/j.1467-8586.1985.tb00185.x

Sheshinski, E., & López-Calva, L. F. (2003). Privatization and its benefits: Theory and evidence. *CESifo Economic Studies*, *49*(3), 429–459.

Shleifer, A. (1998). State versus private ownership. *Journal of Economic Perspectives*, *12*(4), 133–150.

Singer, P. W. (2007). *Corporate warriors: The rise of the privatized military industry* (2nd ed.). Cornell University Press.

Sterlacchini, A. (2012). Energy R&D in private and state-owned utilities: An analysis of the major world electric companies. *Energy Policy*, *41*, 494–506.

Tisdell, C. A. (2003). Efficient public provision of commodities: Transaction costs, bounded rationality and other considerations, University of Queensland working papers, no. 1742-2016-140702.

UK Parliament (2011). *Committee publishes report on Private Finance Initiative funding*. 19 August. https://committees.parliament.uk/committee/158/treasury-committee/news/177569/pfi-report/

UK Parliament (2021). *Foreign involvement in the defence supply chain*. Available at: https://publications.parliament.uk/pa/cm5801/cmselect/cmdfence/699/69902.htm

Vickers, J., & Yarrow, G. (1991). Economic perspectives on privatization. *Journal of Economic Perspectives*, *5*(2), 111–132.

Profit maximization for a monopolist

Firms maximize profits by producing at the point where their marginal revenue—the revenue raised from selling one additional unit of output—equals marginal cost, or the cost of producing that additional unit. For firms in perfectly competitive markets, their marginal revenue just equals the market price because they are price-takers.

For a monopolist, marginal revenue is less than the market price. As the sole supplier in the market, a monopolist faces a downward-sloping demand curve: to increase the quantity of output sold, the monopolist must lower its price, but it must lower it for all units of output sold. So the change in revenue when the firm sells an additional unit of output involves two components: an increase in revenue from the sale of one additional unit; a decrease in revenue because all units previously sold are now being sold at a lower price. So the marginal revenue earned from selling one additional unit will be less than the price at which that unit is sold.

Therefore the marginal revenue curve, *MR*, will lie below the demand curve, as illustrated in Figure 7.5.[43] The firm's profit-maximizing output level is given by Q_M, where marginal revenue equals marginal cost: $MR = MC$. Here we have assumed a constant marginal cost for simplicity. The price at which this output level is sold is given by the market demand curve, at P_M.

To work out the profits the firm earns, we need to look at the average cost of production, *AC*, which tells us the cost of producing each unit of output. The total revenue the firm earns from selling output level Q_M equals: $TR = P_M Q_M$; this is given by the rectangle $0P_MAQ_M$ in

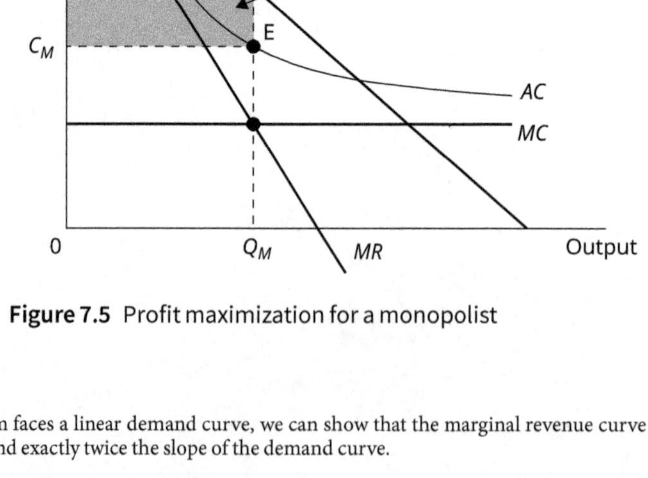

Figure 7.5 Profit maximization for a monopolist

[43] When the firm faces a linear demand curve, we can show that the marginal revenue curve will have the same vertical intercept and exactly twice the slope of the demand curve.

the figure. The total cost of producing this level of output equals the cost per unit multiplied by the level of output: $TC = C_M Q_M$, given by the rectangle $0C_M EQ_M$. Total profits equal the difference between total revenue and total costs, shown by the shaded area in Figure 7.5.

The welfare loss from monopoly

There is an efficiency or welfare loss associated with the monopolist's production decision because at the profit-maximizing level of output, Q_M, marginal benefit (as captured by the demand curve) is greater than marginal cost. As we saw in Chapter 2, efficiency is achieved where marginal benefit and marginal cost are equal. The efficiency loss or deadweight loss is captured by the shaded triangle ABC in Figure 7.6; the magnitude of this efficiency loss can be calculated by calculating the area of that triangle.

Efficiency could be increased by expanding output from Q_M to Q_C, where the marginal benefit from selling one additional unit juts equals the marginal cost of producing it. However, as we saw in the chapter, at output level Q_C the average cost of production is greater than the price at which the output would be sold, and therefore the firm would be making a loss.

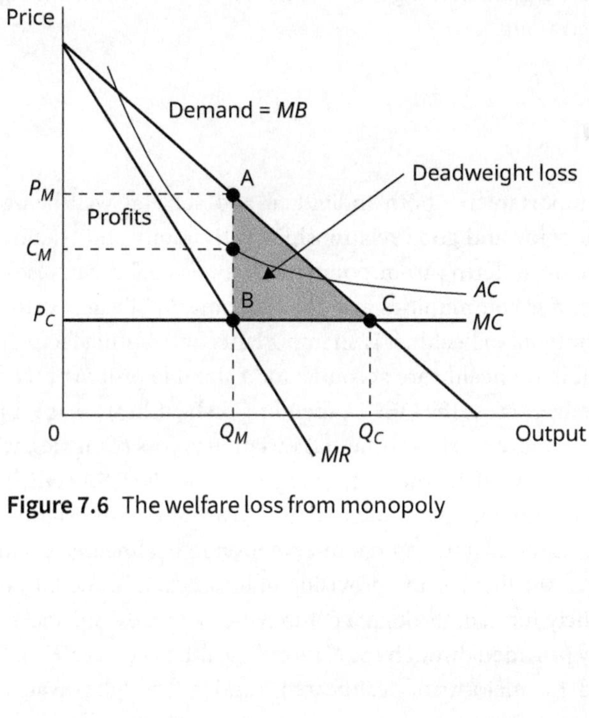

Figure 7.6 The welfare loss from monopoly

8
Healthcare

Learning objectives

By the end of this chapter, you will be able to:

8.1 Explain the objectives of the healthcare system and the challenges involved in measuring these in practice.
8.2 Discuss the arguments for government intervention in healthcare.
8.3 Explain the different ways in which governments intervene in healthcare and how these address the arguments for government intervention.
8.4 Discuss the implications of different types of government intervention for the performance of different healthcare systems.
8.5 Discuss the arguments for government intervention in the funding and/or provision of long-term care.

Introduction

Good health is important for both individual and societal well-being. Having a steady income, a job you enjoy and good relationships with family and friends will bring less life satisfaction if you are suffering from poor health. Poor health can also limit our ability to participate fully in our communities and the economy. While access to good healthcare is not the only determinant of health, it is an important contributing factor. Perhaps unsurprisingly, then, spending on healthcare accounts for a sizeable proportion of GDP across most countries. On average, across the OECD, spending on healthcare was 9.1 per cent of GDP in 2023. However, this figure masks substantial variation across countries, with spending ranging from 4.3 per cent of GDP in Turkey to 16.7 per cent in the USA (OECD, 2023c).

The extent of government involvement in healthcare also varies significantly across countries. When thinking about government intervention in healthcare, it is important to draw a distinction between the finance and provision of healthcare. In the UK, the vast majority of healthcare is publicly funded, through a combination of taxes and social security contributions, and publicly provided through the National Health Service (NHS). In the Netherlands, on the other hand, the majority of healthcare is funded through private insurance and provided by private hospitals and primary care providers, although the government plays a significant role in setting healthcare priorities and regulating and monitoring private providers. Why do governments intervene in healthcare? What do the different forms of government intervention imply for the performance of different healthcare systems?

These are the key questions we will be examining in this chapter. We start by discussing the main objectives of the healthcare system in section 8.1. In section 8.2, we analyse the economic arguments for government intervention in healthcare, and in section 8.3, we look at the different ways in which governments intervene and their implications. Section 8.4 reviews the structure and performance of the healthcare system in three countries: the UK, the USA, and the Netherlands. Section 8.5 briefly discusses the challenges affecting one particular branch of healthcare—long-term care.

8.1 Objectives of the healthcare system

Before we can discuss what the proper role of government in healthcare should be, we need to think about what the objectives of the healthcare system are. The primary aim of the healthcare system is to promote good health and, ultimately, it is good health that matters for well-being, rather than healthcare itself. Healthcare is just one component of health—albeit an important one. Good health depends on a range of other factors including individual lifestyle choices about diet and exercise, individual environments and living conditions, and genetic factors. A well-designed health policy should consider all of these factors, encompassing the diagnosis and treatment of illness, as well as preventive care and information and education about healthy lifestyle habits.

While good health is important for well-being, this does not mean that society should devote all of its resources to promoting good health. Resources are scarce and devoting more resources to healthcare means fewer resources will be available to spend in other areas, such as education. As we saw in Chapter 1, two important social objectives when considering the allocation of resources are efficiency and the promotion of equity or social justice. In this section, we explore each of these objectives and what they mean in the context of healthcare.

8.1.1 Efficiency

Because resources are scarce, we want to ensure that they are used efficiently. In economics, an allocation of resources is efficient if there is no way to change this allocation to make at least one person better off without making anyone else worse off. This is the concept of Pareto or allocative efficiency that we discussed in Chapter 2. In a partial equilibrium context, where we are focusing on a single market, the efficient quantity of a good is given by the point where the value society places on one additional unit of the good—the social marginal benefit (SMB)—just equals the cost of producing it, or social marginal cost (SMC). Applying this concept in the context of healthcare, we might ask, for example, whether a particular hospital should hire an extra 100 nurses. In order to answer this question, we would want to compare the social marginal benefit of hiring these extra nurses with the social marginal cost of doing so; if the SMB is greater than the SMC, then the hospital should hire these additional nurses. In fact, if the goal is to hire the optimal number of nurses, the hospital should continue hiring more nurses up to the point where SMB equals SMC.

More generally, allocative efficiency is concerned with whether we are producing the optimal quantity, quality, and combination of healthcare services.[1] It includes both **macro-efficiency**, which focuses on the size of the healthcare sector relative to the rest of the

[1] This is captured by the three conditions required for allocative efficiency discussed in Chapter 2, section 2.2.3: efficiency in consumption, efficiency in production, and efficiency in product mix.

economy, comparing the allocation of resources to healthcare versus resources allocated to other areas, such as education or public infrastructure; and **micro-efficiency**, which focuses on how resources are allocated within the healthcare sector—for example, whether more resources should be devoted to training nurses or to buying additional MRI scanners. Allocative efficiency also encompasses **productive efficiency**, which focuses on the actual running of medical institutions and whether healthcare goods and services are being produced with the optimal combination of inputs to ensure maximum output for the minimum cost.[2]

Assessing efficiency in healthcare requires a measure of the costs and benefits of different resource allocations. While measuring costs is generally straightforward, measuring benefits is often more challenging. Going back to our earlier example, we could measure the cost of hiring an extra 100 nurses based on the salaries they would be paid, alongside any other financial benefits, and recruitment and administrative costs. But how should we measure the benefits that hiring these additional 100 nurses will provide?

The main benefits of healthcare expenditure are improvements in health, so the question then becomes: how should we measure health and how should we value improvements in health? Traditional health indicators include measures such as life expectancy, infant mortality rates, and the incidence of certain diseases such as cancer or diabetes. As a general measure of improvements in health, life expectancy is a useful but imperfect measure, as it is not just the quantity of additional years of life that matters but also their quality—one extra year of life in good health is not the same as an extra year of life in poor health. For this reason, evaluations of medical interventions and technologies typically use quality-adjusted life-years (QALYs), a measure which combines the quantity and quality of life lived. One QALY is equivalent to one year of life in perfect health.

Another challenge involves how to value improvements in health. What is the monetary value of one additional year in good health, for example? There is no straightforward answer to this question. The benefits of improved health include both economic benefits (e.g. the potential for higher output and earnings if healthier workers are more productive) and individual well-being benefits (e.g. from reduced pain or suffering), and the latter are much harder to quantify. We discussed some of the difficulties involved in measuring intangible benefits in Chapter 5, including the particular challenges involved in placing a monetary value on human life and some of the methods that are used to do this. These include wage-based measures, which value human life based on potential lifetime earnings; contingent valuation measures, which are based on asking people how much they would be willing to pay for an increase or decrease in the probability of death in hypothetical scenarios; and measures that infer the value of a human life based on choices that individuals make that involve a change in the probability of death (e.g. paying to have smoke alarms fitted in their homes or how much more individuals need to be paid to accept a riskier job). Each of these methods has its advantages and limitations, and they tend to arrive at different estimates of the value of a human life.[3]

In spite of the difficulties in measuring the benefits from healthcare, having these measures is important to help ensure consistency in policy decision-making and to guide decisions about how to prioritize health expenditures.[4] Given the range of empirical estimates,

[2] In the context of healthcare, productive efficiency is sometimes referred to as internal efficiency, in contrast to allocative efficiency, which is referred to as external efficiency.

[3] See Chapter 5, section 5.3.2.

[4] In Chapter 5 we discussed particular tools for policy evaluation that mitigate these challenges to some extent, by not requiring monetary measures of benefits—see section 5.5. Two of these tools, cost-effectiveness analysis and cost-utility analysis, are widely used in healthcare policy evaluation.

Box 8.1 How much to save a life?

How much would we be willing to pay to save a life or to reduce the risk of death by 1 per cent? Although some may argue that human life is priceless and trying to place a monetary value on it is immoral, answers to these questions are implicit in decisions that are made about health spending. Making these answers explicit helps ensure transparency in policy decision-making and helps guide decisions about how to prioritize expenditures. In England, these sorts of questions are regularly considered by the National Institute for Health and Care Excellence (NICE), a public body that was set up by the UK government in 1999 with the aim of assessing the clinical effectiveness of healthcare interventions and providing guidance to public healthcare professionals. NICE was originally set up to attempt to counteract the 'post-code lottery' of healthcare in England and Wales, whereby the treatments that were available to patients often depended on where they lived, since they were decided by the local health authorities. NICE's remit has subsequently been extended to cover social care.

NICE provides independent evidence-based guidance on what medical treatments should be available on the NHS, the UK's publicly funded healthcare system. This inevitably requires a value to be placed on lives saved and improvements in health. NICE makes use of QALYs to compare the effectiveness of different drugs and other medical technologies. The threshold value for treatments to be recommended for use on the NHS is between £20,000 and £30,000 per QALY—above this level, treatments are less likely to be recommended (NICE, 2025).

governments will often set values based on a combination of evidence and expert guidance. Box 8.1 provides an illustration for the UK.

8.1.2 Equity

Another objective of the healthcare system is that it should be equitable or fair. But what do we mean by equity or fairness in the context of healthcare? We discussed some of the different concepts of equity in Chapters 1 and 2. In the context of healthcare, it is useful to draw a distinction between equity in the delivery or provision of healthcare and equity in the finance of healthcare. In the provision of healthcare, the focus has tended to be on **horizontal equity** or the 'equal treatment of equals'.[5] Four concepts of equity are often employed:

- **Equal treatment for equal need**: the principle of equal treatment for equal need embodies the notion of full equality—that individuals with the same healthcare needs should receive the same level of treatment and other factors are deemed irrelevant, such as their income, gender, and ethnicity. This concept is intuitively appealing and it is implicit in the healthcare system of many countries. It acknowledges that healthcare expenditure should take into account differences in individual need—society should not devote the same amount of resources to a healthy individual as to someone with a chronic health

[5] The discussion of the various concepts of equity in this section is necessarily brief. See Wagstaff and Van Doorslaer (2000) and other suggestions for further reading at the end of the chapter for a more comprehensive discussion.

condition—and that receipt of medical treatment should not be constrained by ability to pay. However, there is a difficulty in defining precisely what is meant by 'need' or 'treatment'—for example, does equality refer to the quantity of treatment or the value of healthcare to the individual?[6] The concept also ignores the fact individuals may have different preferences over their consumption of healthcare or may value their health differently.

- **Equality of access**: there are different interpretations of 'access', but one widely used interpretation views equality of access as the requirement that individuals should face the same prices or costs when accessing healthcare (Le Grand, 1987). These costs include both monetary and time costs—for example, payments for treatments, lost earnings from having to take time off work to attend appointments, and the cost of travel and waiting times. This equity principle allows for differences in individual preferences over how much healthcare to consume.
- **A minimum standard of treatment for all**: this concept requires that everyone, regardless of income or other characteristics, should have access to the same minimum standard of healthcare. Some individuals may choose to consume more or better healthcare, so this concept is compatible with unequal treatment for equal needs and unequal access to healthcare (beyond the minimum standard).
- **Equality of health or equality of outcomes**: promoting equality of health or eliminating health inequalities is often seen as the ultimate equity goal of health policy. However, health depends on a number of factors, including lifestyle and environmental factors, so eliminating all health inequalities is unlikely to be feasible in practice. Arguably, what matters is not whether everyone achieves the same level of health, but that everyone has the opportunity to achieve the same level of health. Ensuring equality of access or equal treatment for equal need can provide a path to promoting equality of health.

These concepts of equity have different implications for how the government should intervene in healthcare markets, and they are not necessarily mutually compatible. Two individuals may face the same personal costs of accessing healthcare, and may have the same level of need, but may nonetheless receive different levels of treatment because of differences in the perceived benefits of healthcare. For example, an individual with a lower level of education may perceive the benefits of healthcare to be lower and therefore might not seek medical treatment. This would imply equality of access, but also unequal treatment for equal need.

In the finance of healthcare, the focus has tended to be on **vertical equity** or the extent to which payments for healthcare vary with individual ability to pay and whether the finance of the healthcare system is progressive or regressive. If healthcare is financed through a **progressive tax system**, where tax rates rise with income, and everyone (both high- and low-income individuals) consumes the same amount of healthcare, then the health system acts as an equalizing force and redistributes from higher-income to lower-income individuals.

Measuring equity in healthcare is challenging, given the difficulties in measuring health and in measuring inequalities in the distribution of health.[7] Approaches to measuring inequalities in healthcare generally aim to distinguish what are considered 'appropriate' or 'fair' inequalities from 'inappropriate' or 'unfair' inequalities, in order to account for differences in

[6] See, for example, Le Grand (1987) and Wagstaff and van Doorslaer (2000).
[7] See Propper (2024) for a discussion of these challenges.

individual needs and preferences for healthcare. This involves making assumptions about the extent to which individuals with different needs or preferences should be treated differently, which can be problematic. It is also difficult to obtain data on individual healthcare needs.

Measuring vertical equity in healthcare is further complicated by the difficulty in measuring the incidence of various taxes and benefits. If a country has a progressive tax system and healthcare is publicly funded and provided free at the point of use, in principle the system should redistribute from higher-income to lower-income individuals. However, this will depend on whether high- and low-income individuals consume the same amount of healthcare in practice. A study by Le Grand (2018) found that, in England, the top socioeconomic group received a greater proportion of NHS expenditure per person reporting an illness than the bottom group, suggesting that high-income and low-income individuals do not consume healthcare equally.

8.2 Arguments for government intervention

Having reviewed the main objectives of the healthcare system, the next question we want to consider is whether the market system alone can achieve these objectives or whether some form of government intervention in healthcare is necessary. It is sometimes argued that governments should intervene in healthcare because access to adequate healthcare is a basic human right, as laid out in Article 25 of the Universal Declaration of Human Rights.[8] However, food, clothing, and housing are also basic human rights, but these goods are typically not provided by the government. What is it about the nature of healthcare that warrants government intervention?

When thinking about the arguments for government intervention in healthcare, it is useful to start by taking a step back and considering what a competitive private market for healthcare, with no government intervention, would look like (see Box 8.2). In this section, we will first analyse the extent to which a market system for healthcare will be efficient, before turning to the question of whether such a system is compatible with achieving equity in healthcare.

Box 8.2 The libertarian view of healthcare

Governments intervene in healthcare in the majority of countries across the world today, although the nature of this intervention varies considerably across countries and is often the subject of strong political debate. What would a competitive private market for healthcare with no government intervention look like?

- Patients seeking healthcare would be charged a price which would depend on the type and length of treatment, and they would be required to pay for this themselves, either directly or through private insurance.
- Patients would be free to choose which doctor or hospital to go to for treatment (provided they could pay).

(Continued)

[8] Article 25, point 1 reads: 'Everyone has the right to a standard of living adequate for the health and well-being of himself and of his family, including food, clothing, housing and medical care and necessary social services, and the right to security in the event of unemployment, sickness, disability, widowhood, old age or other lack of livelihood in circumstances beyond his control' (United Nations, 1948).

- There would be no mandatory health insurance. People would be free to take out private health insurance if they could pay for it and as long as there was a provider willing to insure them.[9] People without health insurance would need to pay for any medical costs directly, or forgo medical care.
- Doctors and hospitals would be free to maximize profits.

Would this system be efficient? Would it be equitable?

8.2.1 Government intervention to increase efficiency

As we saw in Chapter 2, markets will only lead to an efficient allocation of resources under a fairly strict set of conditions, known as the first-best conditions. These include perfect competition, perfect information, and the absence of externalities or public goods.[10] In healthcare, several of these conditions are likely to fail and therefore a pure market system for healthcare is unlikely to be efficient. We are going to focus on four key market failures in healthcare: imperfect information, bounded rationality and bounded willpower; asymmetric information and incomplete insurance; externalities; and imperfect competition. We discuss each of these problems below.

Imperfect information, bounded rationality, and bounded willpower

Individual choices will maximize welfare if individuals are well informed about the nature of the product and their preferences when making decisions. In healthcare, however, people might be ill without being aware of it, or they might not fully understand the nature of their health problems, and individuals will often lack information about the treatments available and the outcomes of different treatments. So individuals are likely to have imperfect information about the quantity of healthcare they need and the quality of the healthcare available.

Unlike other areas where individuals may have incomplete information—for example, when buying food or household appliances—in healthcare there is limited scope for learning from experience as treatments are typically not repeated. If you break your leg and are dissatisfied with the quality of care provided by your doctor or orthopaedic surgeon, you are unlikely to have the need to find a different orthopaedic surgeon (unless you are very unlucky and break your leg again).[11] There is limited scope for patients to shop around in most cases. If you have broken your leg or suffered some other injury, you are likely to want to get medical treatment as quickly as possible, rather than spending time researching the different healthcare providers available and reading patient reviews. These reviews may also be of limited value, given the individual nature of many health problems and treatments. The cost of making a mistake is also higher in healthcare than in other areas. Choosing a poor-quality healthcare provider or relying on an unqualified doctor for advice could be a matter of life or death.

Patients often rely on doctors and other healthcare professionals for information, which gives these professionals some degree of monopoly power. The ease with which information

[9] This could be a problem for some people, particularly those with pre-existing medical conditions.

[10] See Chapter 2, section 2.2.4.

[11] This argument may not apply to the same extent to more general health services, such as family doctor or GP services.

can now be accessed and disseminated on the internet has reduced the costs of acquiring information. However, information about health and healthcare treatments is often complex and patients' lack of medical expertise can make it difficult for them to assess the information provided, limiting individual choice. Individuals are therefore unlikely to be able to collect and process all relevant information before making a decision that maximizes their utility. Instead, individual choices in healthcare are likely to be characterized by bounded rationality,[12] which recognizes the limited cognitive resources and time that people have to process all this information.

In matters of health, emotions play a big role and may cloud individual decisions. Upon receiving a cancer diagnosis, for example, most people would probably find it difficult to weigh up the costs and benefits of different courses of treatment and different treatment providers, who may present the relevant information in slightly different ways, to make a fully informed decision; and speed in making a decision may be vital. Health problems are very emotionally charged and fear or anxiety may lead individuals to procrastinate and delay seeking treatment. These problems of bounded willpower reflect the fact that, even if individuals know what the welfare-maximizing decision is (i.e. go to the doctor to discuss a health concern, do the necessary tests), they may fail to act accordingly.

Problems of imperfect information, bounded rationality, and bounded willpower limit individuals' ability to make fully informed rational choices when it comes to healthcare and may result in either underconsumption or overconsumption of healthcare. Individuals may underestimate the severity of their health condition and therefore not go and see a doctor, leading to underconsumption. Alternatively, anxiety about their health may lead them to visit their doctor more often than necessary, resulting in an overconsumption of healthcare. Both of these outcomes are inefficient, since in both cases individual estimates of their demand or private marginal benefits from the consumption of healthcare do not reflect their true marginal benefit. Both these scenarios are illustrated in Figure 8.1, where *PMB*

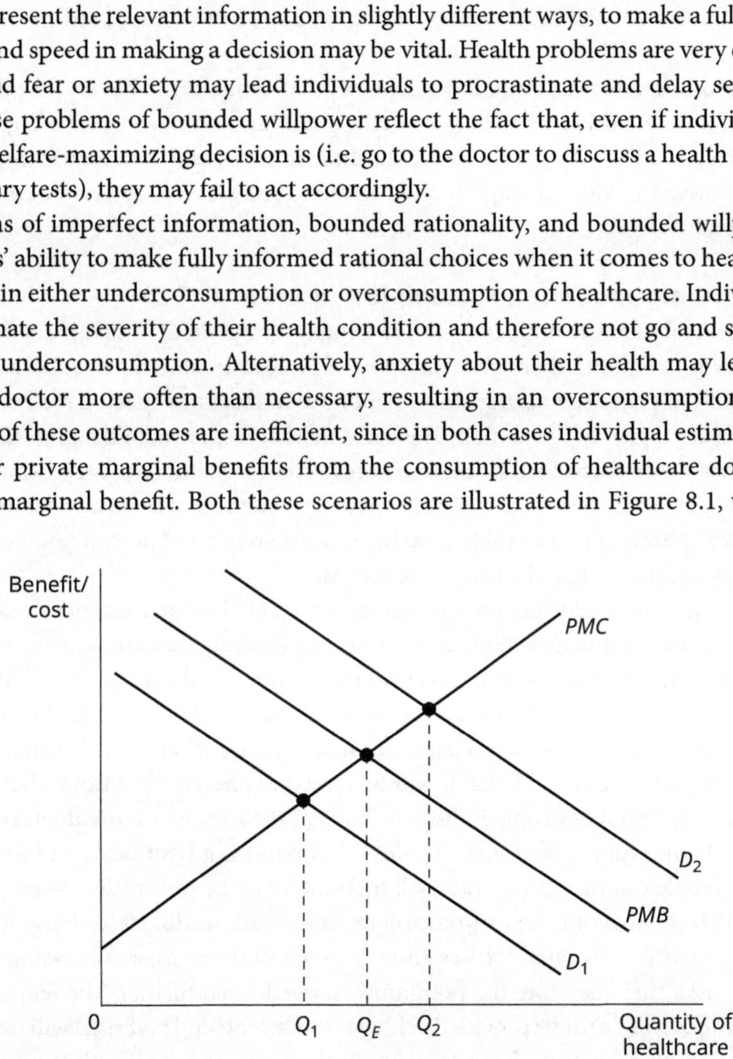

Figure 8.1 Imperfect information, bounded rationality, and the equilibrium quantity of healthcare

[12] See discussion of bounded rationality and bounded willpower in Chapter 2, section 2.3.4.

represents the 'true' private marginal benefit of healthcare consumption. Given the private marginal cost of healthcare represented by *PMC*, the optimal quantity of healthcare is Q_E. However, problems of imperfect information and bounded rationality may lead to individual demands that are either lower (D_1) or higher (D_2) than the 'true' (i.e. fully informed) demand for healthcare, resulting in an equilibrium quantity of healthcare that is lower or higher than the optimal level.

Doctors, in turn, have their own incentives: if they are paid for each treatment, they may have an incentive to overprescribe treatments to increase their revenues; whereas if they are paid for each patient seen, they may have an incentive to underprescribe treatment to maximize the number of patients they treat. It is important to keep in mind, however, that doctors are not necessarily driven purely by financial motives and many would place patient care above money or profits, as well as having an incentive to build and maintain a good reputation.

Problems of imperfect information also mean that competition between healthcare providers will not necessarily lead to better-quality goods and services. Since many individuals may be unable to judge the quality of the healthcare services they are receiving, providers have an incentive to reduce quality in order to offer their services at a lower cost and maximize their profits.

Asymmetric information and incomplete insurance

Demand for healthcare is inherently unpredictable—in general, individuals do not know when they will fall ill and therefore when they will need treatment. It is therefore difficult for individuals to plan their saving and expenditure to meet unexpected medical costs, and medical bills are typically substantial. The usual market response for dealing with problems of uncertainty is insurance. So the question here becomes whether a private health insurance market will operate efficiently. There are two main problems that arise: adverse selection and moral hazard.[13] Both of these problems arise because an insured person knows more about their health and actions than the insurance company.

The problem of adverse selection arises in the context of health insurance because it is difficult for insurance companies to identify good risks (healthy individuals who are less likely to need medical treatment) and bad risks (unhealthy individuals who are more likely to need treatment and therefore cost the insurance company more). This is why problems of adverse selection are often referred to as problems of hidden information. If the insurance company cannot identify good and bad risks, it will be forced to charge a premium that reflects the average risk in the pool of people it insures. Some of the healthier individuals may find this premium to be too high, given their likelihood of requiring treatment, and may therefore decide not to take out insurance. This will then increase the proportion of bad risks being insured, which will drive up the insurance company's costs, leading it to charge a higher premium. This, in turn, may push further good risks out of the market, increasing the proportion of bad risks, and therefore the premiums charged, even further. The end result is that health insurance will be underprovided, which is inefficient, and bad risks will face very high insurance premiums. This also has equity implications, since poor health is often correlated with income.

[13] These concepts were introduced in Chapter 2, section 2.3.3, which includes a discussion of the conditions required for private insurance markets to operate efficiently.

In practice, insurance companies can and do collect information on individuals before providing insurance, and the cost of insurance premiums is typically tied to individual risks. This means that good risks will typically face lower premiums, whereas bad risks are likely to face higher insurance costs or, in some cases, be unable to buy health insurance. There is also scope for **cream-skimming**, whereby private healthcare providers or insurers weed out individuals who are more likely to require treatment (the bad risks), based on their medical histories. Developments in genetic testing could lead to more uninsurable health conditions in the future, by providing insurers with more information about future health conditions (Barr, 2001).

Moral hazard problems are usually referred to as problems of hidden action. They arise in the context of healthcare because the health insurance company is unable to observe the actions of the individuals it insures, and these individuals have an incentive to change their behaviour once they are covered by insurance, resulting in an increase in the insurer's costs. There are essentially three sources of moral hazard problems in health insurance: patients can affect the probability of needing treatment (i.e. by taking less care of their health); patients can affect the cost of healthcare by choosing to consume more healthcare (e.g. by deciding to visit their doctor more often, or through other choices, such as pregnancy); lastly, there is the risk of a **third-party payment problem**. This arises when the insurance company is separate from doctors and patients, and doctors are paid a fee for service. If health insurance covers all patient costs, then healthcare is essentially free at the point of use and patients do not face the true costs of the healthcare they consume. They therefore have an incentive to overconsume healthcare. If doctors are paid a fee for service, they will have an incentive to overprescribe treatments in order to increase the payment they receive from the insurance company. These two effects combined will lead to an overconsumption of healthcare, increasing the insurance provider's costs.[14] Evidence suggests the scale of these moral hazard problems can be significant (see Box 8.3).

Box 8.3 Evidence of moral hazard in health insurance

A number of empirical studies have found that health insurance coverage is associated with an increase in healthcare spending. An early study by Newhouse (1993) looked at the RAND Health Insurance Experiment carried out in the USA in the late 1970s. This experiment varied the degree of consumer cost-sharing across roughly 2,000 families to explore what impact it would have on health spending and health. The results suggest that, when comparing individuals with full health insurance to individuals who had to pay a large deductible, those with full health insurance coverage had healthcare costs which were on average 40 per cent higher, with no significant difference in health outcomes on average. Individuals on low incomes and those with chronic conditions did, however, see an improvement in their health with free healthcare.

(Continued)

[14] One approach to addressing this particular moral hazard problem that is widely used in the USA is through health maintenance organizations (HMOs). These organizations effectively combine the activities of doctors and health insurance companies. Individuals pay a fixed annual fee to their HMO, which in return offers a range of medical services.

More recently, Finkelstein et al. (2012) analysed evidence from the 2008 Oregon Health Insurance Experiment. As part of this experiment, a group of low-income adults without health insurance was selected by lottery to be given the chance to apply for Medicaid.[15] The study found that having access to Medicaid led to an average increase in healthcare spending of $775 in the first year and this increase in spending was seen across different types of healthcare, including hospital admissions, primary care, and preventive care.

Evidence also suggests that healthcare systems which rely heavily on private finance and have few mechanisms in place to limit third-party payment problems tend to have higher rates of treatment, but these are not reflected in improved health outcomes. So both theory and evidence suggest that moral hazard problems do lead to overconsumption of healthcare.

The problem of moral hazard in private health insurance is illustrated in Figure 8.2. If the individual does not have health insurance and faces the full cost of medical care, given by the social marginal cost curve (*SMC*), the equilibrium quantity of healthcare demanded is Q_1. However, if they have health insurance and only have to pay P_2 for each unit of healthcare (e.g. each visit to the doctor), their private marginal cost is given by *PMC* and the equilibrium quantity of healthcare demanded rises to Q_2. Here P_2 is an example of a **co-payment** or 'co-pay', a fixed amount that individuals are required to pay upfront for medical services, as part of their health insurance coverage. This outcome is inefficient as the private marginal benefit from consuming this level of healthcare is less than the social marginal cost of providing it. The size of the inefficiency, or deadweight loss, is captured by the shaded triangle in the figure.

Figure 8.2 also illustrates the third-party payment problem. Given the demand for healthcare and the social marginal cost of providing healthcare illustrated (*SMC*), the optimal level of healthcare is Q_1. However, if both the patient and doctor face zero private costs, then they would choose to consume at Q_3, which again is above the efficient level. In general, the fact

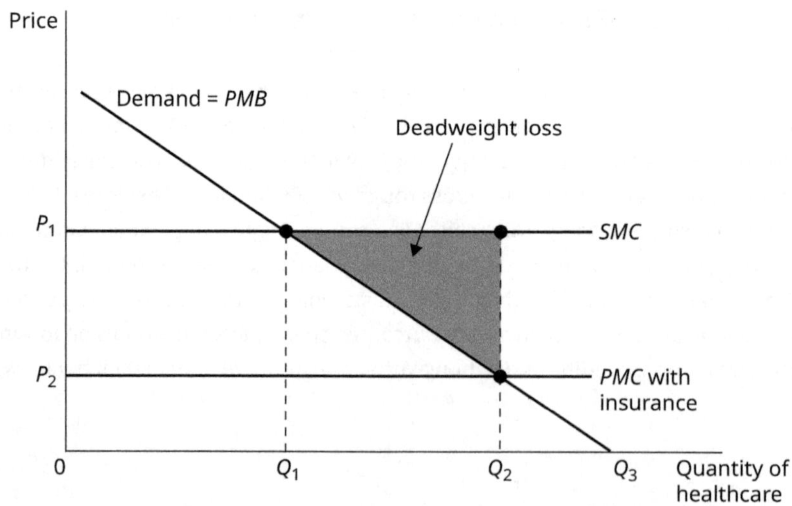

Figure 8.2 Moral hazard in private health insurance markets

[15] Medicaid is the public health insurance programme for individuals on low incomes in the USA.

that doctors have more information than patients can lead to supplier-induced demand, where patients are encouraged to buy more medical care than required. This can be compounded if the medical profession is not regulated and there are no restrictions on who can call themselves a doctor.

Solutions for dealing with moral hazard problems typically involve insurance companies limiting the cover provided—for example, through **deductibles** (where patients pay the first £x of any claim) or through **co-insurance** (where patients are liable for x per cent of any claim). In both cases, because patients are required to meet some of their healthcare costs, the quantity of healthcare demanded should fall, as we saw in Figure 8.2 above. At price P_2, healthcare is still provided to the patient below the social marginal cost, so the quantity of healthcare consumed, Q_2, is above the efficient level, but it is below the level that would prevail in the absence of any cost containment mechanism (i.e. if the price of healthcare were zero). This solution has implications for equity, particularly if those on lower incomes are less likely to be able to afford the deductibles or co-pays, and therefore consume less healthcare. So here there is a trade-off between efficiency (which would call for higher co-pays) and equity (calling for lower or no co-pays).

Externalities

As we saw in Chapter 2, externalities arise when an individual's action has an impact on other individuals and this impact is not reflected in the market price. Externalities cause a divergence between private and social costs and benefits, so the price of a good does not necessarily reflect its social value. As a result, the good in question will be either underprovided, in the case of a positive externality, or overprovided, in the case of a negative externality.

There are two main types of externalities that arise in the context of healthcare: technological externalities and **caring externalities**. An example of a technological externality is vaccination against communicable diseases: this protects the individual from the disease, thus providing a private benefit, but it also reduces the likelihood of other individuals getting that disease, and hence provides an external benefit. In general, individuals will only consider their private costs and benefits when making a decision. When deciding whether to get vaccinated or not, individuals will typically base their decision on whether the private benefit to them from the vaccine exceeds the cost they face. They will not take the wider external benefits into account and therefore the level of vaccination provided will be less than the efficient level.

Figure 8.3 illustrates the positive externalities associated with vaccination against communicable diseases and the inefficiency of the market outcome. The market equilibrium is given by point E, where private marginal benefit (*PMB*) and private marginal cost (*PMC*) are equal, and the equilibrium level of vaccination is Q_1. This is less than the socially optimal level of vaccination, Q_2. Because of the positive externalities associated with vaccination, social marginal benefit (*SMB*) is greater than private marginal benefit, and the socially optimal equilibrium is at point S. The shaded triangle captures the inefficiency of the market outcome: welfare would be increased by expanding the level of vaccination to Q_2, where social marginal benefit equals marginal cost.

It has been suggested that the magnitude of these technological externalities in developed countries is relatively small, and that they are more important in countries where communicable diseases are more prevalent. However, communicable diseases can re-emerge, as the rise in measles cases across Europe illustrates, and new communicable diseases can appear (e.g. Covid).

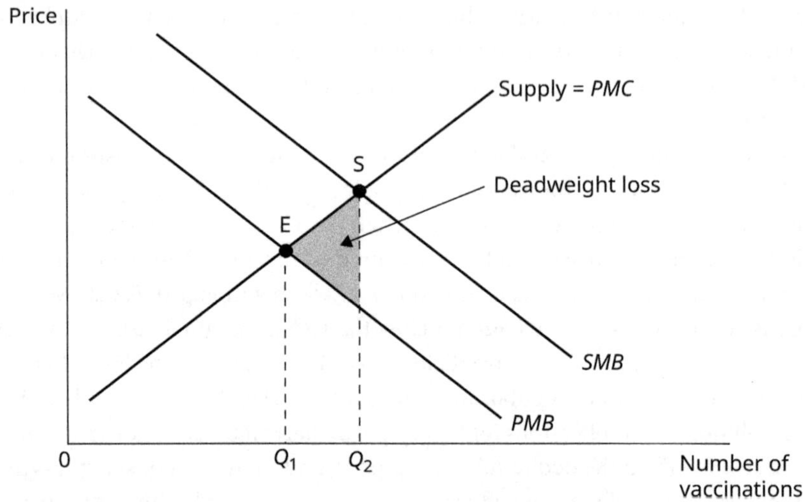

Figure 8.3 Positive externalities associated with vaccination

Caring externalities arise if people care about the well-being of others, so the utility of individuals who are healthy is affected by the level of healthcare consumed by those who are sick. Providing healthcare to individuals who are ill will therefore involve positive externalities and the equilibrium market outcome will again be inefficient. Arrow (1963) recognized the importance of caring externalities in the context of healthcare; however, determining the extent of these externalities in practice is challenging.

Imperfect competition

There are several reasons why a market for healthcare is unlikely to satisfy the assumptions required for perfect competition. There are both **returns to scale** and **returns to scope** in the provision of hospital services, which give hospitals some degree of monopoly power. There is also evidence of economies of scale in some medical treatments, as death rates for certain surgeries tend to fall with the number of surgeries practised (Connolly & Munro, 1999).

Doctors also have some monopoly power over the supply of healthcare, as they need to undergo a significant amount of training and, in most countries, only licensed individuals are allowed to practise medicine. This is compounded by the fact that most licensing bodies are run by doctors, so effectively they are self-governing.[16] Arrow (1963) argued this was effectively a cartel and would therefore lead to rises in the price of medical services. However, doctors are not driven purely by financial motives; they care about the welfare of their patients and their reputations. But if doctors do not face the true costs of their decisions (as illustrated by the third-party payment problem discussed above), this could lead to them overprescribing treatments, with a possible bias towards more interesting or glamorous treatments, which are more likely to enhance their reputations.

The problems of imperfect information discussed above also limit the effective amount of competition in healthcare. If patients lack information on the quality of treatments and

[16] For example, in the UK, the General Medical Council is responsible for maintaining the official register of medical practitioners within the country. It sets the standards for medical schools in the UK and can suspend or remove members if necessary.

Box 8.4 The opioid epidemic in the USA

The opioid epidemic is one of the biggest public health crises to affect the USA in recent decades. Between 1999 and 2022, it is estimated that nearly 727,000 people died from an opioid overdose in the country, and the number of opioid overdose deaths was 10 times higher in 2022 than in 1999 (CDC, 2024). The causes behind the rapid increase in the overuse and misuse of opioids, a class of highly addictive moderate to strong painkillers, are complex. Research suggests the main drivers include inadequate regulation, undue influence by pharmaceutical companies, the overprescription of opioids by medical professionals, and increased use of heroin and synthetic opioids.

An in-depth analysis of the practices of the manufacturer of one such drug, OxyContin, found evidence of aggressive marketing and promotion strategies. Between 1996 and 2000, the company more than doubled its sales force, from 318 sales representatives to 671, and a bonus system was used to encourage representatives to increase sales of OxyContin. More than 40 pain-management and speaker-training conferences were organized at resorts across the USA and these all-expenses-paid symposia were attended by over 5,000 physicians, pharmacists, and nurses. Sophisticated marketing data were also used to influence doctors' prescribing practices. Sales of OxyContin increased from $48 million in 1996 to almost $1.1 billion in 2000 (Van Zee, 2009).

The Stanford–Lancet Commission was launched in 2022 to help tackle the opioid crisis. It has proposed a number of measures, including better drug regulation, education, and restrictions on the prescription of opioids.

Sources: CDC (2024), The Lancet Regional Health—Americas (2023), and Van Zee (2009).

providers, it is harder for them to make price comparisons. For example, a lower-quality provider may be charging lower prices because they are struggling to attract patients. The range of medical treatments available makes price and quality comparisons even more challenging, and there is a risk that providers may sacrifice quality to maximize profits.

Of course, not all private hospitals operate on a for-profit basis, and most doctors care about the well-being of their patients, rather than being driven purely by financial goals. However, the opioid epidemic in the USA illustrates how dangerous market incentives in healthcare can be (see Box 8.4).

8.2.2 Government intervention to promote equity

Having reviewed the efficiency arguments for government intervention in healthcare, we now turn to the question of whether a pure market system for healthcare would be equitable. In the absence of any government intervention, individuals needing medical care would need to pay for this directly or, if available, pay for private health insurance. Their access to healthcare would therefore depend on their ability to pay. Insurance companies would be free to choose whom they insure and what prices they charge. In this section, we are going to explore what such a market system for healthcare would imply for each of the concepts of equity discussed above.

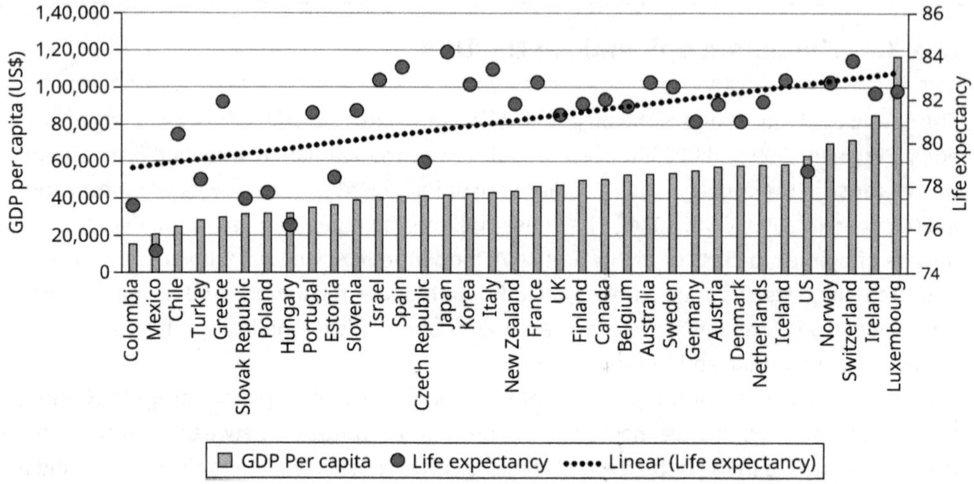

Figure 8.4 Life expectancy and GPD per capita (current PPPs), 2018
Sources: OECD (2023a, 2023d).

Income plays an important role in the distribution of health outcomes. Average life expectancy tends to be higher in countries with a higher GDP per capita, as Figure 8.4 illustrates. This relationship is also true within countries. In England, for example, the life expectancy for a woman living in the poorest areas is five years shorter than for a woman living in the wealthiest areas; for men, this difference is nine years (Watt et al., 2022). However, evidence suggests that income inequality may have a more powerful impact on health outcomes than income itself. Among developed countries, it is generally the most equal societies that have the best health, not necessarily the richest (Wilkinson & Pickett, 2010). The impact of income on health will be mediated by how the healthcare system is structured—in particular, what role the government plays in the finance and provision of healthcare.

A market system for healthcare is incompatible with the principle of equal treatment for equals needs. Because access to treatment depends on ability to pay, individuals on lower incomes are unlikely to receive the same medical care as individuals on higher incomes. Medical care is extremely expensive and medical bills are still a significant cause of financial hardship in the USA, where healthcare is mainly privately funded. In a recent study, 58.5 per cent of debtors in the USA cited medical expenses as a leading contributor to their bankruptcy (Himmelstein et al., 2019), and this is potentially aggravated by loss of work due to illness. Given the correlation between income and health, individuals from poorer backgrounds are likely to face higher health insurance premiums, which may further deter them from buying health insurance. Insurance companies may also refuse to sell insurance to individuals with pre-existing medical conditions.

A market system for healthcare is also unlikely to guarantee equality of access. Even if individuals face the same prices for healthcare, these prices will represent a proportionately larger share of income for low-income households. Other costs of accessing healthcare are also likely to be higher for lower-income individuals. For example, they are more likely to work in occupations that require them to take time off work—and to forgo earnings—to attend appointments or receive medical treatment. The costs of accessing healthcare do not just include the monetary costs: low-income individuals may face higher time costs, particularly if the nature of their lives means they are more heavily time constrained (Propper, 2024). Problems of imperfect information and unequal power are also likely to vary with individual incomes and socioeconomic background, and individuals from poorer backgrounds may be less well equipped to navigate complex healthcare systems and lobby healthcare providers to ensure they receive quality care.

Since the care that individuals have access to will depend on their ability to pay, a pure market system for healthcare is unlikely to guarantee a minimum standard of treatment or level of care for everyone.

In terms of vertical equity, a pure market system for healthcare where each individual pays for the care they receive through out-of-pocket payments or private insurance will be regressive, particularly if individuals from poorer backgrounds face higher insurance costs.

8.2.3 The role of giving and intrinsic motivation

Another argument for some form of government intervention in healthcare—or against a pure market system—is based on the impact that markets have on the nature of the things being traded and on the motivations of individuals who participate in those markets.[17] There is growing evidence to suggest that while a price mechanism can enhance efficiency in some areas, it may not always be morally appropriate and may end up creating inefficiencies.

In the context of healthcare, the argument was originally proposed by Titmuss (1970), who argued that a system of voluntary blood donation like the one that existed in the UK at the time was both morally and economically superior to the US system, where most blood donors were paid. Intuitively, we may expect that by offering payment for something, we encourage more people to supply it, particularly if the marginal cost of doing so is relatively low, as is generally the case with donating blood. However, by introducing a payment, we also change the incentives that people face, encouraging self-interest over altruism, and discouraging individuals from doing something simply because they believe it to be right or a good thing to do. Another interesting example to consider, with added complexities, is organ donation (see Box 8.5).

Humans are not just motivated by monetary incentives; we also do things because we think it is right or because they make us feel good—for example, we might get a warm feeling from helping a neighbour with their shopping. The former is an example of **extrinsic motivation**, where external factors or rewards (e.g. payment, praise, or fame) drive individual actions; whereas the latter reflects the role of **intrinsic motivations**, where internal rewards (e.g. enjoyment or a sense of what is right) influence individual behaviour. Extrinsic motivation can crowd out intrinsic motivation: offering monetary incentives to donate blood, for example, encourages people who want to make money out of donating blood to come forward, but it may at the same discourage people who would donate blood voluntarily from doing so—for them, receiving payment may taint the act of giving blood, so that they no longer derive the same satisfaction from doing so (Frey, 1997). Le Grand (1997) suggests there are different

[17] See, for example, Sandel (2012) on the moral limits of markets and how paying people to do something they might otherwise do for free changes the value of that activity.

Box 8.5 Should we pay for organ donations?

Across the world, countries are struggling with a shortage of organs for donation. According to the Global Observatory on Donation and Transplantation, only 10 per cent of global demand for transplants is being met (Global Observatory on Donation and Transplantation, 2024). The suggestion that paying for organ donations could help address these shortages has been debated for some time; however, there is widespread resistance to this idea, even in cases where live donations are possible, as is the case with kidney donations.

There are concerns that paying for organ donations risks objectifying these exchanges, putting organs into a class of impersonal objects that they should not belong to. Monetizing these transactions might end up crowding out altruistic donations, resulting in a reduction of the supply of organs for transplantation. Offering monetary incentives is also potentially coercive and may leave some individuals, particular those on lower incomes, open to exploitation or feeling as if they have no choice but to donate.

Critics of these views argue that many of the risks could be mitigated by appropriate market regulation. However, there are alternatives to payment that have proved successful in increasing organ donations. Spain has one of the highest deceased donor rates in the world. This success has been attributed to having an opt-out system where everyone is an organ donor by default, as well as strong clinical leadership and a solid legislative framework based on transparency and an equitable organ allocation across regions. In the context of live organ donations, the kidney exchange programme pioneered by the Nobel economics laureate Alvin Roth, together with Tayfun Sönmez and Utku Ünver, has led to a dramatic increase in kidney donations across the world. Under this scheme, pairs of kidney donors who are incompatible are put together with other incompatible pairs so that everyone who is donating a kidney can find a matching recipient.

Sources: Roth (2007), Roth et al. (2004), and The Lancet (2024).

types of people and their different motivations should be taken into account in policymaking: 'knights' are public-spirited altruists who are motivated by intrinsic rewards and a desire to help others; 'knaves' are essentially self-interested and motivated by monetary rewards. Changing rewards will attract more knaves and fewer knights.

Introducing a payment for something that some people were willing to provide for free can have an impact on quality. Going back to our blood donation example, if a person is willing to donate their blood for free, presumably because they want to help others, they have little incentive not to reveal its quality and are unlikely to make a donation if they know they have a medical condition that can be transmitted through blood transfusions, such as HIV/Aids or hepatitis. If individuals are donating blood because they are getting paid for it, then they have an incentive to conceal if it is poor quality, with potentially devastating consequences, as illustrated by the contaminated blood scandal of the 1970s and 1980s.[18]

[18] Several countries struggling to meet demand for blood-clotting treatments imported blood supplies from the USA. Many of these were bought from high-risk donors (e.g. drug users and prison inmates) and at the time blood donations were not routinely screened for viruses such as hepatitis C and, later, HIV. As a result, many countries imported contaminated blood products and used these in treatments.

If the marginal cost of providing the good is also low or close to zero, as is typically the case with blood donations, then having a system of voluntary donations is also more efficient. But this will not be true in general as the marginal cost of providing most healthcare goods and service is significant.

8.3 Types of government intervention

As we have seen, there are strong arguments for some form of government intervention in healthcare, but what form should this intervention take? Governments intervene in healthcare in virtually all countries in the world today; however, the extent and nature of that intervention varies significantly across countries. This section will focus on the different ways in which governments intervene in healthcare, the main arguments behind these interventions, and their implications. We consider three broad types of government intervention: finance, production, and regulation.

8.3.1 Public finance

The finance of healthcare refers to the manner in which the goods and services provided by the healthcare sector are paid for. The main sources of finance of healthcare include: government spending, either through general or local taxes, or social insurance schemes; private health insurance, which may be mandatory or voluntary; and out-of-pocket payments.[19] The majority of OECD countries have some form of national health insurance or statutory health insurance,[20] but these schemes can be operated by the public sector, the private sector, or some combination of the two. Within publicly funded healthcare systems, it is important to distinguish schemes that are funded primarily through taxes, such as the UK system, and those which are funded through social insurance. Under social insurance schemes, benefits are partly related to the contributions that individuals make, whereas in tax-funded systems, entitlement to benefits does not depend on contributions.

Figure 8.5 shows how healthcare is financed across a selection of OECD countries, illustrating the varying degrees of government intervention. Government and compulsory financing schemes account for between 62 per cent of all spending on health in Greece and 86.7 per cent in Germany. Within these schemes, the balance between public and private funding varies widely. For example, in both the UK and the Netherlands, government and compulsory schemes account for over 80 per cent of all healthcare spending. However, whereas in the UK the majority of healthcare is publicly funded through taxation and National Insurance contributions, which accounts for 81.5 per cent of all spending on healthcare, in the Netherlands all residents are required to buy health insurance from private providers. Healthcare funding does include a payroll tax on employers, general tax revenues and government grants, but this accounts for only 10 per cent of healthcare spending.

[19] Out-of-pocket payments (OOPs) are direct payments that individuals make to healthcare providers when healthcare is accessed. For example, if you had to pay £30 to visit your GP, this would constitute an out-of-pocket payment. OOPs are usually not reimbursed.

[20] The USA is currently the only high-income country which lacks universal health coverage.

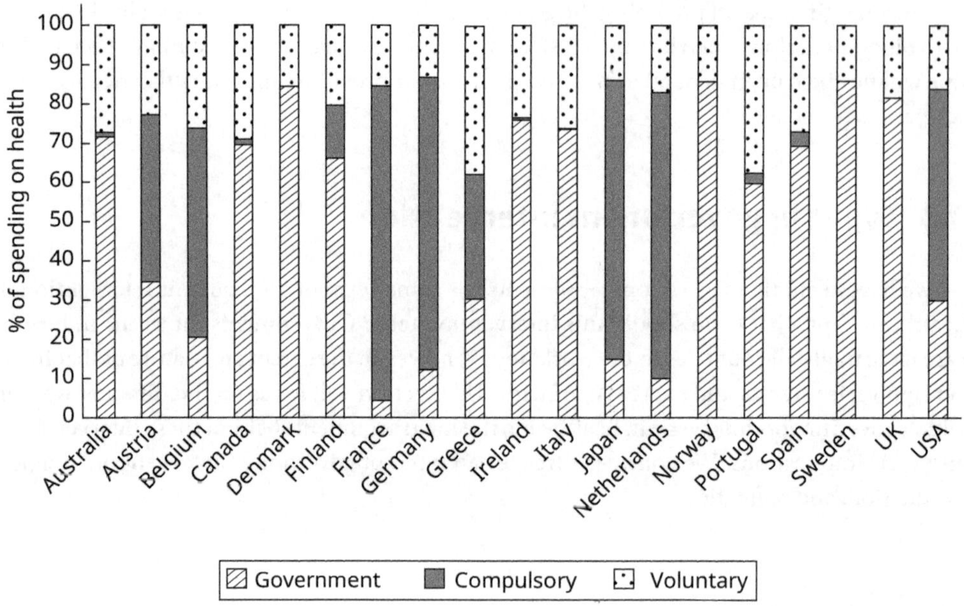

Figure 8.5 Components of health spending in the OECD, 2022
Note: Voluntary schemes include out-of-pocket payments.
Source: OECD (2025a).

The main arguments for some form of government intervention in the finance of healthcare are based on the problem of adverse selection discussed above, as well as equity considerations. Adverse selection problems can be overcome either through mandatory participation in private health insurance schemes or through government-funded schemes. Publicly funded schemes are generally more equitable, particularly if they are financed through progressive taxes, since individual contributions are tied to their ability to pay, but their consumption of healthcare is not. Under a publicly funded system, income does not act as a barrier to accessing healthcare in the same way as it does under a privately funded system.[21]

In schemes with mandatory private insurance, governments will typically regulate health insurance providers—for example, requiring them to accept all applicants, setting caps on the premiums that can be charged, and preventing them from charging higher premiums for pre-existing medical conditions.[22] Voluntary private health insurance schemes are the least equitable, since the benefits received are proportional to the premiums paid, which will depend on income and an individual's health risk.

In healthcare systems that rely largely on private funding, governments can mitigate some of the equity concerns and address the positive externalities associated with healthcare by providing subsidies aimed at specific groups. For example, in the USA, the Medicare and

[21] A study of the redistributive effects of healthcare financing mechanisms found that tax-based systems are more progressive than social and private health insurance systems. Social insurance systems are generally progressive, but may be regressive as a result of contribution ceilings and exemptions for high-income earners (Luyten & Tubeuf, 2025).

[22] Many private health insurance companies also operate on a non-profit basis.

Medicaid programmes provide health coverage for individuals aged 65 and over, as well as some individuals with disabilities (Medicare) and individuals on low incomes (Medicaid). These programmes are mainly funded through payroll, federal, and state taxes. Other countries subsidize private health insurance by making it tax deductible (e.g. Switzerland). Several countries also offer free or subsidized prescription charges for patients on low incomes or with chronic health conditions.

In terms of the finance of healthcare, it is not just whether funding is public or private that matters, but also what the schemes cover. Out-of-pocket payments (OOPs) can account for a sizeable proportion of healthcare expenditure and can push households into financial hardship. The share of total healthcare spending accounted for by OOPs ranges from 9.2 per cent of all healthcare spending in France to 33.5 per cent in Greece (OECD, 2025a). Research by the World Health Organization found that between 1 per cent and 9 per cent of households in Europe are pushed into poverty by out-of-pocket healthcare expenses (Thomson et al., 2019).

Publicly funded systems also have their limitations. In a system that is largely government-funded and where healthcare is free at the point of use, like the UK's NHS, individuals do not face the true cost of their consumption decisions, which can lead to overconsumption of healthcare (see Figure 8.2 above). But some form of rationing is inevitable and in these systems waiting times typically replace prices in rationing access to healthcare (see Box 8.6). This has equity implications since, as we have seen, time costs tend to vary with income.

Box 8.6 Rationing healthcare

In systems where healthcare is mainly privately funded and provided, prices act as a rationing mechanism, bringing together supply and demand. If demand exceeds supply, this pushes prices up, and individuals who cannot afford to pay will not have access to healthcare. In publicly funded systems where healthcare is free at the point of use, patients do not face the cost of treatments directly. This does not mean there is no rationing; rather, waiting times act as a rationing device. Access to healthcare here depends not on ability to pay, but on ability to wait.

The definition and measurement of waiting times varies across countries, and waiting times also vary across different types of health services (e.g. primary care, diagnostic tests, or elective treatment). This can make cross-country comparisons difficult, but the evidence suggests there is a wide variation in waiting times across countries. For example, 25 per cent of people waited one month or more for a specialist appointment in Switzerland, Germany, and the Netherlands, compared with over 60 per cent in Canada and Norway. Long waiting times can have a negative impact on individual health outcomes.

In light of developments in medical technology, more and better treatments are becoming available, and the range of healthcare treatments that can be provided is expanding. This is generally a good thing, but resources are limited, so the question about how to ration the allocation of resources in healthcare is unavoidable.

Source: OECD (2020).

8.3.2 Public production

Healthcare can be provided by publicly owned hospitals and health centres or by private sector hospitals, and these private providers may operate on a for-profit or not-for-profit basis. Even in systems where healthcare is mainly publicly provided, such as the NHS in the UK, the private sector will often provide certain inputs, such as medical equipment, cleaning, and catering services.

If problems of imperfect information and bounded rationality are severe, then government production and allocation of healthcare may be justified as a means of ensuring quality, particularly if quality is more difficult to monitor in the private sector. Public production may also help counteract the inefficient levels of healthcare provision that arise as a result of asymmetric information and the third-party payment problem. If the majority of healthcare is publicly provided, this will give the government some degree of monopsony power, as the main or sole buyer of services from doctors and nurses, and other healthcare inputs, which will enable the government to negotiate lower prices. However, the lack of competition may lead to inefficiencies in public production and weaker incentives to innovate.[23]

Public production and allocation of healthcare may be a more effective way of supporting vertical equity compared with redistributing incomes and allowing individuals to choose how much healthcare they want to consume. As an in-kind transfer, publicly provided healthcare may be favoured by wealthier people (for altruistic or selfish reasons—i.e. healthier people will be more productive) and by poorer people, since it may be more generous than cash transfers and will have a lower level of stigma attached.

8.3.3 Regulation

Government intervention in healthcare may also involve regulating the prices of medical services or the quality of care, mainly to address problems of imperfect information, bounded rationality, and monopoly power. Regulations to control the quality of care include regulating professional standards and the training and qualifications required to practise medicine, as well as regulating drugs and treatments and the practices of healthcare providers to ensure that standards for good medical practice are met. These interventions can also help improve horizontal equity by counteracting problems of unequal access to information.

Regulation of prices is typically imposed in systems where patients are charged fees for accessing medical care, to ensure healthcare providers do not abuse their market power.

8.4 Assessing the performance of different healthcare systems

Healthcare systems vary in the way they are structured and the challenges they face. In this section, we provide an overview and assess the performance of the healthcare system in three countries: England, where healthcare is mainly publicly funded and publicly provided; the

[23] See Chapter 7 for a discussion of the general arguments against public production.

USA, where healthcare is mainly privately funded and provided; and the Netherlands, where healthcare is also largely privately funded and provided, but it is structured very differently from the US system.[24]

When assessing a particular healthcare system it is important to consider multiple indicators. Focusing on healthcare spending alone and not considering health outcomes, for example, tells us little about the quality of healthcare provision or whether this is distributed equitably. In line with our discussion of the objectives of the healthcare system in section 8.1, we base our assessment of these healthcare systems on three criteria:[25]

- **Efficiency**: captured by measures including the level of healthcare spending, the scope for cost containment in the design of the system, measures of administrative efficiency, the quality of care, and whether there is scope for patient choice.
- **Equity**: measured by factors such as access to care—which includes both affordability (coverage) and timeliness of care provision (reflected in waiting times)—and equity in the distribution of healthcare resources.
- **Health outcomes**: measured by indicators including life expectancy, infant mortality, incidence rates of chronic diseases, mortality amenable to healthcare, and disease-specific health outcome measures (e.g. mortality rates following a heart attack or stroke).

Some of these indicators may fall under multiple categories. For example, waiting times could also be considered an indicator of efficiency, and patient choice could be considered an indicator of equity in access to care.

Before we explore each of these three systems, it is useful to start with an overview of how healthcare systems are structured more generally. We also discuss one challenge affecting virtually all healthcare systems today—rising healthcare spending.

8.4.1 The structure of healthcare systems

The distinction between the finance and provision of healthcare suggests one possible way of categorizing healthcare systems, which is summarized in Table 8.1.[26] Healthcare systems may be largely publicly funded and provided, privately funded and provided, or involve a combination of mostly public funding and private provision. Public finance covers systems funded mainly through general taxation (e.g. the NHS in the UK) and public statutory health insurance schemes. In the table, a country's healthcare system is classed as being mainly publicly provided if the majority of hospitals in that country are public, even if primary care involves mainly private providers. For example, in the UK and Denmark, the majority of hospitals are public, but most primary care providers, such as **general practitioners (GPs)**, are private.

[24] See Blumenthal et al. (2024), Schneider et al. (2017), and the individual country profiles on the Commonwealth Fund website (https://www.commonwealthfund.org/international-health-policy-center/countries) for a more in-depth analysis.

[25] See Barr (2020), Propper (2001), and Schneider et al. (2017) for a more detailed discussion of the relevant indicators.

[26] For detailed information on the healthcare systems in various countries, see the Country Profiles section on the Commonwealth Fund website: https://www.commonwealthfund.org/international-health-policy-center/countries.

Table 8.1 Types of healthcare system

Finance	Production	Country
Public	Mainly public	Denmark, Sweden, UK
	Mixed public/private	Australia, France, Germany
	Mainly private	Canada
Private	Mainly private	Netherlands, Switzerland, USA

While the structure of healthcare systems varies across countries, healthcare spending has been rising steadily, both as a share of GDP and in per capita terms, across most of the OECD. In Japan, Portugal, the UK, and the USA, spending on health as a proportion of GDP doubled between 1980 and 2022 (Table 8.2). In other countries, the growth in health spending may not have been as pronounced, but spending on health still accounts for a significant share of GDP.

There are various causes behind this rise in healthcare spending. These include an ageing population and the associated increase in demand for healthcare, lifestyle changes which have contributed to a rise in 'diseases of plenty' such as obesity and diabetes, and increases in wealth, as demand for healthcare typically rises faster than income. Technological changes,

Table 8.2 Healthcare spending as a percentage of GDP

	1980	1990	2000	2010	2022
Australia	5.8	6.5	7.6	8.4	9.9
Austria	7.1	7.7	9.4	10.3	11.2
Belgium	6.2	7.1	8.0	10.4	10.7
Canada	6.5	8.4	8.2	10.7	11.1
Denmark	8.5	8.0	8.1	10.6	9.5
Finland	5.9	7.3	7.1	9.1	9.7
France	6.8	8.1	9.6	11.2	11.8
Germany	8.1	8.0	9.8	10.8	12.4
Greece	–	6.2	7.5	9.6	8.4
Ireland	7.5	5.6	5.9	10.5	6.0
Italy	–	7.0	7.5	8.9	8.9
Japan	6.1	5.7	7.0	9.1	12.3
Netherlands	6.5	7.0	7.7	10.1	10.0
Norway	5.4	7.1	7.7	8.9	7.9
Portugal	4.8	5.5	8.6	10.0	10.5
Spain	5.0	6.1	6.8	9.2	9.7
Sweden	7.7	7.2	7.3	8.3	10.9
UK	5.1	5.1	7.1	9.8	11.1
USA	8.2	11.2	12.5	16.2	16.5

Source: OECD (2025a).

such as developments in medical treatments, have expanded the range of treatments available, leading to increased costs. It has also been suggested that healthcare is prone to Baumol's cost disease,[27] as providing healthcare is typically labour-intensive and there is limited scope for labour-saving technological progress. Productivity increases lead to rises in wages, which become cost increases in the healthcare sector.

These external pressures are combined with factors related to the design of particular healthcare systems which can encourage overconsumption, as we have seen above. Certain institutional features, including the use of primary-care gatekeepers, direct patient payment for care (which is later reimbursed by the insurer), and the public provision of healthcare services are all associated with lower healthcare expenditure. This highlights the importance of micro-incentives in containing costs.

8.4.2 The healthcare system in England

Structure of the healthcare system

The healthcare system in England[28] is mostly publicly financed and publicly provided by the National Health Service, although there is a small private healthcare system which operates alongside the NHS. The system is mainly financed out of general tax revenue, with around 20 per cent deriving from National Insurance contributions. The majority of healthcare is free at the point of use,[29] although there are charges for prescriptions and some ancillary services, such as eye tests. Roughly 11 per cent of the population buy supplementary private insurance coverage for more rapid and convenient access, including to elective treatment in private hospitals. The majority of primary care providers are private, while most hospitals are public.

The NHS was originally set up in 1948, based on the following core principles: that it should meet the needs of everyone; that it should be free at the point of delivery; and that it should be based on clinical need, not ability to pay. Although these are still the guiding principles of the NHS, there have been changes in the mechanisms of provision over time, with a gradual move away from central planning and towards greater competition between providers. Since 2006, the role of non-NHS providers in delivering NHS-funded care has increased dramatically (these include private, voluntary, and local authority providers) and the Health and Social Care Act 2012 paved the way for increasing competition in the provision of health services. The Act led to the creation of Clinical Commissioning Groups, which are groups of general practices (GP surgeries) which were responsible for commissioning the majority of health services in their area, including emergency care, elective hospital care, maternity services, and community and mental health services. In 2022, Clinical Commissioning Groups were abolished and replaced by integrated care systems (ICS) with the Health and Care Act 2022. ICSs are partnerships of organizations responsible for planning and paying for health and care services in a particular area. The government agency NHS England leads the NHS in England and oversees the allocation of funds.

[27] See Chapter 3 for a more detailed discussion.

[28] Healthcare is mostly publicly funded and provided across the UK. However, as healthcare is a devolved matter, there are important differences between the systems in England, Scotland, Wales, and Northern Ireland. This section focuses on the healthcare system in England specifically, although some of the statistics reported refer to the whole of the UK because of the way in which the data are collected and reported.

[29] This includes hospital, physician, and mental health care, but excludes dentistry and opticians' appointments.

Efficiency

Expenditure on healthcare in the UK is modest by international standards, given the UK's level of income: in 2022, spending on health was $5,493 per person, or 11.1 per cent of GDP, just slightly above the OECD average of $4,986 per person (OECD, 2024). Measures to contain costs are built into the system, through the global budget constraint imposed on the NHS. General practitioners also perform a gatekeeping role, since they are responsible for making referrals for specialist treatment. The UK system performs well on administrative efficiency because services are free at the point of delivery and therefore doctors do not bill patients or the government directly for each service (Blumenthal et al., 2024). The system has fared worse on the quality of the care process and measures of patient choice, although recent reforms have attempted to address this by providing more patient choice regarding hospitals and the timing of treatments.

Equity

Since the system is financed primarily through general taxation, it does promote vertical equity. The UK system also performs highly in terms of access to care and horizontal equity, as ability to pay is not a significant barrier to accessing healthcare when needed (Blumenthal et al., 2024). Government and compulsory health insurance schemes accounted for 81.5 per cent of current expenditure on health in 2022, but out-of-pocket expenditures are significant, accounting for 14.4 per cent of all health spending (OECD, 2025a). Waiting times are also a growing problem for the NHS: the number of people waiting for non-emergency care passed 4 million in 2019 (NHS England, n.d.).

Health outcomes

One of the areas where the UK system seems to perform the worst is on health outcomes. By some metrics, the system is doing relatively well: average life expectancy in 2021 was 81 years (above the OECD average of 80.3) and the infant mortality rate was 4 deaths per 1,000 live births, against an OECD average of 3.9 (OECD, 2024, 2025b). However, it performs less well on most commonly used measures of disease-specific health outcomes, with relatively high rates of mortality amenable to healthcare, and relatively high mortality rates following stroke and heart attack. The UK also had the lowest breast and colon cancer five-year survival rates among a selection of high-income countries (Schneider et al., 2017). These outcomes may reflect a lack of resources, given the comparatively low level of spending on healthcare in the UK.

8.4.3 The healthcare system in the USA

Structure of the healthcare system

The US healthcare system is based mostly on private production and financed by private medical insurance, which is provided primarily by employers. Since the 1960s, the federal government has provided funding for the Medicare and Medicaid programmes for adults aged 65 and over, some people with disabilities, and people on low-incomes. In 1997, the Children's Health Insurance Programme (CHIP) was introduced, which is designed to provide health insurance to children and pregnant women on modest incomes who do not qualify for Medicaid. The majority of primary care providers are private and are paid a fee-for-service; there is no gatekeeping role. Healthcare facilities are mostly owned and operated by the private sector, and include a combination of non-profit community hospitals, for-profit hospitals, and some government-owned hospitals. The Patient Protection and Affordable Care Act (ACA) was enacted in 2010 and aimed to increase the quality, affordability, and coverage of health insurance and reduce healthcare costs. The law required insurers to accept all applicants and charge the same rates regardless of pre-existing medical conditions or gender, and resulted in an estimated 20 million people gaining health insurance coverage, reducing the share of uninsured adults aged 19–64 from 20 per cent in 2010 to 12 per cent in 2018.[30]

Efficiency

The USA has one of the highest levels of medical spending in the world: total spending on health was $12,555 per person in 2022, or 16.5 per cent of GDP (OECD, 2024). Healthcare spending per capita is two-and-a-half times the OECD average of $4,986 per person, but this is not reflected in better health outcomes. The payment incentive structure (which is susceptible to third-party payment problems) and high administrative costs explain part of these high levels of expenditure. Insurance companies can set their own benefits packages and cost-sharing schemes, although these are subject to federal and state regulations. This contributes to the high administrative costs of the system (e.g. time wasted by doctors and patients filing bills and filling out insurance claims). The system performs well in terms of the quality of the care process, while competition among healthcare providers helps ensure a good degree of patient choice (Blumenthal et al., 2024).

Equity

In 2022, government and compulsory health insurance schemes accounted for 83.8 per cent of current expenditure on health, while out-of-pocket payments accounted for 11 per cent (OECD, 2025a). However, the USA is the only high-income country that does not have universal health coverage, and 26 million people (7–8 per cent of the population) lack health insurance (Blumenthal et al., 2024). Those with health insurance coverage typically face higher out-of-pocket costs and higher deductibles than in other high-income countries, leaving about a quarter of working-age people underinsured (Blumenthal et al., 2024). Reliance on private insurance also means the system does not promote vertical equity.

Health outcomes

In spite of the high levels of healthcare expenditure, the US system performs poorly in terms of health outcomes. In a ranking of the healthcare systems in 10 developed countries, the USA came last on health outcomes (Blumenthal et al., 2024). The average life expectancy in 2021 was 76.4 years (below the OECD average of 80.3) and the infant mortality rate was 5.4 deaths per 1,000 live births, against an OECD average of 3.9 (OECD, 2024, 2025b). Performance on disease-specific outcomes is generally better, and the US breast and colon cancer five-year survival rates are among the highest in a selection of high-income countries (Schneider et al., 2017). This disparity may reflect the fact that the quality of care provided is high for those who can afford to pay for it, but not everyone can afford to pay for it.

[30] Commonwealth Fund Country Profiles: https://www.commonwealthfund.org/international-health-policy-center/countries/united-states.

8.4.4 The healthcare system in the Netherlands

Structure of the healthcare system

The Dutch healthcare system is based mostly on private production and financed by private medical insurance. Following a major healthcare reform in 2006, which introduced a managed competition model, all adult residents are required to buy statutory health insurance from private insurers. The government regulates and subsidizes insurance—for example, by paying for children's coverage up to the age of 18. Private insurance companies operate on a non-profit basis and are required to accept all applicants and must charge the same premium to all applicants, regardless of age or health status. Private insurance plans provide statutory benefits, but 84 per cent of the population buy complementary coverage for benefits excluded from the statutory package, such as dental care, alternative medicine, physiotherapy, glasses, and contraceptives. Insurance contributions are collected centrally and issued among insurers in accordance with a risk-adjusted capitation formula that considers age, gender, labour force status, region, and health risk. Most hospitals are privately run, but on a not-for-profit basis; primary care providers are private and perform a gatekeeping role. The government sets the main healthcare priorities and monitors access, quality and costs.

Efficiency

Health expenditure in the Netherlands was $6,729 per person, or 10 per cent of GDP, in 2022 (OECD, 2024). This is above the OECD average, but well below the high levels of expenditure seen in the USA, which also operates a mainly privately funded and provided model. Private health insurers are expected to negotiate with private healthcare providers to ensure they are getting the best quality of care at an affordable price. As the Dutch system is a multi-payer one, competition among private insurers and healthcare providers helps to contain costs. Patients are given the freedom to choose their insurance and healthcare providers, which is good for patient choice, but highlights the need to ensure patients have access to good-quality information on prices and quality to enable them to make informed decisions. In comparison with the US model, which also relies on private insurers, the administrative burden in the Dutch model is minimized by offering standardized benefit packages, although administrative efficiency is one of the weak areas of the system (Blumenthal et al., 2024).

Equity

Government and compulsory health insurance schemes accounted for 82.8 per cent of expenditure on health in 2022, while out-of-pocket expenditures accounted for 11.9 per cent (OECD, 2025a). The Dutch system provides universal coverage, which ensures that any co-payments for health services are small, thus supporting both access and affordability (Blumenthal et al., 2024). There is also a requirement that health services be available after regular office hours and general practitioners are required to provide 50 hours of after-hours care each year.

Health outcomes

The Dutch healthcare system performs well on some healthcare outcomes. The average life expectancy in 2021 was 81.4 years (above the OECD average) and the infant mortality rate was 3.3 deaths per 1,000 live births, below the OECD average of 3.9 (OECD, 2024, 2025b). However, performance on most commonly used measures of disease-specific health outcomes is mixed, with relatively high mortality rates following stroke and heart attack, but also high five-year survival rates for breast and colon cancer (Schneider et al., 2017).

8.5 Long-term care

Our discussion so far has focused on healthcare in general. One area of health-related spending which is predicted to become increasingly important in the future, particularly as life expectancy continues to rise, is long-term care. **Long-term care (LTC)**[31] encompasses a range of personal, social, and medical services to support people who face difficulties in carrying out everyday activities over a prolonged period as a result of chronic conditions or disability. These services can vary from fairly minimal support, such as assistance with shopping or cleaning, to full-time nursing care. In 2021, an average of 11.5 per cent of people aged 65 and over across the OECD received LTC, either in care institutions or at home (OECD, 2023b).

Not everyone will require care, and some people may require only minimal support. However, for some individuals care needs may be significant and expensive: estimates for England suggest that 7 per cent of individuals aged 65 will face lifetime care costs of at least £100,000, and for 5 per cent of people these costs will be at least £200,000 (Comas-Herrera et al., 2012). Should these costs be borne by individuals or should the government help finance LTC?

Given that demand for LTC is uncertain, insurance would provide a better mechanism for financing LTC needs than relying on individual savings. However, there are several reasons why a market for private care insurance would be unlikely to operate efficiently.[32] Problems of imperfect information, bounded rationality, and bounded willpower—discussed above—are likely to be significant. Planning for LTC needs involves planning over long time horizons and requires individuals to consider complex medical information about the risks of developing different conditions and the costs associated with these. On the supply side, private insurers may face difficulties in estimating the relevant probabilities. The probability that an individual will need care in the future will depend on medical advances, among other things, which are difficult to predict in the long run. While some medical advances may make it easier for people to be independent for longer and therefore reduce the need for care, others may be more successful in prolonging life and mean people will need more support and for longer. The problem may therefore better be viewed as one of uncertainty rather than risk. It is also possible that the relevant probabilities are not independent across individuals if everyone benefits from the same medical advances.

A market for private care insurance is also susceptible to problems of adverse selection (if premiums reflect average risks) and moral hazard, since individuals who buy LTC insurance are more likely to consume it. In countries where healthcare is free at the point of use, there is the further risk of moral hazard where families may have an incentive to offload care for their elderly relatives on to the state, making use of publicly provided healthcare rather than paying for private care.

The evidence suggests that the take-up of private LTC insurance is low. In the USA, only about 10 per cent of individuals aged 60 and over own a private LTC insurance policy (Brown & Finkelstein, 2009). In some countries, particularly across Europe, strong family ties have been argued to contribute to the lack of development of private markets for LTC insurance (Costa-Font, 2010). The role of informal care by family and friends can be significant, which raises important equity issues as caring responsibilities typically fall on women.

[31] Sometimes referred to as 'social care'.

[32] See Box 2.6 in Chapter 2 for a summary of the conditions required for private insurance markets to operate efficiently.

Government-provided social insurance may therefore provide a more efficient and equitable means of financing LTC needs. Moreover, if such a scheme were to build on existing social insurance schemes—such as those in place to fund healthcare, pensions, or other welfare benefits—the additional administrative costs could be minimized. There is a danger that state support may be used as a substitute for family care. However, the potential to provide an integrated service spanning healthcare and LTC means that more expensive healthcare is not being wasted when what is required is LTC. The costs of providing LTC are significant and are expected to grow in the future, with public spending on LTC projected to reach 4.3 per cent of GDP by 2060 across Europe, up from 1.4 per cent in 2014 (Economic Commission, 2015). This requires countries to explore new ways of dealing with the problem of spiralling care costs (see Box 8.7).

Conclusion

What is the proper role of government in healthcare? This chapter has provided an introduction to some of the key issues within this vast topic. We have discussed the main objectives of the healthcare system and analysed the extent to which a market system for healthcare can achieve these objectives or whether some form of government intervention is necessary.

Box 8.7 Paying for social care in the Netherlands

The Netherlands was the first OECD country to introduce compulsory social health insurance to finance long-term care (LTC) in 1968—known as AWBZ. The AWBZ initially covered primarily nursing home care and institutionalized care, but was subsequently expanded to include other types of care, including home health care and residential care for the elderly. The public financing scheme for LTC was generous and comprehensive compared to other European countries, and both contributions and co-payments were income-related. While initially workers' contributions made up a larger proportion of the LTC budget, with taxes making up the remainder, as LTC expenditures increased faster than wages, the tax share also had to increase. Between 2000 and 2013, public expenditure on LTC grew on average by 4.3 per cent a year in real terms, and by 2015, public spending on LTC accounted for 2.6 per cent of GDP, almost twice the OECD average.

Concerns over rising expenditure led to a series of in-depth reforms in 2015 affecting both the finance and provision of LTC. The reforms essentially involved splitting up the LTC insurance scheme. Some responsibilities were allocated to municipalities and health insurers, and the role of people's social networks in providing care was strengthened to reduce reliance on formal care. The former public LTC insurance scheme (AWBZ) was replaced by a less comprehensive one (WLZ), which would cover institutional care and intense home health care. So the central government retained responsibility for providing care for the most vulnerable people, who required very intensive care, but other care needs were to be met at the municipal level.

Sources: Alders and Schut (2019) and OECD (2013).

We have also reviewed some of the different ways in which governments intervene in healthcare and their implications.

There are strong efficiency and equity arguments for government intervention in healthcare, but this does not necessarily entail public finance or production. Our analysis of the performance of three very different healthcare systems highlights how there is no single right or best way to organize a healthcare system. A well-designed privately funded and provided system, such as exists in the Netherlands, can perform just as well as a mainly publicly funded and provided system, such as exists in the UK. What matters is not so much whether the system is private or public, but how it is designed: what incentives are in place to help guarantee quality and contain costs, and what mechanisms help ensure equity in access to healthcare.

Questions for discussion

1. Should there be a market for blood donations?
2. 'A health system with insurance suffers from the same problem as one with free healthcare, in that there will be an oversupply.' Discuss.
3. Should doctors be allowed to advertise their services?
4. Does adverse selection in healthcare create an efficiency or an equity problem?
5. 'In order to satisfy efficiency and equity goals, a healthcare system must be publicly funded and publicly provided.' Do you agree with this statement? Why or why not?

Further reading

For a more in-depth discussion of the economics of health and healthcare:

Barr, N. (2020). *The economics of the welfare state* (6th ed.). Oxford University Press.

Folland, S., Goodman, A. C., Stano, M., & Danagoulian, S. (2024). *The economics of health and health care*. Routledge.

On the problems of asymmetric information, adverse selection, and moral hazard in health insurance:

Akerlof, G. A. (1978). The market for 'lemons': Quality uncertainty and the market mechanism. In P. A. Diamond & M. Rothschild (Eds.), *Uncertainty in economics* (pp. 235–251). Academic Press.

Cutler, D. M., & Reber, S. J. (1998). Paying for health insurance: The trade-off between competition and adverse selection. *Quarterly Journal of Economics*, *113*(2), 433–466.

Cutler, D. M., & Zeckhauser, R. J. (2000). The anatomy of health insurance. In A. J. Culyer & J. P. Newhouse (Eds.), *Handbook of health economics* (Vol. 1, pp. 563–643). Elsevier.

Einav, L., & Finkelstein, A. (2018). Moral hazard in health insurance: What we know and how we know it. *Journal of the European Economic Association*, *16*(4), 957–982.

On behavioural economics and healthcare:

Rice, T. (2013). The behavioral economics of health and health care. *Annual Review of Public Health*, *34*(1), 431–447.

For a discussion of the theory and measurement of equity in healthcare:

Culyer, A. J. (2015). Equality and equity. In H. Have (Ed.), *Encyclopedia of global bioethics* (pp. 1–11). Springer.

Luyten, E., & Tubeuf, S. (2025). Equity in healthcare financing: A review of evidence. *Health Policy, 152*, art. 105218.

Propper, C. (2024). Socio-economic inequality in the distribution of health care in the UK. *Oxford Open Economics, 3*, Issue Supplement 1, i577–i581.

Wagstaff, A., & Van Doorslaer, E. (2000). Equity in health care finance and delivery. In A. Culyer and J. Newhouse (Eds.), Handbook of *h*ealth *e*conomics (Vol. 1, pp. 1803–1862). Elsevier.

Wagstaff, A., Van Doorslaer, E., Van der Burg, H., Calonge, S., Christiansen, T., Citoni, G., . . . & Winkelhake, O. (1999). Equity in the finance of health care: Some further international comparisons. *Journal of Health Economics, 18*(3), 263–290.

For a discussion of the structure and performance of a selection of healthcare systems:

Blumenthal, D., Gumas, E. D., Shah, A., Gunja, M. Z., and William II, R. D. (2024). *Mirror, mirror 2024: A portrait of the failing US health system—Comparing performance in 10 nations*. Commonwealth Fund. September. Available at: https://www.commonwealthfund.org/publications/fund-reports/2024/sep/mirror-mirror-2024

Schneider, E. C., Sarnak, D. O., Squires D., Shah A., and Doty M. M. (2017). *Mirror, mirror: How the US health care system compares internationally at a time of radical change*. Commonwealth Fund. July. Available at: https://doi.org/10.26099/0mh5-a632

On the role of government intervention in financing long-term care:

Barr, N. (2010). Long-term care: A suitable case for social insurance. *Social Policy and Administration, 44*(4), 359–374.

OECD (2020). *Long-term care and health care insurance in OECD and other countries*. Organization for Economic Cooperation and Development.

Bibliography

Alders, P., & Schut, F. T. (2019). The 2015 long-term care reform in the Netherlands: Getting the financial incentives right? *Health Policy, 123*(3), 312–316.

Arrow, K. J. (1963). Uncertainty and the welfare economics of medical care. *American Economic Review, 53*(5), 941–973.

Barr, N. A. (2001). *The welfare state as piggy bank: Information, risk, uncertainty, and the role of the state*. Oxford University Press.

Barr, N. (2020). *The economics of the welfare state* (6th ed.). Oxford University Press.

Beckert, W., & Kelly, E. (2017). Divided by choice? Private providers, patient choice and hospital sorting in the English National Health service. Institute for Fiscal Studies working papers, no. W17/15.

Blumenthal, D., Gumas, E. D., Shah, A., Gunja, M. Z., and William II, R. D. (2024). Mirror, mirror 2024: A portrait of the failing US health system—Comparing performance in 10 nations. Commonwealth Fund. September. Available at: https://www.commonwealthfund.org/publications/fund-reports/2024/sep/mirror-mirror-2024

Brown, J. R., & Finkelstein, A. (2009). The private market for long-term care insurance in the United States: A review of the evidence. *Journal of Risk and Insurance, 76*(1), 5–29. https://doi.org/10.1111/j.1539-6975.2009.01286.x

CDC (2024). Understanding the opioid overdose epidemic. US Centers for Disease Control and Prevention. Available at: https://www.cdc.gov/overdose-prevention/about/understanding-the-opioid-overdose-epidemic.html.

Comas Herrera, A., Butterfield, R., Fernandez Plotka, J.-L., Wittenberg, R., & Wiener, J. (2012). Barriers to and opportunities for private long-term care insurance in England: What can we learn from other countries? In *The LSE Companion to Health Policy* (p. 258). London School of Economics. Available at: https://doi.org/10.4337/9781781004241.00026

Connolly, S., & Munro, A. (1999). *Economics of the public sector*. FT Prentice Hall.

Costa-Font, J. (2010). Family ties and the crowding out of long-term care insurance. *Oxford Review of Economic Policy*, *26*(4), 691–712. https://doi.org/10.1093/oxrep/grq040

European Commission (2015). The 2015 ageing report: Economic and budgetary projections for the 28 EU member states (2013–2060). ISSN 1725-3217 (online).

Finkelstein, A., Taubman, S., Wright, B., Bernstein, M., Gruber, J., Newhouse, J. P., Allen, H., & Baicker, K. (2012). The Oregon health insurance experiment: Evidence from the first year. *Quarterly Journal of Economics*, *127*(3), 1057–1106.

Frey, B. (1997). *Not just for the money: An economic theory of personal motivation*. Edward Elgar.

Global Observatory on Donation and Transplantation (2024). *International report on organ donation and transplantation activities 2023*. Available at: https://www.transplant-observatory.org/wp-content/uploads/2025/02/2023-data-global-report-20022025.pdf

Himmelstein, D. U., Lawless, R. M., Thorne, D., Foohey, P. & Woolhandler, S. (2019). Medical bankruptcy: Still common despite the Affordable Care Act. *American Journal of Public Health*, *109*, 431–433.

Le Grand, J. (1987). Equity, health, and health care. *Social Justice Research*, *1*(3), 257–274.

Le Grand, J. (1997). Knights, knaves or pawns? Human behaviour and social policy. *Journal of Social Policy*, *26*(2), 149–169.

Le Grand, J. (2006). *Motivation, agency and public policy: Of knights and knaves, pawns and queens*. Oxford University Press.

Le Grand, J. (2018). *The strategy of equality: Redistribution and the social services*. Routledge. Available at: https://doi.org/10.4324/9780429486852

Luyten, E., & Tubeuf, S. (2025). Equity in healthcare financing: A review of evidence. *Health Policy*, *152*, art. 105218.

Meldrum, M. L. (2016). The ongoing opioid prescription epidemic: Historical context. *American Journal of Public Health*, *106*(8), 1365–1366.

Newhouse, J. P. (1993). *Free for all? Lessons from the RAND health insurance experiment*. Harvard University Press.

Newhouse, J. P. (1996). Health reform in the United States. *Economic Journal*, *106*(439), 1713–1724.

NHS England (n.d.) *Referral to treatment (RTT) waiting times*. Available at: https://www.england.nhs.uk/statistics/statistical-work-areas/rtt-waiting-times/ (accessed 5 February 2026).

NICE (2025). *NICE health technology evaluations: The manual*. National Institute for Health and Care Excellence.

OECD (2013). *The Netherlands—A good life in old age*. Organization for Economic Cooperation and Development/European Commission.

OECD (2020). *Waiting times for health services: Next in line*. OECD Health Policy Studies. Organization for Economic Cooperation and Development. Available at: https://doi.org/10.1787/242e3c8c-en

OECD (2023a). *Annual GDP and consumption per capita, US $, current prices, current PPPs*. Organization for Economic Cooperation and Development. Data explorer. https://data-explorer.oecd.org (accessed 5 February 2023).

OECD (2023b). *Health at a glance 2023: OECD indicators*. Organization for Economic Cooperation and Development. Available at: https://doi.org/10.1787/7a7afb35-en

OECD (2023c). *Health spending*. Organization for Economic Cooperation and Development. Available at: https://www.oecd.org/en/data/indicators/health-spending.html

OECD (2023d). *Life expectancy*. Organization for Economic Cooperation and Development. Data explorer. https://data-explorer.oecd.org (accessed 5 February 2023).

OECD (2024). *Society at a glance 2024: OECD social indicators*. Organization for Economic Cooperation and Development. Available at: https://doi.org/10.1787/918d8db3-en

OECD (2025a). *Health expenditure and financing*. Organization for Economic Cooperation and Development. Data explorer. https://data-explorer.oecd.org (accessed 14 July 2025).

OECD (2025b). *Maternal and infant mortality*. Organization for Economic Cooperation and Development. Data explorer. https://data-explorer.oecd.org (accessed 14 July 2025).

Propper, C. (2001). Expenditure on healthcare in the UK: A review of the issues. *Fiscal Studies, 22*(2), 151–183. https://doi.org/10.1111/j.1475-5890.2001.tb00037.x

Propper, C. (2018). Competition in healthcare: Lessons from the English experience. *Health Economics, Policy and Law, 13*, 492–508.

Propper, C. (2024). Socio-economic inequality in the distribution of health care in the UK. *Oxford Open Economics, 3*, Issue Supplement 1, i577–i581.

Roth, A. E. (2007). Repugnance as a constraint on markets. *Journal of Economic Perspectives, 21*(3), 37–58.

Roth, A. E., Sönmez, T., & Ünver, M. U. (2004). Kidney exchange. *Quarterly Journal of Economics, 119*(2), 457–488.

Sandel, M. J. (2012). *What money can't buy: The moral limits of markets*. Penguin.

Schneider, E. C., Sarnak, D. O., Squires D., Shah A., and Doty M. M. (2017). *Mirror, mirror: How the US health care system compares internationally at a time of radical change*. Commonwealth Fund. July. Available at: https://doi.org/10.26099/0mh5-a632

The Lancet (2024). Organ donation: Lessons from the Spanish model. *The Lancet* (London, England), *404*(10459), 1171.

The Lancet Regional Health—Americas (2023). Editorial: Opioid crisis: addiction, overprescription, and insufficient primary prevention. *The Lancet Regional Health-Americas, 23*, 100557.

Thomson, S., Cylus, J., & Evetovits, T. (2019). *Can people afford to pay for health care? New evidence on financial protection in Europe*. World Health Organization.

Titmuss, R. (1970). *The gift relationship: From human blood to social policy*. Policy Press.

United Nations (1948). *Universal Declaration of Human Rights*. Available at: https://www.un.org/en/about-us/universal-declaration-of-human-rights

Van Zee, A. (2009). The promotion and marketing of oxycontin: Commercial triumph, public health tragedy. *American Journal of Public Health, 99*(2), 221–227.

Wagstaff, A., & Van Doorslaer, E. (2000). Equity in health care finance and delivery. In A. Culyer and J. Newhouse (Eds.), *Handbook of health economics* (Vol. 1, pp. 1803–1862). Elsevier.

Watt, T., Raymond, A. & Rachet-Jacquet, L. (2022). *Quantifying health inequalities in England*. Health Foundation. 15 August.

Wilkinson, R. & Pickett, K. (2010). *The spirit level: Why equality is better for everyone*. Penguin.

9
Education

Learning objectives

By the end of this chapter, you will be able to:

9.1 Explain the objectives of the education system and the challenges involved in measuring these in practice.
9.2 Compare different approaches to modelling the demand for education.
9.3 Discuss the arguments for government intervention in education.
9.4 Explain the different ways in which governments intervene in education.
9.5 Discuss some of the particular challenges affecting compulsory education and policies to address these.
9.6 Discuss some of the particular challenges affecting tertiary education and policies to address these.

Introduction

Across the OECD, countries spent an average of 5.1 per cent of GDP on education in 2020 (OECD, 2024e),[1] and the vast majority of this spending came from the government. In 2020, 84 per cent of all funding for education institutions in the OECD across all levels of education, from primary to **tertiary education**, came from government sources (OECD, 2023). Education is typically one of the largest areas of public spending, alongside social protection and health. On average across the OECD, 12 per cent of government spending goes on education (OECD, 2024b). In the UK, the government spent a total of £166 billion on education in 2022/23, equivalent to 4.4 per cent of national income (Drayton et al., 2023).

Why do governments play such a big role in education? Education has benefits for individuals, providing us with the knowledge and skills we need for the world of work, but also to help us manage everyday life. Education is an important determinant of our lifetime incomes, it provides new opportunities, and it can help us lead more fulfilling lives. But education also brings benefits to society as a whole. Education plays an important role in socialization and supports social cohesion. An educated and skilled workforce is more productive, which promotes economic growth. Education can also support social mobility, helping to reduce inequalities in society. What, then, should be the role of government in education? Should governments be responsible for funding and providing all education, from primary

[1] Public and private spending on all levels of education.

to tertiary education, both academic and vocational? Is there a role for private providers and private funding in education, and what are the benefits and risks?

We start by discussing the main objectives of education systems in section 9.1. We then explore how we can model the demand for education in section 9.2, before analysing the economic arguments for government intervention in education in section 9.3. Section 9.4 discusses the different ways in which governments intervene in education and paints a picture of the extent and nature of government intervention in education across countries. Sections 9.5 and 9.6 explore some of the particular policy challenges in **compulsory education** and tertiary education, respectively.

9.1 Objectives of the education system

In order to assess what the proper role of government in education should be, it is helpful first to clarify what we think the education system should achieve. At a very general level, the objective of the education system is to ensure everyone in society achieves a good education. But what do we mean by a 'good education'? Education is not just about conveying technical knowledge and skills; it also plays an important socialization role, transmitting shared norms and values that enable individuals to fully participate in society. Education should instil a sense of curiosity and an interest in learning for the sake of learning. Our understanding of what a good education involves will vary depending on the particular historical, social, political, and economic context. It will also vary depending on the level of education.

Education systems vary significantly across countries, with variations in the length of the different levels of education and how they are structured. Table 9.1 provides one way of classifying different education levels based on the International Standard Classification of Education (ISCED) drawn up by the United Nations Educational, Scientific, and Cultural Organization (UNESCO) and the categorization adopted by the OECD. It is helpful to draw a distinction between compulsory education and tertiary education. Compulsory education refers to the period of education that governments legally require all individuals to complete, and it typically includes primary and lower secondary education. Tertiary education covers all formal post-secondary education, including academic and higher vocational education. Basic literacy, numeracy, and communication skills are an important part of a good education at the compulsory level, whereas critical thinking, intellectual freedom, and vocational skills may be more important components in higher levels of education.

Achieving a good education, however defined, involves thinking about what resources are allocated to producing education, how these resources are allocated within education, and how education itself is distributed across society. As we saw in Chapter 1, two important social objectives when thinking about the allocation of resources are efficiency and the promotion of equity or social justice.[2] We will explore each of these objectives in more detail in this section.

[2] The concepts of efficiency and equity are discussed in Chapter 2.

Table 9.1 A classification of the different levels of education

Education level	Description
Early childhood education (ISCED level 0)	Education programmes designed to develop skills required to participate in school and society.
Primary education (ISCED level 1)	Programmes designed to provide a basic understanding in reading, writing, maths, and some additional subjects. Typical entry age: between five and seven years. Typical duration: six years.
Lower secondary education (ISCED level 2)	Programmes that build on primary education, normally with a more subject-oriented curriculum. In some countries, completing lower secondary education marks the end of compulsory education. Typical duration: three years.
Upper secondary education (ISCED level 3)	Programmes that involve a stronger specialization than at lower secondary level. Programmes may be general or vocational. Typical duration: three years.
Post-secondary non-tertiary education (ISCED level 4)	Programmes that aim to broaden knowledge and skills gained at the upper secondary level. Usually vocationally oriented.
Tertiary education (ISCED levels 5 to 8)	This includes short-cycle tertiary education, bachelor's degree or equivalent level, master's degree or equivalent level, and doctoral or equivalent-level qualifications.

Source: Based on OECD (2023), table B.

9.1.1 Efficiency

How much of a country's resources should be devoted to education, and how should these resources be allocated to different areas within education? Efficiency is about ensuring that society's resources are being put to their best possible use, to maximize social welfare. As we saw in Chapter 1, an efficient allocation of resources is one where the marginal social benefit derived from one additional unit of a good—in this case, education—equals the marginal social cost of producing it.

We can draw a distinction between allocative (or external) efficiency and productive (or internal) efficiency. Allocative efficiency focuses on whether we are producing the optimal quantity, quality, and combination of education activities, whereas **productive efficiency** focuses on how schools, colleges, and universities are run, and whether the inputs used in the production of education goods and services are being used optimally. Allocative efficiency includes both macro-efficiency, which is about how society allocates resources to education relative to other areas, such as health or pensions, and micro-efficiency, which focuses on how resources are allocated within education—for example, how much should be spent on nurseries versus primary, secondary, and tertiary education, and how much should be spent on staff versus buildings and materials.

To measure efficiency, we need to be able to identify and measure the costs and benefits of education. As with healthcare, the costs of education are generally easier to measure. These include, for example, the cost of teacher salaries, buildings, and teaching materials. Our measure of costs should also include the cost of forgone earnings—that is, the income individuals could have earned if they had been working instead of being in education.

The benefits of education are harder to quantify.[3] Education involves a range of individual benefits. It provides us with the knowledge and skills that should help us find good jobs, with higher pay and more job satisfaction. It also equips us with the skills and values that will help us live and manage our lives in society more effectively. Individuals may also derive utility from the process of education itself, deriving enjoyment from learning for the sake of learning, and the fact that education can help us make friends and build our social lives. Education also involves a wide range of external benefits, including promoting economic growth, increasing societal cohesion, and reducing crime (see Box 9.1).

While it is possible to quantify the benefits of education in terms of higher output or higher wages, measuring other benefits is more challenging. How can we quantify the value to individuals of greater job satisfaction, or the enjoyment they may derive from learning for the sake of learning? How can we accurately measure the benefit to society from having more educated citizens?

It is not just the quantity of education that matters, but also education quality. While we can measure the quantity of education through years of schooling, measuring quality is more complicated. Test scores are often used as a measure of education quality, but they offer a very incomplete picture of education performance. Good educational outcomes will also depend on factors other than the quantity and quality of formal schooling, including natural ability, the quality of parenting, and poverty.

Box 9.1 The wider individual and external benefits of education

Education provides a number of benefits, over and above the benefits to individuals in terms of higher incomes. These include the following:

- Benefits to individual health (Cutler & Lleras-Muney, 2006; Feinstein et al., 2008).
- Lower levels of criminal behaviour, including vandalism, shoplifting, and assault (Feinstein et al., 2008; Groot & Van den Brink, 2010; Lochner & Moretti, 2004; Machin et al., 2011).[4]
- Increased civic engagement, including voter participation and support for free speech (Dee, 2004).
- Increased tax revenues: if education makes workers more productive, this will result in higher earnings, which imply higher tax revenues.
- Increased economic growth (Krueger & Lindahl, 2001).[5] By raising individual productivity and making individuals more adaptable, education offers the potential for faster economic growth. However, measuring the impact on growth in practice is challenging, given the difficulty in separating productivity improvements due to education from improvements due to natural ability, physical capital, or institutions.

[3] The benefits of education also depend on what is perceived to be a 'good education'—as already discussed, there is no consensus here.

[4] Groot and van den Brink (2010) do find, however, that the probability of committing tax fraud increases with years of education. They also find that people with higher levels of education have more permissive attitudes and social norms towards criminal behaviour.

[5] However, evidence on the impact of education on growth is mixed and depends on the level of education (see e.g. Wolf, 2004).

9.1.2 Equity

What does it mean for the distribution of education to be equitable? One concept of equity that is particularly relevant in the context of education is the idea of equality of opportunity, which we introduced in Chapter 2—that everyone, regardless of their personal circumstances, gender, ethnicity, and socioeconomic background, should be able to access the same quantity and quality of education.[6] This is not the same as equality of outcomes, as individuals may face the same opportunities but achieve different outcomes due to differences in preferences or ability. It also does not mean that everyone should receive the same level of education, given differences in individual preferences, capabilities, and needs. However, most countries do stipulate a minimum level of education that everyone should receive.[7]

Equality of opportunity is mainly related to the concept of horizontal equity, which is concerned with 'the equal treatment of equals'. Vertical equity is related to how the education system is financed. If the tax system is progressive and education is financed out of general taxation, and everyone consumes the same level of education (e.g. through compulsory education), then the education system will redistribute from those who are better off financially to those who are worse off. However, this is conditional on everyone receiving not only the same quantity, but also the same quality of education; and the latter is much more difficult to guarantee in practice. That the education system should aim to achieve horizontal equity is relatively uncontroversial. However, there is less agreement on whether the education system should aim to redistribute from those who are better off to those who are worse off, or if other channels of government intervention are better suited to achieving this.

To measure equality of opportunity, we need to consider both the distribution of inputs into education (e.g. teachers and school facilities) and the distribution of outcomes (e.g. educational attainment), and how these vary with individual characteristics such as gender, ethnicity, and socioeconomic background.[8] Focusing on the distribution of inputs alone may give a misleading picture because achieving equality of opportunity may require higher levels of spending in some areas or for certain groups to make up for other disadvantages. For example, there is growing evidence of the importance of early childhood education, which supports the argument for devoting more resources to early years education (see Box 9.7). Differences in education outcomes may reflect inequalities, but may also be due to differences in ability, motivation, or individual preferences.

Measuring vertical equity involves analysing how education is financed, how much different groups in society contribute towards financing education, and how much education different groups 'consume'. The measurement of both equality of opportunity and vertical equity are complicated by difficulties in measuring the quality of education.

[6] This is the concept of equity adopted by the OECD (2012: 9): 'in equitable education systems . . . the vast majority of students have the opportunity to attain high level skills, regardless of their own personal and socio-economic circumstances'.

[7] This varies considerably across countries, from 5 years in Bangladesh or Madagascar, to 16 years in Guatemala, and 17 years in Venezuela (UNESCO Institute for Statistics, 2024—processed by Our World in Data).

[8] These distributions may vary across the different levels of education.

9.2 The demand for education

Having looked at the objectives of the education system, the next question we want to consider is whether government intervention is necessary to achieve those objectives. But before we do that, it is helpful first to understand how individuals decide how much education to 'consume'. In this section, we briefly discuss three models of the demand for education: the human capital model; the screening hypothesis; and the capabilities model.

9.2.1 Human capital model

The human capital model explains individual demand for education by treating education as a type of investment, where individuals decide how much to invest in education by weighing up the costs and benefits. The main benefit of investing in education is the expectation of higher earnings in the future, although education may also involve consumption benefits. There may also be non-monetary benefits in the future (e.g. job satisfaction). The costs include both direct costs (e.g. tuition fees, cost of materials, travel costs, and possibly accommodation costs) and the cost of income forgone by spending time in education rather than working—this is the opportunity cost of education. We would expect both the costs and benefits to vary with the individual's age and level of education.

Figure 9.1 illustrates this model by comparing the earnings profile for an individual who starts working after completing compulsory education with the earnings profile of an individual who continues into further education. By entering the workplace right after completing compulsory education, the individual does not incur any additional costs and their earnings profile is illustrated by the dashed line in the figure. If the individual goes into further education, they will incur the direct costs DC (tuition fees, study material, travel costs) and the opportunity cost OC, which represents the income forgone by continuing in education until the age of 22 instead of joining the labour force. However, once they start

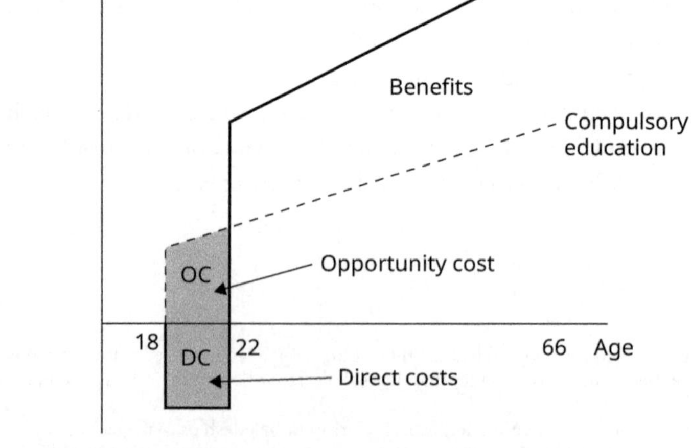

Figure 9.1 Costs and benefits of investing in education

working, they can expect to earn a higher wage. An individual will invest in education if the benefits, in terms of higher lifetime earnings, exceed the sum of the direct costs and opportunity cost.

We can also apply the cost–benefit framework covered in Chapter 5 to model this decision. Let us assume for simplicity that the only benefit of education is the increase in (money) income in the future. We can then calculate the net present value of an additional year of education using the following expression:[9]

$$NPV = \sum_{t=0}^{N} \frac{B_t}{(1+r)^t} - C_0$$

where B_t is the benefit, in terms of higher earnings, from an additional year of education, r is the individual's rate of time preference, and C_0 is the cost of that additional year of education. The individual will invest in education as long as the net present value is positive, or as long as the discounted stream of current and future benefits is greater than the cost.

This simple model, where we assume only monetary benefits to investing in education, essentially sets a lower bound for the optimal level of investment. The model can be extended to allow for consumption benefits, which would have the effect of reducing the cost C_0 and non-monetary benefits of education, which would lead to an increase in B_t.

How likely are individuals to choose the optimal level of investment in education? This would rely on individuals having full information about the current and future costs and benefits of education, as well as being able to borrow to cover the costs. As we will see below, these conditions are unlikely to hold and there is likely to be underinvestment in education in the absence of government intervention.

The human capital model highlights the role of education in developing the skills and knowledge that will enable individuals to be more productive workers and therefore earn a higher wage.[10] There are different approaches to measuring the returns to education, but the evidence suggests that individuals with a higher level of education can expect to earn a higher wage (see Box 9.2). However, this model ignores the intrinsic value of education—it cannot explain, for example, why someone might study a particular subject with no prospect of gaining an economic return from this.

9.2.2 Screening hypothesis

An alternative view of the decision to invest in education questions the crucial assumption underlying the human capital model that education leads to an increase in individual productivity and thereby leads to higher earnings. This view argues instead that investing in education does not improve individual productivity; rather, education acts as a signalling device indicating an individual's pre-existing ability. This perspective is based on the idea that

[9] See section 5.1.2 in Chapter 5 for a discussion of the net present value formula.

[10] The returns in terms of higher earnings from an additional year of education can be estimated using the wage equation proposed by Mincer (1958). This can be applied to all levels of schooling, not only post-compulsory education.

Box 9.2 Measuring the returns to education

There are several different approaches to measuring the private benefits from investing in education.

- **Relative earnings**: one approach is to compare the relative earnings of workers with different levels of education against some benchmark level of education. Across the OECD, workers who do not have upper secondary education earn, on average, 18 per cent less than those who do; while workers with tertiary education earn, on average, 56 per cent more. In Norway, this gap in earnings is much smaller: those with education below upper secondary level earn 14 per cent less, while those with tertiary education earn 18 per cent more, on average. By contrast, in Chile, this gap is much larger: those with below upper secondary education earn 51 per cent less, while those with tertiary education earn 161 per cent more, on average (OECD, 2024b).
- **Private net financial returns**: this widely used measure is based on the net present value of completing a given level of education. Across the OECD, the average private financial returns to tertiary education are US$343,000 for a man and US$292,700 for a woman (OECD, 2024b).[11] The only countries where women have higher private financial returns than men are Australia, Belgium, Denmark, Norway, Spain, Sweden, and Turkey (OECD, 2024b). Here, the benefits to tertiary education include the difference in tertiary-educated workers' estimated lifetime earnings from employment, after paying income taxes and social contributions, relative to the earnings of individuals who enter the labour force at the typical age of upper secondary completion. The costs include the costs of tertiary education and the forgone earnings while completing tertiary education. Student loans and part-time or part-year employment are not taken into account.
- **Benefit–cost ratio**: this measures the financial incentive to invest in education based on total benefits relative to total costs. Across the OECD, the average benefit–cost ratio for a man completing tertiary education was 7.1, compared with 8 for a woman (OECD, 2024b).
- **Internal rate of return**: this is the value of the discount rate, r, which ensures that the discounted benefits equal the discounted costs.[12] The internal rate of return can be interpreted as the interest rate on investing in higher education that an individual could expect to receive each year throughout their working life. On average, across the OECD, the internal rate of return is 15 per cent for men and 18 per cent for women (OECD, 2024b).

These measures of the private rates of return provide an incomplete picture, as they do not capture the non-monetary benefits (and costs) of investing in education.

[11] From a full-time, full-year job, compared to upper secondary and post-secondary education, where future costs and benefits are discounted at a rate of 2 per cent. Choosing the right discount rate is challenging in practice and can have a big impact on the results. It is therefore good practice to present results for various different discount rates. The OECD report discussed here also presents results using discount rates of 3.75 and 8 per cent.

[12] Both the benefit–cost ratio and the internal rate of return were covered in Chapter 5.

individuals have different levels of ability which affect their productivity. There are low-ability workers and high-ability workers, but employers are not able to distinguish between them, so individuals have an incentive to find a way to signal their level of ability to potential employers. Education, particularly post-primary education or education beyond a basic level, acts as such as signal. This is the **screening hypothesis**.

There has been much debate over whether the human capital model or the screening hypothesis provides the more accurate explanation of the role and purpose of education.[13] If the screening hypothesis holds true, this would not necessarily affect the individual decision to invest in education, but it does have implications for what the socially optimal level of spending on education should be, and for the role of the government in funding or providing education. If education acts primarily as a signal of ability, then individual private benefits from education will be greater than the societal benefits, suggesting a lower socially optimal level of spending on education, and a lower degree of government involvement. There is also then a question of whether education is the most efficient screening mechanism—is spending three years at university the best way to signal to a potential employer that the holder of the degree has the ability or characteristics required to be a successful finance manager?

Obvious exceptions to the screening hypothesis include situations where education involves some degree of professional training (e.g. medicine, dentistry, and engineering). It has also been argued that, in practice, individuals have a range of different skills and most jobs will require a combination of different skills. In this context, education can act as a matching device, helping to match workers and jobs.

9.2.3 The capabilities model

Both the human capital model and the screening hypothesis focus on the role of education in a narrow economic sense, where education is tied to individual ability and productivity. More educated workers are considered to be more skilled or to have a higher level of ability, which is associated with a higher level of productivity. The capabilities approach offers a more comprehensive view of the role of education, which focuses on people as individuals, rather than just workers, and where education has value beyond its potential to increase productivity.

The capabilities approach is based on the work of the economist Amartya Sen (2001).[14] Capabilities can be understood as the real opportunities individuals have to achieve various 'doings and beings', such as being healthy, being educated, having a job, or travelling. In the capability approach, education has both intrinsic and instrumental value: having access to an education that allows individuals to flourish is a valuable capability in itself; but being well educated can also help expand other capabilities. For example, education can open up opportunities to earn an income and become financially independent, and to participate more fully in politics and society. The capability approach therefore acknowledges the important role that education and the development of skills play in influencing productivity, but goes beyond this and highlights the impact of education on individual well-being more broadly and in influencing social changes.

[13] Some suggested articles on this debate are provided in the Further Reading at the end of the chapter.

[14] The capability approach was originally proposed by Sen and subsequently developed by the philosopher Martha Nussbaum, among others. See, for example, Nussbaum (2000).

At an individual level, this implies that individuals might not view education purely in financial terms—we might decide to learn a particular subject purely out of interest or for the joy of learning, without expecting to obtain a financial reward in return. The demand for education should not be driven by narrow economic reasoning. In terms of policy, the capability approach highlights the importance of not focusing on narrow policy outcomes when evaluating policies, but rather considering the impact of policies on all affected capabilities.

9.3 Arguments for government intervention

Given the objectives of the education system laid out above, why should the government be involved in funding and/or providing education? Could private markets achieve these objectives? Although it is often publicly provided, education is not a public good in the traditional sense,[15] since it is both rival—my consumption of education will reduce the amount available for others to consume—and excludable—it is possible to prevent someone from consuming education.[16] Education is a merit good—as we saw in Chapter 2, these are goods that individuals are likely to underconsume because they do not realize the full private benefits of consumption. Merit goods may also have wider social benefits associated with them.

In this section, we will start by discussing the arguments for government intervention to increase economic efficiency, before turning to the arguments based on promoting equity or social justice.

9.3.1 Intervention for efficiency reasons

In Chapter 2, we discussed the 'first-best assumptions'—the conditions required for the market to lead to an efficient allocation. These conditions were: perfect competition; the absence of externalities, public goods, or returns to scale; perfect information; utility-maximizing behaviour; complete markets; and no distortionary taxation. To what extent is a market for education likely to satisfy these conditions? This will depend to some extent on the level of education we are considering. In this section, we will be considering education in general.[17] There are five reasons why education markets are unlikely to satisfy these conditions.

Externalities

As we saw above, education may involve external benefits as well as private benefits—for example, increased worker productivity, improved social cohesion, and reduced crime. When consumption of a good or service results in positive spillover effects, the market will not lead to an efficient allocation of resources. The problem is illustrated in Figure 9.2: the positive externalities associated with education mean that the private marginal benefit (*PMB*) from consuming education is lower than the social marginal benefit (*SMB*). Individuals will

[15] Pure public goods were introduced in Chapter 2 and discussed in Chapter 6.

[16] Whether education is strictly rival in consumption depends on how we define it. Teaching, for example, is non-rival up to a point of saturation: a teacher can teach an increasing number of students at a low marginal cost per student as long as the class is not too large; once the class size reaches a point of saturation, then teaching one additional student detracts from the education that can be provided to the other students.

[17] We will consider these arguments in the particular context of compulsory education and tertiary education in sections 9.5 and 9.6, respectively.

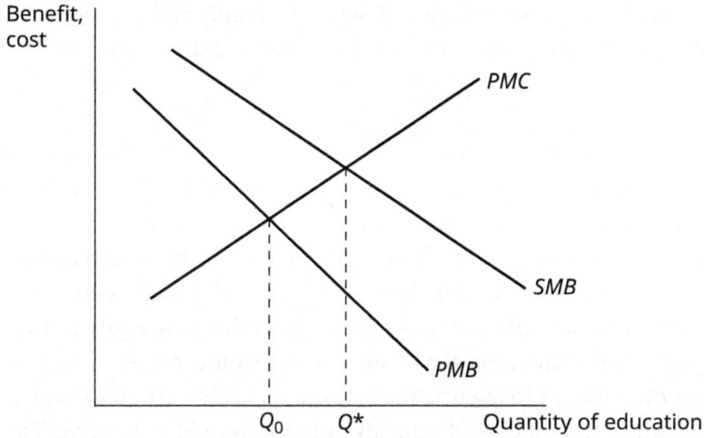

Figure 9.2 Private and social benefits of education

only consider their own private benefit when deciding how much education to consume, so the equilibrium level of education demanded in the market will be Q_0, which is less than the socially optimal level Q^*.

Imperfect information

Will consumers have full information about the nature of the product (education) and prices? In the context of compulsory education, the primary consumers are children and therefore there is reason to suppose they will not be well informed. Decisions about education are likely to be made by their parents or guardians, who may themselves have only limited information. Education is complex; to make a fully informed decision, parents would need information on factors including the quality of the school, staffing and resource levels, and the quality of teaching, as well as a full understanding of the benefits of education. Information on prices may be easier to determine, as information on private school fees is likely to be more readily available. However, information about prices is only really useful in combination with information about the product, as education is by no means a homogeneous good and the quality of education can vary enormously.

Parents therefore might not act in the best interest of their children because they do not have all the necessary information. If there is competition for students among education institutions, then these institutions have an incentive to provide the information to help students/parents make informed choices. However, the scope for mistakes is still significant, and although the costs of making a mistake may not be as high as they potentially are in the context of healthcare, they can still be significant, particularly with early years education. The question is whether the government is in a better position to make decisions about what level (and type) of education is right for children.

Lack of utility-maximizing behaviour

Where parents are making decisions on behalf of their children, they might not have their children's best interests in mind and instead may make decisions based on the interests of the family as a whole, or based on their own private self-interest. Sending a child to school may involve sacrifices on the part of the parent, which they are unwilling to make. For example, there may be costs that need to be financed out of the family budget, such as travel, clothing, or equipment costs, or parents may prefer to have their children at home to help out around the house.

Imperfect competition

Perfect competition requires a large number of buyers and sellers, exchanging goods or services that are homogeneous, and no barriers to enter or exit the market. Are there conditions for perfect competition between schools? In large urban areas, there may be enough schools and students for there to be some degree of competition. However, in smaller rural areas, schools may have some degree of monopoly power, which could result in higher prices. The idea that competition would result in bad schools closing down because they would lose customers (parents/children) assumes that parents are able to realize when the quality of education being provided is poor. The problems of imperfect information discussed above suggest that parents' ability to adequately monitor education quality may be weak.

Incomplete markets

The human capital framework analysed above suggests that as long at the net present value of investing in education is positive, then students (or their parents) should invest in education. If they do not have the savings to fund this investment, they may need to resort to borrowing. With perfect capital markets, students would be able to borrow against their expected future earnings to pay for their education. But capital markets are not perfect and lenders generally require some form of collateral. For example, when someone borrows to buy a house, the house itself acts as collateral, so if the individual fails to keep up with their mortgage repayments, the lender can take their house. Future earnings cannot be offered as collateral. If students (or their parents) cannot provide another form of collateral, they are unlikely to be able to borrow, which will result in underinvestment in education in a pure market system. Since wealthier and higher-income individuals are more likely to have the collateral to offer (e.g. housing or other assets), the problem of incomplete markets for education finance risks exacerbating socioeconomic inequalities.

A further problem relates to the difficulty in drawing up a contract that specifies precisely what schools should deliver, given the complex and multidimensional nature of education. In these circumstances, and particularly if quality is difficult to monitor effectively, there is an argument for government to provide education directly.

Each of these arguments has different implications for the nature of government intervention in education. We return to this point in section 9.4.

9.3.2 Intervention for equity reasons

A pure market system for financing and providing education would be highly inequitable. In a pure market system, individuals (or their parents) would choose how much education to consume based on their preferences and ability to pay, where their ability to pay for education would depend on their income, savings, or ability to borrow. Such a system would be incompatible with the goal of horizontal equity, since access to education would depend on individual incomes.

A lack of income would limit access to education directly, by affecting an individual's ability to pay for education or their ability to borrow to finance education. A lack of income would also limit access to education indirectly, by exacerbating problems of imperfect information, as access to knowledge and information about the value of education and how the education system works—and the ability to make use of that information—can depend on socioeconomic status. Investing in education also means sacrificing income today in the expectation of higher earnings in the future, and individuals who have less money and are less able to borrow may rationally choose to invest less in education. These individuals are likely to come from lower-income backgrounds. As education is linked to higher lifetime incomes, a pure market system would therefore reduce social mobility and perpetuate intergenerational inequality.

A pure market system for education would also not be compatible with vertical equity goals. In a pure market system, each individual (or their parents) only pays for the education they consume, so there is no redistribution. Government involvement in education can provide an effective way of reducing economic inequality. If we believe that the education system should redistribute from those with higher incomes to those with lower incomes, then some form of government intervention will be necessary. In theory, a tax-financed and publicly provided education system, with compulsory free education for all, is redistributive, as those on higher incomes will pay more in taxes, but everyone would receive the same 'amount' of education. In practice, ensuring everyone receives the same amount of education is challenging—while measuring the quantity of education may be straightforward, measuring the quality of education and ensuring everyone receives the same standard of education is difficult.

9.4 Types of government intervention

Having looked at the various arguments for government intervention in education, the next question we need to consider is what form that intervention should take. In this section, we discuss the different ways in which governments intervene in education and how the role of government in education varies across countries.

As we saw in Chapter 1, there are three broad categories of government intervention in the economy:

- **Regulation**: in the context of education, the government might regulate the quantity of compulsory education, school curricula, minimum qualifications for teachers, basic requirements for teaching establishments, inspections to verify quality, and potentially the level of fees that could be charged by private education providers. Government regulations could help address the problems of imperfect information, externalities, failure of utility-maximizing behaviour, and imperfect competition. Setting minimum standards, defining school curricula and teacher qualifications, and monitoring and enforcing these can also be a useful means of achieving horizontal equity goals.
- **Subsidies**: these could be used to encourage consumption of education, helping to promote horizontal equity by expanding access for lower-income students, and addressing some of the problems raised by education externalities and imperfect competition. Types of government subsidies in education include tuition subsidies, interest rate

subsidies, and scholarships or grants to finance other expenses, such as study materials or living expenses. Providing subsidies to students, rather than making the payments directly to education institutions, can help increase competition between institutions. Governments could also provide subsidies to support the development of particular subject areas.

- **Direct production and provision of goods and services**: governments may also finance, produce, and allocate education directly. In many countries, compulsory education is often publicly financed and publicly provided.[18] Public production may be desirable if problems of imperfect information are severe, and if standards and quality are easier to monitor in the public sector. However, it is also important to consider whether public production is more or less efficient than private sector production. This in turn will depend to some extent on whether parents or the state are better placed to make decisions about children's education. The problem of incomplete markets for education finance suggests a role for the government in providing loans for education or creating a framework for privately financed loans.

As in the case of healthcare, it is useful to distinguish different modes of funding and providing education. Education may be publicly funded and publicly provided, publicly funded and privately provided, or privately funded and privately provided. Table 9.2 provides some examples.

Spending on education varies considerably across countries. Across the OECD, average spending on education in 2020 was 5.15 per cent of GDP and the majority of this (4.33 per cent of GDP) was public spending, with average private spending below 1 per cent of GDP (Figure 9.3). Education spending was highest in Norway, the UK, Australia,

Table 9.2 Modes of finance and provision in education

Finance and provision	Example
Public finance and public provision	Compulsory education in most countries is generally funded by general or local taxation, and children attend their local state school.[a]
Public finance and private provision	Government transfers to private entities to provide workplace training or apprenticeship programmes. In Norway, the government provides large subsidies to private companies for vocational education and training (VET) apprenticeships. Private schools in Sweden and New Zealand receive government funding (subject to certain conditions).
Private finance and private provision	Many countries include a small private or independent school sector, where schools are privately run and parents pay tuition fees for their children to attend the school.

[a] Some students may attend private schools instead, which operate alongside state schools.

Source: Based on OECD (2023).

[18] Publicly provided education is an example of a transfer in kind.

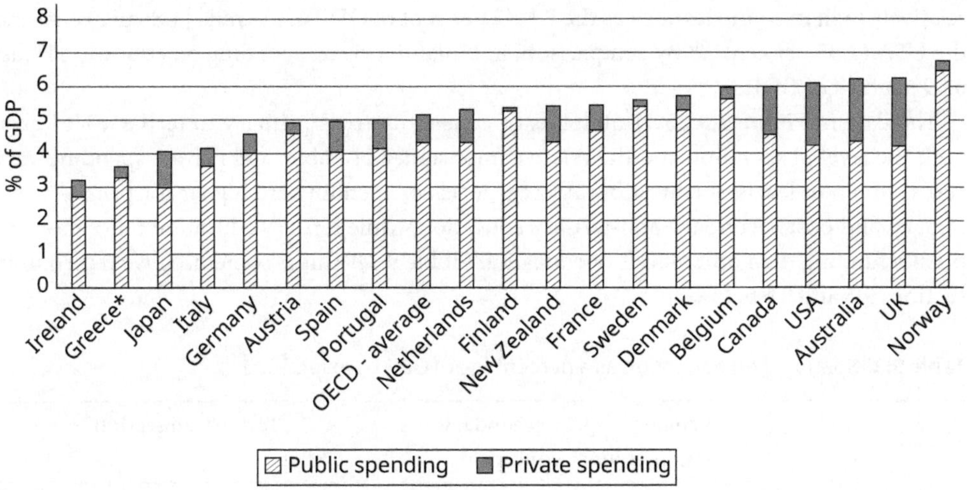

Figure 9.3 Public and private spending on education as a share of GDP for selected OECD countries, 2020

Note: Data for Greece for 2019. All levels of education (primary to tertiary).

Source: OECD (2024e).

the USA, Canada and Belgium, at 6 per cent of GDP or higher. This compares with spending of around 3 per cent of GDP in Ireland. But, of course, it is not just the level of spending that matters, but whether this leads to better education outcomes—a point we return to in section 9.5 below.

Across all countries, the majority of spending on education was public spending, although the relative importance of public spending varies across different levels of education. Public spending includes direct spending by government departments and other public bodies on educational institutions, as well as education-related public subsidies given to households. Public funding plays an important role in compulsory education in most countries, but less so in higher education. In 2020, across the OECD, on average 91 per cent of the funding for primary to post-secondary non-tertiary education institutions came directly from the government, compared with only 67 per cent for tertiary education institutions. Government funding is mostly spent on public institutions, although in some countries a significant proportion of government funding goes towards private institutions. On average across the OECD, government spending on public educational institutions was around $11,600 per student, compared with around $6,700 per student on private institutions.[19] However, in Denmark, for example, average government spending on public institutions was $14,800 per student, whereas average government spending on private institutions was $15,000 per student (OECD, 2023).

Private spending includes all spending by households and other private entities on educational institutions (e.g. school fees and tuition fees), but excluding spending on textbooks, private tutoring, and living costs. As Figure 9.3 shows, private spending on education is

[19] Spending across all levels of education, from primary to tertiary.

relatively high in countries such as the UK (2 per cent of GDP), Australia (1.86 per cent) and the USA (1.85 per cent).[20] By comparison, in Finland, private spending on education is just 0.09 per cent of GDP.

The data in Figure 9.3 cover all levels of education, from primary to tertiary. However, both the level of spending and the relative importance of public and private spending vary across different levels of education. Average levels of spending are higher for primary, secondary, and post-secondary non-tertiary education, while tertiary education relies more on private funding than other levels of education (Table 9.3). This is something we return to in sections 9.5 and 9.6 below.

Table 9.3 Spending on education as a percentage of GDP by level, 2020

	Primary to post-secondary non-tertiary education			Tertiary education		
	Public	Private	Total	Public	Private	Total
Australia	3.69	0.66	4.35	0.68	1.20	1.88
Austria	2.96	0.13	3.09	1.64	0.18	1.82
Belgium	4.25	0.13	4.41	1.37	0.21	1.64
Canada	3.36	0.27	3.63	1.21	1.15	2.37
Denmark	3.70	0.20	3.89	1.59	0.22	1.91
Finland	3.82	0.02	3.84	1.45	0.07	1.60
France	3.53	0.33	3.86	1.17	0.41	1.61
Germany	2.91	0.35	3.26	1.11	0.21	1.34
Greece	2.58	0.20	2.79	0.70	0.12	0.93
Ireland	2.15	0.27	2.42	0.57	0.21	0.81
Italy	3.01	0.15	3.17	0.62	0.37	1.01
Japan	2.49	0.19	2.68	0.49	0.89	1.38
Netherlands	3.13	0.47	3.60	1.21	0.50	1.76
New Zealand	3.40	0.36	3.75	0.95	0.69	1.65
Norway	4.65	0.14	4.80	1.82	0.13	1.98
Portugal	3.38	0.46	3.84	0.77	0.39	1.27
Spain	3.08	0.43	3.51	0.96	0.47	1.46
Sweden	4.05	0.01	4.06	1.34	0.18	1.60
UK	3.70	0.55	4.25	0.51	1.48	2.06
USA	3.29	0.28	3.57	0.94	1.57	2.52
OECD average	3.33	0.31	3.56	0.99	0.50	1.52

Note: Data for Greece from 2019.
Source: OECD (2024e).

[20] Private spending on education is generally higher in English-speaking countries, partly due to a shared neoliberal spirit in public policy that was not quite as entrenched in other European countries.

9.5 Compulsory education

Compulsory education refers to the number of years that children are legally obliged to attend school. Most countries across the world today have some form of compulsory education, but this varies considerably, from 5 years in Bangladesh or Madagascar, to 16 years in Guatemala, and 17 years in Venezuela.[21] In the UK, children are required to attend school for 11 years, from the age of 5 to 16.[22] Compulsory education is often divided into separate levels, including primary and secondary education; secondary education is sometimes split between lower and upper secondary education. How is compulsory education typically funded and provided, and why? What are some of the key issues affecting compulsory education and what policies have governments used to tackle these?

9.5.1 Overview of compulsory education

The majority of spending on education goes towards compulsory education, but this varies across the different levels of education. Table 9.4 shows the average spending per student for early childhood education, primary education, and secondary education across a selection of OECD countries in 2020.[23] Average spend per student tends to rise with the level of education: across the OECD as a whole, average spend per student is $11,942 in secondary education, compared with $10,658 per student in primary education.[24] Of the countries listed, only Greece, Italy, Denmark, and Sweden spend more on primary than on secondary education, on average, and in the latter two countries the difference is marginal. Where data on spending on early childhood education are available, this tends to be lower than average spending on either primary or secondary education. The exceptions here are Denmark, Finland, Norway, and Sweden, where average spend per student is highest for early childhood education.[25]

Of course, it is not just the level of spending that matters, but how this translates into education outcomes. The challenges of meaningfully measuring education outcomes were discussed in section 9.1. One measure that is widely used, particularly for international comparisons, is the Programme for International Student Assessment (PISA) test scores. These are based on an internationally standardized assessment administered to 15-year-olds, covering three areas: reading, maths, and science.[26] Table 9.5 shows the average test scores in these three areas for a selection of countries.

[21] UNESCO Institute for Statistics (2024)—processed by Our World in Data.

[22] In England, students must continue some form of education or training until the age of 18, either by remaining in full-time education, starting an apprenticeship, or spending 20 hours or more a week working or volunteering while in part-time education or training.

[23] The Covid-19 pandemic in 2020 will have affected education spending, as education systems had to adapt to remote learning. This impact varied significantly across countries, but on average across the OECD, total expenditure on primary to tertiary education institutions per full-time equivalent student increased by only 0.4 per cent between 2019 and 2020 (OECD, 2023).

[24] Data on spending on early childhood education are not available for all countries, so comparing this average with average spend on primary and secondary education may be misleading.

[25] This is relevant because, as Box 9.7 highlights, research shows that early childhood education plays a vital role in determining later life outcomes.

[26] See the OECD Programme for International Student Assessment (PISA): https://www.oecd.org/en/about/programmes/pisa.html.

Table 9.4 Average spending per student by level of education, 2020 (US$ per student)

	Early childhood education	Primary education	Secondary education
Australia	8,983	12,673	15,437
Austria	12,698	14,029	17,478
Belgium	n/a	12,813	16,576
Canada	n/a	11,533	14,520
Denmark	16,508	14,273	14,125
Finland	16,016	11,212	12,849
France	9,986	9,673	13,874
Germany	15,049	11,587	15,614
Greece	n/a	7,467	6,901
Ireland	9,580	9,589	11,379
Italy	10,032	12,008	10,569
Japan	8,557	10,057	12,047
Netherlands	11,562	11,188	15,848
New Zealand	n/a	8,438	10,223
Norway	22,386	15,631	17,229
Portugal	n/a	9,340	11,358
Spain	8,742	9,077	11,159
Sweden	16,621	13,997	13,902
UK	6,750	12,513	13,695
USA	n/a	14,321	16,018
OECD average	11,260	10,658	11,942

Note: n/a = not available. Data for Greece from 2019. 'OECD average' refers to average across the whole of the OECD, not just the countries listed in the table.
Source: OECD (2024d).

The data in Tables 9.4 and 9.5 suggest the relationship between education spending and average test scores is weak. Austria, Norway, and the USA are among the highest spenders in primary and secondary education, yet they do not feature in the top three for reading, maths, or science (among the countries listed in Table 9.4). Japan has the highest score for maths and science, yet average spending in primary and secondary education is close to the OECD average. Finland and Canada also perform well in the PISA rankings, yet both have relatively modest levels of spending on primary education. Finland has high average spending on early childhood education, but modest spending on secondary education, while Canada's average spending on secondary education is well above the OECD average, but it is not one of the highest spenders overall. Of course, it is important to keep in mind that these PISA scores are an average for each country and therefore may mask substantial differences within countries—for example, between regions, genders, ethnicities, and socioeconomic groups.

Table 9.5 Education outcomes: Programme for International Student Assessment (PISA) average test scores, 2018

	Reading performance	Maths performance	Science performance
Australia	503	491	503
Austria	484	499	490
Belgium	493	508	499
Canada	520	512	518
Denmark	501	509	493
Finland	520	507	522
France	493	495	493
Germany	498	500	503
Greece	457	451	452
Ireland	518	500	496
Italy	476	487	468
Japan	504	527	529
Netherlands	485	519	503
New Zealand	506	494	508
Norway	499	501	490
Portugal	492	492	492
Spain	n/a	481	483
Sweden	506	502	499
UK	504	502	505
USA	505	478	502
OECD average	487	489	489

Source: OECD (2024f).

High average scores may reflect very high achievement at the top of the distribution, for example. Box 9.3 discusses some of the evidence on the relationship between spending and education outcomes.

How is compulsory education typically funded and provided? Traditionally, the most common system for compulsory education in industrialized countries was for education to be publicly funded, provided, and regulated. Schools were funded by taxation and were typically centrally planned by the government—at either national or regional/local level. The school that children attended was determined by where they lived, and only parents who could afford to move closer to a better school, or could afford a private school, had some element of choice. What students were required to learn in school and the standards they were expected to meet at each level of education were typically set by the government through national curricula. The primary aim was to ensure that all students, regardless of income, had access to a basic minimum level of education, and to ensure a degree of uniformity of content

Box 9.3 Does higher spending lead to better outcomes?

Some studies have suggested that the correlation between spending on education and education outcomes is weak (World Bank, 2019). However, a recent review of 13 different studies from across the USA has found strong evidence to support a significant impact of spending on student outcomes (Jackson, 2020). One study reviewed found that a 10 per cent increase in spending per student per year led to a 0.31 increase in completed years if education, a 7 per cent increase in wages, and a 3.2 percentage point decrease in the annual incidence of poverty. The study also found the effects were more noticeable for children from low-income families. A review of evidence for the UK has similarly found that the amount of spending on education does matter (Department of Education, 2017).

But it is not just the level of spending that matters; how the money is spent is also important, as is the institutional context. Education systems with lower bureaucratic quality and higher corruption are less likely to use resources effectively (World Bank, 2019). Gundlach et al. (2001) compared the cost and quality of schooling across the OECD between 1974 and 1994, using student performance in standardized achievement tests as a measure of education quality. They found a negative relation between the change in the quality of schooling output and changes in the relative price of schooling across OECD countries. They argue these findings imply that it is not just spending on education that matters; the structure of decision-making and the incentives within the education sector are vital determinants of the productivity of schooling. We also know that education outcomes depend not only on spending, but also on the wider socioeconomic context.

and standards in education. As Figure 9.4 shows, government funding is still the dominant source of funding for non-tertiary education.

The arguments reviewed in section 9.3 provide a strong case for government intervention in compulsory education, both to increase efficiency and to promote greater equity.

- The externalities associated with education suggest a role for the government in setting the level of compulsory education, to reduce the risk of underconsumption and to ensure that everyone receives a basic minimum level of education.
- Problems of imperfect information are likely to be particularly significant in the context of compulsory education. Even if parents or guardians are making decisions on behalf of their children, the parents themselves may not have the information needed to make a fully informed decision or they may not make decisions that are in the best interests of their children, which may result in children not receiving the optimal level of education.
- Incomplete markets may mean that some individuals who want to consume more education are unable to do so, particularly those on lower incomes, who have lower savings, or who find it more difficult to borrow. This risks exacerbating problems of horizontal equity.[27]

[27] Even if there are no school fees to be paid, as under a tax-financed education system, there are other costs associated with school attendance (e.g. uniforms, sports equipment, and travel).

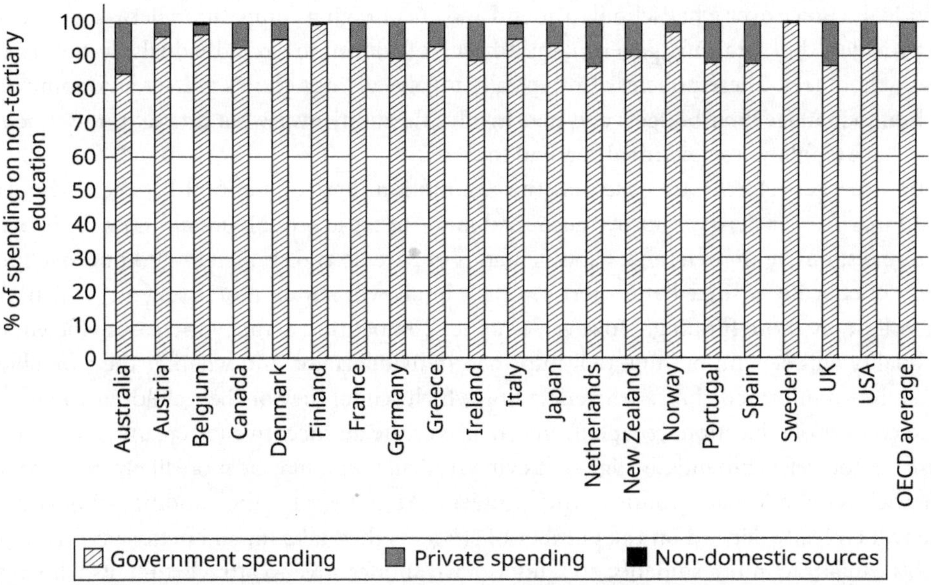

Figure 9.4 Relative share of government and private spending on education in primary, secondary, and post-secondary non-tertiary education, 2020

Notes: For Canada, primary education includes pre-primary programmes. Data for Greece are for 2019. For the USA, figures are for net student loans rather than gross, thereby underestimating public transfers. Figures are after government transfers to the private sector. OECD average is average across all OECD countries, not just those presented here.

Source: OECD (2023), table C3.1.

These arguments provide a case for government regulation and for an active role of government in financing compulsory education. However, they do not necessarily imply governments should be the sole providers of education. As discussed above, whether education should be provided by the public or private sector will depend in part on whether production is more efficient in the public or the private sector, and whether it is easier to regulate standards and quality in the public or the private sector. Publicly provided education has been argued to be less responsive to the preferences or demands of students, parents, and employers, and to leave little room for parental choice. The lack of competition between education providers has also been argued to have contributed to the fall in productivity in education across the OECD (Gundlach et al., 2001).

9.5.2 Government policies to support compulsory education

Given the debate about the role of government in the provision of compulsory education, and the potential benefits of competition between education providers, two policies that have been proposed to promote competition and choice within education are the introduction of 'quasi-market' reforms and school vouchers. We discuss each of these in turn below.

Quasi-markets in education

Quasi-markets essentially involve combining elements of a market system, such as choice and competition, with elements of a non-market system, such as providing goods or services for free at the point of use. In the context of education, quasi-market reforms involve giving individuals choice over what school to attend and encouraging competition between education providers, but retaining government funding of education, so individuals do not have to pay school fees. These policies also typically involve giving schools greater autonomy or freedom to manage their budgets and may involve flexibility over what is taught, so schools do not have to follow a set national curriculum.

Quasi-market reforms are based on the assumption that competition between schools should increase efficiency, improve accountability—because schools should now in theory be more responsive to preferences and demands of parents and students—and improve the quality of education, since better-performing schools will attract more students, which in turn will imply more funding. However, whether competition actually increases efficiency and quality will depend on how well informed individuals are, and whether they are able to exercise an informed choice when deciding which school they or their children attend.[28] In the context of education, competition can also create an incentive for cream-skimming, where schools select potentially high-achieving students, who may be more likely to be from high socioeconomic backgrounds. This problem arises because the funding schools receive will typically depend on the number of students they take in, and better-performing schools can attract more students, so schools have an incentive to attract students who are likely to perform better. Since education performance is heavily influenced by socioeconomic background, schools will have an incentive to try and recruit students from better-off backgrounds.[29]

There is also a question about the desirability of giving schools the freedom to decide what to teach, unencumbered by having to follow a set national curriculum. On the one hand, this gives schools freedom to experiment and allows them to be more responsive to wider societal changes, adapting their curricula accordingly. However, having a set national curriculum and a national testing strategy promotes equality of opportunity and provides a benchmark for parents to compare the performance of different schools.

In England and Wales, the Education Reform Act 1988 paved the way for a quasi-market approach. It introduced a system of open enrolment, where parents could choose what school to enrol their children in,[30] and schools received funding from the government based on their number of students. Schools were also allowed to opt out of local government control, receiving funding directly from the central government. The rise of academy schools illustrates this shift towards quasi-markets in education in England (see Box 9.4). Similar reforms have been followed in countries including Chile, New Zealand and the USA.

[28] There is also the question of whether there is enough flexibility on the supply side for competition to increase efficiency. In practice, schools that are in high demand need to find a way of rationing or allocating places, which may involve prioritizing those who live near the school (particularly if schools are not allowed to select on academic ability). This pushes up house prices in the area (Gibbons & Machin, 2003). This can increase inequality, as it is typically people with higher incomes who can afford to live next to better schools.

[29] This problem is analogous to one that arises in private unregulated health insurance markets, where health insurance companies have an incentive to select healthier clients and not to provide insurance to clients with pre-existing health conditions.

[30] Provided the school was not oversubscribed.

Box 9.4 The rise of academies in England: increasing competition and choice

Academy schools were introduced in England in the early 2000s. By 2023/24 there were over 10,000 academies and more than half of all students in England attended an academy school. Now 43 per cent of primary schools and 82 per cent of secondary schools in England are academies or free schools. Academies are part of a complex system of schools that includes community or local authority maintained schools, foundation schools, free schools, grammar schools, and private schools. Academies receive their funding directly from the government; they do not charge fees and cannot be run for profit. But rather than being run by local authorities, they are run by an academy trust. This means they have more autonomy over how they do things—for example, they are not required to follow the national curriculum and can set their own term times. However, they have to follow the same rules as other state schools on admissions, special educational needs, and exclusions, and their students sit the same exams. Academy trusts are not-for-profit companies, whose trustees are responsible for the performance of the academy. Trusts might have a single academy, or they might run a group of academies.

The freedom with which academies can operate has been argued to lead to better attainment, improved leadership, and more opportunities for innovation. Some academies are sponsored by other organizations, such as businesses, universities, or voluntary groups, which are responsible for appointing the academy's leadership team. This has led to some concerns over conflicts of interest. And because academies are not required to follow the national curriculum and have the freedom to hire unqualified teachers, this has led to concerns over standards. Critics have also argued that, particularly in large multi-academy trusts, individual schools may in fact have less autonomy than when they were under the control of local authorities.

Sources: UK Government (n.d.) and UK Parliament (n.d.).

School vouchers

School vouchers are based on the same rationale of promoting choice and competition as the quasi-market reforms discussed above, but they go one step further. Under this scheme, parents receive a grant or voucher which they can spend on a school of their choice, and these schools can be either public or private.[31] Education vouchers therefore encourage competition not only between public or state schools, but also between public and private schools. The vouchers may involve a flat rate, set at a level intended to cover the average cost of schooling for a child of a particular age; or the value of the voucher may be linked to family income. Some versions of the voucher scheme also allow parents to supplement the value of the voucher with their own money if the fees at their desired school are higher than the value of the voucher.

[31] Charter schools are another example of a mechanism for using public funds to finance private schools.

Under the voucher scheme, schools may be subject to other regulations (or not). Schools that receive vouchers may be subject to government inspections, or schools may be required to follow set allocation rules if they are oversubscribed rather than having the freedom to allocate places to students as they wish. For example, schools that are oversubscribed may be required to give priority to students who live in the area, or to allocate places via a ballot.

Underlying the voucher scheme is the assumption that some education should be produced in the private sector, which may be more efficient or more likely to foster innovation. Proponents of school voucher schemes argue this will improve student performance. A universal voucher scheme would also increase competition for students, which would force public schools to become more productive, thereby leading to improved student outcomes in the public sector as well.

Critics of education vouchers argue that an unconstrained voucher scheme goes against equity goals, by effectively subsidizing parents who are able to afford private education, and does not represent the best use of public resources, since the money could be used to improve public schools instead. Evidence suggests parents use the socioeconomic composition of a school's student body as a proxy for school quality,[32] so any large-scale school voucher programme would risk increasing socioeconomic segregation of schools, as parents try to move their children into schools where students have a higher average socioeconomic background. Private schools typically have more discretion to select which students they accept, whereas public schools have to accommodate a more diverse student body, which will impact on school costs and student performance.

Different models of education voucher schemes have been used in a number of countries, including Chile, Sweden and the USA (see Box 9.5).

Box 9.5 School voucher programmes in practice

This box considers the implementation of school voucher programmes in three countries: Chile, Sweden, and the USA.

Chile

One of the earliest universal school voucher programmes was introduced in Chile in the early 1980s. Under this programme, the government provided a flat subsidy to the school of a family's choice, which could be in the public or private sector. The value of the subsidy did not depend on family income, and private schools were allowed to be selective with their admissions. More than 1,000 private schools entered the market, and the private enrolment rate increased by 20 percentage points (Hsieh & Urquiola, 2006). More than half of urban schools are private and the majority run on a for-profit basis (McEwan et al., 2008). The programme encouraged higher-income and high-ability students out of public sector schools, and about half of all children attend a private school in Chile. The impact on educational performance has been disappointing and Chile's performance in the 2000 PISA ranking was well below the OECD average (McEwan et al., 2008). Research on the impact of competition from private schools on the performance of public schools also found this to be negligible (McEwan, 2000). These poor results motivated a reform introduced in 2008, the Subvención Escolar Preferencial (SEP), which raised the value of school vouchers used to fund private and public

[32] See, for example, the evidence reviewed in Ladd (2002).

schools by 50 per cent for students from lower socioeconomic backgrounds. To be eligible for the vouchers, schools could not charge fees for these students or select students based on academic ability. An assessment of this reform found little evidence that the policy led to a significant reduction in the achievement gap or substantial achievement gains (Feigenberg et al., 2019).

Sweden

Sweden introduced a universal school voucher programme in 1992, alongside reforms to increase parental choice. In the Swedish system, public and private (independent) schools receive funding on almost equal terms, and all schools are eligible for public funding, including religious schools and for-profit schools. Parents can choose between state-run schools and state-funded independent schools. However, to receive public funds, schools cannot charge additional tuition fees and cannot select students based on academic ability. For example, private schools are not able to refuse low-ability students. The number of independent schools increased from 90 in 1991/92 to around 400 in 2001/02. The number of students enrolled in independent schools was only 4 per cent in 2002, but this number was increasing rapidly. Sweden tends to perform well in the PISA rankings and research suggests that these reforms have led to improvements in the standards of public schools (Sandström & Bergström, 2005).

The USA

Smaller-scale publicly funded school voucher programmes have also been introduced across the USA, including in Milwaukee, Cleveland, and Florida, as well as small privately funded programmes providing vouchers for low- and moderate-income students in cities including New York City, Dayton, Ohio, and Washington, DC. It is difficult to draw general conclusions from the studies of the US programmes, since these covered only a fraction of eligible students. A comprehensive review of various voucher programmes (both universal and small scale) found that, although there have been benefits associated with some schemes, there is not enough evidence to support widespread adoption of education vouchers at this stage (Epple et al., 2017).

9.6 Tertiary education

Tertiary education[33] covers all formal post-secondary education, including academic and higher vocational education. Academic education, which includes undergraduate and postgraduate degrees, is sometimes referred to as higher education (HE), while higher vocational education is sometimes referred to as further education or continuing education.[34] How is tertiary education typically funded and provided, and why? What are some of the key challenges affecting tertiary education, and what policies have governments used to address these?

[33] Tertiary education is also sometimes referred to as post-secondary education.

[34] The term 'further education' is often used in the UK, whereas 'continuing education' is more commonly used in the USA.

9.6.1 Overview of tertiary education

Total spending on tertiary education is lower than spending on other levels of education. As we saw in Table 9.3 above, across the OECD, average spending on tertiary education is 1.52 per cent of GDP, which is less than half of the level of spending on primary, secondary, and post-secondary non-tertiary education combined. However this varies across countries, as Table 9.6 illustrates: spending on tertiary education ranges from less than 1 per cent of GDP in Ireland, to more than double that in Canada (2.37 per cent) and the USA (2.52 per cent).

While total spending on tertiary education is lower, average spending per student is generally significantly higher than average spending per student at lower levels of education. Higher levels of education typically require teachers to have more specialist knowledge and more advanced qualifications, which leads to higher salaries. Average spending per student on tertiary education across the OECD was US$18,105 in 2020, compared with US$10,658 for primary education and US$11,942 for secondary education (Tables 9.4 and 9.6).

Table 9.6 Average spending on tertiary education across countries, 2020

	% of GDP	US$ per student
Australia	1.88	22,204
Austria	1.82	21,753
Belgium	1.64	22,555
Canada	2.37	24,363
Denmark	1.91	23,432
Finland	1.60	19,583
France	1.61	18,880
Germany	1.34	20,760
Greece	0.93	4,300
Ireland	0.81	17,400
Italy	1.01	12,663
Japan	1.38	19,676
Netherlands	1.76	21,642
New Zealand	1.65	19,567
Norway	1.98	24,374
Portugal	1.27	12,104
Spain	1.46	14,361
Sweden	1.60	26,215
UK	2.06	29,534
USA	2.52	36,172
OECD average	1.52	18,105

Note: Data for Greece for 2019. 'OECD average' refers to average across the whole of the OECD, not just the countries listed in the table.

Source: OECD (2024c).

Average spending per student on tertiary education was highest in the USA ($36,172) and the UK ($29,534). By comparison, average spending in Portugal was just $12,104 per student, and in Greece this figure was even lower at $4,300 per student.

Do higher levels of spending lead to better outcomes? This question is even harder to answer in the context of tertiary education, as there is no standardized measure of achievement comparable to the PISA test scores we looked at in section 9.5. Tertiary education is more specialized, covering a wide range of areas, both academic and vocational, and different types of institutions, including universities, colleges, technical institutions, and vocational schools. This makes deriving a set of measures for comparing the education outcomes of these different institutions extremely difficult. Global university rankings are published, but these offer an incomplete picture because they tend to be either teaching or research focused and do not cover all the other types of institutions that are involved in providing tertiary education.

The number of people completing tertiary education has been increasing. On average across the OECD, in 2005, 32.17 per cent of people aged 25–34 had a tertiary education qualification; by 2022, this had increased to 47.42 per cent (Figure 9.5).[35] However, there is considerable variation between countries: more than half of people in this age group now have a tertiary qualification in a number of countries, including Spain, Sweden, Ireland, Japan, the UK, and Canada; but in Italy and Germany, the figure is less than 40 per cent. In Portugal, the proportion of people aged 25–34 with a tertiary qualification more than doubled, from 19.11 per cent in 2005 to 44.44 per cent in 2022. These different trajectories reflect, in part, the different policies governments have adopted to support tertiary education.

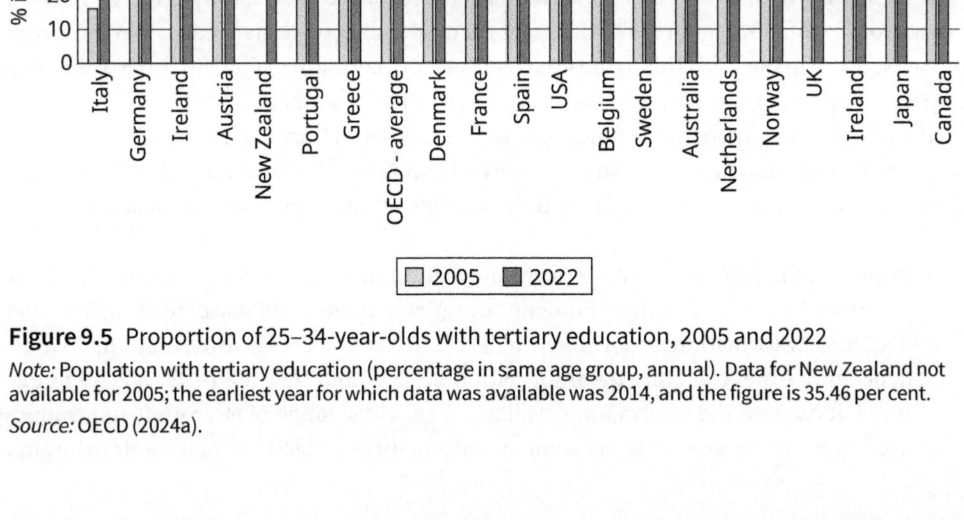

Figure 9.5 Proportion of 25–34-year-olds with tertiary education, 2005 and 2022

Note: Population with tertiary education (percentage in same age group, annual). Data for New Zealand not available for 2005; the earliest year for which data was available was 2014, and the figure is 35.46 per cent.

Source: OECD (2024a).

[35] Tertiary education here includes theoretical programmes leading to advanced research or high-skill professions (e.g. medicine), as well as more vocational programmes leading to the labour market.

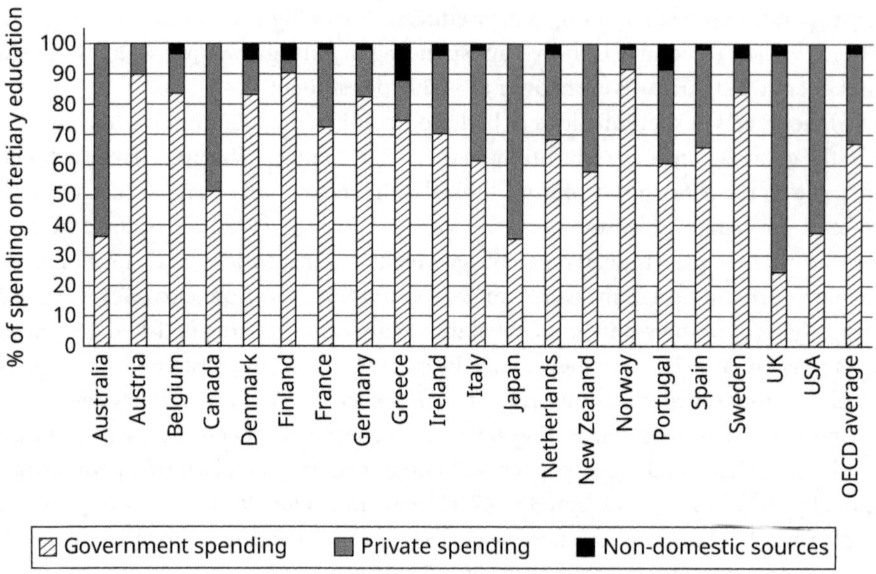

Figure 9.6 Relative share of government and private spending on tertiary education, 2020

Notes: Data for Greece are for 2019. For the USA, figures are for net student loans rather than gross, thereby underestimating public transfers. Figures are after government transfers to the private sector. Non-domestic sources include direct international payments to educational institutions (e.g. research grants).

Source: OECD (2023), table C3.1.

As we saw above, tertiary education relies more heavily on private sources of funding compared to other levels of education, although this varies across countries (Figure 9.6). Private sources of funding include all spending on things such as tuition fees and other payments to education institutions by households, businesses, and non-profit organizations.[36] Private funding also includes spending by companies on training apprentices and students. The UK and the USA both have a high level of average spending per student, but the majority of this comes from private sources of funding. In the UK, 72 per cent of spending on tertiary education came from private sources; in the USA, this figure was 62 per cent. In contrast, in Finland and Norway, over 90 per cent of funding for tertiary education came from government sources.

The role of government in the funding and provision of tertiary education varies considerably across countries, more so than in the case of compulsory education. What do the arguments reviewed in section 9.3 imply for the role of government in tertiary education?

- In theory, the problems of imperfect information may be less severe in tertiary education than in earlier education. Students are older and more capable of making informed decisions. Information is more likely to be readily available (e.g. university guides), students have time to acquire the information needed, and they are better able to understand and assess the information available. The wider range of education and training options available also suggests students may be better placed to make a decision that

[36] The figures are after the flow of transfers, so private spending may include spending that is partly covered by government subsidies.

aligns with their own preferences, compared with a central planner. The costs of making a poor decision can be significant though.

- Most countries have a large number of universities, colleges and other institutions providing tertiary education, so there is some degree of competition in the market. The option of studying abroad and the availability of distance learning programmes further increases competition between providers. However, reputation and prestige play an important role in education, which may give some institutions a degree of monopoly power and could result in higher prices. There is therefore a role for government to regulate prices, as well as regulating standards and quality.
- Diversity of subject matter is also arguably more important than in compulsory education, so a centrally planned system is less likely to be efficient. But will a market for tertiary education produce the mix of education and skills that the economy needs? There may be an argument for targeted government subsidies to encourage the development of certain areas which may be deemed less profitable.
- The problem of incomplete markets and the inability for students to borrow against their future earnings suggests there is an important role for government to play in the funding of tertiary education. However, financing a growing tertiary education sector is expensive and constraints on public finances mean that this spending is competing with growing spending needs in areas such as health, care, and pensions, in the face of demographic change. Financing higher education, in particular, through taxation is also regressive, given that students from better-off backgrounds are more likely to benefit from higher education. Alternative funding options include loans or a graduate tax. We discuss the merits of these different policies for financing tertiary education in section 9.6.2 below.
- Lastly, promoting horizontal equity means that access to tertiary education should not depend on income, socioeconomic background, gender, or ethnicity; it should depend only on an individual's preferences and abilities. If individuals have to rely heavily on private funding, this may discourage potential students from entering tertiary education, particularly those from lower socioeconomic backgrounds, even with a well-functioning student loan market. Problems of imperfect information, discussed above, could also be more severe among students from less well-off backgrounds. A fully government-funded system of tertiary education is unlikely to be affordable and is potentially regressive, as mentioned above. Concerns for horizontal equity goals may instead provide an argument for government grants or other interventions to provide more targeted support for particular groups of students.

9.6.2 Government policies to support tertiary education

The discussion above suggests that governments have an important role to play in tertiary education, in terms of finance, regulating prices, providing quality assurance, promoting access, and possibly providing subsidies for particular subject areas. In this section we are going to focus on higher education, and two policy areas in particular: how higher education should be funded, and what governments can do to promote access and widen participation in higher education.

How should higher education be funded—general taxation, loans, or a graduate tax?

Higher education in several European countries—including Denmark, Germany, Norway, and Sweden—is largely tax-funded. In these countries, students pay no or very low tuition fees to attend university, and the quality of education and research is high. However, the tax-funded model of higher education can be regressive, if individuals from higher socio-economic backgrounds are more likely to go to university and therefore benefit from subsidized higher education. The expansion of higher education and increasing student numbers in many countries have also highlighted how a tax-funded system may not be sustainable, as spending on higher education competes with other spending priorities, such as health and care. Free higher education or low fees may also have a negative impact on the quality of education and/or access, by requiring more rationing of university places.

Wanting to achieve horizontal equity does not mean that higher education should be free, only that it should be free at the point of use, so that everyone has access regardless of income.[37] Evidence suggests there is a substantial private benefit to attending university, and therefore some might argue that individuals who benefit should contribute towards the cost of their education. However, most students are unlikely to have sufficient savings to pay for university. Two alternative funding options have been proposed: student loans and a graduate tax.

Option 1: Student loans

Standard commercial loans—of the sort that would be used to buy a car or house—are not viable in higher education, largely because of the lack of physical collateral. An alternative would be to offer students income-contingent loans where, after graduating, students earning above a certain income level are required to pay a given percentage of their income each month until the loan and outstanding interest have been repaid. The loans should be large enough to cover both the cost of tuition fees and living costs.

Income-contingent loans offer borrowers some protection against the risk of not getting a high-paying job after graduating, as individuals on low incomes would make no, or low, repayments. Because the loans are typically written off after a fixed number of years, individuals with low lifetime earnings would not be required to fully repay their loan.

In order to prevent students from building up excessive debt, some student loan schemes charge a zero or subsidized interest rate. But these interest subsidies are expensive for the government, they open up opportunities for arbitrage,[38] and they are regressive. The cost of the subsidy may reduce the amount of money available for teaching and research, which will negatively impact quality, or it may require loans to be rationed, which will have a negative impact on access.[39] Barr (2020) argues that interest rates should roughly equal the government's cost of borrowing.

There is a danger that loans—and the prospect of taking on a significant amount of debt—may deter students from low-income backgrounds from going to university, exacerbating

[37] Free higher education in itself will also not promote access and widen participation, as the barriers to going to university are determined much earlier in life (see Box 9.7).

[38] The arbitrage opportunities arise as wealthier individuals, who do not need the loan, have an incentive to take out the loan anyway and put the money in a savings account that earns a higher rate of interest.

[39] See Barr (2020: ch. 12) for a good discussion of the arguments against interest subsidies.

existing inequalities. This could be mitigated to some extent by offering grants to low-income students and adopting other policies to promote access and widen participation (discussed below).

Student loans are a staple of higher education funding in countries such as the USA, Australia, and the UK. See Box 9.6 for a discussion of the UK's experience.

Option 2: Graduate tax

The main alternative to an income-contingent loan is a graduate tax. In some respects, a graduate tax operates like an income-contingent loan: once they start working and earning, university graduates pay an extra tax. The graduate tax is only paid by people who have attended university. However, whereas with a loan repayments finish once the loan has been repaid, with a graduate tax repayments are made for as long as the individual is working and earning. Graduate taxes are administratively simpler and cheaper to run. However, there are challenges with collecting payments from graduates who go on to work in a different country.

Box 9.6 The UK student loan system

Student loans are the main channel of direct government support for higher education students in the UK. The loans provide subsidized support to cover tuition fees and living costs, and they are administered by the Student Loans Company, a non-profit, government-owned organization. The Student Loans Company was originally set up in 1990 to provide students with support towards living costs, but the volume of loans increased dramatically after the introduction of tuition fees in 1998. Initially set at £1,000 per year, by 2017 tuition fees had increased to £9,250. In 2023/24, £20 billion was loaned to roughly 1.5 million higher education students across England. The structure of the student finance support system has also changed during this period.

Initially the loans were set up in a similar way to mortgage repayments, where individuals had to start paying back their loan after completing their course, provided they were earning above a certain threshold. Repayments were made in 60 equal instalments over a five-year period. From the late 1990s, the government moved towards an income-contingent repayment system, where graduates paid 9 per cent of their gross annual income above a certain threshold.

Students who started university in 2022/23 were projected to have accumulated an average debt of £45,600 by the end of their course. Graduates start repaying their student loans to the government once their earnings exceed the threshold, which is currently set at £25,000 and due to increase in line with inflation as measured by the Retail Prices Index (RPI). The maximum interest rate on student loans is also set in line with inflation as measured by the RPI. The loans are subject to a maximum term of 40 years, after which they are written off (this term has been increased over the years, from 25 years in 2006/07). Government projections suggest that around 65 per cent of full-time undergraduates starting in 2023/24 will repay their loans in full.

Source: Bolton (2024).

Another drawback of graduate taxes is that the amount an individual pays does not depend on the cost of their degree, but instead will depend on the income they earn, which may act as a work disincentive for high earners.

Both student loans and graduate taxes make financial concerns a leading factor determining young people's choice of career path. Rather than choosing a higher education subject based on their interests, talents, or how they would like to contribute to society, individuals have an incentive to choose subjects that are likely to lead to higher salaries. And these incentives are likely to be stronger for individuals from less privileged backgrounds. Both these policies therefore have the potential to reinforce existing inequalities.

How can we promote access and widen participation in higher education?

The number of students going into higher education has been increasing in many countries, but this has not necessarily been accompanied by an increase in participation of students from diverse backgrounds. Students from high-income backgrounds are more likely to attend university, and more likely to complete their studies and get a degree. In England, a recent study found that only 16 per cent of students eligible for Free School Meals attended university, compared with over 75 per cent of those attending private school and 50 per cent of state school pupils from the least deprived backgrounds (Britton et al., 2021). Low-income students are also far less likely to attend the top universities: in the mid-2000s, students who attended private secondary schools were around 100 times more likely to attend Oxford or Cambridge than students who were eligible for free school meals (Britton et al., 2021). Similar patterns have been found in other countries, including the USA, Australia, and Germany (Blanden et al., 2023). And this is not just being driven by the need to pay tuition fees: in England in 2002, when students from lower-income backgrounds did not pay tuition fees, only 15 per cent of students from manual backgrounds went to university, compared with 81 per cent of children from professional backgrounds (UK Education and Skills Select Committee, 2002).

The arguments discussed above suggest two key barriers preventing individuals from lower socioeconomic backgrounds from participating in higher education: problems of imperfect information and cost. The rigid structure of many higher education programmes can also act as a barrier, whereas more flexible programmes—for example, ones which involve part-time study—can facilitate access for a broader range of students who may otherwise find it difficult to pursue further studies (OECD, 2022).

Research suggests that prior educational attainment is also a significant barrier. Chowdry et al. (2010) found that differences in participation in higher education across socioeconomic groups were significantly reduced once prior educational attainment was taken into account. This suggests that poor attainment in secondary school is a key barrier to participation in higher education, and therefore there is a need for earlier policy interventions.

More recent studies have found that while prior educational attainment is important, an individual's socioeconomic background plays a role, over and above the impact it may have on a child's earlier educational performance. Research by Blanden et al. (2023) found that, conditional on maths and reading scores, the probability of attending university at age 20 was 14 percentage points higher for children of highly educated parents in the USA, and 7 percentage points higher in the UK. In Germany, where there are no tuition fees in public universities, students from more advantaged backgrounds were still 11 percentage points more likely to attend university than their peers with comparable test scores (Blanden et al., 2023).

This suggests policies aimed at widening participation in higher education should focus on the following areas:

- Improving prior educational attainment—for example, by preventing children from dropping out of school and supporting early childhood development (see Box 9.7).
- Addressing problems of imperfect information—for example, by providing more information about the benefits of higher education and the options available to students in schools, or by offering student mentoring schemes.
- Providing access to income-contingent loans and ensuring students have access to information that will enable them to understand the benefits and risks of these loans.
- Offering grants that provide support with tuition fee and/or living costs, to reduce the financial burden of attending university.
- Providing more support for flexible approaches to learning and encouraging institutions to do more to embrace these, particularly part-time and distance learning.

Box 9.7 The importance of early childhood interventions

There is a large body of evidence highlighting the importance of investing in early childhood development programmes for addressing inequalities later in life. Research has found, for example, that about half of the inequality in the present value of lifetime earnings is due to factors determined by age 18 (Cunha & Heckman, 2008). While cognitive abilities are an important driver of socioeconomic inequalities, non-cognitive—or socio-emotional—skills have also been found to play a significant role (Borghans et al., 2008; Heckman et al., 2006). Both cognitive and non-cognitive abilities are heavily influenced by the family environments of young children. Early interventions can improve both cognitive and socio-emotional skills of children from disadvantaged backgrounds, leading to improved school performance, higher workforce productivity, lower crime, and improved health outcomes (Heckman, 2008). These early childhood interventions have a much higher rate of return compared with later interventions, such as smaller student–teacher ratios, public job training, tuition subsidies, and adult literacy programmes (Heckman, 2008).

This suggests that interventions to widen participation in higher education need to start much earlier in life. One example is the Sure Start programme which was launched in England in 1999. This provided investment to set up children's centres across the country which provided a range of services for families with children under five years old, including: healthcare and advice about family health and child health; parenting support; high-quality play and learning experiences for children; and parental employment services. At its peak in 2010, Sure Start received £1.8 billion a year, although spending has since been cut significantly and many centres have been closed (Cattan et al., 2021). Sure Start centres had a strong positive impact on the educational performance of children from disadvantaged backgrounds, increasing their GCSE[40] results by as much as three grades (Carneiro et al., 2024). These centres were also found to have had long-term benefits for children's health: at their peak, they prevented 13,000 hospitalizations a year among 11- to 15 year-olds (Cattan et al., 2021).

[40] The General Certificate of Secondary Education (GCSE) is an academic qualification taken by students in England, Wales, and Northern Ireland, normally at the age of 16. GCSEs are offered in a range of subjects (history, maths, science, etc.).

Conclusion

Governments play an important role in education in most countries across the world today. We have seen how the existence of externalities, problems of imperfect information, and incomplete markets provide strong arguments for some degree of government intervention to increase efficiency in education. Government intervention may also be motivated by a desire to promote equity, particularly equality of opportunity in education. The nature of this intervention may involve finance, regulation, or the production and provision of education, and this is likely to vary across different levels of education. Compulsory education is mostly publicly financed, regulated, and, in many cases, produced, whereas tertiary education relies more heavily on private sources of funding.

The desire to improve educational outcomes in compulsory education has led several countries to experiment with policies to promote competition and parental choice, with mixed results. The extent to which promoting more choice is beneficial depends on how well informed individuals are and what barriers they face (financial or non-financial) in making those decisions. There is no consensus on whether public or privately produced education leads to better student outcomes. Inequalities in education are generally the result of wider socioeconomic inequalities and therefore, in order to address the former, we need policies that focus on the latter.

As technology continues to develop rapidly, and labour markets and the way we work evolve, learning over the course of our lives is becoming increasingly important. What role should government play in encouraging lifelong learning?

Questions for discussion

1. What would a pure private market for education look like? Would this be desirable?
2. What do the different models of the demand for education imply about the role of government in education?
3. Should the government pay for individuals to stay in school?
4. Should the education system aim to promote vertical equity?
5. How much choice should parents and students have over what schools they and attend and what they learn?
6. What should be the role of government in higher education?

Further reading

For a more in-depth discussion of the role of government in education:

Barr, N. (2020). *The economics of the welfare state* (6th ed.). Oxford University Press.

For a review of the structure, financing and performance of education systems across OECD countries:

OECD (2025). *Education at a glance 2025: OECD Indicators*. Organization for Economic Cooperation and Development.

On educational inequality:

Blanden, J., Doepke, M., & Stuhler, J. (2023). Educational inequality. In E. A. Hanushek, L. Woessmann, & S. J. Machin (Eds.), *Handbook of the economics of education* (Vol. 6, pp. 405–497). Elsevier.

Heckman, J. J. (2008). Schools, skills, and synapses. *Economic Inquiry, 46*(3), 289–324.

On modelling the demand for education:

Becker, G. S. (1964). *Human capital.* National Bureau of Economic Research.

Chevalier, A., Harmon, C., Walker, I., & Zhu, Y. (2004). Does education raise productivity, or just reflect it? *Economic Journal, 114*(499), F499–F517.

Leoni, S. (2025). A historical review of the role of education: From human capital to human capabilities. *Review of Political Economy, 37*(1), 227–244.

Layard, R., & Psacharopoulos, G. (1974). The screening hypothesis and the returns to education. *Journal of Political Economy, 82*(5), 985–998.

Riley, J. G. (2001). Silver signals: Twenty-five years of screening and signalling. *Journal of Economic Literature, 39*(2), 432–478.

On the returns to education:

Blundell, R., Dearden, L., & Sianesi, B. (2005). Measuring the returns to education. In S. Machin & A. Vignoles (Eds.), *What's the good of education? The economics of education in the UK* (pp. 117–145). Princeton University Press.

Oreopoulos, P., & Salvanes, K. G. (2009). *How large are returns to schooling? Hint: Money isn't everything.* National Bureau of Economic Research working papers, no. w15339.

On the performance of different schooling systems:

Hanushek, E. A., & Luque, J. A. (2003). Efficiency and equity in schools around the world. *Economics of Education Review, 22*(5), 481–502.

On quasi-markets in education:

Bartlett, W., & Le Grand, J. (1993) *Quasi-markets and social policy*. Palgrave Macmillan.

Bradley, S. (2020). Quasi-markets in education: The case of England. In S. Bradley & C. Green (Eds.), *The economics of education* (2nd ed.) (pp. 455–469). Academic Press.

Burgess, S., Propper, C., & Wilson, D. (2007). The impact of school choice in England: Implications from the economic evidence. *Policy Studies, 28*(2), 129–143.

On school vouchers:

Epple, D., Romano, R. E., & Urquiola, M. (2017). School vouchers: A survey of the economics literature. *Journal of Economic Literature, 55*(2), 441–492.

Ladd, H. (2002). School vouchers: A critical view. *Journal of Economic Perspectives, 16*(4), 3–24.

On funding higher education and widening participation:

Asplund, R., Adbelkarim, O. B., & Skalli, A. (2008). An equity perspective on access to, enrolment in and finance of tertiary education. *Education Economics, 16*(3), 261–274.

Barr, N. (2004). Higher education funding. *Oxford Review of Economic Policy, 20*(2), 264–283.

Jongbloed, B., & Vossensteyn, H. (2016). University funding and student funding: International comparisons. *Oxford Review of Economic Policy, 32*(4), 576–595.

McMahon, W. W. (2009). *Higher learning, greater good: The private and social benefits of higher education*. Johns Hopkins University Press.

Younger, K., Gascoine, L., Menzies, V., & Torgerson, C. (2019). A systematic review of evidence on the effectiveness of interventions and strategies for widening participation in higher education. *Journal of Further and Higher Education, 43*(6), 742–773.

Bibliography

Barr, N. (2020). *The economics of the welfare state* (6th ed.). Oxford University Press.

Blanden, J., Doepke, M., & Stuhler, J. (2023). Educational inequality. In E. A. Hanushek, L. Woessmann, & S. J. Machin (Eds.), *Handbook of the economics of education* (Vol. 6, pp. 405–497). Elsevier.

Bolton, P. (2024). *Student loan statistics* (published 10 July). House of Commons Library. Available at: https://researchbriefings.files.parliament.uk/documents/SN01079/SN01079.pdf

Borghans, L., Duckworth, A. L., Heckman, J. J., & Ter Weel, B. (2008). The economics and psychology of personality traits. *Journal of Human Resources, 43*(4), 972–1059.

Britton, J., Drayton, E., & Van der Erve, L. (2021). *Which university degrees are best for intergenerational mobility*. Research report. Institute for Fiscal Studies and The Sutton Trust. November.

Carneiro, P., Cattan, S., & Ridpath, N. (2024). *The short-and medium-term impacts of Sure Start on educational outcomes*. IFS report R307. Institute for Fiscal Studies.

Cattan, S., Conti, G., Farquharson, C., Ginja, R., & Pecher, M. (2021). *The health impacts of universal early childhood interventions: Evidence from Sure Start*. Institute for Fiscal Studies working papers, no. 21/43. Available at: https://ifs.org.uk/publications/health-impacts-universal-early-childhood-interventions-evidence-sure-start

Chowdry, H., Crawford, C., Dearden, L., Goodman, A., & Vignoles, A. (2010). *Widening participation in higher education: Analysis using linked administrative data*. Institute for Fiscal Studies working papers, no. W10/04.

Cunha, F., & Heckman, J. (2008). A new framework for the analysis of inequality. *Macroeconomic Dynamics, 12*(S2), 315–354.

Cutler, D. M., & Lleras-Muney, A. (2006). *Education and health: evaluating theories and evidence*. National Bureau of Economic Research working papers, no. 12352.

Dee, T. S. (2004). Are there civic returns to education? *Journal of Public Economics, 88*(9–10), 1697–1720.

Department for Education (2017). School funding and pupil outcomes: A literature review and regression analysis. August 2017. Available at: https://assets.publishing.service.gov.uk/media/5a81dcc940f0b62305b91348/School_funding_and_pupil_outcomes.pdf

Drayton, E., Farquharson, C., Ogden, K., Sibieta, L., Tahir, I., and Waltmann, B. (2023). *Annual report on education spending in England: 2023*. IFS report R290. Institute for Fiscal Studies.

Epple, D., Romano, R. E., & Urquiola, M. (2017). School vouchers: A survey of the economics literature. *Journal of Economic Literature, 55*(2), 441–492.

Feigenberg, B., Yan, R., & Rivkin, S. (2019). Illusory gains from Chile's targeted school voucher experiment. *Economic Journal, 129*(623), 2805–2832.

Feinstein, L., Budge, D., Vorhaus, J., & Duckworth, K. (2008). *The social and personal benefits of learning: A summary of key research findings*. Institute of Education, Centre for Research on the Wider Benefits of Learning.

Gibbons, S., & Machin, S. (2003). Valuing English primary schools. *Journal of Urban Economics, 53*(2), 197–219.

Groot, W., & Van den Brink, H. M. (2010). The effects of education on crime. *Applied Economics, 42*(3), 279–289.

Gundlach, E., Wossmann, L., & Gmelin, J. (2001). The decline of schooling productivity in OECD countries. *Economic Journal, 111*(471), C135–C147.

Heckman, J. J. (2008). Schools, skills, and synapses. *Economic Inquiry, 46*(3), 289–324.

Heckman, J. J., Stixrud, J., & Urzua, S. (2006). The effects of cognitive and noncognitive abilities on labor market outcomes and social behavior. *Journal of Labor Economics, 24*(3), 411–482.

Hsieh, C. T., & Urquiola, M. (2006). The effects of generalized school choice on achievement and stratification: Evidence from Chile's voucher program. *Journal of Public Economics, 90*(8–9), 1477–1503.

Jackson, C. K. (2020). Does school spending matter? The new literature on an old question. In L. Tach, R. Dunifon, & D. L. Miller (Eds.), *Confronting inequality: How policies and practices shape children's opportunities* (pp. 165–86). American Psychological Association. Available at: https://doi.org/10.1037/0000187-008

Krueger, A. B., & Lindahl, M. (2001). Education for growth: Why and for whom? *Journal of Economic Literature, 39*(4), 1101–1136.

Ladd, H. (2002). School vouchers: A critical view. *Journal of Economic Perspectives, 16*(4), 3–24.

Lochner, L., & Moretti, E. (2004). The effect of education on crime: Evidence from prison inmates, arrests, and self-reports. *American Economic Review, 94*(1), 155–189.

Machin, S., Marie, O., & Vujić, S. (2011). The crime reducing effect of education. *Economic Journal, 121*(552), 463–484.

McEwan, P. J. (2000). *The impact of vouchers on school efficiency: Empirical evidence from Chile.* Stanford University.

McEwan, P. J., Urquiola, M., Vegas, E., Fernandes, R., & Gallego, F. A. (2008). School choice, stratification, and information on school performance: Lessons from Chile [with comments]. *Economia, 8*(2), 1–42.

Mincer, J. (1958). Investment in human capital and personal income distribution. *Journal of Political Economy, 66*(4), 281–302.

Nussbaum, M. C. (2004). Women's education: A global challenge. *Signs: Journal of Women in Culture and Society, 29*(2), 325–355.

Nussbaum, M. (2000). *Women and human development: The capabilities approach.* Cambridge University Press.

OECD (2012). *Equity and quality in education: Supporting disadvantaged students and schools.* Organization for Economic Cooperation and Development.

OECD (2022). *Education at a glance 2022: OECD indicators.* Organization for Economic Cooperation and Development. Available at: https://doi.org/10.1787/3197152b-en

OECD (2023). *Education at a glance 2023: OECD indicators.* Organization for Economic Cooperation and Development. Available at: https://doi.org/10.1787/e13bef63-en

OECD (2024a). *Adults' educational attainment distribution, by age group and gender.* Organization for Economic Cooperation and Development. Data explorer. https://data-explorer.oecd.org (accessed 7 November 2024).

OECD (2024b). *Education at a glance 2024: OECD indicators.* Organization for Economic Cooperation and Development. Available at: https://doi.org/10.1787/c00cad36-en

OECD (2024c). *Education spending (%GDP and US dollars/student).* Organization for Economic Cooperation and Development. Data explorer. https://data-explorer.oecd.org (accessed 3 November 2024).

OECD (2024d). *Education spending (US dollars/student).* Organization for Economic Cooperation and Development. Data explorer. https://data-explorer.oecd.org (accessed 3 November 2024).

OECD (2024e). *Expenditure on educational institutions as a percentage of GDP.* Organization for Economic Cooperation and Development. Data explorer. https://data-explorer.oecd.org (accessed 3 November 2024).

OECD (2024f). PISA: Programme for International Student Assessment. *OECD Education Statistics* [database]. https://doi.org/10.1787/data-00365-en (accessed 6 November 2024).

Oreopoulos, P., & Salvanes, K. G. (2009). *How large are returns to schooling? Hint: Money isn't everything.* National Bureau of Economic Research working papers, no. w15339.

Robeyns, I. (2003). Sen's capability approach and gender inequality: Selecting relevant capabilities. *Feminist Economics*, *9*(2–3), 61–92.

Robeyns, I. (2006). Three models of education: Rights, capabilities and human capital. *Theory and Research in Education*, *4*(1), 69–84.

Sandström, F. M., & Bergström, F. (2005). School vouchers in practice: Competition will not hurt you. *Journal of Public Economics*, *89*(2–3), 351–380.

Sen, A. (2001) *Development as freedom.* Oxford University Press.

UK Education and Skills Select Committee (2002). *Post-16 student support.* Sixth Report of Session 2001–02, HC445. The Stationery Office.

UK Government (n.d.). *Schools, pupils and their characteristics.* Available at: https://explore-education-statistics.service.gov.uk/find-statistics/school-pupils-and-their-characteristics

UK Parliament (n.d.). *The future of academies and free schools.* Available at: https://www.parliament.uk/business/publications/research/key-issues-parliament-2015/education/academies- and-free-schools/

UNESCO Institute for Statistics (2024). *Duration of compulsory education* [dataset]. *UNESCO Institute for Statistics (UIS)—education* [original data]. Retrieved 6 November 2024 from https://ourworldindata.org/grapher/duration-of-compulsory-education

Wolf, A. (2004). Education and economic performance: Simplistic theories and their policy consequences. *Oxford Review of Economic Policy*, *20*(2), 315–33.

World Bank (2019). *Learning to realize education's promise.* World Development Report.

10
The environment

Learning objectives

By the end of this chapter, you will be able to:

10.1 Discuss the arguments for government intervention to address environmental problems.
10.2 Explain possible market-based solutions to the problem of environmental externalities and discuss their limitations.
10.3 Describe the different ways in which governments can intervene to address environmental problems and discuss the advantages and limitations of these different types of intervention.
10.4 Discuss what policies can be used to tackle the problem of urban traffic congestion.
10.5 Discuss how insights from economics can help develop solutions to address the global threat of the climate crisis.

Introduction

At the turn of the twenty-first century, the Millennium Ecosystem Assessment (MEA) carried out a comprehensive review of the state of the world's ecosystems and the services they provide, including clean water, food, natural resources, and flood control.[1] It concluded that humans have changed ecosystems more rapidly and dramatically in the previous 50 years than in any comparable period in human history. While these changes have contributed to economic development and improvements in human well-being, they have come at a cost in terms of the degradation of many ecosystem services.

In the two decades since the MEA, global carbon dioxide (CO_2) emissions from fossil fuels and industry have continued to rise, reaching an average 4.7 tonnes per person in 2023,[2] driving increases in global temperatures, and threatening human livelihoods and biodiversity. Between 2010 and 2020, an average 4.7 million hectares of forests were lost per year across the world (FAO, 2020), destroying natural habitats, damaging ecosystems, and harming biodiversity. According to the latest *Global Environment Outlook* report, the world is not on

[1] The Millennium Ecosystem Assessment was called for in 2000 by the then Secretary-General of the United Nations, Kofi Annan. It was carried out between 2001 and 2005 and involved the work of more than 1,360 experts from across world. The findings were published in five technical volumes and six synthesis reports, which contain a detailed assessment of the state of and trends in the world's ecosystems, as well as solutions for restoring and enhancing the sustainable use of these systems (MEA, 2005).

[2] Global Carbon Budget (2024); population based on various sources (2024), with major processing by Our World in Data. These global averages mask considerable variation across countries, as we will see in section 10.1.

track to meet the environmental dimension of the Sustainable Development Goals by 2030, or to deliver long-term sustainability by 2050 (UN Environment Programme, 2019).

But there are also some environmental success stories. The hole in the ozone layer, a pressing global problem in the 1990s, has been brought under control, largely due to a concerted international effort. EU funding has supported the restoration of important natural ecosystems across Europe, including Ireland's unique peatlands and the cork oak forests in Portugal (European Commission, n.d.b). Many countries throughout the world have introduced charges for plastic bags and other single-use plastics, in an effort to help reduce global plastic pollution. What role can economics play in informing the design of environmental policies?

We begin in Section 10.1 with an overview of the relationship between the environment, economic growth, and welfare, and analyse the economic rationale for government intervention to help protect the environment. Section 10.2 discusses some of the private market responses to these challenges, and their limitations in practice. In Section 10.3, we analyse the main types of government intervention to address environmental problems, and discuss their advantages and limitations. We then discuss two policy cases studies—urban traffic congestion and the climate crisis—in sections 10.4 and 10.5.

10.1 Arguments for government intervention

Government intervention to help protect the environment and reduce environmental harms can increase social welfare and support equity goals. Before analysing these arguments, it is helpful to take a step back and think about the role of the environment and how it interacts with the economy.

10.1.1 The environment, economic growth, and welfare

A healthy environment is the foundation for human health, well-being, and economic prosperity. We rely on natural resources for our survival, as a source of food, clean air, and water. Natural resources also provide sources of fuel and key inputs in production and, as such, are the basis for economic growth. The concept of **natural capital** reflects this role of the natural environment both as a source of raw materials for production and as essential for human well-being by providing vital goods, such as clean water and fertile soil for agriculture. Natural capital encompasses the stock of renewable and non-renewable resources—air, water, soils, plants, animals, and minerals. Growing awareness of the importance of natural capital for our economies and human well-being has driven efforts to incorporate the value of these natural resources into national accounts (see Box 10.1).

The economy relies on a healthy environment, but economic activity is increasingly putting the health of the environment at risk. The type of economic growth we have witnessed in recent decades is not sustainable—it is contributing to environmental pollution, the destruction of ecosystems, and the depletion of natural resources, including freshwater, forests, and fish stocks. Global CO_2 emissions have increased dramatically since the 1950s, as Figure 10.1 shows. In 1950, the world emitted 5.9 billion tonnes of CO_2; by the end of the twentieth century, this had increased more than fivefold to over 25.5 billion tonnes, and the figure has

Box 10.1 Going beyond GDP: natural capital accounting

GDP is still the most widely used measure of economic progress, but it has its limitations. GDP does not capture the value of natural resources—such as clean air, clean water, and food—that are essential for human well-being. Nor does it account for the costs of economic activity, in terms of human health, resource depletion, and pollution. Growing awareness of the vital importance of natural resources in sustaining not only our economies but also human welfare have driven attempts to incorporate the value of these resources into national accounts.

Natural capital accounting is a framework for measuring and reporting on the stocks and flows of natural capital in a systematic way, which can be better integrated into widely used frameworks, such as the System of National Accounts. Natural capital accounting includes individual environmental resources (e.g. water, minerals, and fish stocks), ecosystems (e.g. forests), biodiversity, and ecosystem services. Measuring and valuing natural resources presents many challenges. The United Nations Statistical Commission of the System of Environmental and Economic Accounts (SEEA) was adopted in 2012 and provides an internationally agreed method for accounting for the environment and its relationship with the economy—both how the environment contributes to the economy and how the economy impacts on the environment. Several countries have started compiling environmental accounting data.[3] Critics have argued, however, that applying market-based calculations to the environment will exacerbate rather than help address environmental problems.

Source: United Nations SEEA (n.d.).

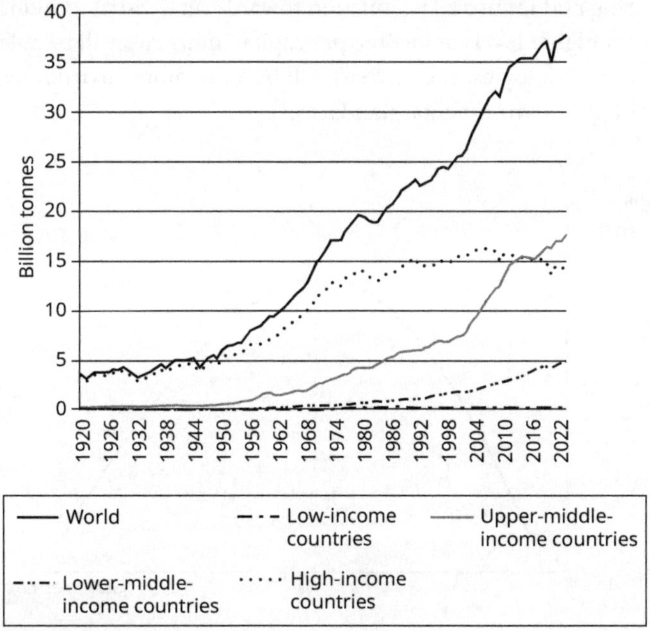

Figure 10.1 Annual carbon dioxide emissions across the world

Note: CO_2 emissions from fossil fuels and industry.

Source: Global Carbon Budget (2024)—with major processing by Our World in Data.

[3] The UN System of Environmental Economic Accounting Global Assessment of Results includes details of countries that have implemented an environmental accounting system and links to the data. See United Nations SEEA (2023).

continued to rise. CO_2 emissions, along with emissions of other greenhouse gases, are one of the leading causes of the rise in global temperatures, which is threatening human livelihood and biodiversity.[4]

Will economic growth inevitably lead to environmental degradation? One hypothesis, originally proposed in the 1990s, suggested that while pollution initially increased as GDP increased, it would eventually start to fall. This hypothesis became known as the **environmental Kuznets curve (EKC)**.[5] The EKC links the intensity of pollution to a country's income or GDP per capita. The EKC is typically assumed to have an inverted U-shape, as illustrated in Figure 10.2. This implies that environmental quality does not deteriorate steadily with economic growth. Instead, as economies grow, pollution intensity initially rises, but once a country reaches a certain level of development, the intensity of pollution then starts to fall.

The concept of the EKC is based on the work of the American economists Gene Grossman and Alan Krueger in the 1990s (Grossman & Krueger, 1995). They analysed data on the evolution of GDP and measures of local air and water pollution across roughly 40 countries and found that this supported the hypothesis of an inverted U-shape, shown in Figure 10.2. Moreover, they attempted to identity the turning point (point X_1 in Figure 10.2) for each of the different pollutants analysed. They found these turning points varied for the different pollutants, but that overall growth would start to lead to environmental improvements once per capita income reached $8,000.

What explains this hypothesized relationship between economic growth and environmental degradation? In the initial stages of growth, industrial production intensifies and more energy is used, leading to an increase in pollution and a greater depletion of natural resources. But once an economy reaches a certain level of development, there will be a structural shift from manufacturing and industrial production towards service-based industries. It has also been argued that at higher levels of income per capita, industries will be able to afford to use better and cleaner technologies, and citizens will become more environmentally aware and start to demand higher environmental standards.

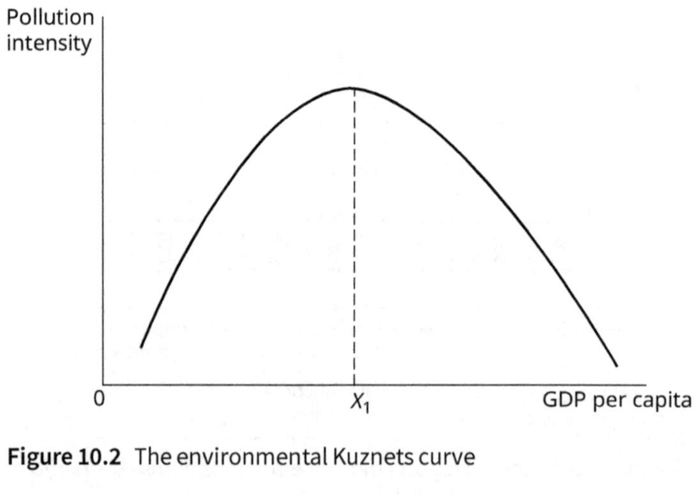

Figure 10.2 The environmental Kuznets curve

[4] See, for example, IPCC (2014).

[5] The original Kuznets curve, named after the economist Simon Kuznets, hypothesized a similar inverted U-shaped relationship between income inequality and economic growth, where inequality would initially increase, but eventually fall, as income per capita increased.

But there is no reason to suppose this inverted U-shape relationship will hold for all pollutants. Depending on the ability of the natural environment to absorb pollutants, the stock of pollutants may accumulate. In some cases the accumulation of pollutants beyond some threshold level may trigger significant environmental changes, as we have seen with CO_2 emissions (Tisdell, 2001).

Although some empirical studies have found evidence to support the EKC, others have been more critical (see Box 10.2). The shift from manufacturing to services also does not eliminate the pollution—it simply moves it (along with the manufacturing industry) to other countries. So even if the relationship depicted by the EKC held true for some countries, it could not hold for all countries across the world. This has led to calls to adopt more comprehensive measures of the environmental impact of economic activity, such as measuring each country's **global material footprint**—the total amount of raw materials required to meet final consumption demands. Between 2000 and 2022, the global material footprint increased by 71 per cent, from 57.4 billion tonnes to 98.0 billion tonnes (United Nations, 2024). Throughout much of the past 20 years, the global material footprint has been increasing at a faster rate than both population and economic output (United Nations, 2019).

10.1.2 Efficiency arguments for government intervention

Arguments for government intervention to protect the environment on efficiency grounds are centred around two main issues: externalities and common-pool resources.

Box 10.2 Does the evidence support an environmental Kuznets curve?

Grossman and Krueger's (1995) early work on the environmental Kuznets curve (EKC) hypothesis relied on data on a small number of local measures of pollution. Subsequent research has explored whether the same relationship holds true for other indicators of environmental degradation, including greenhouse gas emissions, deforestation, and total energy use, and has looked at both indicators measuring levels of pollutant emissions and pollution concentrations.

Early studies did find some support for an inverted U-shaped relationship between local pollutants and income, although not between global indicators such as CO_2 emissions and income (e.g. Shafik & Bandyopadhyay, 1992). Other studies have found that environmental improvements are possible in developing economies, with evidence showing a fall in pollutants in developing countries over time (e.g. Dasgupta et al., 2002). Research also suggests that other factors are likely to play a role. For example, Torras and Boyce (1998) found that environmental quality in fact tends to be higher in countries where income is more equally distributed, where literacy rates are higher, and where civil and political rights are stronger.

Stern (1998, 2004, 2018) reviews a number of studies on the EKC and concludes that the relationship between economic growth and environmental degradation is more complicated that the EKC implies. Overall, the evidence suggests economic growth usually has a negative impact on the environment. Other factors—such as technological change and political freedom—are more likely to help preserve the environment.

Externalities

Externalities are at the heart of many environmental problems. As we saw in Chapter 2, externalities arise when an action by an individual or firm has an impact on other individuals or firms, and this effect is not reflected in the market price. **Production externalities** arise as a result of firms' production decisions. As an example, if a chemical manufacturer releases pollution into the air and water as part of its production process, the air and water pollution are production externalities. If the externality is a result of an individual's consumption decisions, these are referred to as **consumption externalities**—for example, if someone likes to play loud music and this has a negative impact on their neighbours.

Chapter 2 explained that externalities can be positive or negative. Pollution is the classic example of a negative externality, where the action of a firm or individual imposes a cost on other economic agents. Positive externalities arise if the actions of an individual or firm impose a benefit on other individuals or firms—for example, firms investing in R&D can generate positive externalities or spillover effects that other firms benefit from.

When there are externalities, markets will no longer lead to an efficient allocation of resources. Suppose a firm produces chemicals and, as a result of its production process, pollution is released into a local lake. Figure 10.3 illustrates the demand and supply curves, where the demand curve reflects the marginal benefit to individuals from each extra unit of output produced. We assume there are no positive externalities, so demand equals private marginal benefit (*PMB*) and social marginal benefit (*SMB*). The supply curve reflects the private marginal cost (*PMC*) of producing each unit of output. The market equilibrium is given by point E, where marginal benefit equals (private) marginal cost. In the absence of externalities, this equilibrium outcome is efficient as it maximizes the sum of consumer and producer surplus, as we saw in Chapter 2.[6]

If the production of chemicals creates pollution, this will impose a cost on society. Air pollution can have a negative impact on the health of people living nearby, and if pollution is released into local waterways, this can affect fish stocks and local wildlife. But these social costs will not be taken into account by the firms in the industry when deciding their profit-maximizing level of output. The line *SMC* in Figure 10.3 represents the social marginal cost of production, which is greater than the private marginal cost of production. Each unit of output produced involves a cost in terms of raw materials, labour hours, and other factors, which are reflected in the *PMC* curve. But it also involves a social cost as a result of the pollution generated. The *SMC* curve therefore includes the *PMC* and the cost of the externality. Here we assume the level of pollution is proportional to the level of output, and the marginal cost of each unit of pollution is fixed.

The socially optimal or efficient level of output in this case is Q_2, where marginal benefit equals the social marginal cost of production. This is less than the private market equilibrium level, Q_1. Because the firms do not have to take into account the external cost of their production decisions, the level of output produced is too high. The magnitude of the inefficiency created in this example is illustrated by the shaded **deadweight loss** triangle in the figure. This measures the inefficiency or loss in welfare that arises because the level of output produced in the market is above the socially optimal level. For any level of output above Q_2, the social marginal cost is greater than the marginal benefit and therefore expanding production beyond this point will be inefficient.

6 Consumer and producer surplus capture the benefits to consumers and producers from buying/selling goods in the market. See Chapter 2, section 2.2.2, for a review of these concepts.

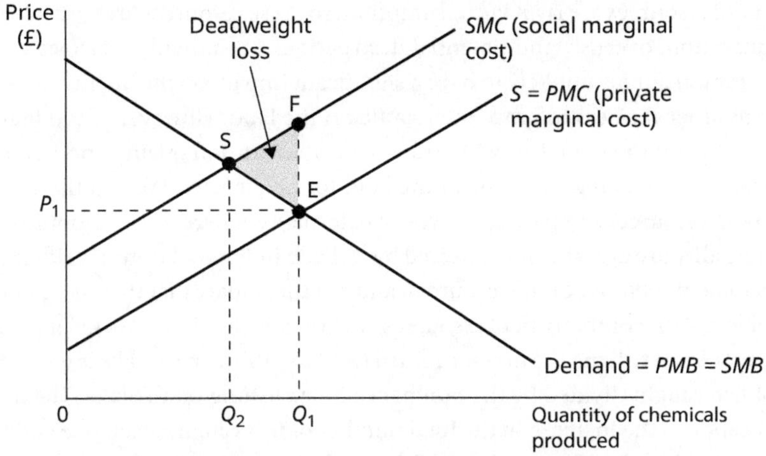

Figure 10.3 Negative production externalities and inefficiency

According to this analysis, the problem with the market outcome is not that it involves pollution, but rather that the level of pollution will be too high, because firms do not take into account the social costs associated with their activities.

Common-pool resources

As we saw in Chapter 2, common-pool resources or 'the commons' are defined by two key characteristics: they are non-excludable, in that it would be impossible or very costly to exclude an individual from consuming or using the resource (either through physical barriers or legal means); and they are rival in consumption, which means the use or consumption of the resources by one individual reduces the amount available for others to consume. They therefore differ from pure public goods which, as we saw in Chapter 5, are both non-excludable and non-rival, so consumption of the good by one person does not reduce the amount available for others to consume. Examples of common-pool resources include fisheries, forests, grazing lands, and water systems.[7]

It is important to distinguish common-pool resources from **common-property resources**, although the terms are sometimes used interchangeably. The term 'common-pool resources' refers to the goods or resources themselves, whereas 'common-property resources' refers to the property regime that determines how these resources are managed. Common-pool resources can be managed under different types of property regimes—they may be owned by national, regional, or local governments, by individuals, firms, or communal groups, or they may be used as **open-access resources** (Ostrom, 2001). Open-access resources are common-pool resources that anyone can access or use and are therefore at risk of being overexploited. In contrast, common-property resources are common-pool resources where the right to access or use these resources is held by a group of individuals, and so their use can be regulated in different ways.

Because it is not possible to exclude individuals from using common-pool resources, there is a risk they will be overexploited, as with pure public goods. But unlike pure public goods,

[7] These are examples of natural common-pool resources. There are also examples of artificially made common-pool resources, such as the internet.

common-pool resources are rival in consumption, so these resources are susceptible to problems of congestion, overuse, and potential destruction. An individual farmer grazing their cattle on common land is unlikely to have a significant impact on the quality of the land, and the ability of other farmers to graze their cattle on the land. However, if too many farmers graze their cattle on the land, this will lead to a decrease in soil quality and fewer plants for cattle to graze on, reducing the value of the land for all farmers. We can therefore think of common-pool resources as a particular type of externality, where those responsible for creating the externality are also the ones affected by it. Each individual only considers the private cost and benefit of their use of the resources, and not the impact that their use has on others.

The problem with common-pool resources is illustrated in Figure 10.4. Suppose there is a lake that anyone can fish in. The average return (*AR*) to fishing in the lake is given by the total number of fish caught divided by the number of boats fishing on the lake. The marginal return (*MR*) captures the increase in the total number of fish caught when one additional boat starts fishing on the lake. The number of fish caught increases with the number of boats on the lake, but less than proportionately, because of diminishing returns. So, the average catch per boat falls as the number of boats increases and the *AR* curve slopes downwards. Each additional boat on the lake reduces the number of fish available for the other boats to catch. For simplicity, the marginal cost of each additional boat is assumed to be constant.

The socially optimal number of boats on the lake is given by the point where the marginal benefit (or marginal return) of another boat just equals the marginal cost. This is shown by point S in the figure—the efficient outcome is where there are Q_2 boats on the lake. However, each individual fisher, when deciding whether or not to start fishing on the lake, will only consider whether the potential benefit to them outweighs the cost. The benefit to each fisher just equals the average return, so individuals will continue fishing on the lake up to the point where the average return equals the marginal, at point E, where there are Q_1 boats on the lake. The result is overfishing on the lake.

This is the **tragedy of the commons**, a problem originally described in a classic article by the ecologist Garret Hardin (1968). The tragedy of the commons highlights how many individuals acting independently and rationally will ultimately lead to the depletion of shared limited resources, even when it is clear that it is in no one's long-term interest for this to happen. However, while open-access resources may be overexploited or overused, this 'tragedy'

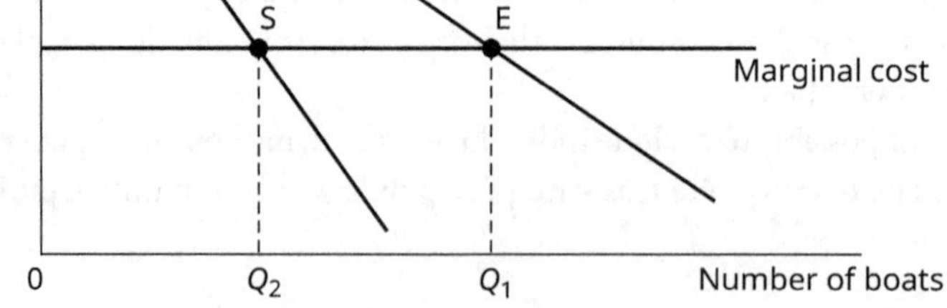

Figure 10.4 Common-pool resources

Box 10.3 The challenge of managing common-pool resources in practice

While we are still grappling with many tragedies of the commons today—whether it is massive overfishing of our oceans, deforestation, or excessive CO_2 emissions in the atmosphere—there have also been some success stories. In the state of Maine in the USA, local fishers and government officials have managed to find effective ways to manage lobster stocks and these are in a better state today than they were a century ago. Lobster stocks dropped sharply in the 1930s, but initiatives including providing effective protection for juvenile lobsters, limiting the number of lobster traps, and rules enabling lobster fishers to monitor each other's harvesting have helped stocks recover and even prosper.

This and other examples of successful local conservation efforts highlight some important lessons for managing common-pool resources. Top-down approaches are rarely successful. It is crucial to work with the users of the common-pool resource and develop a system that is suited to the particular nature of the resource itself and to the culture, practices, and norms of those who depend on the resource for their livelihood. Active and effective monitoring is essential to ensure there is no incentive to free ride on the cooperation of others.

Source: Ostrom (2008).

is not inevitable. As Elinor Ostrom's work has demonstrated, it will depend on the property regime that is in place for managing these common-pool resources. Commons can be successfully managed by well-defined communities with shared rules and sanctions for those who break the rules.[8] There are many different types of common-pool resources and there is no single property regime and resource management system that will work perfectly in all situations, but there are some key principles that should guide effective management of these resources (see Box 10.3).

10.1.3 Equity arguments for government intervention

Environmental problems raise a series of important equity considerations. Environmental justice can be defined as having 'equal access to a clean environment and equal protection from possible environmental harm irrespective of race, income, class or any other differentiating feature of socio-economic status' (Cutter, cited in Mitchell, 1995). In practice, environmental inequalities are widespread, both within and across countries. Individuals with lower levels of income and education are often more likely to be affected by air, water, and noise pollution.

Countries in southern and eastern Europe, where incomes tend to be lower, have been found to be more exposed to air pollutants, including particulate matter and ground-level ozone (EEA, 2018). Wealthier countries have been found to have average higher levels of nitrogen dioxide, mainly due to higher concentrations of traffic, although it is generally poorer

[8] See, for example, Ostrom (1999, 2008). Elinor Ostrom was awarded the Nobel Memorial Prize in Economic Science for her work in this area.

communities within these countries that are more exposed to these higher concentrations of pollutants (EEA, 2018). Developing countries also face greater risks from climate change; average temperatures tend to be higher, and they are more susceptible to extreme weather events (Benyon & Wickstead, 2024).

Environmental problems impose a cost on individuals and communities, but policies to address environmental problems also involve a cost, and these costs are not always fairly distributed. Environmental taxes, for example, may lead to higher prices, which may have a larger impact on lower-income households, particularly in the case of essential commodities such as energy.

One important issue is **intergenerational fairness**, or how the costs and benefits of environmental policies are distributed across generations. Often the costs of addressing environmental problems are borne by current generations, but the benefits will also be experienced by future generations. The standard approach based on welfare economics requires the costs and benefits experienced in the future to be discounted to make them equivalent to costs and benefits experienced today.[9] But choosing an appropriate discount rate is challenging, particularly when dealing with benefits that may be experienced several decades or even hundreds of years into the future. Using a standard discount rate of—for example, 5 per cent—means that little weight will be given to the well-being of future generations. A zero discount rate, so the well-being of current and future generations is weighted equally, may seem like the fairest approach, but it is not practically feasible. One option is to use low but positive discount rates, but even these low rates have serious implications for the weight given to the welfare of future generations. It would be preferable to use methods for evaluating policies that do not require the future to be discounted,[10] but instead take into account the rights and obligations of current and future generations.

There are also a number of broader ethical issues raised by environmental problems. Do animals have rights? Do humans have a duty to preserve the natural world? Anthropocentrism is the view that animals and the natural world only have value insofar as they are valued by specific human individuals. This contrasts with the non-anthropocentric view, which holds that the non-human world has value independent of its benefit to human individuals. The choice of ethical principles will determine how the environment is incorporated into economic models and analysis, and will have implications for the policies adopted.

10.2 Market solutions: the Coase theorem

Can the market solve the externality problem? In the example discussed above, suppose the fishers owned the lake and had a right to clean water. In this case, they could get together and demand the chemical plant stop polluting the lake. If the only way for the chemical plant to stop polluting the lake is to shut down production, the plant may be willing to pay the fishers some compensation, to allow it to produce a given amount of chemicals and emit some pollution into the lake. The chemical plant would be willing to pay compensation to maintain some production, as long as it were profitable for it to do. Meanwhile, the fishers would be willing to accept compensation as long as it were profitable for them to do so.

9 See Chapter 4 for a review of discounting and the difficulty in choosing appropriate discount rates.
10 We discussed some of these alternatives in Chapter 4.

What if instead the chemical plant owned the lake and was therefore entitled to pollute it? In this case, given the impact that the pollution from the plant has on their livelihoods, the fishers may be willing to pay the chemical plant to reduce the amount of pollution it emits. The fishers would be willing to pay as long as the cost to them of doing so was outweighed by the benefit of being able to fish in the lake. And the chemical plant would accept compensation—and reduce production and pollution—as long as this outweighed the cost to them in lost output.

This example suggests that the problem of externalities arises because of a lack of ownership. If property rights over the lake (and clean water) are well defined, then bargaining between the fishers and the chemical plant should lead to a mutually beneficial outcome. This solution to the problem of externalities was originally proposed by Ronald Coase (1960). Moreover, Coase argued that the same solution would be arrived at regardless of who is assigned the property rights. Formally, the **Coase theorem** holds that if property rights are well defined and bargaining is costless, negotiations between the party generating the externality and the party or parties affected by the externality can lead to the socially optimal (efficient) market quantity, and the efficient solution does not depend on who is assigned the property rights. The Coase theorem illustrates one way of **internalizing an externality** or requiring those responsible for generating external costs or benefits to take these into account in their decision-making.

The argument underpinning the Coase theorem is illustrated in Figure 10.5. The horizontal axis measures the quantity of pollution emitted per unit of time. The line BC measures the marginal benefit to the chemical plant of polluting the lake, measured by its **marginal abatement cost (MAC)** or the cost to the plant of each successive unit of pollution abatement or reduction. The chemical plant does not benefit from polluting the lake per se, but from the output it produces, and producing this output inevitably creates pollution. The *MAC* curve is generally downward-sloping because the lowest-cost opportunities for reducing pollution are exploited first. As the level of pollution is reduced (moving from right to left along the horizontal axis in the figure), the technologies and strategies available for reducing pollution further become progressively more expensive, leading to a higher cost for each unit of

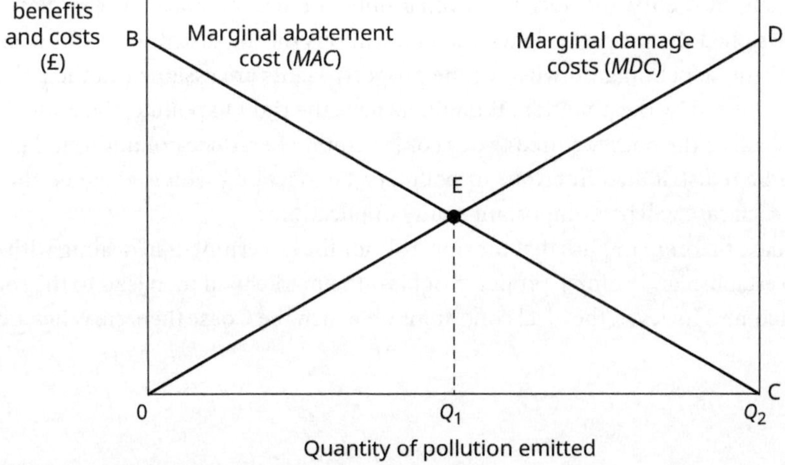

Figure 10.5 Illustration of the Coase theorem

pollution abated. The line 0D is the **marginal damage cost (MDC)** curve, which measures the marginal cost to the fishers of each additional unit of pollution, for example due to declining fish stocks[11]. We assume that the greater the concentration of pollution in the lake, the greater the cost of each additional unit of pollution, so the *MDC* curve in Figure 10.5 slopes upwards.

The socially optimal level of pollution is given by Q_1. For any level of pollution below this level, the marginal benefit to the chemical plant of increasing pollution (because it allows them to produce and sell more of their product) is greater than the cost to the fishers and therefore increasing the level of production (and pollution) would increase social welfare. For levels of pollution above Q_1, the marginal cost to the fishers in terms of depleted fish stocks is greater than the marginal benefit to the chemical plant.

If the chemical plant owned the property right to pollute the lake, it could emit up to Q_2 units of the pollutant. Reducing pollution emitted to Q_1 would impose a cost on the chemical plant equal to the area of the triangle EQ_1C. However, the benefit to the fishers of reducing pollution to Q_1 is equal to the area EQ_1CD, which is greater than the cost to the chemical plant. So, the fishers would be willing to compensate the chemical plant for the loss in earnings due to forgone output. The minimum compensation the chemical plant would accept is equal to the area EQ_1C, while the maximum compensation the fishers would be willing to pay is equal to the area EQ_1CD. The actual level of compensation paid would depend on the bargaining power of the chemical plant and the fishers.

If instead the fishers owned the right to a pollution-free lake, they could require the chemical plant to shut down production, thus ensuring a level of pollution of 0. However, they may be willing to allow some production, if the chemical plant offered compensation for the impact this would have on fish stocks and their livelihoods. To allow the chemical plant to increase production and emit a level of pollution Q_1, the fishers would demand a minimum compensation equal to the area $0EQ_1$. The benefit to the chemical plant of increasing production to this level is given by the area $0BEQ_1$, which is greater than the level of compensation required by the fishers. So, again, the chemical plant and the fishers could negotiate to reach a mutually beneficial agreement. In theory, bargaining between the parties would lead to a level of pollution equal to Q_1, and the level of compensation paid would depend on each party's respective bargaining power.

Although, in theory, the socially optimal outcome will be reached regardless of which party is assigned the property rights, the implications for the distribution of income will be very different, depending on whether the property rights are assigned to the polluter or to the those affected by the pollution. If polluters have the right to pollute, those affected by the pollution will be the ones required to pay compensation to reduce pollution, and income will therefore be redistributed in favour of polluters. So, deciding who is assigned the property rights in each case will have important equity implications.

The Coase theorem implies that the only role for the government in dealing with externalities is to establish and enforce property rights—the market will then lead to the socially optimal outcome. However, the ideal conditions on which the Coase theorem relies are unlikely

[11] Alternatively, we can think of the marginal damage cost curve as measuring the value to the fishers of each successive unit of pollution abatement.

to hold in practice or in the case of many real-world externality problems. There are three key problems:

- **Free rider problem**: many of the goods involved in externalities, such as clean air or clean water, have the characteristics of public goods, in that they are non-rival and non-excludable.[12] If every fisher benefits from a reduction in water pollution, regardless of whether they have contributed towards the necessary compensation, then they will not have an incentive to contribute towards paying the compensation and engaging in the bargaining process. But if every fisher thinks like this, then no compensation will be paid and the chemical plant will continue to pollute the lake.
- **Problems of imperfect information**: for bargaining to lead to the socially optimal outcome, the parties involved must have full information about the relevant costs and benefits. In practice, this is unlikely to be the case, and neither party has an incentive to truthfully reveal the cost of the impact of the externality or the cost of reducing the externality. Those negatively affected by the externality will have an incentive to overstate the negative impact, in the hope of securing a larger compensation. If the property right is assigned to those generating the externality, then they will have an incentive to overstate the cost of reducing the externality. In the case of many real-world externalities, it can also be difficult to accurately quantify the costs of the externality.
- **Transaction costs**: the Coase theorem assumes that bargaining is costless, but in practice there is typically a cost associated with getting all parties together, engaging in negotiations, and reaching an agreement on a mutually beneficial solution.[13] Bargaining costs are likely to be high if there are many individuals involved—since they all need to reach an agreement—and if the nature of the externality is such that individuals have an incentive to free ride and misrepresent their true preferences in the bargaining process. The market may be able to internalize some small-scale localized externalities—for example, where the noise from a construction site has a negative impact on the business at a nearby restaurant. However, the Coase theorem may be less likely to work in the case of large global externalities, which involve multiple individuals or countries, such as global warming triggered by excessive greenhouse gas emissions. The institutional framework (i.e. the rules that govern the bargaining process) will affect the bargaining costs, and therefore the outcome.

An alternative market-based solution to the problem of externalities is **unitization**, which involves creating a single ownership of the activities connected by the externality. In the example above, if the chemical plant and the lake are owned by the same firm, the firm will have an incentive to consider the impact of increasing chemical production on the fish stocks in the lake, since both potentially provide it with a source of revenue. However, in creating single ownership, unitization will lead the firm to enjoy some degree of monopoly power, which will have implications for efficiency and equity. Moreover, many environmental externalities are not easily contained to a specific area, making unitization a less effective solution in practice.

[12] See Chapter 5 for a discussion of public goods. A good is non-rival if consumption of the good by one person does not reduce the amount available for others to consumer. A good is non-excludable if it would be impossible (or extremely costly) to prevent someone from consuming it.

[13] It is worth noting that Coase himself did not believe that transaction costs would be zero in the real world (Desmarais-Tremblay & Stojanović, 2022).

These limitations suggest a potentially greater role for government in addressing the problems created by environmental externalities. We discuss some of the ways in which governments may intervene in the next section.

10.3 Types of government intervention

Government spending on addressing environmental issues is relatively low in most countries. Most environmental interventions take the form of laws or regulations, taxes, and subsidies, and their economic impact is harder to quantify. We analyse the impact of these different types of policy intervention, and discuss their main advantages and limitations, below.

10.3.1 Taxes and subsidies

Corrective taxes

As we saw in section 10.1, the problem with negative externalities arises because the social marginal cost of production is greater than the private marginal cost, but the firm only considers its private costs when deciding how much to produce. One solution to this problem is to impose a tax, which raises the firm's private marginal cost. By forcing the firm to take the social cost of the pollution it generates into account, the tax provides an alternative way of internalizing the externality. These types of taxes are known as **corrective taxes** or **Pigouvian taxes**, after the English economist A. C. Pigou who originally proposed them (Pigou, 1932). There were nearly 400 environmentally related taxes across the OECD in 2006, as well as other environmentally related fees (OECD, 2006). Examples of environmental taxes include fuel duties, air passenger duties, landfill taxes, and plastic bag taxes.

Figure 10.6 illustrates how such a corrective tax would work in the case of the chemical plant discussed above. As we saw, because the firm only takes into account its private marginal cost—and not the social marginal cost—when deciding how much to produce, the level of chemicals produced will be excessive. The plant's profit-maximizing level of output is given by Q_1 in Figure 10.6, where *PMC* equals demand. By imposing a tax t equal to the marginal cost of pollution, the firm's marginal cost curve is increased to match the social marginal cost (*SMC*), and the firm will produce the socially optimal level of output, Q_2.

Rather than imposing the tax on the level of output, the government could impose a tax directly on the level of pollution. The advantage of taxing output is that this is more easily observable, whereas the level of pollution may be harder to measure. Provided there is a clear relationship between the level of output and pollution, output can act as a proxy measure for pollution. However, the firm can reduce the level of pollution emitted either by reducing the level of output produced, or by changing its production process so it emits less pollution. Both these approaches involve a cost in terms of lower output or the cost of investing in new, more environmentally friendly technology. A tax tied to the level of pollution provides an ongoing incentive for firms to reduce their emissions—for example, by investing in technologies that help it reduce its emissions—as each unit of emissions carries a cost.

The cost of reducing pollution is likely to vary across firms, even within the same industry. It will be relatively cheaper for some firms to reduce their emissions than for others. If firms that face lower marginal abatement costs reduce their emissions by more than firms with higher marginal abatement costs, the total costs of reducing pollution to a given a level will

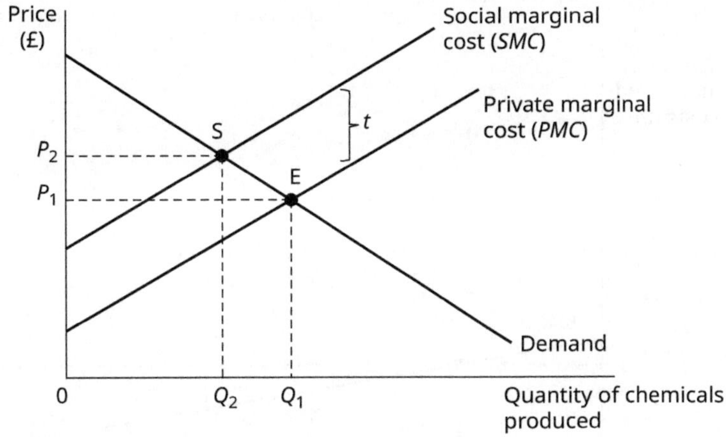

Figure 10.6 The impact of corrective taxation

be lower. A tax on emissions provides an incentive for firms that face lower abatement costs to reduce their emissions by more and will therefore ensure emissions are reduced in a more cost-effective way.

To see why this is the case, consider Figure 10.7, which illustrates the marginal abatement costs (*MAC*) for two firms, one facing a lower cost of reducing emissions (panel a) and one facing a higher cost (panel b). In the absence of government intervention, each firm will produce a level of emissions equal to Q^*. Suppose the government wants to reduce *total* industry emissions to Q^*. It could achieve this by requiring each firm to halve its emissions, so that each is producing a level of emissions equal to Q_1. It will cost the high-cost firm more to achieve this than it will cost the low-cost firm, as we can see from their corresponding marginal abatement cost curves, MAC_L and MAC_H. In fact, at a level of emissions of Q_1, the marginal abatement cost is almost twice as high for the high-cost firm as for the low-cost firm.

Alternatively, the government could impose a uniform tax t on each unit of emissions. Faced with this tax, the low-cost firm will reduce its emissions to Q_L. For any level of emissions above this, it will cost the firm more to pay the tax than to reduce its emissions, as the level of the tax is higher than the firm's marginal abatement cost. But for emissions below Q_L, the cost to the firm of reducing its emissions further is greater than the tax it has to pay, so it does not make sense for the firm to reduce its emissions further. Faced with the same tax on emissions, the high-cost firm will only reduce its emissions to Q_H, as beyond this level, it is cheaper for the firm to pay the tax than to reduce its emissions further. The government therefore achieves the same reduction in total emissions, to Q^*, but at a lower total cost, because the lower-cost firm reduces its emissions by more than the high-cost firm. And crucially, this does not rely on the government having detailed information on each firm's abatement costs.

Taxing pollution—or pollution-generating activities—also provides governments with an additional source of revenue, which could be used to cut other taxes or invest in initiatives that support social and environmental welfare. In fact, it is sometimes argued that environmental taxes involve a **double dividend**: they increase social welfare by reducing the level of pollution (or environmentally harmful activities) *and* by reducing the need for the government to rely on other distortionary taxes.[14] However, this argument ignores the fact that environmental taxes will impose distortions of their own, as they are likely to lead to an increase

[14] The impact of taxes on social welfare is discussed in Chapter 13.

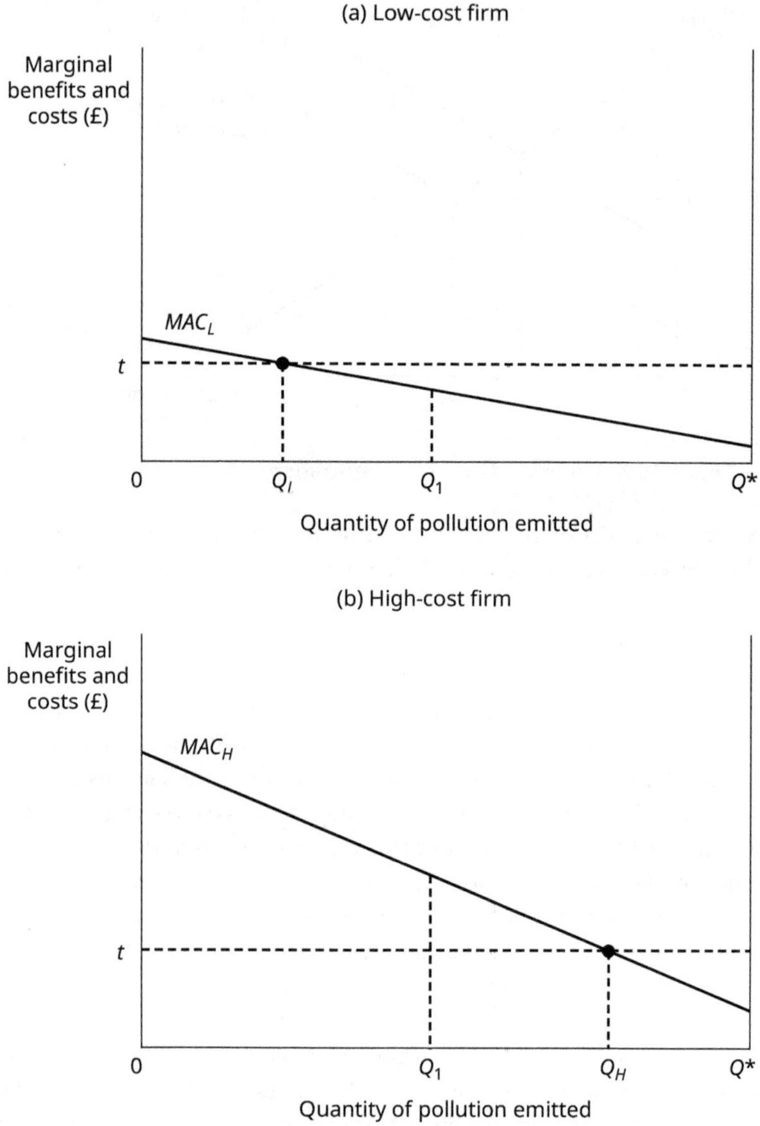

Figure 10.7 A tax on emissions for firms with different costs

in the price of goods, and it is important to consider the distributional consequences of environmental taxes as well (see Box 10.4).

A tax will not guarantee that a target level of pollution will be achieved, since this will depend on how firms respond to the tax, which will only be known imprecisely. Choosing the right level for the tax is also challenging in practice, since it relies on the government knowing the private marginal cost of production (which will probably vary across firms), the social cost of pollution, and market demand. This means the tax may be set either too low or too high and, depending on the political process, changing the level of the tax may be a slow and complex process.[15]

[15] Lobbies and special interest groups may also influence the government's decision over the level at which the tax is set.

Box 10.4 Who pays for environmental taxes?

The importance of environmental taxes—as a share of GDP and as a share of total taxation—varies significantly across countries. In 2022, across the OECD, average revenue from environmental taxes as a share of GDP was 1.3 per cent, but this ranged from 3.7 per cent in Greece to 0.11 per cent in Mexico (OECD, 2025). Environmental taxes are taxes levied on units that have an established negative impact on the environment, such as flights or fuel. The main categories of environmental taxes include energy, transport, resource, and pollution taxes. Evidence suggests that carbon taxes are generally unpopular, but support for carbon taxes is heavily influenced by how the revenues raised are used: support for carbon taxes increases if revenues are used to fund environmental infrastructure, subsidize low-carbon technologies, or reduce income taxes, particularly for the lowest-income households (Dechezleprêtre et al., 2025).

Some environmental taxes are regressive, in the sense that total tax payments make up a larger share of spending for low-income households than for high-income households. Taxes on energy, for example, tend to be regressive because poorer households spend a larger share of their budget on energy than wealthier households (Fullerton et al., 2010). However, taxes on vehicle fuel and aviation are more likely to be progressive, as wealthier households spend a larger share of their budget on these items (Johnson et al. 2012; Leicester & O'Dea, 2008). But even in the case of regressive environmental taxes, the revenues raised could be used to compensate lower-income households through other means.

The impact of taxes is not always easy to determine, particularly if taxes are levied on firms. Who bears the burden of the tax is not necessarily the person or organization who is responsible for making the tax payment to the government.[16] Firms might respond to taxes by increasing their prices, or they may attempt to reduce other costs, such as wages. When thinking about the distributional impact of environmental taxes, it is important to think beyond the immediate impact and consider how firms and individuals might respond to the tax.

Subsidies

An alternative to taxing pollution is to provide subsidies to firms to help reduce their costs of reducing pollution—for example, by subsidizing the adoption of more environmentally friendly technologies. The government could also subsidize activities that involve positive environmental spillovers. A subsidy reduces the firm's marginal cost of production, leading to an expansion of the output or activities that involve positive externalities.

However, whereas taxes provide a source of revenue for the government, subsidies need to be paid for, so the government needs to raise tax revenues from other sources. Environmental subsidies therefore involve an additional social welfare cost.

[16] We discuss this in detail in Chapter 13, where we draw a distinction between the statutory or legal incidence of a tax (which refers to who is responsible for making the tax payment to the tax authorities), and the economic incidence of a tax (which refers to who actually bears the burden of the tax in terms of a loss of welfare).

10.3.2 Regulation

While taxes and subsidies aim to limit environmental harms through the price mechanism, regulations aim to address the quantity of environmental harm directly. Governments have long relied on regulation to help protect the environment. One of the earliest examples of environmental legislation in the UK was the Smoke Nuisance Abatement Act 1853, which fined factories that emitted excessive smoke in London. Some environmental regulations limit emissions of certain pollutants (e.g. vehicle exhaust emission standards), whereas others limit the use of certain products or inputs. In some cases, environmental legislation may ban the use of certain inputs altogether. The use of chlorofluorocarbons (CFCs) was banned across the world in the 1990s to help preserve the ozone layer. The EU implemented a ban on the sale of many single-use plastic products in member countries in 2021 (European Union, 2019), and the sale of new petrol and diesel cars is set to be banned by 2035.

Regulation can provide more certainty. If the government knows the marginal abatement costs and the marginal damage cost of pollution, it can identify the optimal level of pollution and issue **pollution permits** restricting the quantity of pollution that firms can emit. But with a tax, the actual level of emissions will depend on how firms respond to the tax, which is unlikely to be known with certainty.

In the example illustrated in Figure 10.7 above, the government could issue a permit to each firm which allowed it to produce a maximum level of emissions of Q_1. This would achieve the desired overall level of emissions of Q^*. In cases where it is costly (or impossible) to accurately monitor the level of emissions, the government may instead choose to regulate use of a particular input that acts as a proxy for the level of emissions (e.g. fuel). This relies on there being a clear relationship between these inputs and the level of pollution. Regulating inputs rather than the level of pollution reduces the incentive for firms to invest in more environmentally friendly technology.

However, as with taxation, uncertainty about marginal abatement costs and the marginal damage cost of pollution means that it is often difficult for the government to legislate precisely on the optimal level of emissions. The government may not be able to determine Q^* and will therefore set the regulated level of emissions either too low or too high.

Compared to a tax, regulation is a less cost-effective way of reducing pollution. As we saw above, an emissions tax provides an incentive for firms that face lower abatement costs to reduce their pollution by more than firms that face higher abatement costs. In theory, the government could set a different level of emissions for each firm, requiring firms that face lower costs of reducing emissions to reduce their emissions more—for example, limiting emissions by low-cost firms to Q_L and emissions by high-cost firms to Q_H. However, in practice, the government would need detailed information on each firm's abatement costs, and firms (particularly low-cost firms) would have an incentive to overstate their abatement costs. Taxes also provide an ongoing incentive for firms to reduce their emissions, as each unit of emissions carries a cost.

Regulation also raises the possibility of regulatory capture, where the regulator gradually comes to identify itself with the interests of the firm that it regulates, making it vulnerable to bribery and lobbying by the firm's managers. The regulator may then stop acting in the best interests of consumers and society, and instead work to advance the interests of the industry it is supposed to regulate, setting the permissible level of pollution above the socially optimal level. Weak or ineffective regulation can have a serious negative impact on the environment and well-being (see Box 10.5). However, this problem also arises to some extent in

Box 10.5 England's sewage scandal

Water companies in England released raw sewage into rivers, lakes, and the surrounding sea for 3.6 million hours in 2023, compared to 1.75 million hours in 2022. Untreated sewage can cause serious damage to local environments and pose a health risk for people who come into contact with it. Water companies are legally allowed to release untreated sewage when it rains heavily, to prevent homes being flooded, but there is a limit to how much can be released. The Environment Agency is the regulator responsible for monitoring and regulating land and water pollution in England, but its environmental protection budget was halved between 2010 and 2020, severely limiting its ability to enforce regulations. This problem has been compounded by the lack of investment by the privatized water companies in newer and bigger wastewater treatment works.

Source: Grecksch (2024).

the context of taxes, where lobby or special interest groups may influence the government's decision over what level to set taxes at, such that taxes are set too low. Special interest groups and large corporations can also lobby the government to exempt their industry from the tax altogether, arguing for the 'strategic nature' of their industry or the supposed need to protect jobs from unfair international competition.

10.3.3 Tradeable permits

As we saw above, one of the key advantages of taxes over pollution permits is that taxes provide a more cost-effective way of reducing emissions, since they encourage firms that face lower marginal abatement costs to reduce their pollution by more. There is a way in which similar incentives can be built into a system of pollution permits—by creating a market for pollution permits.[17] Under a system of **tradeable permits**, the government sets a limit on the total level of emissions and issues the necessary number of permits, and these permits are then auctioned off, so firms bid for the right to pollute. Firms will be willing to sell permits as long as the price of the permit exceeds their marginal abatement cost; and firms will want to buy permits if the price of the permit is less than their marginal abatement cost. In equilibrium, the level of pollution that each firm emits will be such that the marginal cost to them of reducing pollution just equals the market price of the permit. Firms that face higher marginal abatement costs will be expected to pay a higher price for permits, and to pay to pollute more, since it costs them more to reduce pollution. So as with a pollution tax, firms that face lower marginal abatement costs will reduce their pollution more; but here the price is set by the firms, rather than the government.

One of the challenges with implementing a pollution tax is that the government might not be able to accurately predict how firms will respond, so the level of pollution with a tax might be higher than socially optimal. If the government knows what level of pollution is socially optimal, then a system of tradeable permits is preferable. The government does not need to have detailed information on each firm's marginal abatement costs; it can simply set the

[17] This builds on the insights from the Coase theorem, discussed in section 10.2.

overall target level of pollution and allow the market to determine the price. However, determining this optimal level is challenging in itself.

A system of tradeable permits or **emission trading scheme** has a number of attractive features, and these schemes have become increasingly popular as a way of reducing carbon emissions with a view to achieving climate goals (see Box 10.6). However, there are also challenges. Perhaps one of the biggest challenges involves determining the initial allocation of permits to firms. If permits are issued based on firms' current levels of emissions, then more polluting firms will be favoured and firms that pollute less (and which may have already invested heavily in reducing their emissions) are effectively penalized. The process whereby firms are allocated permits based on their historical level of emissions is known as 'grandfathering'. Firms can then continue polluting at that level, or they can cut their emissions and sell their permits. Grandfathering has the advantage of reducing the initial cost to firms, which may make these schemes easier to implement. However, the biggest polluters are effectively rewarded, as they receive the largest allocation of permits.

Tradeable permits will also only be effective if the geographical location of pollution does not matter. If the aim is to reduce air pollution in urban areas, for example, then enabling firms located in and around urban centres to pollute more by buying up permits will not be very effective. There is also a cost associated with trading permits that needs to be taken into account.

Box 10.6 The rise of carbon markets

Carbon markets are pricing mechanisms that allow governments and non-state actors such as firms and cities to trade greenhouse gas emission or carbon credits. These credits essentially represent the reduction or removal of greenhouse gases from the atmosphere, and firms can buy carbon credits to offset their carbon emissions. Compliance carbon markets include national and regional emission trading schemes (ETSs), where participants are legally required to meet certain emissions targets. However, carbon markets can also be voluntary, where participants are not obliged to achieve specific emissions targets.

The number of emissions trading schemes around the world has been increasing. The world's first international ETS was the European Union Emission Trading Scheme (EU ETS), which was set up in 2005 and which applies to all EU member states, as well as Iceland, Liechtenstein, and Norway (European Commission, n.d.a). The price per ton of carbon increased from just under €10 in 2012 to around €60 in 2021 (ECB, 2021). Although there were concerns that the price of carbon under the EU ETS was low relative to the social cost of carbon, estimates suggest that between 2008 and 2016 the scheme saved about 1.2 billion tons of CO_2 (3.8 per cent) relative to a world without carbon markets (Bayer & Aklin, 2020). This was almost half of what EU governments had committed to reduce under the Kyoto Protocol. The EU ETS is also an important source of revenue for funding the climate transition across member states, raising €43.6 billion in 2023 (European Commission, 2024).

China, South Korea, Mexico, the United Kingdom, and New Zealand have also implemented ETSs at the national level, whereas the USA and Canada have schemes only at the subnational level.

Pollution permits are effectively a type of property right—they allow the owner to emit a certain level of pollution. An important question for policymakers, then, is whether and how these entitlements to pollute can be reduced. Should the government be required to buy back permits if it wishes to reduce the level of pollution allowed (with the cost implications this entails for the government), or should a proportion of permits revert back to the government after a specified period of time?

In deciding which policy tool to use to address environmental problems, the government should not just focus on how it will impact efficiency. It should also consider the likely equity or distributional implications, and whether a particular type of intervention is more or less likely to encourage socially beneficial innovation. This, in turn, is likely to depend on the nature of the problem—for example, is it global or local?—and how easy it is to measure and monitor.

10.4 Policy problem 1: tackling urban traffic congestion

Urban traffic congestion is a growing global problem. In a global ranking published in 2024, the top three most congested cities were Istanbul, New York, and Chicago, with the average driver losing between 102 and 105 hours per year due to traffic congestion. London was the worst-performing city for traffic congestion in Europe, with drivers losing an average of 101 hours per year due to congestion (Inrix, 2024).

Driving has many benefits for individuals, but it also imposes a wider cost on society. Environmental spillovers associated with road transport include local air pollution (including carbon monoxide, nitrogen oxide, and particulates), increased greenhouse gas emissions and noise pollution, increased risk of accidents, and the impact on biodiversity.[18] We are going to focus on the problem of congestion, although we could apply a similar rationale to analyse other negative externalities associated with driving.

Traffic congestion imposes a cost in terms of wasted time and fuel. Estimates for the UK place the total cost of congestion at £7.7 billion in 2024 (Inrix, 2024). We can model traffic congestion as a negative externality, where the social marginal cost exceeds the private marginal cost. The private marginal cost of driving depends on journey time and the opportunity cost of that time, and any additional monetary costs (e.g. fuel and car maintenance). The social marginal cost depends on the level of congestion, which impacts on travel time for all individuals. For each individual, driving involves a money cost and a time cost. The time cost will depend on the length or duration of the journey and the speed of travel, which in turn depends on the number of cars on the road. If there are relatively few cars on the road, increasing the number of cars does not affect travel time or the cost of driving. However, if there are already many cars on the road and the road is congested, then additional drivers will slow travel time and increase the cost of driving for all drivers.

An individual will choose to drive if the private marginal cost is less than the marginal benefit they derive from driving. They will not usually consider the impact that their decision to drive has on other road users. This will result in too many drivers on the road, as illustrated in Figure 10.8. Because there are negative externalities associated with driving, the social

[18] In addition, there are the costs associated with building the roads themselves, which include construction costs, but also land loss, potential loss of natural habitats, loss of landscape, and potential to increase urban sprawl.

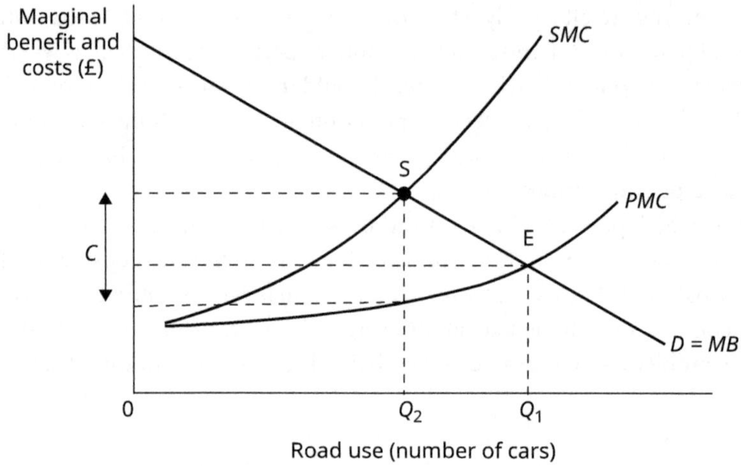

Figure 10.8 Congestion charge to address congestion externalities

marginal cost curve, *SMC*, lies above the private marginal cost, *PMC*. With no restrictions on access, the equilibrium number of drivers will be Q_1, which is above the socially optimal level Q_2.

One possible solution to the congestion problem is to introduce a **congestion charge** or **congestion tax** to internalize the externality. The equilibrium traffic allocation involves too many drivers using the road because each individual driver has no incentive to take into account the social cost of using the road. The congestion charge will ensure individuals face the full social cost of their decision. This is illustrated in Figure 10.8. The socially optimal outcome is S, where there are Q_2 cars on the road. A congestion charge of *C* will increase the private marginal cost to equal the social marginal cost.

The charge leads to a decrease in traffic volume, which will increase travel speed and therefore reduce travel time and travel cost. However, it is important to consider the possible knock-on effects of such a policy. Some individuals may respond to the tax by choosing alternative modes of transport such as buses or trains, or by changing their travel route, and these may in turn become congested. The government may choose to use the revenue raised through the congestion charge to invest in alternative modes of transport. In the longer run, a congestion charge may affect individual decisions about where to work and/or live, in order to reduce their commuting costs.

Traffic congestion tends to be worse in cities and varies over the course of the day. Roads will typically be busier early in the morning and at the end of the afternoon, when people are travelling to and from work. This means the gap between private and social cost will vary across time, so an efficient congestion charge should also vary across time. During peak travel times, the demand or marginal benefit curve will be higher, so there will be a larger gap between social and private cost.[19] An efficient congestion charge will therefore be higher for travel during peak periods. If the congestion charge varies at peak and off-peak times, there is an incentive for individuals to change their time of travel (if they can).

[19] To see this, try drawing a demand curve below the demand curve depicted in Figure 10.8 and determine what the optimal congestion charge would be at this new lower level of demand.

A congestion charge is not the only policy governments can use to tackle problems of traffic congestion. Alternative policies include the following:

- **Fuel taxes**: a fuel tax is a tax imposed on the sale of fuel, which increases the cost of all vehicle travel (not just travel in congested areas). By increasing the cost of driving relative to other modes of transport, a fuel tax can encourage individuals to use alternative modes of travel, such as cycling or taking the bus.
- **Parking taxes**: a parking tax is essentially a charge for parking. Different fares can be charged for different times of day, charging a higher fare when demand for parking is higher. Evidence suggests drivers do respond to changes in the price of parking. A study in Ottawa found that an increase in parking rates led to a fall in workers driving to work and an increase in bus use (DiRenzo et al, 1981). In Paris, drivers of larger cars will face higher parking fees.
- **Public transport subsidies**: providing subsidies for using public transport can encourage more people to use it. But the government will need to raise the revenue to pay for the subsidies, which could introduce distortions and reduce social welfare. It has been argued that public transport subsidies may be less efficient than a congestion charge because they underprice public transport and therefore encourage usage above the optimal level. However, if there are positive externalities associated with public transport use, then the subsidies may help mitigate these.

These policies are often used in combination. Most countries have some form of a fuel tax, and several cities have introduced congestion charging schemes (see Box 10.7). Alongside this, many local governments provide subsidized public transport and there has been a rapid growth in popularity of other shared mobility options in cities across the world, including bike, e-bike, and scooter hire schemes, and car share schemes. When evaluating the impact of these policies, it is important to consider not only how they will affect social welfare and the attainment of environmental goals, but their implications for equity and accessibility.

Box 10.7 Congestion charging in practice

The earliest congestion pricing scheme was introduced in Singapore in 1975. The Singapore Area Licensing Scheme levied a charge on drivers entering the downtown area of Singapore. It was replaced by an electronic road-pricing scheme in 1998, which relies on open road tolling, so vehicles do not have to stop or slow down to pay the charge, as these are collected automatically through a wireless system. Technological developments, such as video surveillance and electronic detection, have made it easier to implement congestion charges, and road-pricing systems have subsequently been implemented in London, Rome, and Stockholm.

The London congestion charge (CC) was introduced in 2003, imposing a charge of £5 for certain types of vehicles entering the CC zone at certain times of day. As of 2024, the charge was £15 a day and applies to vehicles entering the CC zone between 7 a.m. and 6 p.m. weekdays, and 12 to 6 p.m. at weekends and on bank holidays. The two main objectives of the

(Continued)

scheme were to reduce levels of car use and to generate revenue to invest in public transport and other transport projects. The CC was introduced alongside other measures designed to improve transport in the city of London, including investments in the bus network and services, which makes assessing the impact of the CC scheme on congestion complicated. Between 2003 and 2013, about £1.2 billion (46 per cent) of net revenue from the CC was invested in public transport, road and bridge improvement, and walking and cycling schemes. In 2013, Transport for London reported that the congestion charging scheme resulted in a 10 per cent reduction in traffic volumes.

Source: Givoni (2012).

10.5 Policy problem 2: the global threat of the climate crisis

The threat of the climate crisis is the biggest environmental challenge facing the world today. Average temperatures have been rising across the world, as Table 10.1 illustrates. This rise in global temperatures has serious implications for the health and well-being of the population and the planet, with a loss of biodiversity, reduced crop yields, coastal incursion, a rise of weather-related illnesses, as well as an increased likelihood of extreme weather events and the costs these entail. It is now widely accepted that this rise in global temperatures is linked to the increase in emissions of greenhouse gases, particularly CO_2, methane, and nitrous oxide, primarily as a result of human activity.[20]

Greenhouse gas emissions are an example of a negative externality. As we saw above, governments can address negative externalities either through taxes—imposing a tax on the negative externality itself or on the activity generating it—or through permits, which limit the quantity of a particular externality. While taxes provide a more cost-effective way of reducing negative externalities, permits are more appropriate when the goal is to achieve a certain target level of emissions. Several countries have already implemented systems of tradeable pollution permits (see Box 10.6).

However, the climate crisis is a true global commons problem—the damage from excessive greenhouse gas emissions is felt across the world. And it is not just the level of emissions that matters, but the concentration of greenhouse gases in the atmosphere that is driving the increase in global temperatures. The solution therefore requires cooperation between a large number of countries. Each country will have its own particular interests to defend, and the costs and benefits of reducing greenhouse gas emissions are not evenly distributed across countries (see Table 10.2).

Global efforts to address the climate crisis date back to the 1980s, with the Intergovernmental Panel on Climate Change established by the United Nations Environment Programme in 1988. The Kyoto Protocol, an international treaty which aimed to reduce emissions of greenhouse gases that contribute to climate change, was signed in 1997. It came into force in 2005, requiring 41 countries plus the EU to commit to mandatory emission-reduction targets. The Kyoto Protocol paved the way for the establishment of emissions trading schemes, including the EU ETS discussed above. The Kyoto Protocol also acknowledged that countries have different capabilities when it comes to combating climate change due to differences in economic

[20] Global emissions of CO_2, one of the largest contributors to the total volume of greenhouse gas emissions, increased more than fivefold since 1950, as we saw in Figure 10.1.

Table 10.1 Average annual surface temperature, 1950–2024 (°C)

Country	1950	2024	Absolute change
Australia	21.78	22.79	+1.01
Austria	6.25	8.76	+2.51
Belgium	9.32	11.37	+2.05
Canada	−5.98	−1.75	+4.23
Denmark	8.15	9.90	+1.75
Finland	2.61	4.02	+1.40
France	12.63	14.20	+1.56
Germany	8.73	10.95	+2.23
Greece	15.13	16.66	+1.53
Ireland	9.50	10.33	+0.83
Italy	12.74	14.43	+1.69
Japan	10.67	13.45	+2.77
Netherlands	9.52	11.72	+2.21
New Zealand	9.43	10.82	+1.40
Norway	−1.41	2.03	+3.44
Portugal	14.88	16.17	+1.29
Spain	13.49	15.08	+1.60
Sweden	2.83	4.68	+1.85
UK	8.47	10.10	+1.62
USA	8.48	10.71	+2.23
World	13.60	15.09	+1.49

Source: Copernicus Climate Change Service (2025)—with major processing by Our World in Data.

Table 10.2 Top ten CO_2 emitters, 2023

Country	Total annual emissions (million tonnes)	Country	Emissions per capita (tonnes)
China	11,902.5	Qatar	38.8
USA	4,911.4	Bahrain	23.3
India	3,062.3	Trinidad and Tobago	22.8
Russia	1,815.9	Saudi Arabia	22.1
Japan	988.8	United Arab Emirates	21.6
Iran	817.9	Kuwait	20.5
Saudi Arabia	736.2	New Caledonia	17.5
Indonesia	733.2	Oman	15.5
Germany	596.2	Faroe Islands	14.6
South Korea	577.4	Australia	14.5

Source: Global Carbon Budget (2024)—with major processing by Our World in Data.

development. The protocol therefore placed the responsibility for reducing emissions on developed countries, given that these countries were historically responsible for the current concentrations of greenhouse gases in the atmosphere.

This distinction between the responsibilities of developed and developing countries in reducing emissions was abandoned with the Paris Agreement, a legally binding international climate change treaty that was adopted by 196 countries at the UN Climate Change Conference in Paris in 2015 (COP21) and came into force the following year.[21] The goal of this agreement is to limit the increase in the global average temperature by requiring all countries to submit national climate action plans, outlining the measures they intend to adopt to reduce their emissions. World leaders meet each year to discuss these climate commitments and track their progress towards achieving them.[22]

Even where countries are able to reach an agreement, there remains the practical challenge of enforcement. How can countries be persuaded to cooperate and abide by their environmental commitments? Individual countries will also need to persuade their electorates to support environmental policies which are likely to impose a cost on current generations, and voters might not be willing to sacrifice their present welfare for the welfare of future generations.

Economics has a role to play in addressing the threat of the climate crisis. Economic assessments underpin most governmental and private sector policies and strategic decisions related to the climate crisis. However, often these assessments do not adequately reflect the latest scientific evidence on current and future climate changes. Valuing the impacts of the climate crisis is challenging. How can we place a monetary value on the loss of entire species, or population displacement? How can we adequately take into account the uncertainty around possible outcomes, so that extreme outcomes which have a low probability of occurring are not dismissed? We need different models and tools, different ways of presenting information, and to work more closely across disciplines to properly address the climate crisis (see Box 10.8).

Box 10.8 Rethinking the role of economics in understanding the climate crisis

How can we improve the understanding of the economic consequences of the climate crisis? The disconnect between economics and the physical sciences means that often the approaches that underlie economic assessments of the impacts of the climate crisis do not reflect the severity of the consequences (based on the latest physical climate science). Many economic assessments do not take into account the full consequences of extreme weather events or the potential for cascading risks and tipping points. Economic assessments typically rely on past data, and the extrapolation methods used for estimating future economic impacts of the climate crisis are not always appropriate, which means that not all future likely outcomes are considered. The probabilistic way in which uncertainty is treated in economics

[21] The USA withdrew from the Paris Agreement for a second time in 2025, having previously done so in 2020 and rejoined in 2021. The only other countries outside the agreement are Iran, Libya, and Yemen.

[22] These international summits are known as COPs (Conference of the Parties).

means that extreme events which have a low or unknown likelihood of occurring may be understated and potentially overlooked by policymakers.

What needs to change? Nature and health need to be properly integrated into economic assessments. Economic analyses of the climate crisis also need to incorporate ethics, inequality, and justice, recognizing the importance of inclusive wealth, and the vital role of natural and social capital alongside physical and human capital. We need closer interdisciplinary collaboration between physical scientists, economists, and other social scientists. And we need to find new ways of engaging and reporting information to policymakers, such as storyline approaches, particularly on extreme events where the probability of occurring is small or not known.

Source: Royal Society (2023).

Conclusion

Throughout history, humans have made changes to ecosystems to meet a growing demand for food, fresh water, and fuel. These changes have contributed to significant gains in well-being and economic prosperity, but they have come at a cost in terms of the loss and degradation of the natural environment and many ecosystem services. Unless current challenges are addressed, this will continue to impact the well-being of current and future generations.

What role should economic thinking play in the design of environmental policies? In this chapter we have analysed the main arguments for government intervention to address environmental problems and the different types of policies available to governments. Economics provides a useful lens for analysing environmental problems and developing possible policy solutions. But in order to successfully address environmental challenges, particularly global challenges, nature and the environment need to be properly integrated into economic models.

Questions for discussion

1. 'Increased pollution and the deterioration of the environment are an inevitable consequence of economic growth.' Do you agree with this statement?
2. Can markets fully internalize externalities? Why might government intervention beyond establishing and enforcing property rights be necessary?
3. 'Attempts to create a market for pollution are destined to fail because we cannot put a price on nature.' Do you agree with this statement?
4. What weight should be placed on the welfare of future generations?
5. What policy or policies would you propose the government adopts to address the following problems: (a) an increase in food waste; (b) rubbish being dumped at a local park; (c) deforestation in the Amazon; (d) a rise in greenhouse gas emissions? What would be the challenges in implementing these policies? What would be their likely impact?

Further reading

For a more in-depth discussion of the economics of the environment:

Common, M., & Stagl, S. (2005). *Ecological economics: An introduction*. Cambridge University Press.

Tietenberg, T., & Lewis, L. (2009). *Environmental and natural resource economics* (8th ed.). Pearson international edition. Addison Wesley.

On common-pool resources:

Ostrom, E. (1990). *Governing the commons: The evolution of institutions for collective action*. Cambridge University Press.

Ostrom, E. (1999). Coping with tragedies of the commons. *Annual Review of Political Science*, *2*, 493–535. https://doi.org/10.1146/annurev.polisci.2.1.493

For a discussion and critique of the Coase theorem:

Medema, S. G. (2020). The Coase theorem at sixty. *Journal of Economic Literature*, *58*(4), 1045–1128. https://doi.org/10.1257/jel.20191060

On environmental taxation:

European Environment Agency (2023). *The role of (environmental) taxation in supporting sustainability transitions*. Available at: https://www.eea.europa.eu/publications/the-role-of-environmental-taxation

Mirrlees, J., et al. (2011). *Tax by design: The Mirrlees review*. Institute for Fiscal Studies and Oxford University Press. See chapters 10 and 11 on environmental taxation and tax and climate change.

Williams III, R. C. (2016). *Environmental taxation*. National Bureau of Economic Research working papers, no. 22303. Available at: https://doi.org/10.3386/w22303

On the problem of urban traffic congestion:

ECMT (2007). *Managing urban traffic congestion*. European Conference of Ministers of Transport. Organization for Economic Cooperation and Development. https://doi.org/10.1787/9789282101506-en. The executive summary (pp. 11–27) gives a good overview of the problem of traffic congestion and policies that can be used to address it.

Glazer, A., & Niskanen, E. (1992). Parking fees and congestion. *Regional Science and Urban Economics*, *22*(1), 123–132.

Parry, I. W., Walls, M., & Harrington, W. (2007). Automobile externalities and policies. *Journal of Economic Literature*, *45*(2), 373–399.

On individual attitudes towards climate policies:

Dechezleprêtre, A., Fabre, A., Kruse, T., Planterose, B., Sanchez Chico, A., & Stantcheva, S. (2025). Fighting climate change: International attitudes toward climate policies. *American Economic Review*, *115*(4), 1258–1300.

Bibliography

Adams, W., Brockington, D., Dyson, J. & Vira, B. (2003) Managing tragedies: Understanding conflict over common pool resources. *Science*, *302*(5652), 1915–1916.

Bayer, P., & Aklin, M. (2020). The European Union Emissions Trading System reduced CO_2 emissions despite low prices. *Proceedings of the National Academy of Sciences*, *117*(16), 8804–8812. https://doi.org/10.1073/pnas.1918128117

Beynon, J., & Wickstead, E. (2024). *Climate finance: Fair shares revisited*. Center for Global Development, CGD note 371.

Coase, R. H. (1960). The problem of social cost. *Journal of Law and Economics, 3*, 1–44.

Copernicus Climate Change Service information (2025)—with major processing by Our World in Data. *Temperature anomaly* [data set]. Contains modified Copernicus Climate Change Service information, *ERA5 monthly averaged data on single levels from 1940 to present 2* [original data]. Available at: https://ourworldindata.org/temperature-anomaly

Dasgupta, S., Laplante, B., Wang, H., & Wheeler, D., 2002. Confronting the environmental Kuznets curve. *Journal of Economic Perspectives, 16*, 147–168.

Dechezleprêtre, A., Fabre, A., Kruse, T., Planterose, B., Sanchez Chico, A., & Stantcheva, S. (2025). Fighting climate change: International attitudes toward climate policies. *American Economic Review, 115*(4), 1258–1300.

De Moor, T. (2011). From common pastures to global commons: A historical perspective on interdisciplinary approaches to commons. *Natures Sciences Sociétés, 19*(4), 422–431.

Desmarais-Tremblay, M., & Stojanović, A. (2022). Framing institutional choice, 1937–1973: New institutional economics and the neglect of the commons. *Review of Political Economy, 34*(4), 665–691. https://doi.org/10.1080/09538259.2022.2096284

DiRenzo, J. F., Barber, E., & Cima, B. (1981). *Parking management tactics*, Vol. 3: *Reference guide*. Federal Highway Administration.

ECB (2021). EU emissions allowance prices in the context of the ECB's climate change action plan. European Central Bank. *Economic Bulletin*, issue 6/2021.

EEA (2018). *Air quality in Europe—2018 report*. European Environment Agency, report no. 12/2018. ISSN 1977-8449.

European Commission (n.d.a). *Development of EU ETS (2005–2020)*. Available at: https://climate.ec.europa.eu/eu-action/carbon-markets/eu-emissions-trading-system-eu-ets/development-eu-ets-2005-2020_en

European Commission (n.d.b). *Nature restoration success stories*. Available at: https://environment.ec.europa.eu/topics/nature-and-biodiversity/nature-restoration-law/success-stories_en

European Commission (2024). *Report from the Commission to the European Parliament and Council on the functioning of the European carbon market in 2023*. Document 52024DC0538. Available at: https://eur-lex.europa.eu/legal-content/EN/TXT/?uri=celex:52024DC0538

European Union (2019). *Directive (EU) 2019/904 on reducing the impact of certain plastic products on the environment*. Available at: https://eur-lex.europa.eu/legal-content/EN/LSU/?uri=CELEX:32019L0904

FAO (2020). *Global forest resources assessment, 2020: Key findings*. Food and Agriculture Organization. Available at: https://doi.org/10.4060/ca8753en

Fullerton, D., Leicester, A., & Smith, S. (2010). Environmental taxes. In J. Mirrlees et al. (Eds.), *Dimensions of tax design: The Mirrlees review* (pp. 423–547). Oxford: Oxford University Press.

Givoni, M. (2012), Re-assessing the results of the London congestion charging scheme. *Urban Studies, 49*(5), 1089–1105.

Global Carbon Budget (2024)—with major processing by Our World in Data. *Annual CO_2 emissions* [dataset]. Global Carbon Project, *Global Carbon Budget v15* [original data]. Retrieved 23 January 2025 from https://archive.ourworldindata.org/20260119-070102/grapher/annual-co2-emissions-per-country.html. Population based on various sources (2024)—with major processing by Our World in Data. *CO_2 emissions per capita* [data set]. Global Carbon Project, *Global Carbon Budget v15*; various sources, *Population* [original data]. Retrieved 23 January 2025 from https://archive.ourworldindata.org/20260119-070102/grapher/co-emissions-per-capita.html

Grecksch, K. (2024). Renationalising water could fix sewage crisis—but no major party will do it. *The Conversation*. 2 July.

Grossman, G. M., & Krueger, A. B. (1995). Economic growth and the environment. *Quarterly Journal of Economics, 110*(2), 353–377.

Hardin, G. (1968). The tragedy of the commons. *Science, 162*(3859), 1243–1248.

Inrix (2024). *Global traffic scorecard*. Available at: https://inrix.com/scorecard/#form-download-the-full-report

IPCC (2014). *Climate change 2014: Synthesis report. Contribution of working groups I, II and III to the Fifth Assessment Report of the Intergovernmental Panel on Climate Change* [Core writing team R. K. Pachauri & L. A. Meyer (Eds.)]. Intergovernmental Panel on Climate Change.

Johnson, P., Leicester, A., & Stoye, G. (2012). *Fuel for thought: The what, why and how of motoring taxation*. RAC Foundation.

Leicester, A. (2012). Environmental taxes: Economic principles and the UK experience. Institute for Fiscal Studies. Available at: https://ifs.org.uk/sites/default/files/output_url_files/chapter_leicester_uk2.pdf.

Leicester, A., & O'Dea, C. (2008). Aviation taxes. In R. Chote, C. Emmerson, D. Miles, & J. Shaw (Eds.), *The IFS green budget: January 2008* (pp. 187–211). Institute for Fiscal Studies.

Medema, S. G. (2020). The Coase theorem at sixty. *Journal of Economic Literature, 58*(4), 1045–1128. https://doi.org/10.1257/jel.20191060

MEA. 2005. *Ecosystems and human well-being: Synthesis report*. Millennium Ecosystem Assessment/Island Press. Available at: https://www.millenniumassessment.org/en/index.html

Mirrlees, J., Adam, S., Besley, T., Blundell, R., Bond, S., Chote, R., Gammie, M., Johnson, P., Myles, G., & Poterba, J. M. (2011). *Tax by design: The Mirrlees review*. Oxford University Press/Institute for Fiscal Studies.

Mitchell, G. (2005). Forecasting environmental equity: Air quality responses to road user charging in Leeds, UK. *Journal of Environmental Management, 77*(3), 212–226.

OECD (2006). *The political economy of environmentally related taxes*. Organization for Economic Cooperation and Development.

OECD (2025). *Environmentally related tax revenue*. Organization for Economic Cooperation and Development. Data explorer. https://data-explorer.oecd.org (accessed 3 October 2025).

Ostrom, E. (1990). *Governing the commons: The evolution of institutions for collective action*. Cambridge University Press.

Ostrom, E. (1999). Coping with tragedies of the commons. *Annual Review of Political Science, 2*, 493–535. https://doi.org/10.1146/annurev.polisci.2.1.493

Ostrom, E. (2001). Environment and common property institutions. In N. J. Smelser & P. B. Baltes (Eds.), *International encyclopaedia of the social and behavioural sciences* (pp. 4560–4566). Elsevier.

Ostrom, E. (2008). The challenge of common-pool resources. *Environment: Science and Policy for Sustainable Development, 50*(4), 8–21.

Ostrom, V. & Ostrom, E. (1999). Public goods and public choices. In M. McGinnis (Ed.), *Polycentricity and local public economies* (pp. 75–106). University of Michigan Press.

Pigou, A. C. (1932) *The economics of welfare* (4th ed.). Macmillan.

Raworth, K. (2017). *Doughnut economics: Seven ways to think like 21st century economist*. Penguin Random House.

Ritchie, H. (2022) CO_2 emissions dataset: Our sources and methods. Published online at OurWorldinData.org. Retrieved from: https://ourworldindata.org/co2-dataset-sources

Royal Society (2023). New horizons for understanding economic consequences of climate change—A summary report. October. Available at: https://royalsociety.org/news-resources/publications/2023/climate-change-economics/

Samborska, V. (2024) How much have temperatures risen in countries across the world? Published online at OurWorldinData.org. Retrieved from: https://ourworldindata.org/temperature-anomaly

Shafik, N., & Bandyopadhyay, S. (1992). *Economic growth and environmental quality: Time series and cross-country evidence*. Background paper for the *World development report 1992*. World Bank.

Stern, D. I. (1998). Progress on the environmental Kuznets curve? *Environment and Development Economics*, *3*(2), 173–196.

Stern, D. I. (2004). The rise and fall of the environmental Kuznets curve. *World Development*, *32*(8), 1419–1439.

Stern, D. I. (2018). The environmental Kuznets curve. In N. Castree, M. Hulme, & J. D. Proctor (Eds.), *Companion to environmental studies* (pp. 49–54). Routledge.

Tisdell, C. (2001). Globalisation and sustainability: Environmental Kuznets curve and the WTO. *Ecological Economics*, *39*(2), 185–196.

Torras, M., & Boyce, J. K. (1998). Income, inequality, and pollution: A reassessment of the environmental Kuznets curve. *Ecological Economics*, *25*(2), 147–160.

UN Environment Programme (2019). *Global environment outlook 6* (published 4 March). Available at: https://www.unep.org/resources/global-environment-outlook-6

United Nations (2019). *The Sustainable Development Goals report 2019*. Available at: https://unstats.un.org/sdgs/report/2019/goal-12/

United Nations (2024). *The Sustainable Development Goals report 2024*. Available at: https://unstats.un.org/sdgs/report/2024

United Nations SEEA (n.d.). *What is the SEEA?* United Nations System of Environmental Economic Accounting. Available at: https://seea.un.org/content/homepage

United Nations SSEA (2023). *2023 global assessment results*. United Nations System of Environmental Economic Accounting. Available at: https://seea.un.org/content/2023-global-assessment-results

11
Retirement and pensions

Learning objectives

By the end of this chapter, you will be able to:

- 11.1 Explain the objectives of old-age pensions.
- 11.2 Explain the different types of pension schemes and the structure of national pension systems.
- 11.3 Discuss the arguments for government intervention in the provision of old-age pensions.
- 11.4 Discuss the different ways in which governments can intervene in old-age pensions and their implications.
- 11.5 Discuss the key challenges affecting many pension systems across the world today and their implications for the design of pension policy.

Introduction

Across the OECD, the average retirement age is currently 64 for both men and women, whereas average life expectancies are 83 and 86 respectively (OECD, 2023).[1] This means that a man retiring today can expect to have to fund his retirement for approximately 19 years, while women will need to fund their retirement for even longer, at 22 years. Pensions provide a mechanism for individuals to finance their consumption after they have stopped working. They can be provided by the government or employers, or they can be based on private savings that individuals have built up throughout their working lives.

Pensions represent a significant component of government expenditure, accounting for 18.5 per cent of total government spending across the OECD in 2021 (OECD, n.d.b). In Spain, Austria, Portugal, Greece, and Italy, public pensions accounted for over a quarter of total government expenditure. This is set to rise over the coming years as many public pension schemes face the pressures of an ageing population, driven by increases in life expectancy and falling fertility rates. As people are living longer, their retirement incomes need to be sustained for longer. But retirement is a largely predictable event, so, in theory, individuals should be able to finance their consumption needs in retirement by saving during their working lives. Why should governments intervene in the provision of old-age pensions? What form should government intervention take?

We start by discussing the main objectives of old-age pensions in section 11.1. Section 11.2 provides an overview of the different types of pensions and the structure of pension systems.

[1] Life expectancy at the age of 65.

The economic arguments for government intervention in the provision of old-age pensions are laid out in section 11.3, while section 11.4 explores the different forms government intervention can take. Section 11.5 discusses the key challenges facing pension systems today and the implications for pension policy.

11.1 Why do we need pensions?

Pensions as we know them today are a relatively recent invention. Until the mid-twentieth century, in most countries individuals had to rely on their own savings, or support from family, friends, or charitable institutions once they were no longer able to work (see Box 11.1).

Pensions serve a number of objectives. They enable individuals to transfer income from periods when they are working to periods when they are not working, thus allowing them to smooth their consumption over the course of their lives. Pensions act as a form of insurance against uncertainty over how long individuals will live for and the risk they may outlive their resources. Public pensions can also be used as a tool to protect against the risk of poverty in old age or to redistribute income between different groups in society. We discuss each of these objectives below.

11.1.1 Consumption-smoothing

Over the course of our lives, most of us will have periods when we are working and periods when we are not working—for example, in retirement. How should we allocate our income across our lives to maximize our lifetime welfare? We can answer this question using Fisher's **intertemporal choice model**. Because individuals can save and borrow, how much they can spend in a given period is not constrained by what they earn in that period. The simplest version of this model assumes individuals live for two periods: period 1, when they are working;

Box 11.1 The first pension system

It is difficult to pinpoint the precise historical origins of public old-age pension schemes, partly due to disagreements over what constitutes an old-age pension programme. The general consensus is that the German pension system was the first state pension system in the world, although governments in some European countries had provided smaller-scale support to protect civil servants against the risk of old age, and some private employers had also offered workplace pensions to their employees. However, the German state pension system was the first public pension system that covered a wider population. It was designed by Otto von Bismarck and introduced in 1889. By 1910, only five countries offered formal old-age protection schemes, but this expanded dramatically following the First and Second World Wars and the period of decolonization. Prior to this, individuals would have to rely on support from family members or charity, or just keep working, in order to fund their consumption in later life.

Source: Grünewald (2021).

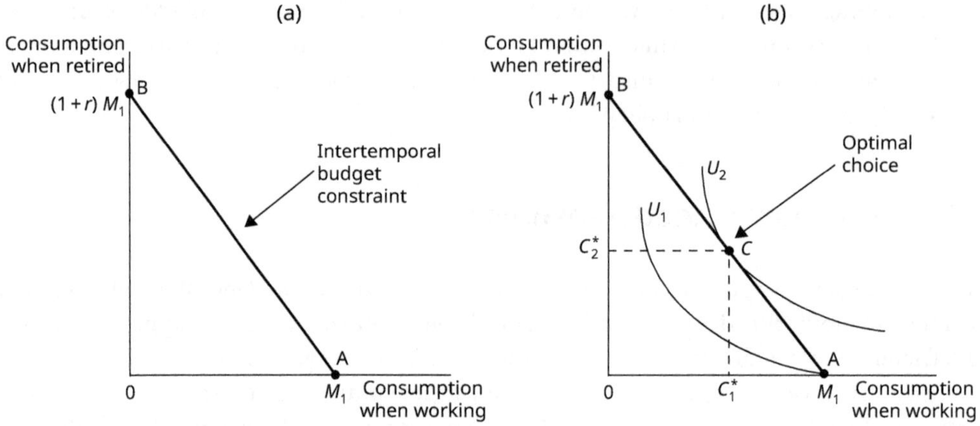

Figure 11.1 Intertemporal choice model

and period 2, when they retire. Individuals are rational and forward-looking and they choose the level of consumption in each period that will maximize their lifetime utility.

The model is illustrated in Figure 11.1. Panel (a) depicts the **intertemporal budget constraint**. This is analogous to the budget constraint in the rational choice model we introduced in Chapter 2, but here we are measuring consumption when working, C_1, along the horizontal axis and consumption when retired, C_2, along the vertical axis. Individuals receive an income M_1 when they are working, in period 1.[2] They could spend all of their income on consumption in that period, which would leave them with no money to spend and therefore no consumption in period 2. This is illustrated by point A in the figure. If they saved all of their income in period 1 and used it to finance their consumption in period 2, the maximum level of consumption they could afford would be $(1+r)M_1$, where r is the interest rate, illustrated by point B. Of course, individuals do not have to save all of their income—they could save any amount of their period 1 income and would receive $(1+r)$ pounds/euros for every pound or euro saved today. The intertemporal budget constraint is the line that connects the maximum level of consumption in period 1 and the maximum level of consumption in period 2. The slope of the budget constraint is $-(1+r)$. As in the model discussed in Chapter 2, the slope of the budget constraint can be interpreted as a relative price ratio, but here it reflects the relative price of present and future consumption.[3]

The utility-maximizing choice will depend on individual preferences over consumption in each period. Panel (b) depicts one possible set of preferences, illustrated by the two indifference curves U_1 and U_2. Clearly, point A will not maximize individual utility, as it is on a lower indifference curve. The utility-maximizing choice is given by the point where the budget line is tangent to the highest attainable indifference curve, illustrated by U_2. Utility is maximized by consuming C_1^* in period 1 and C_2^* in period 2, which implies saving some of the income earned in period 1 (given by the difference $M_1 - C_1^*$) to consume in period 2.

[2] Here we assume individuals can only earn an income when they are working, in period 1, but the model can be extended to allow for other sources of income. The model can also be extended to cover more than two periods.

[3] For simplicity we are assuming individuals face a constant interest rate, but the model can be extended to allow for variations in the interest rate.

This model illustrates how welfare can be increased by allowing individuals to redistribute some of their income from period 1, when they are working, to period 2, when they are retired. Consumption will not necessarily be the same in all periods, as consumption needs vary over an individual's life. For example, when they are working, individuals are likely to have expenses associated with travelling to work, or their consumption needs may be higher if they have small children. Once they retire, individuals might not face these costs, but they may face higher costs associated with healthcare. Individuals also do not place the same weight on consumption in all periods. Typically, individuals value consumption in the present more than consumption in the future—in other words, individuals discount the future. This discounting matters because it means that consumption is likely to be skewed towards the present, as individuals value £1 spent today more than £1 saved for the future.

11.1.2 Insurance against longevity risk

Another objective of pensions is to provide insurance against **longevity risk**. Most people do not know how long they will live for, which makes it difficult to determine how much they will need to save for their retirement and how to spread their savings over their retired years. If individuals have to rely only on their personal savings to finance their retirement, there is a risk that they may outlive their savings, potentially leaving them destitute in later life, or, if they die earlier than expected, they may leave behind large unintended bequests. Insurance provides a means for dealing with this uncertainty. While the life expectancy of any one individual is generally not known, the life expectancy for a group can be predicted. By **pooling** individual savings, pensions can provide insurance against this uncertainty over how long individuals will live for. Pensions can also provide a mechanism to insure against disability (invalidity pensions) and can provide protection to spouses or young children if a worker dies prematurely (survivors' pensions).

11.1.3 Poverty relief

State pensions can help tackle poverty in later life by providing a basic level of income for all individuals in retirement. Old-age income poverty varies significantly across countries, ranging from 4 per cent of the population in Norway to 34 per cent in New Zealand (OECD, 2020).[4] In several countries, old-age poverty rates are in fact lower than the poverty rate for the population as a whole, suggesting the pension system in these countries does a reasonably good job in providing sufficient income for individuals to sustain a minimum standard of living in retirement. However, by providing this income security in later life, there is a risk this might discourage individuals from actively saving more towards their own retirement. Old-age poverty is usually measured in relative terms, as the proportion of people aged 65 or over earning less than some fraction of the median income, typically 50 or 60 per cent. By defining old-age poverty relative to the median income of the entire population, we are ignoring the different consumption needs of retired individuals. What matters is not the income that people receive per se, but the standard of living they can sustain with that income.

[4] Income poverty rate for people aged 65 and over, after taxes and transfers. Poverty line at 50 per cent of median income.

11.1.4 Redistribution

State pensions can also be used as a tool to redistribute resources across different groups in society, thereby reducing inequalities. This redistribution can happen on various levels. Pensions can redistribute from high-income to low-income individuals, by requiring individuals to make contributions that are relative to their income, while paying out a flat-rate pension that does not depend on earnings. Pensions can redistribute across generations, by adjusting the contribution rates and pensions received by different generations.[5] Pensions can also redistribute from men to women, particularly if women have fewer years of contributions, perhaps as a result of earlier retirement or having taken years out of the labour market to care for children, but end up receiving pension payments for longer due to higher average life expectancies.[6] Lastly, pensions can redistribute towards couples, by paying out a higher amount to couples even if only one spouse made pensions contributions.

We have looked at the different objectives that pensions can achieve. The extent to which a particular pension system achieves each of these objectives will depend on how it is designed. This is the question we turn to next.

11.2 The design of pension systems

There are different ways of categorizing pensions. We can classify them based on how they are financed, drawing a distinction between funded and unfunded pension schemes. Or we can classify them based on the relationship between contributions, what individuals pay in, and the benefits they receive. Pension schemes can be public or privately run and participation can be mandatory or voluntary. We begin by discussing these different types of pension schemes below, before focusing on the structure of national pension systems as a whole.

11.2.1 Funded and unfunded schemes

A **fully funded pension scheme** is one where the value of the pension that individuals receive when they retire is tied to their contributions. Individuals pay into a fund during their working lives and these contributions are invested in assets, with any interest or dividends earned added to the fund. The pension individuals receive when they retire is based on the contributions they have made throughout their working lives, together with interest and dividends earned, minus any pension scheme administration costs. When an individual retires, the fund built up from their contributions is typically converted into an **annuity**. An annuity is a financial product that converts pension savings into a steady income stream that individuals receive until the end of their lives. An annuity therefore helps mitigate the uncertainty over how long an individual will live for.

An **unfunded** or **pay-as-you-go (PAYG) pension scheme** is one where pensions are paid out of current contributions. The current working age population pays into the pension scheme and these payments are used to fund the pensions of the current retired population.

[5] Particularly in the case of unfunded pay-as-you-go pension schemes, which we discuss below.

[6] Although different retirement ages for men and women have been a feature of state pension systems for several decades, most countries have reformed their systems to equalize retirement ages across men and women.

In most countries, public pension systems operate on this basis, whereas most privately run schemes are fully funded. For individuals, a PAYG pension represents a promise from the government to pay them a certain income once they retire. At the aggregate level, a PAYG scheme effectively operates as an income transfer, where the state taxes one group of people (current workers) and uses these funds to pay another group of people (retirees).

Under PAYG schemes, the benefits enjoyed by each generation are not constrained by their contributions, so there is scope to redistribute across generations and share in the benefits of economic growth. Fully funded schemes, on the other hand, should hold sufficient reserves to meet all outstanding financial liabilities, and each generation receives what they have paid in, plus any interest earned on investments made. Because of this, full pension rights can be built up more quickly in PAYG schemes than in funded schemes, since an individual's pension does not have to rely on their own past contributions.

It is sometimes argued that PAYG schemes are more vulnerable to demographic change driven by increases in life expectancy and falling fertility rates. Since current pensions are paid by current workers, an increase in the ratio of retirees to workers—the **old-age dependency ratio**—will mean fewer people paying into the system relative to the benefits that need to be paid out, which can put a financial strain on the scheme. However, funded pension schemes are also vulnerable to changes in the dependency ratio, as we discuss in section 11.5.

11.2.2 Defined benefit and defined contribution schemes

In a **defined benefit (DB) scheme**, the value of the pension that will be received is defined in advance. These schemes can be run by the government or by firms, and they promise to pay members a given income in retirement. In final-salary schemes, the retirement income depends on the worker's earnings in the final year of work (or sometimes an average of the last few years), along with the length of time spent working. Other defined benefit schemes link the value of retirement income to average earnings over a longer period—for example, average lifetime earnings.

In a **defined contribution (DC) scheme**, individual members pay in a proportion of their earnings, which is used to invest in assets. At retirement, the value of the pension paid to members depends on how much they paid into the scheme and how the investments performed. These benefits can be paid as a lump sum or can be used to buy an annuity, which will provide a steady income stream in retirement. DC schemes can be funded or notional. In a **funded defined contribution (FDC) scheme**, individual contributions and investment returns build up in an individual account, which is then converted into an individual pension at retirement. **Notional defined contribution (NDC) schemes** operate in a similar way, but an individual's contributions are only *notionally* or hypothetically accumulated. Individuals pay a proportion of their earnings into the scheme and a notional rate of return is applied to these contributions, thereby mimicking FDC schemes. These accounts are notional in the sense that the balance only exists on the books of the institution that is managing the accounts. When they retire, individuals receive a retirement income based on this notionally accumulated value. NDC schemes typically operate on a PAYG basis.

An important difference between FDC and DB schemes is that in FDC schemes the risk of unexpected changes in the real rate of return on assets is borne by the individual, whereas in DB schemes this risk is borne by the firm or institution that provides the pension.[7] These risks can be mitigated to some extent by including a provision for a guaranteed minimum pension, where the institution commits to paying a minimum level of benefits regardless of the financial performance of the assets that the pension funds were invested in.

A number of OECD countries have introduced **points-based schemes**. Under these schemes, workers earn pension points based on their earnings and contributions. Once they retire, the value of their pension equals the sum of all the pension points they have accumulated multiplied by a pension-point value. The pension-point value is usually linked to average earnings and can be adjusted to take into account wage growth or changes in the dependency ratio.

11.2.3 The structure of national pension systems

We have looked at different types of pension schemes. In this section, we are going to focus on the organization of a country's pension system as a whole. Pension systems are complex and vary across countries. Most countries operate a multi-tier or multi-pillar model which acknowledges the different objectives of pensions discussed above and how the role of the government in achieving each of these objectives varies. Different taxonomies for national pension systems have been proposed, although there is now a significant amount of overlap between them.[8] Here we adopt the taxonomy proposed by the OECD. This involves three tiers (see Figure 11.2).

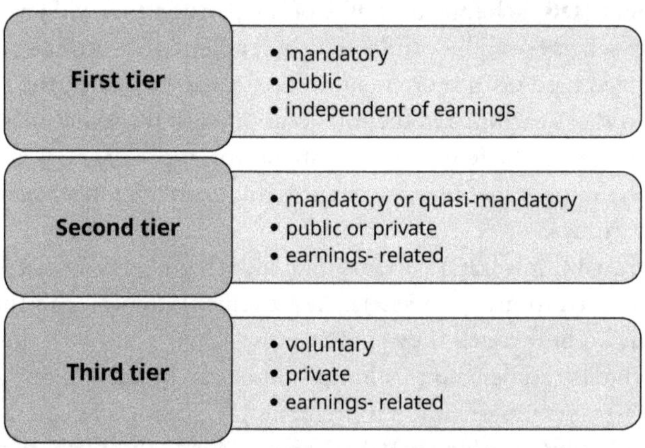

Figure 11.2 Design of national pension systems

[7] The UK recently introduced **collective defined contribution (CDC) pension schemes**, which provide an alternative balance of risk to existing DB and DC schemes. The contribution rates are defined in advance, as in a regular DC scheme, but the risks are shared collectively between the scheme's members. CDC schemes also provide an income for life in retirement instead of a pot of savings that need to be converted into an annuity, as in DC schemes.

[8] The World Bank proposed its original three-pillar model in 1994 in its report *Averting the Old Age Crisis: Policies to Protect and Promote Growth*. This was subsequently extended to five pillars: a non-contributory social assistance pillar financed by the state; a mandatory earnings-related pillar; a mandatory defined contribution plan with independent investment management; a voluntary savings pillar; and a social support pillar which includes formal social support provided by the state, such as healthcare or housing, and informal support mechanisms (World Bank, 2008). The OECD classification covers similar areas, although these are referred to as tiers rather than pillars.

First tier

The first tier involves mandatory publicly provided schemes. Eligibility for first-tier pensions may depend on individuals satisfying certain residency or minimum contribution requirements, but the level of pension paid is independent of the level of past earnings. These pension schemes focus on poverty relief and redistribution, aiming to ensure everyone has a minimum level of income in retirement. First-tier pensions may involve an element of targeting, where the value of the pension received depends on whether individuals have income from other sources or the value of any assets held. This ensures poorer retirees receive higher benefits than those who are better off.

Countries that operate first tier pensions on a **contributory** basis include Austria, France, Ireland, Spain, and the UK. Countries such as Australia, New Zealand, the Netherlands, South Africa, and Chile have first-tier pensions that operate on a **non-contributory** basis, where pensions are financed through taxation.

Second tier

The second tier involves mandatory or quasi-mandatory membership of either public or private pension schemes. It is earnings-related, so contributions and pension benefits are tied to individual incomes, and it is aimed primarily at supporting consumption-smoothing. Public schemes may be defined benefit, defined contribution, or points-based. Private schemes are generally defined benefit or defined contribution.

The range of schemes varies across countries. For example, Austria, Belgium, Canada, Spain, and Portugal have public DB schemes, while Germany operates a public points-based scheme. France has a public DB and points-based system. Australia, the Netherlands, and the UK operate mandatory or quasi-mandatory private FDC schemes.[9] Not all countries have mandatory second-tier pensions—for example, Ireland and New Zealand.

Third tier

The third tier involves voluntary contributions to private funded pension schemes and is aimed primarily at boosting consumption-smoothing. Contributions and pensions entitlements are earnings-related, and schemes may operate on a defined benefit or defined contribution basis. Schemes may be organized at the firm or industry level, or at an individual level.

All of these tiers help meet the insurance objective of pensions. Box 11.2 illustrates two different ways in which this multi-tier system has been implemented. There is generally little disagreement over the need for the first tier, to help alleviate poverty and ensure everyone can achieve a basic standard of living in retirement. The main point of contention concerns the second tier—in particular, whether membership of these additional schemes should be mandatory or voluntary. There are strong arguments for making membership mandatory, as we discuss in the next section, but this can also be seen as an infringement on individual freedom and choice.

[9] Quasi-mandatory schemes are based on collective agreements but with a high coverage rate.

Box 11.2 Alternative pension systems

Australia

Australia's pension system involves the following:

- First tier: a means-tested[10] Age Pension, which is funded through general tax revenues.
- Second tier: a mandatory occupational savings pension, known as the Superannuation Guarantee.
- Third tier: voluntary superannuation contributions and other private savings.

There is no earnings-related social insurance scheme in Australia. The Age Pension is designed to provide a safety net for people unable to save enough for their retirement. It is paid at a flat rate and aims to ensure all retired individuals are able to achieve a basic standard of living in retirement. The Age Pension is payable to all qualifying individuals from the age of 67. The current maximum basic rates are AU$1,051.30 per fortnight for an individual and AU$1,585.00 for a couple.[11] Eligibility for the Age Pension is tied to individual income and assets (excluding the family home), and many people spend their assets in order to qualify for the Age Pension. Individuals also need to have lived in Australia for at least 10 years.

The Superannuation Guarantee requires employers to contribute 12 per cent of employee earnings to their employees' superannuation fund (a private pension plan).[12] Employees do not need to contribute to the scheme, but they can make additional voluntary contributions if they want to.

The UK

The pension system in the UK involves the following:

- First tier: a contributory basic state pension, funded through National Insurance contributions.
- Second tier: quasi-mandatory contributions to a workplace or occupational pension.
- Third tier: additional voluntary private pension savings.

A new state pension was introduced in April 2016. It is paid at a flat rate of £230.25 per week[13] to all qualifying individuals who reach the **state pension age**[14] after this date. For individuals retiring before this, the state pension involves two tiers: a flat-rate basic pension and an earnings-related additional pension. In order to qualify for the full new state pension, individuals need to have 35 years of National Insurance contributions and the minimum qualifying period is 10 years. Individuals over the state pension age who are on very low incomes are

[10] Means-testing refers to the process of assessing an individual's income and assets to determine whether they are eligible to receive government assistance or welfare benefits.
[11] Figures for 2025.
[12] Figures for 2025/26.
[13] In 2025/26.
[14] The state pension age is the age at which individuals are eligible to receive their state pension.

also eligible for Pension Credits, an income-related benefit which is not based on National Insurance contributions. The state pension age is currently 66 for both men and women and it is not possible to claim the state pension early.

The second tier operates on a quasi-mandatory basis. All individuals over the age of 22 who are in employment and earning over £10,000 a year are automatically enrolled into their employer's workplace pension scheme, although they have a right to opt out of the scheme. Both employees and employers contribute to the pension and the minimum contribution is 8 per cent, which includes 4 per cent from employees, 1 per cent from the government in tax relief, and 3 per cent from employers. Automatic enrolment was introduced by the government in 2012. To ensure all employers had access to a quality low-cost pension scheme, the government also set up the National Employment Savings Trust (NEST), a trust-based occupational defined contribution scheme, although employers can invest in other pension schemes.

Source: OECD (n.d.a).

11.3 Arguments for government intervention

As we have seen, pensions can serve a range of objectives. To what extent will a pure market system for pensions achieve these objectives? Section 11.3.1 considers whether, in a pure market system, the conditions for efficient consumption-smoothing and insurance are met, while section 11.3.2 looks at whether the market system is compatible with equity objectives such as poverty relief and redistribution.

11.3.1 Government intervention to increase efficiency

The conditions required for the market outcome to be efficient are unlikely to hold in the case of old-age pensions.[15] Optimal consumption-smoothing requires individuals to solve a complex intertemporal allocation problem, where they would need vast amounts of information, including on their expected future earnings, the rate of return on different investments, and their life expectancy. In practice, individual decisions are marred by problems of imperfect information, bounded rationality, and bounded willpower, and evidence suggests that many people are not saving enough for their retirement (see Box 11.3). On the supply side, private markets are unable to insure against **social risks** including inflation and unexpected increases in life expectancy, and typically involve significantly higher transaction costs. We discuss each of these problems below.

Imperfect information

Pensions are incredibly complex, with hundreds of personal pensions plans that individuals can choose from, and individuals need to decide not just how much to save, but also what assets to invest in and how to balance different risks. Yet many individuals have a weak understanding of probabilities and struggle to understand basic finance concepts. Levels of **financial literacy** are low across many countries, particularly among women, some ethnic

[15] See Chapter 2, section 2.2.4, for an overview of these conditions.

Box 11.3 Do people save enough for retirement?

Researchers have adopted different approaches to measuring 'enough'. Some studies measure the optimality of retirement savings by solving lifecycle models and then comparing the implied wealth accumulated with actual reported wealth levels in household surveys. Other studies have focused on the adequacy of retirement savings, either defined as the level of income required to meet basic needs (i.e. based on the poverty line), or based on a particular **replacement rate**. The replacement rate measures the proportion of pre-retirement income that individuals will have available once they retire.

Early studies for the USA suggested that the majority of the population were well prepared for their retirement.[16] Engen et al. (2005) estimate that around 65 per cent of households have adequate retirement wealth; estimates in other studies are slightly higher, at around 70–80 per cent. However, these studies all assume that households will make full use of their housing wealth in retirement, whereas in practice few households do. Under the assumption that households only use half of their housing wealth, the estimates of Engen et al. (2005) fall to 56 per cent. Poterba et al. (2012) study the wealth of older retirees in the US Health and Retirement Study, finding that almost half of respondents died with virtually no financial assets. Many of these households also had no housing wealth and relied almost entirely on income from social security. Individuals in this group are also more likely to be in poor health.

For the UK, research suggests that just over half (57 per cent) of private sector employees who are saving into a defined contribution pension scheme will have an adequate replacement rate in retirement (O'Brien et al., 2024). This implies that around four in ten people may be undersaving for retirement. People on higher incomes are more likely to be undersaving, by this measure, than those on lower incomes, although lower earners are less likely to reach a minimum living standard (O'Brien et al., 2024). Private pension wealth is very unequally distributed: the 10 per cent of individuals with the most pension wealth have, on average, £874,000, whereas the 10 per cent with the least have, on average, just £48,000 (Banks et al., 2005). Increasing levels of household debt, particularly among younger households, suggest that these households may be more financially vulnerable in retirement than the current generation of retirees.

Establishing how much individuals should be saving for their retirement is complicated. It is not simply an economic question, but involves issues in psychology and health (Skinner, 2007). People are different and are therefore likely to experience different consumption needs in retirement. It is also impossible for most households to save enough to guard against all possible contingencies, such as dramatically lower rates of return or significant unexpected health or care costs.

minorities, and people with lower levels of education (Lusardi & Mitchell, 2011a).[17] Financial literacy has been found to play an important role in retirement income security, as people with higher levels of financial literacy are more likely to plan for retirement, and retirement planning has been shown to have a significant impact in explaining differences in wealth levels as individuals approach retirement (Lusardi & Mitchell, 2011b, 2011c). Information

[16] See, for example, Gomes et al. (2021) for a discussion of some of the evidence for the USA.

[17] Financial literacy measures individual understanding of key financial concepts, including interest compounding, inflation, and risk diversification.

Box 11.4 The UK pensions mis-selling scandal

In 1988, employees in the UK were allowed for the first time to save for their retirement in a personal pension instead of an occupational pension offered by their employer or the State Earnings Related Pension Scheme (SERPS) provided by the government. Following these changes, commission-driven salespeople persuaded millions of individuals to opt out of their more generous and safer occupational pensions and take up riskier personal pensions, facing the risk of significantly lower incomes in retirement. Between 1988 and 1994, over 5 million personal pensions were sold. The total cost of compensating individuals who had been mis-sold personal pensions has been estimated at between £8.4 and £11 billion by the Financial Services Authority.

Source: UK Parliament (1998).

poverty and financial poverty tend to be highly correlated, and therefore these differences in financial knowledge will also have equity implications.

Financial advisers could potentially help mitigate these problems of imperfect information, by providing individuals with good-quality impartial advice on the benefits and risks of different pension products. However, this requires that financial advisers have their clients' best interests at heart, which may not be the case, particularly if advisers receive a commission for the investment products they recommend. These problems of asymmetric information, where financial advisers and the sellers of pension products have more information about the benefits and risks of these products than the buyers, can be exploited to the detriment of individuals, with potentially severe consequences (see Box 11.4).

Evidence suggests that individuals will often turn to family, friends, and work colleagues for information and advice about retirement plans and how to invest their retirement savings, even though these individuals are not necessarily better informed. Studies of workers in the USA suggest that peer effects play an important role in influencing retirement savings decisions (Duflo and Saez, 2002, 2003).

Unlike other large financial decisions individuals make, such as buying a house or a car, there are limited opportunities to learn from experience and the costs of making a mistake can be very high. If individuals fail to save enough for their retirement, they could end up destitute in later life.

Bounded rationality

The intertemporal choice model discussed above assumes individuals are rational and forward-looking. In practice, individual behaviour often departs from this ideal, resulting in suboptimal or inconsistent saving behaviour. Some examples include the following:

- **Reliance on heuristics or rules of thumb**: evidence suggests that people are unlikely to calculate their optimal savings rate and instead rely on heuristics or rules of thumb, such as choosing contribution rates that are multiples of 5 per cent, or saving the maximum allowed, or contributing the minimum amount required to get the full employer match (Benartzi & Thaler, 2007). While rules of thumb can be useful and help save time, they can also lead to systematic biases.

- **Framing effects**: individual decisions about how to allocate their savings across different assets are influenced by the order or manner in which options are presented. Benartzi & Thaler (2007) found that small variations in the framing of a problem can lead to dramatically different portfolio choices, with significant implications for accumulated saving.
- **Familiarity**: individuals are more likely to invest in the stock of their employer or hold a substantial amount of their employer's stock in their pension plans (Meulbroek, 2005). This increases their exposure to risk, since if their employer goes bankrupt they lose not only their source of income but also their pension savings[18]. This behaviour demonstrates a general lack of understanding of the importance of diversification. In fact, when deciding how to allocate savings across assets, individuals tend to follow simple or naïve diversification strategies, for example by dividing their contributions equally across the funds offered in a plan (Benartzi & Thaler, 2001, 2007).
- **Immobilization**: too much choice can also lead to immobilization or passive behaviour. Reforms to the pension system in Sweden in the late 1990s introduced a component of funded individual accounts which offered individuals a wide range of investment funds to choose from to build their investment portfolio. But faced with roughly 700 different funds, the vast majority of individuals made no choice, thus being assigned to the default fund (Sundén, 2006). In the US, Iyengar et al. (2004) looked at the impact of the number of funds offered in 401(k) savings plans on participation rates and found that individuals are less likely to participate in a retirement plan as the number of investment options available increases.

Bounded willpower

Most people know they need to save more for their retirement, but in practice find it difficult to do so. Evidence shows that people do not join retirement plans even when it is clearly in their interests to do so (Benartzi & Thaler, 2007). One possible explanation is that individual preferences over consumption in different time periods are not consistent over time. In particular, preferences tend to be **present-biased**, favouring short-term gratification and more immediate consumption.

The rate at which the future is discounted has also been found to vary over time. Individuals tend to be patient for the future, but impatient in the present. When faced with the choice of receiving £100 today or £120 in a month's time, most individuals would prefer the lower amount today; however, when faced with the choice of receiving £100 in a year's time or £120 in a year and a month, most people would be willing to wait the extra month to receive the higher amount (Thaler, 1981). These preferences exhibit **time-inconsistency** because eventually the future becomes the present and the individual would then again prefer to receive £100 today rather than waiting another month to receive £120. This is an example of **hyperbolic discounting**, the tendency of people to prefer a smaller reward received sooner over a larger reward received later, if the time gap is smaller (Laibson, 1997).[19] Hyperbolic discounting often leads to procrastination, which in turn can lead to **inertia**, or the tendency of individuals to accept the status quo or default option.

[18] The collapse of the American energy, commodities and services company Enron in 2001 highlighted the real and significant dangers of this approach.

[19] These preferences imply a higher discount rate in the short run, with a tendency to favour immediate gratification and to consume more today rather than saving, and a lower discount rate in the medium or longer run.

In the context of retirement saving, present-bias and hyperbolic discounting help explain the gap between what people feel they should save and what they actually save: you might plan today to start saving next month, but at the start of next month you will want to postpone this plan for another month (Laibson et al., 1998). The focus on short-term gratification may also result in individuals retiring as soon as they can, even if this means they will have an inadequate income to live on in retirement.

Inertia may make it more difficult for individuals actually to start saving or rebalance their investment portfolios to ensure they are maximizing their returns. However, inertia is a feature that has been exploited by policies designed to encourage individuals to save more. Evidence suggests that designing retirement saving plans based on **automatic enrolment**, where individuals have the option to opt out, can have a dramatic effect on participation rates (Cribb & Emmerson, 2016; Madrian & Shea, 2001). This is something we return to in section 11.4.

Pensions as a merit good

Some individuals might choose not to save enough for their retirement, either because their preferences for present consumption are very strong or because they simply do not care about their future. But this imposes a cost on society, particularly if the rest of society cares if some retirees are living in abject poverty. In this sense, pensions are a sort of merit good, and individual pension saving generates positive externalities for the rest of society. This provides an argument for the government to make some level of retirement saving mandatory, but it does not imply that the government should be responsible for *providing* pensions.

Incomplete insurance

Problems arise in the supply of pensions because there are some risks that private markets are unable to fully insure against. These are known as **social risks** (or **aggregate risks**) because they are risks faced by society as a whole. They include the risk of unexpected increases in life expectancy, which affects the provision of annuities, and the risk of unanticipated inflation, which will affect the real value of individual pensions.

When they reach retirement, individuals can use their pension savings to buy an annuity, which will guarantee them a fixed income every month until they die, regardless of how long they live for. Annuities essentially provide insurance against longevity risk.[20] Annuity markets work because the annuity provider can pool risks across individuals. Although it does not know how long each individual will live for, the annuity provider knows the average life expectancy for a cohort of individuals. Some individuals will live for longer after they retire (these are bad risks, since they will cost the annuity provider more), whereas other individuals will die sooner (these are good risks, as they imply lower costs for the annuity provider). Provided that the annuity provider's predictions regarding the average life expectancy of the cohort are reasonably accurate, then it will be able to pool good and bad risks to cover its costs. However, evidence suggests that projections have tended to underestimate increases in life expectancy. If *everyone* lives longer than expected, this will lead to an unanticipated increase the annuity provider's costs and these costs are likely to be borne by the annuitant through lower annuity payments.

[20] The conditions required for insurance markets to operate efficiently are reviewed in Chapter 2, Box 2.6. These include: independent probabilities across individuals; probabilities being known or estimable, and less than 1; and no problems of adverse selection or moral hazard.

Annuity markets are also susceptible to problems of adverse selection and moral hazard. If annuity providers cannot identify good and bad risks, in a competitive equilibrium they will charge each individual a premium that reflects the average risk (i.e. the average life expectancy for the cohort). Good risks are then essentially subsidizing bad risks, or those who expect to have shorter lives are subsidizing those who expect to live for longer. If individuals know how long they are going to live for, those who know they are likely to die sooner may choose not to buy an annuity. This would leave the annuity provider with mainly bad risks, or people with long life expectancies, and therefore unable to pool risks. In the extreme, the annuity market would collapse. In practice, most people do not know how long they will live for, although evidence does suggest that people who buy annuities do tend to live longer (Finkelstein & Poterba, 2002).[21] The potential for moral hazard problems arises because individuals who have larger pensions will be able to spend more on their health and are therefore likely to live longer. This suggests that access to healthcare matters. In countries that provide good healthcare that is free at the point of use, the risk of moral hazard is less significant.

Another type of aggregate risk that affects pensions is **inflation**. For individual consumption-smoothing what matters is the real value of the pension they receive, which is affected by inflation. Private markets can provide some insurance against inflation. This is achieved through **indexation**, where the value of the pension is tied to increases in prices to maintain purchasing power. However, this is normally capped at a maximum inflation rate, usually 5 per cent. Without this cap, pension providers would face significant increases in costs if the inflation rate increased faster than expected, given that inflation is an aggregate risk. For individuals, though, the lack of full indexation means that large increases in inflation will imply a permanent loss in real pension income, and this loss can be significant.

The government is better placed to cope with aggregate risks, as it can raises taxes to cover its obligations and can spread these risks across generations. But, as we will see below, government-provided pensions are not the only option for addressing these problems.

High transaction costs

Private pension providers offer consumers more choice and this is generally considered a good thing. But choice is costly. Individual funded accounts generally involve high management and administrative costs, often including commissions for salespeople. For the USA, the administrative costs for social security are estimated at less than 1 per cent of benefits paid, whereas for private pensions this number is closer to 6 per cent (Department of Labor cited in Stiglitz & Rosengard, 2015). These higher administrative costs will lead to lower pension incomes for individuals. For an individual funded account, an annual management charge of 1 per cent reduces an individual's accumulated pension wealth by 20 per cent over a full career (Barr & Diamond, 2008). There is therefore a trade-off between choice and administrative costs.

In summary, in the absence of government intervention, problems of imperfect information, bounded rationality, and bounded willpower suggest that many individuals risk not

[21] A separate issue is how annuity providers handle different average life expectancies for men and women. Since women tend to live longer than men, should they be charged a higher premium? This raises important equity issues. The EU Gender Directive of 2012 includes provisions for gender-neutral pricing of insurance products, which means that annuity providers within the EU cannot charge different prices based on differences in average life expectancy between men and women.

saving enough for their retirement.[22] The inability of private markets to fully insure against inflation and other aggregate risks, combined with the high administrative costs of private providers, risk eroding the value of private pensions even further.

11.3.2 Government intervention to promote equity

In a pure market system, individuals would be responsible for deciding how much to save during their working lives and how to manage their incomes in retirement. But some people might not earn enough over the course of their lives to be able to save enough for retirement. Requiring these individuals to work for longer might not be feasible, as poor health in later life may prevent them from working, and might also be considered unfair. There is therefore an argument for governments to intervene to mitigate the risk of poverty in later life by providing a minimum income in retirement to individuals who are unable to save enough due to low lifetime earnings. In practice, it would be very difficult and costly to distinguish individuals who have not saved enough for retirement because their income was too low from those who have chosen not to save, so it may be fairer—and administratively simpler—to provide everyone with a minimum guaranteed income in retirement. This is the rationale behind the first tier of the pension system in many countries, as we saw in section 11.2.

A public pension scheme can also support vertical equity goals. Schemes that operate on an unfunded PAYG basis generally involve some redistribution from high-income to low-income individuals if contributions are linked to individual earnings but everyone receives the same flat-rate pension regardless of income.[23] In contrast, in voluntary DC schemes, the pensions received must be proportional to contributions, so the scope for redistribution is limited.

Public pensions are not limited to redistributing resources from higher-income to lower-income individuals. Unfunded PAYG systems can redistribute resources across generations, thereby allowing everyone to share in the benefits of economic growth. In an unfunded scheme, the pensions received by a particular generation are not constrained by their contributions and the benefits received may exceed the sum of their past contributions. However, this redistribution is not inevitable, as these schemes can be designed to ensure that the benefits received by each generation are more closely linked to their contributions, as in notional DC schemes. In private funded schemes, whether there is redistribution between generations will depend on the level of unanticipated inflation.

Although most countries across the OECD have taken steps to reduce or remove differential retirement ages for men and women,[24] many mandatory pension schemes still redistribute from men to women. This is because men and women typically face the same contribution rates and are entitled to the same pension benefits, but women have higher life expectancies and therefore will receive their pension for longer. This may seem inequitable, but overall

[22] However, there is also a risk that some people may end up saving too much for retirement, which could impact their quality of life during their working years.

[23] However, higher-income individuals tend to have higher life expectancies and are also more likely to be in education for longer, and therefore will start contributing to their pensions later and receive their pensions for longer (Barr, 2020).

[24] In 2023, only six OECD countries had lower normal retirement ages for women who were just entering the labour market: Colombia, Costa Rica, Hungary, Israel, Poland, and Turkey (OECD, 2023).

Box 11.5 The gender pension gap

Although pension systems may have traditionally redistributed from men to women, in virtually all countries across the world women have lower private pension wealth and receive a lower pension income in retirement than men, on average. Across the EU, women aged over 65 received a pension that was on average 29 per cent lower than their male counterparts in 2019. And this average masks substantial differences across countries: in Luxembourg, Malta, and the Netherlands, women received a pension income on average more than 40 per cent lower than their male counterparts, whereas in Denmark and Estonia this difference was less than 10 per cent.

What are the causes of this gender pension gap? In part, it is due to the different labour market experiences of men and women. Women typically have lower lifetime earnings than men, partly because they are often paid less, but also because they are more likely to take time out of the labour force to care for young children or other family members. Women are also more likely to work part-time. These different work experiences mean that women are more likely to be unable to save in certain pension schemes due to eligibility restrictions that may require a minimum salary or minimum number of work hours. The gender pension gap may also reflect differences in saving rates between men and women or different investment strategies. Women may also suffer financially if pension rights are not split evenly following a divorce, particularly if during the partnership women have taken time out of the labour force to care for children, which will have reduced their ability to accumulate pension savings.

Different causes will play a different role in different countries, but understanding the causes behind the gender pension gap is important in order to be able to design appropriate policies to address it.

Sources: Cribb et al. (2023) and Eurostat (2021).

women still tend to fare worse than men when it comes to their income in retirement (see Box 11.5). In order to abolish this redistribution completely, women would either need to be required to pay higher contributions for the same level of benefit, or need to receive a lower level of benefit if paying the same pension contributions as men.

While some redistribution may be argued to be desirable on equity grounds, there is a question as to whether the pension system is the right mechanism for achieving redistribution or whether this is best achieved through income transfers.[25] Redistributing income through the pension system lacks transparency and restricts individual choice. Direct income transfers are less prescriptive about how much people should save for their retirement, allowing individuals who have a stronger preference for current consumption to save less. However, given the problems of imperfect information and imperfect optimization discussed above, it is not clear whether individuals would save optimally for their retirement even if given the resources to do so.

Moreover, there is a high correlation between information poverty and financial poverty: individuals on lower incomes are more likely to face difficulties accessing the necessary

[25] See Barr (2020).

information to make fully informed decisions regarding their retirement savings (Barr, 2012). Evidence also suggests that levels of financial literacy tend to be lower among individuals from poorer socioeconomic groups (Lusardi & Mitchell, 2014; Lusardi & Tufano, 2009). Here, the equity and efficiency arguments for government intervention complement one another and there is a role for government, at a minimum, to regulate the information provided by pension providers to ensure it is accurate and accessible. This will help safeguard horizontal equity.

11.4 Types of government intervention

There are strong efficiency and equity arguments for some degree of government intervention in the provision of old-age pensions, but what form should that intervention take? We are going to focus on three ways in which governments can intervene in old-age pensions: direct provision; regulation; and subsidies.

11.4.1 Direct provision

To address some of the problems discussed above, governments can provide an income to those in retirement directly, through either social insurance-based schemes or **means-tested benefits**. Governments can also provide specific financial products to address some of the causes of incomplete insurance, or provide financial education.

Social insurance-based schemes

The vast majority of countries across the OECD provide an insurance-based pension scheme where everyone receives a state pension in retirement regardless of income, provided they meet certain eligibility criteria.[26] These criteria typically involve having made a specified number of contributions and may also include minimum residence requirements. Such public schemes may operate on an unfunded PAYG basis or they may be funded.

Publicly provided pensions address the various problems discussed in section 11.3. However, they also involve challenges. One such challenge relates to the level or generosity of pension benefits. If the level of the pension is set too low, this may not be enough for individuals to maintain an adequate standard of living in retirement. But if the level is set too high, this may put pressure on public finances. The generosity of state pensions varies across countries and many countries have been forced to reform their retirement income systems to ensure their financial sustainability in the face of demographic change.[27]

Another challenge of publicly provided pensions involves their impact on individual incentives to save. Publicly provided pensions may act as a substitute for private saving, effectively crowding out the savings individuals would otherwise have set aside for their retirement. In the absence of a state pension, individuals would have to rely on their own savings to fund their consumption in retirement, or rely on support from family, friends, or

[26] A notable exception here is Australia, where the basic state pension is funded through taxation.
[27] We return to this point in section 11.5.

Box 11.6 How significant is the crowding -out effect?

The earliest study on the impact of the state pension on private savings was carried out by Feldstein (1974). He focused on the impact of Social Security wealth on private savings in the USA and his results suggested that Social Security led to a 50 per cent reduction in private saving. Subsequent studies analysing the magnitude of this crowding-out effect have identified several flaws in his approach, but overall the evidence seems to suggest that the state pension does crowd out private saving to some extent, but not on a one-for-one basis.

Attanasio and Rohwedder (2003) explored the impact of partial reforms to the state pension in the UK on private saving. They found that the earnings-related tier of the state pension had a negative impact on private savings, although the magnitude of this impact varied by age; they found no effect for the basic state pension.[28] A study by Attanasio and Brugiavlni (2003) analysing an Italian pension reform in 1992 found that individual saving rates increased in response to reductions in pension wealth, and that this effect also varied with age. For the USA, Engelhardt and Gruber (2004) analysed the evolution of living standards among the elderly. They found that old-age poverty rates fell the most for cohorts who benefited more from the expansion of Social Security, suggesting that these individuals had not saved enough for their retirement and that therefore the crowding-out effect was probably minimal or non-existent for these individuals.

charities. If individuals know they will receive a pension from the government when they retire, they have less of an incentive to save themselves, and lower saving rates may have a negative impact on a country's economic growth. This has traditionally been considered a strong argument against state provision. However, as we saw in section 11.3, there are many reasons why individuals are unlikely to save enough for their retirement, which would reduce the impact of this crowding-out hypothesis. Several studies have estimated the extent to which state pensions crowd out private savings and have found evidence to support some—though partial—crowding out of private saving (see Box 11.6).

Publicly provided pensions can also have an impact on incentives to work, influencing individual decisions about when to retire. In most countries, individuals can choose to continue to work after they reach the state pension age—the age at which they are eligible to start receiving the state pension. The question is whether they benefit financially from doing so. By continuing to work beyond the state pension age, an individual will continue to earn an income (on which they will need to pay taxes), but they will be forgoing their state pension during that period. The value of the state pension may be increased for people who delay their retirement, but this may not be done actuarially.[29] The additional income from working and the increase in the level of the state pension both have a positive effect on the likelihood of working past the state pension age, while the tax paid on earned income and the forgone state pension benefits will have a negative effect. The net effect on the likelihood of working past the state pension age will therefore depend on the relative size of these two effects, along

[28] Before 2016, the UK's state pension involved two tiers: a flat-rate basic pension and an earnings-related additional pension.

[29] If the pension is increased less than actuarially, this will create an incentive for people to retire at the point at which their pension wealth is maximized.

with other factors such as an individual's health. Publicly provided pensions can therefore act as an implicit tax or a subsidy for remaining in work. The design of the pension system—in particular, how the state pension is adjusted for individuals who choose to delay their retirement—plays a crucial role here.[30]

While publicly provided pensions provide some security in retirement, a unified public scheme does not allow for differences in individual preferences. A less generous state pension may be preferred if there is a concern that individuals may be forced to save too much (more than they would like) for their retirement. But given the problems of imperfect information, bounded rationality, and bounded willpower discussed above, determining individuals' true preferences regarding retirement saving is a challenge.

Means-tested benefits

An alternative to providing a state pension to the whole population would be to adopt a more targeted approach and provide benefits to individuals above a certain age who meet specific income and wealth eligibility criteria. Australia's Age Pension scheme operates on this basis, where benefits are paid to individuals who have reached the pension age provided their income and assets fall below certain limits. In the UK, Pension Credit is a means-tested benefit that supplements the state pension for people on very low incomes.

Means-tested benefits provide a mechanism for supplementing the retirement income of individuals with low or no income, but at a lower cost to the government, since the benefits are only paid to those deemed to need it. However, these schemes create a potential moral hazard problem: by providing a safety net for people who cannot save enough for their retirement, they potentially reduce the incentive to save for all individuals, and the government is unable to distinguish those who genuinely cannot afford to save from those who simply choose not to. In practice, this moral hazard problem is unlikely to be pervasive, particularly if the level of retirement income provided is low, as some individuals will want to save to ensure a higher income in retirement. Countries can also adopt other policies to mitigate the risk of moral hazard—for example, by making pension saving compulsory for those who can afford it, as is the case in Australia.

Financial products

Governments can also intervene by providing specific financial products to help mitigate some of the supply-side problems affecting the provision of pensions. These could include the following:

- **State-provided annuities**: annuities are typically provided by private firms, including banks, financial services companies and insurance companies, but governments can also provide annuities directly. This allows the government to take on some of the uncertainty around future increases in life expectancy.
- **Longevity bonds**: these are a mechanism for dealing with the problem of longevity risk. Longevity bonds involve no repayment of principal, but pay a coupon that is linked to the survivorship of a cohort.[31] If a higher than expected proportion of the cohort

[30] See Gruber and Wise (2008) for a discussion of how the design of the social security system impacts retirement decisions in a number of industrialized countries.

[31] The principal is the amount of money that the bond issuer will pay to bondholders when the bond matures. The coupon is the annual interest rate paid on a bond.

survives to a given age (which would lead to an unexpected increase in the annuity provider's costs), the coupon rate will increase, offsetting some of the annuity provider's costs. By issuing longevity bonds for annuity providers to buy, the government is taking on the uncertainty surrounding increases in life expectancy, whereas the annuity provider takes on the risk.

- **Inflation-indexed or inflation-linked bonds**: the government can help markets cope with unanticipated inflation by providing inflation-indexed bonds. These are bonds where the principal is indexed to the inflation rate and therefore provide a hedge against inflation.

Financial education

Given that one of the barriers preventing individuals from saving optimally for retirement relates to low levels of financial literacy, the government could support individuals to make better choices by investing in financial education programmes. However, evidence on the effectiveness of such programmes is mixed. Lusardi and Mitchell (2014) review several studies that have assessed the effectiveness of financial education programmes across the world and find some promising results. Their work suggests these programmes can be effective in promoting financial literacy and influencing financial behaviours, although the authors acknowledge both the theoretical and empirical limitations of the studies examined. Another comprehensive review by Fernandes et al. (2014) of roughly 200 studies covering the relationship between financial literacy, financial education, and financial outcomes such as saving, debt, planning, and investment found that financial education interventions have a negligible effect on individuals' financial behaviours, explaining only 0.1 per cent of the variance in financial behaviours. They also found these effects tend to be weaker among low-income households. These authors suggest that 'just-in-time' financial education tied to specific financial behaviours is likely to be more effective.

11.4.2 Regulation

Regulation can help address problems of imperfect information, bounded rationality, and bounded willpower by making it easier for people to save and, in some cases, actively encouraging or nudging people to save. There are different types of regulation. Here we are going to focus on two examples: automatic enrolment and financial market regulation.

Automatic enrolment

One of the big barriers to individual saving discussed above involves the difficulty in actually implementing saving plans. Policy can exploit people's inertia by encouraging them to start saving and to save more by introducing pension plans that involve automatic enrolment. Under automatic enrolment, eligible individuals are enrolled into a pension scheme by their employer and monthly pension contributions are deducted from their salary automatically, but individuals can opt out of the scheme if they wish to.[32] Automatic enrolment pension

[32] In some automatic enrolment schemes, such as the one introduced in the UK, eligible individuals are enrolled into the relevant pension scheme by default. Other schemes require individuals to make a decision about whether or not to join the company's retirement plan when they join a company (see e.g. Carroll et al., 2009).

schemes have been introduced in countries including Italy, New Zealand, Turkey, and the UK. Other countries have introduced automatic enrolment schemes at the firm level.[33] Evidence suggests that these initiatives have had a significant impact in increasing individual saving towards retirement (see Box 11.7).

One of the big challenges with automatic enrolment programmes involves choosing the appropriate default contribution rate, since most individuals are unlikely to deviate from the default rate and may interpret it as representing the right level at which they should save. A lower default contribution rate may help discourage individuals from opting out of the plan, but if the default rate is set too low, individuals may end up with insufficient savings to fund their retirement. Choosing the appropriate saving rate is complicated because this is likely to vary across individuals depending on their age, family composition, and what other assets they hold—in particular, whether they are homeowners or not. The Save More Tomorrow scheme in the USA mitigates this problem to some extent by linking planned increases in the savings rate to future pay rises.

Box 11.7 Does automatic enrolment encourage people to save more?

The KiwiSaver plan introduced in New Zealand in 2007 was the first example of automatic enrolment on a national scale. By 2018, it had achieved a coverage rate of 80 per cent. Italy also introduced an automatic enrolment programme in 2007, although this covered private sector employees only and participation rates have been more modest. Automatic enrolment was introduced in the UK in 2012 and gradually rolled out to all employers. By 2018, 46 per cent of the working-age population was covered by an employer-sponsored plan. Turkey, Germany, Lithuania, and Poland have all recently introduced automatic enrolment schemes. Automatic enrolment is also encouraged by regulation in Canada and the USA, but at the firm level.

For the USA, Madrian and Shea (2001) find that participation in 401(k) plans[34] is significantly higher under automatic enrolment, although they also find that individuals are likely to retain the default contribution rate and fund allocation. This can partly be explained by inertia, but it is also likely that some individuals perceive the default as investment advice. In the UK, private sector pension membership had been falling since the late 1990s, with just 32 per cent of private sector workers enrolled in a private pension scheme in 2012. Following the introduction of automatic enrolment, pension participation increased dramatically, reaching 75 per cent of private sector employees in 2021 (Cribb & Emmerson, 2016; Karjalainen, 2022). Overall, the evidence suggests that automatic enrolment does lead to much higher participation in workplace pension saving schemes. However, savers tend to stick to default levels of contribution and therefore, if these defaults are not set at an appropriate level, there is a risk that individuals may still be undersaving for retirement.

Sources: Cribb and Emmerson (2016), Karjalainen (2022), Madrian and Shea (2001), and OECD (2019).

[33] For example, the Save More Tomorrow programme in the US (Thaler & Benartzi, 2004).

[34] A 401(k) plan is a defined contribution personal pension plan offered by employers in the USA.

Regulating financial products and services

Governments can use a range of regulations to help mitigate the problems of imperfect and asymmetric information discussed above, including regulating disclosure requirements, requiring firms to provide standardized information about the products they sell, and specifying standards for financial advisers selling or promoting products.

Governments can also regulate the financial products and services available. Research suggests that reducing the number of options and simplifying choice or the investment selection process can boost participation in retirement plans (Iyengar et al., 2004). In the UK, in 1999 the government introduced stakeholder pensions, a type of individual pension offered by some employers, which must meet minimum standards set out by the government, including a limit on charges, low minimum contributions, and being able to stop and start contributions at any point. Other examples include using penalties and fees to discourage individuals from accessing their savings before retirement.[35]

Regulation can be used effectively to simplify the choices that individuals face and provide them with the tools to make informed decisions. But is regulation enough? As the financial crisis of 2008 highlighted, financial markets can be unpredictable and individual funded accounts are subject to greater risk. Workers retiring just a few years apart may receive very different DC pensions, even if they have followed virtually identical investment strategies (Burtless, 2010). Investment professionals are also prone to error and may not always act in the best interests of their clients (as we saw in Box 11.4). To mitigate some of these risks, countries have introduced additional safeguards for workers. In the UK, for example, the government introduced the Pension Protection Fund in 2005, which guarantees a minimum level of pension provision if an employer goes bankrupt or if a pension fund is underfunded.

11.4.3 Subsidies

Governments can also encourage individuals to save more for their retirement by subsidizing pension savings. In most countries this is achieved by offering some form of tax relief on pension contributions, whereby contributing to a personal pension lowers the amount of tax an individual has to pay.[36]

In theory, the impact of these tax incentives on savings is ambiguous. In the context of the intertemporal choice model (see Figure 11.1), tax relief on savings will increase the rate of return, which should encourage people to save more. However, tax relief also effectively gives individuals an income boost, allowing them to consume more in both periods, which implies a reduction in saving today. So the net effect—whether individuals will save more (or, equivalently, consume less) in the current period—will depend on which of these two effects is greater.[37] It will also depend on whether the tax relief makes saving in a pension more

[35] Government legislation can also go in the opposite direction. Pension legislation passed in the UK in 2014 and 2015 included provisions that made it easier for individuals aged 55 or over to access pension wealth held in DC pension schemes. Prior to these reforms, most people were required to buy an annuity with their DC pension wealth.

[36] For example in the UK, the government provides 1 per cent tax relief at the minimum contribution rate.

[37] In the context of the intertemporal choice model in Figure 11.1, tax relief on savings can be modelled as an increase in the interest rate, so the intercept on the vertical axis will increase and the budget constraint becomes steeper. The total effect on saving (or period 1 consumption) can be broken down into a substitution effect, which captures the change in the relative price of current and future consumption, and an income effect, which captures the change in the individual's purchasing power. We introduced these concepts in Chapter 2, and they are discussed in the context of taxation in Chapters 13 and 14. See the suggested Further Reading for an application of these concepts in the intertemporal choice model.

attractive than other forms of saving. Evidence suggests the impact of tax relief on savings is small (Chetty et al. 2014; Crawford et al. 2012). Income tax relief on pension saving is also highly regressive. This is partly because wealthier individuals tend to save more in pensions, but also because tax relief applies at the individual's **marginal tax rate**, which is higher for wealthier individuals.

11.5 The changing pension landscape

We have looked at the objectives of pensions and the extent to which government intervention may be required to help achieve these objectives, as well as the various forms government intervention can take. In this section, we are going to focus on two of the key challenges facing many pension systems today and what they imply for pension policy.

11.5.1 What are the challenges facing pension systems?

There are two key challenges facing pension systems today: how to ensure the sustainability of public pension schemes in the face of demographic change; and how to ensure the adequacy of pension provision to prevent poverty in later life.

The sustainability of public pension schemes

Public spending on pensions and other old-age related cash benefits accounts for a significant proportion of all government spending. Across the OECD, average public spending on pensions was 18.5 per cent of all government expenditure in 2021, although as Figure 11.3 shows, this varies significantly across countries. In new Zealand and Australia, public spending

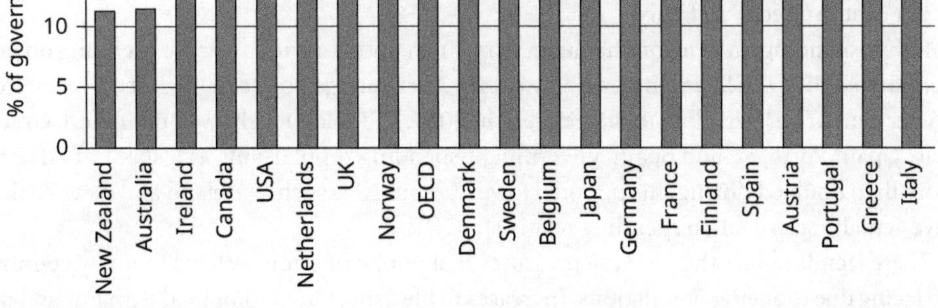

Figure 11.3 Public spending on old-age and survivor benefits as a percentage of total general government expenditure, 2021

Note: 'OECD' represents the average across all OECD countries.

Source: OECD (2025b).

Table 11.1 Public spending on old-age pensions and cash benefits (% of GDP)

	1980	1990	2000	2010	2020
Australia	3.6	3.1	4.7	3.8	4.2
Austria	10.4	11.8	12.3	13.1	14.3
Belgium	9.1	9.4	9.1	9.9	11.5
Canada	3.4	4.5	5.0	5.1	6.4
Denmark	5.7	6.1	6.3	7.1	8.2
Finland	5.4	7.2	7.4	9.8	12.6
France	9.3	10.5	11.5	13.2	14.4
Germany	10.4	9.5	10.9	10.7	11.2
Greece	5.2	9.6	10.5	14.4	17.9
Ireland	5.0	4.8	3.1	5.2	3.3
Italy	8.5	11.3	13.5	15.3	17.4
Japan	3.7	4.6	6.9	9.5	9.6
Netherlands	6.9	7.5	5.7	5.9	6.8
New Zealand	6.9	7.1	4.6	4.5	5.1
Norway	4.5	5.5	4.7	5.3	7.6
Portugal	3.7	4.8	7.8	12.0	13.6
Spain	6.0	7.7	8.1	9.1	12.8
Sweden	6.6	7.2	7.4	8.0	8.5
UK	6.5	6.8	7.3	8.3	7.8
USA	6.0	5.8	5.7	6.6	7.4
OECD	5.6	6.3	6.7	7.7	8.5

Notes: Data include spending on old-age pension and early retirement pensions, survivor's pension, and other cash benefits. Spending on old-age pensions accounts for the majority of all spending in the area. 'OECD' represents average across all OECD countries.

Source: OECD (2025b).

on pensions was around 11 per cent of total government expenditure, compared with over 28 per cent in Greece and Italy.

Public spending on pensions has been rising in many countries. Average spending on pensions across the OECD has increased by nearly 3 percentage points in the last 40 years, from 5.6 per cent of GDP in 1980 to 8.5 per cent in 2020, as Table 11.1 shows. In Finland, Greece, Italy, Japan, Portugal, and Spain, government spending on pensions as a share of GDP has more than doubled during this period. However, countries such as Ireland and New Zealand have actually seen a fall in spending relative to GDP.

These trends reflect the growing pressures that public pension systems in many countries are facing due to ageing populations. Increases in life expectancy combined with low and falling fertility rates in many countries are leading to increases in the old-age dependency ratio,[38]

[38] Sometimes referred to as the old-age to working-age ratio.

Table 11.2 Old-age dependency ratios across selected OECD countries (%)

	2000	2010	2020	2050	2075
Australia	20.6	22.1	27.7	41.6	48.4
Austria	24.9	29.0	31.3	56.0	63.1
Belgium	28.3	28.6	33.1	51.3	54.0
Canada	20.5	22.5	29.8	44.9	54.5
Denmark	24.2	28.2	34.9	44.6	53.4
Finland	24.8	28.5	40.1	51.4	54.7
France	27.3	28.6	37.3	54.5	55.8
Germany	26.5	34.4	36.5	58.1	63.1
Greece	26.7	30.9	37.8	75.0	75.2
Ireland	18.0	18.5	25.0	50.6	50.9
Italy	29.2	33.4	39.5	74.4	67.0
Japan	27.3	38.9	52.0	80.7	75.3
Netherlands	21.9	25.3	34.3	53.3	59.7
New Zealand	20.3	22.0	28.3	43.8	54.5
Norway	25.9	25.2	29.6	43.4	51.2
Portugal	26.8	29.2	38.6	71.4	77.6
Spain	26.9	27.1	32.8	78.4	70.4
Sweden	29.5	31.2	35.9	45.5	51.6
UK	27.0	27.8	32.0	47.1	53.0
USA	20.9	21.8	28.4	40.4	49.3
OECD average	22.5	24.8	30.4	52.7	58.6

Source: OECD (2022).

which measures the proportion of people aged 65 and over relative to the working-age population.[39] As Table 11.2 shows, old-age dependency ratios have been rising across the OECD and are predicted to continue increasing. In 2010, across the OECD, there were on average 25 peopled aged 65 or over for every 100 people of working age; by 2020, this had increased to 30, and it is forecast to increase to over 50 by 2050. In some countries, these predicted increases are even more dramatic: forecasts suggest that in Italy, Greece, Japan, Portugal, and Spain there will be more than 70 people aged 65 and over for every 100 working-age individuals by 2050.

These increases in the old-age dependency ratio put pressure on public unfunded PAYG schemes, since a smaller working-age population is needed to support an increasing number of retired people. However, evidence suggests that these longevity gains may be slowing. Even

[39] Working-age individuals are defined as those aged 20 to 64. The old-age dependency ratio is expressed as a percentage.

before the Covid-19 pandemic, life expectancy had been growing less rapidly than between the mid-1990s and 2010 (OECD, 2021).

The adequacy of retirement incomes

Another challenge facing national pension systems is the adequacy of the retirement income provided, which is reflected in old-age poverty rates. In some countries, old-age poverty rates are in fact lower than the poverty rate for the population as a whole, suggesting the pension system in these countries does a reasonably good job in providing sufficient income for individuals to sustain a minimum standard of living in retirement. However, in other countries, such as Australia, Japan, Sweden, the UK, and the USA, old-age poverty rates are substantially higher than for the rest of the population, particularly for individuals aged 76 and over. Old-age poverty rates also tend to be higher among women.

Pension replacement rates provide another means for assessing how effective a country's pension system is in sustaining individual living standards in retirement. Pension replacement rates measure an individual's pension income as a percentage of their pre-retirement income. They therefore give an indication of the extent to which individuals will be able to sustain the same standard of living once they retire.[40] For the OECD as a whole, the average net pension replacement rate is 69 per cent. This means that an individual who has spent their working life employed in a job that paid average earnings could expect to

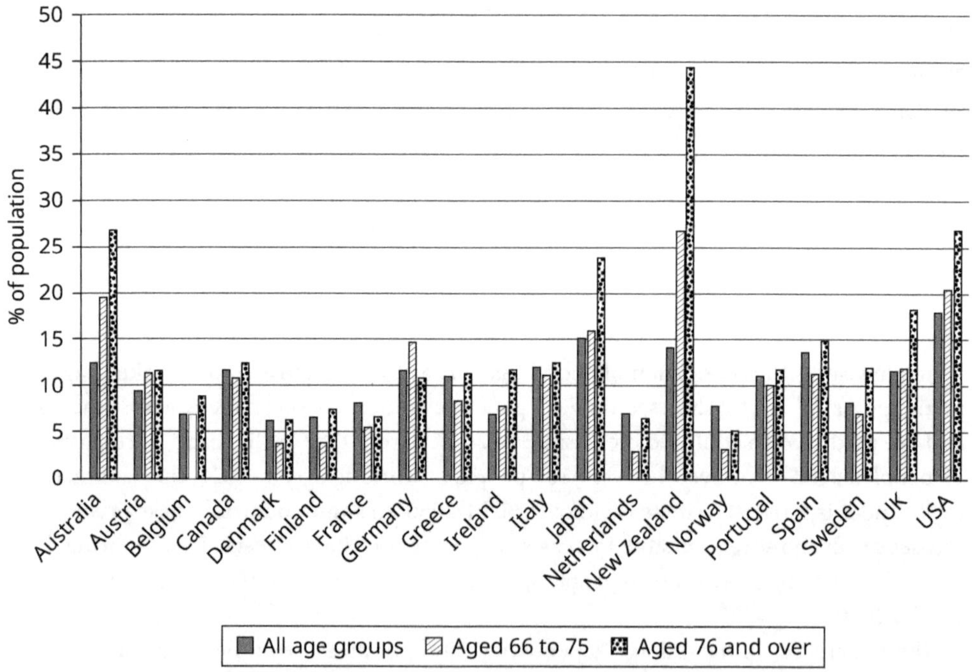

Figure 11.4 Old-age income poverty rates for a selection of OECD countries, 2022

Notes: Poverty rate after taxes and transfers. Poverty line at 50 per cent of median income. Data for Australia are for 2020, and for Germany and Japan are for 2021.

Source: OECD (2025a).

40 However, it is important to keep in mind here that spending needs are also likely to change in retirement.

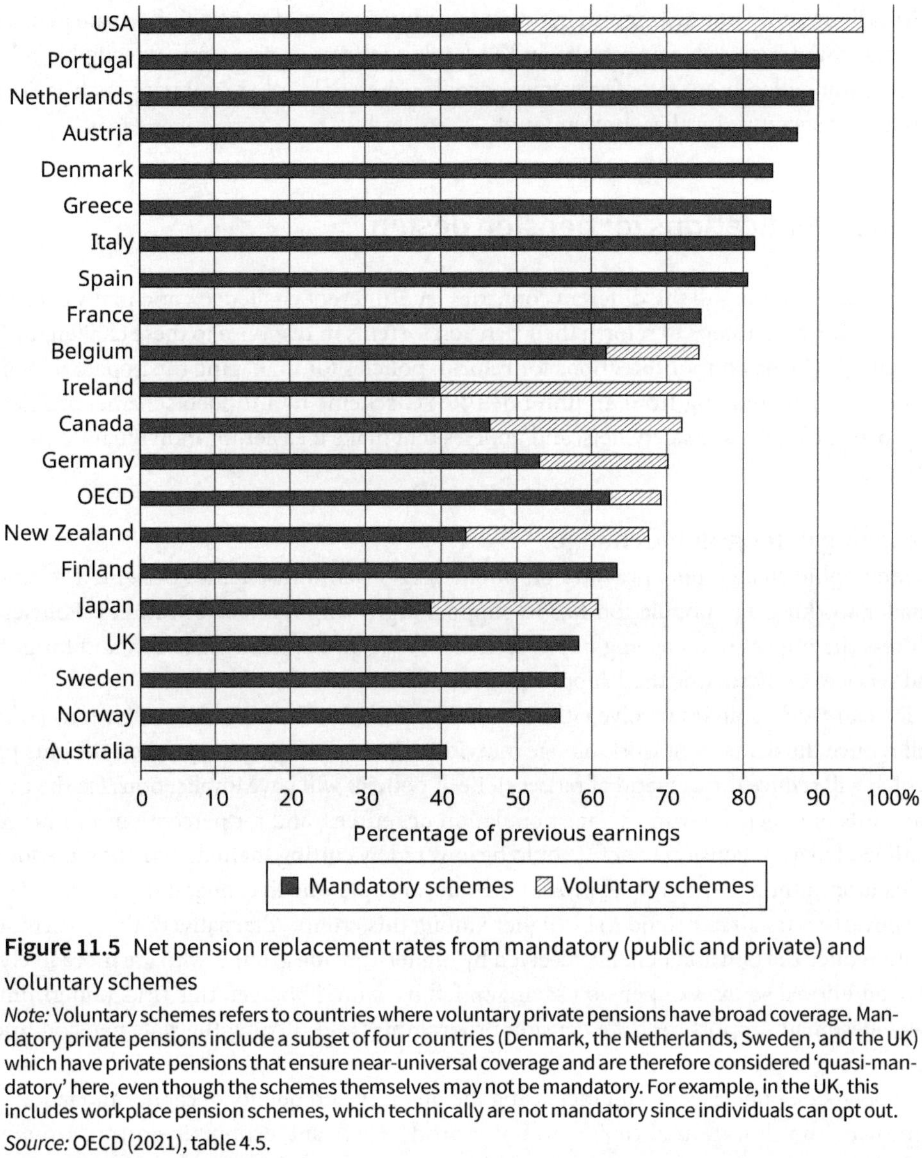

Figure 11.5 Net pension replacement rates from mandatory (public and private) and voluntary schemes

Note: Voluntary schemes refers to countries where voluntary private pensions have broad coverage. Mandatory private pensions include a subset of four countries (Denmark, the Netherlands, Sweden, and the UK) which have private pensions that ensure near-universal coverage and are therefore considered 'quasi-mandatory' here, even though the schemes themselves may not be mandatory. For example, in the UK, this includes workplace pension schemes, which technically are not mandatory since individuals can opt out.

Source: OECD (2021), table 4.5.

receive 69 per cent of their income once they retire, with the bulk of this (62.4 per cent) being made up of contributions to mandatory pension schemes (see Figure 11.5).[41] So, if their pre-retirement income was £1,500 a month, they could expect to receive just over £1,000 in retirement. The average net pension replacement rate ranges from 41 per cent in Australia to over 90 per cent in the USA. However, in the USA, the average pension replacement rate from mandatory pension schemes is only 50 per cent, with the remainder reliant on voluntary schemes.

[41] The net pension replacement rate is defined as the individual net pension entitlement divided by net pre-retirement earnings, taking into account personal income taxes and social security contributions paid by workers and retirees. These are modelled pension replacement rates, based on what a typical retiree would receive if they earned average earnings over their working lives, assuming they work for a full career and assuming today's pension rules remain unchanged. They are therefore not necessarily the same as the pensions that those currently retired receive. Further information on the modelling assumptions can be found in OECD (2023: ch. 4).

This figure does not distinguish between the contribution of public and private pensions. In some countries, such as Australia and Iceland, public provision plays a negligible role in net pension replacement rates for average earners, whereas in other countries, such as France and Italy, it accounts for the whole amount.

11.5.2 Implications for pension design

As the data above highlight, different countries face different challenges, and many countries have already taken steps to reform their pension systems in response to these challenges. We are going to focus on four directions for reform: policies for managing the impact of demographic change; moving from an unfunded PAYG scheme to a funded scheme; policies to improve public old-age safety nets; and policies that make it easier for individuals to save for retirement.

Managing demographic change

Demographic change puts pressure on public PAYG pension schemes because a relatively smaller working-age population has to support a growing number of retirees. Policies to address the impact of an ageing population can focus on decreasing the demand for goods and services or increasing their supply.

Demand-side policies involve either increasing individual pension contributions (which will reduce the demand of working-age individuals) or decreasing the pension benefits paid (which will reduce the demand of retirees). Both policies will have implications for the living standards of either the working-age population or retirees, and for perceptions of intergenerational fairness. Pension benefits could be lowered by cutting them directly or by reducing indexation, although the latter approach will affect people who live longest the most, and old-age poverty rates already tend to be higher among this group. Alternatively, the government could reduce the pension benefits received by higher-income groups, who are more likely to have additional sources of pension saving to fall back on. However, this risks undermining the widespread support for state pension programmes and turning the state pension into a welfare programme.

Supply-side policies focus on increasing the quantity and quality of capital and labour, or improving the allocation of capital, to boost productivity and economic growth. Examples include:

- investing in education and training to boost labour productivity and improve labour mobility;
- increasing labour force participation—for example, by improving nursery care to support young mothers in returning to work;
- increasing the quantity of labour by promoting immigration;
- increasing the labour supply of current workers by raising the retirement age and/or making it more attractive for individuals to work beyond the retirement age.

Most countries have introduced changes to the retirement age in recent years, although these policies tend to be politically unpopular. But the demographic landscape has changed dramatically: a man retiring in 1950 could expect to spend about 53 years of their life in work

Box 11.8 Automatic adjustment mechanisms

Automatic adjustment mechanisms (AAMs) are predefined rules that specify how pension parameters or pension benefits should be adjusted in response to changes in demographic, economic, or financial indicators. These include pension indexation to protect pension adequacy against inflation, linking the statutory retirement age to life expectancy, or adjusting benefits to changes in life expectancy, demographic ratios, or the wage bill. About two-thirds of OECD countries employ AAMs as part of their mandatory or quasi-mandatory pension schemes.

AAMs originally emerged as a tool to maintain pension adequacy through wage or price indexation, but they can also be useful tools to prevent pension schemes from becoming financially unsustainable in the face of population ageing. They minimize some of the uncertainty involved in discretionary adjustments and can provide a better way of including the interests of future generations—who are less likely to have a voice—in decisions involving pensions.

Source: OECD (2021).

and 11 years in retirement; whereas a man retiring in 2004 could expect to spend on average 48 years in work and 20 years in retirement (Barr, 2006). Raising the retirement age addresses the problem not by reducing living standards in retirement but by reducing the duration of retirement.

Changes to pensions to cope with demographic pressures can be made on a discretionary basis—for example, by changing the legal retirement age—or they can be incorporated into the design of pension schemes by setting rules about how pension parameters should be adjusted in response to changes in the wider economic and financial environment. Many countries now have such automatic adjustment mechanisms built into their pension systems (see Box 11.8).

Switching from a PAYG to a funded scheme

As we have seen, PAYG schemes are better equipped to cope with inflation and allow retirees to share in economic growth. However, they are perceived to be more vulnerable to demographic change and this perception lies at the heart of calls for governments to move from unfunded PAYG schemes to funded schemes.

In an unfunded pension scheme, the pensions of current retirees are paid for by the contributions of current workers. This requires the total contributions paid by current workers to equal the total pension benefits paid out:

$$t.w.L = p.R$$

where L represents the number of current workers, t is the rate of tax and w is their income, p is the individual pension benefit, and R is the number of retirees. This implies the relevant tax rate is determined by:

$$t = \frac{p}{w}.\frac{R}{L}$$

where $\frac{R}{L}$ represents the old-age dependency ratio. For the system to be financially sustainable if the old-age dependency ratio is increasing, the tax paid by the current working age population will also have to increase if the relative generosity of pension benefits is to be maintained.

In a funded scheme, each individual saves towards their own pension, so the old-age dependency ratio is irrelevant. However, this argument misses one important point: by focusing on the funding or financial side of pensions, it ignores the fact that what matters to society is not funding per se, but the amount of goods and services available to consume, which depends on the number of workers available to produce them (Barr, 2020). If the current workforce is shrinking relative to the number of retirees, then in the absence of significant productivity improvements, the total amount of goods and services being produced will fall. So a funded scheme is not immune to the problem of demographic change.

Whether the choice between a funded or unfunded scheme matters depends on the extent to which funding affects economic growth. This in turn will depend on whether funding affects saving, and whether this saving leads to higher investment and growth. The link between saving, investment, and growth is not automatic.[42] It is also not clear whether moving towards a funded scheme will increase national saving, particularly if individuals simply offset any mandatory private pension saving by decreasing their voluntary saving (as we saw in Box 11.6).

Moving from an unfunded to a fully funded scheme would imply a significant cost, since it would require a generation of workers to save for their own retirement while also financing the retirement of the current retired population, with implications for intergenerational fairness. In a private funded scheme, individually funded accounts also involve much higher administrative costs due to the administrative inefficiencies of managing smaller investment pools, profits earned by administrators, and advertising costs.

An alternative would be to move towards a partially funded notional DC scheme, as in Sweden. Being partially funded would provide a buffer against demographic change, but if the scheme is centrally administered, it will involve lower administrative costs than individual funded accounts, as well as involving less risk. The scheme would also be better equipped to spread risk compared to individually funded accounts, given the notional aspect.

Improving old-age safety nets

The problem of old-age poverty can be addressed by introducing a non-contributory basic pension, sometimes referred to as a **citizen's pension** or **social pension**. This is a pension that is financed through taxation and is paid at a flat rate based on age and residence, rather than contributions, and is designed to ensure everyone receives a minimum level of income in retirement.

The nature of work and family structures has changed. Many societies have moved away from the norm of a job for life and have seen an increase in part-time and precarious work, more periods out of the labour force to care for children or elderly relatives, as well as increases in divorce rates. These changes mean that it is often more difficult for individuals to amass the required contributions to be eligible for a full state pension, and it is typically women who are more likely to have fragmented contribution records. In the UK, prior to 2010, men needed 44 years' worth of contributions to be entitled to the full state pension,

[42] See Barr (2020) for a detailed discussion of this point.

whereas women needed only 39 years. Even with this lower requirement, only 35 per cent of women had a full record of contributions (Barr, 2012).

A non-contributory basic pension would address the problem of old-age poverty and the associated gender inequities. Since the benefit is paid out at a flat rate, the impact on work incentives is likely to be less severe than with income-tested poverty relief programmes. However, implementing such a scheme would involve a heavy cost, particularly if benefits were to be set at a high enough level to address the risk of poverty in later life. Excluding wealthier individuals from receiving this basic pension would help reduce the cost of the scheme, although it could potentially have a negative impact on incentives to work and save.

Countries including Australia, Canada, Chile, the Netherlands, and New Zealand all have non-contributory pension schemes.

Making retirement saving easier

The discussion in section 11.3.1 highlighted the prevalence of information and behavioural problems in hindering individuals' incentives and ability to save for retirement. This suggests that a useful avenue for government intervention would involve making retirement saving easier. Policies could include the following:

- **Reducing the amount of choice**: offering a small number of simple, low-cost saving plans for individuals to choose from.
- **Introducing automatic enrolment schemes**: evidence from countries that have introduced such schemes suggests they can be very effective in boosting saving rates (see Box 11.7). These schemes can also be implemented at the level of individual firms, as with the Save More Tomorrow scheme in the USA.
- **Ensuring good default options to mitigate the problem of individual inertia**: default options should make use of lifecycle profiling, where savings of young people are invested in stocks, which are riskier in the short term but historically have had higher rates of return in the long run, and shifted towards government bonds as individuals move closer to retirement (Beshears et al., 2009).

Conclusion

How should individuals finance their consumption to ensure they can maintain a suitable standard of living in retirement? What role should the government play in this process? In this chapter, we have looked at the various objectives of pension systems and discussed why government intervention might be necessary to achieve these objectives. Problems of imperfect information, bounded rationality, and bounded willpower suggest that many individuals are unlikely to save enough for their retirement. Some people simply might not earn enough over the course of their lives to be able to save enough for retirement. Private markets are also unable to fully insure against social risks, including the risk of unexpected increases in life expectancy and the risk of unanticipated inflation. There is therefore potential for government intervention to increase both efficiency and equity.

We have also seen that there are many different ways of organizing pension systems and different ways in which governments can intervene. Governments have a range of policy tools available, including providing social insurance-based pension schemes or means-tested pension benefits, introducing automatic enrolment into pension saving schemes, and regulating pension providers and products. There is no single best pension system that will be suitable for all countries. Each country faces its own particular challenges and its own economic, political, and institutional constraints, which will influence the optimal design of their pension system.

Questions for discussion

1. 'Retirement is an entirely predictable event, so people should self-insure through private savings and insurance.' Do you agree with this statement? Why or why not?
2. Should reducing old-age poverty be an objective of government policy? What are the challenges associated with achieving this?
3. Should governments make pension saving compulsory?
4. In the UK, it used to be compulsory for individuals to use their defined contribution pension savings to buy an annuity when they retired. What are the advantages and disadvantages of this policy?
5. What are the main challenges facing pension systems and how can these be addressed?

Further reading

For a more in-depth discussion of the economics of old-age pensions:

Barr, N. (2020). *The economics of the welfare state* (6th ed.). Oxford University Press.

On the problems of imperfect information, bounded rationality, and bounded willpower in pensions decision-making:

Benartzi, S., & Thaler, R. (2007). Heuristics and biases in retirement savings behavior. *Journal of Economic Perspectives*, *21*(3), 81–104.

Lusardi, A., & Mitchell, O. (2011a). Financial literacy around the world: An overview. *Journal of Pension Economics and Finance*, *10*(4), 497–508. https://doi.org/10.1017/S1474747211000448

Lusardi, A., & Mitchell, O. S. (2014). The economic importance of financial literacy: Theory and evidence. *Journal of Economic Literature*, *52*(1), 5–44. https://doi.org/10.1257/jel.52.1.5

For a discussion of the impacts of public pensions on incentives to work and save:

Attanasio, O. P., & Brugiavini, A. (2003). Social security and households' saving. *Quarterly Journal of Economics*, *118*(3), 1075–1119.

Attanasio, O. P., & Rohwedder, S. (2003). Pension wealth and household saving: Evidence from pension reforms in the United Kingdom. *American Economic Review*, *93*(5), 1499–1521.

Disney, R. (2004). Are contributions to public pension programmes a tax on employment? *Economic Policy*, *19*(39), 268–311.

Engels, B., Geyer, J., & Haan, P. (2017). Pension incentives and early retirement. *Labour Economics*, *47*, 216–231.

Gruber, J., & Wise, D. A. (2008). *Social security and retirement around the world.* University of Chicago Press.

For an analysis of the impact of tax subsidies on saving using the intertemporal choice model:
Frank, R., & Cartwright, E. (2021). *Microeconomics and behaviour* (3rd ed.). McGraw-Hill. See chapter 16.

On the options for reforming pension systems:
Barr, N., & Diamond, P. (2008). *Reforming pensions: Principles and policy choices.* Oxford University Press.
Barr, N., & Diamond, P. (2010). *Pension reform in China: Issues, options and recommendations.* MIT Press.

On the effectiveness of financial education programmes:
Benartzi, S., & Thaler, R. (2007). Heuristics and biases in retirement savings behavior. *Journal of Economic Perspectives, 21*(3), 81–104.
Fernandes, D., Lynch, J. G., & Netemeyer, R. G. (2014). Financial literacy, financial education, and downstream financial behaviors. *Management Science, 60*(8), 1861–1883. https://doi.org/10.1287/mnsc.2013.1849
Gomes, F., Haliassos, M., & Ramadorai, T. (2021). Household finance. *Journal of Economic Literature, 59*(3), 919–1000.
Lusardi, A., & Mitchell, O. S. (2014). The economic importance of financial literacy: Theory and evidence. *Journal of Economic Literature, 52*(1), 5–44. https://doi.org/10.1257/jel.52.1.5

Bibliography

Attanasio, O. P., & Brugiavini, A. (2003). Social security and households' saving. *Quarterly Journal of Economics, 118*(3), 1075–1119.

Attanasio, O. P., & Rohwedder, S. (2003). Pension wealth and household saving: Evidence from pension reforms in the United Kingdom. *American Economic Review, 93*(5), 1499–1521.

Banks, J., Emmerson, C., Oldfield, Z., & Tetlow, G. (2005), *Prepared for retirement? The adequacy and distribution of retirement resources in England.* Institute for Fiscal Studies, report no. 67.

Barr, N. (2006). Pensions: Overview of the issues. *Oxford Review of Economic Policy, 22*(1), 1–14.

Barr, N. (2012). *Economics of the welfare state* (5th ed.). Oxford University Press.

Barr, N. (2020). *Economics of the welfare state* (6th ed.). Oxford University Press.

Barr, N., & Diamond, P. (2008). *Reforming pensions: Principles and policy choices.* Oxford University Press.

Benartzi, S., & Thaler, R. H. (2001). Naive diversification strategies in defined contribution saving plans. *American Economic Review, 91*(1), 79–98. https://doi.org/10.1257/aer.91.1.79

Benartzi, S., & Thaler, R. (2007). Heuristics and biases in retirement savings behavior. *Journal of Economic Perspectives, 21*(3), 81–104.

Beshears, J. L., Choi, J. J., Laibson, D., & Madrian, B. C. (2009). The importance of default options for retirement saving outcomes: Evidence from the United States. In J. Brown, J. Liebman, & D. A. Wise (Eds.), *Social security policy in a changing environment* (pp. 167–195). University of Chicago Press. Available at: http://www.nber.org/chapters/c4539

Bourquin, P., Emmerson, C., & Cribb, J. (2020). Who leaves their pension after being automatically enrolled? Institute for Fiscal Studies briefing notes, no. BN272.

Burtless, G. (2010). Lessons of the financial crisis for the design of national pension systems. *CESifo Economic Studies, 56*(3), 323–349. https://doi.org/10.1093/cesifo/ifq001

Carroll, G. D., Choi, J. J., Laibson, D., Madrian, B. C., & Metrick, A. (2009). Optimal defaults and active decisions. *Quarterly Journal of Economics, 124*(4), 1639–1674. https://doi.org/10.1162/qjec.2009.124.4.1639

Chetty, R., Friedman, J. N., Leth-Petersen, S., Nielsen, T. H., & Olsen, T. (2014). Active vs. passive decisions and crowd-out in retirement savings accounts: Evidence from Denmark. *Quarterly Journal of Economics, 129*(3), 1141–1219. https://doi.org/10.1093/qje/qju013

Crawford, R., Disney, R., & Emmerson, C. (2012). *Do up-front tax incentives affect private pension saving in the United Kingdom?* Institute for Fiscal Studies working papers, no. W12/05.

Crawford, R. & O'Dea, C. (2012). *The adequacy of wealth among those approaching retirement.* Institute for Fiscal Studies, report R72.

Cribb, J. & Emmerson, C. (2016). *What happens when employers are obliged to nudge? Automatic enrolment and pension saving in the UK.* Institute for Fiscal Studies working papers, no. W16/1. https://doi.org/10.1920/wp.ifs.2016.1619

Cribb, J., Karjalainen, H., & O'Brien, L. (2023). *The gender gap in pension saving.* Institute for Fiscal Studies, report R250. Available at: https://doi.org/10.1920/re.ifs.2023.0250

Duflo, E., & Saez, E. (2002). Participation and investment decisions in a retirement plan: The influence of colleagues' choices. *Journal of Public Economics, 85*(1), 121–148. https://doi.org/10.1016/S0047-2727(01)00098-6

Duflo, E., & Saez, E. (2003). The role of information and social interactions in retirement plan decisions: Evidence from a randomized experiment. *Quarterly Journal of Economics, 118*(3), 815–842. https://doi.org/10.1162/00335530360698432

Engelhardt, G. V., & Gruber, J. (2004). *Social security and the evolution of elderly poverty.* National Bureau of Economic Research working papers, no. 10466.

Engen, E. M., Gales, W. E, & Uccello, C. E. (2005). Lifetime earnings, Social Security benefits, and the adequacy of retirement wealth accumulation. *Social Security Bulletin, 66*(1), 38–57.

Eurostat (2021). *Closing the gender pension gap?* Available at: https://ec.europa.eu/eurostat/web/products-eurostat-news/-/ddn-20210203-1

Feldstein, M. (1974). Social security, induced retirement, and aggregate capital accumulation. *Journal of Political Economy, 82*(5), 905–926.

Fernandes, D., Lynch, J. G., & Netemeyer, R. G. (2014). Financial literacy, financial education, and downstream financial behaviors. *Management Science, 60*(8), 1861–1883. https://doi.org/10.1287/mnsc.2013.1849

Finkelstein, A., & Poterba, J. (2002). Selection effects in the United Kingdom individual annuities market. *Economic Journal, 112*(476), 28–50. https://doi.org/10.1111/1468-0297.0j672

Gomes, F., Haliassos, M., & Ramadorai, T. (2021). Household finance. *Journal of Economic Literature, 59*(3), 919–1000.

Gruber, J., & Wise, D. A. (2002). *Social security programs and retirement around the world: Micro estimation.* National Bureau of Economic Research working papers, no. 9407. Available at: https://doi.org/10.3386/w9407

Gruber, J., & Wise, D. A. (2008). *Social security and retirement around the world.* University of Chicago Press.

Grünewald, A. (2021). From benefits and beneficiaries: The historical origins of old-age pensions from a political regime perspective. *Comparative Political Studies, 54*(8), 1424–1458.

Iyengar, S., Huberman, G., & Jiang, W. (2004). How much choice is too much? Contributions to 401(k) retirement plans. In O. Mitchell & S. P. Utkus (Eds.), *Pension design and structure: New lessons from behavioral finance* (pp. 83–95). Oxford University Press.

Karjalainen, H. (2022). *On a roll? The first decade of automatic enrolment into workplace pensions*. Institute for Fiscal Studies. Available at: https://ifs.org.uk/articles/roll-first-decade-automatic-enrolment-workplace-pensions

Laibson, D. (1997). Golden eggs and hyperbolic discounting. *Quarterly Journal of Economics, 112*(2), 443–478. https://doi.org/10.1162/003355397555253

Laibson, D. I., Repetto, A., Tobacman, J., Hall, R. E., Gale, W. G., & Akerlof, G. A. (1998). Self-control and saving for retirement. *Brookings Papers on Economic Activity, 1998*(1), 91–196. https://doi.org/10.2307/2534671

Lusardi, A., & Mitchell, O. (2011a). Financial literacy around the world: An overview. *Journal of Pension Economics and Finance, 10*(4), 497–508. https://doi.org/10.1017/S1474747211000448

Lusardi, A., & Mitchell, O. S. (2011b). *Financial literacy and planning: implications for retirement wellbeing*. National Bureau of Economic Research working papers, no. 17078. Available at: https://doi.org/10.3386/w17078

Lusardi, A., & Mitchell, O. S. (2011c). *Financial literacy and retirement planning in the United States*. National Bureau of Economic Research working papers, no. 17108. Available at: https://doi.org/10.3386/w17108

Lusardi, A., & Mitchell, O. S. (2014). The economic importance of financial literacy: Theory and evidence. *Journal of Economic Literature, 52*(1), 5–44. https://doi.org/10.1257/jel.52.1.5

Lusardi, A., & Tufano, P. (2009). *Debt literacy, financial experiences, and overindebtedness*. National Bureau of Economic Research working papers, no. 14808.

Madrian, B. C., & Shea, D. F. (2001). The power of suggestion: Inertia in 401(k) participation and savings behavior. *Quarterly Journal of Economics, 116*(4), 1149–1187. https://doi.org/10.1162/003355301753265543

Meulbroek, L. (2005). Company stock in pension plans: How costly is it? *Journal of Law and Economics, 48*(2), 443–74. https://doi.org/10.1086/430807

O'Brien, L., Sturrock, D., & Cribb, J. (2024). *Adequacy of future retirement incomes: New evidence for private sector employees*. Institute for Fiscal Studies, report R331.

OECD (n.d.a) *Country profiles of pension systems*. Organization for Economic Cooperation and Development. Available at: https://www.oecd.org/els/public-pensions/oecd-pensions-at-a-glance-19991363.htm.

OECD (n.d.b). *Social expenditure database (SOCX), public expenditure on old-age and survivors benefits (% total government expenditure)*. Organization for Economic Cooperation and Development. Available at: http://dx.doi.org/10.1787/220615515052

OECD (2019). *Pensions at a glance 2019: OECD and G20 indicators*. Organization for Economic Cooperation and Development.

OECD (2020). *Income distribution database*. Organization for Economic Cooperation and Development. Data explorer.

OECD (2021). *Pensions at a glance 2021: OECD and G20 indicators*. Organization for Economic Cooperation and Development. Available at: https://doi.org/10.1787/ca401ebd-en

OECD (2022). *Old-age dependency ratio*. Organization for Economic Cooperation and Development. Data archive. https://www.oecd.org/en/data/indicators/old-age-dependency-ratio.html (accessed 19 February 2022).

OECD (2023). *Pensions at a glance 2023: OECD and G20 indicators*. Organization for Economic Cooperation and Development. Available at: https://doi.org/10.1787/678055dd-en

OECD (2025a). *Income distribution database*, Organization for Economic Cooperation and Development. Data explorer. https://data-explorer.oecd.org (accessed 27 July 2025).

OECD (2025b). *Social expenditure aggregates*. Organization for Economic Cooperation and Development. Data explorer. https://data-explorer.oecd.org (accessed 27 July 2025).

Poterba, J. M., Venti, S. F., & Wise, D. A. (2012). *Were they prepared for retirement? Financial status at advanced ages in the HRS and AHEAD cohorts*. National Bureau of Economic Research working papers, no. 17824.

Skinner, J. (2007). Are you sure you're saving enough for retirement? *Journal of Economic Perspectives*, *21*(3), 59–80.

Stiglitz, J., E., & Rosengard, J. K. (2015). *Economics of the public sector* (4th ed.). W. W. Norton.

Sundén, A. (2006). The Swedish experience with pension reform. *Oxford Review of Economic Policy*, *22*(1), 133–148.

Thaler, R. (1981). Some empirical evidence on dynamic inconsistency. *Economics Letters*, *8*(3), 201–207. https://doi.org/10.1016/0165-1765(81)90067-7

Thaler, R. H., & Benartzi, S. (2004). Save More Tomorrow™: Using behavioral economics to increase employee saving. *Journal of Political Economy*, *112*(S1), S164–S187. https://doi.org/10.1086/380085

UK Parliament (1998). *The mis-selling of personal pensions*. Treasury Select Committee ninth report. 17 November. Available at: https://publications.parliament.uk/pa/cm199798/cmselect/cmtreasy/712/71203.htm

World Bank (1994). *Averting the old age crisis: Policies to protect and promote growth*.

World Bank (2008). *The World Bank pension conceptual framework*. World Bank Pension Reform Primer Series. https://openknowledge.worldbank.org/handle/10986/11139

12

Inequality, poverty, and redistribution

Learning objectives

By the end of this chapter, you will be able to:

12.1 Explain how income can be used as a measure of welfare.

12.2 Describe how inequality can be measured and discuss the advantages and limitations of those measures.

12.3 Describe how poverty can be measured and discuss the advantages and limitations of those measures.

12.4 Explain the arguments for government intervention to address inequality and poverty.

12.5 Describe the different ways in which governments intervene to address inequality and poverty.

12.6 Discuss the challenges involved in designing effective redistributive policies.

12.7 Discuss the advantages and limitations of universal basic income and Universal Credit as policies for addressing inequality and poverty.

Introduction

The last century has brought about dramatic gains in economic growth and development across the world, but these gains have not been uniformly distributed. While global income inequality has been falling since the 1980s, within many OECD countries the gap between the rich and poor has grown, and many countries have also seen an increase in poverty rates. Technological changes, particularly increased automation, and changes in the structure of labour markets, with an increase in flexible work arrangements and the rise of the 'gig economy', have the potential to further exacerbate poverty and inequality.

Governments have provided some form of social safety net in most Western countries since the early twentieth century, providing protection against income losses due to sickness, disability, unemployment, and retirement, and supporting the welfare of those on very low incomes. Today, social spending is one of the largest areas of government spending across the OECD, accounting for nearly half of all government expenditure. Why should governments intervene to redistribute resources and support individual incomes? What policies can governments use to reduce poverty and inequality?

This chapter starts with a discussion of the concept of individual welfare in section 12.1. Sections 12.2 and 12.3 explore how we can define and measure inequality and poverty, and analyse how they vary across countries. Section 12.4 looks at the main economic arguments for government intervention to reduce poverty and inequality, and Section 12.5 provides an overview of the different types of policies that governments can use to tackle inequality and poverty. Section 12.6 explores some of the challenges involved in designing effective redistributive policies, and section 12.7 looks at two particular policies to support individual incomes: a universal basic income and a UK-based policy, Universal Credit.

12.1 Measuring welfare

Before we can discuss the concepts of inequality and poverty, we need to think about how we define and measure individual welfare or well-being. Inequality and poverty are closely linked to the notion of welfare, but welfare itself is a fuzzy concept. Welfare is tied to income and wealth, while also including less tangible elements.[1] We therefore need a broad concept of income which goes beyond purely monetary aspects.

The classic definition of income used by public finance economists is the **Haig–Simons income** definition, based on the work of the American economists Robert M. Haig and Henry Simons. According to this concept, income is defined as the amount that individuals could have spent over a given period without changing their net wealth position (Atkinson, 1983). Income is therefore a measure of *potential* consumption, given by the sum of an individual's actual consumption over a given period and any change in their stock of wealth. By this definition, an individual's income is increased if their opportunity to consume has increased, regardless of whether their actual consumption increased.[2] The Haig–Simons definition of income provides a comprehensive concept of income, which includes both money income—from wages, interest, or dividends—and the **capital gains** from owning assets,[3] as well as various forms of non-money income. These include any benefits in kind that individuals receive from their employers, such as employer-provided health insurance and company cars, and wider non-monetary benefits such as job satisfaction, as well as the value of goods and services that individuals produce themselves (e.g. cooking, cleaning, childcare), the value of leisure time, and the value of the services derived from physical assets such as housing.

Although the Haig–Simons concept of income is comprehensive, there are important aspects of individual welfare that are not captured by it. This definition of income does not factor in the uncertainty that often surrounds the consumption opportunities available to individuals and which can have a negative impact on their welfare. Individual welfare also depends on the extent to which we are free or able to make choices concerning the consumption opportunities available to us, and the extent to which our consumption represents a genuine choice.[4] This is a point that was highlighted by the economist Amartya Sen, who proposed a broader concept of well-being based on individual freedom and our capability to make choices regarding our education, health, employment, security, and participation

[1] It is important to be aware here of the distinction between income and wealth. Wealth is defined as a stock variable, which gives rise to a flow of income. In its broadest sense, wealth includes physical assets (e.g. housing, land, and consumer durables), financial assets (e.g. savings accounts, stocks, and shares) and human capital or our set of marketable skills and knowledge. Each of these sources of wealth generates a flow of income, be it in the form of interest payments, wages, or the flow of services that arise from the physical assets we own, such as housing services.

[2] This is also known as an accretion concept of income, which captures what an individual can spend over a period without affecting their net wealth.

[3] Capital gains are the profits earned from owning an asset, such as a house or piece of artwork.

[4] For example, in countries without adequate state-provided healthcare, poor health can lead to large medical expenditures which are outside of an individual's control. Should such medical expenditures be included in our measure of income?

(Sen, 1993). For Sen, well-being is not just about wealth or happiness, but about having the freedom to choose a life we have reason to value.

The Haig–Simons definition of income is also difficult to implement in practice. While some non-monetary benefits can be easily measured, such as the value of employer-provided private health insurance or a company car, this is more challenging (or even impossible) with others. For example, how should we value job satisfaction, or how can we consistently estimate the value of all own production or unpaid services, such as housework or caring for children or relatives? Because of these challenges, most measures of welfare tend to focus on money income, including all earnings from employment and self-employment, interest income from savings, and dividends.[5] However, this provides an incomplete measure of welfare and it is important to be aware its limitations.

When using income as a measure of welfare, it is important to be aware of what our unit of analysis is. Income is usually measured at the level of the household rather than at the individual level, but households vary in their size and composition. A couple with two young children, for example, will need a different level of income to achieve a given level of well-being than a couple without children. **Equivalence scales** provide a means for comparing household incomes across different types of households, by scaling household incomes to factor in differences in the number of adults in a household, and the number and age of any dependants (see Box 12.1). There is no question about the need to use equivalence scales, but the choice of equivalence scale is important, as different equivalence scales are based on different assumptions about the available economies of scale in consumption.[6] Equivalence scales also assume that resources are shared equally or fairly within a household, which may not always be true in practice. For example, a couple where one partner earns significantly more than the other may choose not to pool their incomes completely. There is evidence of significant gender inequality across countries and there are different pooling and sharing patterns across households, leading to inequality within households.[7]

It is also important to consider the time period over which income is measured. If an individual has a job that pays a regular monthly income, then focusing on annual income will give a

Box 12.1 Comparing household incomes across different types of households

Two households might earn the same income, but if one is a single-person household and the other is a couple with two young children, then comparing their incomes alone will tell us little about their standard of living. A larger household will necessarily need a higher income to achieve a given level of welfare—the question is: how much higher? To answer this question we can use equivalence scales. Equivalence scales are a tool for adjusting household income to take into account the different resource requirements of different types of households. Larger households will typically need a higher income than smaller households to achieve

(*Continued*)

[5] Capital gains and certain more easily measurable fringe benefits from work may sometimes be included in measured income.

[6] There are returns to scale in household formation, given that a couple do not face twice the costs to meet their basic needs as a single-person household. The question is: how much more income does a couple need to achieve the same standard of living as a single person?

[7] See, for example, Sauer et al. (2021).

an equivalent standard of living, but there are also economies of scale when individuals can share housing and other consumption (e.g. energy). A couple do not face twice the costs to meet their basic needs compared to a single-person household. Household composition will also affect resource needs because, for example, living costs for adults are typically higher than for children.

There are three main approaches for computing equivalence scales:

- **Minimum needs approach**: this involves identifying a basket of goods and services which are required to meet the basic needs of different types of households. The cost of each of these baskets is then computed and the equivalence scale is based on the ratio of these costs for different types of households.
- **Engel approach**: this is based on the principle that a household's welfare depends on the proportion of income that is spent on food. According to Engel's law, the share of household spending that goes towards food should fall as income rises. Household equivalence scales can be derived by calculating the income levels at which different households have the same share of expenditure on food.
- **Utility approach**: this aims to derive equivalence scales directly from preferences and the household's utility maximization problem, by determining the level of income required for different households to achieve the same level of utility.

Table 12.1 illustrates the OECD modified equivalence scale.[8] A single adult household is assigned a value of 1 and each additional adult in the household is assigned a value of 0.5. Children aged 14 and over are assumed to have the same living costs as an adult and are also given a value of 0.5, whereas children under 14 are assigned a value of 0.3. Using the OECD modified equivalence scale, a family of two adults and two children, aged 8 and 14, would have an equivalence value of 2.3. This suggests this family would need marginally more than twice the income of a single adult household to achieve the same standard of living. If this family had an annual income of £40,000, their equivalized income would be £17,391, which is just their annual income divided by the equivalence value. A single-person household with an annual income of £40,000 would have an equivalized income of £40,000 (since their equivalence value is 1).

Table 12.1 OECD modified equivalence scale

Household member	Equivalence value
First adult	1.0
Additional adult	0.5
Child aged 14 and over	0.5
Child aged under 14	0.3

Source: ONS (2015).

[8] The OECD equivalence scale is used by Eurostat and various UK government departments.

reasonably good picture of their standard of living. But for many people, earnings can fluctuate considerably from month to month, or even week to week.[9] In these cases, annual income can give a misleading picture of individual welfare, particularly if these individuals are on low incomes and have limited opportunities to save and build up a buffer against these fluctuations in income.

When analysing government policies, we are often interested in how they affect particular groups (e.g. those on low incomes, single parents), but we also want to understand their impact on the welfare or well-being of society as a whole. In Chapter 2, we saw how we can aggregate the welfare of individuals using a **social welfare function**, which summarizes the welfare of society as a function of the welfare of the individuals in that society. There are different forms of social welfare functions, which reflect different concepts of equity.[10]

While money income is widely used as a measure of individual welfare, the discussion in this section has highlighted some of the limitations of relying on money income. It is important to have these in mind when analysing measures of poverty and inequality which are based on money income. This is the focus of the next two sections.

12.2 Inequality

Inequality is a concept that most people have an intuitive understanding of, but it can be defined and measured in different ways. In this section, we review some of these definitions and measures of inequality, before looking at how inequality varies across countries and how it has changed over time.

12.2.1 Defining and measuring inequality

The first question we need to think about is: inequality or equality of what? Inequality is not just about income and wealth, although these are typically the more widely used indicators of inequality. There are other important dimensions of equality, including life expectancy and health, education, physical safety, and political participation. These different dimensions are often related and are likely to reinforce one another—for example, income inequalities tend to be closely related to inequalities in health. In this chapter, we will focus mainly on income inequality, but it is important to be aware of these other dimensions of inequality.

It is useful to draw a distinction between equality of opportunity and equality of outcomes. We introduced the concept of equality of opportunity in Chapter 2. It captures the idea that everyone should have fair and equal access to the same chances in life, whether in access to healthcare, education, employment, security, and so on. Whether this translates into equality of outcomes will, in part, depend on individual effort and the choices people make. Individual incomes depend on people's endowments (of human capital, financial assets, and physical

[9] The rise of the gig economy, characterized by flexible and temporary jobs, is likely to make this more common in the future.

[10] We saw two examples in Chapter 2: the utilitarian and the Rawlsian social welfare functions. A detailed discussion of the properties of social welfare functions is beyond the scope of this chapter, but suggestions for further reading are provided at the end of the chapter.

assets), their preferences or tastes, and the choices they make—for example, how much time they spend in education and whether they work fewer hours to enjoy more leisure time. Differences in individual incomes due to different preferences and choices need not imply inequality. However, incomes also depend on external factors and chance: people with the same opportunity sets and preferences, and who have made the same life choices, may experience very different outcomes in life due to bad luck or other external factors, such as discrimination. In this case, differences in individual incomes are a sign of inequality.[11] Distinguishing choice and chance factors in practice is not always easy.

There are two main approaches to measuring inequality: one involves working with descriptive statistical measures that capture certain features of the income distribution; the other approach starts from explicit welfare assumptions about what an equal income distribution should look like and derives a measure of inequality based on these assumptions. Our discussion below focuses on the first of these approaches.[12] Even when working with established statistical measures, each inequality measure relies on implicit welfare assumptions and it is possible to derive a social welfare function from these inequality measures.

Commonly used descriptive statistical measures of inequality include the following:

- **Income shares**: these involve dividing households into quantiles (e.g. quartiles, quintiles, or deciles) and calculating the share of income going to each quantile of the population. For example, we may be interested in examining how the income share of the poorest 20 per cent of the population has evolved over time.
- **Quantile ratios**: these measure the gap between the poorest and the richest households. Two widely used quantile ratios are the **S80/S20 ratio** and the **Palma ratio**. The S80/S20 ratio measures the ratio of the income share of the richest 20 per cent of the population divided by the income share of the poorest 20 per cent of the population. The Palma ratio takes the ratio of the income share of the richest 10 per cent of the population divided by the income share of the poorest 40 per cent.[13]
- **Range**: a measure of the difference between the highest and lowest income, as a proportion of total income. Mathematically, this is given by $R = \frac{y_H - y_1}{H\mu}$, where y_H is the highest income and y_1 is the lowest income, μ is the mean income in the population, and H is the number of households. Dividing the income difference by total income means that this measure will be independent of the units in which income is measured.
- **Coefficient of variation (CV)**: a measure of the variability of income in relation to mean income.[14] Formally, the coefficient of variation is calculated as the standard deviation, σ, divided by mean income, μ: $CV = \frac{\sigma}{\mu}$. This normalization ensures that the measure is not dependent on the scale of income or the units in which income is measured, and both the CV and squared coefficient of variation are bounded between zero and infinity.
- **Lorenz curve**: this provides a graphical representation of the entire income distribution, by arranging the population in increasing order of income and plotting the proportion of income going to each proportion of the population.

[11] See Barr (2020) for a more comprehensive discussion of these issues.

[12] See the appendix at the end of the chapter for a brief discussion of inequality measures derived from explicit welfare assumptions.

[13] If the Palma ratio is 1 or below, this suggests less inequality, as it means that the top 10 per cent of the population do not receive a larger share of income than the bottom 40 per cent. A Palma ratio greater than 1 suggests more inequality.

[14] In some cases, the squared coefficient of variation (SCV) is used: $SCV = (\frac{\sigma}{\mu})^2$.

- **Gini coefficient**: this provides a measure of the area between the Lorenz curve and the line of perfect equality, as a proportion of the entire area below the line of perfect equality.

A Lorenz curve is illustrated in Figure 12.1, where the horizontal axis measures the cumulative proportion of the population, while the vertical axis measures the cumulative share of income. If income were equally distributed across the population—so that the bottom 20 per cent of the population received 20 per cent of income, the next 20 per cent of the population received 20 per cent of income, and so on—then the Lorenz curve would coincide with the diagonal line of perfect equality. The degree of inequality is therefore captured by the distance between the Lorenz curve and the line of perfect equality. We can use the Lorenz curve to compare the extent of inequality across countries, or within a country over time. However, if two Lorenz curves cross, then they cannot provide an unambiguous ranking of two income distributions. This is one of the main limitations of this measure.

The Gini coefficient goes some way towards addressing this limitation. Based on Figure12.1, the formula for the Gini coefficient is:

$$G = \frac{\alpha}{\alpha + \beta}$$

Because the Gini coefficient is based on the size of the area between the Lorenz curve and the line of perfect equality, it provides a complete ranking of income distributions even if the Lorenz curves cross. The Gini coefficient has the added advantage of being naturally bounded between

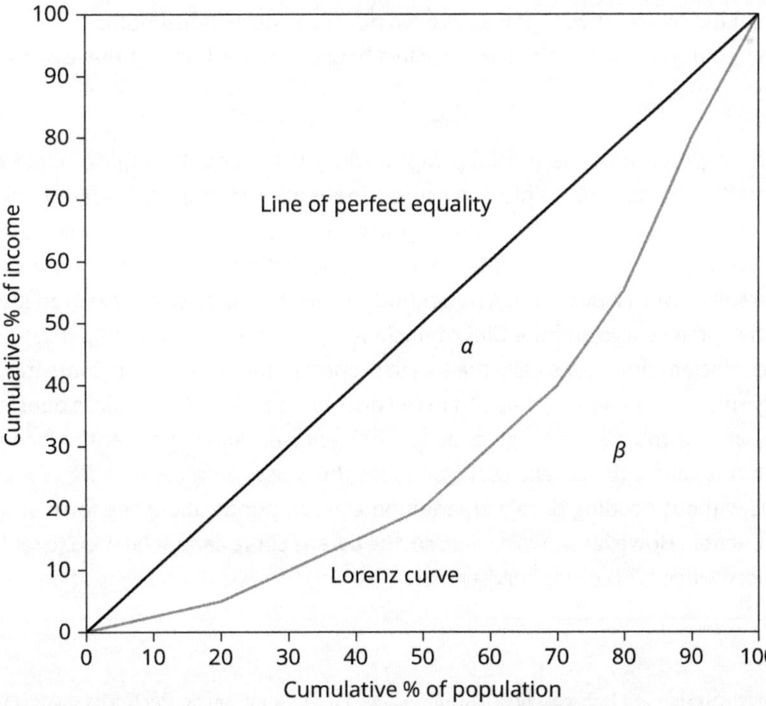

Figure 12.1 Lorenz curve

zero (complete equality) and 1 (complete inequality). However, one of the key limitations of this measure is that it treats deviations from equality the same regardless of where they happen in the income distribution. For example, a transfer of income between two households in the lowest decile of the income distribution will have the same impact on measured inequality as a transfer of equal size between two households in the highest decile, whereas we would expect a good measure of inequality to be more sensitive to transfers between households on lower incomes, which are lower in the income distribution (see Box 12.2).

The discussion above has focused on how incomes vary across the population as a whole. But inequalities also cut across categories such as gender, ethnicity, geography, and generations. For example, there is evidence of a gender pay gap in every OECD country, with women who work full-time earning, on average, only 88 cents to every euro earned by full-time working men (OECD, 2023a). Women also tend to receive lower incomes in retirement—this is known as the gender pension gap.[15] Within countries, some racial and ethnic groups are persistently disadvantaged and face higher levels of poverty and unemployment.[16] Understanding the extent of these inequalities is vital for designing policies that promote more equitable societies.

Box 12.2 Properties of a good inequality measure

There are certain properties that a good measure of inequality should satisfy, which include the following:

1. Anonymity: it should not depend on the labelling of households.
2. It should capture information about the entire income distribution.
3. It should be sensitive to transfers from richer to poorer households.
4. It should be more sensitive to transfers between households at the lower end of the distribution.

The third property above is formally captured by the Pigou–Dalton principle of transfers. According to this principle, measured inequality should decrease if there is an income transfer from a richer to a poorer household that preserves the ranking of the two households in the income distribution and does not affect total income. Conversely, any income transfer from a poorer to a richer household must increase measured inequality.

Both the Lorenz curve and the Gini coefficient satisfy the first three properties. However, the Gini coefficient does not satisfy the fourth property, since it regards income transfers the same regardless of where they happen in the distribution. The Lorenz curve does not suffer from the same problem, since it gives us a visual representation of the entire income distribution. In this sense, the Lorenz curve provides the most complete ranking of income distributions without needing to rely on additional assumptions about the form of the social welfare function. However, as we have seen, the Lorenz curve cannot be used to rank income distributions when two Lorenz curves cross.

[15] The gender pension gap is discussed briefly in Chapter 11. See, for example, Ponthieux & Meurs (2015) for a more complete discussion of gender inequalities.

[16] See, for example, Mirza & Warwick (2024) for the UK.

12.2.2 Trends in inequality

Global income inequality started to grow during the nineteenth century, with the onset of industrialization in north-western Europe. By the 1970s, the world was effectively split between a group of poor developing countries and a group of very wealthy countries. Since the 1980s, there has been a move towards a global convergence in incomes, with incomes in many poorer countries, particularly in South-East Asia, growing at a faster rate than in richer countries. Although there are still significant differences in income between countries, these are not nearly as stark as they were a couple of centuries ago.[17]

Within the OECD, the picture has been different, with the gap between the rich and poor tending to grow since the 1980s in most countries. The richest 10 per cent in the OECD now earn roughly 9.5 times the income of the poorest 10 per cent, whereas in the 1980s this ratio was 7.1 (Cingano, 2014). Table 12.2 shows how income inequality has changed since the 1980s for a selection of OECD countries based on the Palma ratio (before taxes and benefits). In the UK, the income share of the richest 10 per cent was 1.8 times the income share of the bottom 40 per cent in 1981; by 2023, this had increased to 2.8. Income inequality measured by the Palma ratio

Table 12.2 Palma ratio before taxes and benefits for selected OECD countries

	1981	1990	2000	2010	2023
Australia	2.1	2.4	3.0	3.2	3.2
Austria	–	–	–	2.1	2.1
Belgium	–	–	2.5	2.2	2.2
Canada	2.0	2.6	3.5	3.5	3.4
Denmark	1.6	1.4	1.7	2.0	2.1
Finland	1.6	1.6	2.0	2.0	2.1
France	1.9	2.1	2.4	2.5	2.6
Germany	1.6	2.2	2.1	2.6	2.8
Greece	3.1	2.5	4.4	2.7	2.6
Ireland	1.8	1.8	2.7	2.1	2.4
Italy	2.0	2.7	3.5	3.3	3.8
Japan	2.7	3.5	3.7	3.8	3.8
Netherlands	1.5	1.6	1.4	1.8	1.7
New Zealand	3.6	4.3	3.4	3.1	2.6
Norway	1.3	1.0	1.7	1.8	1.9
Portugal	2.1	2.5	3.1	3.1	2.7
Spain	2.6	3.0	2.6	2.3	2.2
Sweden	1.4	1.3	1.6	2.1	1.8
UK	1.8	2.6	2.9	2.5	2.8
USA	2.7	3.6	4.5	5.1	5.5

Source: World Inequality Database (2025)—with major processing by Our World in Data.

[17] See Hasell et al. (2022) and Hasell et al. (2023).

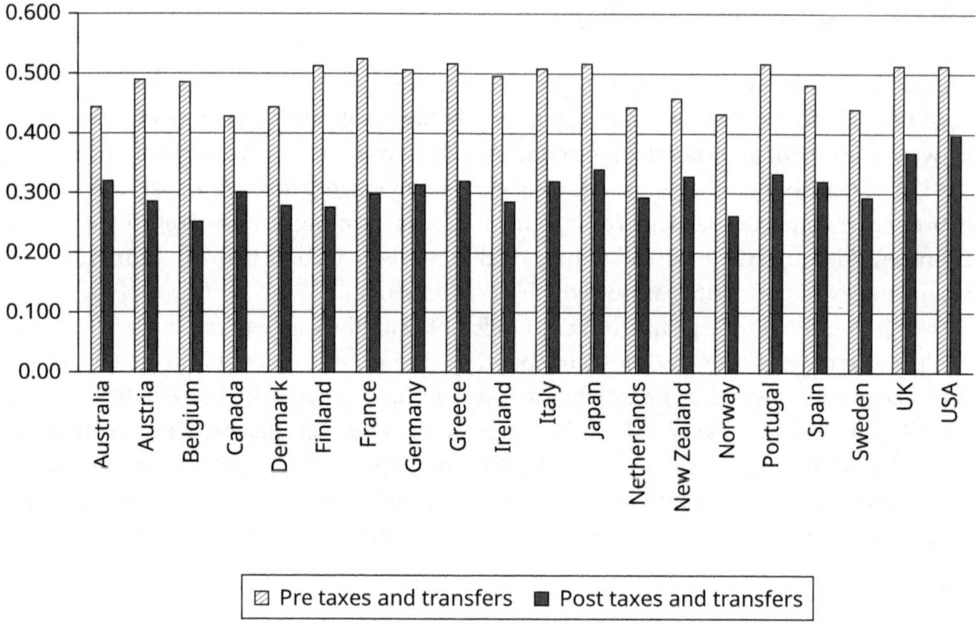

Figure 12.2 Gini coefficient for selected OECD countries (pre and post taxes and transfers), 2022
Note: Data for Australia are from 2020, and for Germany and Japan are from 2021.
Source: OECD (2025a).

has increased in most countries listed, although this increase has been greater in some countries than others. In Greece, New Zealand, and Spain, income inequality has actually decreased.

Figure 12.2 illustrates the level of inequality across the same subset of OECD countries measured using the Gini coefficient. The figure shows the Gini coefficient estimates before and after taxes and transfers, and therefore gives an indication of the extent to which government policies help reduce measured inequality. Before taxes and transfers, the Gini coefficient ranges from 0.427 in Canada to 0.524 in France; post taxes and transfers, the Gini coefficient is lowest in Belgium, at 0.250, and highest in the USA, at 0.396. Looking at the difference between the two measures, it is clear that taxes and transfers are effective in reducing measured inequality in all of these countries, although they play a much greater role in reducing inequality in Finland and Belgium than they do in the USA and Australia.

Wealth inequality is often greater than income inequality and is an increasingly important driver of economic inequality (Piketty, 2014). A study of the distribution of household wealth across 28 OECD countries found that 52 per cent of total household wealth is concentrated in the hands of the wealthiest 10 per cent of households, while the 60 per cent least wealthy households hold, on average, a little over 12 per cent (Balestra & Tonkin, 2018). These wealth differences will have a knock-on effect on income inequality and poverty, since they increase individuals' vulnerability to shocks to their income and may increase their risk of being pushed into poverty.

12.3 Poverty

As with the concept of inequality, most people have an intuitive understanding of what poverty means, but arriving at a precise definition is difficult. At a very general level, poverty can be understood as having fewer resources than are necessary to achieve an acceptable standard of living. The challenge then is to determine what counts as 'an acceptable standard of living' and whether this can be determined independent of time and place. Below, we review some of the definitions and measures of poverty, and then explore how poverty varies across countries.

12.3.1 Defining and measuring poverty

Poverty is a multidimensional concept. It is not just about the income or financial resources an individual has, but about their well-being more broadly—their health, education opportunities, sense of security, and ability to participate in society. Some authors use the concept of **social exclusion** rather than poverty, as a broader concept of deprivation which encompasses low income, poor health, education, and housing conditions, among other factors.

The challenge with adopting these multidimensional concepts lies in determining how each dimension should be measured, and how the different dimensions can be combined. This is why, in practice, researchers often rely on money income to measure poverty. Income and other dimensions of poverty also tend to be closely correlated. Recent work by the UK's Social Metrics Commission has adopted a more holistic approach and has proposed a new framework for measuring poverty which goes beyond simple income-based measures (see Box 12.3).

While it is important to be aware of the limitations of using income as a measure of welfare, in this chapter we will focus mainly on income-based measures of poverty. It is important to draw a distinction between two concepts of poverty:

- **Absolute poverty** assumes there is a fixed minimum level of consumption that constitutes poverty independent of time or place. For example, the World Bank has set the current international measure of absolute poverty at $3.00 per person per day,[18] based

Box 12.3 A new measure of poverty for the UK

Traditional measures of poverty often rely heavily on income and the UK no longer has an official measure of poverty for children, adults, or pensioners. The Social Metrics Commission was brought together to develop a new approach to measuring poverty that more accurately reflects how different families and individuals experience poverty, and which will provide a valuable basis for guiding policy.

The new poverty measure proposed by the commission takes into account resources aside from income—for example, by including any assets that households own. The measure also takes into account any inescapable costs that households may face which may make them more susceptible to experiencing poverty, such as the extra costs related to disabilities, costs of childcare, or housing costs, as well as including an assessment of housing adequacy as part of poverty measurement. This measurement framework provides insights into the depth and persistence of poverty, as well as exploring the wider factors that can have an impact on the lives of people in poverty.

Source: Social Metrics Commission (2018).

[18] As of June 2025, based on 2021 purchasing power parities (PPPs).

on the cost of buying basic necessities, including food, clothing, and shelter. Anyone earning below $3.00 per day is considered to be poor.

- **Relative poverty** assumes that the definition of poverty depends on the prevailing standard of living in a particular society, and therefore poverty can only ever be defined in terms of a given society and a given time period. The official poverty measure used in the UK is based on this relative concept of poverty, defining individuals as being poor if their incomes are below 60 per cent of the median income. The OECD uses the lower threshold of 50 per cent of median income.

A complete measure of poverty should capture how many people are poor, by how much they are poor (the depth of poverty), and how long they have been poor for (the persistence of poverty). The starting point for any measure of poverty is to define a **poverty line**, which determines who is in poverty. A poverty line can be set for both absolute and relative concepts of poverty. The World Bank criterion of $3.00 per day is an example of an absolute poverty line. In the UK and many European countries, the poverty line is set at 50 per cent or 60 per cent of median income; these are examples of relative poverty lines. The incomes used to set the poverty line should be equivalized household incomes, to take into account any differences in household size or composition.

There are two limitations with setting a poverty line in this way. First, if an individual is earning just below the poverty line, they are considered poor; but as soon as they earn even marginally above the poverty line, they are no longer considered poor. In reality, poverty is more nuanced and complex than this. The second limitation concerns relative definitions of poverty which base the poverty line on median income. If incomes fall, as they normally do during a recession, then median income will also fall and the number of households counted as poor will decrease, which seems counterintuitive. For this reason, it may be preferable to set a relative poverty line which depends on average median income over a number of years, as suggested by the UK's Social Metrics Commission.

Some commonly used measures of poverty include the following:

- **Headcount ratio**: a measure of the number of households with incomes below the poverty line, as a proportion of the population. Formally, this is given by: $E = \frac{q}{H}$, where q is the number of households whose incomes fall below the poverty line and H measures the total population. While the headcount ratio may be a useful indicator of who is poor, it tells us little about the extent or depth of poverty. For example, if the poverty line is set at £300 a week, a household earning £290 per week and a household earning £100 per week are treated as equally poor.
- **Income gap**: a measure of how far below the poverty line an individual's income is. We can express the income gap g_h as: $g_h = z - y_h$, where z is the poverty line and y_h is the income level of household h.
- **Aggregate poverty gap**: this equals the sum of the income gaps for all households whose incomes fall below the poverty line and provides an estimate of the depth of poverty or how much income would be required to eliminate poverty. One of the limitations of the aggregate poverty gap is that it gives equal weight to all households that are poor, regardless of how far their income falls below the poverty line. It also does not directly capture the number of households in poverty.

- **Income gap ratio**: a measure of the average normalized income shortfall among the poor. This is given by the aggregate poverty gap divided by the number of households in poverty, and this value is then divided by the poverty line z:

$$I = \frac{1}{z}\frac{\sum_{h=1}^{q} g_h}{q}$$

One limitation of the income gap ratio is that it is not sensitive to regressive transfers: an income transfer from a household below the poverty line to another household below the poverty line will not affect measured poverty.
- **Sen poverty measure** or Sen index: a measure that combines information on the number of households in poverty, their income level, and a measure of the distribution of income among the poor. Formally, this is given by:

$$P_{SEN} = E(I + (1 - I)G_P)$$

where E is the headcount ratio, I is the income gap ratio, and G_p is a measure of the Gini coefficient among the poor. The Sen poverty measure therefore combines information on the number of poor, the depth of poverty, and the relative deprivation among those in poverty, giving a higher weighting to households furthest from the poverty line. In this way, the Sen poverty measure is sensitive to regressive transfers. If there is no inequality among the poor, then G_p is zero and the Sen poverty measure reduces to EI, which is the product of the headcount ratio and the income gap ratio—this is commonly referred to as the **poverty gap.**[19]

Each of these measures has its advantages and limitations. However, none of them captures an important aspect of poverty, which is its persistence or how long people have been poor for (see Box 12.4). Understanding the duration of poverty has important implications not only for individual welfare, but for policy as well. There is currently no single measure which distinguishes between persistent and transient poverty, although recent work on income dynamics aims to capture some of this information.[20]

Box 12.4 Properties of a good poverty measure

There are certain features that a good poverty measure should possess. These were summarized by Sen (1976):

1. The measure of poverty should not depend on who is poor (anonymity axiom).
2. Income transfers between households above the poverty line should not have an impact on the measure of poverty (focus axiom).

(Continued)

[19] The headcount ratio and the poverty gap are part of a class of decomposable poverty measures known as the Foster–Greer–Thorbecke (or FGT) poverty measures (Foster et al, 1984). See the appendix at the end of the chapter for details.

[20] See, for example, Jenkins (2011).

3. Measured poverty should increase if the income of a household below the poverty line decreases (monotonicity axiom).
4. Measured poverty should be sensitive to income transfers among the poor (weak transfers axiom).

The final feature implies that a regressive income transfer among the poor should lead to an increase in measured poverty. Among the measures discussed above, the headcount ratio satisfies the first two properties, while the poverty gap also satisfies the monotonicity axiom. The Sen poverty measure is the only measure that satisfies all four properties.

A further desirable property of a poverty measure is subgroup consistency. This holds that, if poverty increases in a subgroup of the population and remains unchanged in the rest of the population, then measured poverty should increase overall. The Foster–Greer–Thorbecke class of poverty measures, which include the headcount ratio and the poverty gap, satisfy this property.[21]

12.3.2 Trends in poverty

Global extreme poverty is at historically low levels. However, poverty rates across the OECD have increased since the mid-1980s, although the experience has not been uniform across countries (OECD, 2009). Figure 12.3 illustrates the extent to which poverty rates vary across countries. The figure includes two measures of the poverty rate: before and after taxes and transfers, again highlighting the effectiveness of government policies in reducing

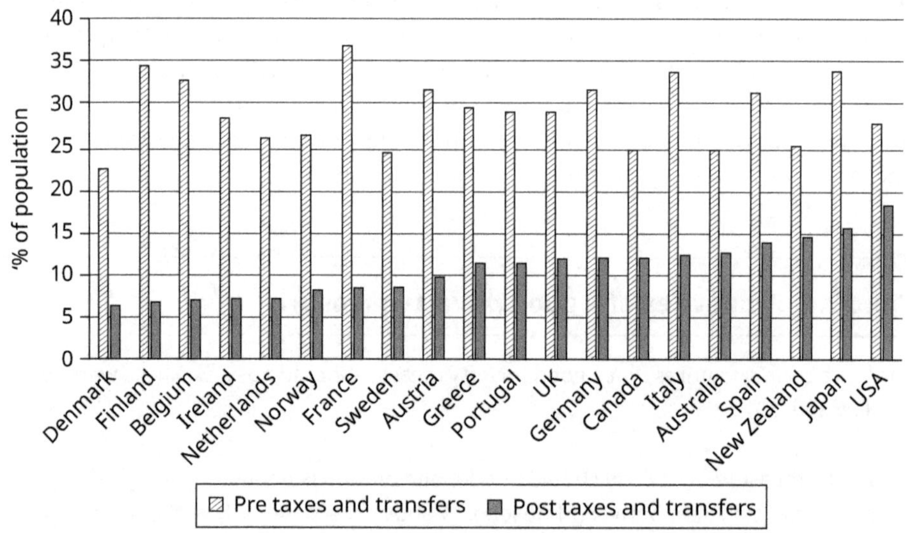

Figure 12.3 Poverty rate in selected OECD countries, 2022

Note: Data for Australia are from 2020, and for Germany and Japan are from 2021. The poverty rate is measured as the share of the population with an income below 50 per cent of the respective national median income.

Source: OECD (2025a).

[21] See the appendix at the end of the chapter for a description of this class of poverty measures.

poverty. Poverty rates before taxes and transfers range from 22.2 per cent of the population in Denmark to 36.5 per cent in France. This means that in France, more than a third of the population has an income which is less than half of the national median income. The poverty rate after taxes and income transfers are taken into account is again lowest in Denmark, at 6.3 per cent, and highest in the USA, at 18.1 per cent. The tax and transfer system is particularly effective at reducing poverty rates in countries such as Finland and Belgium, where the pre-taxes and transfers poverty rate is over 30 per cent, compared to less than 7 per cent after taxes and transfers.

The poverty rate provides a measure of the number of people who are poor, as measured by the poverty line. But, as we saw above, we are also interested in the depth of poverty or understanding by how much they are poor. Figure 12.4 illustrates the poverty gap for a selection of OECD countries, which provides a measure of the extent to which the mean income of the poor falls below the poverty line (measured here after taxes and transfers). In Ireland and Belgium, the average income of people in poverty was around 20 per cent below the poverty line; in Norway and the USA, this gap was nearly 40 per cent. In some countries, both the extent of poverty (measured by the poverty rate) and the depth of poverty (measured by the poverty gap) are high. This is the case in Spain, Japan, and the USA. But countries with the lowest poverty rates do not necessarily have the lowest poverty gaps—for example, the poverty rate in Denmark is around 6 per cent (post taxes and transfers), while the poverty gaps is 29.5 per cent.

Poverty can vary significantly within countries as well as across countries, with certain groups more at risk of experiencing poverty. Table 12.3 shows how poverty rates vary across different age groups. Poverty rates tend to be lowest among working-age adults, while children under 18 and older adults are more at risk of poverty. In some cases, the differences can be significant. For example, in Australia and New Zealand, the poverty rate for people aged 65 and over is more than double the poverty rate among

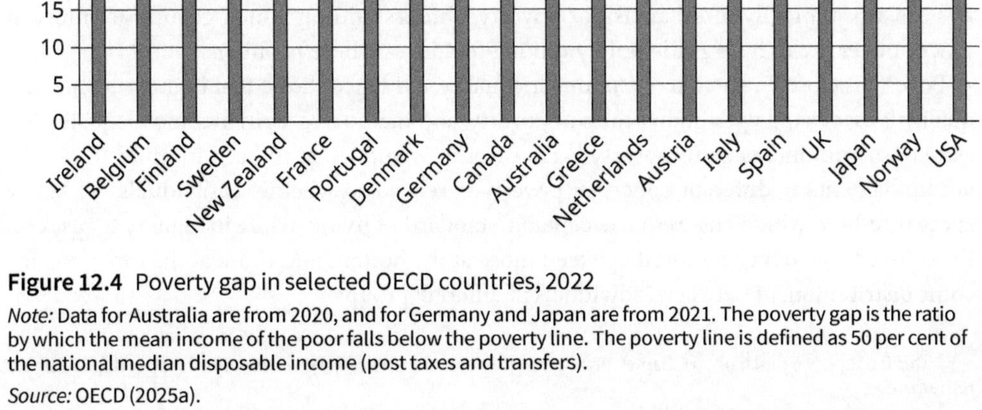

Figure 12.4 Poverty gap in selected OECD countries, 2022

Note: Data for Australia are from 2020, and for Germany and Japan are from 2021. The poverty gap is the ratio by which the mean income of the poor falls below the poverty line. The poverty line is defined as 50 per cent of the national median disposable income (post taxes and transfers).

Source: OECD (2025a).

Table 12.3 Poverty rates by age group for selected OECD countries, 2022

	Under 18	18 to 65	Over 65
Australia	13.3	10.1	22.6
Austria	11.7	8.4	11.6
Belgium	7.6	6.4	7.7
Canada	12.5	11.7	11.6
Denmark	4.2	7.4	5.0
Finland	3.8	8.0	5.5
France	11.2	8.0	6.1
Germany	11.1	11.7	12.6
Greece	13.0	11.1	10.0
Ireland	7.9	6.1	9.5
Italy	14.0	11.9	12.0
Japan	11.5	12.7	20.0
Netherlands	9.2	7.2	4.4
New Zealand	13.9	9.8	33.7
Norway	7.0	9.4	4.1
Portugal	14.3	10.5	11.0
Spain	20.7	12.1	13.1
Sweden	8.5	7.9	9.4
UK	13.6	10.2	14.9
USA	20.8	15.8	23.1

Note: Data for Australia are from 2020, and for Germany and Japan are from 2021. The poverty rate is measured as the share of the population with an income below 50 per cent of the respective national median income.

Source: OECD (2025a).

the working-age population.[22] In countries such as Denmark and Finland, on the other hand, poverty rates are highest for working-age people. But poverty rates do not just vary by age group; other groups, including women, single parents, and some ethnic minorities are also typically more at risk of poverty. Understanding which groups are more at risk of poverty can help guide policymaking to address these problems.

Poverty is closely related to economic inequality. Evidence shows that higher income inequality is associated with higher rates of poverty, and that increases in income inequality are associated with increases in poverty.[23] However, it is important to keep in mind that these are fundamentally different concepts: poverty is related to whether individuals fall below some threshold which ensures an acceptable standard of living, while inequality focuses on the difference in living standard between those at the bottom and those at the top of the income distribution, or between individuals in different groups.

[22] This is a topic we touch on in Chapter 11, where we discuss the role of the government in supporting saving for retirement.

[23] See, for example, Hills et al. (2019).

12.4 Arguments for government intervention

Most Western countries have provided some form of poverty relief for centuries, although the modern welfare state is a relatively more recent creation (see Box 12.5). Today, government interventions to reduce poverty and inequality include **social insurance** schemes to cover periods of sickness, unemployment, or retirement, as well as benefits to support individuals on low incomes, and publicly provided services such as education or healthcare. These policies help raise living standards and narrow the gap between the rich and the poor. But why should governments adopt policies to reduce poverty and inequality? One answer is that governments should adopt redistributive policies because societies care about fairness and because it seems wrong that, in wealthy developed countries, some people are not able to meet their basic needs. These equity arguments are powerful, but there are also important efficiency arguments for government intervention. We discuss each of these below.

12.4.1 Government intervention to increase efficiency

As we saw in Chapter 2, markets will lead to an efficient outcome under certain conditions, which include perfect competition, perfect information, and the absence of externalities or public goods.[24] In the context of poverty and inequality, there are two leading sources of market failure: asymmetric information and externalities.

Box 12.5 A very brief history of the modern welfare state

Germany was one of the first countries to introduce a social insurance system in the 1880s, under the Chancellor Otto von Bismarck. This scheme provided retirement benefits and disability benefits to workers. Participation in the scheme was mandatory and both employees and employers were required to contribute. In the UK, the foundations of the modern welfare state date back to the introduction of the Old-Age Pensions Act in 1908. A National Insurance system was introduced in 1911, providing basic unemployment and sickness protection.

The economic devastation caused by the Great Depression in 1929 and the Second World War helped spur the development of the welfare state in several countries. President Roosevelt introduced the social security scheme in the USA in 1935, as part of his New Deal programme. In the UK, the economist William Beveridge published *Social Insurance and Allied Services*—commonly known as the Beveridge Report—in 1942. In this report, Beveridge called for widespread reforms to banish poverty and 'want', one of the 'five giants' he identified, alongside disease, squalor, ignorance, and idleness. Beveridge's recommendations to tackle these problems included the setting up of a National Health Service, which would be free at the point of use, and a social insurance scheme that individuals would pay into while working and which would provide benefits if they were ill, unemployed, or once they retired. The principles outlined in the Beveridge Report are considered to be the foundation of the modern welfare state, based on the idea that the government should play a key role in promoting the economic and social well-being of citizens.

[24] See Chapter 2, section 2.2.4, for a review of these concepts.

Asymmetric information and incomplete insurance

We discussed the problem of asymmetric information and incomplete insurance in the context of healthcare and old-age pensions in Chapters 8 and 11. These problems also arise in the context of poverty relief. There are certain risks—for example, the risk of unemployment, sickness, or disability—that lead to income losses that can push individuals into poverty. Because most people do not know if or when they may become unemployed, or sick and unable to work, it is difficult for them to plan their saving and expenditure to smooth their consumption when these income losses occur. The usual market response for dealing with risk is insurance. However, as we saw in Chapter 2, for private insurance markets to operate efficiently, a number of conditions are required: the probability of the risk being insured against must be independent across individuals (i.e. the probability of one individual suffering a loss must be independent of the probability of anyone else suffering a loss); these probabilities must be known or estimable, and less than 1; and there must be no problems of adverse selection or moral hazard. These conditions are unlikely to hold in the case of private insurance against unemployment, ill-health, or disability, and therefore private markets may fail to provide insurance to everyone who wants it or may provide too low a level of insurance.

Social or aggregate risks are risks that private markets are unable to fully insure against because they are risks faced by society as a whole, so the probabilities are not independent across individuals. Inflation is an example of an aggregate risk. An economic recession, resulting in an increase in unemployment, is another example.[25] In the event of a recession, many people would lose their jobs at the same time. Because everyone faces the same level of risk, private insurance markets cannot pool these risks and therefore cannot provide insurance against them.

Private markets for insurance against unemployment also suffer from the problems of adverse selection and moral hazard that we discussed in Chapter 8 in the context of health insurance.[26] In the case of unemployment insurance, the problem of adverse selection arises if individuals who believe they are at a low risk of becoming unemployed feel that the premium charged by the insurance provider is too high, and therefore opt out of unemployment insurance. This will leave the insurance company with a pool of individuals who face a high risk of becoming unemployed, forcing it to raise its premiums further to cover its costs, thus driving lower risks out of the market. In the extreme, the insurance company is faced only with a pool of individuals that face a high risk of unemployment to insure and the market will collapse.

The problem of moral hazard arises because individuals can affect their probability of becoming unemployed or how long they remain unemployed for. If an individual knows that unemployment insurance will cover their full wages if they lose their job, they have an incentive to invest less time and effort in looking for a new job if they are unemployed. This raises the costs of the insurance provider, leading it to increase its premiums, thus making private insurance less attractive.

In the absence of private insurance to protect against the risk of unemployment, there is a role for government-provided support in the form of social insurance.[27] Simply making insurance compulsory would address the problem of adverse selection, but not the problem of aggregate risks or the moral hazard problem. By pooling risk across many individuals, social

[25] High housing costs are another example of an aggregate risk that is often correlated with poverty.

[26] See also Chapter 2 for a review of these concepts.

[27] Note that the same arguments may not apply to the same extent to other risks which are typically covered by social insurance, such as the risk of illness or disability.

insurance also provides a more efficient way of smoothing consumption than relying on individual saving, since individuals are likely to either save too much or too little. However, there is a risk that social insurance may crowd out private saving.[28] And publicly provided insurance is not immune from the problem of moral hazard, as we discuss in section 12.6.

Alongside these problems of asymmetric information, there are also problems of imperfect information. These arise because individuals who are buying insurance against unemployment or ill-health may not be well informed about the costs and benefits of the different insurance policies available. While individuals can often acquire more information, this may be costly, resulting in suboptimal decisions. This can have equity implications, particularly if problems of imperfect information are correlated with individuals' incomes.

Externalities

There are negative externalities associated with poverty.[29] High poverty rates may lead to increased crime and social unrest, which imposes an additional cost on society in terms of increased policing. Poverty is often associated with malnutrition, which contributes to poor health, leading to increased healthcare costs and a deterioration in the quality of the labour force. In the case of child poverty, malnutrition will impair children's development and educational attainment, limiting their future life outcomes. There may also be psychic costs associated with poverty. For example, if individuals care about the well-being of everyone in society, then individual utilities will be lower if there are people in society who cannot afford an acceptable standard of living. These external costs provide an argument for making insurance against unemployment, sickness, and disability compulsory.

There are also positive externalities associated with the provision of certain goods, such as health and education. Investing in health and education involves wider social benefits over and above the benefits to individuals, and therefore these goods are likely to be underprovided by the market, providing a further argument for government intervention. This is discussed in more detail in Chapters 8 and 9.

12.4.2 Government intervention to promote equity

When we think about equity or social justice, most of us probably have in mind the concept of equality of opportunity, rather than equality of outcomes. As we saw in section 12.2, unequal outcomes may be the result of choices that individuals make and therefore might not be considered unfair. But equality of outcomes is important for both ethical and practical reasons. On an ethical level, it seems wrong that individual living standards should vary so widely within society. On a practical level, high levels of inequality are associated with higher crime rates and lower social cohesion, and risk weakening democracy as wealthier individuals have more power to influence government policies to suit their own interests. High inequality of outcomes may also limit the possibilities of achieving equality of opportunity, as higher-income individuals will typically be better placed to ensure their children have better opportunities in life—for example, in terms of education or employment.

[28] The problem of crowding out was discussed in Chapter 6, in the context of government provision of public goods.

[29] See Chapter 2 for a review of the concept of externalities.

A pure market system is unlikely to lead to a distribution of resources that satisfies either equality of outcomes or equality of opportunity. As we saw at the beginning of this chapter, individual incomes depend on individual endowments and the choices individuals make, as well as chance or external factors. Individual endowments include people's stock of human capital, physical capital, and financial assets, and chance plays a significant role in determining the allocation of these initial endowments. An individual's level of ability and their access to inherited wealth are largely determined by chance and are outside of an individual's control. However, governments can affect this initial allocation, through policies such as inheritance taxes and investments in education and health.

Individual incomes will also depend on the prices for which people can sell their assets, including their human capital. These market prices are not always set fairly and will depend on individuals' bargaining power, and some individuals will have more power than others to influence the wages they are paid. Chief executives and directors are likely to have more power to influence their salaries than many employees, particularly low-skilled workers. Individuals may also be subject to discrimination based on gender, ethnicity, age, or disability, and have unequal access to information (e.g. about job or training opportunities, or financial products). This provides a further justification for government intervention to promote horizontal equity[30]—for example, by addressing labour market discrimination or guaranteeing minimum wages.

12.4.3 Inequality and economic growth

The discussion so far has focused on arguments for government intervention to reduce poverty. While reducing poverty will, by definition, affect inequality by increasing low incomes, there is a separate question about whether governments should adopt policies aimed specifically at reducing inequality. Alongside arguments based on equity or fairness, there are also arguments based on the impact of inequality on economic growth.

Early work on the relationship between inequality and economic growth focused on the impact of growth on inequality. This relationship is captured by the famous **Kuznets curve**, based on the work of Simon Kuznets. Having analysed data for several countries in the 1950s, Kuznets suggested that, as an economy develops, inequality will initially increase and then decrease, resulting in an inverted U-shaped relationship between economic growth and inequality. However, more recent evidence does not support this hypothesis and, as we saw in section 12.2, inequality has continued to rise in many countries in spite of economic growth.

What about the impact of inequality on economic growth? On the one hand, inequality can be seen to have a positive impact on growth: it increases incentives for individual effort, innovation, and entrepreneurship, and the higher propensity to save among high-income individuals can lead to more investment, which will boost economic growth. On the other hand, too much inequality can be harmful for growth by discouraging risk-taking and encouraging social and political unrest. High-income individuals are also more likely to save in non-productive assets such as housing and luxury goods, which have a limited potential to have a positive impact on the wider economy. Overall, the evidence suggests there is no strong correlation between inequality and economic growth.[31]

[30] As we saw in Chapter 2, horizontal equity concerns the equal treatment of individuals who are equal in all relevant respects.

[31] See Hills et al. (2019) for a review of the theory and evidence on the relationship between inequality and growth.

12.5 Types of government intervention

Social spending is one of the largest areas of government spending across the OECD, accounting for nearly half of all government expenditure, on average (see Figure 12.5).[32] In countries such as Japan, Ireland, and Spain, this figure is closer to 60 per cent. Social spending includes all spending on financial support provided to individuals and households who are unemployed, sick, disabled, or retired, as well as spending on healthcare, family assistance, and housing support, and tax breaks with a social purpose. The largest areas of social spending in most OECD countries are old-age and survivor pensions and health (OECD, 2024). But government interventions to tackle inequality and poverty are broader than this. They include other publicly provided goods, such as education and public transport, as well as legislation such as minimum wages. These policies can help narrow the gap between the rich and the poor, and increase the incomes of the poor, thereby helping to reduce both inequality and poverty.

There are different ways of classifying government interventions to address inequality and poverty. In Chapter 1 we distinguished three broad types of government intervention: direct provision of goods and services; regulation; and taxes and subsidies. This classification is useful in helping us understand the range of ways in which governments intervene to affect the distribution of resources. Table 12.4 gives some examples of policies that fall under each of these categories:

- **Direct provision**: this includes the provision of social insurance schemes that aim to protect individuals against income losses that may arise as a result of unemployment, injury, sickness, disability, maternity, widowhood, or retirement.[33] These benefits can help prevent people from falling into poverty. Alongside social insurance, some have

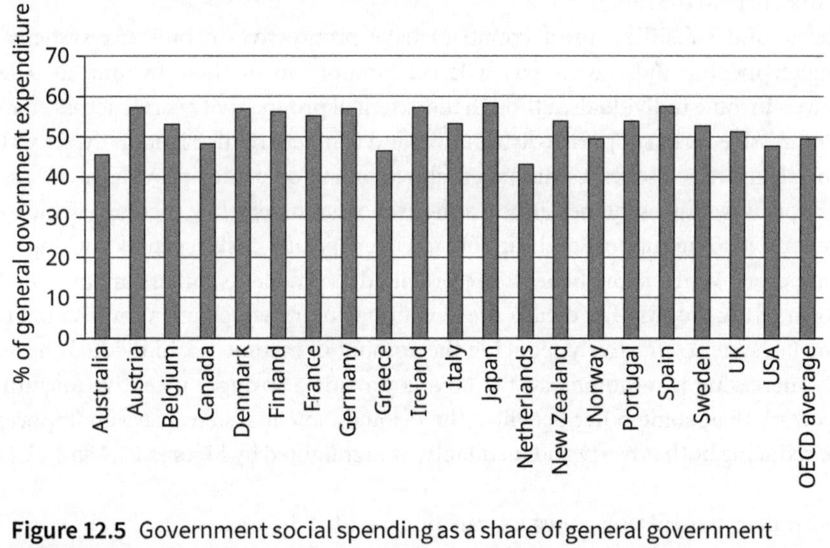

Figure 12.5 Government social spending as a share of general government expenditure, 2021

Note: 'OECD average' is for all OECD countries. Social expenditure includes cash benefits, in-kind goods and services, and tax breaks with a social purpose.

Source: OECD (2025b).

[32] The data in the figure refer to 2021, which was an unusual year as the Covid-19 pandemic led to an increase in government spending in areas such as health. However, data on government social spending as a share of general government expenditure in 2018 (pre-pandemic) was at a similar level for most countries.

[33] Old-age pensions are discussed in Chapter 11. Social insurance schemes differ from social assistance or welfare schemes that are aimed primarily at poverty relief.

Table 12.4 Different types of government intervention

Type of policy	Examples
Direct provision	Social insurance (e.g. unemployment, disability, old-age pensions) Asset-based welfare Free education
Regulation	Minimum wage legislation Equal pay legislation Quotas for minorities
Taxes and subsidies	Progressive income taxes Inheritance taxes Income support, housing benefit, child benefit

argued for **asset-based welfare** policies, which involve providing individuals with financial assets that can provide a buffer against income shocks.[34] Direct provision also includes the provision of public services such as healthcare and education, as well as facilities including public libraries and sports facilities, and subsidized public transport. The provision of public services supports redistribution, as individuals on lower incomes are typically more likely to benefit from them and, in most countries, these services are funded through progressive taxation.[35]

- **Regulation:** this includes policies such as minimum wages, which provide a minimum rate of pay that earnings cannot fall below, as well as equal pay legislation and quotas for minorities which aim to promote both equality of opportunity and equality of outcomes—for example, by ensuring that men and women doing essentially the same work are paid the same.
- **Taxes and subsidies**: most countries have progressive income tax systems, where higher-income individuals pay a larger proportion of their income in taxes than lower-income individuals, although the extent of progressivity varies across countries.[36] Progressive taxes support redistribution and can help reduce inequality. As well as the social insurance schemes discussed above, many countries provide social assistance or **social welfare** schemes aimed at households on very low incomes, which include general income support and support to cover specific costs, such as housing or childcare costs. While some benefits are provided as payments, others are provided in the form of **tax credits**. Tax credits are benefit payments which are administered through the tax system, effectively reducing the amount of income tax individuals have to pay. By increasing take-home pay, tax credits provide a stronger incentive for individuals to work than some other benefits. The tax and benefit system plays an important role in reducing both poverty and inequality, as highlighted by Figures 12.2 and 12.3 above.

Government benefits or transfers can be provided in cash or in kind, as we saw in Chapter 1. **Cash transfers**, as the name suggests, refer to programmes that provide cash benefits to recipients. Examples include old-age pensions, unemployment benefits, and sickness and disability benefits. **In-kind transfers** involve providing certain goods and services

[34] In 2002, the UK government introduced Child Trust Funds, which provided every child born in the UK with £250, which they could access when they turned 18. The scheme was abolished in 2011.

[35] See Chapter 13 for a discussion of progressive taxation.

[36] See Chapters 13 and 15 on taxation.

directly to recipients, such as healthcare, education, housing, and food stamps. In-kind transfers ensure that support is targeted where it is considered most needed, guaranteeing the consumption of or access to a minimum level of education, healthcare, or housing. This can be particularly important when there are problems of imperfect information or bounded willpower (e.g. a lack of self-control),[37] which may prevent individuals from making socially optimal choices if given transfers in cash. However, in-kind benefits are distortionary, as it would be possible to achieve the same gain in individual well-being at a lower cost to the government, and they are often more costly to administer.

Some benefits are only available to individuals who fall within a certain category, such as being unemployed or retired, or having a disability. These are known as **categorical benefits**. Categorical benefits may be universal, in the sense that everyone who qualifies is entitled to receive the same level of benefit, regardless of their income, or they may be means-tested. Entitlement to **means-tested benefits** depends on an individual or household's financial situation—that is, their level of income or wealth. The state pension in many countries is an example of a categorical benefit that is universal, since everyone above the state pension age typically receives the same level of the state pension. In the UK, the Winter Fuel Payment was a **universal benefit** paid to all individuals over the state pension age to help them meet the costs of heating their homes in winter, but eligibility to this benefit was restricted in 2025 to people with an income below £35,000. Means-tested benefits are better targeted towards those in need and are less costly to deliver, although they are often more costly to administer, given the need to ensure that only those who are entitled to the benefits receive them. Means-tested benefits also risk creating a social divide between those who receive the benefits and those who do not. While universal benefits are more expensive to provide, they may receive wider support (and voter approval) because everyone is entitled to them. Determining the best way of targeting benefits is also challenging in practice (see Box 12.6).

Box 12.6 Targeting benefits

There are three main approaches to targeting benefits:

1. **Income test**: this involves identifying individuals eligible for benefits based on their income. One of the main challenges with income targeting involves determining the rates at which benefits are reduced once individual incomes increase, which will have implications for individual incentives to work. If eligibility for benefits or the level of benefits is reduced too quickly, this may discourage individuals from working. Income targeting can also imply high costs, both administrative (in terms of carrying out detailed income assessments) and personal, given that income assessments can be quite intrusive.
2. **Indicator targeting**: this approach involves using certain poverty indicators which may be more easily measured than income, such as the number of children. Indicator targeting can be less costly and less liable to disincentive effects. However, it may

(Continued)

[37] See Chapter 2 for a review of these concepts.

result in gaps in coverage if all eligible individuals do not satisfy a given indicator. Ideal indicators should be highly correlated with poverty, easily observable, and exogenous or outside of the individual's control. In practice, it is difficult to find indicators that satisfy all of these criteria.

3. **Self-targeting:** this approach involves creating an incentive mechanism which induces individuals to identify themselves as eligible for a particular benefit. This may involve subsiding the prices of certain commodities which are usually consumed disproportionately by the poor (e.g. public transport in some contexts) or making access to benefits conditional on certain actions (e.g. workfare programmes where recipients' access to benefits is conditional on their participating in certain training schemes or actively looking for work).

A further important distinction is between contributory and non-contributory benefits. With **contributory benefits**, what individuals are entitled to receive depends on the number and level of their contributions, whereas access to **non-contributory benefits** does not depend on previous contributions. Social welfare schemes usually operate on a non-contributory basis and are financed through general taxation, but they tend to be means-tested. Social insurance schemes tend to operate on a contributory basis.

As we have seen, government intervention to tackle inequality and poverty can take many different forms. Some of these interventions will help promote equality of outcomes (e.g. tax and subsidy policies), whereas others can help promote equality of opportunity, targeting the underlying causes of poverty and inequality (e.g. labour market and education policies).

12.6 Challenges of designing effective redistributive policies

We touched on the problem of moral hazard in the provision of private unemployment insurance in section 12.4. Social insurance and social welfare schemes face the same problem, which has implications for economic efficiency. Both social insurance and social welfare schemes provide benefits to individuals, and these benefits can affect individual incentives to work and save. We discussed the impact of publicly provided pensions on the incentives to save in Chapter 11. In this section, we are going to focus on how welfare benefits affect individual incentives to work. We then explore how insights from the field of behavioural economics can inform the design of redistributive policies. Lastly, we discuss some of the economic and political limits to redistribution.

12.6.1 Impact of welfare benefits on incentives to work

The level of benefits provided and the rate at which benefits are tapered or reduced as an individual's income increases can affect both the number of hours an individual chooses to work and the decision whether to work at all (the participation decision), resulting in a **poverty trap** or an **unemployment trap**. Although these terms are often used interchangeably, they refer to slightly different things:

- The **unemployment trap** arises when an individual who is unemployed has little financial incentive to look for work, as the rate at which benefits are withdrawn when they start working means that the increase in their total income is marginal.
- The **poverty trap** arises when an individual has no financial incentive to work longer hours because for every additional pound/euro earned, they are losing a pound/euro or more in means-tested benefits (i.e. they face a high implicit tax rate).

We can illustrate these problems using the neoclassical model of labour supply.[38] In this model, individuals do not derive utility from working directly; instead, they derive utility from the complementary good, leisure, and from the income they receive from working. Rather than modelling labour supply directly, we model an individual's choice over two goods—hours of leisure and income—and then derive their labour supply from their optimal choice of leisure. We assume individuals spend their time either working or enjoying leisure, so their labour supply (the number of hours worked) is just the difference between the total hours available and their utility-maximizing hours of leisure.

This model is illustrated in Figure 12.6, where hours of leisure h, are measured along the horizontal axis, and income M, is measured along the vertical axis. Individuals are assumed to have a total time endowment of T, which they can allocate between leisure and working. Hours of leisure are measured from left to right, while hours of work are measured from right to left along the horizontal axis. Suppose that, initially, the only income Alfie can earn is by working at a constant hourly wage rate w. If Alfie spends all of his time working, his leisure time will be zero and he will receive a maximum income of $w \cdot T$ (point P in the figure). If instead Alfie decides not to work at all, he will enjoy total leisure time T and his income will be zero (point Q in the figure). We assume Alfie can choose to work any number of hours between zero and T, and the line connecting these two extremes, PQ, is Alfie's budget constraint, which represents the various possible combinations of hours worked and income.[39] The slope of the budget line is given by the wage rate w, which is the price of leisure.[40] Alfie's utility-maximizing choice is the point where the budget line is tangent to his highest possible indifference curve, illustrated by point A in the figure. Here, Alfie enjoys h_1 hours of leisure, which implies l_1 hours of work (where $l_1 = T - h$), and receives an income $M_1 = w \cdot l_1$.

Now suppose the government introduces a scheme where individuals receive a guaranteed benefit level S, but face a benefit reduction rate (or implicit tax rate) of 100 per cent, so the level of benefits received falls by £1 for every £1 in earnings. With this programme, Alfie's new budget constraint is given by CBP. If Alfie decides not to work ($l = 0$), he will receive an income of S and enjoy T hours of leisure. For any number of hours worked between zero and l_2, Alfie's income will still equal the guaranteed benefit level S because of the 100 per cent benefit reduction rate, so working more hours will not increase his income. If Alfie works more than l_2 hours, he will not receive any of the benefit and his income will be determined by the number of hours worked and the wage rate.

[38] The set-up of this model is similar to the consumer choice model discussed in Chapter 2. See section 2.2.3 for a review of the relevant concepts.

[39] For example, suppose we are analysing Alfie's decision over the course of a day, so the maximum number of hours of work or leisure is 16 (assuming he has to sleep 8 hours). If the hourly wage is £20 per hour, the maximum income Alfie can earn in a day is $w \cdot T = 20 \cdot 16 = 320$ and the maximum hours of leisure he can enjoy is 16 hours. The budget line will be the line connecting these two points.

[40] The cost of one additional hour of leisure time is just the income Alfie would have earned if he had chosen to work instead.

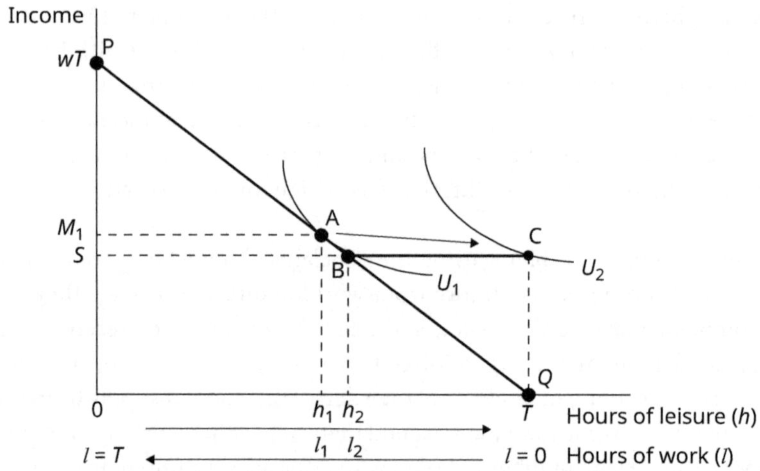

Figure 12.6 Welfare benefits and individual labour supply

How will this programme affect the number of hours Alfie chooses to work? Point A is no longer Alfie's utility-maximizing choice, since his old indifference curve U_1 passes below the new budget constraint CBP. To maximize his utility, Alfie should choose point C on the higher indifference curve U_2. This implies zero hours of work and an income equal to S. So in this example, the introduction of the welfare programme would encourage Alfie not to work. This would also be true for any individual whose initial utility-maximizing choice involved working fewer than l_2 hours, along the line segment BQ—they would be better off by not working and taking the guaranteed benefit income S. However, for individuals working more than l_2 hours, along the line segment BP, the programme might not affect their labour supply decision; this will depend on their preferences and the shape of their indifference curves.

In reality, the budget constraints that individuals face when they are eligible for multiple benefits are far more complex than the one illustrated in Figure 12.6. Different benefits may be reduced at different rates, and individuals will be liable to start paying taxes once their earnings exceed a certain threshold. This can result in budget constraints with multiple flat segments where the financial incentives to increase hours worked are removed. The **effective marginal tax rate** is the tax rate individuals face on each additional pound or euro earned taking into account both the impact of income taxes and the withdrawal of means-tested benefits.

So, as well as the cost of providing the welfare benefits themselves, there is an additional efficiency cost that arises as a result of the impact of benefits on incentives to work. Evidence on the extent of these incentive effects has been mixed, but it suggests that both the level of the benefits and their duration can have an impact on labour supply (see Box 12.7). There is also the cost associated with raising the revenues required to fund these government programmes. In most cases, these are funded by taxes, which introduce further distortions.[41]

However, there are steps governments can take in designing redistributive policies to help minimize these disincentive effects. One option is to lower the benefit reduction rate, so that the benefit to individuals from increasing their hours of work is increased. Whether this

[41] See Chapters 13 to 15.

reduces the disincentives to work will depend on individual preferences and where along the budget constraint their initial utility-maximizing choices lie. Other strategies governments can use include reducing the generosity of benefits by reducing the replacement rate,[42] adopting better targeting of benefits, and increasing the costs of accessing benefits—for example, by requiring individuals to attend appointments or complete training courses. While these strategies may help reduce the efficiency cost of providing benefits, they also have implications for equity. Several countries have introduced policies which subsidize employment rather than unemployment—for example, through the use of tax credits—and evidence suggests that these can be effective in increasing employment, at least for single people (Millar, 2008). However, these policies do not support individuals who are out of work.

Box 12.7 Do unemployment benefits increase unemployment?

Over 70 countries worldwide provide some form of unemployment insurance, including all countries in the OECD. The programmes vary across countries, but the majority are based on mandatory social insurance and eligibility for benefits depends on having made a minimum level of contributions. Individuals may face a waiting period before being eligible to receive benefits and both the level and duration of the benefits varies across countries. Across the OECD, the duration of unemployment benefits ranges from under six months in Hungary, the USA, and the Czech Republic to four years or more in Chile and Belgium (OECD, 2023b). The level of unemployment benefits is measured as a percentage of pre-unemployment earnings—the replacement rate—and is often subject to a maximum benefit level. Replacement rates for single low earners range from 50 per cent to 80 per cent of previous earnings, and tend to be lower for higher earners (OECD, 2023b). In most countries, individuals are required to actively look for work to receive unemployment benefits.

Estimating the impact of unemployment insurance on labour supply in practice is challenging. Studies have focused on estimating duration elasticities, which measure how sensitive the duration of unemployment is to changes in either the level of unemployment benefits or their duration (i.e. the length of time individuals can receive benefits for). The results suggest that unemployment is slightly more sensitive to the level of benefits than the duration of benefits, but this varies across countries. Unemployment duration elasticities with respect to the level of unemployment benefits range from 0.1 to 2, with a median value of 0.53.[43] Elasticities with respect to the duration of benefits range from 0.1 to 1, with a median value of 0.37 (Schmieder & Wachter, 2016).

In practice, people are not only motivated to work by monetary incentives. Individuals may derive utility from work itself, over and above the income earned. For example, work can contribute positively to individual identify or sense of self, and provide a basis for developing wider social networks. Welfare support also means that individuals can turn down bad jobs and devote time to developing new skills.

[42] The replacement rate measures the income individuals receive when not working as a proportion of their income when working.

[43] An estimated elasticity of 0.5 means that a 1 per cent increase in the level of benefits leads to a 0.5 per cent increase in the duration of unemployment, on average.

12.6.2 Insights from behavioural economics

The key to designing effective redistributive policies lies in understanding how individuals are likely to respond to these policies. While the neoclassical model discussed above can help us understand individual behaviour, it relies on a set of fairly strong assumptions and its predictions about how individuals should behave do not always match how individuals actually behave.[44] Behavioural economics recognizes that individual decisions are shaped by a range of factors and can provide a more holistic view of individual behaviour, which can help inform the design of redistributive policies.[45] These include the following:

- **Bounded rationality**: real-world decisions will often fall short of the utility-maximizing ideal because individual rationality is limited by the information individuals have available and their ability to process that information. This, in turn, will depend on the complexity of the information, and individual time and cognitive limitations. This suggests that designing a more complex benefit system can help reduce costs by deterring fraudulent claims, discouraging people who are not eligible for benefits from applying for them. This may involve the use of screening processes (e.g. requiring individuals to provide evidence of their entitlement to benefits, or carrying out interviews) or increasing the ordeal associated with particular screening processes (e.g. making forms more complex). While this might reduce fraudulent benefit claims, it also increases the scope for mistakes to be made and may discourage eligible individuals from applying.
- **Framing**: the way in which information is presented affects the choices individuals make. The framing of benefits is not neutral, and the label attached to benefits affects how they are used. For example, evidence suggests that Winter Fuel Payments[46] are more likely to be used to fund household energy consumption when compared with other sources of income.
- **Time inconsistency**: the frequency and timing of benefit payments can have an impact on behaviour. Providing benefits in larger but less frequent instalments (e.g. monthly rather than weekly payments) can help households develop important budgeting skills. However, many individuals are prone to problems of self-control, which may result in hardship if benefit payments are spent too soon and households are left with little or no resources to support them until they receive their next payment.
- **Social preferences**: evidence suggests that individuals are only imperfectly self-interested: they care not only about their own well-being, but also about the well-being of others. These social preferences can influence the extent to which individuals support redistributive policies, potentially reducing the distortionary effects of the taxes raised to finance redistributive schemes.

[44] See the discussion in Chapter 2.

[45] See Congdon et al. (2011) and Leicester et al. (2012) for a more complete discussion of these issues.

[46] The Winter Fuel Payment was a universal benefit paid to all individuals over the state pension age in the UK to help them meet the costs of heating their homes in winter.

12.6.3 The limits to redistribution

The economist Arthur Okun compared the process of income redistribution to a 'leaky bucket'. When redistributing income, he argued:

> The money must be carried from the rich to the poor in a leaky bucket. Some of it will simply disappear in transit, so the poor will not receive all the money that is taken from the rich. (Okun, 1975: 91)

There are three sources of 'leakages': the reduced incentives to work for those who receive welfare benefits; the reduced incentives to work and save as a result of the taxes required to fund redistributive programmes; and the administrative costs, which in the case of means-tested benefits can be significant. If these disincentive effects are sufficiently strong, this can have a significant impact on the economy as a whole, reducing economic growth. And lower growth implies fewer resources available to redistribute. This highlights the possible trade-off between achieving greater equity, through redistribution, and promoting economic efficiency.

There are also political barriers to redistribution. High-income and wealthy groups typically enjoy greater political influence than lower-income groups, who are the main beneficiaries of redistributive policies, and wealthier groups will have greater incentives to oppose redistributive policies, since they will bear most of the burden of financing these policies. Information plays a vital role in politics, and wealthy individuals are better positioned to acquire it. Combined, these factors may lead to strong political opposition to more redistributive policies. However, this ignores the negative externalities associated with poverty and inequality, and the potential for social preferences to increase support for redistributive policies. Society as a whole stands to benefit from lower levels of poverty and inequality.

12.7 Policy applications

Well-designed redistributive policies can play an important role in reducing poverty and inequality. However, welfare benefits can undermine incentives to work and save, as well as potentially being open to abuse and fraud. Social spending is one of the largest areas of government expenditure; it is therefore important to ensure policies are designed in a way that maximizes their effectiveness. But how should the effectiveness of redistributive policies be assessed? Box 12.8 outlines four criteria that are useful for assessing tax and transfer-based policies.[47] In this section, we apply these criteria to two particular policies: a **universal basic income** and a UK-based policy, Universal Credit.[48]

[47] These criteria are based on Barr (2020).

[48] See suggestions in the Further Reading at the end of the chapter for more in-depth discussions of these policies.

Box 12.8 Criteria for assessing redistributive policies

There are different ways of assessing the effectiveness of redistributive policies. Four useful criteria comprise the following (Barr, 2020):

- **Adequacy**: is the level of benefits sufficient to allow households to achieve an acceptable standard of living and reduce poverty? This will depend in part on how poverty is defined—in particular, whether we adopt an absolute or a relative measure of poverty. Adequacy covers both the money value of the benefits and any costs attached to receiving benefits, such as stigma costs, which will decrease individual utility for a given level of benefits.
- **Coverage**: this includes whether the benefits go to all individuals who need them, leaving no gaps in coverage (horizontal efficiency); and whether the benefits go only to individuals who need them, ensuring there are no leakages in the system (vertical efficiency). There may be gaps in the coverage of benefits for supply-side reasons—for example, some eligible individuals may not be awarded benefits due to financial pressures on the organization responsible for awarding them. Take-up of benefits may also be incomplete for demand-side reasons, where eligible individuals may not claim benefits due to ignorance (not being aware they are entitled to them) or the costs of claiming benefits—which include stigma costs, as well as the time costs of accessing relevant information, gathering necessary paperwork, and filling out forms. Coverage will depend on how well the benefits are targeted. More tightly targeted benefits will help reduce leakages, but this involves a cost (see Box 12.6).
- **Cost**: this includes the cost of the benefits themselves and administrative costs. Administrative costs can be significant, particularly in the case of means-tested benefits, because of the cost of measuring individual incomes and the need to review entitlements on a regular basis.
- **Incentive effects**: how do benefits affect individual incentives to work and save? This will depend on factors including the level of benefits, how long individuals can claim benefits for, and how different benefits within the system interact with one another.

There may be trade-off between achieving different criteria. For example, ensuring welfare payments are set at a level which is adequate to reduce poverty has implications for costs.

12.7.1 Universal basic income

A universal basic income (UBI) is a flat payment provided by the government to all individuals regardless of age, gender, race, labour market status, or income. The idea of a UBI has a long history and it is a policy that has been gaining in popularity in recent years, particularly as the rise in automation threatens to displace many jobs. UBI experiments have been carried out in a wide range of countries, including Kenya, Finland, Namibia, India, the USA, and Canada.

UBI policies vary depending on the level of the payment made to individuals and how the scheme is funded. In its simplest form, UBI operates as a **negative income tax**, where all individuals are guaranteed a minimum level of income: individuals earning below this level receive payments from the government, while individuals earning above this level pay a proportional or progressive tax.[49]

We can apply the criteria discussed above to assess the effectiveness of a UBI:

- **Adequacy**: this will depend on the level at which the UBI is set, but is it financially (and politically) feasible to set a UBI at a sufficiently high level to provide an acceptable standard of living? As a UBI is by definition universal, there should be no stigma costs attached to it.
- **Coverage**: as the UBI is universal, it is paid to all individuals regardless of their level of income, wealth, or individual need. This ensures horizontal efficiency, but it also means the benefit is poorly targeted—it is not only being paid to individuals who need it, and therefore does not support vertical efficiency.
- **Cost**: a UBI would imply lower administrative costs, as the benefit is universal and therefore would not involve the costs usually associated with administering and monitoring means-tested benefits. However, the cost of providing the UBI itself would be substantial. The OECD estimated the cost of introducing a UBI in a selection of countries and found that tax revenues would need to increase significantly to provide a UBI at a meaningful level (OECD, 2017a). Estimates for the UK suggest the cost of providing a UBI would range from £140 billion to £427 billion, depending on the level of the benefits provided (Martinelli, 2017).[50]
- **Incentive effects**: the impact of a UBI on incentives to work will depend on individual labour supply elasticities, which are likely to vary with individual income levels. In a UBI experiment carried out in Finland, 2,000 unemployed Finns were selected at random to receive a flat monthly payment of €560. There was no evidence of a significant increase or decrease in unemployment, although there was a lower incidence of reported health problems, suggesting the policy did have a positive impact on well-being (De Wispelaere et al., 2023).

12.7.2 Universal Credit

Universal Credit (UC) is a UK-based welfare policy which was introduced in 2013 and gradually rolled out across the country. The policy aimed to simplify the UK benefits system by combining six of the previously existing means-tested benefits for working-age adults into a single benefit called Universal Credit.[51] The benefit is paid monthly in arrears, and it can take up to five weeks after making a claim to receive the first payment. A single payment is made to families rather than being paid to individuals within families. In 2025, the standard allowance was £400.14 for single individuals aged 25 or over, and £628.10 for couples.[52]

[49] See Figure 15.8 in Chapter 15 for an illustration of a negative income tax.

[50] By comparison, total spending on benefits in the UK in 2016/17 was £210 billion.

[51] These six benefits were Income Support, income-based Job Seekers Allowance, income-related Employment and Support Allowance, housing benefit, child tax credit, and working tax credit.

[52] The allowances for individuals or couples aged under 25 are slightly lower.

Individuals may be eligible for additional payments depending on whether they have children and whether they have a health condition or disability. Additional support with housing and childcare costs is also available in some cases.

Assessing Universal Credit against the criteria above:

- **Adequacy**: there are concerns that the level of benefits provided under UC is not high enough to guarantee an acceptable standard of living. While some individuals saw their benefit payments increase under UC, many receive less than they would have under the previous benefits system. The fact that UC is paid in arrears and that it can take up to five weeks to receive the first payment can lead to significant financial hardship. However, the labelling of the benefit as Universal Credit means that stigma costs should be reduced.
- **Coverage**: since access to UC is conditional on meeting certain requirements, issues of coverage still arise and it is not clear whether the benefit is going to everyone who needs it. The majority of claims are made online, which has led to an increase in the number of fraudulent claims, while at the same time potentially excluding some individuals from accessing the benefit, namely those who do not have access to a computer or the internet.
- **Cost**: by combining multiple benefits into a single benefit and requiring most claims to be made online, this has the potential to reduce administrative costs. However, administrative costs increased during the initial transition period.
- **Incentive effects**: there are no limits on how many hours a week individuals can work if they are claiming UC. The amount received will gradually reduce as people's earnings increase, but benefits are not all lost at once. This helps strengthen incentives to work.

Conclusion

Income inequality and poverty remain pressing problems in many countries across the world today. Widening income gaps and stagnant or falling living standards matter for individual well-being, but also for social cohesion, as high levels of income inequality are associated with a decrease in political trust and threaten to undermine democracy. Government intervention to tackle inequality and poverty can take many different forms, ranging from income support and social insurance schemes to cover periods of sickness, unemployment, or retirement, to minimum wages and publicly provided services such as education and healthcare. But designing effective redistributive policies is challenging. Should policies focus on redistributing income or should they focus on developing human capital by investing in education and health? Should benefits be provided in cash or in kind? Should benefits be universal or targeted to those who need them? How can welfare benefits be designed to minimize distortions on individual incentives to work and save?

We also need to consider the broader economic and political context in which policies are designed and enacted. If the disincentive effects of policies are substantial, this can have a negative impact on economic growth, and lower growth implies fewer resources available to redistribute. High-income and wealthy groups typically enjoy greater political influence than lower-income groups, and wealthier individuals may have greater incentives to oppose redistributive policies, thus making it more difficult for governments to tackle the problems of poverty and inequality.

Questions for discussion

1. Suppose there are two individuals, Anna and Bill, who each earn an income of £30,000. Are they necessarily equal? What if Anna earns £40,000 and Bill earns £20,000. Are they necessarily unequal?
2. Will policies aimed at reducing poverty always help reduce inequality?
3. Why do government provide social insurance against the risk of unemployment, sickness, and disability, rather than simply making private insurance mandatory?
4. Should there be a maximum wage as well as a minimum wage?
5. Why might universal benefits be more effective in alleviating poverty than means-tested benefits that are targeted at those most in need?

Further reading

For a more in-depth discussion of inequality, poverty, and redistributive policies:

Atkinson, A. B., Piketty, T., & Saez, E. (2011). Top incomes in the long run of history. *Journal of Economic Literature*, *49*(1), 3–71. https://doi.org/10.1257/jel.49.1.3

Barr, N. (2020). *The economics of the welfare state* (6th ed.). Oxford University Press.

Deaton, A., Attanasio, O., Banks, J., Berkman, L., Besley, T., Blundell, R., Goldberg, P., Johnson, P., Joyce, R., Kiernan, K., Platt, L., Rasul, I., Satz, D., & Tirole, J. (Eds.). (2024). *Dimensions of inequality: The IFS Deaton Review*, Vol. 3, Issue Supplement 1. Oxford University Press.

Hills, J., McKnight, A., Bucelli, I., Karagiannaki, E., Vizard, P., Duque, M., & Rucci, M. (2019). *Understanding the relationship between poverty and inequality: Overview report* (no. 119). Centre for Analysis of Social Exclusion.

Piketty, T. (2014). *Capital in the twenty-first century*. Harvard University Press.

For a discussion of the properties of social welfare functions:

Cowell, F. A. (2011). *Measuring inequality* (3rd ed.) Oxford University Press.

On the effectiveness of redistributive policies in tackling inequality:

Doerrenberg, P., & Peichl, A. (2014). The impact of redistributive policies on inequality in OECD countries. *Applied Economics*, *46*(17), 2066–2086.

On gender inequality and public policy:

Gornick, J. C. (2004). Women's economic outcomes, gender inequality and public policy: Findings from the Luxembourg Income Study. *Socio-Economic Review*, *2*(2), 213–238.

Ponthieux, S., & Meurs, D. (2015). Gender inequality. In A. B. Atkinson & F. Bourguignon (Eds.), *Handbook of income distribution* (Vol. 2, pp. 981–1146). Elsevier.

Sauer, P., Rehm, M., & Mader, K. (2021). Gender and income inequality. In K. F. Zimmermann (Ed.), *Handbook of labor, human resources and population economics* (pp. 1–24). Springer.

On race and ethnic inequalities in the UK:

Mirza, H. S., & Warwick, R. (2024). Race and ethnic inequalities. *Oxford Open Economics*, *3*(Supplement 1), i365–i452.

On the implications of behavioural economics for the design of redistributive policies:

Congdon, W. J., Kling, J.R., & Mullainathan, S. (2011). *Policy and choice: Public finance through the lens of behavioural economics*. The Brookings Institution.

Leicester, A., Levell, P., & Rasul, I. (2012). Tax and benefit policy: Insights from behavioural economics. Institute for Fiscal Studies commentary C125. Available at: https://www.ucl.ac.uk/~uctpimr/research/IFScomm125.pdf

On a universal basic income:

Banerjee, A., Niehaus, P., & Suri, T. (2019). Universal basic income in the developing world. *Annual Review of Economics, 11*, 959–983.

Hoynes, H., & Rothstein, J. (2019). Universal basic income in the United States and advanced countries. *Annual Review of Economics, 11*, 929–958.

Martinelli, L. (2017). *Assessing the case for a universal basic income in the UK*. IPR policy brief. Institute for Policy Research, University of Bath.

OECD (2017a). *Basic income as a policy option: Can it add up?* Policy brief on the future of work. Organization for Economic Cooperation and Development.

OECD (2017b). *Basic income as a policy option: Technical background note illustrating costs and distributional implications for selected countries*. Jobs and Income Division, Organization for Economic Cooperation and Development.

On Universal Credit:

Brewer, M., Browne, J., & Jin, W. (2012). Universal Credit: A preliminary analysis of its impact on incomes and work incentives. *Fiscal Studies, 33*(1), 39–71.

Brewer, M., Dang, T., & Tominey, E. (2024). Universal Credit: Welfare reform and mental health. *Journal of Health Economics, 98*, art. 102940.

Bibliography

Aaberge, R., Langørgen, A., & Lindgren, P. (2013). *The distributional impact of public services in European countries*. Econstor working papers, no. 746. Available at: https://www.econstor.eu/handle/10419/192728

Atkinson, A. B., Piketty, T., & Saez, E. (2011). Top incomes in the long run of history. *Journal of Economic Literature, 49*(1), 3–71. https://doi.org/10.1257/jel.49.1.3

Atkinson, A.B. (1970). On the measurement of inequality. *Journal of Economic Theory, 2*, 244–63.

Atkinson, A. B. (1983). *The economics of inequality* (2nd ed.). Clarendon Press.

Balestra, C., & R. Tonkin (2018). *Inequalities in household wealth across OECD countries: Evidence from the OECD wealth distribution database*. Organization for Economic Cooperation and Development statistics working papers, no. 2018/01. Available at: https://doi.org/10.1787/7e1bf673-en

Barr, N. (2020). *The economics of the welfare state* (6th ed.). Oxford University Press.

Brewer, M., Browne, J., & Jin, W. (2012). Universal Credit: A preliminary analysis of its impact on incomes and work incentives. *Fiscal Studies, 33*(1), 39–71.

Cingano, F. (2014). *Trends in income inequality and its impact on economic growth*. Organization for Economic Cooperation and Development social, employment and migration working papers, no. 163.

Congdon, W. J., Kling, J. R., & Mullainathan, S. (2011). *Policy and choice: Public finance through the lens of behavioural economics*. The Brookings Institution.

Deaton, A., Attanasio, O., Banks, J., Berkman, L., Besley, T., Blundell, R., Goldberg, P., Johnson, P., Joyce, R., Kiernan, K., Platt, L., Rasul, I., Satz, D., & Tirole, J. (Eds.). (2024). *Dimensions of inequality: The IFS Deaton review*, Vol. 3, Issue Supplement 1. Oxford University Press.

De Wispelaere, J., Halmetoja, A., & Pulkka, V.-V. (2023). A primer on the Finnish basic income experiment: From design and implementation to evaluation and impact. In M. Torry (Ed.), *The Palgrave international handbook of basic income* (pp. 413–435). Springer.

Foster, J. E. (1984). On economic poverty: A survey of aggregate measures. *Advances in Econometrics*, 3, 215–251.

Foster, J. E., Greer, J., and Thorbecke, E. (1984). A class of decomposable poverty measures. *Econometrica, 52*, 761–767.

Foster, J. E., & Shorrocks, A. F. (1991). Subgroup consistent poverty indices. *Econometrica*, *59*(3), 687–709.

Giddens, A. (1999). Notes on social justice and the welfare state. In R. Walker (Ed.), *Ending child poverty: Popular welfare for the 21st century*. Policy Press.

Hasell, J., Rohenkohl, B., Arriagada, P., Ortiz-Ospina, E., & Roser, M. (2022). *Poverty*. Available at: https://ourworldindata.org/poverty

Hasell, J., Rohenkohl, B., Arriagada, P., Ortiz-Ospina, E., & Roser, M. (2023). *Economic inequality*. Available at: https://ourworldindata.org/economic-inequality

Hills, J., McKnight, A., Bucelli, I., Karagiannaki, E., Vizard, P., Duque, M., & Rucci, M. (2019). *Understanding the relationship between poverty and inequality: Overview report* (no. 119). Centre for Analysis of Social Exclusion.

Hindriks, J., & Myles, G. D. (2013). *Intermediate public economics*. MIT Press.

Jenkins, S. P. (2011). *Changing fortunes: Income mobility and poverty dynamics in Britain*. Oxford University Press.

Le Grand, J., Propper, C., & Smith, S. (2008). *The economics of social problems* (4th ed.). Palgrave Macmillan.

Leicester, A., Levell, P., & Rasul, I. (2012). Tax and benefit policy: Insights from behavioural economics. Institute for Fiscal Studies commentary C125. Available at: https://www.ucl.ac.uk/~uctpimr/research/IFScomm125.pdf

Martinelli, L. (2017). *Assessing the case for a universal basic income in the UK*. IPR policy brief. Institute for Policy Research, University of Bath.

Millar, J. (2008). Making work pay, making tax credits work: An assessment with specific reference to lone-parent employment. *International Social Security Review*, *61*(2), 21–38.

Mirza, H. S., & Warwick, R. (2024). Race and ethnic inequalities. *Oxford Open Economics*, *3*(Supplement 1), i365–i452.

OECD (2009). *OECD factbook 2009: Economic, environmental and social statistics*. Organization for Economic Cooperation and Development.

OECD (2017a). *Basic income as a policy option: Can it add up?* Policy brief on the future of work. Organization for Economic Cooperation and Development.

OECD (2023a). *Reporting gender pay gaps in OECD countries: Guidance for pay transparency implementation, monitoring and reform*. Organization for Economic Cooperation and Development.

OECD (2023b). *Income support for jobseekers: Trade-offs and current reforms*. Organization for Economic Cooperation and Development.

OECD (2024). *Society at a glance 2024: OECD social indicators*. Organization for Economic Cooperation and Development.

OECD (2025a). *Income distribution database*. OECD data explorer. https://data-explorer.oecd.org (accessed 29 August 2025).

OECD (2025b). *Social expenditure aggregates*. OECD data explorer. https://data-explorer.oecd.org (accessed 20 September 2025).

Okun, A. (1975). *Equality and efficiency: The big tradeoff.* The Brookings Institution.

ONS (2015). *Family spending in the UK: Calendar year 2014.* Chapter 3: Equivalised income. Office for National Statistics. Available at: https://www.ons.gov.uk/peoplepopulationandcommunity/personalandhouseholdfinances/incomeandwealth/compendium/familyspending/2015/chapter3equivalisedincome

Piketty, T. (2014). *Capital in the twenty-first century.* Harvard University Press.

Ponthieux, S., & Meurs, D. (2015). Gender inequality. In A. B. Atkinson & F. Bourguignon (Eds.), *Handbook of income distribution* (Vol. 2, pp. 981–1146). Elsevier.

Roemer, J. (2000). *Equality of opportunity.* Harvard University Press.

Sauer, P., Rehm, M., & Mader, K. (2021). Gender and income inequality. In K. F. Zimmermann (Ed.), *Handbook of labor, human resources and population economics* (pp. 1–24). Springer.

Schmieder, J. F., & Wachter, T. von. (2016). The effects of unemployment insurance benefits: New evidence and interpretation. *Annual Review of Economics*, *8*, 547–581.

Sen, A. (1976). Poverty: An ordinal approach to measurement. *Econometrica*, 44(2), 219–231.

Sen, A. K. (1993). Capability and Well-being. In M. Nussbaum & A. Sen (Eds.), The Quality of Life (pp. 30–53). Oxford: Clarendon Press.

Sen, A. K. (1997). *On economic inequality.* Oxford University Press.

Sen, A. K. (1998). Economic policy and equity: An overview. In V. Tanzi, K. Chu, & S. Gupta (Eds.), *Economic policy and equity* (pp. 44–48). International Monetary Fund.

Social Metrics Commission (2018). *A new measure of poverty for the UK.*

Work and Pensions Committee (2019). *Universal credit: Natural migration.* Available at: https://publications.parliament.uk/pa/cm201719/cmselect/cmworpen/1884/188402.htm

World Inequality Database (WID.world) (2025). *Income inequality: Palma ratio (before tax)—World inequality database* [original data]. Retrieved 20 September 2025 from https://archive.ourworldindata.org/20250909-093708/grapher/palma-ratio-s90s40-ratio.html (archived 9 September 2025).

Inequality measures derived from explicit welfare assumptions

The second approach to deriving measures of inequality involves starting from explicit assumptions about the form of the social welfare function—in particular, how the welfare of the individuals in society should be combined to determine social welfare. For example, should social welfare be a function of the sum of the welfare of all individuals (as with a utilitarian social welfare function), or should social welfare be a function of the welfare of the least well-off individual in society (as in the Rawlsian social welfare function)?

One of the best-known measures of inequality derived using this approach is the Atkinson measure of inequality, named after the British economist Anthony Atkinson. This is given by:

$$A(\varepsilon)=1-\left[\frac{1}{H}\sum_{h=1}^{H}\left(\frac{y_h}{\mu}\right)^{1-\varepsilon}\right]^{\frac{1}{1-\varepsilon}}$$

Here, ε captures the sensitivity to transfers between rich and poor, or the extent of inequality aversion, H is the number of households, y_h is the equivalized household income for household h, and μ is mean income. The Atkinson measure of inequality will equal zero either if income is equally distributed (y_h equals μ for all households) or if society is not concerned with the distribution of income (ε equals zero). Measured inequality will be greater, the higher the value of ε or the greater the deviation between household incomes y_h and mean income μ.

The Atkinson measure of inequality provides a complete ranking of income distributions and makes the underlying welfare assumptions explicit. The main criticism of this measure is the fact that it relies on an additive social welfare function and assumes that social welfare is simply the sum of individual utilities.

The Foster–Greer–Thorbecke poverty measures

The headcount ratio and the poverty gap are part of a class of decomposable poverty measures known as the Foster–Greer–Thorbecke (FGT) poverty measures (Foster et al., 1984). This class of measures have the general form:

$$P_\alpha=\frac{1}{H}\sum_{h=1}^{q}\left(\frac{z-y_h}{z}\right)^{\alpha}$$

where z is the poverty line, H is total population, $(z-y_h)/z$ is the normalized income gap, and α is a poverty aversion parameter. P_α is then a measure of average poverty in the population. If $\alpha=0$, then the measure reduces to the headcount ratio, whereas if $\alpha=1$, then the average poverty measure becomes the product of the income gap and the headcount ratio, or the poverty gap. Increasing α increases the weight given to the poorest of the poor in the average measure of poverty.

One important property of the FGT poverty measure is its decomposability. In empirical applications, we are often interested in estimating poverty rates for different groups of the population—for example, working adults and pensioners, or men and women. We therefore want a measure that will allow us to determine the poverty level of each group and to aggregate the poverty levels of different groups into a single measure of poverty for the whole population. Aggregate measured poverty should increase if poverty increases for one of the groups and does not decrease in any of the other groups. A poverty measure is subgroup-consistent if it satisfies this property. The FGT poverty measure is subgroup-consistent.

PART III
FINANCING THE GOVERNMENT

13
Introduction to taxation

Learning objectives

By the end of this chapter, you will be able to:

13.1 Explain the role of taxes in the economy and the different types of taxes that governments can use.
13.2 Discuss the properties of a good tax system and whether these properties are always mutually compatible.
13.3 Explain the challenges involved in determining the fairness of a tax system and what determines who bears the burden of a tax.
13.4 Explain how taxes affect economic efficiency and the wider economic costs of taxation.
13.5 Discuss whether income or consumption should form the basis of taxation.
13.6 Discuss some of the key challenges facing the design of tax policy today.

Introduction

Taxation is central to the existence of modern governments. In order to finance their activities, governments need to raise revenue, and in most countries the primary source of revenue is taxation. Taxes can be used to finance public spending that will have a positive impact on welfare—for example, building roads, bridges and cycle paths, or funding schools and hospitals. However, taxes also impose a significant cost on society. Taxes accounted for 34 per cent of GDP on average across the OECD in 2022 (OECD, 2025a), which represents a significant transfer of resources from individuals to the government. Taxes reduce individual spending power, raising the cost of goods and services or reducing disposable income. By changing the relative prices that individuals face, taxes also influence behaviour, affecting individual decisions about what to buy, how much to work and save, and when to marry or retire, as well as businesses' decisions about how much to invest and how to finance their investments. How can the costs of taxation be minimized? Who bears the burden of taxation? What makes a good tax system?

To answer these questions, we start by reviewing the purpose of taxation and the different types of taxes that governments use in section 13.1. We then discuss the properties of a good tax system in section 13.2. In section 13.3, we look at how we can measure the fairness of a tax system and explore the question of tax incidence, or who bears the burden of taxation. Section 13.4 focuses on the costs of taxation—in particular, the impact of taxes on economic efficiency—and in section 13.5, we discuss what the appropriate basis of taxation should be. Section 13.6 looks at some of the challenges of designing tax policy in the twenty-first century.

13.1 The purpose and main types of taxation

13.1.1 Why do we need taxes?

Taxation has a long history, dating back to Ancient Greek and Roman times (see Box 13.1). It has three principal purposes, described below.

Raising revenue

The primary purpose of taxation is to raise revenue to fund government expenditures.[1] Maintaining law and order, administering the legal system, enforcing property rights, defending a country's interests in an international context, providing vital infrastructure such as roads and bridges, investing in health and education—all of these government activities need to be financed. Taxation provides a means of requiring the individuals and firms that live or operate in a country to contribute towards the publicly provided goods and services that they benefit from.[2]

Income redistribution

Taxes can also be used alongside government transfers to redistribute income and help reduce poverty and inequality. As we saw in Chapter 12, income inequality has been rising across the OECD and government taxes and transfers play an important role in reducing measured inequality. A progressive tax system is one in which individuals earning a higher income pay a higher share of their income in taxes than lower-income individuals. This can be combined with a range of government transfer programmes, including unemployment and sickness benefits, child benefits, and housing subsidies, to redistribute income from higher-income to lower-income individuals. However, not all taxes are progressive, as we will see in section 13.3.

Corrective taxes

Finally, taxes (and subsidies) can be used to discourage or encourage consumption of certain goods and services. These are known as corrective taxes or Pigouvian taxes and are typically used to address externalities.[3] Externalities arise when the consumption or production of a good or service imposes a cost (or benefit) on society over and above the cost (or benefit) to the individual. Taxes can be used to bridge this gap between private and social costs, raising the price of the good or service and thereby discouraging consumption. Examples include environmental taxes on motor fuels or transport taxes, as well as various **sin taxes** on goods such as alcohol, tobacco, and sugary drinks. In other cases, subsidies or tax credits may be used to encourage certain types of behaviour, as in the case of R&D tax credits to encourage firms to invest in research and development.[4]

[1] Although the economist Abba Lerner (1903–1982) would argue that the main purpose of taxation is in fact to maintain the level of total spending in the economy relative to total output, to keep inflation and unemployment in check. If total spending is too high, the government can raise taxes to reduce private spending, and if total spending is too low, the government can cut taxes to boost private consumption (Lerner, 1943).

[2] Some of these are goods and services that would otherwise not be provided by the market, or would be under-provided. This is the case with public goods, which we discussed in Chapter 6.

[3] The concept of externalities was introduced in Chapter 2 and is discussed in more detail in the context of the environment in Chapter 9.

[4] Whereas taxes can be used to address a mismatch between private and social costs, subsidies are used to address mismatches between private and social benefits.

Box 13.1 A very brief history of taxation

The history of taxation dates at least as far back as Ancient Greek and Roman times, with taxes levied on consumption and property to raise additional revenues in times of war. For example, a 1 per cent general sales tax was introduced during the time of Julius Caesar. In the Middle Ages, taxes included land and property taxes, custom duties and aids,[5] head taxes (poll taxes) for the poor, and net worth taxes on the rich. These taxes were often levied to provide revenues for specific expenditures, such as military campaigns. Income taxes as we know them today are a more recent creation, normally attributed to the British prime minister William Pitt the Younger, who introduced a tax on income in 1799 to help fund the Revolutionary Wars against France.

As governments have grown, so too has the need to raise revenue through taxation, and while some taxes have been abandoned—such as the window tax introduced in England in 1696 and the newspaper tax adopted in 1712—others have grown in importance. Administrative considerations, related to the ease of collecting different types of taxes, have played an important role in explaining patterns of taxation throughout history. These help explain why import duties were among the earliest taxes, since imported products were easier to tax than domestic output, or why real estate was more often taxed than other assets. Administrative considerations continue to be important today, as changes in technology have made some types of taxes simpler and therefore less costly to collect.

Source: Britannica (n.d.).

13.1.2 Types of taxes

In theory, anything that can be measured can be taxed. Table 13.1 illustrates the range of different taxes, based on the classification system adopted by the OECD. This classification is particularly useful for comparing tax systems across countries. Taxes on income, wealth, and profits are generally referred to as **direct taxes**, whereas taxes on goods and services are known as **indirect taxes**. We discuss some of these different types of taxes below.

Direct taxes

Direct taxes are taxes imposed directly on the earnings of individuals and corporations, and include the following:

- **Income tax**: a tax levied on individual net income (i.e. gross income minus any tax reliefs); this includes income from employment and self-employment.
- **Social security contributions**: compulsory payments which are levied on individual income and which confer an entitlement to social security benefits, such as unemployment and disability insurance.
- **Capital gains tax**: a tax levied on the profits from selling capital assets, such as stocks, property, real estate, and artwork.

[5] An aid was a tax levied in medieval Europe, which was paid by individuals or communities to someone in authority, such as a feudal lord or the Crown.

Table 13.1 The OECD classification of taxes

1000	**Taxes on income, profits, and capital gains**			
	1100	Taxes on income, profits, and capital gains of individuals		
		1110. On income and profits		
		1120. On capital gains		
	1200	Corporate taxes on income, profits, and capital gains		
	1300	Unallocable as between 1100 and 1200		
2000	**Social security contributions**			
	2100	Employees		
	2200	Employers		
	2300	Self-employed or non-employed		
	2400	Unallocable as between 2100, 2200, and 2300		
3000	**Taxes on payroll and workforce**			
4000	**Taxes on property**			
	4100	Recurrent taxes on immovable property		
		4110. Households		
		4120. Other		
	4200	Recurrent taxes on net wealth		
		4210. Individual		
		4220. Corporate		
	4300	Estate, inheritance, and gift taxes		
	4400	Taxes on financial and capital transactions		
	4500	Other non-recurrent taxes on property		
	4600	Other recurrent taxes on property		
5000	**Taxes on goods and services**			
	5100	Taxes on the production, sale, transfer, leasing, and delivery of goods and rendering of services		
		5110	General taxes	
				5111. Value-added taxes
				5112. Sales taxes
				5113. Turnover and other general taxes on goods and services
		5120	Taxes on specific goods and services	
		5130	Unallocable as between 5110 and 5120	
	5200	Taxes on use of goods, or on permission to use goods or perform activities		
	5300	Unallocable as between 5100 and 5200		
6000	**Other taxes**			

Note: Some categories are subdivided further. See OECD (2021b) for full details. Taxes on specific goods and services (5120) include excises, customs and import duties, and taxes on exports.

- **Wealth taxes**: taxes levied not on the income earned from an asset, but on the asset value itself. These include **property taxes**, which are levied on the value of real estate owned, and **estate and inheritance taxes**, which are levied on any bequests (property, money, etc.) that are transferred when someone dies. In many countries, a separate tax applies to gifts, which are transfers of property, money, or other assets above a certain value made from a living person.
- **Corporate income** or **corporation tax**: a tax levied on the income of a corporation; the tax is normally levied on net profits (i.e. profits net of allowances for interest payments and depreciation costs).

Taxing individual income and wealth raises a series of important questions. How should individual income be defined and measured for tax purposes? Clearly it should include all earnings from employment or self-employment, but employers often offer additional fringe benefits, such as private health insurance or a company car—should these be covered by the income tax? What should be the appropriate unit of taxation—should it be the individual, married couples, or entire family units? Should everyone pay the same rate of tax or should this vary depending on income? If there are varying tax rates, how many different tax rates should there be? Should there be some form of tax relief—that is, a level of tax-free income that all individuals can earn? Should individuals be able to claim tax relief on certain expenditures—for example, donations to charity, work-related expenditures, mortgage interest payments, or pension payments? Some of these questions are discussed below, and others we return to in Chapter 15.

Direct taxes also include taxes on the income or net profits of corporations. In practice, *people* pay taxes, not corporations, so a corporation tax will either reduce the incomes of shareholders through after-tax lower profits and dividends, or the incomes of workers through lower wages, or the real incomes of consumers through higher prices. Who actually bears the burden of corporation taxes—is it shareholders, workers, or consumers? What expenses should corporations be allowed to deduct from their earnings for tax purposes? This can have an impact on their investment decisions. If firms can deduct interest payments from their taxable income, for example, they have an incentive to finance their investments by borrowing rather than through equity. Corporate taxes can also be used to encourage investment, by offering tax credits or tax allowances for capital expenditure.

Indirect taxes

Indirect taxes on goods and services include the following:

- **Sales tax**: a tax levied as a percentage of the price of goods and services, which consumers pay to sellers at the point of sale.
- **Value-added tax** (VAT): a general sales tax which is levied on the value added to goods and services at each stage in the production and distribution process.
- **Excise tax**: a special tax on the sale or use of a particular good, such as alcohol, tobacco, or energy.
- **Custom duties**: taxes on goods imported into a country.

Since they are levied on household consumption expenditures, indirect taxes generally suffer from fewer measurement problems compared to taxes on income and wealth, although this relies on the sellers of goods and services fully declaring all of their sales. Indirect taxes are generally regressive, since all individuals pay the same rate regardless of their income, although some goods and services may be exempt from tax or may be taxed at a lower rate. Should all goods and services be taxed and should they all be taxed at the same rate? If not, which goods should attract a lower or no tax rate? Is consumption a better basis for taxation than income? We return to these questions below and in Chapter 14, where we focus on taxes on goods and services.

The importance of these different taxes for government revenue varies across countries, as illustrated in Figure 13.1. The majority of government tax revenues come from individual income taxes, social security contributions, and taxes on goods and services, which together account for 80 per cent of government tax revenues for the OECD as a whole. The proportion of revenues raised from individual income taxes ranges from 13.6 per cent in Greece to over 50 per cent in Denmark, whereas corporate income taxes play a much less significant role in most countries, with the exception of Norway, where corporate income taxes accounted for over 40 per cent of all tax revenues in 2022. Indirect taxes on goods and services are an important source of government revenues across virtually all countries, accounting for, on average, just over 30 per cent of total tax revenues across the OECD, and over 40 per cent in Greece.

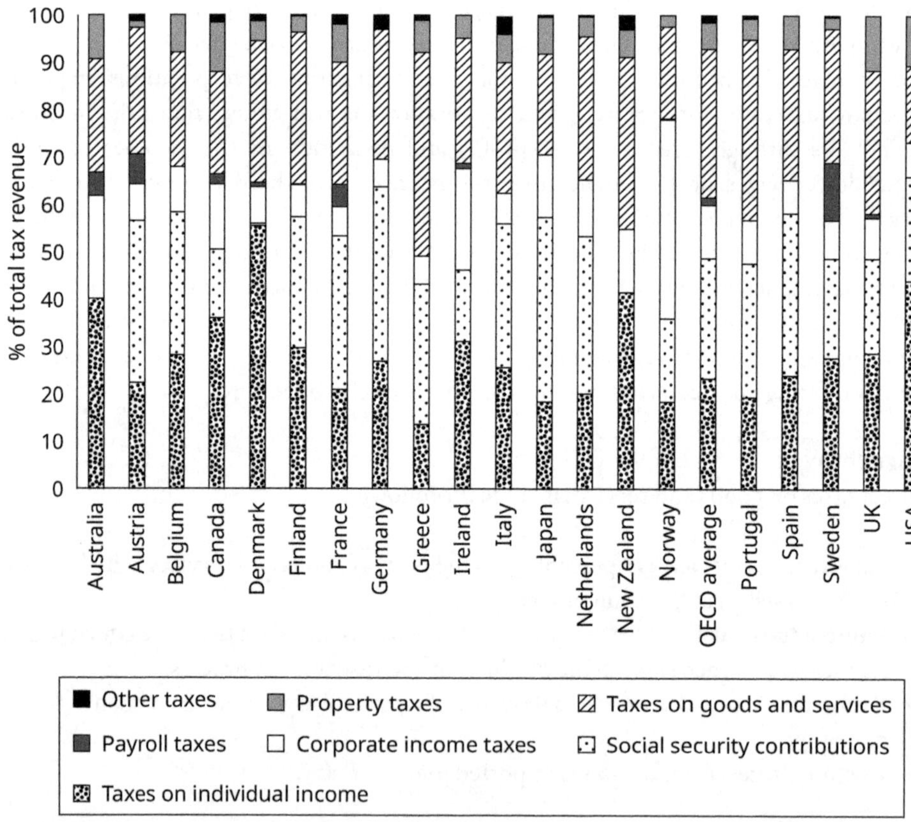

Figure 13.1 Sources of government tax revenue for selected OECD countries, 2022

Note: Figures as a percentage of total tax revenue for 2022. 'OECD average' represents average across all OECD countries.

Source: OECD (2025a).

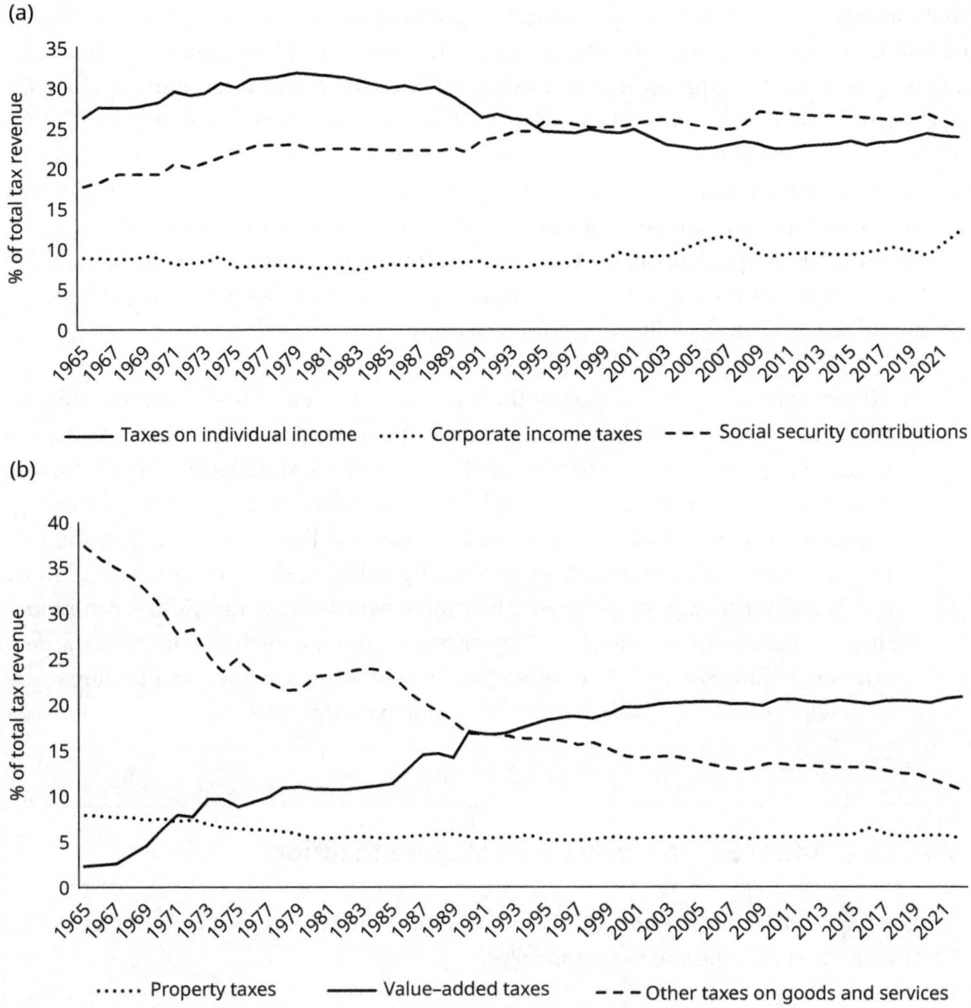

Figure 13.2 Evolution of the tax structure across the OECD, 1965–2022
Source: OECD (2025a).

The importance of these different sources of tax revenue has also changed over time, as Figure 13.2 shows. Across the OECD, the share of total tax revenues accounted for by taxes on personal and corporate income was not significantly different in 2022 compared to 1965, but the importance of social security contributions has increased during this period, from 17.6 per cent to 24.8 per cent of total tax revenues. In terms of indirect taxes, value-added taxes have clearly increased in importance, while the contribution of other taxes on goods and services to total tax revenue has declined steadily since 1965. The share of property taxes fell from 7.9 per cent to 5.3 per cent of total tax revenues.

13.2 Properties of a good tax system

What are the characteristics of a good tax system? To be able to answer this question, we first need to think about what society wants the tax system to achieve; we can then think about how best to design a tax system to achieve these objectives. As we saw above, aside from raising revenue to finance government expenditure, taxes can also be used to influence behaviour, discouraging activities that are deemed harmful to society, such as smoking or pollution, and encouraging socially beneficial activities, as well as to promote a fairer distribution of income. Which activities society wishes to encourage or discourage are likely to vary across time and place, and different societies will have different preferences for redistribution, and a different understanding of what a 'fair' distribution of income looks like. Given this, can we identify any general properties that all good tax systems should have?

Adam Smith famously laid out the four canons of taxation in *The Wealth of Nations* (1776) (see Box 13.2), which subsequent work has built on. It is generally agreed that a good tax system should be based on the following four properties:[6]

1. **Efficiency**: the negative impact of the tax system on welfare and economic efficiency should be minimized. All taxes reduce spending power and therefore have a negative impact on individual welfare. However, the vast majority of taxes are also **distortionary** because individuals and firms can reduce their tax liability by changing their behaviour. Taxes on goods and services are distortionary because individuals can reduce the amount of tax they pay by reducing their consumption of those goods and services. Income taxes are distortionary because individuals can reduce their tax liability by working less. Distortionary taxes are inefficient because the government could raise the same amount of revenue while having a smaller impact on individual welfare. We will return to this point in section 13.4.

Box 13.2 Adam Smith's principles of good taxation

In his work *The Wealth of Nations* (1776), Adam Smith argued that a good tax system should be based on the following four basic principles:

1. **Fairness**: 'The subjects of every state ought to contribute towards the support of the government, as nearly as possible, in proportion to their respective abilities . . .'
2. **Certainty**: 'The tax which each individual is bound to pay ought to be certain, and not arbitrary . . .'
3. **Convenience**: 'Every tax ought to be levied at the time, or in the manner, in which it is most likely to be convenient for the contributor to pay it . . .'
4. **Efficiency**: 'Every tax ought to be so contrived as both to take out and keep out of the pockets of the people as little as possible over and above that which it brings into the public treasury of the state . . .'

These four principles are widely accepted. However, putting them into practice is challenging given the potential conflicts or trade-offs between them.

Source: Smith (1776), book V, part II.

[6] See, for example, Mirrlees et al. (2011).

2. **Low administrative and compliance costs**: collecting taxes is costly and a good tax system should aim to minimize these costs. Taxes involve both direct costs, such as the cost of running the revenue service, and indirect costs, which include costs borne by taxpayers in filling out forms, keeping records, and paying accountants. The level of these costs will in part depend on the complexity of the tax system, but they can be significant. If the tax system involves a lot of exemptions and different tax rates for different types of income, the administrative and compliance costs will be higher.
3. **Transparency**: the tax system should be easily understandable; people should know what taxes they are liable for and why, and what benefits they receive as a result. Moreover, any changes in the tax structure should be a result of legislation rather than chance or taxation by 'stealth'. For example, in a progressive tax system, if tax brackets rise more slowly than earnings, then government revenues can rise in real terms during periods of particularly high inflation, a phenomenon known as **fiscal drag**. In the UK, fiscal drag played an important role in increasing the number of income taxpayers from below 26 million in 1996/97 to 32.5 million in 2007/08, as well as a doubling of the number of individuals paying the higher 40 per cent rate from 2 million to nearly 4 million during the same period (Mirrlees et al., 2011).
4. **Fairness**: the tax system should be fair. But what does a fair tax system look like? There are several concepts of fairness that are relevant here: the tax system should treat people who are the same equally (horizontal equity); individuals with a higher ability to pay should pay higher taxes (vertical equity or distributional fairness); and there should be fairness of procedures, to avoid discrimination. These concepts raise a series of questions. For example, what does it mean for two people to be equal? And what does it mean to treat them the same? Who should pay higher taxes and how much more should they pay? We return to these questions in section 13.3.

So, a good tax system is one that raises revenue for the government and helps it achieve its desired distributional objectives, while having low administrative and compliance costs, being fair and transparent, and having a minimal impact on economic efficiency. These objectives will not always be mutually compatible. If the government wants to minimize the efficiency cost of taxation, it should adopt non-distortionary or lump-sum taxes, but these taxes are highly inequitable, as we will see in section 13.4.[7] How can we manage the trade-offs between different objectives, and what should we do when different objectives conflict? This is the focus of **optimal tax theory**.[8] Optimal tax theory provides a framework for analysing the trade-offs between objectives—in particular, the desire for redistribution (equity) and the desire to minimize the impact on individual welfare (efficiency). Optimal taxation theory identifies the objectives of policy and the constraints under which policy operates, and then aims to build a tax system that best achieves the stated objectives subject to the constraints. We will analyse the key insights of optimal tax theory for the design of taxes on goods and services and taxes on income in Chapters 14 and 15.

[7] A head tax, a tax individuals have to pay regardless of their income, is an example of a lump-sum tax.

[8] The seminal work on optimal tax theory was developed by Mirrlees (1971). Subsequent economists have built on this early work—for example, by highlighting the need to incorporate administrative and compliance costs (Shaw et al., 2010).

Alongside these properties, Mirrlees et al. (2011) identify three rules of thumb which should guide the design of a tax system:

- **Simplicity**: a simple tax system is likely to have lower administrative costs and be more transparent.[9]
- **Neutrality**: a neutral tax system treats similar activities in the same way. For example, a neutral consumption tax would tax all consumption the same. A neutral system therefore minimizes distortions over the choices people make and will tend to minimize welfare losses. But neutrality may not always be desirable, particularly if society wants to discourage certain harmful behaviours.
- **Stability**: a stable tax system is one where changes are not being continually made. Regularly changing the tax system increases compliance costs and makes it harder for individuals and firms to make long-term saving and investment decisions.

These rules of thumb differ from the properties discussed above in that they are not ends in themselves, or goals that a tax system should be designed to achieve—as, for example, efficiency and fairness are—but rather provide guidelines that should inform the design of a good tax system. More complex and less neutral tax systems will in general be more distortionary and have higher costs, as well as being more susceptible to **tax avoidance.**[10] However, in some cases complexity or non-neutrality may be necessary to help achieve greater fairness.

The properties described above provide a basis for assessing tax systems, by analysing the extent to which a particular tax system achieves or falls short of these properties. It is important to keep in mind that these properties should be applied to the tax (and transfer) system as a whole, rather than using them to assess individual taxes in isolation.[11] It is not necessary for every single tax to be progressive—what matters is the redistributive impact of the system of taxes and transfers as a whole. We must also not forget the constraints under which governments operate when designing or making changes to the tax system. These include various information constraints—for example, the fact the government cannot directly observe all income that individuals earn, as well as political constraints. There may be a tension between what is economically desirable in terms of tax reform and what is politically feasible.

We will now discuss two of these properties—fairness and efficiency—in more detail.

13.3 Measuring the fairness of a tax system

A good tax system should be fair, but what do we mean by the fairness of a tax system and how can we measure it? The concepts of horizontal and vertical equity, which we introduced briefly in Chapter 2, are useful for assessing the fairness of a tax system. We begin by discussing these concepts below, before turning to the question of tax incidence or who bears the burden of taxation.

[9] Tax legislation in the UK amounts to over 8,000 pages (Mirrlees et al., 2011).

[10] This is a point we will return to in Chapter 17.

[11] An exception here relates to horizontal equity or the principle that people who are equal should be treated equally. Individual taxes should be assessed against the principle of horizontal equity.

13.3.1 Horizontal and vertical equity

Horizontal equity requires that individuals who are equal in all relevant aspects be treated equally. In the context of taxation, this implies that individuals who earn the same income should pay the same amount in taxes or face the same tax burdens. Intuitively, this seems an appealing concept. It implies that the tax system should not discriminate based on characteristics such as age, gender, or ethnicity, and that preferential treatment should not be given to certain individuals. If a man and a woman each earn £30,000 a year, it would seem fair that they should both face the same tax burden. However, what if one of them has two young children to look after—would we still think fairness dictates that they should both pay the same amount in taxes, or would we want the tax system to make allowances for the fact that one of them only needs to support themselves with that income, whereas the other needs to support three people? Or suppose there are two individuals who earned the same income during their working lives, but while one of them saved towards their retirement in a private pension, the other spent all their income. Is it fair that the person who saved pays tax on their pension income, whereas the individual who didn't save receives benefits from the state? Although both individuals received the same income during their working lives, once they retire they will receive different incomes, which warrants differences in taxes paid.[12]

These examples highlight the difficulty in defining what it means for two people to be equal in all relevant aspects. It is also not always clear exactly what is meant by treating people equally. We saw in Chapter 11 how the state pension system often discriminates in favour of women, since mandatory pensions are normally based on unisex lifetables, so women pay the same premium as men, but will typically benefit more because they tend to live longer. Does treating men and women equally here require women to pay higher contributions or to receive a lower monthly pension, to account for the fact that they tend to live longer? Most tax systems do include allowances and exemptions, to help mitigate the impact of differences in needs or circumstances. The concept of horizontal equity raises the challenging question of what the basis for these exemptions should be.[13]

While horizontal equity requires that individuals who are equal be treated equally, **vertical equity** requires that individuals with higher incomes, who have a greater ability to pay, pay higher taxes. But who should pay the higher taxes and how much more should they pay? Should higher-income individuals pay more in absolute terms or should they pay a higher fraction of their income? This ability-to-pay approach to taxation contrasts with the benefit approach to taxation, whereby the amount of tax that individuals pay should be proportionate to the benefits they receive from the public expenditures funded by those taxes.

Two concepts which are particularly useful for describing the degree of redistribution or progressivity of taxes, in particular income taxes, are the **marginal tax rate** and the **average tax rate**. The marginal tax rate is the percentage of the next unit of currency earned (pound, euro, etc.) that is paid in tax. The average tax rate is the percentage of total income that is paid in tax. The example below illustrates the difference between these two concepts, and how they are related.

[12] This example illustrates the importance of how we define 'income' for tax purposes, which we discuss in section 13.5. Some economists have argued in favour of taxing individuals based on their lifetime income rather than annual income, in part to address some of these anomalies.

[13] We discuss this issue further in Chapter 15, where we focus on the taxation of income and wealth.

Table 13.2 Income tax rates and bands for the UK, 2025/26

Tax band	Taxable income (annual)	Tax rate (%)
Personal allowance	Up to £12,570	0
Basic rate	£12,571 to £50,270	20
Higher rate	£50,271 to £125,140	40
Additional rate	over £125,140	45

Table 13.2 shows the income tax schedule for the UK.[14] We can see that the marginal tax rate rises with income: for incomes between £12,570 and £50,270, the marginal tax rate is 20 per cent; this rises to 40 per cent for incomes up to £125,140; and for incomes over £125,140, the marginal tax rate is 45 per cent. The average tax rate a person pays will depend on their income. Suppose someone earns an income of £65,000 a year, so their marginal tax rate is 40 per cent. This does not mean they pay 40 per cent in tax on all of their income. They would pay no tax on the first £12,570 they earn. They would then pay the basic rate of 20 per cent on the £37,700 they earn between £12,571 and £50,270; and they would pay the higher rate of 40 per cent on the final £14,730 of their income. So their total tax bill would be:

$$(0.2 \times 37{,}700) + (0.4 \times 14{,}730) = 13{,}432$$

And their average tax rate would be calculated as follows:

$$\text{Average tax rate} = \frac{13{,}432}{65{,}000} \times 100 = 20.66$$

Whereas their marginal tax rate is 40 per cent, their average tax rate is just under 21 per cent.

For a tax system to satisfy the principle of vertical equity, individuals with a higher ability to pay taxes should pay higher taxes. This will be the case if the tax system is progressive or proportional. A **progressive tax system** is one where the average tax rate rises with income, which implies that richer households pay a higher share of their income in taxes than poorer households. The example illustrated in Table 13.2 represents a progressive tax system. A tax system where the marginal tax rate is higher than the average tax rate will be progressive, as the marginal tax rate will pull the average tax rate upwards. However, this is not required for the tax system to be progressive. A tax system with a flat tax (an income tax charged at a single constant rate) is progressive, provided there is a tax-free allowance. In contrast, a **proportional tax system** is one where the average tax rate does not increase with income, so all taxpayers pay the same proportion of their income in taxes. Higher earners will still pay more in taxes in absolute terms under a proportional tax system, as their incomes are higher. A **regressive tax system** is one where the average tax rate falls with income. For a complete understanding of how redistributive a particular system is, we need to assess the redistributive impact of the tax and benefit system as a whole, rather than focusing on individual taxes in isolation.[15]

[14] Tax rates and tax bands for the 2025/26 tax year.

[15] In theory, we should also assess the distributional effect of the tax system over a person's entire lifetime, rather than focusing on a single year, although this is challenging in practice.

Our discussion above highlights the importance of thinking about what the appropriate tax unit is—should taxes be levied on individuals, couples, or households? What are the implications of using different tax units for the fairness of the tax system? And should we judge the redistributive effect of taxes based on their impact on individuals or entire households? These questions are particularly important in the context of income taxes, and we return to them in Chapter 15.

We have also focused on income as a measure of individual welfare, as a basis for determining who is better off or who has a greater ability to pay. But, as we saw in Chapter 12, in practice income is an imperfect proxy for welfare, and other factors, such as health, play an important role.

13.3.2 Tax incidence

One fundamental question when thinking about the redistributive impact of taxation is the question of **tax incidence**, or who actually bears the burden of the tax. The **statutory or legal tax incidence** of a tax refers to who is responsible for making the tax payment to the tax authorities. For example, if a tax is levied on the producers of sugary soft drinks, then these producers are responsible for paying the tax to the authorities. However, this concept ignores the fact that taxes change behaviour and these responses need to be taken into account when determining the ultimate burden of taxation. The **economic tax incidence** refers to who actually bears the burden of the tax or who is made worse off by the tax. As we will see below, who bears the burden of the tax is not necessarily the person or organization who is responsible for making the tax payment to the government.

Another important distinction is between current and lifetime tax incidence. **Current tax incidence** is concerned with the incidence of a tax or taxes in relation to an individual's current resources, say in a particular year. In contrast, **lifetime tax incidence** is concerned with the incidence of taxes over an individual's entire lifetime resources. Although lifetime tax incidence is virtually impossible to measure in practice, it is worth keeping this distinction in mind when assessing the fairness of different taxes through the lens of tax incidence, since a tax that may appear deeply regressive when analysed in the context of a particular year may be less so—or even progressive—when analysed in the context of a person's lifetime.[16]

There are three fundamental principles of economic tax incidence. These principles are illustrated below using a **specific excise tax**—that is, a fixed tax that is levied on a good or service.[17]

[16] Even assessing tax liability over a small number of years might affect the distribution of the tax burden. For example, if many people lose their job in one year but are employed again the following year, the tax system may appear more regressive at the lower end of the income distribution (as there will be more individuals in a lower income bracket), unless income and tax liabilities are averaged over a few years.

[17] The same principles apply in the case of an **ad valorem tax**, which is levied as a fixed percentage of the sales price. In this case, the demand or supply curves will shift proportionally rather than by a fixed amount. For a comparison of specific and ad valorem taxes, see Chapter 14, section 14.1.1.

1. The statutory burden of the tax is not necessarily the same as the economic burden

To illustrate this principle, suppose the government imposes a fixed tax t per litre on sugary soft drinks, which is to be paid by soft-drink manufacturers. What impact will this tax have on the market for soft drinks?

Figure 13.3 illustrates the impact of a tax paid by producers. The initial market equilibrium is shown in panel (a). Assuming the market is perfectly competitive, then the quantity that producers are willing to supply at any given price just equals their marginal cost of production, so the supply curve, *S*, coincides with the marginal cost curve, *MC*. The demand curve, *D*, equals the marginal benefit, *MB*, that individuals derive from consuming soft drinks. The initial market equilibrium is given by point E in panel (a), where the demand and supply curves intersect: the equilibrium price is P_0 and the equilibrium quantity is Q_0.

The impact of the tax is to increase the producers' marginal cost by the value of the tax, t. For any given quantity of soft drinks, the cost to producers equals the sum of the production cost plus the tax, so the supply curve will shift up by the value of the tax and the new supply curve is S_1 in panel (b). At the initial equilibrium price P_0 there is now excess demand: consumers want to buy a quantity Q_0 of soft drinks, but producers are only willing to supply quantity Q_1. This excess demand will push up the price of soft drinks, until a new equilibrium is reached at point F, where the quantity of soft drinks sold in the market has fallen to Q_T, consumers pay a price P_T while producers receive a price P_1. The difference between the price consumers pay and the price producers receive (net of the tax) is the **tax wedge**. As this example illustrates, while the responsibility for paying the tax to the tax authorities falls on producers, they do not bear the entire burden of the tax: part of the burden of the tax falls on producers, as they now receive a lower price, but consumers also share in this burden by paying a higher price for soft drinks. The fact that market prices need not rise by the exact amount of the tax (i.e. firms absorb part of the increase) means that the economic incidence of the tax can be difficult to identify in practice.

Who ultimately bears the burden of the tax is not necessarily the individual or organization responsible for paying the tax to the tax authorities. This applies in the case of indirect taxes on goods and services, as well as in the case of direct taxes on income. As we will see in Chapter 15, the even though income taxes are often paid by employers, part of the economic incidence of these taxes fall on employees.

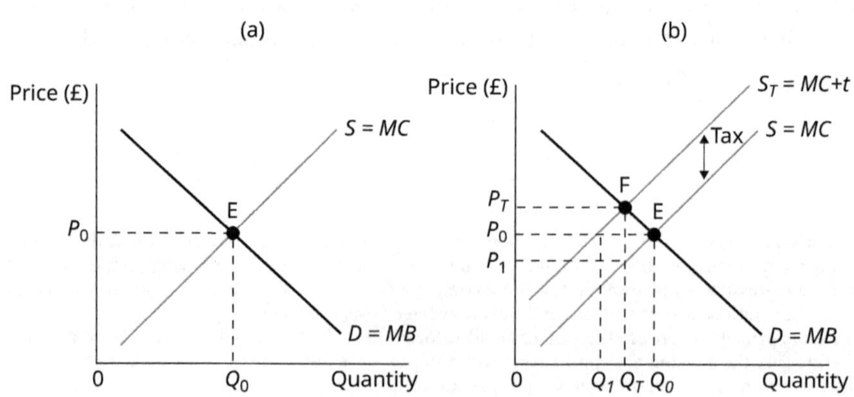

Figure 13.3 Tax incidence of a tax paid by producers

2. The side of the market on which the tax is levied is irrelevant to who bears the economic burden of the tax

In the example above, the soft-drink manufacturers were responsible for making the tax payment to the government. Would the outcome be different if the statutory burden of the tax fell on consumers instead?

Figure 13.4 illustrates the impact of a tax that is paid by consumers. The market demand curve D_1 represents consumers' willingness to pay for different quantities of sugary soft drinks, and the initial market equilibrium is at point E. If consumers are now required to pay a tax t in addition to the price charged by producers, they will now be willing to pay t less for each quantity, so the entire demand curve shifts down by the amount of the tax and is now given by D_2. At the initial equilibrium price P_0 there is now excess supply: producers want to supply a quantity Q_0 of soft drinks, but consumers now only want to buy quantity Q_1. This excess supply will push down the price of soft drinks, until a new equilibrium is reached at point G. Producers will receive the lower price P_1, but consumers will need to pay the tax t on the soft drinks that they buy—so the price plus tax that consumers pay is given by P_T.

Even though in this case the consumers are responsible for paying the tax to the government, both consumers and producers bear some of the economic burden of the tax—and the way the economic burden is shared between producers and consumers is exactly the same as in the example above, where the tax was paid by producers.

3. Who bears more of the burden of the tax will depend on the relative elasticities of supply and demand

In general, the economic burden of the tax will not be shared equally between consumers and producers but will depend on the relative **price elasticities of demand and supply.**[18] Whichever side of the market is less responsive or sensitive to changes in the price will bear a greater burden of the tax. Suppose the government is planning to tax a good for which

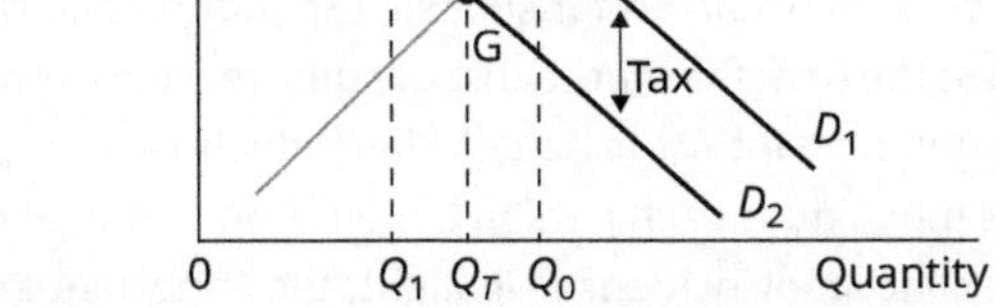

Figure 13.4 Tax incidence of a tax paid by consumers

[18] The price elasticity of demand/supply measures how sensitive demand/supply is to changes in price. Formally this is given by the percentage change in the quantity demanded/supplied in response to a 1 per cent increase in price.

demand is fairly elastic, such as sugary soft drinks, where a small change in price will lead to a large change in the quantity demanded. If firms raise their prices, then consumers will reduce their demand significantly and buy goods that are close substitutes, such as soft drinks that have a lower sugar content. The majority of the burden of the tax will therefore be borne by producers, in the form of lower prices. If, on the other hand, the government plans to tax a good for which demand is fairly inelastic, such as insulin, then the majority of the burden of the tax will fall on consumers, since they have limited options other than to buy that good, and therefore will have to pay a higher price for it. Similar arguments apply if we consider the elasticity of supply.[19]

Allocating the economic incidence between firms and consumers only tells us part of the story. As we have seen, organizations do not pay taxes; only individuals pay taxes. Therefore, any tax that is borne by producers will ultimately be borne by their shareholders or employees. We have also focused on the question of tax incidence in a partial equilibrium setting, where we have analysed the impact of a tax in a single market. In Chapter 14, we will see how we can extend this to a general equilibrium setting, where we consider the spillover effects from a tax in one market on other markets, as well as analysing tax incidence when markets are not perfectly competitive.

For a more complete understanding of tax incidence, we should also consider who benefits from the spending financed from the revenues raised through taxation (see Box 13.3).

Box 13.3 A more comprehensive view of tax incidence

Our analysis so far has focused only on the incidence of taxes in terms of who pays for them, but taxes are used to raise revenues to finance government expenditure. A more complete analysis of who bears the burden of taxation should consider not only the distribution of the tax burden, but also the distribution of the benefits from the associated government expenditure. This is the focus of budget incidence.

This is related to the benefit approach to taxation, which holds that individuals should pay taxes in proportion to the benefits they receive from government expenditure, so that those who benefit more from the goods and services provided by the public sector are required to pay more towards them. For example, car and fuel taxes are only paid by individuals who drive or own a car, and the revenues generated from these taxes may go towards funding improvements in the road network, which will primarily benefit drivers. In practice, the revenues from taxes are rarely earmarked for specific expenditures in this way. It is also difficult to accurately assess the benefits that each individual receives from taxation, and it is not always clear how we should quantify the benefits individuals receive, particularly in the case of public goods—how much does each person benefit from national defence or streetlighting? Nonetheless, this concept of incidence highlights the importance of considering how tax revenues are spent and who benefits from these expenditures if we want to assess the true burden—and hence the fairness—of a tax system.

[19] We analyse this issue in more detail in Chapter 14.

13.4 The costs of taxation

Taxation is the main source of government revenue in the vast majority of countries, providing the means to finance government expenditures which have the potential to increase social welfare. However, taxes also involve costs. They reduce spending power, by making goods more expensive or reducing disposable income. Taxes also affect individual behaviour by changing relative prices and, therefore, the incentives that individuals face, leading to inefficiency. In this section, we will explore some of the costs of taxation, starting with the impact of taxes on economic efficiency.

13.4.1 Taxation and economic efficiency

Tax revenues account for a significant proportion of GDP across most of the OECD, although this varies across countries, as illustrated in Figure 13.5. Between 1965 and 2022, total tax revenues ranged from under 30 per cent of GDP in Australia, Ireland, and the USA, to over 45 per cent of GDP in France. This measure of the burden of taxation has also increased over time across most countries, with the exception of Ireland. However, there is no clear relationship between the size of the tax burden and a country's economic performance. The USA and Denmark both enjoy similar levels of GDP per capita,[20] but whereas tax revenues amounted to 27.6 per cent of GDP in the USA in 2022, they were over 40 per cent in Denmark.

As we saw in Chapter 2, under specific circumstances, perfectly competitive markets will lead to an efficient allocation of resources, where total welfare is maximized. When governments introduce a tax, this will—in general—create an incentive for individuals to change

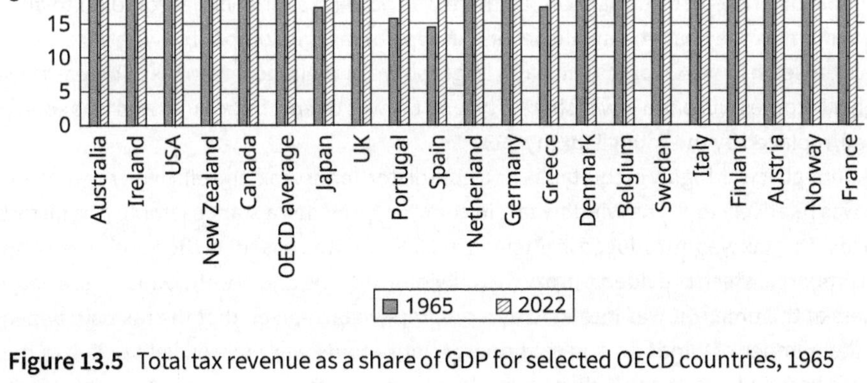

Figure 13.5 Total tax revenue as a share of GDP for selected OECD countries, 1965 and 2022
Source: OECD (2025a).

[20] In 2022, GDP per capita was US$77,004 in Denmark and US$77,778 in the USA (OECD, 2025b). Figures in US dollars per person, PPP converted.

their behaviour to minimize the amount of tax they have to pay, which will move the market away from the competitive equilibrium, resulting in a loss of welfare.

It is in this sense that most taxes are distortionary—they drive a wedge between the price that buyers pay and that sellers receive, distorting price signals and preventing otherwise mutually beneficial trades from taking place. Taxes on consumption goods mean people pay more for goods than sellers receive, while taxes on income mean employers pay more for labour than employees receive, and both lead to a reduction in the quantities traded. Individuals can reduce their tax liability by changing their behaviour—if the government raises the tax on sugary items, individuals can reduce the amount of tax they pay by reducing their consumption of these goods. But this reduction in the quantity demanded will lead the market away from the socially efficient outcome. Distortionary taxes are inefficient because the government could raise same amount of revenue with a smaller impact on individual welfare.[21]

Non-distortionary or lump-sum taxes, on the other hand, are taxes where there is nothing an individual or firm can do to alter their tax liability. Examples of lump-sum taxes include a head tax (or poll tax), a flat tax that all taxpayers must pay regardless of income, or taxes that are tied to an individual characteristic that cannot be changed, such as age. These types of taxes are problematic in practice because they are not tied to an individual's ability to pay, raising concerns about fairness and making them politically unpopular (see Box 13.4). Another example of a non-distortionary tax is a tax on pure **economic rents**. This term refers to the income generated by a resource in excess of its next best alternative use. Taxing pure economic rents should not create a distortion, since the tax is only applied to the excess income. Economic rents are often associated with the return on land, which derives its value in large part from its location (and the location cannot be changed).

Box 13.4 Distortionary and non-distortionary taxes

The Community Charge, commonly known as the poll tax, was a tax introduced in England and Wales in 1990. The tax was levied as a fixed sum on every adult resident, regardless of their income or resources, and was intended to fund local council services. The poll tax is an example of a non-distortionary tax, as there was nothing an individual could do to alter the amount of tax they had to pay. However, this type of tax is incompatible with vertical equity, since those on lower incomes will pay a larger share of their income in tax, whereas those on higher incomes will pay a lower share. The poll tax was deeply unpopular and was soon abolished, replaced by the council tax in 1993.

Although it was highly inequitable, as a non-distortionary tax, the efficiency cost of the poll tax was relatively low. The window tax, in contrast, provides a stark example of a distortionary tax. This tax was introduced in England in 1696 and was based on the number of windows in a property, which provided a proxy for individual income and wealth, which were harder to assess at the time.[22] It was intended as a progressive tax—given that the tax paid depended on the number of windows and that poorer households were more likely to live in houses with fewer windows, they would be taxed less. However, the tax resulted in many households

[21] This is a point we will explore in more detail in Chapter 14.

[22] The window tax also avoided the vexation of having tax collectors intruding into individuals' privacy, highlighting the important role that social norms play in the acceptability of different taxes.

boarding up their windows and houses being built with fewer windows, with serious negative effects on health, all in order to reduce tax liabilities. This tax provides a dramatic example of the potentially distorting effects of taxation.

Sources: Cullis et al. (1993) and Oates and Schwab (2015).

We can illustrate the impact of taxation on economic efficiency using a supply and demand diagram. As we saw in Chapter 2, in a perfectly competitive market, efficiency is maximized at the point where the demand curve (which measures the social marginal benefit of consumption) and the supply curve (which measures the social marginal cost of production) intersect. This is given by point E in Figure 13.6, where the equilibrium price is P_0 and the quantity traded is Q_0. All quantities of the good for which the social marginal benefit of consumption exceeds the social marginal cost of production are produced and consumed.

Suppose the government now introduces a tax which is paid for by producers, shifting the supply curve upwards, to S_2, and leading to a new market equilibrium at F. The tax drives a wedge between the price that consumers pay, P_T, and the price that producers receive, P_1, reducing the quantity sold from Q_0 to Q_T. By increasing prices and reducing quantities bought and sold, taxes impose a loss on both consumers and producers: consumer surplus falls by the amount P_TP_0EF, while producer surplus falls by the amount P_1P_0EG.[23] Part of this reduction in consumer and producer surplus is transferred to the government in the form of tax revenues, given by the rectangle, P_TP_1GF. But part is lost to society—the triangle EFG. This is the **deadweight loss** of the tax: a measure of the decrease in efficiency or loss in welfare that arises because mutually beneficial trades are not taking place.[24] The impact of the tax on efficiency would be exactly the same if the tax were levied on consumers rather than producers.[25]

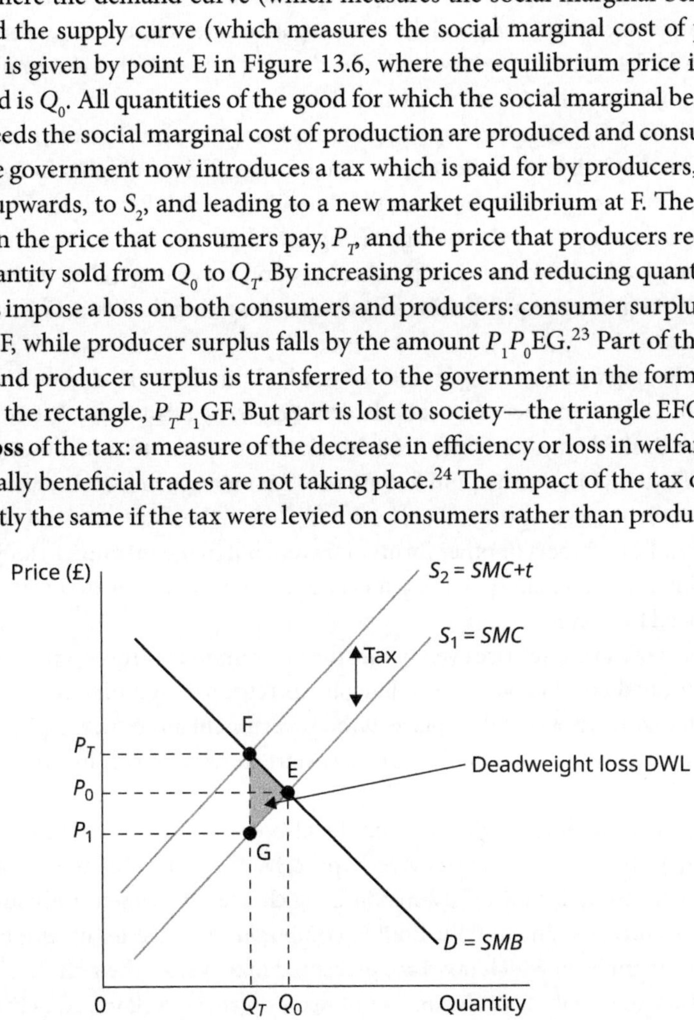

Figure 13.6 Deadweight loss of a tax

[23] Recall from Chapter 2 that consumer surplus is measured by the area below the demand curve and above the equilibrium price, whereas producer surplus is measured by the area above the supply curve and below the equilibrium price.

[24] Technically, we should be using the compensated demand curve when measuring the deadweight loss of a tax. The compensated demand curve measures the demand for a good where the individual is compensated for any price changes so that their utility is constant. We expand on this point in our analysis of the efficiency loss from taxation in Chapter 14.

[25] You can try checking this out for yourself.

The deadweight loss of the tax arises because the tax leads to a reduction in the quantities traded in the market. As such, the size of the deadweight loss will depend on how sensitive supply and demand are to changes in prices—that is, it will depend on the elasticities of supply and demand. For example, if demand is very elastic, then a tax will have a large impact on reducing the quantity demanded, resulting in a large deadweight loss. This suggests that in order to minimize the efficiency cost of taxation, governments should levy higher taxes on goods for which demand is more inelastic or reduce taxes on individuals who are more responsive to higher taxes. However, these strategies may conflict with the pursuit of other social objectives, such as equity. Reducing the quantity of a good may also be desirable if consumption or production of the good involves negative externalities. We will explore the role of elasticities in determining the size of the deadweight loss and what this implies for optimal tax policy in more detail in Chapters 14 and 15.

So far, we have focused on the impact of a tax in a single market in isolation, but in practice a tax in one market will have spillover effects in other markets. A higher tax on drinks with a high sugar content may lead individuals to demand more drinks with lower sugar contents. A tax on interest income may discourage saving, which in turn may reduce the supply of capital, which may lead to a reduction in productivity and lower wages. It is therefore important to consider these **general equilibrium** effects when assessing the impact of a tax. We explore these in Chapter 14.

When evaluating a tax, it is important to consider both the short-run and long-run effects on behaviour. The full impact of a tax is also unlikely to be immediate. Whereas in the short run there are limited ways in which individuals can respond to a tax, they generally have much more flexibility in the medium to long run. An increase in fuel taxes may lead individuals to reduce their consumption of fuel by driving less in the short run (and perhaps increase reliance on public transport or other forms of travel), but in the medium to long run they may be able to switch to more energy-efficient cars or even move closer to their place of work to reduce the need for travel.

Some effects of a tax may arise even before the tax is imposed. These announcement effects arise when individuals change their behaviour in response to a planned change in policy, even if the change has not yet taken place. If the government announces a plan to increase the tax on fuel in the next quarter, individuals may start stocking up on fuel now, or looking for ways to drive less.

Our analysis of the deadweight loss from taxation assumes that individuals are responding optimally to the tax: that they correctly perceive the impact of the tax and are able to accurately work out their new utility-maximizing choice. In practice, individuals might not perceive taxes correctly, due to their limited computational abilities or limited attention, or the context or manner in which taxes are presented may distort their choices. This will have implications for our analysis of the impact of taxes on social welfare, something we explore further in the context of indirect and direct taxes in Chapters 14 and 15.

13.4.2 Administrative and compliance costs

In addition to the efficiency costs discussed above, there are also various administrative and compliance costs associated with taxation. These include the direct costs associated with running the tax revenue service (e.g. paying staff to ensure taxes are being correctly paid, or setting up systems) and the indirect costs individuals and companies incur, such as filling out tax returns, keeping records, or paying accountants. The size of these costs varies across individuals and companies, and depends on what the basis of taxation is. The compliance costs for self-employed individuals, who need to submit their own tax returns, are generally higher than for individual employees, whose taxes are deducted automatically from their wages. Compliance costs are also generally higher for smaller than for larger organizations, as well as varying across countries—compliance costs tend to be higher in countries with weak institutional set-ups.[26]

More complex tax systems, with different tax bands, different tax rates for different types of income, and more exemptions, will tend to have higher administrative and compliance costs, although there may be strong equity arguments for setting up a tax system in this way. Having different tax rates for different types of income can also create incentives for individuals to try and shift income into categories that are taxed at a lower rate. More generally, taxes—in particular, high tax rates—may encourage individuals to devote time and resources to minimizing the amount of taxes they have to pay, rather than engaging these resources in productive activities.

When the mechanisms individuals use to reduce their tax burden are legal, such as channelling funds to offshore jurisdictions or creating separate legal entities such as trusts or foundations and transferring assets, they engage in what is known as **tax avoidance**. When individuals intentionally fail to declare part or all of their taxable economic activity—for example, by underreporting their true income to the tax authorities—they engage in what is known as **tax evasion**. Tax avoidance is legal, whereas tax evasion is not, although in practice the distinction between the two is not always clear-cut. Both tax evasion and tax avoidance reduce the tax revenue the government can collect and impose costs on the economy in terms of wasted resources. They also have implications for horizontal and vertical equity. This is something we explore in Chapter 17.

While the discussion of tax incidence above focused on the impact of taxes on market prices, this section has focused on the impact of taxes on quantities and how they move the economy away from the competitive market equilibrium and reduce efficiency.

13.5 What should be the basis of taxation?

As we have seen, countries rely on many different types of taxes. The **tax base** is the area of economic activity on which a tax is payable. The majority of taxes are paid by individuals, and individuals can be taxed either on their resources—their income, savings, and wealth—or on their consumption expenditure. Is it fairer to tax income or consumption? What are the implications of these different tax bases for efficiency?

13.5.1 Taxing income

Income taxes are an important source of government revenue for most countries today, but the income tax as we know it is a relatively recent creation. As we have seen, it was originally

[26] In some areas there is a trade-off between administrative and compliance costs—for example, depending on whether the tax authority or individual taxpayers are responsible for calculating the tax liability. Compliance costs can be reduced by providing support and guidance, but this increases administrative costs (Shaw et al., 2010).

introduced in Britain at the end of the eighteenth century to finance the Revolutionary Wars, but it did not become a permanent fixture until the late nineteenth century, when it was also introduced in other countries as governments expanded and the need for revenue increased. Income is generally perceived to be a fair basis for taxation because it measures an individual's ability to pay: people with higher incomes have a higher ability to pay and therefore should pay more in taxes.[27] Income taxes therefore have the potential to be more progressive, as well as minimizing the distortions associated with having many different taxes on different goods.

But is income a good measure of ability to pay? This will depend on how income is defined and what allowances are made for individual circumstances within this definition. The classic definition of income used by public finance economists is the Haig–Simons income definition, which we introduced in Chapter 12.[28] According to this definition, income is the amount of money an individual is able to spend over a given period without changing their net wealth position. This is a comprehensive concept of income, which includes both monetary income and any benefits in kind that individuals receive from their employers, such as employer-provided health insurance and company cars, as well as wider non-monetary benefits such as job satisfaction. Of course, not all of these benefits can be readily measured, as discussed in Chapter 12, and therefore income measures used in practice will provide an incomplete measure of ability to pay and individual well-being.

This definition treats all consumption the same, regardless of whether it is a genuine a choice. For example, in countries without adequate state-provided healthcare, poor health can lead to large medical expenditures which are outside of an individual's control. Two individuals may earn the same income, based on the Haig–Simons definition, but if one has a serious chronic health condition, is it fair for both to pay the same income tax? In practice, most tax systems include a range of tax deductions or exemptions which mean that the income tax base is often less than total income. Allowable deductions may include certain 'non-voluntary' expenses, such as medical expenses and local tax payments, as well as business expenses and expenses related to behaviours governments may want to encourage, such as charitable donations.[29]

Compared to taxes on consumption, any allowances or deductions are more easily applied to an income tax: the tax owed can simply be adjusted to take into account medical expenditures or the number of dependants, for example. The practice of withholding tax, where an employer deducts tax directly from an employee's earnings and pays this directly to the government, means that collecting income tax is administratively more straightforward and minimizes the risk of individuals not paying the full amount of income tax they owe. The scope for non-compliance is typically higher for self-employed individuals.

However, basing taxes on individual's actual income risks unfairly penalizing certain behaviours. Suppose we have two individuals with the same level of education and skills, but one takes a higher-paying job and works longer hours, whereas the other takes a lower-paying job and works fewer hours/enjoys more leisure time—is it fair that the person working longer hours should pay more in taxes? In theory, it would be fairer to tax an individual's earning potential or earning ability, but in practice governments can only tax people based

[27] The question of whether they should pay more in absolute terms or as a fraction of their income is one we will return to in Chapter 15.

[28] However, it has been argued that Haig believed consumption expenditure to be a better measure of 'true' income and would have favoured a tax on consumption expenditure over an income tax (Wildasin, 1990).

[29] We discuss the reasons behind these exemptions in Chapter 15.

on what they actually earn. This risks penalizing individuals who work more, potentially discouraging work and saving.[30] But by taxing individuals based on what they actually earn, we are also mitigating the effect that chance plays in securing a good job—two people with the same level of education and skills may end up in very different jobs due to chance, rather than choice. There are also many low-paying jobs which are fundamental to society, and a high wage is not equivalent to high social value.

So income is an imperfect measure of ability to pay and well-being. Taxing income also means we are taxing individuals on the basis of what they contribute to society, which may seem unfair. If the return to savings, or interest income, is taxed, this will reduce the incentive to save. And if different forms of saving are taxed at different rates, this will create an incentive for individuals to save in assets that are subject to lower tax rates, creating distortions and potentially reducing efficiency.[31]

13.5.2 Taxing consumption

Consumption may seem to be a fairer basis for taxation since by taxing consumption we are taxing people based on what they take out of the economy, rather than what they contribute. A tax on consumption would, in theory, be simpler to administer, as it avoids the problems of defining and measuring income discussed above. Since the difference between income and consumption is given by savings, a pure tax on consumption implies savings should be exempt from taxation.[32] Taxing consumption would therefore encourage saving and minimize distortions to saving decisions, potentially boosting investment and economic growth.

However, consumption is arguably a less equitable tax base for two reasons. First, not taxing savings will benefit primarily higher-income individuals who are more likely to save more over the course of their lives. Estimates for the USA suggest that individuals in the lowest income quintile save only 3 per cent of their lifetime income, compared to 25 per cent for those in the highest income quintile (Dynan et al., 2004). By accumulating more savings, wealthier individuals are more likely to leave large inheritances or bequests to their relatives when they die, further entrenching inequalities. While these wealth transfers can be subject to inheritance or estate taxes, in practice these taxes tend to be hugely politically unpopular and countries that have inheritance taxes tend to apply them at low rates or only on very high levels of wealth.[33] But whether a tax on consumption implies that all savings should be exempt from taxation will depend on the particular form of the consumption tax.[34]

A consumption tax is also more likely to be regressive. Individuals consuming the same goods and services will pay the same rate of tax, regardless of their income, and the share of

[30] We will return to these points in Chapter 15, where we also discuss some of the evidence on the impact of income taxes on working hours and saving.

[31] In many countries, the tax system has an inbuilt bias towards saving in real estate rather than equity, by exempting imputed rents from owner-occupied housing and capital gains from tax, but taxing interest income and dividends.

[32] Formally, income Y equals the sum of consumption C and savings S: $Y = C + S$. This implies, $C = Y - S$. However, this ignores the role of inheritances and bequests.

[33] We discuss some of the types of wealth taxes in Chapter 15.

[34] There are different versions of a consumption tax, including the flat tax originally proposed by Hall & Rabushka (1995), the X tax proposed by Bradford (2004), and the personal expenditure tax. Most versions of the consumption tax would imply a zero effective tax rate on the normal returns to capital, but they would also imply a tax on economic rents and the excess return to risk-taking. See, for example, Auerbach (2006).

income spent on consumption is much higher for lower-income individuals. As poorer individuals consume more of their income over the course of their lives, they will end up paying more in taxes (see Box 13.5). The regressive nature of a consumption tax can be addressed to some extent by levying different tax rates on different types of goods—for example, by exempting or charging lower tax rates on essential items such as staple foods, and higher tax rates on luxury goods, such as foreign holidays.[35] This will, however, make the tax system more complex and therefore more costly to administer. There is the further challenge of determining what goods should be exempt from tax or should attract a lower rate.[36]

Further problems with taxing consumption may arise depending on how the tax itself is structured. If the tax is levied on items bought as business inputs, rather than just on final retail sales, this gives rise to the cascading problem, where businesses pay sales taxes on their business inputs, and then again when they sell their outputs. The more stages there are in the production and distribution process, the worse the problem becomes. This problem can be mitigated to some extent by having a value-added tax in place of a retail sales tax, as we discuss in Chapter 14.

Lastly, moving to a tax system where only consumption is taxed would require consumption to be taxed at a very high rate. Estimates for the USA suggest that replacing income tax with a sales tax would require a sales tax in the order of 35 per cent to finance existing levels of government expenditure (Gale, 1999). Such high tax rates have the potential to encourage non-compliance, creating an incentive for individuals to collaborate with retailers to avoid paying the tax—for example, by not making purchases official or by buying and selling goods in the black market.

13.5.3 Equivalence between taxing income and consumption

The difference between income and consumption as a tax base is smaller than it may initially appear. In any given year, an individual's level of consumption may differ from their income. A couple with young children will have high consumption needs and may need to borrow against their future income, whereas an older homeowner living alone may find their income more than covers their current consumption needs, allowing them to save any excess. However, over the course of their lifetime, an individual's total income and total consumption should be roughly equivalent. To see this, suppose an individual lives for two periods, receiving earnings of w_1 and w_2 in each. The present discounted value of their total lifetime income will be:[37]

$$Y = w_1 + \frac{w_2}{(1+r)}$$

[35] Most countries do this in practice, allowing for exemptions for goods such as food, children's clothing, and education.

[36] We return to this point in Chapter 14.

[37] The concept of present value was introduced in Chapter 5. In order to make payments in the future comparable to payments today, we need to discount future payments by multiplying them by the discount factor, $\frac{1}{1+r}$, where r is the rate of interest or discount rate. This captures the fact that a pound or euro received next year is worth $(1+r)$ times less than a pound or euro received today, because that pound or euro could earn interest of r per cent if it were received today and invested.

Box 13.5 The incidence of income and consumption taxes in the UK

The impact of direct and indirect taxes on households varies with household income. Whereas indirect taxes on goods and services tend to be more regressive, disproportionately affecting lower-income households, direct taxes on income tend to be more progressive, particularly when combined with government transfers.

Panel (a) in Figure 13.7 shows how the impact of indirect taxes falls with household income in the UK. Indirect taxes accounted for over 20 per cent of the disposable income

(a)

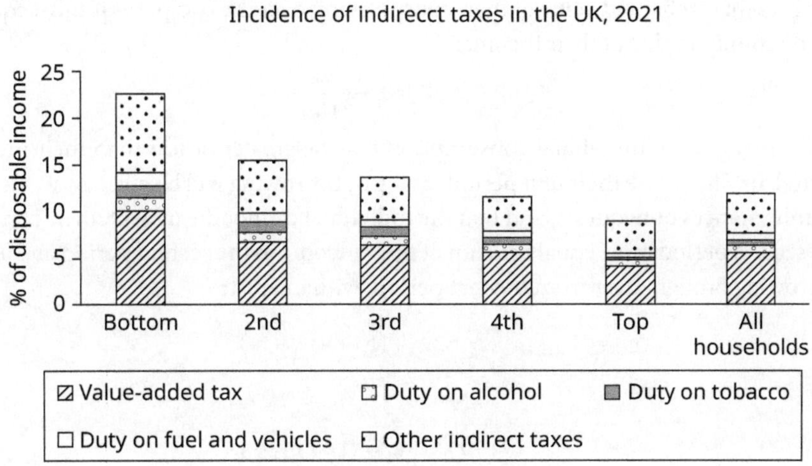

(b)

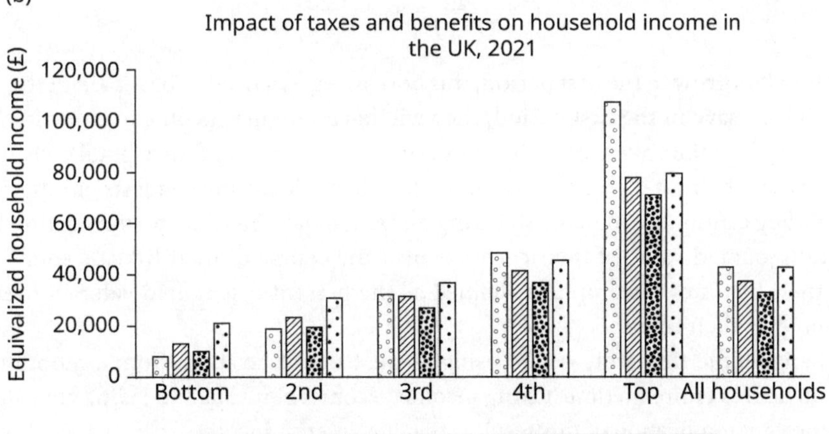

Figure 13.7 Impact of indirect and direct taxes and benefits on households in the UK, by income quintile, 2021
Source: ONS (2022).

(*Continued*)

of households in the poorest income quintile, compared with just 9 per cent of disposable income for households in the wealthiest income quintile. However, direct taxes, together with government transfers, do work to redistribute income across households, as illustrated in panel (b). While the richest fifth of households had an average income before taxes and benefits of £107,600 (which was over 13 times larger than the poorest fifth at £8,200), after considering all taxes and benefits, this gap was reduced to 3.7 times, with households in the top income quintile having an average final income of £79,200, compared with £21,400 for those in the lowest quintile.

The present discounted value of their consumption over the two periods must equal the present discounted value of their income:

$$Y = c_1 + \frac{c_2}{(1+r)}$$

In the first period, individual consumption may be greater or less than their income in that period, in which case their first period saving or borrowing will be given by $w_1 - c_1$. Assuming no inheritances or bequests, and that the individual cannot die in debt, their consumption in the second period must equal the sum of their income in the second period and any saving or borrowing brought over from the first period, with interest:

$$c_2 = w_2 + (1+r)(w_1 - c_1)$$

This is equivalent to:

$$(1+r)c_1 + c_2 = (1+r)w_1 + w_2$$

Dividing both sides by $(1+r)$ we get:

$$c_1 + \frac{c_2}{(1+r)} = w_1 + \frac{w_2}{(1+r)}$$

If individuals borrow in the first period, this borrowing will need to be repaid in the second period. If they save in the first period, they will have a higher income to enjoy in the second period. Over the course of their two-period lifetime, though, their total consumption cannot exceed their total income, assuming they do not leave any bequests or inheritances, and that they cannot die in debt. So taxing an individual's lifetime income, defined as the present discounted value of their earnings over the course of their lives, is equivalent to taxing their lifetime consumption, defined as the present discounted value of their consumption over their lifetime.

By changing the time unit we are using as the basis of taxation, from a month or year to an individual's entire lifetime, taxing income becomes equivalent to taxing consumption. One important implication of this result is that any interest income from savings should not be taxed. As we saw above, whether exempting interest income from taxes is fair is open to debate.

Focusing on lifetime income also provides a more accurate understanding of the progressivity of the tax system. Because people's incomes change over the course of their lives, focusing on snapshots of income and tax paid at a particular point in time can give a misleading picture of the distributional impact of the tax system. Of course, in practice we do not normally observe an individual's lifetime income, but this suggests that looking at income and consumption expenditure together—and analysing income taxes as a proportion of current income, and consumption taxes as a proportion of current consumption—will provide a better sense of how progressive the tax system is. However, as we have discussed above, income—whether annual or lifetime—is a flawed measure of an individual's ability to pay.

13.6 Designing tax policy in the twenty-first century

We discussed the general properties of a good tax system in section 13.2. When it comes to the specific details—for example, the balance between direct and indirect taxes, the different income tax rates, and tax bands—the tax system should be designed to fit the particular context of the country in question. Developing countries tend to rely more on indirect taxes, partly due to issues around the collectability of taxes, whereas developed economies rely more on direct taxes on income and social security contributions. Countries with a federalized political structure need to balance taxes collected at the national and subnational levels. Different countries will also have different social objectives, which will affect the focus given to redistribution within the system and the balance between equity and efficiency objectives.

This also means that the tax system should change in response to changes in the economic and social context. Many aspects of the tax systems of today were designed for economies of the past. Globalization and technological developments have led to changes in the structure of economies and in the world of work, changing the nature of the productive activities on which taxes are based. Meanwhile, new challenges such as rising inequality and climate change place new demands on national tax systems. In this section, we review some of the key challenges for the design of tax policy today.

13.6.1 Globalization and technological change

Globalization and technological change, including the growing digitalization of the economy, have increased capital mobility, creating incentives for potentially harmful tax competition between countries and opening up opportunities for tax avoidance by large multinational corporations. Rates of corporation tax influence the location decisions of firms and, in our globalized world, countries have an incentive to lower their corporate tax rates to attract investment from multinational companies, risking a race to the bottom in corporation tax rates.

There has been a clear downward trend in statutory corporate tax rates across the OECD in the last forty years (see Table 13.3), although revenues from corporation taxes have remained relatively stable. Across the OECD, average corporate income tax revenues fluctuated between 7 per cent and 9 per cent of total tax revenues between 1965 and 2003, rising to a high of 11.3 per cent in 2007 before falling to 9 per cent in 2010, and remained between 9 per cent and 10 per cent of total revenues until 2020 (OECD, 2021b). However, falling corporate tax rates have led to a widening gap between corporate and personal income tax rates in several countries, creating incentives for individuals to incorporate and recharacterize wage income as corporate income (OECD, 2018).

Globalization also raises new challenges for the tax treatment of multinational companies. Changes in the nature and structure of production processes, particularly the increasing role of knowledge-based assets and global value chains, complicate how companies should be taxed.

Table 13.3 Statutory corporate income tax rates

	1980	1990	1996	2000	2010	2020
Australia	50	39	36	34	30	30
Canada	46	38	38	29.1	18	15
France	50	37	33	37.8	34.4	32
Germany	56	50	45	42.2	15.8	15.8
Ireland	45	10	10	24	12.5	12.5
Italy	25	36	37	37	27.5	24
Japan	40	40	37.5	30	30	23.2
Spain	33	35	35	35	30	25
Sweden	57	30	28	28	26.3	21.4
UK	52	34	33	30	28	19
USA	46	34	35	35	35	21

Sources: Data for 1980 to 1996 from Dilnot and Giles (1997), table 5.1; these are national corporate income tax rates, ignoring special surtaxes and local corporate income taxes. Data for the remaining years from OECD (2022).

In theory, tax policies should try and ensure that the amount of tax paid in a particular country reflects the economic activity carried out in that country, but this is often difficult in practice. For example, how should one tax a Swiss company that develops a drug using research facilities based in the UK, manufactures it in Belgium, and sells it mainly in the USA?[38]

The increased mobility of capital has made it easier for multinational companies to engage in strategic tax planning to reduce their tax burdens, by shifting their profits from high-tax to low-tax jurisdictions. Domestic tax base erosion and profit shifting (BEPS), whereby multinational companies exploit gaps between different countries' tax systems, imposes significant costs on all countries—the OECD estimates between $100 billion and $240 billion are lost each year to tax avoidance by multinational companies (OECD, n.d.). These are challenges that no country can solve on its own and addressing these issues will require international cooperation.[39]

Globalization and technological change have also had an impact on the world of work. Developments in automation have increased job precarity in some sectors, while technological changes have led to growing wage gaps between high- and low-skilled workers, exacerbating inequality (OECD, 2018). Increased labour mobility, particularly among high-skilled workers, raises the prospect of increased tax competition and falling income tax rates, particularly in higher bands, making the tax system less progressive and reducing overall income redistribution (Causa & Hermansen, 2017).

[38] Example given by John Kay at a conference at the London School of Economics in May 2011, cited in Mirrlees et al. (2011: 15).

[39] In October 2021, a significant reform of the international tax system to address some of these issues was finalized at the OECD, with over 136 countries and jurisdictions signing up to a plan to reform international tax rules. This global minimum tax agreement will not eliminate tax competition, but it will help to limit it, by ensuring a global minimum corporate tax rate of 15 per cent and including provisions for a fairer distribution of profits and taxing rights among countries (OECD, 2021c).

While globalization and technological change present clear challenges for the design of tax systems, they also offer up new opportunities. The digitalization of transactions and increased data storage capacity also provide new opportunities to streamline tax collection and administration processes, reducing the costs associated with taxation.

13.6.2 Increasing inequality in income and wealth

In spite of a move towards global convergence in incomes since the 1980s, income inequality across the OECD has been increasing and is now at its highest level in the last 50 years: the average income of the richest 10 per cent of the population is over nine times the income of the poorest 10 per cent, whereas in the 1980s this ratio was 7.1 (Cingano, 2014). High levels of inequality threaten social cohesion and the perceived legitimacy of government. The level of inequality in society also matters because the impact of a given tax system in raising revenue will depend on the underlying income distribution: the impact of a higher rate of income tax on incomes over £100,000 will depend on the number of individuals in a country with incomes above that level (Mirrlees, 2011).

Technological developments, such as increased automation, and changes in the structure of labour markets, with an increase in flexible work arrangements and non-standard employment (the rise of the 'gig economy'), have the potential to further exacerbate inequalities, while also presenting new challenges for tax collection. Tax policies should be responsive to changes in labour markets, including changes in the levels of non-employment or low-wage employment, and changes in the labour force participation of different groups in society, particularly women with children.

The tax and transfer system can be a powerful tool for redistributing income and tackling inequality, as we saw in Chapter 12. However, there is a risk that the promotion of equity may come at the cost of efficiency, as high taxes may reduce incentives to work, save, and invest, hampering economic growth.[40] The challenge for tax policy is to design a system that helps to tackle growing levels of inequality without sacrificing efficiency, through policies that encourage investment in education, skills, and innovation.

Moreover, it is not just inequality in income that matters. Household wealth has grown in importance relative to income, and wealth is very unequally distributed. Across the OECD, the wealthiest 10 per cent of households own on average 52 per cent of total net wealth, while households in the bottom half of the wealth distribution own little or no net wealth (OECD, 2021a). However, in many countries, wealth-related taxes such as inheritance taxes and property taxes have failed to keep up with the increasing importance of household wealth and the role it plays in driving inequality, leading to calls for the reform of wealth taxes.

13.6.3 New and growing fiscal pressures

In Chapter 11, we saw how increases in life expectancy combined with falling fertility rates are contributing to rising old-age dependency ratios across most of the OECD, putting pressure on

[40] This is a point we will return to in Chapter 15, where we discuss the theory and evidence on the impact of taxes on individual incentives to work and save.

state pension systems as more revenue is required to maintain existing standards of pensions. An ageing population will also increase demands on health and social care, adding to the fiscal pressures that governments face. The Covid-19 pandemic has put further pressure on public finances in many countries, with countries amassing significant debts that will need to be repaid.

New technologies and changes in the world of work are leading to new social risks, placing new demands on social protection systems. While there is scope to debate the extent to which we believe governments should intervene to address these various challenges, these examples illustrate how discussions about reforming tax systems need to be considered alongside the changing demands on government expenditure.

13.6.4 Climate change

The tax system has an important role to play in tackling one of the greatest challenges the world faces today: climate change. Emissions of carbon dioxide and other greenhouse gases as a result of human activities are a leading cause of climate change, and taxes can play a role by discouraging the activities that are driving increases in greenhouse gas emissions and encouraging more environmentally friendly behaviours. Environmental taxes have the potential to promote economic efficiency by reducing pollution, while at the same time reducing the costs associated with the tax system, by reducing the need to rely on other distortionary taxes. This is known as the double dividend hypothesis. However, if environmental taxes are indeed effective in discouraging environmentally harmful behaviour, then alternative sources of revenue will need to be found to fill the gap. Estimates for the UK suggest the shift to electric vehicles will lead to a potential loss to the Treasury of £35 billion a year in lost fuel duty and vehicle excise duty by 2050 (Corlett, 2019: 62).[41]

These challenges will not affect all countries equally. Their impact, and the implications for tax policy, will depend on each country's specific economic, social, political, and institutional context. There is no one-size-fits-all optimal tax policy. But economic theory, combined with empirical research, can help inform the design of effective tax policies. When planning tax reforms, it is important not to focus on changes to individual taxes in isolation, but rather to consider the tax and transfer system as a whole (Slemrod & Gillitzer, 2014; Mirrlees et al., 2011). And, of course, it is not enough to identify the appropriate reforms from an economic perspective—there is then the challenge of overcoming the political barriers to implementing tax reform.

Conclusion

Taxes are necessary to finance government expenditure programmes, which can bring significant benefits to individuals and to society. There are different types of taxes that governments can use, including taxes on individual incomes and corporate incomes, taxes on savings and consumption, taxes on property, and fuel duties. But all taxes involve a cost: they reduce spending power and, by changing relative prices, they distort individual behaviour, moving the market away from the socially optimal outcome. Taxes therefore impact not just the distribution of welfare in society, but also the size of the economic cake.

[41] We discuss some of these issues in Chapter 9.

The design of the tax system has significant implications for social welfare and should balance three core objectives: promoting equity and reducing inequalities, minimizing the impact of taxes on efficiency, and raising revenue. There is no one-size-fits-all optimal tax system that is right for all countries and all time periods. The appropriate tax policies will depend on each country's specific economic, social, political, and institutional circumstances. Tax systems also need to be responsive to their changing environments. Technological changes have changed the nature of the economy on which taxes are levied, making it easier to administer taxes, but also making it easier to structure economic activities in a way to avoid taxes. Increased globalization, changes in labour markets, ageing populations, and climate change all pose new challenges for governments and societies, placing new demands on national—and international—tax policies. The shape of the economy and society will influence the appropriate tax system; but tax systems and tax policy can also help shape the economy and society.

Questions for discussion

1. Is it possible to design a tax a system that will satisfy all of the properties of a good tax system? Why?
2. What would a fair tax system look like?
3. Why are most taxes distortionary? How can we measure these distortions?
4. Is it fairer to tax income or consumption?
5. Do globalization and technological change reduce governments' ability to raise revenue?

Further reading

For a more in-depth discussion of issues related to the economics of taxation:

Auerbach, A. J., & Smetters, K. A. (2017). *The economics of tax policy*. Oxford University Press.

Mirrlees, J., Adam, S., Besley, T., Blundell, R., Bond, S., Chote, R., Gammie, M., Johnson, P., Myles, G., & Poterba, J. M. (2011). *Tax by design: The Mirrlees Review*. Oxford University Press. Available at: https://ifs.org.uk/publications/5353

On the costs of taxation and the impact of taxation on economic growth:

Alinaghi, N., & Reed, W. R. (2021). Taxes and economic growth in OECD countries: A meta-analysis. *Public Finance Review*, *49*(1), 3–40. https://doi.org/10.1177/1091142120961775

Gale, W. G., & Samwick, A. A. (2014). *Effects of income tax changes on economic growth* Social Science Research Network scholarly papers, no. 2494468. Available at: https://doi.org/10.2139/ssrn.2494468

Oates, W. E., & Schwab, R. M. (2015). The window tax: A case study in excess burden. *Journal of Economic Perspectives*, *29*(1), 163–180.

On the choice between income and consumption as the basis of taxation:

Atkinson, A. B., & Stiglitz, J. E. (1976). The design of tax structure: Direct versus indirect taxation. *Journal of Public Economics*, *6*(1–2), 55–75.

Auerbach, A. (2006). *The choice between income and consumption taxes: A primer*. National Bureau of Economic Research working papers, no. 12307. Available at: https://doi.org/10.3386/w12307

Correia, I. (2010). Consumption taxes and redistribution. *American Economic Review, 100*(4), 1673–1694. https://doi.org/10.1257/aer.100.4.1673

Hall, R., & Rabushka, A. (1995). *The flat tax* (2nd ed.). Hoover Institution Press.

On optimal tax theory and the design of tax policy:

Brys, B., et al. (2016). Tax design for inclusive economic growth. Organization for Economic Cooperation and Development tax policy working papers, no. 26.

Diamond, P., & Saez, E. (2011). The case for a progressive tax: From basic research to policy recommendations. *Journal of Economic Perspectives, 25*(4), 165–190. https://doi.org/10.1257/jep.25.4.165

Loretz, S. (2008). Corporate taxation in the OECD in a wider context. *Oxford Review of Economic Policy, 24*(4), 639–660.

Mankiw, N. G., Weinzierl, M., & Yagan, D. (2009). Optimal taxation in theory and practice. *Journal of Economic Perspectives, 23*(4), 147–174. https://doi.org/10.1257/jep.23.4.147

Slemrod, J., & Gillitzer, C. (2014). Insights from a tax-systems perspective. *CESifo Economic Studies, 60*(1), 1–31.

Bibliography

Auerbach, A. (2006). *The choice between income and consumption taxes: A primer*. National Bureau of Economic Research working papers, no. 12307. Available at: https://doi.org/10.3386/w12307

Bradford, D. F. (2004). *The X tax in the world economy*. National Bureau of Economic Research working papers, no. 10676. https://doi.org/10.3386/w10676

Britannica (n.d.). *History of taxation*. Available at: https://www.britannica.com/topic/taxation/History-of-taxation

Causa, O., & Hermansen, M. (2017). *Income redistribution through taxes and transfers across OECD countries*. Organization for Economic Cooperation and Development, Department of Economics working papers, no. 1453. Available at: https://doi.org/10.1787/bc7569c6-en

Cingano, F. (2014). *Trends in income inequality and its impact on economic growth*. Organization for Economic Cooperation and Development social, employment and migration working papers, no. 163. Available at: https://doi.org/10.1787/5jxrjncwxv6j-en

Corlett, A. (2019). *The shifting shape of UK tax: Charting the changing size and shape of the UK tax system*. Resolution Foundation.

Cullis, J., & Jones, P. (2009). *Public finance and public choice: Analytical perspectives* (3rd ed.). Oxford University Press.

Cullis, J., Jones, P., & Morrissey, O. (1993). Evaluating the poll tax as a tax reform. *Local Government Studies, 19*(1), 77–91.

Dilnot, A., & Giles, C. (Eds.). (1997). *The IFS green budget: Summer 1997*. Institute for Fiscal Studies. Available at: https://ifs.org.uk/publications/ifs-green-budget-summer-1997

Dynan, K. E., Skinner, J., & Zeldes, S. P. (2004). Do the rich save more? *Journal of Political Economy, 112*(2), 397–444.

Gale, W. G. (1999). The required tax rate in a national retail sales tax. *National Tax Journal, 52*(3), 443–457. https://doi.org/10.1086/NTJ41789734

Gruber, J. (2013). *Public finance and public policy* (4th ed.). Worth Publishers.

Hall, R., & Rabushka, A. (1995). *The flat tax* (2nd ed.). Hoover Institution Press.

Hubbard, R. G. (1997). How different are income and consumption taxes? *American Economic Review, 87*(2), 138–142.

Lerner, A. P. (1943). Functional finance and the federal debt. *Social Research, 10*(1), 38–51.

Mirrlees, J. A. (1971). An exploration in the theory of optimum income taxation. *Review of Economic Studies, 38*(2), 175–208. https://doi.org/10.2307/2296779

Mirrlees, J., Adam, S., Besley, T., Blundell, R., Bond, S., Chote, R., Gammie, M., Johnson, P., Myles, G., & Poterba, J. M. (2011). *Tax by design: The Mirrlees review*. Oxford University Press/Institute for Fiscal Studies.

Musgrave, R., & Musgrave, P. (1989). *Public finance in theory and in practice* (5th ed.). McGraw-Hill.

Oates, W. E., & Schwab, R. M. (2015). The window tax: A case study in excess burden. *Journal of Economic Perspectives, 29*(1), 163–180.

OECD (n.d.). *Base erosion and profit shifting (BEPS)*. Organization for Economic Cooperation and Development. Available at: https://www.oecd.org/tax/beps/about/ (accessed 20 July 2022).

OECD (2018). *Tax challenges arising from digitalisation—Interim report 2018: Inclusive framework on BEPS*. OECD/G20 Base Erosion and Profit Shifting Project, Organization for Economic Cooperation and Development. Available at: http://dx.doi.org 10.1787/9789264293083-en

OECD (2021a). *Inequalities in household wealth and financial insecurity of households*. Centre on Wellbeing, Inclusion, Sustainability, and Equal Opportunities, Organization for Economic Cooperation and Development. Policy insights. July.

OECD (2021b). *Revenue statistics 2021: The initial impact of Covid-19 on OECD tax revenues*. Organization for Economic Cooperation and Development. Available at: https://doi.org/10.1787/6e87f932-en

OECD (2021c). *Statement on a two-pillar solution to address the tax challenges arising from the digitalisation of the economy* (release date, 8 October). Available at: https://www.oecd.org/content/dam/oecd/en/topics/policy-issues/beps/statement-on-a-two-pillar-solution-to-address-the-tax-challenges-arising-from-the-digitalisation-of-the-economy-october-2021.pdf

OECD (2022). *Corporate income tax statutory and targeted small business rates*. Organization for Economic Cooperation and Development. Data explorer. https://data-explorer.oecd.org (accessed 14 July 2022).

OECD (2025a). *A comparative table of tax revenues for revenue statistics in OECD member countries*. Organization for Economic Cooperation and Development. Data explorer. https://data-explorer.oecd.org (accessed August 2025).

OECD (2025b). *National accounts at a glance*. Organization for Economic Cooperation and Development. Data explorer. https://data-explorer.oecd.org (accessed 24 August 2025).

ONS (2022). *Effects of taxes and benefits on UK household income: Financial year ending 2021*. Office for National Statistics. *Statistical Bulletin*, 29 July. Available at: https://www.ons.gov.uk/peoplepopulationandcommunity/personalandhouseholdfinances/incomeandwealth/bulletins/theeffectsoftaxesandbenefitsonhouseholdincome/financialyearending2021

Shaw, J., Slemrod, J., & Whiting, J. (2010). Administration and compliance. In Mirrlees, J., Adam, S., Besley, T., Blundell, R., Bond, S., Chote, R., Gammie, M., Johnson, P., Myles, G., & Poterba, J. (Eds.), *Dimensions of tax design: The Mirrlees review* (pp. 1100–1162). Oxford University Press.

Slemrod, J., & Gillitzer, C. (2014). Insights from a tax-systems perspective. *CESifo Economic Studies, 60*(1), 1–31. https://doi.org/10.1093/cesifo/ift015

Smith, A. (1776). *The wealth of nations*. Various modern editions available.

Stiglitz, J. E., & Rosengard, J. K. (2015). *Economics of the public sector* (4th ed.). W. W. Norton.

Wildasin, D. (1990). R. M. Haig: Pioneer advocate of expenditure taxation? *Journal of Economic Literature, 28*(2), 649–654.

14
Taxes on goods and services

Learning objectives

By the end of this chapter, you will be able to:

14.1 Analyse the incidence of commodity taxes and explain how it varies with the price elasticities of demand and supply, in markets with imperfect competition, and in general equilibrium contexts.
14.2 Explain what factors determine the size of the efficiency loss of taxes on goods and services.
14.3 Explain the Ramsey rule and the inverse elasticity rule and their limitations.
14.4 Explain how insights from behavioural economics can help inform the design of commodity taxes.
14.5 Discuss the arguments for and against the use of value-added taxes (VAT).

Introduction

Taxes on the consumption of goods and services have a long history, dating at least as far back as Ancient Greek and Roman times. Today, these indirect taxes are an important source of government revenue, accounting for nearly 32 per cent of total tax revenues across the OECD on average (OECD, 2025). Taxes on goods and services include both general consumption taxes and specific taxes on the consumption of certain goods, such as tobacco, alcohol and fuel, and customs duties. While the importance of these specific taxes has declined over time, general consumption taxes have grown and now account for around two-thirds of all indirect tax revenues. Among them, the value-added tax, or VAT, has become the most important general consumption tax in use today, with 170 countries across the world having some form of VAT system in place. What are the implications of these changes in the composition of indirect taxes for the economy? Should all goods and services be taxed? And should they all be taxed at the same rate?

In order to answer these questions, we need to take a closer look at how indirect taxes affect the economy. We will start in section 14.1 by exploring what factors determine who bears the burden of indirect taxes in an economy and how this depends on the structure of the market. In section 14.2, we will shift our focus to how indirect taxes affect the level of welfare in the economy: how we can measure the efficiency loss from taxation and what determines the size of this loss. Building on these insights, section 14.3 focuses on the question of how to design a tax system that will minimize these welfare losses to society, while raising a given amount of revenue for the government. Section 14.4 explores how insights from behavioural economics can enhance our understanding of how people actually respond to taxes, and section 14.5 discusses some of these concepts in the context of one particular tax, VAT.

14.1 Tax incidence

As we saw in Chapter 13, in economics, the incidence of a tax refers to who bears the burden of a tax, which is not necessarily the same as the person or organization responsible for making the tax payment to the tax authorities. This concept is fundamental for understanding the redistributive impact of taxation. In this section, we are going to explore this in more detail. We will start by analysing the equivalence between specific and ad valorem taxes in perfect competition. We will then explore the impact of elasticities on tax incidence. Lastly, we will look at two extensions of our model of tax incidence—how tax incidence differs in markets that are not perfectly competitive and what happens when we go beyond a single market to consider the incidence of a tax in several closely related markets.

14.1.1 Specific and ad valorem taxes

There are two main types of indirect taxes: specific taxes and ad valorem taxes. A **specific or unit tax** is a tax that is levied as a fixed amount per unit sold—for example, a 30p tax per can on sugary drinks, or a tax of £5.26 per packet of cigarettes. An **ad valorem tax** is levied as a percentage of the sales price—for example, a tax of 15 per cent on the price of soft drinks. The value-added tax (VAT) is the most widely used ad valorem tax in the world today, with over 160 countries having some form of VAT (OECD, 2020). In Chapter 13, we illustrated the three fundamental principles of tax incidence for the case of a specific tax, but the same principles apply in the case of an ad valorem tax. In perfectly competitive markets, it does not matter whether the tax is levied as a percentage of the price or as a fixed amount per unit of output—both have the same effect on output, while raising the same amount of revenue.

To illustrate this point, suppose we are analysing a tax levied on consumers.[1] A specific tax is modelled as a parallel shift in the entire demand curve, since the tax is the same regardless of the level of output. An ad valorem tax, however, causes the demand curve to rotate downwards, as the tax is a proportion of the price: when the price is zero, the tax is also zero and the two demand curves coincide; but as the price increases, as we move from right to left along the demand curve, the gap between the before and after-tax demand curves will also increase.

This is illustrated in Figure 14.1, where the initial pre-tax equilibrium is E_1. The introduction of an ad valorem tax levied on consumers causes the demand curve to rotate downwards, to D_2, leading to a new market equilibrium, E_T, with a lower equilibrium quantity Q_T. The price buyers pay is P_T, but sellers receive only P_N, and the difference between the two represents the level of the tax. It is possible to design a specific tax that is of the same magnitude as the ad valorem tax at the equilibrium E_T, and which will therefore have the same impact on prices, output, and tax revenues as the ad valorem tax. This is illustrated by demand curve D_3. The magnitude of the tax at the equilibrium is given by the difference $P_T - P_N$, so this is the amount by which the after-tax demand curve for the specific tax is shifted downwards, as illustrated by D_3.

In theory, we can design specific and ad valorem taxes that will have the same impact if the market is perfectly competitive. In practice, there are some important differences between

[1] The outcome would be the same in the case of a tax levied on producers. Recall the second principle of tax incidence covered in Chapter 13: the side of the market on which the tax is levied is irrelevant to who bears the economic burden of the tax.

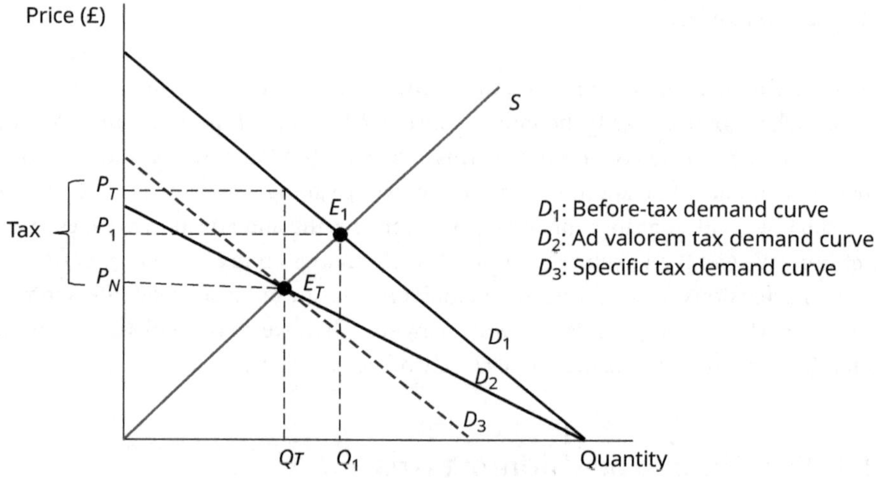

Figure 14.1 Specific and ad valorem commodity taxes

these types of taxes. A specific tax can be more effective in reducing demand, since it increases the price of all goods (both cheap and expensive) equally. An ad valorem tax is proportionately higher for more expensive goods, which can encourage consumers to switch from more expensive to cheaper varieties of the good on which the tax is levied (e.g. switch to cheaper soft drinks or cigarettes). However, a specific tax is also more regressive, since the tax is proportionately higher for lower-priced products, so will hit those consuming the cheaper products more, whereas ad valorem taxes hit those buying expensive varieties more.

14.1.2 Elasticities and tax incidence

According to the third principle of tax incidence, the incidence of a tax on consumers and producers will ultimately depend on how sensitive the quantity demanded or supplied is to changes in prices—in order words, it will depend on the relative price elasticities of demand and supply.[2] To understand why, it is helpful to analyse the extreme cases, where demand or supply is perfectly inelastic or perfectly elastic.

Demand

How does the elasticity of demand affect who bears the burden of a tax? Intuitively, we might think that this will depend on how willing or able consumers are to switch their consumption from the good that is being taxed to other goods—in other words, how sensitive their demand is to changes in price. And our intuition would be right.

When demand is perfectly inelastic, quantity demanded does not change when the price changes, so the market demand curve is vertical. Tap water, or some prescription medications, are examples of goods which have a low elasticity of demand. This is illustrated in panel (a) of Figure 14.2. The initial equilibrium is illustrated by point E_1, where price is P_1

[2] This was originally demonstrated by Harberger (1962), on whose work the modern study of tax incidence is based.

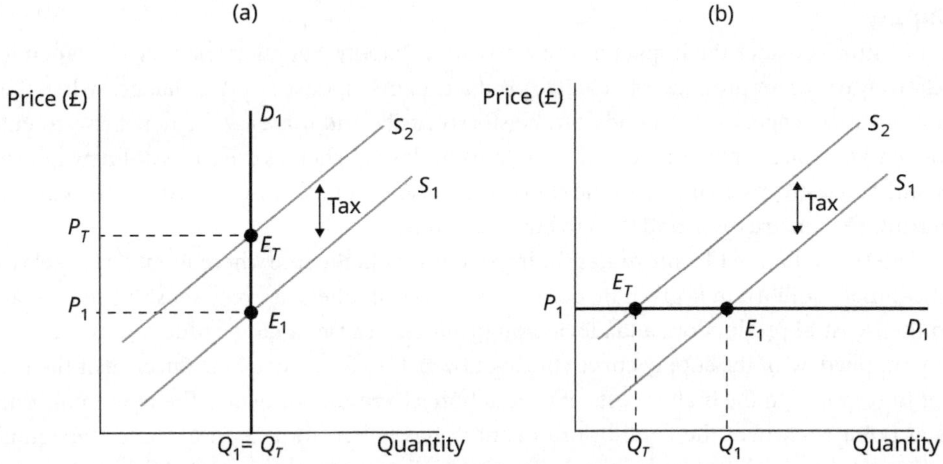

Figure 14.2 Tax incidence and the elasticity of demand

and quantity is Q_1. With a tax levied on producers, this is equivalent to an increase in their marginal cost, so the quantity supplied falls and the supply curve shifts left, from S_1 to S_2. The new equilibrium is now E_T and we can see that the whole of the tax has been passed on to consumers in the form of a higher price, P_T. So, when demand is perfectly inelastic, the entire burden of the tax falls on consumers.

If demand is perfectly elastic, then any increase in the price would lead demand to fall to zero, and the demand curve is horizontal, as illustrated in panel (b) of Figure 14.2. Examples of goods for which demand is very elastic include particular brands of goods, such as ice-cream and breakfast cereal. The initial equilibrium is given by point E_1, where the equilibrium quantity is Q_1 and the equilibrium price is P_1. A tax levied on producers again shifts the supply curve from S_1 to S_2, but now the equilibrium quantity falls to Q_T, and producers bear the full burden of the tax. Will this fall in quantity make consumers worse off? Not necessarily, because each point on the demand curve represents how much consumers are willing to pay for a good, which depends on the next best alternative use of their budget. If the price of a good—say, a particular brand of breakfast cereal—increases enough, consumers will stop buying that good and switch their consumption to an alternative that provides them with an equivalent level of utility. This highlights the important point regarding tax incidence that we saw in Chapter 13: tax incidence is fundamentally about prices, not quantities.

Based on our analysis of these two extreme cases, we can draw an important general conclusion: the greater the elasticity of demand, the lower the burden of the tax borne by consumers. So, if the government were to raise the tax on a good such as hamburgers, for which demand is relatively elastic, then firms in this sector would be unlikely to pass all of the tax on to consumers in the form of higher prices—if they did, consumers could simply switch to consuming a substitute good. On the other hand, if the government were to raise the tax on a good with a fairly inelastic demand, such as tap water or insulin, firms would be able to pass almost the entirety of the tax onto consumers, since they would have few (or no) substitute goods available to consume instead (see Box 14.1).

Supply

Let us now consider the impact of the elasticity of supply. Supply is more elastic when it is relatively easier for producers to change production in response to price changes, when there is more spare capacity and goods can be stored easily, and it is easy for new firms to enter the market. The supply of notebooks is relatively elastic, whereas the supply of new housing is fairly inelastic, particularly in the short run, because it takes time to acquire the land and permits for construction, and then to build the houses.

Panel (a) in Figure 14.3 illustrates the impact of a tax in the case where supply is very elastic. The initial equilibrium is given by point E_1. Because suppliers are very sensitive to increases in their cost of production, a tax levied on producers causes a large reduction in the quantity supplied, with the supply curve shifting upwards to S_2, as many producers exit the market in response to the higher costs of production as a result of the tax. The new equilibrium is at point E_T, where the equilibrium quantity has fallen from Q_1 to Q_T, and the equilibrium price has increased from P_1 to P_T. In this case, consumers bear most of the burden of the tax in the form of higher prices.

What if supply is more inelastic? In this case, producers have fewer options to diversify their production activities in response to the tax and the supply curve is steeper. The initial equilibrium is given by point E_1 in panel (b) of Figure 14.3. In response to the tax, producers may decrease the quantity supplied only slightly, and the supply curve shifts from S_1 to S_2, and the new equilibrium is now point E_T. The equilibrium quantity has fallen by a small amount and the price has risen, but only marginally, which shows that most of the tax will be borne by the producers.

As with the elasticity of demand, we see that the greater the elasticity of supply, the lower the tax burden borne by producers. In sum, consumers will bear more of the burden of the tax if demand is more inelastic or supply is more elastic; producers will bear more of the burden of the tax if supply is more inelastic or demand is more elastic. Although the analysis above focused on a tax levied on producers, the conclusions would be the same if the tax were levied on consumers.[3]

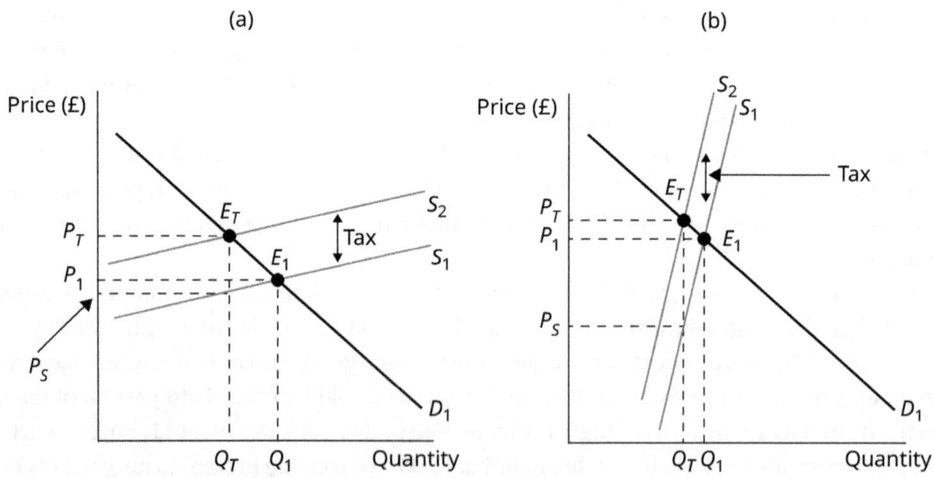

Figure 14.3 Tax incidence and the elasticity of supply

[3] Recall the second principle of tax incidence covered in Chapter 13.

Box 14.1 Tax incidence in practice

Understanding who bears the burden of taxation in practice is important for understanding what impact taxes have on social welfare and, in the case of sin taxes,[4] how effective these taxes are likely to be in discouraging consumption. Economic theory suggests that the incidence of a tax will depend on the elasticities of supply and demand: the more inelastic supply or demand is, the greater the share of the tax it will carry.

Because of their addictive nature, demand for cigarettes is fairly price inelastic, so we would expect consumers to bear most of the burden of these taxes. However, in a study of the incidence of cigarette taxes in the USA, Harding et al. (2012) found that taxes were not fully passed through to consumer prices: on average, a 1 cent increase in taxes led to a 0.85 cent increase in prices. Therefore, while consumers bear most of the burden of cigarette taxes, some of this burden is passed on to producers. But these estimates varied significantly across regions: in areas on the border with low-tax states, a 1 cent increase in cigarette taxes led to a price increase of 0.49 cents. In the USA, cigarette taxes vary considerably across states: in 2008, the average state-level cigarette tax was $1.10 per pack, but this ranged from $0.07 in South Carolina to $2.58 in New Jersey. These large variations in cigarette taxes create opportunities for tax avoidance, since individuals can drive to a state with lower taxes and buy cigarettes there. Harding et al. (2012) also found that the prices consumers paid varied depending on their level of income and education. This study highlights how any assessment of tax incidence should take into account individuals' socioeconomic background and any opportunities individuals (or firms) may have for avoiding taxes.[5]

14.1.3 Tax incidence in imperfectly competitive markets

Our analysis of tax incidence so far has assumed that markets are perfectly competitive, where we have a large number of buyers and sellers, selling virtually identical products, with minimal barriers to enter or exit the market. In reality, few real-world markets match this ideal—what happens when we move away from perfect competition?

The polar opposite of perfect competition is pure monopoly, where there is a single seller in the market. Although few firms have pure monopoly power on a global scale, there are several firms whose market share is large enough for them to be considered virtual monopolies. For example, although its market share has been falling, Microsoft still has significant monopoly power in the computer operating systems market. There are many other examples of local monopolies, where firms have a high degree of market power over specific geographical areas. Examples include a single grocery shop on a university campus, motorway petrol stations, and water companies providing household water and sewerage services.

Monopolists aim to maximize profits, just as firms in perfect competition do. But unlike firms in a perfectly competitive market, which take the market price as given, a monopolist,

[4] As we saw in Chapter 13, a sin tax is a tax levied on a good that is considered harmful to individuals or society, such as alcohol or cigarettes.

[5] See, for example, Besley and Rosen (1999) and Poterba (1996) for other estimates of pass-through rates of sales taxes to prices in the USA.

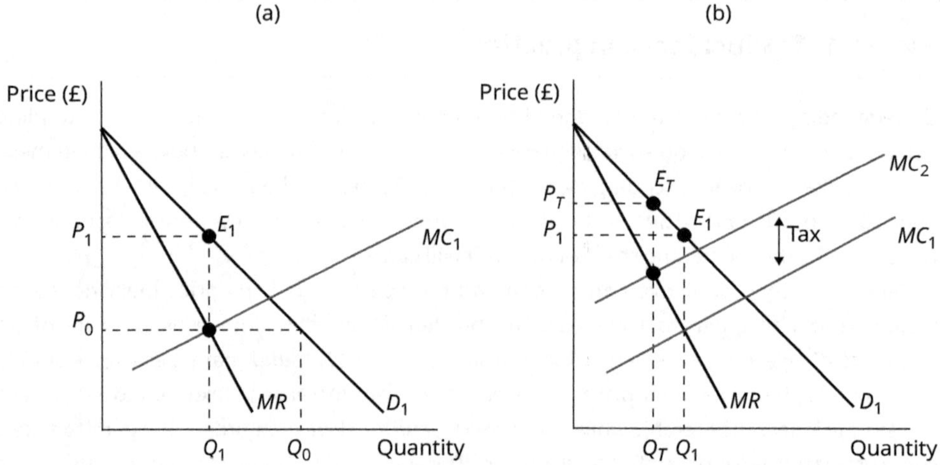

Figure 14.4 Tax incidence in monopoly markets

as the sole supplier in the market, has some control over the market price. Does this control give the monopolist an advantage when it comes to avoiding the burden of taxation?

Panel (a) in Figure 14.4 illustrates the profit-maximizing decision for a monopolist. The monopolist faces the downward-sloping demand curve D_1. Because the monopolist is the only seller in the market, to sell more output it will need to lower its price, but it will need to lower it for *all* units sold.[6] This is why, for a monopolist, the marginal revenue curve (MR) lies below the demand curve. **Marginal revenue** captures the change in total revenue from selling one additional unit. To sell another unit of output, the monopolist will need to lower its price, so the change in the firm's total revenue will be the additional revenue gained from selling that one extra unit, minus the loss in revenue from the fact that the firm has to sell all units of output at the new lower price.

The profit-maximizing condition for a monopolist is the same as for firms in perfect competition: profit is maximized where the additional revenue from selling one extra unit of output just equals the additional cost of producing it, in other words, where marginal revenue equals marginal cost. This provides the firm's profit-maximizing level of output, Q_1 in panel (a), sold at the market price P_1, which is how much consumers are willing to pay for this level of output given the market demand curve. If the monopolist were to charge the price P_0, for example, consumers would demand the higher level of output Q_0. The monopolist's profits are captured by the difference between the price that consumers pay, P_1, and the firm's marginal cost, multiplied by the level of output.

What happens if the government introduces a tax on the monopolist's product? Panel (b) illustrates the impact of a tax levied on the monopolist. The tax effectively raises the firm's marginal cost of production, shifting the marginal cost curve to the left, to MC_2. The new profit-maximizing level of output is Q_T and consumers now pay a higher price P_T. Although the price consumers pay has increased, this does not fully offset the amount of the tax, so the monopolist bears some of the burden of the tax, even though they have market power.

[6] Here we are assuming the monopolist charges the same price to all consumers, ignoring cases of **price discrimination**, where firms charge different prices to different consumers, or for different quantities of the good.

The three principles of tax incidence covered in Chapter 13 apply equally in the case of a monopoly:

1. The statutory burden of the tax is not necessarily the same as the economic burden.
2. The side of the market on which the tax is levied is irrelevant to who bears the economic burden of the tax.
3. Who bears more of the burden of the tax will depend on the relative elasticities of supply and demand.

However, the impact of the elasticities of supply and demand under monopoly is not always the same as their impact under perfect competition. If supply is very inelastic, so the marginal cost curve is almost vertical, any change in output following the imposition of a tax will be small and therefore so will be the change in price. This means the bulk of the tax is borne by producers, as happens in the case of perfect competition. If supply is very elastic, so the marginal cost curve is close to horizontal, then who bears the burden of the tax will depend on the shape of the demand curve. If the demand curve is linear, consumers and producers will share the burden of the tax;[7] but in some cases, the price may rise by more than the amount of the tax.[8]

Another difference between tax incidence in monopoly markets and perfectly competitive markets concerns the impact of ad valorem and specific taxes. As we saw above, when markets are perfectly competitive, it does not matter—for price, output, or tax revenue—whether the government adopts a specific or an ad valorem tax, provided they are set at the same rate in equilibrium. In the case of a monopolist, this difference matters: in general, for a given amount of tax revenue, an ad valorem tax will imply a smaller fall in output than a specific tax.

As an alternative to a commodity tax, the government may wish to levy a tax on the monopolist's profits, either as a lump-sum tax or as a proportion of profits.[9] In both cases, the tax will have no impact on the profit-maximizing level of output, and therefore the price at which the firm sells it output will not change, meaning the entire burden of the tax will fall on the firm. A lump-sum profit tax is equivalent to raising the monopolist's fixed cost, which will have no impact on the firm's marginal cost and therefore will not affect the profit-maximizing decision. A proportional profit tax will likewise have no impact on the firm's profit-maximizing decision: the level of output that maximizes profits before the tax will be the same level of output that maximizes profits after the tax.

Tax incidence in oligopoly markets

In between the two extremes of perfect competition and pure monopoly, there are other types of market structure, such as **oligopoly** and **monopolistic competition**. In oligopoly markets, a small number of large sellers dominate the market—for example, Boeing and Airbus dominate the commercial aircraft manufacturing industry. In the UK, for a long time, the supermarket sector was dominated by four key brands—Tesco, Sainsbury's, Asda, and

[7] As an experiment, you can try analysing the extreme case where supply is almost perfectly elastic and the marginal cost curve is horizontal: how is the burden of the tax distributed between consumers and the monopolist in this case? How does this compare with the perfectly competitive case analysed in Figure 14.3?

[8] This will happen in the case of a constant marginal cost and constant elasticity demand curves, where the price elasticity of demand is constant regardless of the price level.

[9] For example, a windfall tax on energy companies.

Morrisons—which together accounted for over 70 per cent of the market. When a small number of large firms dominate a market, their decisions regarding output and prices are interdependent—they depend on what other firms in the market do.

There is no single agreed model or theory for modelling oligopoly markets like there is for perfect competition and monopoly markets. There is disagreement over whether firms in oligopoly markets compete over prices or quantities, and whether they make their price and output decisions simultaneously or sequentially, with one firm setting its price or output level first and other firms then setting their prices or output in response. This makes analysing tax incidence in oligopoly markets more challenging: if a firm raises its price in response to a tax, will other firms in the market follow suit or will they bear the burden of the tax and keep their prices low in order to try and gain market share? Economists disagree over the answer to this question and therefore it is difficult to predict with any degree of certainty what the tax incidence in oligopoly markets will be.

14.1.4 Tax incidence in general equilibrium

The models of tax incidence we have looked at above have focused on the impact of a tax in a single market in isolation. These are known as **partial equilibrium** models. In practice, markets are interrelated: a tax on fuel will have a direct impact on the demand for fuel by drivers, but it will also have a knock-on effect on the demand for public transport and cycling; this in turn may lead to higher prices in those sectors, which will have an impact on the returns to the factors of production in those sectors, labour and capital. A more complete understanding of who bears the burden of a tax calls for a **general equilibrium** model of tax incidence.

To illustrate the implications of moving from a partial to a general equilibrium set-up, consider a city that has decided to impose a local tax on bets placed in betting shops, in an effort to discourage problem gambling. Assuming online and in-person gambling are close substitutes, then the demand for bets in betting shops will be fairly elastic. For simplicity, we will assume that demand is perfectly elastic, so the demand curve is horizontal. Based on our insights from section 14.1.2, we know the tax in this case will be borne entirely by the betting shops themselves: the betting shops will not raise their prices, since any increase in prices will cause consumers to place their bets somewhere else.

However, as we saw in Chapter 13, firms and organizations do not pay taxes; only people pay taxes—consumers, workers, and shareholders. Firms are essentially a technology for combining inputs (e.g. capital and labour) to produce a given output. So, the burden of the tax on betting shops will fall on the owners of the relevant factors of production, labour and capital. Who will bear most of the burden in this case: workers (labour) or shareholders (the owners of capital)? To answer this question, we need to shift our focus onto the markets for labour and capital used by betting shops.

The supply of labour is likely to be fairly elastic, since betting shop workers always have the option of working in other shops or in nearby cities if the betting shop reduces their wages. The demand for labour by betting shops will fall as a result of the tax, as these firms are now willing to pay less per worker since the benefits derived from each worker have fallen as a result of the tax. If we assume that labour supply is perfectly elastic, then this fall in demand will lead to a reduction in the number of workers hired, but no change in the wage rate. This is illustrated in panel (a) of Figure 14.5. The initial equilibrium in the market for labour is

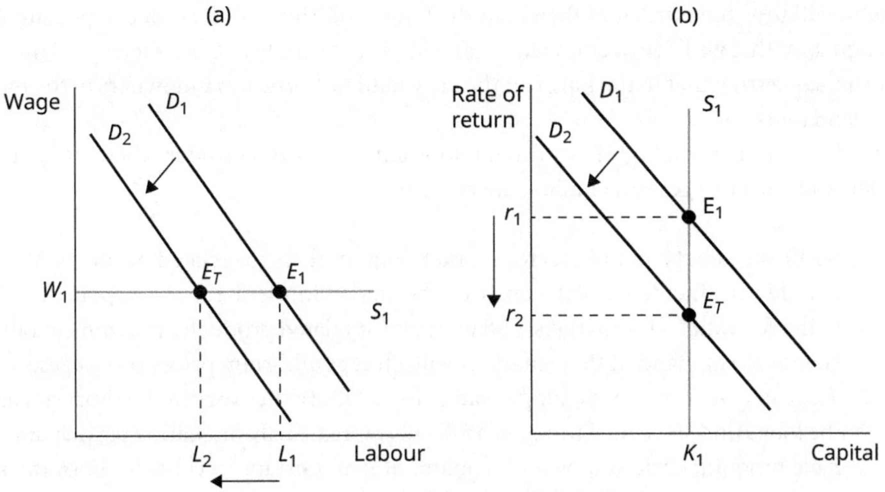

Figure 14.5 Tax incidence in the markets for labour and capital

at E_1. The tax causes the demand for labour to fall, from D_1 to D_2, and the new equilibrium is at E_T, where the equilibrium quantity of labour has fallen, but there has been no change in the equilibrium wage. So workers do not bear the burden of the tax—if the betting shop tried to lower their wages, they would simply go and work somewhere else.

If workers do not bear the burden of the tax, then it must fall on the owners of the other key input: capital. Capital includes the physical inputs such as betting machines, buildings and desks, and the financial capital that is used to buy these inputs. In the short run, the supply of capital is fairly fixed—the owner of the betting shop will have bought the necessary equipment and paid the lease on the building. As a result of the tax, the demand for capital will fall, but as the supply of capital is fairly inelastic, the owners of the capital will bear the burden of the tax in the form of a lower return on their investment in the betting shops. This is illustrated in panel (b) of Figure 14.5. The tax causes the demand for capital to fall, from D_1 to D_2, and the capital market equilibrium shifts from E_1 to E_T. The equilibrium quantity of capital is unchanged, but the rate of return falls from r_1 to r_2.

This example highlights how, although the tax was levied on bets placed in betting shops, ultimately the burden of the tax falls on the owners of the capital invested in the betting shops—so there are spillover effects from the market in which the tax is levied onto the associated factor markets. There may be additional spillover effects in related markets: a tax on bets placed in betting shops may mean more people stay at home and place bets online, which may lead to an increase in demand for home delivery services. In practice, neither demand nor supply is likely to be perfectly elastic or inelastic, so the burden of the tax is unlikely to fall on a single side of the market. But this does not affect our general conclusion: parties or factors with more elastic supply or demand avoid taxes.

Short-run elasticities are also likely to differ from long-run elasticities: once investments have been made in physical capital, these can be hard to change in the short run, but they are easier to change in the long run, as business owners look for additional capital funds to finance their investments. If a tax lowers the return to capital in a particular sector, then investors will choose to invest their money elsewhere, where they can get a higher return.

So, who will bear the burden of the tax in the long run? There is one other important input in production that we have overlooked so far—land. The supply of land is fixed and therefore inelastic, suggesting that in the long run the tax would be borne by landowners in the form of lower land rents.

The discussion above highlights three important factors to consider when analysing the incidence of a tax in a general equilibrium context:

1. **Spillover effects**: in both factor markets and markets for related products. We need to follow the incidence of the tax from the market in which the tax is applied, through to the relevant factor markets, and markets for related products, and think about how changes in demand in these markets will affect equilibrium prices and wages.
2. **Time period**: how do the supply and demand elasticities vary in the short run and in the long run? Since the burden of a tax falls more heavily on market participants who have more inelastic supply and demand, it is important to consider both the short run and the long run when analysing the incidence of a tax. Factors that are fixed in the short run may be varied in the long run.
3. **Scope of the tax**: which goods and services are covered and what is the geographical coverage of the tax? In general, the broader the tax base, the harder it is to avoid the tax, which will affect the elasticities of supply and demand. If instead of levying a tax on bets placed in betting shops in a single city, the tax was levied on all betting (whether in person or online) across a country, individual demand would be less elastic and consumers would bear more of the burden of the tax.

In theory, a complete general equilibrium analysis should take all relevant spillover effects into account and consider both short-run and long-run impacts. This is unlikely to be feasible in practice, but this discussion highlights the importance of looking beyond the market in which a tax is applied when analysing the incidence of a tax, and of remembering that firms do not pay taxes—only people pay taxes.

14.2 Consumption taxes and economic efficiency

When the government imposes a tax on goods and services, this creates an incentive for individuals and firms to change their behaviour in order to reduce their tax burden: consumers may switch to consuming alternative goods, while producers may switch to producing alternative products. These changes in behaviour are a source of inefficiency because they lead to a reduction in the quantity traded in the market, moving the market away from the competitive equilibrium, and meaning that trades that would have been mutually beneficial—where the marginal benefit exceeds the marginal cost—are no longer taking place.

Whereas our discussion of tax incidence above focused on the impact of taxes on prices (or who bears the burden of the tax in the form of changes in prices), our discussion of the efficiency implications of taxes focuses on their impact on quantities—because it is the reduction in quantities traded that is the source of inefficiency. In this section, we will analyse what factors determine the size of this inefficiency, which will provide a basis for our discussion of optimal commodity taxation in section 14.3.

14.2.1 Elasticities and the inefficiency of taxation

We saw above how the price elasticities of supply and demand play an important role in determining who bears the burden of a tax. They also play an important role in determining the inefficiency of a tax. In Chapter 13, we introduced the concept of deadweight loss as a measure of the inefficiency of taxation.[10] The deadweight loss of the tax arises because the tax leads to a reduction in the quantities traded in the market.[11] If the government were to introduce a tax on orange juice and, in response, most consumers switched to buying apple juice instead, this tax would raise very little revenue, but it would impose a cost on individuals because they were no longer consuming their preferred flavour of juice. As such, the magnitude of the deadweight loss will depend on how sensitive the quantities supplied and demanded are to changes in prices—that is, it will depend on the elasticities of supply and demand.

This is illustrated in Figure 14.6. Panel (a) illustrates the case where demand is more inelastic—for example, for a good such as tap water. A tax levied on producers would shift the supply curve from S_1 to S_2. This would lead to a large increase in the market price, from P_1 to P_T, but only a relatively small reduction in quantity, from Q_1 to Q_T. As we saw in Chapter 13, the tax leads to a reduction in both consumer and producer surplus, and while some of this is transferred to the government in the form of tax revenues, part of it is lost to society—the shaded triangle ABC. This is the deadweight loss of the tax: the loss in social welfare as a result of the reduction in mutually beneficial trades. Because the reduction in quantities, from Q_1 to Q_T, is relatively small, the size of the deadweight loss is also small.

We can compare this to panel (b), which illustrates the case where demand is more elastic. The tax on producers shifts the supply curve from S_1 to S_2, but we now have a comparatively smaller increase in the market price, from P_1 to P_T, and a larger reduction in quantity, from Q_1 to Q_T. The deadweight loss of the tax is therefore much larger in this case.

So, the inefficiency of the tax depends on the extent to which individuals change their behaviour to avoid the impact of the tax, which in turn depends on the elasticities of supply

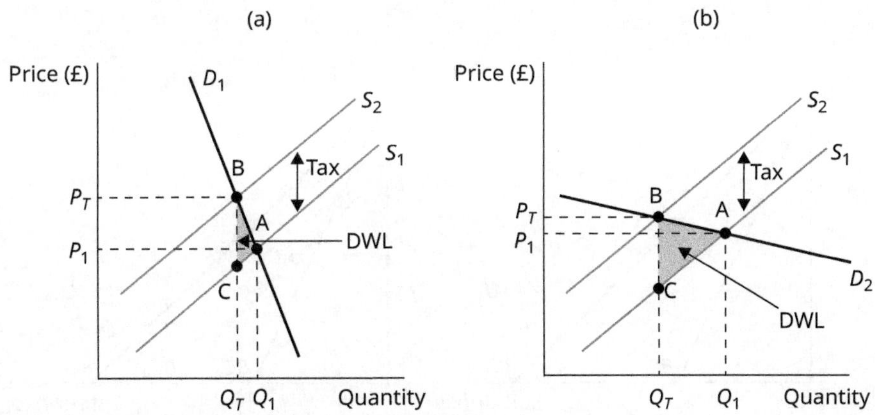

Figure 14.6 Elasticities and deadweight loss

[10] See section 13.4.1.

[11] Measuring the deadweight loss of taxation is not just a theoretical exercise: Hausman (2000) estimated the deadweight loss from taxes on wireless communication services in the USA and found that these taxes imposed an efficiency loss on the economy of $0.53 for every $1 raised in taxes. In aggregate, he found the taxes analysed cost the US economy $2.56 billion more than the $4.79 billion raised in revenues.

and demand.[12] Although we have focused on demand elasticities, the same conclusion would apply to supply elasticities: the greater the elasticity of supply, the more sensitive the quantity supplied will be to changes in prices (as a result of the tax) and therefore the larger the deadweight loss of the tax. The same conclusions would hold if the tax were levied on consumers rather than producers.

We will analyse the role of elasticities more formally in section 14.2.3, but before we do, we are going to explore the source of the efficiency loss from taxation in more detail.

14.2.2 Measuring inefficiency using indifference curves

There is an alternative way of measuring the deadweight loss or efficiency cost associated with a tax which builds on the rational choice model.[13] This analysis will help shed light on what determines the deadweight loss of a tax and help clarify why our focus should be on compensated rather than uncompensated demand curves (and when this distinction does not matter).

Suppose the government introduces a tax on sugary soft drinks. For simplicity, we will assume that the tax is paid entirely by consumers. Individuals have a fixed budget that they spend either on soft drinks or on tea.[14] The line BC_1 in panel (a) in Figure 14.7 illustrates their budget constraint—that is, the various combinations of tea and soft drinks that they can afford given their income. Given their budget and their preferences, illustrated by indifference curve U_1, their initial utility-maximizing choice is given by point A—this tells us what quantities of the two goods they should buy to maximize their utility. If the government introduces a tax on soft drinks, this will raise the price of soft drinks, causing the budget line to rotate inwards to BC_2. The tax on soft drinks has made them relatively more expensive, so bundle A is no longer affordable. The new utility-maximizing choice is given by point B, on the lower

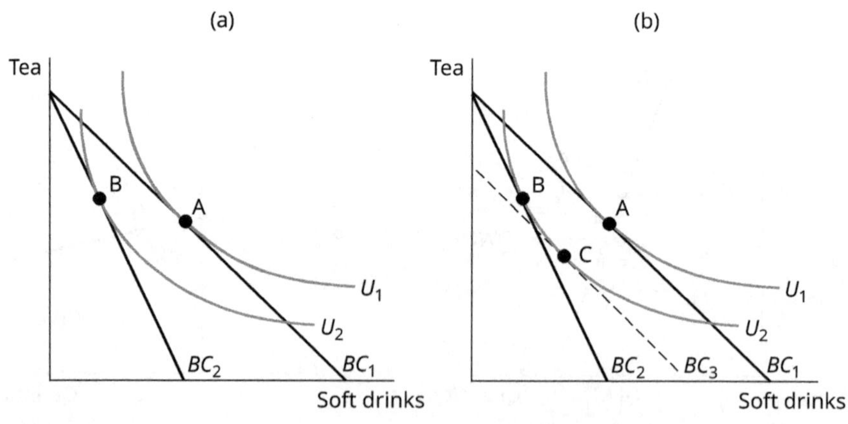

Figure 14.7 Income and substitution effects of a tax on sugary drinks

[12] Strictly speaking, we should be working with the compensated demand curve and compensated elasticities. This point is explored further in section 14.2.2.

[13] See Chapter 2 for a review of the rational choice model.

[14] We could extend this simple model to any number of goods by assuming that the vertical axis measures the money spent on all other goods.

indifference curve U_2. At B, this individual is consuming fewer soft drinks and more tea than they were before the tax.

There are two reasons why the tax will lead to a fall in the consumption of soft drinks. The tax reduces the individual's disposable income, leaving them with less money to spend on both soft drinks and tea—this is the income effect of the tax. But the tax also makes soft drinks more expensive relative to other goods (in this example, tea) and when goods are more expensive, individuals will usually try and find ways to reduce their consumption of these goods, by looking for alternatives—this change in consumption as a result of the change in relative price is the substitution effect.

Panel (b) in Figure 14.7 shows how we can decompose the impact of the tax into these two effects. To isolate the income effect, we need to ask: how would the individual's consumption of soft drinks change if we took away enough income from the individual to have the same effect on their utility as the tax (i.e. moving them onto the lower indifference curve U_2), but without changing the relative prices of the two goods? We can answer this question with the aid of a hypothetical budget line, BC_3. This budget line has the same slope as the original budget line BC_1 (and therefore reflects the same relative prices), but it is tangent to indifference curve U_2 (and therefore it has the same impact on the individual's utility as the tax). The move from A to C in panel (b) therefore captures the income effect of the tax. The substitution effect is reflected in the move from C to B, which shows how the consumption of soft drinks changes due purely to the change in relative prices. In this case, both the income and substitution effect work in the same direction, leading to a reduction in the consumption of soft drinks.

How does this help us understand the distortionary impact of the tax? To answer this question, it is helpful to compare the impact of the (distortionary) tax on soft drinks with the impact of a (non-distortionary) lump-sum tax that has the same impact on individual welfare.[15] In Chapter 13, we saw that a lump-sum tax is a type of tax that individuals cannot avoid by changing their behaviour[16]. The impact of a lump-sum tax is illustrated by the budget line BC_3 in Figure 14.8. The vertical axis in the figure now measures expenditure on all other goods. The lump-sum tax effectively reduces the individual's spending power, causing the budget line to shift inwards. This tax has the same impact on the individual's welfare as the distortionary tax, illustrated by budget line BC_2, because in both cases the individual's utility-maximizing choice lies on indifference curve U_2 and therefore yields the same level of utility.

How do the two taxes fare in terms of the amount of revenue raised? The amount of revenue raised by each tax is simply the distance between the pre and post-tax budget constraints. The lump-sum tax raises revenue equivalent to the distance CD, whereas the distortionary tax raises revenue EB. Because the budget lines BC_1 and BC_3 are parallel to one another, the distance CD is equivalent to the distance EF. So the lump-sum tax raises a larger amount of revenue than the distortionary tax, even though they both have the same impact on the individual's welfare. This additional revenue that could be raised by an equivalent lump-sum tax

[15] The value of the lump-sum tax in this case is sometimes also referred to as the equivalent variation—that is, the maximum amount of income the consumer would sacrifice to leave them indifferent between paying that amount of income and facing the distortionary tax.

[16] If the government introduced a lump-sum tax of £20, for example, this would mean that everyone would have to pay £20 to the government, regardless of individual circumstances.

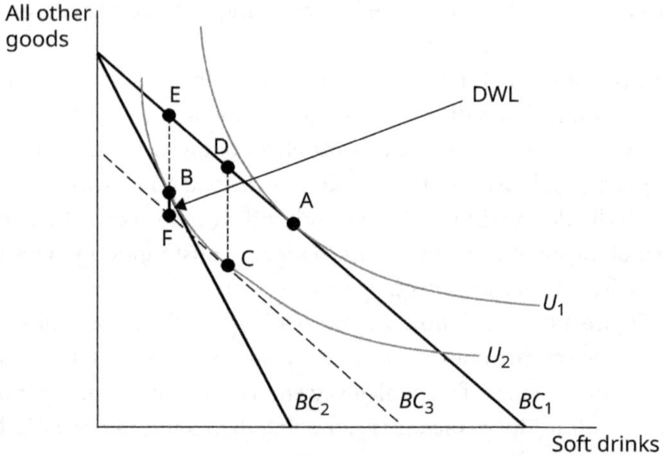

Figure 14.8 Measuring the deadweight loss of a tax using the rational choice model

provides a measure of the inefficiency or deadweight loss associated with the distortionary tax and is given by the distance BF in the figure. This is also known as the **excess burden of taxation.**

It is clear from the analysis above that the magnitude of the deadweight loss will depend on the size of the substitution effect, which, in turn, depends on how easy it is for the individual to substitute the taxed good for other goods. If the taxed good has many close substitutes (e.g. a particular type of soft drink), then the substitution effect will be large, and so too will the deadweight loss. If the taxed good has few close substitutes (e.g. housing), then the substitution effect and deadweight loss of the tax will be small. This is reflected in the shape of the indifference curves: the flatter the indifference curve, the easier it is to substitute the taxed good for other goods.[17]

This analysis provides an alternative way of representing the efficiency loss from taxation, as the difference between the revenue raised by a lump-sum tax and a distortionary tax. It also highlights why we should be using the compensated demand curve when measuring the deadweight loss of a tax using a supply and demand diagram. The compensated demand curve measures how demand for a good changes as the price changes, assuming that money is given to or taken away from the individual to ensure their utility from buying the good is unchanged; it therefore measures the substitution effect only. We want to use this demand curve because we want to know how much extra revenue we could raise with a non-distortionary tax, while having the same impact on the individual's welfare. Calculating the deadweight loss using uncompensated demand curves will tend to overestimate the efficiency cost of taxation. In practice, it can be difficult to separate income and substitution effects, so empirical work often relies on the uncompensated demand curve when estimating the size of the deadweight loss. If the income elasticity of demand is small, or if the good accounts only

[17] You can check this out for yourself by drawing a diagram similar to Figure 14.8 with very flat indifference curves, and one with less flat indifference curves, and comparing the size of the substitution effect in each case. You can also consider the extreme case where there is no scope for substitution between goods—that is, when goods are perfect complements and therefore have L-shaped indifference curves. What is the size of the substitution effect in this case?

for a small proportion of the individual's budget, then estimates based on uncompensated demand curves will be a reasonable approximation of the true deadweight loss of a tax.[18]

14.2.3 The determinants of the deadweight loss

The deadweight loss of a tax depends on the tax itself, as well as on the elasticities of supply demand. In the appendix to this chapter, we show how we can derive the following formula for the deadweight loss (DWL):

$$DWL = -\frac{1}{2} \bullet \frac{\eta_s \eta_d}{\eta_s - \eta_d} \bullet t^2 \bullet \frac{Q}{P}$$

where η_s and η_d represent the price elasticities of supply and demand, respectively, t is the tax rate, and Q and P are quantity and price. This formula highlights the two key factors that determine the size of the deadweight loss:

- **The elasticities of supply and demand:**[19] the greater these elasticities, the more sensitive supply and demand are to changes in prices, and the greater the size of the deadweight loss, because individuals and firms will have more opportunities to consume or produce alternative goods, leading to a larger reduction in quantity and moving the market further away from the socially efficient outcome.
- **The square of the tax rate:** this implies that high tax rates are more distortionary than low tax rates—for example, the efficiency loss from a tax rate of 20 per cent will be about four times larger than the efficiency loss of a tax rate of 10 per cent. This suggests it is preferable to have several smaller taxes than one very large tax.

The fact that the deadweight loss increases with the square of the tax rate means that the **marginal deadweight loss** increases with the tax rate, where the marginal deadweight loss captures the increase in the deadweight loss when the tax rate increases by one unit. This point is illustrated by Figure 14.9. The initial equilibrium is given by point A, with equilibrium quantity and price given by Q_1 and P_1, respectively. An initial tax by the government (Tax 1) causes the supply curve to shift from S_1 to S_2, leading to a new equilibrium at B. The reduction in quantity traded from Q_1 to Q_T implies a deadweight loss equal to the area ABC. Now suppose the government were to introduce an additional tax of the same size as the original tax (Tax 2). This causes the supply curve to shift further, up to S_3, resulting in a new equilibrium D, where quantity traded is now Q_{T2}. The deadweight loss associated with this additional tax is given by the area DBCE, and it is clear that this area is significantly larger than the initial deadweight loss, ABC.

[18] Stiglitz and Rosengard (2015) provide a nice example to illustrate this, which is adapted here. Suppose an individual buys 100 cans of coke a year; a 10p increase in their price would make them worse off, to the value of £10, so that if they were given £10, they would be fully compensated for the price increase. This is the principle behind a compensated price increase: the effect is the combined direct effect of the price change, plus the change in consumption from giving them an extra £10. If the proportion of an individual's income that is spent on the good is small, then there should be little difference between the impact of a compensated and uncompensated change in price because the extra income given as compensation will lead to only a small increase in spending on the good.

[19] The relevant demand elasticities here are the compensated elasticities, which reflect only the substitution effects, as discussed above.

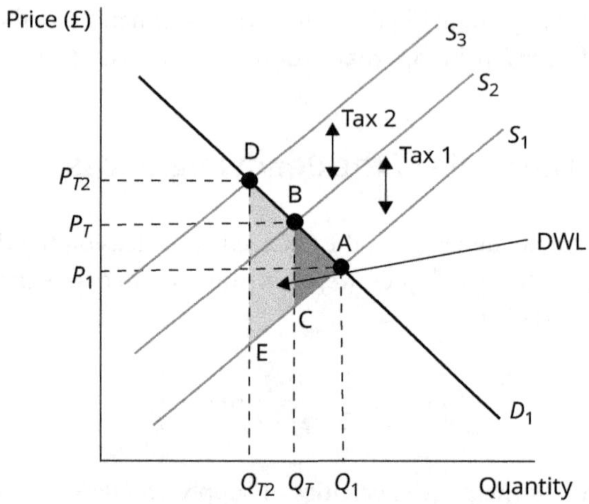

Figure 14.9 Marginal deadweight loss and the tax rate

This increase in the marginal deadweight loss arises because as we increase the tax rate, we are moving the market further away from the initial equilibrium, leading to a larger gap between demand (marginal benefit) and supply (marginal cost) and a greater loss in social surplus. But what if our initial equilibrium is not socially efficient? This will happen, for example, if there are pre-existing distortions in the market or market failures, such as imperfect competition or externalities. In markets with imperfect competition, the level of output will typically be below the competitive equilibrium output level, so imposing a tax in this market will compound the inefficiency already in place, leading to an even larger deadweight loss. This would also be the case in markets with positive externalities, where the output level will also be below the socially optimal level.[20] So, the cost of imposing a tax in these markets with pre-existing distortions will be larger than the cost of imposing a tax in a perfectly competitive market. However, if the market in question involves a negative externality, then the tax may result in no, or at least a smaller, deadweight loss (see Box 14.2).

Box 14.2 Taxing economic bads: the case of a sugar tax

Sugar taxes have become an increasingly popular means to help tackle obesity. Figure 14.10 illustrates the impact of a sugar tax levied on the sugar content of soft drinks. The initial equilibrium in the market is given by point A, with equilibrium quantity of sugary drinks Q_1 and equilibrium price P_1. This is above the socially optimal level of consumption, Q_S, because individuals only take into account their own private marginal benefit (*PMB*) and do not consider the impact their consumption has on the rest of society. With this negative consumption externality, the social marginal benefit (*SMB*) is below the private marginal benefit. So, there is excess consumption of sugary drinks, generating a deadweight loss given

[20] See Chapter 2 for a review of the inefficiency associated with these types of market failure.

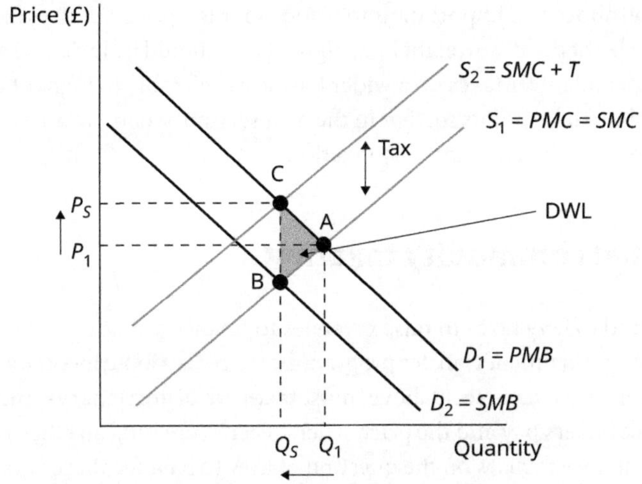

Figure 14.10 Tax in a market with pre-existing distortions

by the area ABC. A tax on sugary drinks levied on producers will shift the supply curve from S_1 to S_2, raising the price consumers pay to P_s and decreasing the quantity of sugary drinks consumed to Q_S. In this way, the tax counteracts the inefficiency generated by the negative externalities and the deadweight loss is eliminated. In practice, it would be very difficult for the government to identify the exact level of the tax required to completely eliminate the deadweight loss, but the general point remains: taxes can enhance market efficiency in the case of economic bads.

In 2016 the UK government announced a sugar tax (the Soft Drinks Industry Levy), which was brought into effect in 2018. The levy involved a tax of 24p per litre for drinks containing 8 grams of sugar per 100 millilitres, which fell to 18p per litre if the sugar content was between 5 and 8 grams; drinks with less than 5 grams of sugar per 100 millilitres were exempt from the levy. The goal was both to increase prices to discourage consumption of sugary drinks, and to raise revenue for the government to help fund healthy foods. Dickson et al. (2021) analysed the impact of this levy and found it has been very effective, but perhaps not for the reasons initially envisaged. They found that the levy led to a substantial reduction in calorie intake—6,500 calories per resident per year. However, most of this reduction happened before the levy even came into effect, as producers responded to the tax by changing their recipes to reduce the sugar content of their drinks below 5g/100ml, substituting artificial sweeteners for some of the sugar, to avoid the levy. For those producers that did not change their recipes, the levy was passed on to consumers, leading to a significant increase in prices and a fall in sales. While the Treasury has estimated the levy would raise £520 million per year, in 2019/20 the revenue raised for the government by the levy was only £336 million. This study highlights the importance of thinking about how producers (and not just consumers) will respond to a tax, and the trade-off between the effectiveness of a tax in discouraging consumption and the goal of raising revenue.

Source: Dickson et al. (2025).

The discussion above has important implications for tax policy: if the goal of tax policy is to minimize the size of the deadweight loss, higher taxes should be levied on goods with more inelastic demand; and lower taxes on a wider base are preferable to higher taxes on a narrow tax base. We explore these points further in the next section, where we analyse the key principles in the theory of optimal commodity taxation.

14.3 Optimal commodity taxation

Governments need to levy taxes to raise revenues to finance public spending. Taxes can also be used alongside government transfer programmes to redistribute income and achieve equity goals. However, as we have seen above, most taxes are distortionary—they drive a wedge between the price buyers pay and the price sellers receive, creating an efficiency cost for society. Optimal tax theory focuses on the question of how to balance these various objectives—namely, how to design a tax system that raises a given amount of revenue for the government, while minimizing efficiency losses and achieving the desired level of redistribution.

In this section, we are going to focus on the key questions that arise in the context of optimal commodity taxation. How should commodity taxes be set to minimize efficiency costs while raising a given amount of revenue? Should all goods be taxed at the same rate? Which goods should attract a higher tax rate? Building on our insights from section 14.2.3, we are going to analyse two key results in the field of optimal commodity taxation: the Ramsey rule and the inverse elasticity rule.[21]

14.3.1 The Ramsey rule

The theory of optimal commodity taxation has its origins in the work of the economist Frank Ramsey (1927). He focused on the question of how a government should set tax rates across different goods in order to minimize the efficiency cost associated with raising a given amount of revenue. The key insight from Ramsey's model is summarized in the following rule:

> **Ramsey rule**: In order to minimize the efficiency cost of raising a given amount of revenue, the government should set taxes across different goods so that the ratio of the marginal deadweight loss to marginal revenue raised is the same across all goods.

Effectively, the Ramsey rule states that the tax rates should be chosen so that the following condition should hold, for any good i:[22]

$$\frac{MDWL_i}{MR_i} = \lambda$$

where $MDWL_i$ is the marginal deadweight loss or the increase in deadweight loss from increasing the tax on good i; MR_i represents the marginal revenue or the additional revenue raised by that tax increase; and λ is the value of the additional government revenues raised. This implies that tax rates should be chosen so that the increase in deadweight loss for each extra pound or euro raised in taxes is the same across all goods.

[21] For an application of the principles of optimal commodity taxation, see, for example, Deaton (2019) for an analysis of price reforms in Pakistan, and Nicita (2004) for a similar analysis for Mexico.

[22] The derivation of this condition is covered in the appendix to this chapter.

To understand the intuition behind this result, it is helpful to think about what would happen if this condition did not hold. Suppose the government sets taxes for two goods, A and B, such that the ratio of marginal deadweight loss to marginal revenue for good A is less than for good B:

$$\frac{MDWL_A}{MR_A} < \frac{MDWL_B}{MR_B}$$

This means that the tax on good B creates more inefficiency relative to the additional revenue raised than the tax on good A. As we saw above, the marginal deadweight loss increases with the tax rate. This means that, to reduce the inefficiency associated with these taxes, the government should reduce the tax on good B, which will lead the associated marginal deadweight loss to fall, and increase the tax on good A, causing its marginal deadweight loss to rise—until the ratios for the two goods are equal.

The level at which these ratios should be set will depend on λ, the value of the additional government revenues or the marginal benefit of taxation. If the value of additional government revenues is high, implying a high λ, then the ratio of marginal deadweight loss to marginal revenue should also be high, implying high tax rates across all commodities. In other words, greater inefficiency is warranted if the benefits from government expenditure are also high (and conversely if the value of additional government revenues is low). However, determining the value of additional government revenues in practice is difficult.

It is important to note that the focus here is on minimizing the distortions of taxes in terms of quantities rather than prices, so taxes should not be set in a way that raises the prices of all goods by the same proportion. This rule implies a potentially large number of different tax rates, depending on the marginal deadweight loss and marginal revenues from taxing different commodities. As we saw above, the size of the deadweight loss associated with a tax depends on the price elasticity of demand of the good on which the tax is levied. So, this rule suggests that the tax rates levied on different goods should depend on their price elasticities of demand and, in particular, that goods with a low price elasticity of demand should be taxed more highly, since they will have a lower marginal deadweight loss.

14.3.2 The inverse elasticity rule

If we assume that markets are perfectly competitive, so the price elasticity of supply is infinite and the supply curve is horizontal (perfectly elastic), we can use the Ramsey rule to derive the following condition for the optimal tax rate for any good i, τ_i^*:[23]

$$\tau_i^* = -\frac{1}{\eta_i} \bullet \lambda$$

where η_i is the compensated price elasticity of demand for good i and λ is the value of additional government revenue.[24] This is the **inverse elasticity rule**, which states that for any

[23] If the supply curve is not infinitely elastic, then the optimal tax rate will be proportional to the sum of the reciprocals of both the elasticities of supply and demand. These results hold under a set of simplifying assumptions—in particular, the assumption that the demands for the goods are independent of one another.

[24] The price elasticity of demand is usually negative, so including the minus sign in the equation ensures the optimal tax rate will be positive.

given value of λ, the greater the elasticity of demand, the lower the tax rate should be. In other words, goods for which demand is very sensitive to changes in price should be taxed less than goods for which demand is less sensitive to changes in price. This is consistent with our analysis in section 14.2, where we saw that the deadweight loss from a tax is higher when the price elasticity of demand is higher, suggesting that if we want to minimize the deadweight loss of taxation, we should tax inelastically demanded goods more than elastically demanded goods.

While this rule may ensure the impact of taxes on efficiency is minimized, it has quite unpalatable equity implications. This result essentially says that high tax rates should be levied on necessities such as food, water, housing, and prescription medications, which typically have a low price elasticity of demand, and lower tax rates should be levied on luxury items such as perfumes and sports cars, which have a higher price elasticity of demand. These goods with low price elasticities will often have low income elasticities as well, representing a larger share of the budget for lower-income households. So, if a high tax is levied on these goods, this will impact lower-income individuals more heavily. Goods with high price elasticities and high income elasticities, such as luxury items, will attract lower taxes, benefiting primarily high-income individuals.

Subsequent research has built on Ramsey's seminal work to incorporate redistributive concerns into optimal commodity taxation.[25] If the government cares about equity as well as efficiency, then optimal tax policy should also take into account how commodity taxes affect individuals in different income groups, by considering not only the price elasticity of demand of different goods, but also the income level of the individuals who consume those goods, when designing optimal tax rates. Goods that are consumed more by higher-income individuals (i.e. have a higher income elasticity) should attract a higher tax rate than that implied by the inverse elasticity rule alone. The extent to which this is done will depend on the government and society's willingness to sacrifice efficiency for greater equity.

The system of differential taxes implied by these rules would also be very complex and costly to administer, and these additional costs should be considered alongside any equity concerns.

14.4 Insights from behavioural economics for commodity taxation

Our analysis above suggests that the magnitude of the efficiency losses associated with commodity taxation, as well as who bears the burden of these taxes, depends on how individuals and firms respond to taxes, as reflected in the elasticities of demand and supply. However, individuals respond to taxes based on how they *perceive* them. While the rational choice model, which underlies our analysis so far, assumes that people correctly perceive and understand the changes in prices due to taxes, evidence suggests that in practice there are several reasons why individuals may fail to perceive taxes correctly, or may fail to respond in a fully rational, self-interested manner. This section reviews some of these reasons and what they imply for the design of commodity taxes.

25 See, for example, Atkinson & Stiglitz (1976), Diamond (1975), Diamond & Mirrlees (1971), and Stiglitz (2015).

14.4.1 Bounded rationality, inattention, and social preferences

The standard model of individual behaviour assumes that individuals are rational, self-interested, fully informed utility maximizers. In practice, **bounded rationality** implies that we do not always have the ability to collect and process all the information required to make a utility-maximizing decision. Our limited information-gathering and computational abilities mean that, in many cases, rather than responding optimally to taxes we may rely on rules of thumb, or we may make mistakes, particularly when the information we are faced with is complex. This is supported by research by Fochmann et al. (2010) which suggests that individual judgements and the quality of decisions made tends to be worse when tax systems are more complex. The fact that individuals may make mistakes or rely on rules of thumb when responding to taxes means that the observed response, as captured by the elasticity of demand, will not reflect an optimal outcome. These mistakes and rules of thumb may lead individuals to respond more or less to taxes than they would if they understood the taxes correctly, and therefore the true excess burden from the tax may be higher or lower than the measured efficiency loss. This also has implications for individual welfare, since it means individuals are not consuming the bundles of goods that would maximize their utility.

There are other costs associated with more complex tax systems. The costs of administering such a system are likely to be higher, and there will be more scope for costly tax avoidance. If the extent of bounded rationality is correlated with individual characteristics such as income, then complexity will also involve negative distributional implications.

How individuals perceive taxes will depend on how salient or visible they are. For example, in the USA, sales taxes are not normally included in the prices posted to consumers in stores and are only added at the till, making them less salient than taxes such as VAT, as most countries show VAT-inclusive prices on the labels in stores. If individuals are less aware of sales taxes because they are less visible, then their response to these taxes will be muted, which will affect the efficiency cost of these taxes, as well as the burden of the tax that falls on consumers. When taxes are less salient, the observed elasticity of demand will be lower, and therefore the efficiency loss from the tax will also be lower. But the fact that individuals are unaware of the tax will again move them away from their utility-maximizing optimum, reducing individual welfare. The salience of taxes depends on factors including their size and frequency—with larger and more frequently collected taxes being more salient—the complexity of the tax system, and whether taxes are paid automatically.[26] Evidence suggests that salience effects of commodity taxes can be significant (see Box 14.3).

Individuals might evaluate taxes not in absolute terms, but relative to a particular reference point. These reference points may be the current situation (or status quo), past states, expected future states, or social comparisons—for example, their income or their average weekly food budget. This means that tax schemes that are otherwise identical may lead to different individual responses if they are evaluated against different reference points, and tax changes may be perceived as gains or losses depending on how they are presented. How individuals respond to a tax—in particular, the magnitude of that response—might depend on the reference point against which the tax change is evaluated, or whether the tax change represents a gain or loss relative to a particular reference point.

[26] For example, Finkelstein (2009) found that drivers were less responsive to road tolls when these were collected electronically rather than manually.

Box 14.3 Salience and commodity taxes

Chetty et al. (2009) carried out an experiment in a grocery store in the USA to test the extent to which the salience of taxes affects individual responses. They wanted to test whether a commodity tax had a larger impact on demand if it was included in the posted price that individuals saw while shopping, and was therefore more salient, when compared with a sales tax that was added at the till. Their experiment involved posting tax-inclusive prices for 750 products subject to a sales tax over a three-week period and comparing the changes in sales for these products with the change in sales for products which did not have tax-inclusive prices added to the label. They also compared these changes in sales with sales of the same products in nearby stores, where no products were given new labels. Using scanner data, they found that posting tax-inclusive prices on the label reduced demand by about 8 per cent, suggesting individuals were unaware of or were ignoring the sales taxes if these were only applied at the till. Their findings clearly show that consumers will underreact to taxes that are not salient, which has implications for the efficiency cost of taxation. Their findings also have implications for the incidence of taxation, since if consumers are inattentive and underreact to tax changes, then firms will be able to pass a greater proportion of any tax increase onto consumers.

The standard model of individual behaviour also assumes individuals typically care only about their own wellbeing, but evidence suggests that many individuals have **social preferences**. We care not only about our own well-being, but also about the well-being of others, and value things such as fairness and conforming to social norms. These social or other-regarding preferences mean that individuals may have an intrinsic willingness to pay taxes, which will influence their response to taxes and will therefore affect the excess burden and incidence of taxation. With social preferences, the legal incidence of a tax may in fact be related to the economic incidence of a tax—contrary to one of the fundamental principles of tax incidence we identified in Chapter 13. The legal incidence of a tax makes visible or reinforces social norms about who should pay the tax, which in turn may change how individuals respond to the tax.

14.4.2 The design of commodity taxes

So what does this mean for tax policy, and the design of commodity taxes in particular? According to the standard model, if the government wants to minimize the efficiency losses from taxation, it should tax goods with more inelastic demands more highly. However, this is based on the assumption that the observed responses, as reflect in the demand elasticities, are optimal, whereas individuals' lack of responsiveness to taxes may reflect mistakes or a lack of awareness of taxes, and the true efficiency losses from a tax may be higher or lower. Tax policy should not only look at observed elasticities but also consider the salience of taxes and whether people may be making mistakes. Taxing goods with more inelastic demand more heavily may no longer be an optimal policy response if it is the lack of salience (or the existence of mistakes) that is driving individuals' unresponsiveness to taxes.

Tax policy can affect the salience of taxes, and therefore the efficiency loss from taxation and the distribution of the burden of those taxes, although it is not clear whether more or less salient taxes are better for welfare. When taxes are less salient, the observed elasticity of demand will be lower, and therefore the efficiency loss from the tax will also be lower. But less salient taxes will also imply a higher welfare cost because of the mistakes individuals are making in their optimization by ignoring the tax. The process of passing the legislation required to make a particular tax less salient would also draw attention to it, effectively making it more salient (Leicester et al., 2012); such a move could also undermine public trust in taxation.

Governments can increase the salience of taxes by requiring taxes to be included in posted prices. Higher taxes are also more likely to be salient, but as we have seen above, they are also likely to result in a larger excess burden, as the measure of the deadweight loss of taxation depends on the square of the tax rate.[27] So, there is a trade-off between setting low tax rates across a wide range of goods to minimize the deadweight loss of taxation, and ensuring taxes are high enough that they are salient and minimize the chances of people making mistakes. Changing the salience of taxes will also affect their incidence, so tax policy can shift the burden of taxation. Who bears the burden of a tax depends on who responds to the tax, so the less an individual changes their behaviour in response to a tax, the more of the tax they will end up paying.

If individuals have social preferences and care about the well-being of others, then the form and object of the tax may also influence how people respond to it. People are more likely to be willing to pay taxes if they believe the tax revenues are going to be used for something they support. This suggests a possible role for **hypothecation** in tax policy, whereby revenue from particular taxes is tied to particular expenditures. However, in practice, it is very difficult to verify that tax revenues have been spent in a particular way.

Being aware of these behavioural aspects when designing tax policy is important, since they suggest that predictions regarding the efficiency cost or incidence of taxes based on the standard rational choice model are not always accurate. However, there are also costs associated with using this information in the pursuit of a more efficient tax system: more complex tax systems are more costly to administer and open up more opportunities for costly tax avoidance; there may be negative distributional implications to consider; and public support for taxation may be undermined if people believe that the government is exploiting biases—for example, by attempting to make taxes less salient. And, as we saw in Chapter 13, transparency is one of the key properties of a good tax system.

14.5 Application: the value-added tax

The value-added tax (VAT) is one of the most important indirect taxes in use today. Originally introduced in France in 1954, VAT is currently employed in 170 countries across the world—including all countries in the OECD, except for the USA. But is VAT a 'good' tax? How does it work in practice? What are the main criticisms of this tax? These are the questions we will be focusing on in this section.[28]

[27] The excess burden of taxation may even increase by more than the square of the tax rate, since as the tax rate rises, it becomes more salient and individuals will respond more to it.

[28] In terms of the challenges associated with VAT, we will be focusing on one particular issue, namely the use of differentiated rates and exemptions. For a more in-depth discussion of this issue and the other key challenges associated with VAT, readers are advised to consult the excellent discussion in Mirrlees et al. (2011).

14.5.1 What is VAT and how does it work?

VAT is a tax on the value added at each stage in the production process. It is a tax levied on all sales—both wholesale and retail[29]—but registered traders are able to claim back any tax charged on their inputs. This means that the tax base (the total value added) equals the value of final sales. It is therefore effectively a tax on final consumption only, and not on inputs. The popularity of VAT has increased steadily over time, as Figure 14.11 illustrates.

The main alternative to VAT is a retail sales tax (RST), which is currently used in most states in the USA. An RST makes a distinction between wholesale and retail sales, and the tax is levied only on retail sales—that is, sales of goods for final consumption. In theory, this approach would seem more straightforward than spreading tax liabilities across the supply chain, as VAT does. However, in practice, making the distinction between wholesale and retail sales is difficult.[30] Sellers need to check whether their buyers will be using the goods they buy for consumption or for business use, and charge tax only on the former, but there is little incentive for sellers to do this.

Because VAT is collected at various stages in the production process—and not only when goods are sold to final consumers—the scope for tax evasion is more limited than with a general sales tax. But the complex structure of VAT means that compliance costs for businesses are high, including the costs to firms of determining their VAT liabilities, keeping records, and so on.[31] The administrative costs to the government, of monitoring and enforcing compliance, are also significant, and tax evasion and fraud are still a problem in the administration of VAT (as well as the cost of honest mistakes). For the UK, estimates of the VAT gap—the difference between the amount of tax collected and what would have been collected if all individuals and businesses complied with the law—was £9 billion in 2020/21 (HM Revenue and Customs, 2022).

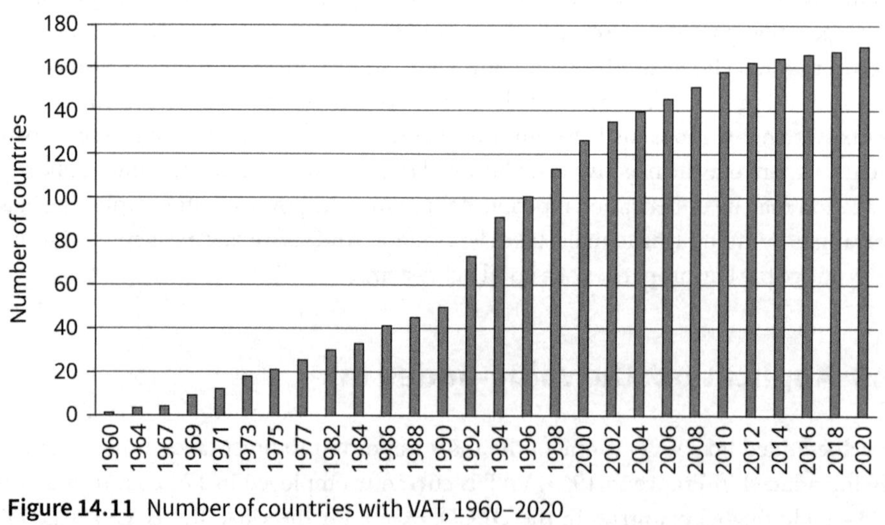

Figure 14.11 Number of countries with VAT, 1960–2020

Source: OECD (2020).

[29] 'Wholesale' refers to the sale of goods to other businesses or shops, rather than to consumers; 'retail' refers to the direct sale of goods to end consumers.

[30] However, VAT is not completely immune from this issue. In practice, it is not always easy to distinguish business expenditure from consumption expenditure. For example, with many more people working from home, should energy consumption be classed as a business expenditure?

[31] To help address these high costs, most countries have in place VAT thresholds—a level of taxable turnover beyond which businesses need to register for VAT. In the UK, this threshold was £85,000 in 2021/22. Businesses earning below this threshold in any given year do not need to register for VAT.

VAT rates vary across countries. In the OECD, the standard rate ranges from 5 per cent in Canada to 25 per cent in Sweden, Norway, and Denmark, and 27 per cent in Hungary (OECD, 2020). In most countries, alongside the standard rate, there are also categories of goods and services which are subject to a lower VAT rate, or which are exempt from VAT. In the UK, the standard rate is 20 per cent, but some goods are subject to a lower rate of 5 per cent, while other goods are zero-rated or exempt from VAT.[32] These differential rates are motivated primarily by equity concerns and the desire to encourage the consumption of certain goods, but there are also disadvantages, as we will discuss below.

The range of goods and services which are either zero-rated, subject to a reduced VAT rate, or exempt from VAT, can be extensive, as Table 14.1 illustrates. These broad categories mask the substantial challenges involved in determining which goods and services should qualify for lower rates or be exempt—should all food items be zero-rated, including caviar? Why are children's clothes zero-rated, but adult clothes are subject to a 20 per cent rate? The table also shows the estimated cost of these differential rates, measured as the revenue forgone by not charging the standard VAT rate on these goods and services. The revenue losses implied by having these differential VAT rates are quite significant. Are the benefits of having these differential rates sufficient to justify these costs?

14.5.2 The tax base

In Chapter 13, we considered the question of whether income or consumption should be the basis of taxation. Within consumption taxes, there are a wide range of goods and services which could be taxed, and taxes can be levied on goods and services destined for final consumption or on goods and services to be used as inputs in the production process. As we saw above, VAT is a tax on consumption—it is paid by final consumers; businesses do not pay VAT on the inputs they buy to use as part of their production process.[33] Are final consumption goods the appropriate tax base, or should inputs be subject to taxation as well?

The answer to this question is based on an important result in public economics known as the **Production Efficiency Theorem** (Diamond & Mirrlees, 1971). This theorem states that the optimal commodity tax system should not distort production efficiency and it implies that intermediate goods (i.e. inputs) should not be taxed. So, an optimal commodity tax system is one where taxes are only levied on final consumption goods, which will ensure production efficiency.

To understand the intuition behind this result, note that production efficiency means that the economy is producing on the boundary of its production possibility frontier, which represents all possible combinations of two goods that an economy can produce, using a given set of inputs and technology.[34] When the economy is producing on the boundary of the PPF, available resources are being used efficiently and it is not possible to increase the output of one good without decreasing the output of the other good. If we are not on the boundary of

[32] Both zero-rating and exemption imply no VAT is levied on the final product, but there is an important distinction between the two. Zero-rating means that registered traders can reclaim any VAT paid on inputs used in the production process, so the final product price does not include any tax. Exemption means producers cannot reclaim any VAT paid on inputs used as part of production, so although no VAT is levied on the final product, the VAT charged on inputs will feed into the final price.

[33] Technically they do pay VAT, but registered traders can then claim back any tax charged on inputs bought.

[34] See Chapter 2.

Table 14.1 Estimated revenue cost of VAT zero-rating, reduced rating, and exemptions in the UK, 2010/11

	Estimated cost (£m)
Zero-rated	
Food	14,250
Construction of new dwellings	5,400
Domestic passenger transport	3,250
International passenger transport	150
Books, newspapers, and magazines	1,600
Children's clothing and footwear	1,300
Water and sewerage services	1,700
Drugs and supplies on prescription	1,850
Supplies to charities	200
Certain ships and aircraft	550
Vehicles and other supplies to people with disabilities	450
Reduced rate	
Domestic fuel and power	4,250
Women's sanitary products	50
Energy-saving materials	50
Residential conversions and renovations	200
Exempt	
Rent on domestic dwellings	4,850
Supplies of commercial property	350
Education	1,150
Health services	1,500
Postal services	200
Burial and cremation	150
Finance and insurance	9,050
Betting, gaming, and lottery duties	1,150
Businesses below registration threshold	1,650

Note: The standard VAT rate during this period was 17.5 per cent, rising to 20 per cent in January 2011.

Source: HM Revenue and Customs statistics (table 1.5) in Mirrlees et al. (2011: 172).

the PPF—that is, if there is inefficiency in production—then the amount of one good could be increased without sacrificing the amount of other goods produced, simply by reallocating inputs. If the government taxes inputs, this will change their relative prices, distorting the choices that firms make regarding what combination of inputs to use in production, which will reduce production efficiency.[35] What matters for the level of welfare in a society is the

[35] The process here is analogous to what we saw in section 14.2, where we analysed how taxes on consumption goods distort the choices that individuals make about what bundle of goods to consume to maximize their utility.

total amount of goods and services produced, and by not taxing intermediate goods, we can ensure that this is maximized.

However, the Production Efficiency Theorem holds for an economy with no market failures and where there are constant returns to scale. Importantly, this result does not rule out the possibility of taxing inputs which are harmful to society and the environment, such as certain pesticides, fertilizers, or toxic metals.

14.5.3 Should all goods be taxed at the same rate?

Most countries with a VAT regime do not apply the same rate to all goods and services. There are multiple categories of goods that are either exempt or attract reduced rates, as illustrated for the UK by Table 14.1 above. But these reduced rates and exemptions involve a cost. The **VAT revenue ratio** measures the difference between the actual VAT revenues collected and the revenues that would be collected if VAT were applied at the standard rate to all consumption. In 2018, the average VAT revenue ratio for the OECD was 0.56, suggesting that 44 per cent of potential VAT revenue is not collected (OECD, 2020).[36] Given these costs, what are the arguments for having these differential rates?

Efficiency

We have already encountered one key argument above, in our discussion of optimal commodity taxation in section 14.3. Both the Ramsey rule and the inverse elasticity rule suggest that in order to minimize the efficiency costs of taxation, tax rates should vary depending on the price elasticity of demand of different goods: goods with more elastic demand should attract lower taxes, whereas those with more inelastic demand should attract higher taxes. Aside from the obvious troubling equity implications of this result, there are also practical difficulties involved in basing tax rates on price elasticities, such as determining the level of disaggregation for individual goods (e.g. should cakes be in a different category from biscuits?) and identifying the appropriate elasticities, as well as managing a complex tax system with many different rates. Having a large number of categories of tax rates also opens up more opportunities for fraud.

Uniform VAT rates, on the other hand, will minimize the distortions to individual choices, as well as reducing administrative and compliance burdens for businesses, reducing the need to spend time and effort—and in some cases, legal fees[37]—determining what category a particular good falls into.

Equity

Perhaps the strongest arguments in favour of differential VAT rates are based on concerns about equity. Individuals on lower incomes spend a larger share of their incomes on certain goods, including necessities such as food, housing, and energy, and therefore these should

[36] This ratio includes the effect of lost revenues as a result of exemptions and reduced rates, as well as fraud and non-compliance.

[37] In 1991, the British biscuit manufacturer McVitie's went to court to defend the status of its Jaffa cakes (small, biscuit-shaped cakes with a sponge base, orange filling, and chocolate topping). In the UK, chocolate-covered biscuits are subject to VAT, but chocolate-covered cakes are not. McVitie's believed that Jaffa cakes should be considered cakes, whereas HM Revenue and Customs felt they should be considered biscuits for tax purposes. Ultimately, the VAT tribunal ruled in McVitie's favour.

attract a lower tax rate. It does not seem fair that basic food items such as rice and eggs should attract the same rate of tax as caviar or luxury chocolate. Caution is needed here over what goods should warrant a lower rate, though. Lower-income individuals also typically spend a disproportionate share of their income on cigarettes and alcohol, but it would be difficult to argue that these should attract a lower rate of tax. For goods considered essentials, the government (and society) may want to encourage their consumption, and lower VAT rates can make these items more affordable.

However, one could argue that if the main concern is about equity, indirect taxes are not the most effective tool. It is important to consider the tax and welfare system as a whole, rather than focusing on specific taxes in isolation. In countries with well-established direct tax and transfer systems, redistributive goals are better achieved through those means, rather than through indirect taxation, since the support can be better targeted to those who need it. While it may seem unfair to levy the same rate of VAT on bread and caviar, is it not also unfair that both rich and poor benefit from the lower VAT rates on bread? In countries where the direct tax and transfer system is less well developed, there may still be an argument for using indirect taxes to achieve redistributive goals.

Differential VAT rates may also have a negative impact on horizontal equity. In Chapter 13, we saw that horizontal equity is about treating individuals who are equal in all relevant aspects equally. This implies that individuals earning the same income should pay the same taxes. But people with the same level of income may have different tastes, and taxing goods at different rates will end up penalizing some individuals while subsidizing the consumption of others. In the UK, individuals with a preference for reading will benefit from the zero rate of VAT on books, while those who prefer to watch films or series will have to pay 20 per cent VAT on their subscription to online streaming services.

The setting of the different VAT rates also raises some challenging questions: why should children's clothes be zero-rated, while child car seats attract a rate of 5 per cent, and educational toys a 20 per cent rate? What if a child is big and has to wear adult-sized clothes, on which VAT is charged at a 20 per cent rate?[38]

Taxes on goods and services are already differentiated to some extent in most countries as a result of excise duties. These taxes are levied on particular goods considered to be harmful to individuals or society, such as cigarettes, alcohol, and petrol/diesel, where governments want to discourage their consumption. The availability of excise duties may therefore weaken the argument for charging different VAT rates.

So, is VAT a good indirect tax? From the perspective of production efficiency, yes—since it taxes only goods and services for final consumption and not if they are to be used as inputs in production. As it is collected at various stages in the production process, the scope for tax evasion is more limited than with a retail sales tax. However, the structure of the tax means that it is complex and costly to administer, both for businesses and for the government, as it requires careful auditing and enforcement. Tax non-compliance is still a problem, particularly in an international context. While having reduced rates and exemptions provides a means for addressing equity concerns, it can generate distortions that will ultimately reduce social welfare. An alternative tax on consumption that could be designed to address both equity and efficiency concerns is an **expenditure tax**, a tax levied on household expenditures.

[38] This example is borrowed from Mirrlees et al. (2011).

Box 14.4 An expenditure tax as an alternative to VAT?

An expenditure tax is a tax levied on annual consumption expenditures, rather than on individual sales. Under an expenditure tax, households would submit an annual tax return in which they report their income, minus saving, plus any spending out of existing savings. This would provide an estimate of a household's total expenditure in a given year, which could then be taxed at progressive rates.[39] The arguments for an expenditure tax were originally developed by the economist Nicholas Kaldor in the 1950s.[40] Kaldor argued that taxing expenditure was preferable to taxing income, as taxing income would benefit wealthier individuals and discourage saving and risk-taking, and therefore investment.

In theory, an expenditure tax could be designed to be as progressive as any income tax system, by varying the tax rates for different levels of expenditure. In practice, the information requirements for an expenditure tax would be significant: implementing an expenditure tax would require detailed information on the annual consumption expenditures of households, supported by evidence (e.g. receipts). Ensuring compliance with the tax would place significant demands on tax authorities, increasing the complexity and administrative burden of taxation. On Kaldor's advice, two countries, India and Sri Lanka, adopted expenditure taxes in the late 1950s, but these experiments were quickly abandoned. However, technological developments in recent decades combined with the move towards a cashless economy in many countries may help overcome some of the administrative burdens of implementing an expenditure tax. Is it time to reconsider the expenditure tax?

However, attempts to implement expenditure taxes have ultimately failed, in large part due to the complex information requirements (see Box 14.4.). Given these challenges, should governments rely more on taxes on income? This is the focus of the next chapter.

Conclusion

Indirect taxes on goods and services have become an increasingly important source of government revenue, highlighting the importance of understanding how these taxes affect the economy and social welfare. In this chapter, we saw that who bears the burden of these taxes, as well as their impact on economic efficiency, depends on how responsive individuals and firms are to taxes: the more sensitive supply and demand are to taxes, the greater the efficiency loss of taxation; but the more sensitive individuals or firms are to changes in prices, the lower the burden of the tax they will bear. This illustrates the trade-off between efficiency and equity in the design of commodity taxes.

The early theory of optimal commodity taxation suggested that to minimize efficiency losses, governments should levy higher taxes on goods with more inelastic demand. However, as discussed above, this has stark implications for equity. More recent research has built

[39] Recall that income Y equals the sum of consumption C and savings S: $Y = C + S$. This implies $C = Y - S$. An expenditure tax would therefore be equivalent to an income tax, but where all savings are deducted.

[40] See Kaldor (1955).

on this work to incorporate redistributive concerns. If the government cares about equity as well as efficiency, then optimal tax policy should also take into account how commodity taxes affect individuals in different income groups. Insights from the field of behavioural economics have also highlighted that what matters is how individuals *perceive* taxes, and there are several reasons why individuals may fail to perceive taxes correctly, or may fail to respond in a fully rational, self-interested manner. These insights will affect the welfare implications of taxation and, as a result, the appropriate design of commodity taxes. But it is important to take a holistic view and consider the tax and welfare system as a whole, rather than focusing on specific taxes in isolation.

Questions for discussion

1. How does the impact of a specific tax differ from the impact of an ad valorem tax?
2. When will a tax be borne entirely by consumers? And by producers?
3. How does tax incidence in monopoly markets differ from tax incidence under perfect competition?
4. If the government is taxing a monopolist, should it levy a tax on the firm's output or profits? Why?
5. What are the limitations of a partial equilibrium analysis of the impact of taxation? When is a partial equilibrium analysis more likely to be useful?
6. How can we measure the deadweight loss of taxation? How does the deadweight loss depend on whether goods are complements or substitutes?
7. Should all goods be taxed? Should bread and luxury cars be taxed at the same rate?

Further reading

The classic study of tax incidence is:

Harberger, A. C. (1962). The incidence of the corporation income tax. *Journal of Political Economy*, *70*(3), 215–240.

For a recent review of the tax incidence literature:

Fullerton, D., & Metcalf, G. E. (2002). Tax incidence. In A. J. Auerbach & M. Feldstein (Eds.), *Handbook of public economics* (Vol. 4, pp. 1787–1872). Elsevier. Available at: https://doi.org/10.1016/S1573-4420(02)80005-2

For a review of the tax incidence literature with a particular focus on empirical results that highlight limitations of the canonical model of tax incidence:

Benzarti, Y. (2025). Tax incidence anomalies. *Annual Review of Economics*, *17*, 615–634. https://doi.org/10.1146/annurev-economics-081324-085805

On optimal commodity taxes:

Atkinson, A. B., & Stiglitz, J. E. (1976). The design of tax structure: Direct versus indirect taxation. *Journal of Public Economics*, *6*(1–2), 55–75.
Diamond, P. A., & Mirrlees, J. A. (1971). Optimal taxation and public production II: Tax rules. *American Economic Review*, *61*(3), 261–278.

Mankiw, N. G., Weinzierl, M., & Yagan, D. (2009). Optimal taxation in theory and practice. *Journal of Economic Perspectives, 23*(4), 147–174.

Ramsey, F. P. (1927). A contribution to the theory of taxation. *Economic Journal, 37*(145), 47–61.

Stiglitz, J. E. (2015). In praise of Frank Ramsey's contribution to the theory of taxation. *Economic Journal, 125*(583), 235–268.

On the application of the principles of optimal commodity taxation:

Deaton, A. (2019). *The analysis of household surveys: A microeconometric approach to development policy* (reissued ed.). World Bank.

Nicita, A. (2004). *Efficiency and equity of a marginal tax reform: Income, quality, and price elasticities for Mexico*. World Bank policy research working papers, no. 3266.

On the insights from behavioural economics for the design of commodity taxes:

Chetty, R., Looney, A., & Kroft, K. (2009). Salience and taxation: Theory and evidence. *American Economic Review, 99*(4), 1145–1177.

Finkelstein, A. (2009). E-ztax: Tax salience and tax rates. *Quarterly Journal of Economics, 124*(3), 969–1010.

Leicester, A., Levell, P., & Rasul, I. (2012). *Tax and benefit policy: Insights from behavioural economics*. Institute for Fiscal Studies commentary C125. Available at: https://www.ucl.ac.uk/~uctpimr/research/IFScomm125.pdf

On the value-added tax and options for reform:

Mirrlees, J., Adam, S., Besley, T., Blundell, R., Bond, S., Chote, R., Gammie, M., Johnson, P., Myles, G., & Poterba, J. M. (2011). *Tax by design: The Mirrlees review*. Oxford University Press/Institute for Fiscal Studies. See, in particular, chapters 7 and 9.

Thomas, A. (2022). Reassessing the regressivity of the VAT. *Fiscal Studies, 43*(1), 23–38. https://doi.org/10.1111/1475-5890.12290

Thomas, A. (2024). *VAT rate structures in theory and in practice*. World Bank policy research working papers, no. 10677.

Bibliography

Atkinson, A. B., & Stiglitz, J. E. (1976). The design of tax structure: Direct versus indirect taxation. *Journal of Public Economics, 6*(1–2), 55–75.

Besley, T. J., & Rosen, H. S. (1999). Sales taxes and prices: An empirical analysis. *National Tax Journal, 52*(2), 157–178.

Chetty, R., Looney, A., & Kroft, K. (2009). Salience and taxation: Theory and evidence. *American Economic Review, 99*(4), 1145–1177.

Congdon, W. J., Kling, J. R., & Mullainathan, S. (2011), Policy and choice: Public finance through the lens of behavioural economics, The Brookings Institution.

Deaton, A. (2019). *The analysis of household surveys: A microeconometric approach to development policy* (reissued ed.). World Bank.

Diamond, P. A. (1975). A many-person Ramsey tax rule. *Journal of Public Economics, 4*(4), 335–342.

Diamond, P. A., & Mirrlees, J. A. (1971). Optimal taxation and public production II: Tax rules. *American Economic Review, 61*(3), 261–278.

Dickson, A., Gehrsitz, M., & Kemp, J. (2021). *Does a spoonful of sugar levy help the calories go down? An analysis of the UK Soft Drinks Industry Levy*. Institute of Labor Economics (IZA) discussion papers, no. 14528.

Dickson, A., Gehrsitz, M., & Kemp, J. (2025). Does a spoonful of sugar levy help the calories go down? An analysis of the UK Soft Drinks Industry Levy. *Review of Economics and Statistics, 107*(6), 1754–1763. https://doi.org/10.1162/rest_a_01345

Epley, N., Mak, D., & Idson, L. C. (2006). Bonus of rebate? The impact of income framing on spending and saving. *Journal of Behavioral Decision Making, 19*(3), 213–227.

Finkelstein, A. (2009). E-ztax: Tax salience and tax rates. *Quarterly Journal of Economics, 124*(3), 969–1010.

Fochmann, M., Kiesewetter, D., Blaufus, K., Hundsdoerfer, J., & Weimann, J. (2010). *Tax perception: An empirical survey*. Arbeitskreis Quantitative Steuerlehre (arqus) discussion papers in quantitative tax research, no. 99.

Gruber, J. (2013). *Public finance and public policy* (4th ed.). Worth Publishers.

Harberger, A. C. (1962). The incidence of the corporation income tax. *Journal of Political Economy, 70*(3), 215–240.

Harding, M., Leibtag, E., & Lovenheim, M. F. (2012). The heterogeneous geographic and socioeconomic incidence of cigarette taxes: Evidence from Nielsen Homescan data. *American Economic Journal: Economic Policy, 4*(4), 169–198. https://doi.org/10.1257/pol.4.4.169

Hausman, J. (2000). Efficiency effects on the US economy from wireless taxation. *National Tax Journal, 53*(3), 733–742.

HM Revenue and Customs (2022). *Measuring tax gaps 2022 edition: Tax gap estimates for 2020 to 2021*. Section 2. Tax gaps: VAT. https://www.gov.uk/government/statistics/measuring-tax-gaps

Kaldor, N. (1955). *An expenditure tax*. Allen & Unwin. Republished by Routledge, 2003.

Leicester, A., Levell, P., & Rasul, I. (2012). *Tax and benefit policy: Insights from behavioural economics*. Institute for Fiscal Studies commentary C125. Available at: https://www.ucl.ac.uk/~uctpimr/research/IFScomm125.pdf

Mirrlees, J., Adam, S., Besley, T., Blundell, R., Bond, S., Chote, R., Gammie, M., Johnson, P., Myles, G., & Poterba, J. M. (2011). *Tax by design: The Mirrlees review*. Oxford University Press/Institute for Fiscal Studies.

Nicita, A. (2004). *Efficiency and equity of a marginal tax reform: Income, quality, and price elasticities for Mexico*. World Bank policy research working papers, no. 3266.

OECD (2020). *Consumption tax trends 2020: VAT/GST and excise rates, trends and policy issues*. Organization for Economic Cooperation and Development. Available at: https://doi.org/10.1787/152def2d-en

OECD (2025). *A comparative table of countries in the global database*. Organization for Economic Cooperation and Development. Data explorer. Revenue statistics. https://data-explorer.oecd.org (accessed 11 August 2025).

Poterba, J. M. (1996). Retail price reactions to changes in state and local sales taxes. *National Tax Journal, 49*(2), 165–176. https://doi.org/10.1086/NTJ41789195

Ramsey, F. P. (1927). A contribution to the theory of taxation. *Economic Journal, 37*(145), 47–61.

Stiglitz, J. E. (2015). In praise of Frank Ramsey's contribution to the theory of taxation. *Economic Journal, 125*(583), 235–268.

Stiglitz, J. E., & Rosengard, J. K. (2015). *Economics of the public sector* (4th ed.). W. W. Norton.

The mathematics of tax incidence

As we have seen in this chapter, tax incidence is about prices, not quantities. So how does imposing a tax affect the market price? Suppose we have a tax levied on consumers. The total change in the price as a result of the tax is $\Delta P + t$, where t is the tax and ΔP is the change in market price. To see how this change in price is related to the elasticities of demand and supply, note that the price elasticity of demand is given by:

$$\eta_d = \frac{\Delta Q}{(\Delta P + t)} \bullet \frac{P}{Q}$$

And the formula for the price elasticity of supply is:

$$\eta_s = \frac{\Delta Q}{\Delta P} \bullet \frac{P}{Q}$$

Since the tax is levied on consumers, the change in price for producers is just given by the change in market price as a result of the tax, ΔP.

We can rearrange both equations so we have the same expression on the left-hand side:

$$\eta_d = \frac{\Delta Q}{(\Delta P + t)} \bullet \frac{P}{Q} \Leftrightarrow \frac{\Delta Q}{Q} = \eta_d \bullet \frac{(\Delta P + t)}{P}$$

and

$$\eta_s = \frac{\Delta Q}{\Delta P} \bullet \frac{P}{Q} \Leftrightarrow \frac{\Delta Q}{Q} = \eta_s \bullet \frac{\Delta P}{P}$$

We can now set these two expressions equal to one another:

$$\eta_d \bullet \frac{(\Delta P + t)}{P} = \eta_s \bullet \frac{\Delta P}{P}$$

$$\Leftrightarrow \Delta P = \frac{\eta_d}{\eta_s - \eta_d} \bullet t$$

This equation gives us the change in price as a function of the tax, and the elasticities of demand and supply.

If instead the tax were levied on producers, we can show that the change in price is given by:

$$\Delta P = \frac{\eta_s}{\eta_d - \eta_s} \bullet t$$

Deriving the formula for the deadweight loss

From Figure 14.6, we can see that the deadweight loss of a tax is given by a triangle where the base equals the change in quantity following the tax and the height of the triangle is the size of the tax. We can therefore calculate the size of the deadweight loss (DWL) using the following formula:

$$DWL = -\frac{1}{2} \bullet \Delta Q \bullet t$$

where we have included a minus sign to account for the fact that the deadweight loss is positive, even though the change in quantity, ΔQ, is negative.

From our analysis above of tax incidence we have:

$$\frac{\Delta Q}{Q} = \eta_s \bullet \frac{\Delta P}{P}$$

and

$$\Delta P = \frac{\eta_d}{\eta_s - \eta_d} \bullet t$$

We can combine these two equations to derive an equation for ΔQ, the change in quantity following the introduction of the tax:

$$\Delta Q = \frac{\eta_s \eta_d}{\eta_s - \eta_d} \bullet t \bullet \frac{Q}{P}$$

We can then substitute this into the formula for the DWL:

$$DWL = -\frac{1}{2} \bullet \frac{\eta_s \eta_d}{\eta_s - \eta_d} \bullet t^2 \bullet \frac{Q}{P}$$

15
Taxes on income, savings, and wealth

Learning objectives

By the end of this chapter, you will be able to:

15.1 Explain how income is defined and measured for tax purposes and discuss the implications of using individual or household income as the unit of income taxation.
15.2 Discuss the equity implications of income taxes.
15.3 Assess the impact of income taxes on individual labour supply and economic efficiency.
15.4 Discuss the insights of optimal tax theory for the design of income taxes.
15.5 Critically discuss the impact of taxes on individual saving behaviour.
15.6 Describe the main types of wealth taxes that governments use and discuss the arguments for and against taxing individual wealth.

Introduction

Taxes on individual income are the largest source of government revenue for most governments across the world today. Across the OECD, individual income taxes and social security contributions combined accounted for almost half (48.4 per cent) of all government tax revenues in 2022 (OECD, 2025a).[1] As well as providing a key source of revenue to finance government spending, these direct taxes are one of the main mechanisms for redistributing income, alongside the benefit system, helping to reduce poverty and inequality.[2] Compared with indirect taxes on the consumption of goods and services, income taxes are also often considered fairer because they are more closely linked to an individual's ability to pay. But there is a trade-off between redistribution and the need to promote economic efficiency, as income taxes affect incentives to work and save, and high tax rates may lead individuals to try and find ways to minimize their tax burden.[3] How do income taxes affect the distribution of income? What impact do they have on individual decisions about how much to work and save?

Before we can answer these questions, we need to think about how we define income for tax purposes, which is our focus in section 15.1. We then go on to discuss the implications of income taxes for equity in section 15.2. In section 15.3, we analyse how income taxes affect individual labour supply decisions, discussing both the theory and empirical evidence.

[1] Individual income taxes include taxes on the earned income, profits, and capital gains of individuals.

[2] Other direct taxes include taxes on property and wealth and corporate income taxes. In this chapter, we will focus only on direct taxes on individual income, savings, and wealth, and not taxes paid by corporations. See Chapter 13 for an overview of the main types of taxes.

[3] We return to this point in Chapter 17 where we discuss the problems of tax evasion and tax avoidance.

Section 15.4 looks at the theory of optimal income taxation and what it implies for the design of the income tax system. In section 15.5, we turn to taxes on savings, analysing how they affect individual incentives to save, while section 15.6 briefly considers the taxation of individual wealth.

15.1 What is the basis for income taxation?

The answer to this question may seem obvious: the basis for income tax is just income. However, as we saw in Chapters 12 and 13, defining precisely what we mean by income, and how we measure it, is more challenging than it may at first appear. What should be included in our measure of income for tax purposes? Should this include income from savings as well as labour income? Should employer-provided benefits, such as health insurance or a company car, be part of taxable income? What—if any—exemptions should be allowed? Should donations to charity be tax deductible? And should income tax be levied on individuals or households? These are the questions we will be focusing on in this section. How we define the income tax base, and how we tax income from different sources, has implications both for equity—as it may benefit individuals earning an income from lower-taxed sources—and efficiency—as it creates an incentive for individuals to shift their income into lower-taxed forms.

15.1.1 Defining the income tax base: theory and practice

The tax base refers to the area of economic activity on which tax is payable. In Chapter 13, we saw that the two main bases for taxation are income and consumption. The classic definition of income used for income tax purposes is the Haig–Simons definition, which we introduced in Chapter 12. This defines income as an individual's *potential* consumption in a given period while keeping their wealth intact. It is the amount of money an individual could have spent on consumption without affecting their net wealth over a given period (Atkinson, 1983). According to this definition, the source of income is irrelevant. To calculate total income, we should add up income from all sources, including both money income (from wages, interest on savings, and dividends) and non-money income (e.g. non-monetary or fringe benefits from work, such as employer-provided health insurance, and the value of own production).[4]

The Haig–Simons definition of income provides a useful benchmark for defining the income tax base, but it is difficult to implement in practice. While some non-monetary benefits can be easily monetized, such as the value of private health insurance, this is more difficult (or perhaps impossible) to do with others. For example, how should we value job satisfaction, or how can we consistently estimate the value of all own production, such as housework or caring for children or relatives? In practice, total income for tax purposes will therefore typically include all earnings from employment and self-employment, plus measurable fringe benefits from work, interest income from savings, dividends, and capital gains.[5]

[4] See Chapter 12 for a more complete discussion of the Haig–Simons definition of income.

[5] Capital gains are the profits earned from owning an asset, such as a house or piece of artwork. We discuss the taxation of capital gains in section 15.6.

Most tax systems also include a series of allowances or deductions, which mean that the income tax base is often less than total income. There are several reasons for these exemptions:

- **Allowing for the necessary costs of earning an income**: costs that people need to incur in order to do their jobs, and which are not reimbursed by their employer, should be deductible from their income before tax is paid. This is particularly important for people who are self-employed or run their own businesses. But it is not always easy to determine what these costs are. Can travel for business purposes be fully distinguished from travel for leisure? If a business trip includes some hours of sightseeing, should the trip be tax deductible? Should buying a new laptop which is primarily used for work, but can also be used to watch TV series, be tax deductible? What about childcare costs—should these be considered a necessary cost of working?
- **Consumption is not always a choice**: some categories of deductions are designed to make the tax system fairer. The Haig–Simons definition of income is based on an individual's potential consumption, but consumption is not always a choice. Ill health can lead to substantial medical costs in countries that do not have publicly provided healthcare or mandatory health insurance, and this will limit a person's ability to pay. A person facing significant healthcare expenses that need to be paid for privately will have lower potential consumption, and therefore a lower ability to pay taxes. This is why medical expenses are tax deductible in countries such as the USA. However, some medical spending is optional and should be classed as consumption. The challenge is distinguishing these discretionary medical expenses from necessary medical expenses.
- **Encouraging socially desirable behaviours**: some tax allowances are motivated by a desire to encourage certain types of behaviour. Where consumption of certain goods involves positive externalities, reducing the tax paid should encourage people to consume more of these goods, which will benefit society as a whole. In many countries, charitable contributions are tax deductible for this reason. Mortgage interest is also tax deductible in some countries, as there are presumed positive externalities associated with homeownership (e.g. better cared-for properties, improved social connection). Some countries allow private pension contributions to be deducted before income tax is calculated to encourage saving for retirement.

These adjustments to the income tax base can be applied in the form of deductions, exemptions, or tax credits. A **tax deduction** or **tax relief** decreases an individual's taxable income, whereas a **tax credit** directly reduces the amount of taxes owed.[6] Tax deductions imply higher benefits for people with higher incomes, who are in higher tax brackets, and they are therefore more inequitable. What deductions or exemptions are allowed, and how they are applied, varies across countries (see Box 15.1).

[6] A tax deduction lowers the price of an activity or behaviour to $(1-t)$, where t is the marginal tax rate. Suppose your monthly income is £1,000 and you face a single tax rate of 20 per cent, so you would normally pay £200 in tax. If you make a £100 donation to charity that is fully tax deductible, then your taxable income is now £900 and the amount of tax paid falls to £180. So effectively the price of donating to charity is now $1-t=0.8$. A tax credit of £100, in contrast, would reduce the amount of tax paid by £100.

Box 15.1 Tax deductions and exemptions across countries

What can be deducted from income for tax purposes varies across countries. Japan allows contributions made to government, local authorities, and scientific research centres to be deducted from taxable income, as well as social security contributions and compulsory contributions to private pensions. The US tax system includes allowances for various exemptions and deductions, including mortgage interest, some medical expenses, philanthropic contributions, and state and local income and property taxes. Mortgage interest is also tax deductible in Belgium, Chile, Italy, Luxembourg, and the Netherlands. In Germany, interest on loans is tax deductible, as are local taxes. In France, interest on loans is also deductible, as are life insurance premiums (up to a certain amount). Contributions to social security and compulsory contributions to private pensions are also deductible in France, Belgium, and the Netherlands. The UK provides tax relief on contributions into workplace pensions and self-employed people can deduct some of their running costs from their taxable income, including office costs, travel costs, clothing expenses, and advertising and marketing. Individual donations to charity or amateur sports clubs are tax-free, and the tax that would have been paid can go either to the individual or to the charity.

Sources: Britannica (n.d.), OECD (2023), and UK government (n.d.).

15.1.2 What should be the unit of income taxation?

Another important question related to the tax base is whether income tax should be levied on individuals or households—in other words, what should be the tax unit for income taxation? While taxes on consumption are generally paid by the individual (or individuals) making a particular purchase, income taxes can be levied on the individual, couples, or entire households. This matters because taxing couples or households will have very different implications for work incentives and redistribution, compared to taxing individuals.

To illustrate the problem, suppose we have a tax system that includes a personal tax-free allowance of £12,500 per person, and a basic tax rate of 20 per cent on incomes up to £50,000, which rises to 40 per cent on incomes above £50,000. And suppose we have two couples: Chris and Ana, who earn £45,000 a year each, so their total household income is £90,000; and Zoe and Ben, who also have a total household income of £90,000, but Zoe earns £80,000, while Ben earns £10,000. This is illustrated in Table 15.1.

One option would be for the government to tax these couples on an individual basis. In this case, Chris and Ana would each pay £6,500 in tax, so the total tax paid would be £13,000.[7] Zoe would pay £19,500 in tax, while Ben would pay no tax, since his income falls below the tax-free personal allowance.[8] The total amount of tax paid by Zoe and Ben's household is substantially higher, even though their total household income is the same as Chris and Ana's. This contradicts the principle of horizontal equity because two families with equal incomes are not paying the same in tax.[9]

[7] To calculate the amount of tax paid by each individual, note that the first £12,500 earned is not taxed, and the tax rate on earnings between £12,500 and £50,000 is 20 per cent. So Chris and Ana would each pay $T = 0.2(45{,}000 - 12{,}500) = 6{,}500$.

[8] The amount of tax Zoe pays is given by $T = 0.2(50{,}000 - 12{,}500) + 0.4(80{,}000 - 50{,}000) = 19{,}500$.

[9] We introduced the concept of horizontal equity in the context of taxation in Chapter 13. Horizontal equity requires that individuals who are equal in all relevant aspects be treated equally.

Table 15.1 The impact of marriage on the tax burden

Household	Tax unit	Individual income (£)	Total household income (£)	Tax paid by individual (£)	Tax paid by couple (£)	Total tax paid (£)
Chris and Ana	Individual	45,000 45,000	90,000	6,500 6,500		13,000
	Couple	45,000 45,000	90,000		23,500	23,500
Zoe and Ben	Individual	80,000 10,000	90,000	19,500 0		19,500
	Couple	80,000 10,000	90,000		23,500	23,500

The alternative is for the government to tax the couples as a family unit, in which case the tax paid by each couple would be £23,500. So both couples pay the same in tax, but they are now paying more in tax than if they were not married—so there is effectively a marriage tax.

This problem arises because of the progressive nature of the tax system, where marginal tax rates rise as incomes rise. This means that families with a more equal distribution of income between them pay lower taxes. The only way to avoid this problem is to have a proportional or flat tax, but then the system is no longer progressive.[10] This example illustrates a more general point: a tax system cannot be simultaneously progressive, neutral towards marriage/cohabitation, and tax all families with the same joint income equally.

Marriage allowances, where the personal tax allowance is transferable within the couple when two people marry, can help mitigate this problem. The effective tax on marriage could be removed by providing a greater personal allowance to married couples than is provided to singles. However, it is not possible to design a tax system that is marriage neutral (i.e. that does not involve either a marriage tax or subsidy). This has obvious equity implications, and will also impact the labour supply decisions of secondary earners in the household.[11] If couples are taxed on their combined income, secondary earners are likely to face a higher marginal tax rate, which may have a negative impact on their labour supply. Approaches to the tax treatment of marriage have changed over time, but still vary across countries (see Box 15.2).

Box 15.2 Marriage taxes in practice

Historically, in many countries, higher tax allowances were given to married couples, as women were treated as dependants. This created an incentive for couples to marry rather than just live together. In the UK, husband and wife were treated as a single tax unit until 1990 and any income the wife earned was added to the husband's income for tax purposes when they married. Married men were entitled to a tax allowance worth one a half times a single person's allowance. The system of independent taxation was introduced in 1990, but a married couple's allowance was introduced, equal to 0.6 of a single person's allowance. This meant married couples had a

(Continued)

[10] See Chapter 13 for a discussion of progressive, proportional, and regressive taxes. Under a proportional income tax, the average tax rate does not increase with income, so all taxpayers pay the same proportion of their income in taxes.
[11] The secondary earner within the household is typically the spouse who earns the lower income.

tax advantage over unmarried couples. This married couple's allowance was abolished in 2000. From 2015, married couples and civil partners have been able to transfer a fraction (roughly 10 per cent) of their personal tax-free allowance to their partners, provided neither of them is a higher-rate taxpayer; this allowance was worth up to £252 in 2023/24.

In France, in contrast, the tax unit is the family and there is a single rate schedule. Couples submit a joint income tax declaration, which means their incomes are combined and taxed jointly. This applies both to couples who are married and to those in a civil partnership. In Germany, married couples are assessed jointly for tax purposes, but they can choose to have their taxes assessed individually. The USA similarly has a family-based tax system where married couples have the option of filing their taxes separately or jointly. In countries including Argentina, India, and Japan, couples have to file separate tax returns.

Sources: Christl et al. (2023) and House of Commons Library (2023).

15.2 Income tax and fairness

One of the properties of a good tax system is that it should be fair. But, as we saw in Chapter 13, there are different ways of defining and measuring fairness in the context of taxation. Building on the concepts introduced in that chapter, in this section we explore their implications for income taxes. We start with a discussion of horizontal and vertical equity, before turning to the question of who bears the burden of income taxes.[12]

15.2.1 Horizontal and vertical equity

In the context of taxation, horizontal equity implies that individuals who are equal in all relevant respects—who have the same income or ability to pay—should pay the same taxes, whereas vertical equity requires that individuals with higher incomes, who have a higher ability to pay, pay more in taxes. How we define and measure income for tax purposes therefore has important implications for the fairness of the income tax system.[13]

The Haig–Simons income definition discussed above supports both horizontal and vertical equity, as it does not discriminate between income from different sources. It implies that two people who receive the same income should pay the same in taxes, and that individuals receiving a higher income should pay more in tax, regardless of the form in which that income is received. If Alfie receives an annual income of £25,000 and Leni receives an annual income of £24,000 plus employer-provided health insurance valued at £1,000 per year, their annual incomes are identical under the Haig–Simons definition, and they should both pay the same in taxes. If Alfie and Leni both receive an annual income of £25,000, but Leni also receives health insurance valued at £1,000 and a company car, then under the Haig–Simons definition of income Leni should pay more in taxes.

However, as we saw above, measuring all the different sources of income is not always feasible in practice and therefore the income measure used for tax purposes will typically be less

[12] See Chapter 13, section 13.3, for a review of these concepts. Throughout this section and the next, our focus is on labour income. The taxation of savings and wealth is covered in sections 15.5 and 15.6.

[13] An alternative to this ability-to-pay approach is the benefit approach to taxation, whereby the amount of tax that individuals pay should be proportionate to the benefits they receive from the public expenditures funded by those taxes. We discuss some of the difficulties with this benefit approach in Chapter 13.

comprehensive than the Haig–Simons definition. This concept of income also fails to take into account the fact that not all consumption is a choice. Two individuals may earn the same income, but if one of them has a chronic health condition which means they face significant healthcare bills, is it fair to say they both have the same ability to pay? In section 15.1, we saw how most tax systems include various allowances and exemptions, which goes some way towards mitigating this issue. The challenge then lies in determining what should be covered by these allowances to ensure the system is equitable. That they should cover essential healthcare costs may seem fairly uncontroversial, but what about childcare costs? Should childcare expenditure be viewed as a necessary cost of work?

Income taxes, alongside the benefit system, are one of the main tools for achieving redistribution. Table 15.2 illustrates how effective the tax and transfer system is in reducing inequality, measured by the Gini coefficient.[14] Most countries have progressive income tax

Table 15.2 Income inequality across countries (Gini coefficient), 2022

Country	Gini coefficient pre taxes and transfers	Gini coefficient post taxes and transfers
Australia	0.441	0.319
Austria	0.490	0.285
Belgium	0.481	0.250
Canada	0.427	0.300
Denmark	0.442	0.276
Finland	0.512	0.274
France	0.524	0.297
Germany	0.503	0.313
Greece	0.514	0.316
Ireland	0.493	0.285
Italy	0.508	0.319
Japan	0.513	0.338
Netherlands	0.441	0.292
New Zealand	0.457	0.326
Norway	0.434	0.262
Portugal	0.514	0.332
Spain	0.480	0.316
Sweden	0.439	0.290
UK	0.512	0.365
USA	0.512	0.396

Note: Data for Australia are from 2020, and for Germany and Japan are from 2021.
Source: OECD (2025c).

[14] A Gini coefficient of zero represents perfect equality, while a Gini coefficient of 1 represents perfect inequality.

schedules, where the marginal tax rate rises with income.[15] But the top marginal tax rate has fallen significantly in many countries since the late 1970s and early 1980s. In 1978, the top marginal tax rate in the UK was 98 per cent; it was 75 per cent in Japan and 70 per cent in the United States. By 2017, the top marginal income tax rate had fallen to 45 per cent in the UK, 40 per cent in the USA, and 56 per cent in Japan (Our World in Data, 2024). Part of the rationale for reducing marginal tax rates was based on the impact they have on individual incentives to work, a question we explore in section 15.3.

Progressive tax schedules involve setting different marginal tax rates for different income bands. If the tax thresholds—the income levels at which different rates of income tax are levied—are not uprated in line with inflation, this can lead to the problem of **fiscal drag** (see Box 15.3).

The discussion above has focused on marginal tax rates. But ultimately what matters for welfare is the *effective* tax rate—that is, the total amount of income that is taken in tax and reduced benefits.[16] The **effective marginal tax rate** takes into account the withdrawal of benefits as income rises. Suppose benefits are withdrawn at a rate of 60p for every additional £1 earned (in gross earnings) and the marginal tax rate is 20p per £1. The effective marginal tax rate is then 80 per cent.

Box 15.3 Fiscal drag

Fiscal drag arises when tax thresholds are frozen or when they are increased more slowly than the rate at which incomes are increasing. This means individuals' taxable income increases even if marginal tax rates are unchanged, which allows the government to increase the revenue it raises, as more individuals are 'dragged' into paying tax, or paying tax at a higher marginal tax rate. Suppose the personal allowance—the level at which individuals start paying income tax—is set at £12,000. An individual earning £11,500 a year will not have to pay any income tax. Now suppose that both income and prices increase by 10 per cent, but the personal allowance threshold does not change. This individual's nominal income will increase to £12,650, and they will have to start paying taxes, even though their real income has not changed.

The impact of fiscal drag is significant. The increase in the number of income taxpayers in the UK from under 26 million in 1996/97 to 32.5 million in 2007/08 has been attributed to fiscal drag (Mirrlees et al., 2011). A number of tax thresholds in the UK have been frozen since April 2022 and are expected to remain frozen until April 2028. This freeze in income tax thresholds is estimated to raise over £33.5 billion per year in 2028/29. This is why fiscal drag is sometimes referred to as a 'stealth tax'.

Source: House of Commons Library (2024).

[15] See Chapter 13 for a review of progressive, proportional, and regressive tax systems. A tax is progressive as long as the average tax rate rises with income. The average tax rate is the percentage of total income that is paid in tax, whereas the marginal tax rate is the percentage of the next pound/euro/dollar earned that is paid in tax. A tax system with a constant marginal tax rate can also be progressive, provided it includes a tax-free allowance.

[16] See Chapter 12.

15.2.2 The incidence of income tax

The economic incidence of a tax refers to how the burden or impact of a tax is shared between consumers and producers in a market. As we saw in Chapter 13, this is not necessarily the person or organization who is responsible for making the tax payment to the government.[17] We analysed this concept in the context of commodity taxation in Chapter 14. Here we briefly discuss the incidence of income taxes in the context of labour markets. The analysis of tax incidence in labour markets is similar to the general analysis we carried out in Chapter 13, but now the consumers are the firms that employ workers and the producers are the individuals who supply their labour in the market.

Figure 15.1 illustrates the equilibrium in the market for labour, where the quantity of labour in hours worked is measured along the horizontal axis and the hourly wage is measured along the vertical axis. The demand for labour by firms is given by D_1 and the labour supply curve is given by S_1. The initial equilibrium is at A, where the equilibrium wage is W_0 and H_0 hours of labour are supplied.

Suppose a tax t of £1 per hour is levied on workers. This will effectively reduce the return to work by £1 per hour, so workers will now require a higher wage (by £1) for every hour worked. The supply curve therefore shifts up from S_1 to S_2, as illustrated in panel (a) of Figure 15.1. Demand for labour is unchanged, so at the initial equilibrium wage W_0 there is now excess demand for labour, which puts upward pressure on wages. The new equilibrium wage is W_1 at point B, and hours worked fall to H_1. Workers now receive the higher wage W_1, but they need to pay the tax to the government, so their take-home wage is the lower wage W_2. Firms have to pay the higher wage, and therefore employ fewer workers. If the supply and demand elasticities are equal, the burden of the tax is shared equally between workers and firms: firms now pay the higher wage W_1 instead of W_0, and workers receive the lower wage W_2 instead of W_0. If the elasticities of supply and demand are different, then whichever side of the market is less sensitive to changes in the price will bear a greater burden of the tax.[18]

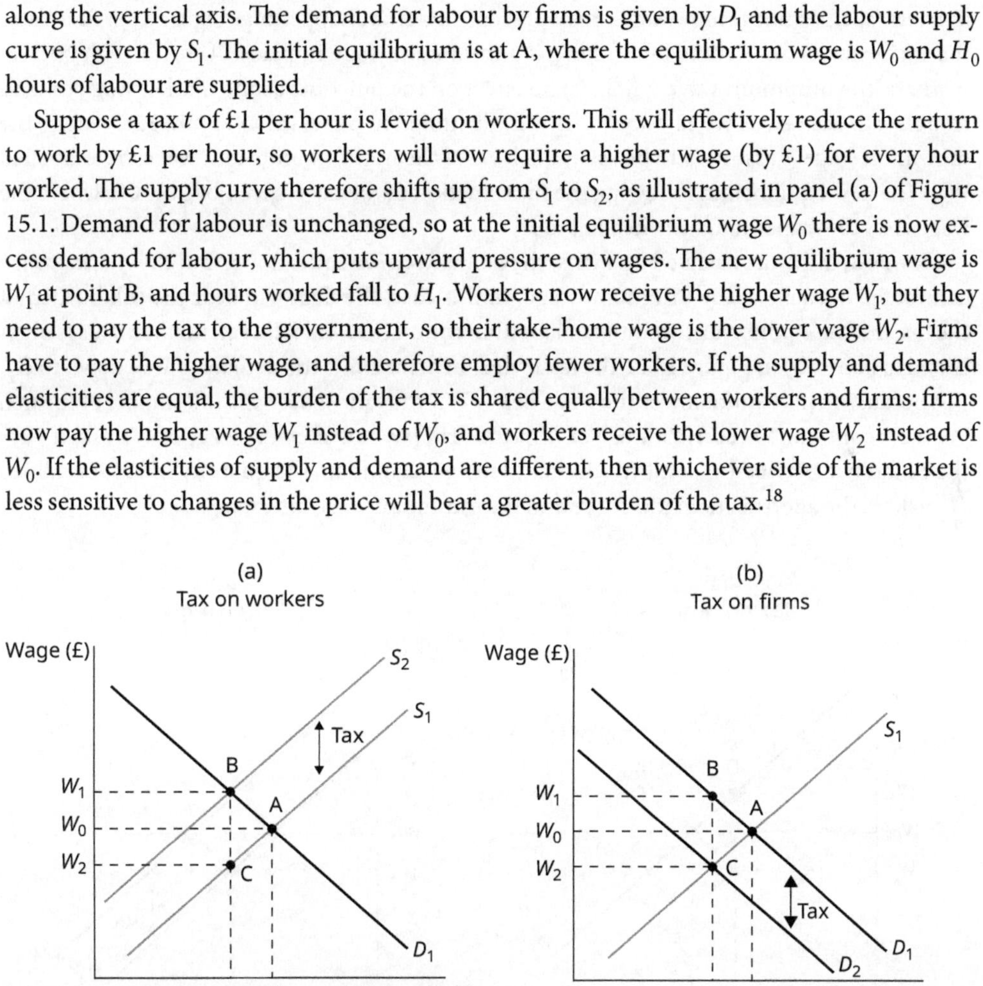

Figure 15.1 Tax incidence in factor markets

[17] See Chapter 13 for a review of this concept and the three principles of tax incidence.

[18] See Chapter 13 for an explanation of the intuition behind this result, and Chapter 14 for an illustration in the context of taxes on goods and services.

Now suppose that instead the tax is levied on firms, so the firm is responsible for paying the tax to the government. How will this change our analysis? This case is illustrated in panel (b) of Figure 15.1. The tax now raises the effective price of labour, so the firm's demand for labour falls and the demand curve shifts down from D_1 to D_2. The supply of labour is unchanged and at the original wage W_0 there is now excess supply of labour, which will put downward pressure on wages. The new equilibrium wage is W_2 at point C, and hours worked fall to H_1. The burden of the tax is again shared equally between workers and the firm.[19] Workers receive the lower wage W_2 instead of W_0, while firms effectively pay the higher wage W_1 instead of W_0 (W_2 goes to the workers and the difference between W_1 and W_2 is the tax paid to the government).

Our analysis above is analogous to the general case we covered in Chapter 13. However, this relies on the market being able to fully adjust to the new equilibrium. In practice, certain barriers, such as minimum wages, may prevent this from happening. Figure 15.2 illustrates the incidence of an income tax if there is a minimum wage in place. If the tax is levied on workers, the minimum wage will have no effect on the outcome as the market wage rises in response to the tax, as we saw above. This is illustrated in panel (a) in Figure 15.2, where the minimum wage is assumed to be set at the level of the initial equilibrium wage, now labelled W_M. The new equilibrium following the introduction of the tax is given by point B, where the wage rises to W_1 and hours worked fall to H_1.

However, if the tax is levied on firms, the demand curve shifts down, but the market wage cannot fall because of the minimum wage. In this case, the firm will bear the full burden of the tax and the equilibrium quantity of labour in the market will fall even further. This is illustrated in panel (b) in Figure 15.2. The tax levied on firms shifts the demand curve down to D_2. But because firms cannot lower the wage below W_M they must bear the full impact of the tax. Workers continue to receive a wage of W_M, the firm pays an after-tax wage of W_3, and it pays the difference between W_3 and W_M in tax to the government. The quantity of labour falls to H_2, where the after-tax demand curve and the minimum wage intersect.

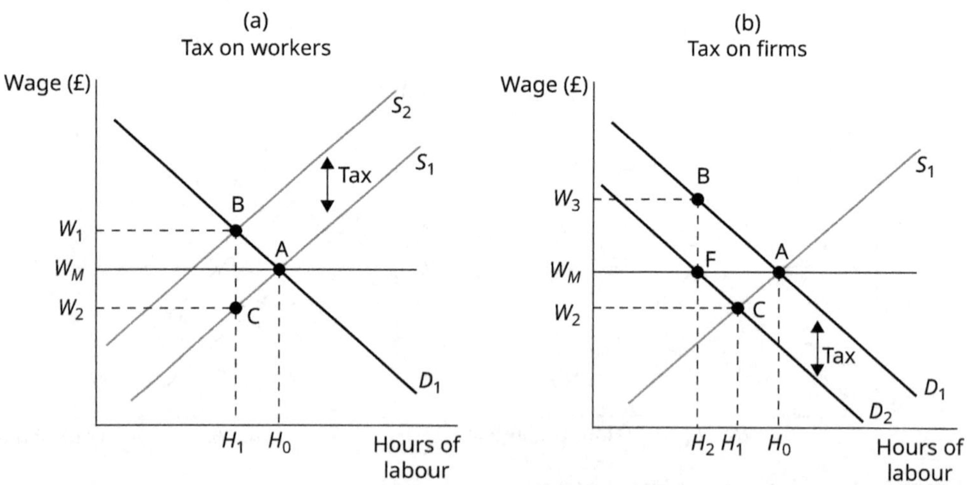

Figure 15.2 Tax incidence in factor markets with a minimum wage

[19] This result will still hold if the tax is an ad valorem or proportional tax rather than a fixed tax. The only difference is that instead of the demand or supply curve shifting, they would now rotate to reflect the percentage change in the price/wage. See Chapter 14 for an illustration in the context of commodity taxes.

15.3 Income tax and economic efficiency

When governments introduce a tax, this creates an incentive for individuals to change their behaviour to minimize the amount of tax they have to pay, and these changes in behaviour are a source of inefficiency. Income taxes can affect labour supply in different ways: they can affect how many hours we work and whether we choose to work at all, the amount of effort we put into our work, how long we spend in education, and when we choose to retire. In this section, we will focus on the first two aspects: hours worked, which is sometimes referred to as the decision at the intensive margin; and the decision to work, which is known as the decision at the extensive margin. We start by analysing the impact of taxes on these decisions using the neoclassical labour supply model and then discuss some of the empirical evidence on how income taxes affect labour supply.

15.3.1 Income tax and labour supply

In the neoclassical labour supply model, labour or work is assumed to be a 'bad': individuals do not derive utility from working directly; instead, they derive utility from the complementary good, leisure, and from the income they receive from working. So in this framework we do not model labour supply directly. Rather, we model an individual's choice over two goods—hours of leisure and income—and then derive their labour supply from the optimal choice of leisure. We assume individuals spend their time either working or enjoying leisure, so their labour supply (the number of hours worked) is just the difference between the total hours available and their utility-maximizing hours of leisure.

The basic set-up of this model is depicted in panel (a) of Figure 15.3. This illustrates Alfie's choice between hours of leisure h, measured along the horizontal axis, and income M, measured along the vertical axis. We assume Alfie has a total time endowment of T, which he can allocate between leisure and working. Hours of leisure are measured from left to right, whereas hours of work are measured from right to left along the horizontal axis. For simplicity, we assume the only income Alfie receives is from working, which is paid at a constant hourly wage rate w.[20]

If Alfie spends all of his time working, his leisure time will be zero and he will receive a maximum income of $w \cdot T$. If instead Alfie decides not to work at all, he will enjoy total leisure time T and his income will be zero. We assume Alfie can choose to work any number of hours between zero and T, and the line connecting these two extremes, BC_1, is Alfie's budget line, which represents the various possible combinations of hours worked and income.[21] The slope of the budget line is given by the wage rate w, which is the price of leisure. The cost of one additional hour of leisure time is just the income Alfie would have earned if he had chosen to work instead. Alfie's utility-maximizing choice is given by point where the budget line is tangent to his highest possible indifference curve, illustrated by point A in panel (a).[22]

[20] The model can be extended to allow for other sources of income and to allow for a wage rate that varies with hours worked.

[21] For example, suppose we are analysing Alfie's decision over the course of a day, so the maximum number of hours of work or leisure is 16 (assuming he has to sleep 8 hours). If the hourly wage is £20 per hour, the maximum income Alfie can earn in a day is $w \cdot T = 20 \cdot 16 = 320$ and the maximum hours of leisure he can enjoy is 16 hours. The budget line will be the line connecting these two points.

[22] See Chapter 2 for a review of an individual's utility maximization problem in the context of consumption, including a brief review of concepts including indifference curves and budget lines.

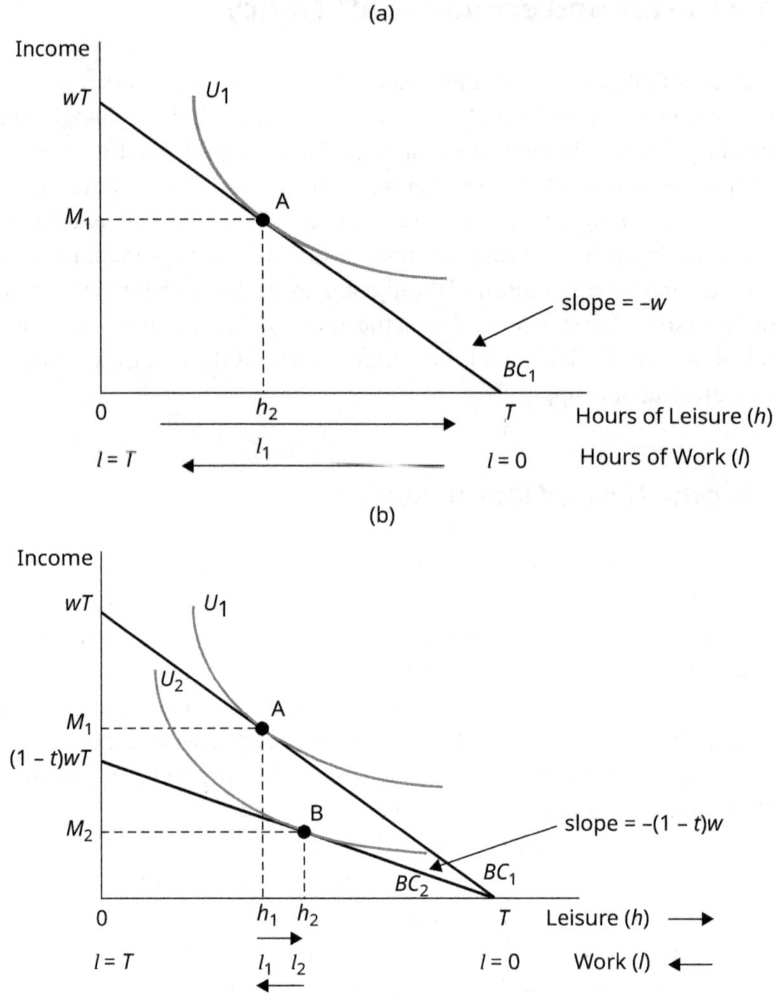

Figure 15.3 Impact of an income tax on individual labour supply

Here, Alfie enjoys h_1 hours of leisure, which implies l_1 hours of work (where $l_1 = T - h$), and receives an income $M_1 = w \bullet l_1$.

Now suppose the government introduces a tax of 20 per cent on each pound or euro earned, so $t = 0.2$. This will cause the budget line to rotate downwards to BC_2, as illustrated in panel (b) of Figure 15.3. If Alfie now spends all of his time working, the maximum take-home pay he will receive is $(1-t)wT$. The price of each hour of leisure has fallen to $-(1-t)w$, the after-tax wage rate, which is the slope of the new budget line.[23] Point A on his original indifference curve U_1 is no longer attainable, and Alfie now maximizes his utility at point B on the lower indifference curve U_2. As a result of the tax, Alfie's utility is lower and he now enjoys more leisure time h_2, which means he spends less time working. His income is also lower, at M_2, partly because he is working fewer hours, but also because part of this is paid in tax to the government. The amount of revenue raised by the tax is given by the difference between the pre- and post-tax budget lines, BC_1 and BC_2, at the level of hours worked.

[23] If the wage is £20 per hour, the after-tax wage per hour is $(1-t)w = (1-0.2)20 = 16$.

In this example, the tax has led to a reduction in hours worked, but will this always be the case? To answer this question, it is helpful to break up the impact of the tax into two separate effects: the income effect and the substitution effect. The tax reduces the effective price of leisure, encouraging individuals to consume more leisure as it is now relatively cheaper (and hence to work less)—this is the substitution effect. The substitution effect is always negative: as the effective wage falls, leisure becomes cheaper and demand for leisure increases.[24] But the tax will also lead to a reduction in the income that individuals earn from a given number of hours of work, which means that they can 'afford' less leisure—this is the income effect. The income effect is always positive, as the change in the wage and in the demand for leisure move in the same direction: as the wage falls (rises), demand for leisure falls (rises).[25] As these two effects work in opposite directions, the net impact of the tax on leisure and hours worked will depend on their relative magnitudes. If the income effect is larger than the substitution effect, then the tax will lead to a decrease in leisure and an increase in hours worked; if the substitution effect is larger than the income effect, then the tax will lead to an increase in leisure and a reduction in hours worked.

These two cases are illustrated in Figure 15.4. In both panel (a) and panel (b), the initial optimal choice is at point A. The tax causes the budget line to rotate inwards, from BC_1 to BC_2, and the new optimal choice is given by point B. To isolate the substitution effect, we need to analyse how demand for leisure changes in response to the change in the price of leisure following the introduction of the tax, but holding real income and utility constant at the original level U_1. In this way, we are focusing just on the impact of the change in the price of leisure, abstracting from how this price change affects the individual's purchasing power. We do this by adding in a hypothetical budget line which has the same slope as the budget line following the introduction of the tax—as the slope of the budget line reflects the price of leisure—but which is tangent to the original indifference curve U_1, to ensure the utility level is unchanged. This hypothetical budget line is the dashed line BC' in the figure.[26] The substitution effect is captured by the move from point A to C in both panels in Figure 15.4. In both cases, demand for leisure increases from h_1 to h'.

To isolate the income effect, we need to look at how demand for leisure changes in response to the reduction in purchasing power, but now keeping the price of leisure constant. This is shown by the inward shift of the budget line, from BC' to BC_2, and the move from point C to B. In both cases, demand for leisure falls, from h' to h_2. In panel (a), the substitution effect is larger than the income effect and the net effect of the tax is to increase hours of leisure from h_1 to h_2, which implies a reduction in hours worked. In panel (b), the income effect is larger and the net effect of the tax is to reduce hours of leisure, or equivalently increase hours of work.

Income tax systems in practice are far more complex than in this simple example, as Box 15.4 illustrates.

[24] Conversely, if the effective wage were to rise, leisure would become more expensive and demand for leisure would fall. Because the change in the demand for leisure has the opposite sign to the change in the wage rate, the effect is negative.

[25] Assuming leisure is a **normal good**, for which demand falls (rises) as income falls (rises).

[26] Another way of thinking about this is to imagine that, following the introduction of the tax, the government gave individuals enough money to restore their original level of utility. This would effectively push their budget line out from BC_2 to BC'.

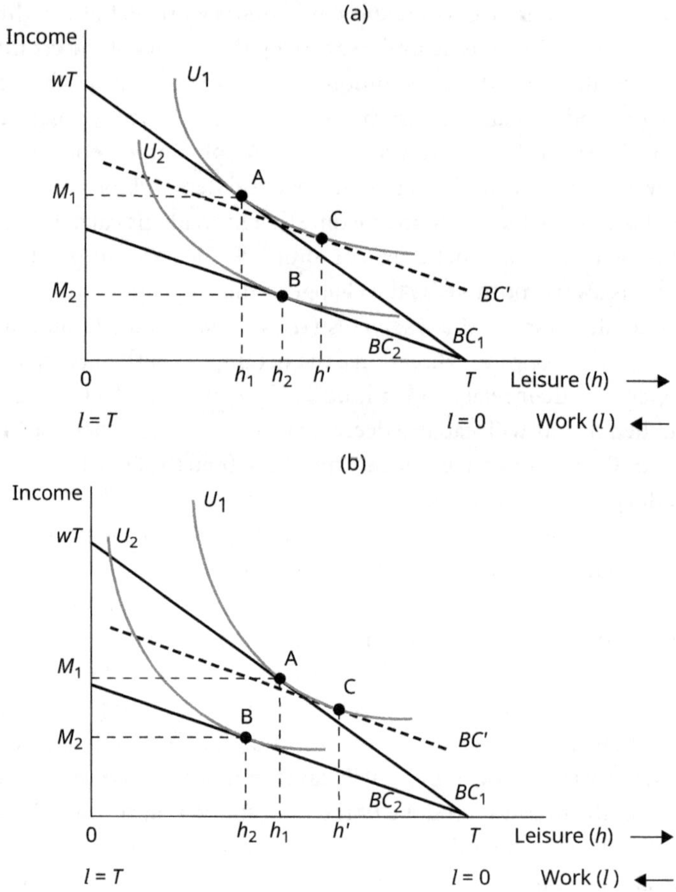

Figure 15.4 Income and substitution effects of an income tax

Note: In panel (a), the substitution effect is larger than the income effect; in panel (b), the income effect is larger.

Box 15.4 A progressive tax system

Progressive real world income tax systems typically include a combination of a personal tax-free allowance and higher marginal tax rates for higher earners. Figure 15.5 illustrates the budget line for the UK tax schedule for 2025/26. The tax-free personal allowance is £12,570 per year, which is the amount of income individuals do not have to pay tax on. A marginal tax rate of 20 per cent is levied on annual incomes between £12,571 and £50,270; incomes between £50,271 and £125,140 attract a marginal tax rate of 40 per cent; and for incomes above £125,140, the marginal tax rate is 45 per cent. The figure shows how these varying marginal tax rates affect the shape of the budget line, which is now made up of various segments with different slopes according to the marginal tax rates in the different income bands. There is one detail of the UK income tax schedule that is not reflected in this figure: the personal allowance is gradually withdrawn from individuals earning an income over £100,000 a year, so the effective tax rate on incomes between £100,000 and £125,140 is 60 per cent.

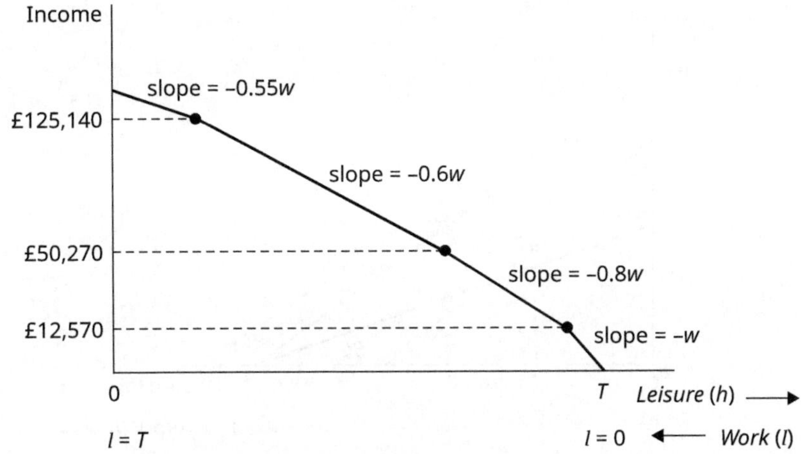

Figure 15.5 The UK income tax schedule, 2025/26

With a non-linear budget constraint, small changes in marginal tax rates can lead to big changes in the optimal number of hours worked.

The deadweight loss from income taxes

The income tax discussed above is an example of a distortionary tax, as it changes the relative prices and, therefore, the incentives individuals face. Distortionary taxes are inefficient because the government could raise the same amount of revenue while having a smaller impact on individual welfare. Or, equivalently, the government could raise more revenue while having the same impact on individual welfare. We can assess the distortionary impact of a tax by looking at how much additional revenue the government could raise through a lump-sum tax which has the same impact on individual welfare.[27] This difference in revenues provides a measure of the deadweight loss, or additional loss in welfare, from the tax.

In panel (a) of Figure 15.6, the initial utility-maximizing choice is at point A. Following the introduction of an income tax, the budget line rotates downwards from BC_1 to BC_2 and the new utility-maximizing choice is at point B. A lump-sum tax will shift the budget line inwards, without affecting its slope. This is illustrated by the budget line BC_3 in the figure, which is parallel to the original budget line BC_1. The lump-sum tax has been chosen at a level to ensure the individual is indifferent between the lump-sum tax and the proportional tax, since in both cases their utility-maximizing choice is on the same indifference curve, U_2, and therefore yields the same level of utility.[28] With the proportional income tax, the new optimal choice is at B and demand for leisure increases (and hence hours worked decrease), whereas with the lump-sum tax, the new optimal choice is at C and demand for leisure falls (and hours worked increase). This will be true more generally, since the lump-sum tax involves only an income effect and no substitution effect, and the income effect is positive as long as

[27] We introduced the concept of a lump-sum or non-distortionary tax in Chapter 13. For a more detailed explanation of the difference between distortionary and non-distortionary taxes, see Chapter 13.

[28] The difference between BC_3 and BC_1 provides a measure of the equivalent variation, or how much money would need to be taken away from an individual at the original wage level to have an equivalent effect on their welfare as the tax.

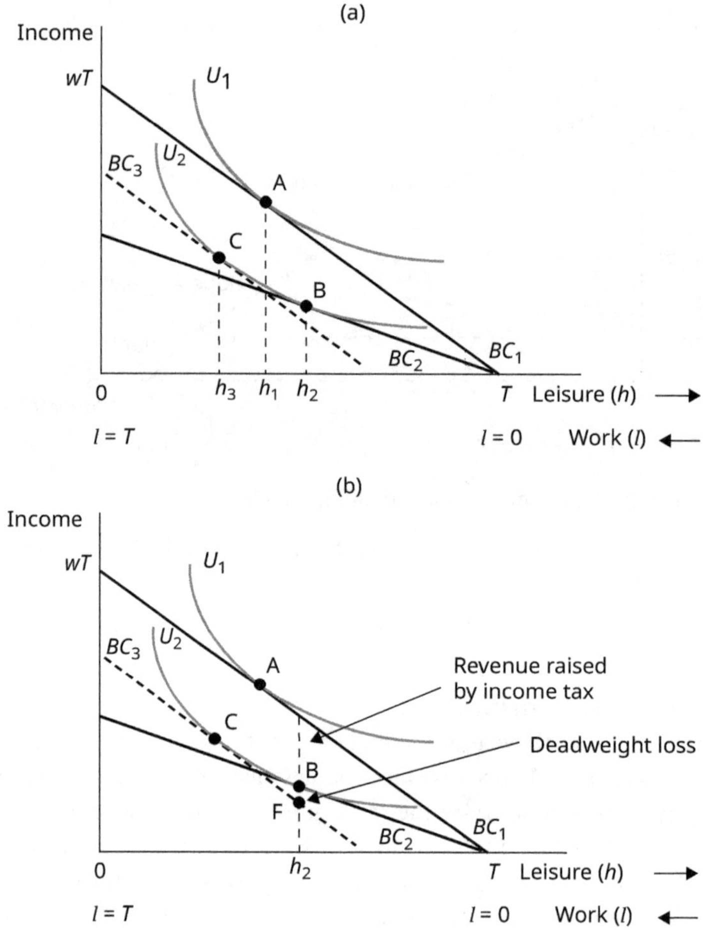

Figure 15.6 Measuring the deadweight loss of an income tax

leisure is a normal good. So demand for leisure will always fall, and hence labour supplied will always increase, in response to a lump-sum tax.

To measure the deadweight loss from the income tax, we need to compare the revenues raised by each tax.[29] This is illustrated in panel (b). With the proportional tax, the revenue raised is shown by the dotted line between the original budget line BC_1 and BC_2, at point B. The revenue raised by the lump-sum tax is given by the vertical distance between the budget lines BC_1 and BC_3. Under the lump-sum tax, the amount of revenue raised is constant and does not depend on the number of hours worked. We can see that the lump-sum tax would raise more revenue, while having the same impact on individual welfare. The income tax is therefore inefficient and the deadweight loss from the tax is given by the vertical distance BF, which measures the loss in revenue.

The size of the deadweight loss will depend on the size of the substitution effect, and the larger the substitution effect, the larger the deadweight loss from the tax. But even in cases where the income and substitution effects offset one another, so there is no change in hours

[29] The amount of revenue raised by a tax is given by the distance between the pre- and post-tax budget lines at the optimal choice.

worked, the tax will still be distortionary. As long as there is a substitution effect, there will be an efficiency cost associated with the tax.

The deadweight loss captured here may understate the true economic cost of the tax. If the tax creates a significant disincentive for people to work and enough individuals reduce their labour supply—either directly through hours worked or through their work effort—this will have an impact on economic growth. Reducing hours worked and earnings may also mean lower consumption and therefore lower revenues from indirect taxes such as VAT.

15.3.2 How sensitive is labour supply to changes in the tax rate?

As we have seen, the income and substitution effects work in opposite directions, so whether income taxes lead to an increase or decrease in hours worked will depend on the relative size of these two effects. Whether the income or the substitution effect dominates is, ultimately, an empirical question. In this section, we review some of the evidence on the impact of taxes on labour supply decisions.

There has been extensive empirical work on the impact of taxes on labour supply, using a range of approaches:

- **Surveys**: where individuals are asked directly about how income taxes affect their work effort or how they feel about higher income taxes.
- **Experiments**: these include randomized experiments, where individuals are randomly divided into a treatment group (i.e. a group that experiences a higher marginal tax rate) and a control group (i.e. a group that does not experience the higher tax rate), and the labour supply decisions of the two groups are compared to assess the impact of the tax. Examples include the various negative income tax experiments in the USA in the late 1960s and 1970s.[30] There are also studies based on quasi-experimental evidence, which analyse the impact of actual policy changes.
- **Statistical analysis of existing datasets**: where econometric techniques are used to analyse how labour supply responds to changes in the after-tax wage rate, while controlling for other variables which may influence labour supply decisions.

Each of these approaches has its advantages and limitations.[31] Even well-designed surveys run the risk of people saying what they think the interviewer wants to hear, and how people respond in a survey will not necessarily match how they behave in practice. If people know they are taking part in an experiment, they may change their behaviour, leading to potentially misleading results. Existing datasets typically collect information on hours worked at different after-tax wage rates, which is not the same as having data on how hours worked vary with different tax rates—people may respond differently to changes in taxes than they do to changes in wages. Having said this, empirical work in this area has become increasingly sophisticated, with steps being taken to mitigate the potential drawbacks of the different methods.

[30] See, for example, Allen (n.d.).
[31] See Atkinson and Stiglitz (2015) in the Further Reading at the end of the chapter for a more thorough discussion.

Table 15.3 Estimates of labour supply elasticities

Study	Sample	Uncompensated wage elasticity	Compensated wage elasticity	Income elasticity
Married women				
Arellano and Meghir (1992)	UK			
	No children	0.37	0.44	−0.13
	Young children (aged 2 or under)	0.29	0.50	−0.40
	Older children (5–10)	0.71	0.82	−0.21
Blundell et al. (1998)	UK			
	No children	0.14	0.14	0.00
	Youngest child aged 2 or under	0.21	0.30	−0.19
	Youngest child aged 3–4	0.37	0.44	−0.17
	Youngest child aged 5–10	0.13	0.17	−0.10
	Youngest child 11+	0.13	0.16	−0.06
Bourguignon and Magnac (1990)	France	1.00	–	−0.30
Hausman (1981)	USA	0.45	0.90	−0.45
Married men				
Blundell and Walker (1982)	UK	−0.23	0.13	−0.36
Bourguignon and Magnac (1990)	France	0.10	–	−0.07
Flood and MaCurdy (1992)	Sweden	0.16	–	−0.10
MaCurdy et al. (1990)	USA	0		−0.01
Hausman (1981)	USA	0.03	0.95	−0.98
Lone mothers				
Hausman (1981)	USA	0.53	0.65	−0.18
Jenkins (1992)	UK	1.44	–	−0.24
Bingley et al. (1992)	UK	0.76	1.28	−0.52

Note: Some of these studies account for the impact of benefits as well as taxes, while others focus solely on taxes.

Sources: Blundell (1992), Blundell and MaCurdy (1999), Blundell et al. (1998), and Meghir and Phillips (2010).

Most empirical work has focused on estimating **labour supply elasticities**, which capture how hours worked respond to changes in the wage rate. Table 15.3 summarizes some of the empirical results in this area. Because individuals are likely to respond differently to changes in the wage rate depending on their circumstances, studies have tended to estimate labour supply elasticities separately for different groups—for example, married women and married men, with and without children, and single mothers. In the table, separate estimates are given for: compensated wage elasticities, which capture the substitution effect; income elasticities, which capture the income effect; and uncompensated wage elasticities, which capture the combined income and substitution effects. It is important to keep in mind that here we are focusing on the impact of wages on labour supply, whereas in our discussion of the theoretical model above we were focusing on the impact of taxes (or changes in the wage rate) on the demand for leisure.[32]

There is some variation in the results across the different studies, but a few general conclusions can be drawn:

- The compensated wage elasticities, which capture the substitution effect, are all positive, which is consistent with the theory—higher wages lead to an increase in hours worked.[33]
- The income elasticities, which capture the income effect, are negative, suggesting leisure is a normal good—as income rises, demand for leisure also rises, and hours worked fall.
- The substitution effect tends to be larger than the income effect, so taxes reduce labour supply, but the size of this effect varies across groups. It is largest for married women and single mothers, and varies with the number of children. The labour supply of married men appears to be fairly unresponsive to changes in the wage rate.[34]

The results summarized above focus on the decision over how many hours to work, but some of these studies have also analysed the impact of taxes on the participation decision or the decision to work. Here research suggests that participation is quite sensitive to taxes, particularly for women and low earners (Blundell & Shephard, 2012; Meghir & Phillips, 2010). While these studies have focused on how labour supply responds to income taxes within a country, a growing body of research has started to explore how taxes affect migration into or out of countries. High-skilled, high-earning individuals typically have more flexibility to choose which country they want to work in, and high top marginal tax rates might encourage them to emigrate to countries with lower top marginal tax rates.[35]

More recent empirical work in public finance has focused on estimating **taxable income elasticities** rather than labour supply elasticities. Taxable income elasticity measures how taxable income changes in response to a change in the tax rate and, as such, it provides a direct measure of the welfare cost or deadweight loss of taxation. The greater the elasticity, the lower the revenue generated from a tax change and the larger the welfare loss per unit of revenue. Taxable income elasticities provide a more complete picture of how taxes affect government revenues and welfare by taking into account how individuals may change their sources of income, or engage in tax evasion and tax avoidance, in response to higher taxes.[36]

[32] So a negative substitution effect in the context of the leisure demand decision implies a positive substitution effect in the context of labour supply (e.g. a decrease in the wage leads to an increase in the demand for leisure, but a decrease in hours worked). A positive income effect in the context of leisure demand implies a negative income effect in the context of labour supply.

[33] This is consistent with the theory because here we are focusing on the impact on labour supply, rather than on the demand for leisure. See previous footnote.

[34] Research has tended to distinguish the responses of primary and secondary earners, where primary earners are the members of the household who are the main source of labour income, and secondary earners are other workers in the household. Traditionally, primary earners were men and secondary earners were women, who were in charge of childcare and other household activities. Evidence suggests the working decisions of primary earners are not very responsive to changes in wages, whereas secondary earners have been found to be much more responsive to changes in their wages.

[35] Analysing the impact of taxes on international labour mobility is challenging, but evidence suggests that offering preferential tax rates for certain types of workers can have a significant impact on migration. In a study of a preferential tax scheme for highly paid foreigners introduced in Denmark in 1991, Kleven et al. (2014) found this led to a doubling of the number of high-earning foreigners in the country.

[36] See, for example, Gruber and Saez (2002) and Saez et al. (2012).

15.3.3 How can we reconcile the theory and the evidence?

The evidence discussed above clearly shows that the labour supply response to taxation varies across groups, but overall labour supply appears not to be as sensitive to taxation as we might expect. Possible reasons for this include the following:

- **Labour supply is a multidimensional concept**: the decision to work and the number of hours worked are one aspect of labour supply, but we also need to consider other aspects, such as the amount of effort people put into each hour worked, their choice of occupation, and their decision about when to retire.[37] All of these aspects are likely to be influenced by taxation: individuals may respond to higher taxes by reducing their work effort, choosing a job with lower pay but higher non-monetary benefits, or retiring earlier. Some groups of people may also respond to higher marginal tax rates by moving into untaxed areas—for example, by working in the **hidden economy** or engaging in tax avoidance or tax evasion, or moving to work abroad.[38]
- **Non-monetary benefits of work**: alongside receiving an income, there are many potential non-monetary benefits of work. Individuals might be motivated not only by the monetary rewards, but also by job satisfaction, the prestige associated with a particular job, the flexibility it offers, or the opportunities to develop social connections.
- **Lack of control over hours worked**: the decision over how many hours to work may be more constrained than the theory assumes. For many jobs, the number of hours of work are set and individuals have very little flexibility to choose the number of hours they want to work each week. However, the rise of the gig economy has started to change this in some sectors.
- **Lack of awareness of taxation**: the theory assumes that individuals make their decisions over how many hours to work based on full information about tax rates and how the amount of tax they pay varies with the number of hours worked. In practice, research suggests most people are not fully aware of tax rates and how much income tax they are paying (Blaufus et al., 2022).

Ultimately, work incentives are likely to vary between different types of households—whether single or couple, with or without children, young or old—and the decision to work, and how many hours to work, will be influenced by social, family, and attitudinal factors, and not just purely financial factors.

15.4 Optimal income taxation

We have seen how taxes on labour income affect incentives to work and can therefore be a source of inefficiency. But income taxes (along with transfers) also provide a useful tool for governments to redistribute income. If society cares about inequality and poverty, then it will be willing to sacrifice some efficiency for greater equity. This equity–efficiency trade-off

[37] There is also the issue of absenteeism, so the actual hours a person works may differ from their contracted hours.

[38] This is a point we will return to in Chapter 17.

is at the heart of the optimal income tax problem. An optimal tax system is one that enables the government to achieve its desired redistributive goals in the least distortionary (or most efficient) way possible, while raising a given amount of revenue.[39]

The field of optimal income tax theory is complex.[40] In this section, we are going to draw on some of the key insights from the theory, with a view to answering three questions. What is the relationship between the income tax rate and the level of tax revenues raised? Should everyone pay the same rate of income tax or should there be different rates for people with different incomes? If there are different tax rates, how should these rates be set?

15.4.1 The Laffer curve

When designing optimal income taxes, the government needs to consider how the marginal tax rate affects the amount of revenue it can raise. The total amount of revenue the government raises from a tax is determined by the tax rate and the tax base. In the case of an income tax, the tax base will depend on the amount of labour supplied or hours worked in the economy. When the marginal tax rate increases, there are two effects on tax revenues: for a given level of labour income, tax revenues will increase as the tax rate increases; however, if a higher marginal tax rate discourages work, then the tax base will shrink and revenue raised will fall. The extent to which revenue falls will depend on the size of the substitution effect, as this effect captures by how much individuals reduce their working hours in response to a tax (as we saw in section 15.3).

This relationship between the tax rate and the level of tax revenue is captured by the **Laffer curve**, illustrated in Figure 15.7. The tax rate is measured along the horizontal axis and total tax revenue is measured along the vertical axis. When the tax rate is zero, no revenue is raised. As the tax rate increases, tax revenue initially increases, as the government is collecting a larger proportion of labour income. However, beyond a certain point—represented by t^* in the figure—raising the tax rate further will lead to a decrease in revenue, as the substitution effect outweighs the income effect and workers reduce hours worked and/or exit the labour

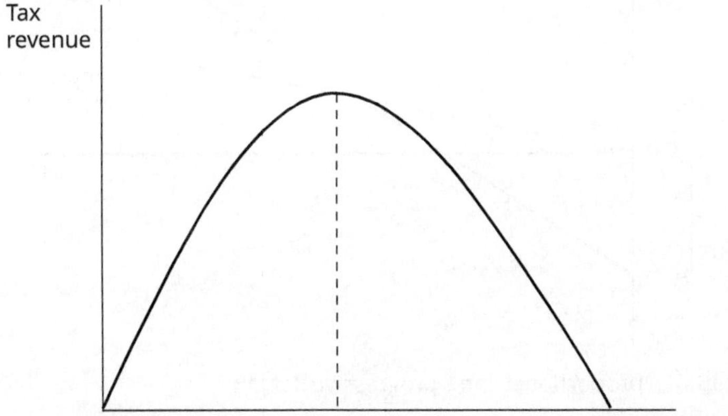

Figure 15.7 The Laffer curve

[39] Governments may also have other priorities—for example, the government may care about the well-being of the working poor over the non-working poor, or the well-being of married parents over people who are cohabiting.

[40] See suggestions in the Further Reading at the end of the chapter.

force. When the tax rate is 100 per cent, no one has an incentive to work and the tax raises no revenue.[41] So lower tax rates may actually lead to an increase in tax revenue because existing workers work more hours, more people join the labour force, or the incentives for avoiding or evading taxes are reduced.[42]

Whether lowering tax rates increases tax revenue will depend on what side of the Laffer curve the economy is on. This theory provided the motivation for tax cuts in several countries in the 1980s, particularly for higher earners. In 1978, the top rate of income tax in the UK was 98 per cent; by 1988, this had been cut to 40 per cent. However, evidence on whether this cut led to an increase in tax revenues has been inconclusive (Dilnot & Kell, 1988).[43]

15.4.2 Linear and non-linear progressive income tax schedules

We now turn to the question of whether everyone should pay the same rate of income tax or whether there should be different rates for people with different incomes.

Under a proportional tax system, everyone pays the same proportion of their income in tax, regardless of their level of income. Individuals with higher incomes pay more in absolute terms, but the average and marginal tax rates are the same for everyone.[44] Intuitively, it might seem fairer for people with higher incomes to pay proportionately more in tax. A proportional tax can be progressive if it includes a grant or lump-sum payment made to all individuals. This ensures that although the marginal tax rate is constant, the average tax rate increases with income, so those on higher incomes pay proportionately more in tax. This type of progressive flat tax is sometimes referred to as a **negative income tax**.[45] Figure 15.8 illustrates a

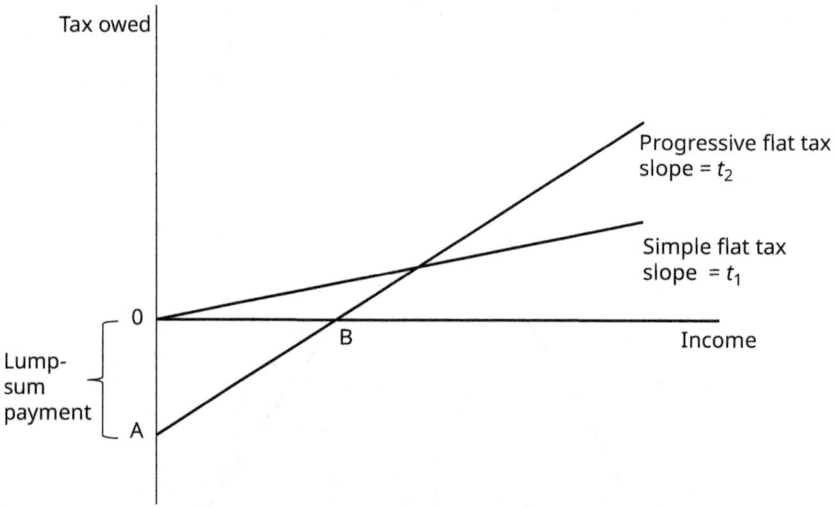

Figure 15.8 A proportional and a progressive flat tax

[41] In reality, the higher rate at which tax revenues are zero is likely to be below 100 per cent.

[42] This is a point we will return to in Chapter 17, where we discuss tax evasion and tax avoidance.

[43] Lundberg (2017) provides estimates of the Laffer curve peak tax rate for a selection of OECD countries. These suggest that for many countries, their current top marginal tax rate is below this peak rate.

[44] Recall from Chapter 13 that the marginal tax rate is the percentage of the next pound/euro/dollar earned that is paid in tax, while the average tax rate is the percentage of total income that is paid in tax. See section 13.3.1 for an example.

[45] A linear income tax of this form is defined by $T = (t \cdot w \cdot l) - G$, where t is the marginal tax rate, w is the hourly wage rate, l is hours worked, and G represents the lump-sum transfer received from the government.

progressive flat tax and a simple proportional flat tax. Pre-tax income is measured along the horizontal axis and the amount of tax paid, as a function of income and the marginal tax rate, is measured along the vertical axis. The progressive flat tax involves a lump-sum transfer paid to everyone, represented by 0A,[46] and a constant marginal tax rate of t_2 levied on all other income. Point B is the break-even point, where the individual pays back in tax exactly the amount received in the lump-sum transfer.

There is scope for significant redistribution with a progressive flat tax, but invariably this comes at a cost: more redistribution requires a larger lump-sum transfer, which in turn will require a higher marginal tax rate to finance it. Most estimates suggest that the tax rate necessary to sustain a reasonable basic income, and finance other public services, would be very high (see Box 15.5). And as we have seen, a higher marginal tax rate implies a larger deadweight loss.[47] The challenge facing policymakers is therefore to choose at what level to set the lump-sum transfer and the marginal tax rate to manage this trade-off between redistribution and work incentives. This will depend on the government or society's preference for equity, as reflected in the **social welfare function**.[48] While poorer individuals benefit from a larger transfer, wealthier individuals lose out as a result of a higher tax. But the social value of the benefits to lower-income individuals may outweigh the social value of the losses to wealthier individuals.

In practice, most countries have non-linear progressive tax schedules, where the marginal tax rate rises with income. In the UK, the marginal tax rate ranges from zero for incomes up to £12,570, to 45 per cent for incomes above £125,140. This type of progressive schedule aligns with most people's intuitive understanding of fairness: those who can afford to pay more should pay more. These non-linear tax schedules are more complex, which potentially opens up more opportunities for tax avoidance,[49] but they can also imply a smaller deadweight loss than an equivalent progressive flat tax. What can we say about how these different marginal tax rates should be set?

Box 15.5 Financing a negative income tax

Milton Friedman was one of the early advocates of a negative income tax in his book *Capitalism and Freedom* (1962). He believed that, rather than discouraging work, such a system would help target poverty directly by providing a universal programme, and potentially at a lower cost than existing welfare programmes. The simplicity and transparency of a negative income tax have made it appealing, but the cost of financing such a programme would probably be significant. Mirrlees et al. (2011) estimate that the total flat tax required to provide a basic income equal to one-third of average income, and finance existing public services, would be 67 per cent—and this is before any behavioural responses are taken into account. This is why in practice most tax and welfare systems withdraw benefits at a high rate once people start working. This reduces the need for higher tax rates on middle- and high-income workers, but it also reduces the incentive to work for people on lower incomes.

[46] This lump sum is also referred to as a social dividend, basic income, or citizen's income. An alternative way to view the progressive flat tax is as a system that imposes a proportional tax on the difference between an individual's income and some critical level of income B. If an individual's income is below B, they receive a grant from the government equal to the tax rate multiplied by the difference between their income and the critical level of income.

[47] See the appendix at the end of this chapter for a formal explanation.

[48] See Chapter 2 for a discussion of this concept.

[49] This is something we will discuss in Chapter 17.

A schedule of tax rates is optimal if there is no change in the tax rates that will raise the same amount of revenue and make society better off. The theory of optimal non-linear income taxation is based on the seminal work by Mirrlees (1971), although the implications for policy from this work have been limited. More recent work on optimal income taxation has focused on the role of the elasticity of earnings[50] with respect to taxes in determining the pattern of optimal income taxes.[51] This works also highlights the importance of the shape of the income distribution—in particular, the number of individuals in each income band—and social marginal welfare rates, which capture the relative value placed by society on the consumption of individuals in each income band.

In a progressive tax schedule, where there are different marginal tax rates for different income bands, we need to think about how changing the marginal tax rate in one band will impact individuals in other income bands. Suppose the government is considering increasing the marginal tax rate for people earning between £12,570 and £50,270. For individuals in this income band, the change in the marginal tax rate will involve both an income and a substitution effect, as we saw in section 15.3. For individuals earning less than £12,570, this change will have no impact, but it will have an impact on those earning above £50,270, as it will lead to an increase in their average tax rate (although their marginal tax rate remains unchanged). This increase in the average tax rate will involve an income effect, encouraging these higher earners to work more, and the number of higher earners in this income band will affect the scale of this effect.

15.4.3 Insights from behavioural economics for optimal income taxation

The discussion above has highlighted that understanding how individuals respond to taxes is key to optimal tax theory and policy. We know the efficiency cost of taxation will depend on the size of these behavioural responses, but individuals will not always behave in accordance

Box 15.6 Minimizing the distortions of income taxes through tagging

Should people be taxed based on their height? This may seem a bizarre suggestion, but height is a good predictor of individual earnings and it is a characteristic that individuals cannot easily change. A tax based on height would therefore reduce the distortions associated with taxing income. This is an example of tagging, which involves basing taxes on personal characteristics, such as gender or height, as a way of reducing the efficiency cost of taxation because there is little scope for individuals to reduce the amount of tax they pay by changing their behaviour (or characteristics). Tagging therefore provides a mechanism for achieving redistribution without distorting incentives to work. Although such a policy may be optimal from the perspective of efficiency, it is unlikely to be socially acceptable, not least because of its implications for horizontal equity.

Source: Mirrlees et al. (2011).

[50] This elasticity measures how sensitive earnings are to changes in the tax rate.

[51] See, for example, Saez (2001) and Piketty and Saez (2012) in the Further Reading. These papers are quite technical, but the intuition behind the results is also explained. See Diamond and Saez (2011) in the Further Reading for a discussion of key policy implications from the theory.

with the predictions of neoclassical theory. Research in behavioural economics can shed light on other aspects of individual behaviour which can help inform the design of optimal income taxes.[52] We highlight three particular issues here.

- **Complexity and mistakes**: individuals respond not to tax rates as they are, but as they *perceive* them, and their perceptions may be mistaken, particularly given the complexity of modern income tax systems. If individuals are not aware of the marginal tax rates they face and this leads them to be less responsive to tax rates, then complexity can actually enhance efficiency. Research suggests that some individuals may behave as if their average tax rate is their marginal tax rate, and individuals who use their average tax rate tend to supply more labour and raise more revenue (De Bartolome, 1995).
- **Social preferences**: how individuals respond to income taxes might reflect not just their preferences over income and leisure, but also whether they perceive the tax system to be fair and how they believe tax revenues are used. If people have a preference for fairness, tax policy can make use of this by highlighting the importance of paying taxes and the social benefits this entails. Making these points more explicit or salient may enhance efficiency.
- **Myopic labour supply**: individuals may place more weight on the present than the future when making labour supply decisions, which can affect the level of effort they put into their work and reduce tax revenues. In most jobs, wages are paid in arrears—that is, after workers have put in the effort. These wages are then used to finance the consumption that increases individual utility. If worker preferences are present-biased, the disutility they get from work today will weigh more than the utility they expect to get from consumption in the future, leading to a reduction in their work effort today.

15.5 Taxes on household savings

We have seen how taxes on labour income can affect individual behaviour, but earnings from work are not the only source of income. Most individuals will rely on savings over the course of their lives, putting some money away to draw on when they need it in the future, and income saved will earn interest.[53] How should this interest income be treated for tax purposes? How savings are taxed will influence individual decisions about how much to save, when to save, and how to save. If the return to savings, or interest income, is taxed, this reduces the incentive to save, and if different forms of saving are taxed at different rates, this creates an incentive for individuals to save in assets that are subject to lower tax rates. By affecting the total amount of saving in an economy, these taxes can affect the amount of capital invested and how it is invested, which will have implications for economic growth.

In this section, we start by reviewing the intertemporal choice model, which is the model traditionally used to explain individual saving behaviour. We then apply this model to analyse how taxes affect the saving decision and review some of the evidence on how responsive saving is to taxation. We finish with a brief discussion of some of the reasons for saving not captured by the intertemporal choice model.

[52] See Kaplow (2024) and Congdon et al. (2009) in the Further Reading.

[53] Income not used to finance consumption can also be invested rather than saved. The key difference between saving and investing is in the level of risk and potential returns. In this chapter, we will focus on saving.

15.5.1 The intertemporal choice model

The intertemporal choice model assumes that people save (or borrow) to smooth their consumption over time. Our income will vary over the course of our lives. Saving and borrowing allow us to redistribute our income over time so that our consumption in each period is not constrained by the income we receive in that period. For example, saving some money today will allow us to spend more when our incomes fall when we reach retirement. So the choice about how much to save in this model is essentially a choice about how to spread our consumption over time.

The intertemporal choice model extends the rational choice model we have discussed previously in this book and that we used to analyse individual labour supply above. But instead of analysing the choice between two goods, or between income and leisure, we are analysing consumption in two different time periods: period 1, which we can think of as consumption today or current consumption; and period 2, which we can think of consumption in the future.[54] The model is illustrated in Figure 15.9, where current consumption is measured along the horizontal axis and future consumption is measured along the vertical axis.

Suppose Leni receives income M_1 today and will receive income M_2 in the future. She could choose to spend exactly her income in each period. Alternatively, if she has a strong preference for consumption today, she may want to borrow against her future income to spend more today; or she might prefer to save some of her income today so that she can spend more in the future. If she saves, her savings will earn interest; whereas if she borrows, she will have to pay interest on the amount borrowed. For simplicity, we will assume that she can save and borrow at the same constant rate of interest, r.[55]

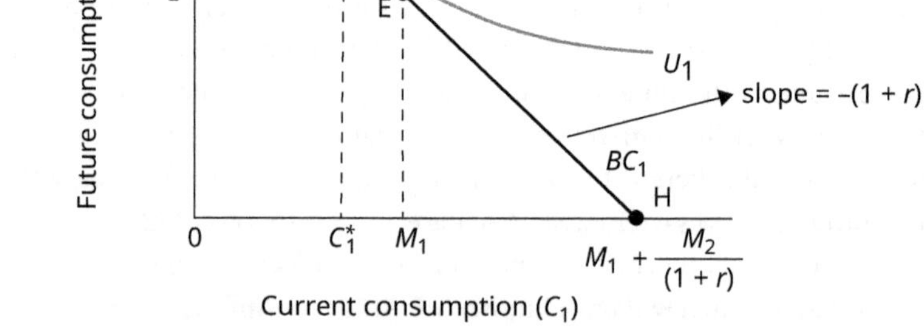

Figure 15.9 Intertemporal choice model

[54] The model can be extended to cover multiple time periods, but two periods is sufficient for the purpose of our analysis.

[55] In practice, the interest rate on saving is different from the interest rate on borrowing, and individuals have access to many different types of assets with different saving rates. This model can be extended to allow for different types of assets and different interest rates, but for our purposes this simple version of the model is sufficient.

[56] We are assuming here that individuals could borrow against all of their future income—that is, there are no constraints on borrowing. In practice, individuals often face borrowing constraints, which the model can be extended to accommodate.

If Leni were to save all of her income in period 1, the income she would receive in period 2 is given by:

$$M_1(1+r)+M_2$$

—that is, the sum of her period 1 income M_1, plus any interest earned on her period 1 income, and her period 2 income M_2. This is illustrated by point G in Figure 15.9.

If, instead, Leni wanted to increase her consumption in period 1, she could borrow against some of her income from period 2. If she borrowed all of her period 2 income in period 1 at the interest rate r, the maximum amount she could borrow would be:[56]

$$\frac{M_2}{(1+r)}$$

So the maximum income she could spend in period 1 is the sum of her period 1 income and her period 2 income, minus any interest she would have to pay for borrowing against her period 2 income:

$$M_1+\frac{M_2}{(1+r)}$$

This is given by point H in Figure 15.9. However, Leni is not restricted to saving or borrowing *all* of her current/future income; she could save or borrow a fraction of her current/future income. The intertemporal budget constraint BC_1 represents all possible combinations of current and future consumption that are feasible given Leni's income in each period and the interest rate. The intertemporal budget line must pass through the initial income point E, since Leni always the option of consuming exactly her income in each period. The slope of the budget line is determined by the relative price of first-period consumption, which is $(1+r)$. This is the opportunity cost of first-period consumption, which is determined by the interest forgone on savings for consumption in period 2. For every pound not spent today, Leni will have $(1+r)$ times that pound in the future—so this is the price of consumption today.

Leni's intertemporal budget constraint represents her **opportunity set**. The indifference curve U_1 represents her preferences for consumption in both periods—that is, it depicts all possible combinations of current and future consumption which give Leni the same level of utility. The shape of her indifference curves will depend on her degree of patience/impatience, or how much she values consumption today versus consumption in the future.

Leni's initial utility-maximizing choice is given by point A in Figure 15.9, where the intertemporal budget constraint is tangent to the highest possible indifference curve. Her consumption in period 1 is C_1^* and her consumption in period 2 is C_2^*. We can see in the figure that her consumption in period 1 is less than her income in that period, M_1, which means she saves some of her period 1 income to increase consumption in period 2. If, instead, the utility-maximizing choice were to the right of point E in the diagram, then Leni would be borrowing against her future income in period 1. However, we are not modelling Leni's saving/borrowing decision directly; instead, we are working out what her utility-maximizing consumption in each period is, and deriving the level of saving/borrowing from this.

Now suppose the government introduces a tax t on interest income. This will cause the after-tax return on savings to fall, since part of the return on savings is now paid to the government. The slope of the budget line falls to $[1+(r-rt)]$ and the budget line becomes flatter, as illustrated by BC_2 in panel (a) of Figure 15.10. Unlike in the labour supply model discussed

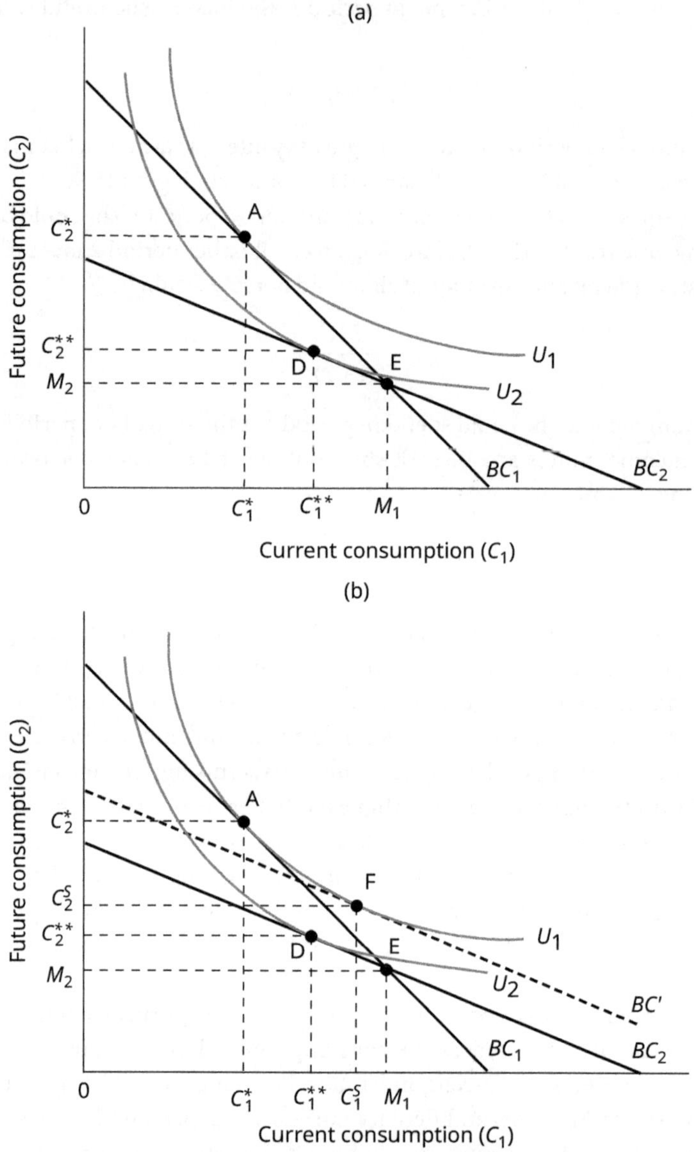

Figure 15.10 Income and substitution effects of a tax on savings

above, in this case both the horizontal and vertical intercepts of the budget line change. The vertical intercept changes because the return on saving has fallen, so maximum period 2 consumption falls. The horizontal intercept changes because borrowing is now cheaper (as we are assuming the same interest rate on saving and borrowing). If Leni borrows against all of her period 2 income, the maximum amount she can consume in period 1 is now greater than it was before, so the horizontal intercept of the budget line lies further to the right in the figure. The budget line will still pass through point E, since Leni always has the option of just consuming the income she earns in each period.

The introduction of the tax effectively reduces the price of consumption in period 1 from $(1+r)$ to $(1+r-rt)$. The price of consumption in period 1 has fallen because the return on each pound saved is now lower. Following the introduction of the tax, Leni's new utility-maximizing choice is given by point D in the figure, on the lower indifference curve U_2. Her consumption in the first period is now higher than before the introduction of the tax, at C_1^{**}, and consumption in the second period has fallen to C_2^{**}. Intuitively, this makes sense: since the return on saving is lower, people save less. But will this always be the case?

To answer this question, it is helpful to understand what is happening when the relative price of period 1 consumption falls as a result of the tax. As in our analysis of the labour supply decision above, we can decompose this price change into two effects: an income effect and a substitution effect. The fact that period 1 consumption is now relatively cheaper means that individuals will want to increase their period 1 consumption and, as a result, save less—this is the substitution effect. The substitution effect captures the impact of the change in relative prices, while holding real income (and utility) constant. But the introduction of the tax on the return to savings means that the individual's after-tax income will fall, which means they can afford less consumption in both periods—this is the income effect.

These two effects are illustrated in panel (b) of Figure 15.10. To capture the substitution effect, we want to analyse how consumption changes purely as a result of the price change, assuming the individual could be compensated for the loss in income associated with the tax. The dashed line BC' represents this hypothetical budget constraint; it has the same slope as the new budget line BC_2 (and therefore reflects the new price of period 1 consumption) but is tangent to the original indifference curve (thus holding the original level of utility constant). The substitution effect is illustrated by the move from A to F in panel (b), where period 1 consumption increases from C_1^* to C_1^S. The income effect captures the impact of the change in purchasing power on consumption and is illustrated by the move from F to D. As the tax leads to a decrease in income, the whole budget line shift inwards from BC' to BC_2, and period 1 consumption falls from C_1^S to C_1^{**}.

The income and substitution effects move in opposite directions. As a result of the tax, period 1 consumption is now relatively cheaper and therefore the substitution effect leads to an increase in period 1 consumption. The income effect, however, leads to a decrease in period 1 consumption, as the tax reduces the individual's purchasing power. The net effect of the tax will therefore depend on the relative magnitude of these two effects. In the example illustrated in panel (b), the substitution effect is larger than the income effect, so the net effect of the tax is to increase period 1 consumption, which implies a decrease in saving. If the income effect were larger, then period 1 consumption would decrease and the individual would save more. In both cases, consumption in period 2 falls, but the size of this reduction will depend on whether period 1 consumption falls or increases. In the example illustrated, period 1 consumption increases, so the individual is saving less which, combined with the lower after-tax return on savings, means that period 2 consumption will fall by a lot.

The intertemporal choice model can help us understand the impact of a tax on savings in theory. Box 15.7 discusses some of the empirical evidence on how these taxes affect saving in practice.

Box 15.7 How do taxes on savings affect saving in practice?

The theory cannot tell us conclusively whether savings are likely to increase or decrease as a result of a tax on the return to saving. What can empirical research tell us about how responsive saving behaviour is to taxes?

Assessing the impact of taxes on saving is challenging. With the empirical analysis of labour supply, researchers have access to data on individual workers' wages. However, with saving, we do not typically observe the interest rate that any individual saver gets. There will be different saving opportunities available and different savings accounts will have different interest rates. For example, an instant access savings account typically attracts a lower rate of interest than a savings account where you put your money away for a longer period.

Early empirical work focused on the impact of interest rates on aggregate consumption and saving, and found little evidence of a clear significant impact. Howrey and Hymans (1978) found that interest rates had little impact on saving, while Blinder and Deaton (1985) found nominal interest rates had a negative impact on consumption (and hence increase saving), but that real interest rates had no effect. Hall (1988) similarly found that saving was not very responsive to changes in the interest rate.

There is a small but growing empirical literature focusing on the effects of changes in the interest rates offered by specific saving products on saving behaviour using household-level data.[57] Retirement savings attract preferential tax treatment in many countries, making them an ideal type of saving to focus on. Several studies have explored whether the favourable tax treatment of retirement saving encourages individuals to save more, but there has been little consensus on this issue (Attanasio & Wakefield, 2008). Some have found that only a small proportion of the savings being channelled into tax-advantaged savings vehicles can be considered 'new' saving (Attanasio et al., 2005). By making some forms of saving more attractive through preferential tax treatment, the government creates an incentive for individuals to channel their savings into these assets rather than increasing saving overall. The fact that there are different savings vehicles available, and that people have different reasons for saving, means that there is unlikely to be a straightforward answer to the question of how interest rates affect saving behaviour.

15.5.2 Beyond the simple intertemporal choice model

The standard intertemporal choice model relies on strong assumptions about the information individuals have and their ability to make complex decisions about how much to save and borrow in each period based on this information. In practice, there are several reasons why saving behaviour might deviate from the predictions of the model. These include the following:

- **Limited information**: the intertemporal choice model assumes individuals have full information about their current income and interest rates, and well-founded expectations about how their income and interest rates are likely to evolve in the future. In reality, individual expectations are unlikely to be fully informed and rational, and

[57] See Attanasio and Wakefield (2008) for a review.

individuals are likely to make decisions based on incomplete information about both current and future income and interest rates.

- **Problems of self-control**: individual decisions are not always rational and forward-looking. When making decisions about how much to save, individuals have to weigh up their consumption and well-being today against their future consumption and well-being. While their long-run preferences may be more patient and favour saving today to ensure a reasonable level of consumption in the future, their short-run preferences may be more impatient and prioritize immediate consumption and gratification.[58]
- **Precautionary saving motives**: the intertemporal choice model assumes that the only reason people save is to smooth consumption over the course of their lives. In reality, there are many other reasons why people save.[59] One reason for saving that has received a substantial amount of attention in the literature is the precautionary saving motive. Within this framework, people save not only to smooth consumption, but also to insure against uncertain adverse events in the future—for example, potential health problems or becoming unemployed or divorced—which will have a negative impact on their income. If individuals face borrowing constraints, or restrictions on how much they can borrow, then they have an incentive to build up a buffer stock of savings which they can draw on in the event of one of these unforeseen adverse events. Individuals who are younger, who have lower incomes, and who have fewer assets that can act as collateral for borrowing are particularly likely to face borrowing constraints in practice.

While the intertemporal choice model can be extended to accommodate some of these limitations, they serve to highlight why interest rates may be less important for understanding saving behaviour than the standard model implies.

15.6 Taxes on wealth

So far, we have focused on the taxation of earned income—that is, income earned from labour or interest income from savings. In this section, we will briefly discuss taxes that are levied not on the flow of income, but on the stock or value of individual wealth. There are three main types of wealth taxes: capital gains taxes, transfer taxes, and property taxes.[60] **Capital gains taxes** are levied on **capital gains**, the difference between the price for which an asset was bought and the price at which it is sold. For example, if you bought a house for £250,000 and then sold it for £350,000, your capital gains from the sale would be £100,000. Capital gains also arise with other assets, such as stocks and shares, or artwork. **Transfer taxes** are taxes levied when an asset is transferred from one individual to another

[58] Individuals are assumed to be both far-sighted when it comes to planning, but also myopic or short-sighted when it comes to doing (Thaler & Shefrin, 1981). See Chapter 11 for a discussion of the problems of bounded rationality and bounded willpower, and how they can affect saving behaviour.

[59] People may save with a specific goal in mind—for example, to buy a car, build up a deposit to buy a home, or save for a holiday. People may also want to build up savings to have something to leave to their children or grandchildren. See Browning and Lusardi (1996) for a discussion of the different reasons for saving.

[60] Some countries also have separate wealth taxes, where a tax is levied on individual wealth holdings (e.g. Norway, Spain, and Switzerland).

and include **gift taxes** and **inheritance or estate taxes**. The main difference between the two is that gift taxes apply to assets that are given while a person is still alive, whereas estate or inheritance taxes are levied on assets that are transferred after a person dies—for example, in the form of bequests. **Property taxes** are taxes levied on the value of real estate, including land and buildings such as homes or offices. We are going to focus only on capital gains taxes and transfer taxes.

The importance of capital gains taxes and transfer taxes for government revenue varies across countries, as illustrated in Table 15.4. Across the OECD as a whole, marginally more revenue is raised through capital gains taxes than through taxes on gifts and inheritances, but on average only 0.4–0.5 per cent of total tax revenues were sourced from these types of taxes in 2022. Belgium, France, and Japan have the highest shares of revenue raised through taxes on gifts and inheritance, at between 1.5 per cent and 1.6 per cent. In Sweden and the USA, capital gains taxes are far more important, with these countries raising 3.7 per cent and 4.8 per cent of tax revenues through taxes on the capital gains of individuals.

Table 15.4 Capital gains and transfer taxes across the OECD, 2022

Country	Capital gains taxes (% of total revenue)	Estate, inheritance and gift taxes (% of total revenue)
Australia	0.0	0.0
Austria	0.0	0.0
Belgium	0.0	1.5
Canada	0.0	0.1
Denmark	0.0	0.6
Finland	0.0	0.8
France	0.0	1.6
Germany	0.0	0.6
Greece	0.1	0.3
Ireland	1.7	0.6
Italy	0.0	0.1
Japan	0.0	1.5
Netherlands	0.1	0.7
New Zealand	0.0	0.0
Portugal	–	0.0
Spain	–	0.7
Sweden	3.7	0.0
UK	1.7	0.8
USA	4.8	0.6
OECD average	0.5	0.4

Note: 'OECD average' represents average across all OECD countries that levy these taxes.
Source: OECD (2025b).

15.6.1 Taxing capital gains

Capital gains are generally **taxed on realization**, which means that the tax is paid only when the asset is sold. This differs from the taxation of savings discussed in the previous section, as savings are **taxed on accrual**—that is, as the interest is being earned (over a given period). With capital gains, because taxes are paid only when the asset is sold, individuals can earn more in interest. If you have a regular savings account, each year you will pay tax on any interest earned above a certain limit, and this tax payment reduces the amount you have in your savings account earning interest. In contrast, if you own an asset such as housing or company shares, your tax liability is lower because you only pay tax when the asset is sold, so you can earn interest on what would have been your tax liability if you were paying tax on accrual or as the value of the asset was increasing.[61]

This preferential tax treatment of capital gains arises partly because taxing on accrual is not feasible for all assets. It may be possible to track the change in value of stocks and shares, but this is more difficult with other assets, such as artwork and housing, where the value of the asset can only be accurately determined when the asset is sold. Even if governments could tax capital gains on accrual, individuals might not have the funds to finance these tax payments if these gains have not been realized (i.e. by selling the asset).[62]

However, taxing capital gains at a lower rate has implications for both equity and efficiency. Capital gains taxes are progressive, since wealthier individuals are more likely to benefit from capital gains. Lower capital gains tax rates will therefore benefit those with more wealth. These lower tax rates also distort incentives. If different sources of income are taxed at different rates, this creates an incentive for individuals to convert their income into the forms that attract these lower tax rates. For example, in some sectors, workers have the option of receiving part of their salary in company shares. If capital gains taxes are lower than taxes on labour income, workers have an incentive to receive more of their salary in shares as opposed to wages, which is inefficient.

15.6.2 Taxing wealth transfers

Not all countries levy taxes on wealth transfers. Among those that do, the design and implementation of inheritance, estate, and gift taxes varies widely (see Box 15.8). Inheritance and estate taxes tend to be controversial, with frequent calls to abolish or reform them, even though most estates are not subject to inheritance or estate taxes.[63]

[61] Suppose you have £100 in a savings account earning 10 per cent interest per year and your annual interest income is taxed at a rate of 20 per cent. After 10 years you will have earned £116 in interest, as the value of your savings pot after 10 years is given by $A = (1 + r - tr)^{10} \times 100$, where the interest rate $r = 0.1$ and the tax $t = 0.2$. If, instead, you had bought £100 worth of stocks which also increased in value by 10 per cent per year, at the end of 10 years your stocks would be worth £259. If you sold the stocks and paid 20 per cent capital gains tax on the difference between the sale price and purchase price, you would pay just under £32 in tax, leaving you with a gain of £127.

[62] A homeowner's house might increase in value by £20,000 in a year. With a capital gains tax rate of 18 per cent, they would face a tax bill of £3,600 if the tax were charged on accrual, and they would need to draw on their savings or borrow to pay this (or sell their home).

[63] In a recent OECD study, the share of estates that were subject to inheritance or estate taxes ranged from 0.2 per cent in the USA to 48 per cent in Belgium (OECD, 2021b).

Box 15.8 Inheritance taxes across the OECD

Inheritance and estate taxes vary significantly across countries. While most countries have progressive inheritance tax schedules, countries including Italy, Ireland, Portugal, the UK, and the USA have flat inheritance tax rates. These flat rates vary from 4 per cent in Italy (for close family members only) to 40 per cent in the UK (where the same flat rate applies to all heirs). Progressive inheritance tax rates range from 1 per cent in Chile to 80 per cent in Belgium. The majority of countries with progressive inheritance tax schedules have different schedules depending on the proximity between the donor and the beneficiary. Tax rates for spouses and children tend to be lower than for siblings, aunts and uncles, and non-related individuals.

Inheritance and estate taxes are not levied on the full value of inheritances, but the tax exemption thresholds typically depend on the relationship between the donor and the beneficiary, with closer family members benefiting from more favourable exemption thresholds. Spouses enjoy the most generous tax exemption thresholds and the surviving spouse is fully exempt from inheritance or estate taxes in most countries. Where this is not the case, the tax exemption threshold for spouses ranges from US$17,133 in Belgium to US$2,541,778 in Korea.

Source: OECD (2021b).

There are several arguments for taxing gifts and inheritances:[64]

- **Supporting equity goals**: transfer taxes are generally very progressive, as higher-wealth households are more likely to receive substantial gifts or inheritances. Across the OECD, 12 per cent of households in the lowest wealth quintile reported receiving a substantial gift or inheritance compared with 51 per cent of households in the wealthiest quintile (OECD, 2021b).[65] The implications of transfer taxes for horizontal equity are less clear-cut: from the perspective of donors, inheritance taxes violate horizontal equity because, among donors with the same level of wealth, these taxes discriminate based on how that wealth is spent; but from the perspective of recipients with the same level of pre-inheritance wealth, these taxes reduce inequality and promote horizontal equity (Gale & Slemrod, 2001).
- **Preventing the excessive concentration of wealth**: wealth inequalities have been increasing throughout most of the world since the 1980s. Across the OECD, the wealthiest 10 per cent of households own on average 52 per cent of total net wealth, while households in the bottom half of the wealth distribution own little or no net wealth (OECD, 2021a). Wealth transfers reinforce the concentration of wealth. The share of inherited wealth as a proportion of private wealth has increased significantly in several countries in recent decades, and in France, Germany, the UK, and the USA, inherited wealth now accounts for over 50 per cent of private wealth (Alvaredo et al., 2017). Taxing wealth transfers helps reduce wealth inequalities by preventing wealth from

[64] In practice, taxing inheritances is generally easier than taxing gifts, since levying these taxes relies on individuals reporting the value of gifts or inheritances received.

[65] These wealth levels refer to the time when households responded to the survey, not when they received the inheritance, so it is possible that a household received a substantial inheritance when its own wealth was lower.

becoming even more concentrated, but to be effective these taxes need to be progressive and should encompass both wealth and capital income.[66]

- **Increasing work incentives**: large inheritances can have a negative impact on labour supply by reducing individual incentives to work. Evidence on this effect has been mixed. An early study by Joulfaian and Wilhelm (1994) found that inheritances did not lead to large reductions in labour supply either for men or for married women. However, a more recent study by Doorley and Pestel (2020) found that women were less likely to work full-time after receiving an inheritance, and Brown et al. (2010) found that receiving an inheritance increased the probability of retirement.

However, some see inheritance and estate taxes as a form of double taxation. Individuals are already taxed on their income as they earn it, either through work or interest on their savings. Estate and inheritance taxes mean that their spouses or children are then taxed on this income again when they die. The problem with this argument is that it views the issue from the perspective of the donor. From the perspective of those who receive an inheritance, it would seem odd to tax individuals on money they earn through work but then not to tax them on money they have received essentially through no effort of their own. A further criticism of inheritance taxes has to do with compliance, since there are mechanisms individuals can use to avoid paying inheritance taxes—for example, setting up trusts for their children.[67] This has obvious implications for the fairness of the tax system. Those benefiting from an inheritance may also need to sell the assets to be able to pay the tax, which could cause problems in the case of some assets, such as inherited homes or family farms.

Conclusion

Income taxes play an important role in the economy. They are the largest source of government revenue in many countries and, alongside the benefit system, are one of the key tools for redistributing income, helping to tackle poverty and inequality. But income taxes can also be a source of inefficiency. In this chapter, we have seen how taxes on labour income affect individual incentives to work and how taxes on savings affect incentives to save. We have analysed both the predictions of the standard neoclassical theory and some of the empirical evidence on these effects. The evidence suggests that while income taxes do affect individual incentives, the impacts on behaviour may not be as clear-cut as the standard theory would suggest.

The design of the income tax system needs to balance a society's desire for more redistribution against potential efficiency losses. How we define and measure income for tax purposes—and how we tax income from different sources—has important implications for both equity and efficiency, as it creates an incentive for individuals to shift their income into lower-taxed forms.

[66] See, for example, the discussion in Fize et al. (2022) in the Further Reading.
[67] We return to this in Chapter 17 where we discuss the issue of tax avoidance.

Questions for discussion

1. Select a country of your choice and find out what items can be deducted from income tax in that country. What is the rationale for these deductions? What implications do they have for equity and efficiency?
2. Should everyone pay the same rate of income tax? Why or why not?
3. Do income taxes discourage people from working?
4. Using the individual labour supply model, illustrate and explain the impact on hours worked of: (a) increasing the personal allowance; (b) reducing the marginal rate of income tax.
5. How do taxes on savings affect individual saving behaviour?

Further reading

For a more in-depth discussion of the taxation of income, savings, and wealth, see the relevant chapters in:

Mirrlees, J., Adam, S., Besley, T., Blundell, R., Bond, S., Chote, R., Gammie, M., Johnson, P., Myles, G., & Poterba, J. M. (2011). *Tax by design: The Mirrlees review*. Oxford University Press/Institute for Fiscal Studies.

For a discussion of the income tax base and a comprehensive discussion of the optimal taxation of capital and labour income:

Banks, J. W., & Diamond, P. A. (2008). *The base for direct taxation*. Social Science Research Network scholarly papers, no. 1112821. Available at: https://doi.org/10.2139/ssrn.1112821

On the implications of the choice of the tax unit:

Christl, M., De Poli, S., & Ivaškaitė-Tamošiūnė, V. (2023). Does it pay to say 'I do'? Marriage bonuses and penalties across the EU. *Journal of European Social Policy*, *33*(3), 317–336.

For a review of empirical studies on the impact of taxes on labour supply:

Atkinson, A. B., & Stiglitz, J. E. (2015). *Lectures on public economics* (updated ed.). Princeton University Press.

Meghir, C., & Phillips, D. (2010). Labour supply and taxes. In J. Mirrlees, S. Adam, T. Besley, R. Blundell, S. Bond, R. Chote, M. Gammie, P. Johnson, G. Myles, & J. Poterba (Eds.), *Dimensions of tax design: The Mirrlees review* (pp. 202–274). Oxford University Press/Institute for Fiscal Studies.

On optimal income tax theory and the design of income taxes:

Alm, J. (1996). What is an 'optimal' tax system? *National Tax Journal*, *49*(1), 117–133.

Congdon, W. J., Kling, J. R., & Mullainathan, S. (2009). Behavioral economics and tax policy. *National Tax Journal*, *62*(3), 375–386. https://doi.org/10.17310/ntj.2009.3.01

Diamond, P., & Saez, E. (2011). The case for a progressive tax: From basic research to policy recommendations. *Journal of Economic Perspectives*, *25*(4), 165–190. https://doi.org/10.1257/jep.25.4.165

Kaplow, L. (2024). Optimal income taxation. *Journal of Economic Literature*, *62*(2), 637–738. https://doi.org/10.1257/jel.20221647

Mankiw, N. G., Weinzierl, M., & Yagan, D. (2009). Optimal taxation in theory and practice. *Journal of Economic Perspectives*, *23*(4), 147–174. https://doi.org/10.1257/jep.23.4.147

Piketty, T., & Saez, E. (2012). *Optimal labor income taxation*. National Bureau of Economic Research working papers, no. 18521.

Saez, E. (2001). Using elasticities to derive optimal income tax rates. *Review of Economic Studies, 68*(1), 205–229. https://doi.org/10.1111/1467-937X.00166

On the taxation of wealth and property:

Fize, E., Grimprel, N., & Landais, C. (2022). Can inheritance taxation promote equality of opportunities? *LSE Public Policy Review, 2*(4). https://doi.org/10.31389/lseppr.73

Kopczuk, W. (2013). Taxation of intergenerational transfers and wealth. In A. J. Auerbach, R. Chetty, M. Feldstein, & E. Saez (eds.), *Handbook of public economics* (Vol. 5, pp. 329–390). Elsevier.

OECD (2021b). *Inheritance taxation in OECD countries*. Organization for Economic Cooperation and Development tax policy studies, no. 28. Available at: https://doi.org/10.1787/e2879a7d-en

OECD (2022). *Housing taxation in OECD countries*. Organization for Economic Cooperation and Development tax policy studies, no. 29. Available at: https://doi.org/10.1787/03dfe007-en

Bibliography

Allen, J. (n.d.). *Negative income tax*. Econlib. Available at: https://www.econlib.org/library/Enc1/NegativeIncomeTax.html

Alvaredo, F., Garbinti, B., & Piketty, T. (2017). On the share of inheritance in aggregate wealth: Europe and the USA, 1900–2010. *Economica, 84*(334), 239–260. https://doi.org/10.1111/ecca.12233

Arellano, M., & Meghir, C. (1992). Female labour supply and on-the-job search: An empirical model estimated using complementary data sets. *Review of Economic Studies, 59*(3), 537–559.

Atkinson, A. B. (1983). *The economics of inequality* (2nd ed.). Clarendon Press.

Attanasio, O. P., Banks, J., & Wakefield, M. (2005). *Effectiveness of tax incentives to boost (retirement) saving*. Organization for Economic Development, *Economic Studies*, special issue: Tax-favoured retirement saving, no. 39, pp. 145–172.

Attanasio, O. P., & Wakefield, M. (2008). *The effects on consumption and saving of taxing asset returns*. Prepared for the report of a Commission on Reforming the Tax System for the 21st Century, chaired by Sir James Mirrlees. Published in J. Mirrlees, S. Adam, T. Besley, R. Blundell, S. Bond, R. Chote, M. Gammie, P. Johnson, G. Myles, & J. Poterba (Eds.), *Dimensions of tax design: The Mirrlees review* (pp. 675–736). Oxford University Press/Institute for Fiscal Studies, 2010.

Bingley, P., Symons, E., & Walker, I. (1992). *The labour supply of UK lone mothers: The effects of maintenance, and the welfare system*. Institute for Fiscal Studies.

Blaufus, K., Chirvi, M., Huber, H.-P., Maiterth, R., & Sureth-Sloane, C. (2022). Tax misperception and its effects on decision making—Literature review and behavioral taxpayer response model. *European Accounting Review, 31*(1), 111–144. https://doi.org/10.1080/09638180.2020.1852095

Blinder, A. S., & Deaton, A. (1985). The time series consumption function revisited. *Brookings Papers on Economic Activity, 1985*(2), 465–521. https://doi.org/10.2307/2534444

Blundell, R. (1992). Labour supply and taxation: A survey. *Fiscal Studies, 13*(3), 15–40.

Blundell, R., Duncan, A., & Meghir, C. (1998). Estimating labor supply responses using tax reforms. *Econometrica, 66*(4), 827–861.

Blundell, R., & MaCurdy, T. (1999). Labor supply: A review of alternative approaches. *Handbook of Labor Economics, 3*, 1559–1695.

Blundell, R., & Shephard, A. (2012). Employment, hours of work and the optimal taxation of low-income families. *Review of Economic Studies, 79*(2), 481–510. https://doi.org/10.1093/restud/rdr034

Blundell, R., & Walker, I. (1982). Modelling the joint determination of household labour supplies and commodity demands. *Economic Journal, 92*(366), 351–364. https://doi.org/10.2307/2232445

Boadway, R., & Wildasin, D. (1994). Taxation and savings: A survey. *Fiscal Studies, 15*(3), 19–63.

Bourguignon, F., & Magnac, T. (1990). Labor supply and taxation in France. *Journal of Human Resources, 5*(3), 358–389.

Britannica (n.d.). *Personal deductions*. Available at: https://www.britannica.com/money/income-tax/Personal-deductions

Brown, J. R., Coile, C. C., & Weisbenner, S. J. (2010). The effect of inheritance receipt on retirement. *Review of Economics and Statistics, 92*(2), 425–434. https://doi.org/10.1162/rest.2010.11182

Browning, M., & Lusardi, A. (1996). Household saving: Micro theories and micro facts. *Journal of Economic Literature, 34*(4), 1797–1855.

Christl, M., De Poli, S., & Ivaškaitė-Tamošiūnė, V. (2023). Does it pay to say 'I do'? Marriage bonuses and penalties across the EU. *Journal of European Social Policy, 33*(3), 317–336.

Congdon, W. J., Kling, J. R., & Mullainathan, S. (2011). *Policy and choice: Public finance through the lens of behavioural economics*. The Brookings Institution.

De Bartolome, C. A. M. (1995). Which tax rate do people use: Average or marginal? *Journal of Public Economics, 56*(1), 79–96. https://doi.org/10.1016/0047-2727(93)01409-4

Dilnot, A., & Kell, M. (1988). Top-rate tax cuts and incentives: Some empirical evidence. *Fiscal Studies, 9*(4), 70–92.

Doorley, K., & Pestel, N. (2020). Labour supply after inheritances and the role of expectations. *Oxford Bulletin of Economics and Statistics, 82*(4), 843–863. https://doi.org/10.1111/obes.12353

Flood, L., & MaCurdy, T. (1992). Work disincentive effects of taxes: An empirical analysis of Swedish men. *Carnegie-Rochester Conference Series on Public Policy, 37*, 239–277. https://doi.org/10.1016/0167-2231(92)90009-8

Friedman, M. (1962). *Capitalism and freedom*. University of Chicago Press.

Gale, W. G., & Slemrod, J. B. (2001). *Rethinking the estate and gift tax: Overview*. National Bureau of Economic Research working papers, no. 8205. Available at: https://doi.org/10.3386/w8205

Gruber, J. (2013). *Public finance and public policy* (4th ed.). Worth Publishers.

Gruber, J., & Saez, E. (2002). The elasticity of taxable income: Evidence and implications. *Journal of Public Economics, 84*(1), 1–32.

Hall, R. E. (1988). Inter-temporal substitution and consumption. *Journal of Political Economy, 96*, 339–357.

Hausman, J. A. (1981). Labor supply. In H. Aaron and J. Pechman (Eds.), *How taxes affect economic behavior*. The Brookings Institution.

House of Commons Library (2023). *Income tax allowances for married couples*. Research briefing. 18 April. Available at: https://commonslibrary.parliament.uk/research-briefings/sn00870/

House of Commons Library (2024). *Fiscal drag: An explainer*. 5 April. Available at: https://commonslibrary.parliament.uk/research-briefings/cbp-9687/

Howrey, E. P., & Hymans, S. H. (1978). The measurement and determination of loanable-funds saving. *Brookings Papers on Economic Activity, 1978*(3), 655–685. https://doi.org/10.2307/3217954

Jenkins, S. P. (1992). Lone mothers' employment and full-time work probabilities. *Economic Journal, 102*(411), 310–320. https://doi.org/10.2307/2234516

Joulfaian, D., & Wilhelm, M. O. (1994). Inheritance and labor supply. *Journal of Human Resources, 29*(4), 1205–1234. https://doi.org/10.2307/146138

Kleven, H. J., Landais, C., Saez, E., & Schultz, E. (2014). Migration and wage effects of taxing top earners: Evidence from the foreigners' tax scheme in Denmark. *Quarterly Journal of Economics*, *129*(1), 333–378. https://doi.org/10.1093/qje/qjt033

Lundberg, J. (2017). *The Laffer curve for high incomes*. Uppsala University, Department of Economics working paper, no. 2017:9.

MaCurdy, T., Green, D., & Paarsch, H. (1990). Assessing empirical approaches for analyzing taxes and labor supply. *Journal of Human Resources*, *25*(3), 415–490. https://doi.org/10.2307/145990

Meghir, C., & Phillips, D. (2010). Labour supply and taxes. In J. Mirrlees, S. Adam, T. Besley, R. Blundell, S. Bond, R. Chote, M. Gammie, P. Johnson, G. Myles, & J. Poterba (Eds.), *Dimensions of tax design: The Mirrlees review* (pp. 202–274). Oxford University Press/Institute for Fiscal Studies.

Mirrlees, J. A. (1971). An exploration in the theory of optimum income taxation. *Review of Economic Studies*, *38*(2), 175–208. https://doi.org/10.2307/2296779

Mirrlees, J., Adam, S., Besley, T., Blundell, R., Bond, S., Chote, R., Gammie, M., Johnson, P., Myles, G., & Poterba, J. M. (2011). *Tax by design: The Mirrlees review*. Oxford University Press/Institute for Fiscal Studies.

OECD (2021a). *Inequalities in household wealth and financial insecurity of households*. Centre on Wellbeing, Inclusion, Sustainability, and Equal Opportunities, Organization for Economic Cooperation and Development. Policy insights. July.

OECD (2021b). *Inheritance taxation in OECD countries*. Organization for Economic Cooperation and Development tax policy studies, no. 28. Available at: https://doi.org/10.1787/e2879a7d-en

OECD (2023). *PH2.2 Tax relief for homeownership*. Organization for Economic Cooperation and Development, Directorate of Employment, Labour, and Social Affairs—Social Policy Division. Available at: https://www.oecd.org/els/family/PH2-2-Tax-relief-for-home-ownership.pdf

OECD (2025a). *A comparative table of countries in the global database*. Organization for Economic Cooperation and Development. Data explorer. Revenue statistics. https://data-explorer.oecd.org (accessed 11 August 2025).

OECD (2025b). *Global revenue statistics—Comparative tax revenues*. Organization for Economic Cooperation and Development. Data explorer. Revenue statistics. https://data-explorer.oecd.org (accessed 20 August 2025).

OECD (2025c). *Income distribution database*. Organization for Economic Cooperation and Development. Data explorer. https://data-explorer.oecd.org (accessed 29 August 2025).

Our World in Data (2024). *Top marginal income tax rate 1900–2017*. Available at: https://ourworldindata.org/taxation#taxation-today (accessed May 2024).

Saez, E. (2001). Using elasticities to derive optimal income tax rates. *Review of Economic Studies*, *68*(1), 205–229. https://doi.org/10.1111/1467-937X.00166

Saez, E., Slemrod, J., & Giertz, S. H. (2012). The elasticity of taxable income with respect to marginal tax rates: A critical review. *Journal of Economic Literature*, *50*(1), 3–50. https://doi.org/10.1257/jel.50.1.3

Simons, H. (1938). *Personal income taxation*. Chicago: University of Chicago Press.

Slemrod, J. (2002). Tax systems. *The Reporter*, no. 3, September. National Bureau of Economic Research.

Stiglitz, J. E., & Rosengard, J. K. (2015). *Economics of the public sector* (4th ed.). W. W. Norton.

Thaler, R. H., & Shefrin, H. M. (1981). An economic theory of self-control. *Journal of Political Economy*, *89*(2), 392–406. https://doi.org/10.1086/260971

UK government (n.d.). *Income tax: Introduction*. Available at: https://www.gov.uk/income-tax

Deriving the formula for the deadweight loss of a tax on income

The size of the deadweight loss of the tax will depend on the elasticity of the compensated labour supply curve and the tax rate. Figure 15.11 illustrates a compensated labour supply curve, where H_0 denotes hours of labour supplied at the wage w, and H_1 denotes the hours of labour supplied at the after-tax wage $(1-t)w$. The deadweight loss of the tax is shown by the shaded triangle in the figure.

The area of this triangle is given by:

$$DWL = \frac{1}{2}(\Delta w \bullet \Delta H)$$

where $\Delta w = t{\bullet}w$. To determine ΔH, note that the elasticity of the compensated labour supply curve is given by

$$\eta_L = \frac{\Delta H}{\Delta w} \bullet \frac{w}{H}$$

which implies

$$\Delta H = \eta_L \bullet \frac{H}{w} \bullet \Delta w$$

So our formula for the deadweight loss becomes,

$$DWL = \frac{1}{2}(\Delta w \bullet \eta_L \bullet \frac{H}{w} \bullet \Delta w) = \frac{1}{2}(t \bullet w \bullet \eta_L \bullet \frac{H}{w} \bullet t \bullet w)$$

$$DWL = \frac{1}{2}(t \bullet \eta_L \bullet H \bullet t \bullet w)$$

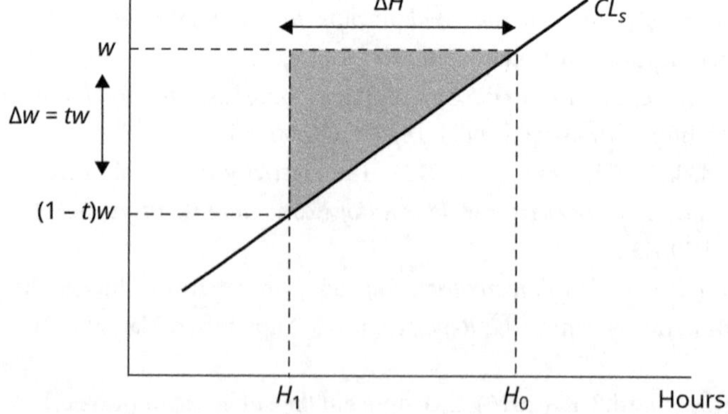

Figure 15.11 Compensated labour supply curve

If we define the revenue raised by the tax as $R = H \cdot t \cdot w$, then the expression for the deadweight loss becomes,

$$DWL = \frac{1}{2}(t \cdot \eta_L \cdot R)$$

So the size of the deadweight loss depends on the tax rate t, and the elasticity of the compensated labour supply schedule η_L, which captures the size of the substitution effect.

If the tax rate were 20 per cent and the compensated **labour supply elasticity** were 0.1, then the DWL would equal 1 per cent of revenue raised. If the labour supply elasticity were 0.5, then the DWL would be 5 per cent of revenue raised. A higher tax rate would similarly lead to a higher DWL.

16
Government borrowing

Learning objectives

By the end of this chapter, you will be able to:

16.1 Explain the difference between the budget deficit and government debt, and how they are measured.
16.2 Explain some of the reasons why governments borrow and their implications for social welfare.
16.3 Describe how government borrowing has evolved over time and how it varies across countries.
16.4 Discuss the consequences of government deficits.
16.5 Critically discuss whether borrowing and taxes are equivalent as means of financing government spending.
16.6 Discuss the challenges governments face in reducing their borrowing.

Introduction

The majority of government spending is financed by tax revenues, but these are not always enough to cover all government expenditure. Economic crises, pandemics, and wars can lead to a significant shortfall in tax revenues, at a time when public spending needs are high. During the Covid-19 pandemic, governments across the world were able to roll out mass vaccination programmes, subsidize businesses and provide financial support to households, all while tax revenues were falling. When government spending exceeds the revenues it can raise through taxes and other sources, it runs a **budget deficit** and must borrow to cover the deficit. On average, across the OECD, government borrowing reached 7 per cent of GDP in 2020 (OECD, 2024). In the UK, the government borrowed £314.4 billion in 2020/21, the highest level since the Second World War (OBR, 2025). Many other countries saw similar historically high levels of borrowing.

Outside of times of crisis, governments might borrow to finance public infrastructure such as roads or digital infrastructure, or to invest in education and healthcare, which will boost productivity and foster economic growth. Governments might also borrow to stimulate economic recovery during a recession. But borrowing comes at a cost. What are the consequences of government borrowing? What impact does borrowing have on the economy? How do we know if government borrowing is too high?

We start by explaining the difference between the government deficit and government debt, and how they can be measured, in section 16.1. In section 16.2, we explore the various reasons why governments borrow. In section 16.3, we look at how borrowing varies across countries and how it has evolved over time. Section 16.4 discusses the consequences of government borrowing, and section 16.5 analyses the Ricardian Equivalence Theorem, according to which government borrowing and taxes are equivalent as means of financing government spending. Section 16.6 explores the challenges involved in reducing government borrowing.

16.1 Government borrowing: definition and measurement

In order to analyse the implications of government borrowing for the wider economy, we need to be clear about what we mean by government borrowing and how it is measured. It is important to draw a distinction between the concepts of deficit and debt. The **budget balance** measures the difference between government revenues and expenditure over a period of time, normally a year. As we have seen, when expenditure is greater than revenues, the government runs a budget deficit; when expenditure is less than revenues, the governments runs a **budget surplus. Government debt** is a measure of the total amount of money the government owes at a particular point in time, accumulated from borrowing to cover budget deficits.

Governments typically finance any difference between the revenues raised and spending by selling bonds, which are bought by institutional investors, such as banks, insurance companies or pension funds, and individual investors.[1] In the UK, government bonds are known as gilts, whereas in the USA they are known as treasury bills or T-bills, and in Germany federal government bonds are known as bunds. By selling bonds/issuing debt, the government is committing to pay a regular interest to the investors who buy their bonds, as well as committing to buy back these bonds when they reach maturity.

In this section, we briefly review some of the different ways of defining and measuring the budget deficit and government debt.

16.1.1 The budget deficit

The budget deficit is a flow measure; it arises if the government spends more than it raises through taxes and other public sector receipts over a given period. The budget deficit typically fluctuates in line with fluctuations in economic activity. During a recession, tax revenues will usually be lower, as more people are out of work and consumer spending is lower, while government spending on welfare will typically be higher, leading to a larger deficit. Conversely, when the economy is strong, tax revenues will be higher and welfare spending will generally be lower, resulting in a smaller deficit or even a budget surplus.

A **cyclical budget deficit** will reflect these fluctuations in tax revenues and spending over the economic cycle. It is a temporary or short-term budget deficit that arises during economic downturns, but should disappear once the economy recovers. This contrasts with the **structural budget deficit**, which takes these fluctuations into account and provides an estimate of the size of the deficit if the economy were operating at a normal level of employment and activity.[2] A structural budget deficit will persist even when the economy is at full employment. It is therefore more of a cause for concern as it suggests that the government's tax and spending policies are not sustainable in the long run. The structural budget deficit provides a

[1] Governments could also finance the deficit by printing money, although this is less common in practice.

[2] The structural deficit is sometimes referred to as the **cyclically adjusted budget deficit**.

useful measure of the government's fiscal stance, but it is difficult to measure in practice as it relies on an estimate of the normal level of economic activity.

The budget deficit captures the flow of government borrowing over a period of time, normally a fiscal year. There may be differences in how the deficit is measured across countries due to differences in how government spending and revenues are defined, or differences in what is included in the definition of 'the government'. The OECD measure of the budget deficit, for example, is narrower than the definition used by the UK government, since it excludes borrowing by public corporations. In the UK, the public sector deficit covers the whole of the public sector, which includes central and local government and public corporations. The budget deficit can be measured in nominal terms—for example, in 2023, the UK's budget deficit was £135.4 billion.[3] However, it is often useful to measure the deficit as a share of GDP, since this gives a better indication of how much the government owes relative to the size of the economy, and makes it easier to make comparisons over time and across countries.

The **primary balance** measures the difference between government revenues and government spending, but excluding net interest payments on government debt. If government spending (excluding net interest payments) is greater than revenues, the government runs a primary deficit. The primary balance therefore provides a more accurate reflection of a government's current fiscal policy, since it ignores the impact of inherited debt.

Governments will typically announce their tax and spending plans—and what they mean for government borrowing—once a year, although the specific details of this process vary across countries. Box 16.1 provides an overview of the budgetary process in the UK.

Box 16.1 The budgetary process in the UK

Each year, the UK government sets out its plans for taxes and spending in the Budget, a statement that the Chancellor of the Exchequer makes to the House of Commons. This speech will normally start with an overview of the state of the economy and the public finances, and will then be followed by an announcement of the government's plans for taxes and spending, an estimate of the cost or yield of these proposals, and their implications for government borrowing. The Budget will also include independent economic forecasts from the Office for Budget Responsibility (OBR). The Chancellor's speech is normally followed by four days of debates on the measures announced in the Budget—the budget resolutions—in the House of Commons. Following these debates, a new Finance Bill, which enacts the proposals made in the Budget, is presented to Parliament, to translate these proposals into law.

The Budget must take place at least once every fiscal year, since two key taxes—income tax and corporation tax—are annual taxes, which need to be reapproved each year. A new Budget will also usually be delivered in election years by the incoming Chancellor of the Exchequer.

Traditionally, the Chancellor carries their speech in a red budget box. The original box was handcrafted for William Gladstone in 1860 and was used by successive chancellors for over 100 years, but it has now been replaced by a newer—though still red—box. The longest continuous Budget speech was delivered by William Gladstone in 1853 and lasted 4 hours and 45 minutes. In contrast, Benjamin Disraeli's Budget speech in 1867 was only 45 minutes long.

Source: UK Parliament (n.d.).

[3] In the UK, the budget deficit is also referred to as 'public sector net borrowing'. Figure from ONS (2024).

16.1.2 Government debt

Government debt—or national or sovereign debt—is a stock measure which captures the total amount the government owes. Each year's deficit is added to the stock of debt from the previous year to derive the new level of debt owed. We analyse the relationship between the deficit and debt in more detail in section 16.4.3. In this section, we are going to focus on how the debt is measured. Should our measure of debt focus only on what the government owes or should it include the debts of public corporations? Should we measure debt in absolute terms or relative to the size of the economy? Should our measure take into account government assets as well as liabilities?

The most widely used measure of government debt is the **debt-to-GDP ratio**, which measures total government nominal debt as a percentage of a country's GDP. Since the same level of debt will be more of a burden for a smaller economy than for a larger one, it is useful to express our measure of government debt relative to the size of the economy. This measure is also useful for analysing the evolution of a country's debt over time and for comparing the burden of debt across countries.

In some cases, measuring debt relative to government revenues may give a better indication of what the government can afford. As we saw in Chapter 13, most countries raise the majority of their revenues through taxation, but levels of tax revenues as a share of GDP vary significantly across countries. For example, tax revenues were 47.3 per cent of GDP in France in 2021, compared with 17.6 per cent in India (UNU–WIDER Government Revenue Dataset, 2023). A country that is raising more in revenues will have more resources to finance expenditure and repay its debts.[4]

It is important to draw a distinction between gross and net debt. **Gross government debt** measures the total debt or liabilities owed by the government at a given point in time, whereas **net government debt** subtracts any financial assets the government owns from these liabilities. These government assets may include bank deposits, loans to the private sector, and foreign exchange reserves. In addition to these financial assets, governments also own physical assets such as land and buildings. However, these physical assets are harder to value accurately and are also more illiquid, making them harder to sell, particularly if the government needs to raise revenues quickly during a crisis. Therefore measures of net debt tend to focus on financial assets only.

Because these financial assets represent a source of income or resources that the government can draw on, incorporating them into our measure of government debt will give a more accurate picture of the government's ability to satisfy its financial obligations. But calculating net government debt is challenging in practice and there is no internationally agreed definition or measurement.[5] The OECD measure of general government financial net worth provides a proxy measure for net government debt (OECD, 2021). In the UK, 'public sector net debt' is the most widely used measure of debt, which subtracts financial assets owned by the government from the gross debt total.

[4] Some countries raise a substantial proportion of their revenues through the sale of natural resources such as oil—for example, Angola, Norway, and Saudi Arabia.

[5] For example, how different governments record unfunded liabilities, such as pension payments to future retirees, will have an impact on their financial net worth. Central banks typically hold a large amount of government debt, but this would not normally be removed from net debt figures.

Another important distinction is between **central government debt** and **general government debt**. General government debt includes debt issued by the central government, as well as debt issued by state and municipal governments. In federal countries, the difference between these two measures can be quite large. In Switzerland, general government debt is almost twice as large as central government debt.

Other factors that are relevant for the measurement of government debt include whether government debt is predominantly long-term or short-term, the currency in which the debt is held, and who holds the debt, as these will affect the volatility of debt-servicing costs. If a significant amount of debt is held by foreign investors, this debt is likely to be denominated in foreign currency, and therefore changes in exchange rates will affect the debt burden. If the domestic currency depreciates, the cost of servicing the debt will increase. Long-term debt usually attracts higher interest rates, but there is more scope for governments to allow inflation to erode the real value of the debt. However, this will depend on whether the interest rate paid by the government is linked to inflation: with index-linked government bonds, the interest rate paid increases in line with inflation and therefore the real value of the debt cannot be inflated away. If domestic banks own a substantial share of a country's government bonds, this can pose risks for domestic financial stability in times of crisis. If the government is having difficulty servicing its debt, this will become a problem for the banks, whereas if banks are in difficulty and need to liquidate their holdings of government bonds, this can then cause problems for the government.[6]

Alternative measures of the government debt burden focus on the cost of servicing the debt, rather than the stock of debt itself. The **debt interest-to-GDP ratio** and the **debt interest-to-revenue ratio** have the advantage of comparing two flow measures—the flow of interest payments this year with the flow of GDP or government revenues this year—and provide a measure of the cost of financing the debt in any given year. However, these measures do not help us understand how the debt burden is likely to evolve in the future (Eichengreen & Panizza, 2022).

16.2 Why do governments borrow?

While different schools of economic thought have very different views on the role (and desirability) of government borrowing (see Box 16.2), government borrowing can be a useful tool for economic policy. During the Covid-19 pandemic, governments across the world were able to increase healthcare spending, roll out mass vaccination programmes, and provide subsidies to businesses and financial support to households, all while tax revenues were falling. Following the 2008 financial crisis, several governments adopted large fiscal stimulus packages, increasing spending and reducing taxes, to stabilize their economies and boost demand. In both cases, governments were able to pursue these policies because they could borrow to cover their expenditure. But governments do not only borrow to address large negative shocks or to finance extraordinary expenditures. There are a number of reasons why governments borrow, discussed below.[7]

[6] This is the sovereign-bank 'diabolic loop', which was one of the hallmarks of the euro area financial crisis between 2009 and 2012.

[7] See Fatás et al. (2019) for a more in-depth discussion of these (and additional) rationales for government borrowing.

Box 16.2 Different perspectives on the economic role of government borrowing

The role and potential impact of government borrowing on the economy is viewed very differently by different schools of economic thought. For classical economists, inspired by the work of Adam Smith and David Ricardo, government borrowing should be avoided or reduced, since borrowing leads to economic instability. Market forces can be trusted to lead to economic growth. Keynesian economists, on the other hand, see government deficits as a strategic macroeconomic tool which can be used during economic recessions. Keynes' **paradox of thrift** highlights how, while increasing saving may be rational for an individual, if everyone decides to increase their saving, this will lead to a fall in aggregate demand and a reduction in output. This suggests that it may be wise for governments to borrow to finance an expansionary fiscal policy during economic recessions—increasing public spending and/or reducing taxes—in order to stimulate economic growth. For the Keynesian school of economic thought, balancing the budget is not always prudent for governments. In contrast, political economy approaches to government borrowing highlight the role of increased political polarization in explaining the increase in government borrowing seen in recent decades.

16.2.1 Tax smoothing

According to the principle of tax smoothing, the government should run a deficit during periods of exceptionally high spending—for example, due to wars or natural disasters. This is partly because financing such large expenditures by raising taxes may not be feasible given the magnitude of the costs. Moreover, as we saw in Chapter 15, raising the tax rate beyond a certain level will actually lead to a decrease in the tax revenues raised.[8] But there is a further argument for financing these expenditures by borrowing rather than by increasing taxes. If the only taxes available to the government are distortionary taxes, and if the size of the distortions increases at an increasing rate with the marginal tax rate, then increasing taxes significantly to cover large or unexpected expenditures will lead to larger distortionary costs and the government should instead borrow to smooth taxes over time.[9] Borrowing allows the government to spread the costs and ensures the expenditures will be financed out of future tax revenues. Crucially, tax smoothing only applies to temporary changes in expenditure. If the change is permanent, then the government should not run a deficit to cover it, as this will imply the need for even higher taxes in the future. Tax smoothing also implies governments should run a budget surplus and pay down their debt during periods of economic expansion.

[8] This relationship between the tax rate and the level of tax revenue is captured by the Laffer curve, discussed in Chapter 15.

[9] This result was originally formulated by Barro (1979). He showed that, for a given tax base, minimizing the distortionary impact of taxes implied that the tax rate should be constant over time. See Chapter 13 for a discussion of distortionary and non-distortionary taxes. In Chapter 14, we saw why high tax rates are more distortionary than low tax rates.

16.2.2 Stabilization policy

Government borrowing can be used as a stabilization tool, helping to lessen the impact of economic fluctuations. Borrowing allows the government to pursue countercyclical fiscal policies during economic recessions—for example, increasing government spending or cutting taxes to help stimulate economic recovery by increasing employment, output, and disposable incomes. Some of the changes in the budget balance will be the result of discretionary policy changes, whereas others will be the result of **automatic stabilizers**. Automatic stabilizers are features built into the tax and welfare system (e.g. income taxes and welfare benefits) that automatically dampen economic fluctuations, without requiring the government to adopt new tax or spending laws. This rationale for government borrowing is consistent with the tax-smoothing rationale and, as with that rationale, government debt should not increase in the long run. Government borrowing during recessions or when economic growth is below average should be counteracted by budget surpluses and the repayment of debt during periods of economic expansion.

16.2.3 Financing long-term investments

Governments may also borrow to finance large public investment projects—for example, investing in transportation networks, power plants, or social infrastructure such as schools and hospitals. This rationale for government borrowing is consistent with the tax-smoothing principle, but here the government is also borrowing to invest in assets that will provide a flow of services in the future. Many public sector and private sector investments are **complements**. Investment in infrastructure such as roads, bridges, and digital technology infrastructure increase a country's productive capacity and support private sector activity. Investments in education and health enhance human capital and boost labour productivity. So government borrowing has the potential to boost economic growth, but this will depend on the social return of each particular project. Government borrowing may also be used to invest in projects that facilitate the transition to a low-carbon economy, helping countries meet their climate change targets. If the benefits of these investments will be shared with future generations, then it is fair that part of the cost of financing them should also be shared, rather than being paid for by current generations through higher taxes.

16.2.4 Providing a safe asset

Another reason for government debt is to provide financial markets with a risk-free asset. Historically, government debt has played an important role in the development of financial markets. In many countries, providing a safe asset may be secondary to the need to meet the government's borrowing requirements. However, in Singapore, for example, the government has run persistent budget surpluses, but still issues debt in order to provide financial markets with a safe asset (Fatás et al., 2019).

16.2.5 Dynamic inefficiency

If the economy is dynamically inefficient, government borrowing can provide a means for transferring wealth across generations. An economy is dynamically inefficient if saving and investment levels are too high relative to the return to capital. In this case, the welfare of all generations could be improved by reducing the saving rate.

16.2.6 Political budget cycles

As we saw in Chapter 4, governments are made up of individuals who will have their own interests and motivations, and these might not always align with the goal of promoting social welfare. Politicians may reduce taxes and increase public spending to increase the likelihood of being re-elected. They may also engage in public expenditure that is more visible or has more immediate benefits, rather than investing in projects that may be of greater long-term benefit to the economy.

16.2.7 Strategic manipulation

Governments may also use borrowing to influence and constrain the actions of future governments. A study by Persson and Svensson (1989) showed that, in a system with two political parties with different preferences over spending and taxation, a left-of-centre party which prefers more public spending and higher taxes might run a budget surplus and try and keep debt low. This is to ensure that if it is followed by a right-of-centre party, this party will not have a strong incentive to reduce public spending. Conversely, the right-of-centre party may increase the level of debt so that the left-of-centre party is forced to limit its spending when in power.

While borrowing to smooth taxes, stabilize the economy, finance large investment projects or provide a safe asset all have the potential to increase social welfare, the same is not true if borrowing is driven mainly by political budget cycles or strategic manipulation. In these cases, there is a risk that governments may borrow more than is socially optimal, where the socially optimal level of borrowing is given by the point where the social marginal cost of an additional unit of debt equals the social return of an additional unit of government expenditure financed by that debt. We discuss the risks of excessive government borrowing in section 16.4.

16.3 Evolution of government borrowing across countries

Having discussed some of the main reasons for government borrowing, in this section we explore how borrowing has evolved over time across countries. Historically, government borrowing has been driven by the need to pay for wars. But from around the eighteenth century, as incomes increased and towns and cities grew, borrowing shifted towards funding education and public works, including water and sewer works, railways, ports, and canals (Eichengreen et al., 2019). The development of global capital markets in the late nineteenth century reinforced this focus of borrowing to finance public investment.

Wars, recessions, and economic crises explain the sharp increases in borrowing throughout the twentieth and twenty-first centuries. Figure 16.1 plots the evolution of the UK government deficit since the early 1900s. Government borrowing peaked at the time of the First and Second World Wars, when the government deficit reached over 25 per cent of GDP. The deficit also increased following the 2007–2008 financial crisis and more recently during the Covid-19 pandemic, when it reached 15 per cent of GDP. These increases in borrowing are consistent with the tax-smoothing and stabilization rationales for government borrowing discussed above. However, both of these motives for government borrowing imply that governments should run large budget surpluses and repay the debt during periods of economic expansion. As Figure 16.1 highlights, the UK government has only run a budget surplus during 18 years since 1900. And this pattern is not unique to the UK.[10]

The extent of government borrowing varies across countries and can fluctuate significantly over time, particularly in response to large negative shocks. Figure 16.2 shows the general government fiscal balance for a selection of OECD countries during the period around the Covid-19 pandemic. In 2018, before the pandemic hit, half of the countries illustrated were running a budget surplus, with Norway running a surplus of almost 8 per cent of GDP. By 2020, all of these countries—with the exception of Denmark—were running a budget deficit, although the size of the deficit varied across countries. While the budget deficit in Norway in 2020 was 2.6 per cent of GDP, in the UK and the USA, the budget deficit was over 10 per cent of GDP. Across the OECD as a whole, the average budget deficit in 2020 was 10.2 per cent of GDP. This was a period when governments were faced with increasing demands for healthcare and for financial support for businesses and households, all while tax revenues were falling as many people were unable to work and many businesses were unable to operate as normal. Borrowing enabled governments to continue to provide essential

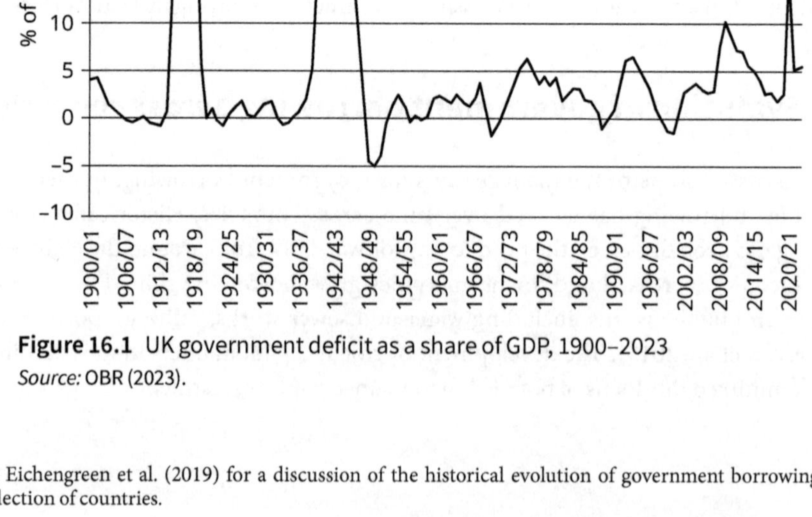

Figure 16.1 UK government deficit as a share of GDP, 1900–2023
Source: OBR (2023).

[10] See Eichengreen et al. (2019) for a discussion of the historical evolution of government borrowing across a wider selection of countries.

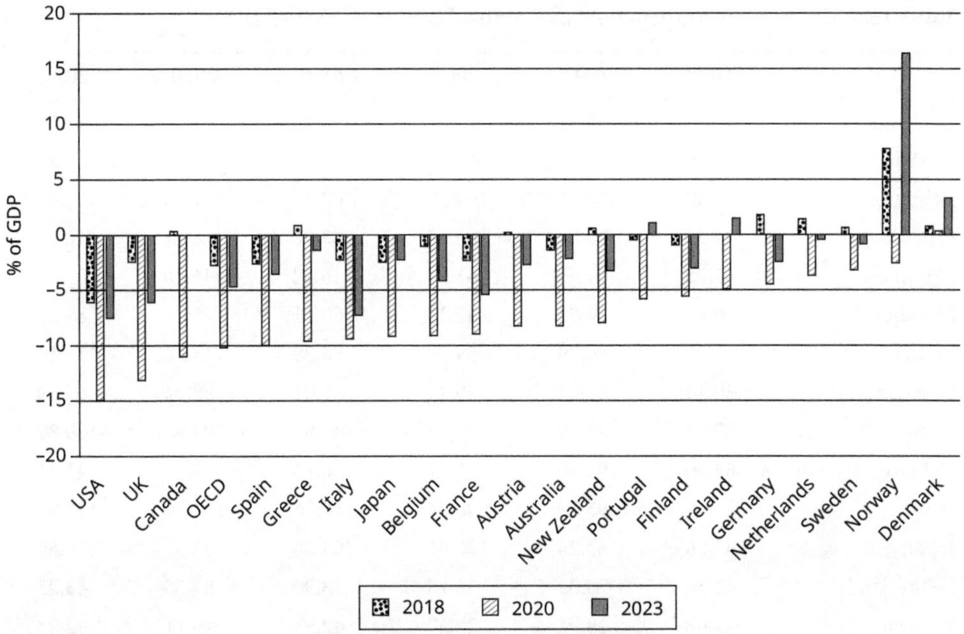

Figure 16.2 General government fiscal balance as a share of GDP
Note: 'OECD average' refers to all OECD countries, not just those listed here.
Source: OECD (2025b).

services and support social welfare. While most of the countries depicted were still running a budget deficit in 2023, the scale of borrowing had fallen and the average budget deficit across the OECD had more than halved, falling to 4.6 per cent of GDP.

As we saw in section 16.1, it is not just the annual flow of borrowing that matters, but also how this impacts on the stock of government debt—the total amount the government owes. Table 16.1 shows how government debt varies across countries and how it has changed over the last 50 years. Overall, there has been a tendency for debt to increase over this period, and this increase has been quite significant in some countries. In Japan, for example, government debt increased from just under 50 per cent of GDP in 1980 to over 230 per cent of GDP in 2024. In the UK, government debt has more than doubled, increasing from 43.71 per cent of GDP in 1980 to just over 100 per cent of GDP in 2024. This long-term increase in debt is not consistent with tax smoothing.

However, in some countries, including the Netherlands, Norway, and Sweden, government debt has remained relatively stable throughout this period, save for a few peaks in borrowing. In Denmark and Ireland, government borrowing has actually decreased significantly since the 1980s, although this decrease has not been linear. Many countries saw government borrowing rise sharply during the Covid-19 pandemic, but government debt has started to fall back from its peak during the pandemic.

Focusing on government debt alone gives an incomplete picture of a country's financial situation, since it ignores any financial assets the government owns. These assets represent a source of income or resources that the government can draw on, and incorporating them into our measure of government debt will give a more accurate picture of the government's ability to satisfy its financial obligations. Figure 16.3 compares the level of general government debt and financial net worth as a share of GDP for a selection of OECD countries, where financial net worth is given by the difference between government-owned financial assets and their

Table 16.1 General government debt as a share of GDP, 1980–2024 (%)

	1980	1990	2000	2010	2020	2024
Australia	–	16.41	19.50	20.35	57.09	49.83
Austria	35.59	56.24	66.11	83.65	83.18	81.21
Belgium	76.80	130.31	109.59	100.25	111.10	104.47
Canada	44.59	73.74	80.44	83.98	118.07	110.77
Denmark	45.75	69.40	53.55	46.12	46.28	27.99
Finland	10.89	13.85	42.45	50.11	75.41	82.53
France	21.30	36.79	59.72	86.28	114.90	113.11
Germany	30.14	40.74	59.24	81.01	68.04	63.89
Greece	22.84	74.19	108.85	147.85	209.93	150.89
Ireland	64.60	92.66	36.41	86.13	57.01	41.11
Italy	55.09	95.30	108.74	118.76	154.38	135.33
Japan	47.78	63.23	135.61	205.88	258.37	236.66
Netherlands	43.56	75.02	52.15	58.90	53.35	43.23
Norway	47.68	28.94	28.67	42.95	46.11	42.72
Portugal	35.00	60.21	54.19	100.08	134.10	94.93
Spain	16.11	41.30	57.84	60.27	119.18	101.82
Sweden	39.81	38.97	50.44	38.59	40.14	32.64
UK	43.71	28.26	37.69	75.86	105.84	101.29
USA	41.27	62.16	53.17	95.35	132.03	120.79

Note: Data for New Zealand were not available.
Source: IMF (2025b).

liabilities. While the difference between financial net worth and debt is relatively small for many of these countries, for some countries the difference is significant. A small number of countries, including Norway, Finland, and Sweden, have positive financial net worth.

16.4 The consequences of government deficits

As we saw in section 16.2, budget deficits and the accumulation of debt can support economic growth and increase social welfare. But government borrowing also involves a cost. In this section, we review three key consequences of government borrowing: the impact of borrowing on future generations; the risk that government borrowing may lead to excessive government growth; and the impact of persistent deficits on accumulated debt.

Public debates about the consequences of government borrowing often draw on an analogy with household borrowing. This household budget analogy suggests that, just as households will go bankrupt if they continually spend more than their income, continuous government borrowing is also unsustainable. But this analogy is misleading, as the constraints facing governments and households are very different (see Box 16.3).[11]

[11] See, for example, Vickrey (1998).

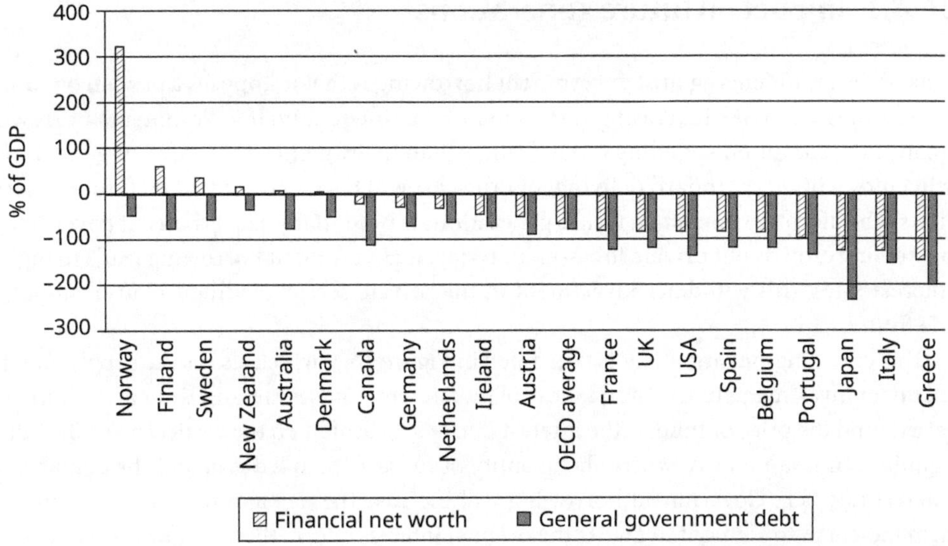

Figure 16.3 General government financial net worth and general government debt as a share of GDP, 2019

Note: Data for Australia, Canada, Sweden, and the USA are adjusted to exclude unfunded pension liabilities.

Source: OECD (2021).

Box 16.3 Is government borrowing the same as household borrowing?

Government borrowing is often compared to borrowing by households. Many households can and do borrow to meet occasional shortfalls in income or to finance a large purchase such as a domestic appliance, car, or house. But eventually households need to repay the money they have borrowed. Similarly, it is argued, governments cannot continually spend more than the revenues they raise through taxation and government assets, otherwise their debt will become unsustainable and the government will be bankrupt. But how accurate is this analogy?

The government budget is far more complicated than household budgets. A household will typically have income coming in from a small number of sources, and relatively few categories of expenditure, whereas the government has several hundred ways of raising revenues and many expenditure programmes, and some of these programmes span far into the future (e.g. future pension liabilities). Government cuts to spending will have a very different impact to when a household cuts its spending, affecting employment, wages, and output in the economy. Drastic cuts to government spending risk exacerbating economic crises. The government also has a licence to print money, although its ability to print money when needed is constrained by the threat of inflation. And while individuals and households have finite lifespans and therefore must eventually repay their debts, governments have indefinite planning horizons and can, in theory, roll over their debt indefinitely.

16.4.1 Impact on future generations

One of the arguments against government borrowing is that it imposes a burden on future generations and risks increasing intergenerational inequality. If governments borrow to finance consumption spending today (rather than investment), then current generations will enjoy a higher standard of living, but the cost will have to be repaid by future generations. This negative impact on future generations is potentially exacerbated if government borrowing crowds out private investment today: if government borrowing leads to higher interest rates, this will deter investment in the private sector, leading to lower output in the future.

This crowding-out argument is illustrated in Figure 16.4, which shows the supply and demand for investment funds. The quantity of investment funds is measured along the horizontal axis and the price of funds—the interest rate—is measured on the vertical axis. The initial equilibrium is at point A, where the quantity of funds demanded is q_1 and the equilibrium interest rate is r_1. Government borrowing will increase the demand for funds, causing the demand curve to shift out to D_2. At the original interest rate, r_1, there is now excess demand for investment funds. This excess demand pushes the interest rate up to r_2, where the new equilibrium level of investment funds is q_2. The higher interest rate increases the cost of borrowing, thereby reducing investment by private firms that rely on borrowing to finance their investments. Higher interest rates also mean that future revenues from investment projects are discounted more heavily, which reduces their net present value, making investment less profitable.[12]

The magnitude of the impact of government borrowing on interest rates and private investment will depend on how sensitive the supply of investment funds is to changes in the interest rate, as reflected in the slope of the supply curve in Figure 16.4. If the supply of investment funds is very sensitive to changes in the interest rate—that is, if it is more elastic—the supply curve will be flatter, and an increase in government borrowing will have a small

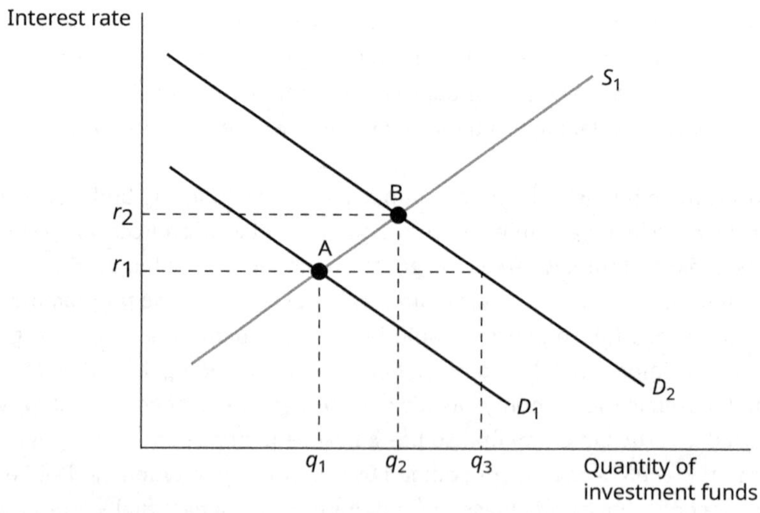

Figure 16.4 Demand and supply of investment funds

[12] The concept of net present value is discussed in Chapter 5.

impact on the interest rate. However, if the supply of investment funds is more inelastic, then the increase in government borrowing will lead to a large increase in the interest rate. The impact of government borrowing on private investment will also depend on how sensitive private investment is to changes in the interest rate. In general, we might expect private investment to fall if interest rates go up, as the cost of borrowing to firms has increased. But during a recession, when firms may be reluctant to invest, government borrowing may have little impact on firms' investment decisions.

The globalization of capital markets also means that, for many countries, the interest rate that firms face will be determined internationally and will be influenced by interest rates in other countries. The size of the government deficit may therefore have little impact on the interest rate firms have to pay and the level of domestic investment. Research by Ardagna et al. (2004) looked at the effects of government deficits and debts on long-term interest rates for a panel of 16 OECD countries. They found that an increase in the primary deficit relative to GDP led to an increase in long-term interest rates; however, an increase in government debt only affected the interest rate in countries with above-average levels of debt.

In assessing the impact of government borrowing on future generations and intergenerational inequality, it is important to consider what the borrowing is used for. If government deficits are used to finance investments that boost the productive potential of the economy, or investments in areas such as rental housing that over time may become fully self-financing, then future generations are likely to enjoy higher living standards as a result. Any burden of borrowing on future generations needs to be weighed against these potential benefits. One approach that attempts to compare the net contributions to the government budget of different generations is the generational accounting approach (see Box 16.4), although this approach is not without its critics.[13]

Box 16.4 Generational accounts: an alternative for measuring fiscal sustainability?

An alternative measure for assessing the sustainability and intergenerational fairness of a country's spending and tax programmes is based on generational accounts. Generational accounts summarize the net lifetime discounted contributions that individuals are expected to make to public finances depending on their age, for a given set of tax and spending rules.

Table 16.2 summarizes the generational accounts for the UK as a function of individual ages in 2010. Based on this, a newborn in 2010 would be expected to make an average net contribution to the public purse of £68,375 over the course of their life. This is based on the difference between the total amount of taxes they are expected to pay over their lifetime, and the public spending they are expected to benefit from, including spending on health, education, welfare, and pensions. An individual aged 50 in 2010, on the other hand, would be expected to receive a net benefit of £105,011 over the remaining course of their life. The final

(Continued)

[13] See, for example, Williamson and Rhodes (2011) for a critical assessment of the generational accounting approach.

Table 16.2 UK generational accounts, 2010

Age in 2010	Net contribution (2008 prices)
0	68,375
5	79,151
10	106,868
15	143,165
20	157,700
25	124,486
30	67,684
35	29,832
40	−11,925
45	−58,601
50	−105,011
55	−155,058
60	−198,930
65	−223,183
70	−206,912
75	−177,732
80	−143,375
85	−114,636
90	−86,040
95	−57,721
Future generations	159,668

Source: McCarthy et al. (2011: 15).

row shows the present value of the net contribution that every future newborn will need to make to ensure the government is able to repay all its debts.

An intergenerational budget gap arises if the net contribution of future generations is larger than the net contribution of current newborns. Generational accounts therefore provide a measure of intergenerational equity, or the extent to which future generations are expected to make larger contributions to the government's finances than today's generations. However, developing these estimates relies on a set of very strong assumptions, and if these assumptions no longer hold, then the estimates will no longer be valid. Generational accounts also assume a future in which the government will fully repay its debts. However, as we saw in Box 16.3, government borrowing is not the same as borrowing by households, and continually rolling over debt is an option that governments have that is not available to households.

Sources: McCarthy et al. (2011) and OBR (2012).

16.4.2 Fiscal illusion and excessive government

Another criticism of government borrowing has to do with its impact on the size of the public sector and, in particular, the potential that borrowing may lead to excessive government growth. This is based on the rational choice models of government growth that we discussed in Chapter 3. According to these models, the size of the public sector reflects the preferences of voters and the public sector grows because people have a preference for larger government. If the government finances part of the goods and services it provides by borrowing, then this will lower the tax price of these goods and services, leading to an increase in the quantity provided. However, if individuals underestimate how much they are paying for government-provided goods and services (because they are not facing the true costs in the form of higher taxes), this may lead them to demand a higher level of expenditure than they otherwise would.

Deficit finance can therefore lead to a problem of **fiscal illusion** or, more precisely, **debt illusion**, where individuals are unaware of the true cost of government-provided goods and services if these are paid for through public-sector borrowing rather than taxation.[14] Utility-maximizing politicians may exploit these opportunities to increase spending, expand the size of the public sector, and increase their chances of re-election. In theory, the greater the degree of political competition, the greater the incentive politicians have to rely on budget deficits to increase public expenditure, with a view to attracting more votes. This has motivated calls for constitutional constraints on government borrowing—for example, requiring governments to maintain a balanced budget over the course of the business cycle. However, Holcombe and Mills (1995) found that the increased security of incumbents actually contributed to increases in deficit finance in the USA, increasing the overall level of government expenditure. In this view, political competition would in fact act as a constraint on deficit finance, while increased electoral safety weakens this constraint.

In practice, determining whether budget deficits lead to a larger public sector is challenging, and the evidence to date on fiscal illusion has been mixed. While some studies have found a positive relationship between deficit finance and government spending, establishing whether deficit finance *causes* an increase in government spending is difficult as the need to increase government spending may itself lead governments to borrow.[15]

Some authors have pointed out that fiscal illusion may lead voters to overestimate as well as underestimate the cost of government-provided goods and services. This implies that budget deficits could lead to a decrease or an increase in the size of the public sector (Alesina & Perotti, 1995). It is also not clear whether fiscal illusion can explain the large differences in budget deficits across countries.

16.4.3 Persistent deficits and accumulated debt

If the government runs a budget deficit year after year, then it must borrow each year to cover the deficit, and the cumulative value of this borrowing will increase government debt. As national debt increases, so too will the interest payments required to service that debt,

[14] Technically, the term 'fiscal illusion' encompasses five different hypotheses: the revenue-complexity hypothesis, the revenue-elasticity hypothesis, the flypaper effect, renter illusion, and debt illusion. See, for example, Dollery and Worthington (1996) for a discussion.

[15] For example, Tridimas (1992) and Gemmell et al. (1999) find that deficit finance is associated with higher government spending in the UK, but this is consistent with both fiscal illusion and other explanations.

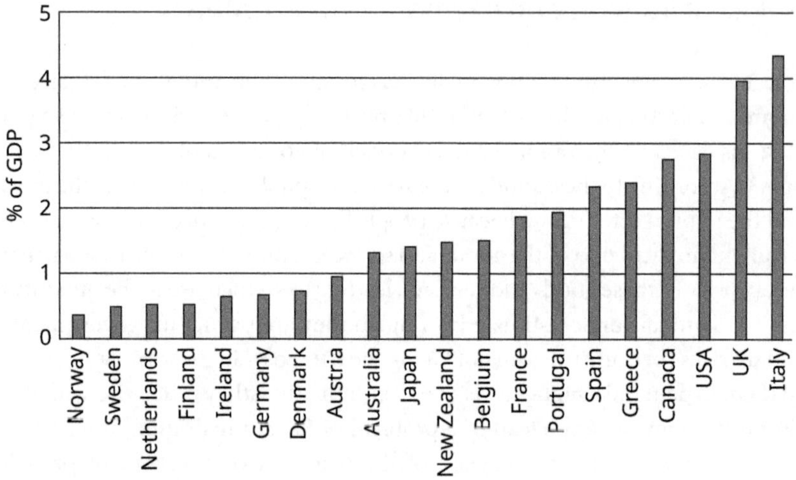

Figure 16.5 Debt interest payments as a share of GDP, 2022
Source: IMF (2024).

and these interest payments will in turn feed back into the annual deficits. The cost of meeting these interest payments can be significant, as Figure 16.5 illustrates. In the UK, net debt interest payments are projected to cost £105.2 billion in 2024/25, which is more than projected government spending on education for that year, at £89.2 billion (OBR, 2025). A larger debt also leaves the government more exposed to interest rate changes, and means less flexibility to meet future challenges, such as the financial pressures of an ageing population and the need to meet climate change targets.

High levels of government debt can also have a negative impact on economic growth. Reinhart and Rogoff (2010) studied economic growth and government debt for a sample of forty-four countries spanning roughly 200 years. They found that government debt has a negative impact on economic growth, but only for very high debt levels where the debt-to-GDP ratio is above 90 per cent.[16] Woo and Kumar (2015) analysed the impact of public debt on long-run growth rates for a sample of advanced and emerging countries covering a shorter period of 40 years. They also found that higher initial debt levels were associated with slower growth. However, they argued this was largely a result of slower labour productivity growth due to lower investment.

Debt dynamics

At what point does the level of government debt become a concern? To answer this question, we need to understand what factors influence the evolution of government debt over time. Current debt, B_t, is given by the sum of the debt carried over from last year, B_{t-1}, plus any government spending minus government revenues raised this year. It is helpful to separate debt interest payments from other government spending (or primary expenditure), since the government can change the primary deficit by changing taxes or expenditure, whereas interest payments are determined by the size of the accumulated debt and the interest rate. Given this, we can express current debt as:

$$B_t = B_{t-1} + INT + D_t$$

[16] This work has also attracted some criticism due to the methodology adopted.

where INT denotes the interest owed and D_t is the primary deficit (the difference between primary expenditure and government revenues).

As we saw above, it is useful to analyse government debt relative to the size of the economy using the debt-to-GDP ratio. We can rewrite the equation above as:

$$b_t = b_{t-1} + r \bullet b_{t-1} + d_t$$

where b_t denotes the current debt-to-GDP ratio,[17] b_{t-1} represents last year's debt-to-GDP ratio, r is the real interest rate (the interest rate net of inflation), and d represents the primary deficit relative to GDP.[18] We can rearrange this equation to get an expression for the change in the debt-to-GDP ratio from one period to the next. Using Δ to denote 'change',[19] we have:

$$\Delta b_t = r \bullet b_{t-1} + d_t$$

This equation tells us that the change in the debt-to-GDP ratio from one year to the next is given by the sum of the real debt interest payments as a share of GDP plus the primary deficit as a share of GDP. However, this ignores the impact of economic growth on the debt-to-GDP ratio. If the economy is growing, GDP is increasing and therefore, for a given level of debt, the debt-to-GDP ratio will be smaller. If we denote the rate of GDP growth by g, we can show that the change in the debt-to-GDP ratio is given by:[20]

$$\Delta b_t = r \bullet b_{t-1} + d_t - g \bullet b_{t-1}$$

This equation can be simplified to:

$$\Delta b_t = d_t + (r - g) b_{t-1}$$

This equation tells us that the evolution of the government debt-to-GDP ratio over time is driven by the relationship between the rate of economic growth and the real interest rate. If the economy is growing, the government will have more resources to repay its debt and, for a given level of debt, the debt-to-GDP ratio will fall. For example, if the initial debt-to-GDP ratio is 50 per cent, the primary deficit is 2 per cent, the real interest rate is 4 per cent, and the growth rate is 3 per cent, then the debt-to-GDP ratio will increase by 2.5 per cent.[21] If the rate of GDP growth is only 1 per cent, then the debt-to-GDP ratio will increase by 3.5 per cent.

For a given interest rate and level of economic growth, we can work out what the primary deficit needs to be in order to keep the debt-to-GDP ratio stable. As long as the economy is

[17] That is, the level of debt divided by the level of GDP.

[18] Here we have replaced the debt interest payments with $\bullet\ b_{t-1}$, since the real debt interest payments as a share of GDP just equal the real interest rate multiplied by the debt-to-GDP ratio carried over.

[19] This is the Greek letter 'delta', which is normally used in economics to denote 'change'.

[20] For an in-depth analysis of debt dynamics, see Eichengreen and Panizza (2022).

[21] Substituting these numbers into the equation we have: $\Delta b_t = d_t + (r - g) b_{t-1} = 0.02 + (0.03 - 0.04)0.5 = 0.025$.

growing at a faster rate than the real rate of interest, the government can still have a primary deficit without this causing the debt-to-GDP ratio to rise. Conversely, if the rate of economic growth is lower than the real rate of interest, then the debt-to-GDP ratio may continue to rise, even of the government is running a primary surplus.[22]

This equation can also help us understand how inflation affects the evolution of government debt. The real interest rate r is a function of the nominal interest rate, i, and the rate of inflation, π.[23] Substituting this into the previous equation, we have:

$$\Delta b_t = d_t + (i - \pi - g)b_{t-1}$$

This tells us that an increase in inflation will have a negative effects on the debt-to-GDP ratio, so high rates of inflation will effectively erode the value of government debt. However, this is not the whole story, since if inflation is higher than expected, this will lead to a higher nominal interest rate, which will mitigate the negative impact of inflation on the value of the debt. So, in general, only unexpected inflation will reduce the debt-to-GDP ratio. After the First World War, Germany successfully inflated away the value of its government debt. The debt-to-GDP ratio was 100 per cent at the end of the war, but the high rate of inflation meant that by 1923 this ratio was close to zero (Eichengreen et al., 2021). But the German government then faced very high rates of interest to be able to borrow again.

What does all this mean for the optimal or sustainable level of government debt? The answer to this question will depend on a complex mix of economic, political, and institutional factors. Box 16.5 discusses some of the challenges in setting reasonable debt targets for governments.

Box 16.5 What constitutes a 'reasonable' debt target?

Determining the sustainable level of government borrowing is challenging in practice. Different approaches to setting targets for government debt have been proposed. One option is for governments to aim for a constant debt-to-GDP ratio. However, this implies no redistribution of income between generations. Alternatively, governments could aim to achieve full-cycle balanced budgets, where the government aims to balance its budget over the course of the economic cycle. This assumes that budget surpluses when the economy is growing will fully offset budget deficits during recessions, so debt is fully repaid out of taxation and the level of debt relative to GDP should fall over time as GDP increases. Under this target, the tax burden on future generations should be lower.

These targets do not consider what government borrowing is used for. If government borrowing is used to finance public investment in physical infrastructure or social infrastructure such as schools and hospitals, then borrowing can help stimulate economic growth. This is the principle that underlies the Golden Rule target. According to the Golden Rule, government borrowing should only be used to finance investment or capital expenditure, and not

[22] Try plugging some numbers into the equation to check this out for yourself.
[23] Formally, $r = i - \pi$. This result is known as the Fisher equation, named after the American economist Irving Fisher.

current consumption. The deficit should therefore not exceed net capital spending by the public sector. Under this target, current generations are not benefiting at the expense of future generations.

Fiscal rules have become increasingly popular. In the 1990s, fewer than 20 countries had a fiscal rule, whereas today almost 100 countries worldwide follow some type of fiscal rule.[24]

Sources: Bailey (2002) and Fatás et al. (2019).

16.5 Is government borrowing equivalent to taxation?

We have looked at some of the arguments against government borrowing, but there is an alternative perspective that sees government borrowing and taxation as essentially equivalent means of financing government spending. Taxes reduce individual disposable income, but if the government borrows to finance its expenditure, this borrowing—plus any interest—will need to be repaid in the future, and therefore taxes will need to rise in the future. Rational forward-looking individuals know this and will increase their private saving today in anticipation of these future tax rises. So from an individual's perspective, using deficit finance to fund government expenditure is equivalent to financing that expenditure through taxes. This is the **Ricardian Equivalence Theorem.**[25]

The theorem takes its name from the nineteenth-century British political economist David Ricardo,[26] and the argument was subsequently developed by Barro (1974). According to the theorem, individuals are altruistic and care not only about their own welfare, but also about the welfare of their children. Individuals will therefore increase their saving to leave bequests for their children, in order to offset any increase in government borrowing which will have a negative impact on their children in the future. This increase in household saving will offset any increase in the deficit, so total national saving is unchanged.

The Ricardian Equivalence Theorem implies that government dissaving is fully offset by the increase in private saving. However, the theorem relies on some fairly strong assumptions:

- **Non-distortionary taxation**: the theorem assumes that the taxes the government will impose in the future are lump-sum or non-distortionary taxes.[27] If, instead, the government has to rely on distortionary taxes, this will change the incentives individuals face. For example, a proportional tax on consumption, by raising the relative price of future consumption, will create an incentive for individuals to increase their consumption today and therefore save less than the theorem would predict.
- **Perfect capital markets**: the theorem relies on the assumption of perfect capital markets, where individuals can borrow and lend at the same rate as the government.

[24] See Eyraud et al. (2018) for a discussion of fiscal rules. The IMF also has a comprehensive database of fiscal rules (IMF, 2025a).

[25] This is sometimes referred to as debt neutrality.

[26] Ricardo is credited with proposing this theorem, although it is not clear whether he actually believed it to be the case or if it was merely a conjecture (Ricardo, 1951, vol. 1: 244–249).

[27] See Chapter 13 for a review of the distinction between distortionary and non-distortionary taxation, and a discussion of how distortionary taxes affect individual behaviour.

If, however, the government were able to borrow at a lower interest rate than that available to individuals, then the present value of government debt would be lower, and so the future repayment would also be lower.

- **No fiscal illusion**: as we saw above, fiscal illusion arises when individuals are not fully aware of or do not understand the implications of the government's tax and spending decisions. In this case, individuals are unlikely to fully offset government borrowing through private saving because they might not expect that government borrowing will lead to higher taxes in the future.
- **No uncertainty**: if uncertainty about future incomes increases as a result of government borrowing, then individuals may save more than is necessary to offset government borrowing. By saving more, current period consumption—and therefore individual utility or welfare—will fall by more than if the government had increased current period taxation to fund its expenditure. So in the presence of uncertainty, government borrowing may have a larger negative impact on individual welfare than taxation.
- **Infinite lives**: individuals will only choose to save to fully offset government dissaving if they expect to be alive when the government raises taxes to repay its debt. However, Barro (1974) shows that Ricardian equivalence may still hold even when individual lives are finite, if the current generation care about the welfare of their children. The current generation will save to offset government borrowing, and pass this saving on to their children in the form of bequests.

Although the theorem has received a lot of attention among economists, there is limited empirical evidence to support it. The Ricardian Equivalence Theorem essentially assumes that individuals are fully rational and altruistic, and will fully take public liabilities into account in their decision-making, increasing their saving one-for-one with public borrowing. In practice, private saving does not fully offset government dissaving. Individuals are not as rational as the theory assumes; they do not fully understand or take into account government borrowing in their decision-making. Nor are they fully altruistic. Many individuals also face borrowing constraints and would like to consume more than they do, so if their disposable income increases (as a result of a tax cut), this is more likely to be consumed than saved.[28]

However, the theorem is potentially useful for policymakers as it highlights how the saving decisions of individuals may offset decisions made by the government. This is particularly relevant in the context of pensions and government efforts to boost private saving for retirement.[29]

16.6 The challenge of reducing government debt

Government borrowing can support economic growth and increase social welfare. However, high levels of government debt can make an economy less resilient to shocks, limiting the scope for using counter-cyclical fiscal policies, and potentially weakening economic growth. In extreme cases, high levels of public debt can lead to sovereign debt crises, where a country is

[28] See the suggested Further Reading at the end of the chapter for a more detailed discussion of Ricardian equivalence.
[29] This is a topic we discuss in Chapter 11.

unable to repay its debt, which may result in the government defaulting on its debt. So how can governments reduce their debt burdens? Our discussion of debt dynamics in section 16.4.3 suggests three main strategies for reducing government debt: raising taxes, cutting expenditure, and promoting economic growth.[30] We briefly discuss each of these strategies below.

16.6.1 Raising taxes

Government debt is the result of accumulated deficits, and deficits arise when government spending exceeds the amount of revenues the government can raise through taxes and other receipts, such as charges for public sector outputs. Therefore, one strategy for reducing the debt is to run a primary budget surplus and use the excess revenues to repay the outstanding debt. To run a primary surplus, governments will need either to cut expenditure or to increase taxes (or both). But, as we saw in Chapters 14 and 15, most taxes are distortionary and can have a negative impact on incentives to work, save, and invest. Taxes on income and consumption reduce individual spending power, potentially reducing aggregate demand and leading to a fall in output. Higher taxes may also encourage individuals to engage in tax evasion or tax avoidance.[31] Therefore simply raising tax rates will not guarantee an increase in tax revenues.

The government would also face the challenge of deciding which taxes to increase and by how much to increase them. Should it increase taxes on consumption or income or wealth? Who should pay the higher taxes? These decisions should consider not only how an increase in taxes will affect economic efficiency, but also how it will affect equity and the distribution of resources.

Although economic theory suggests taxes may have a negative impact on economic growth, the evidence is inconclusive.[32] There is no clear relationship between the size of the tax burden and a country's economic performance. For example, Denmark and the USA enjoy similar levels of GDP per capita, but have very different tax burdens. In 2021, Denmark's GDP per capita was US$69,355, compared with US$71,221 in the USA (OECD, 2025a), but while tax revenues amounted to 27 per cent of GDP in the USA, they were 47 per cent of GDP in Denmark (OECD, 2025c).

In practice, there are few instances where countries have managed to sustain substantial budget surpluses for extended periods of time. A study by Eichengreen and Panizza (2016) found only three examples of countries that had managed to run a budget surplus of 5 per cent of GDP for 10 consecutive years.

16.6.2 Cutting expenditure

An alternative to raising taxes would be to reduce government expenditure. For a given level of tax revenues, cutting government spending can help generate a primary surplus, which will enable the government to repay its debt. The difficulty for governments is deciding what to cut.

[30] Governments can also use inflation to erode the value of the debt, or strive to keep the interest rate on government debt low. Following the Second World War, some governments used statutory regulations to depress the interest rate, a practice known as 'financial repression'.

[31] This is a topic we return to in Chapter 17.

[32] See Chapters 14 and 15 for a discussion of the evidence on the impact of taxes on consumption, income and saving.

It is generally easier for governments to cut capital expenditure rather than current expenditure, as cutting current expenditure is often more challenging politically. But cutting capital expenditure is more likely to have a negative impact on economic growth in the medium to long term, as investment is reduced. The government also does not have direct control over all expenditure. In many areas of welfare spending, for example, expenditure can only be reduced by changing the laws around who is entitled to receive certain benefits and how much they are entitled to receive, and these changes need to be approved by Parliament or another legislative body. At the same time, the pressures of an ageing population and the threat of the climate emergency pose new challenges for governments looking to cut their public spending.

While excessive government borrowing may be harmful for economic growth, the method chosen to reduce borrowing can also have a negative impact on growth, as the example of several euro area countries following the 2008 financial crisis demonstrates (see Box 16.6).

16.6.3 Promoting economic growth

A final strategy governments can use to reduce their debt is to promote economic growth. As we saw in our analysis of the debt dynamics equation, the evolution of the debt-to-GDP ratio is partly driven by the difference between the interest rate the government pays on its debt and the rate of economic growth. As long as the economy is growing at a faster rate than the real rate of interest, the government can still run a primary budget deficit without this

Box 16.6 The impact of austerity in Europe in the wake of the 2008–2009 financial crisis

Government borrowing increased dramatically across Europe following the 2008–2009 financial crisis. Countries including Greece, Portugal, Ireland, Spain, and the UK adopted a series of tough austerity packages in an attempt to bring their borrowing under control. In some cases, austerity measures were also externally imposed by the EU and the International IMF, as part of their financial support packages. These austerity measures included a combination of tax increases and public spending cuts, and cuts to planned public investment programmes.

Rather than stimulating these economies, austerity resulted in economic stagnation, leaving these countries struggling to repay their debts. Austerity policies had a negative impact on economic performance by reducing GDP, inflation, consumption, and investment. For about a third of European countries, GDP fell between 2009 and 2014. In Greece, GDP per capita was 25 per cent lower in 2014 than it had been in 2009. As a result, debt-to-GDP ratios continued to rise. Greece's government debt increased from 130 per cent of GDP in 2010 to 180 per cent in 2014, while Portugal's sovereign debt increased from 106 per cent of GDP to 151 per cent over the same period. Austerity also imposed a human cost: with rising poverty, cuts to health spending leaving many people unable to access care, and an increase in the number of suicides.

Sources: McKee et al. (2012), OECD (2025b), and Proebsting et al. (2017).

causing the debt-to-GDP ratio to rise. If the economy is growing, tax revenues will be higher, which will help reduce the budget deficit or generate a budget surplus. Economic growth also means that, for a given level of debt, the debt-to-GDP ratio will be falling.

The high rates of economic growth in several Western countries following the Second World War played a significant role in helping these countries reduce their debt-to-GDP ratios. However, it is unlikely that these growth rates could be repeated today, particularly given the global slowdown in productivity since the 1970s. Will technological developments—in particular, the rapid growth of generative AI—open up new possibilities for boosting productivity and economic growth in the future? Or will these new technologies ultimately displace workers, increase demands for financial support from governments, and reduce revenues from income taxes?

Conclusion

Government borrowing has a long history. Governments have borrowed to finance wars, to mitigate the impacts of economic crises and smooth economic cycles, and to tackle public health crises. But governments have also borrowed to invest in public infrastructure and human capital, to support the development of their economies and societies, and boost economic growth. During the Covid-19 pandemic, without access to borrowing, most governments are unlikely to have been able to afford to roll out the vaccination programmes and provide the financial support to households and business that they did, and society would undoubtedly have been worse off as a result.

But borrowing also involves a cost. Deficits have the potential to drive up interest rates and crowd out private investment, and the stock of debt has implications for the taxes that will need to be paid by future generations. A larger government debt implies higher interest payments, and leaves the government more exposed to interest rate changes. It also means less flexibility to meet future challenges—for example, financial pressures as a result of an ageing population and the need to meet climate change targets.

Questions about government borrowing are at the heart of the discussion about what the purpose and role of government in the economy should be. When evaluating government borrowing, it is important to think not just about the total level of borrowing, but how it is being used. Ultimately, what matters is what borrowing means for economic growth and living standards—will it improve the well-being of generations today and in the future?

Questions for discussion

1. How should government borrowing be measured?
2. Why is it not always optimal for governments to balance their budgets?
3. Does government borrowing increase intergenerational inequality?
4. Are taxation and deficit finance equivalent means of financing government spending?
5. 'Governments should prioritize reducing their debt, even if this implies higher taxes and cuts to public expenditure.' Do you agree with this statement?

Further reading

For a more in-depth discussion of government debt:

Abbas, S. A., Pienkowski, A., & Rogoff, K. S. (Eds.). (2020). *Sovereign debt: A guide for economists and practitioners*. Oxford University Press.

Eichengreen, B. J., El-Ganainy, A., Esteves, R., & Mitchener, K. J. (2021). *In defense of public debt*. Oxford University Press.

For a broader fiscal picture that combines information on public assets and debt:

IMF (2018). *Fiscal monitor: Managing public wealth*. International Monetary Fund.

On the motives for government borrowing:

Fatás, A., Ghosh, A. R., Panizza, U., & Presbitero, A. F. (2019). *The motives to borrow*. International Monetary Fund working papers, no. WP/19/101.

Yared, P. (2019). Rising government debt: Causes and solutions for a decades-old trend. *Journal of Economic Perspectives*, *33*(2), 115–140.

On the historical evolution of borrowing across countries:

Eichengreen, B., El-Ganainy, M. A. A., Esteves, R. P., & Mitchener, K. J. (2019). Public debt through the ages. In S. Ali Abbas, A. Pienkowski, & K. Rogoff (Eds.), *Sovereign debt: A guide for economists and practitioners* (pp. 7–55). Oxford University Press. Also available as a National Bureau of Economic Research working paper, no. 25494.

Lanskey, L., & O'Loughnan, C. (2023). *300 years of UK public finance data*. Office for Budget Responsibility. Available at: https://articles.obr.uk/300-years-of-uk-public-finance-data/index.html

On the consequences of government borrowing:

Hubbard, G. (2012). Consequences of government deficits and debt. *International Journal of Central Banking*, special supplementary issue, January. Available at: https://www.ijcb.org/journal/ijcb12q0a11.htm

For a discussion of the theory and evidence on the Ricardian Equivalence Theorem:

Barro, R. J. (1996). *Reflections on Ricardian equivalence*. National Bureau of Economic Research working papers, no. 5502. Available at: https://doi.org/10.3386/w5502

Barro, R. J. (1974). Are government bonds net wealth? *Journal of Political Economy*, *82*(6), 1095–1117.

Bernheim, B. D. (1987). Ricardian equivalence: An evaluation of theory and evidence. *NBER Macroeconomics Annual*, *2*, 263–304. https://doi.org/10.1086/ma.2.4623723

On reducing government debt:

House, C. L., Proebsting, C., & Tesar, L. L. (2020). Austerity in the aftermath of the great recession. *Journal of Monetary Economics*, *115*, 37–63.

Pina, Á., Hitschfeld, M., & Miyahara, T. (2025). *Drivers of public debt reductions: Lessons from past episodes in OECD countries*. Organization for Economic Cooperation and Development, Economics Department working papers, no. 1841. Available at: https://doi.org/10.1787/89a45c05-en

Yared, Pierre. (2019). Rising government debt: Causes and solutions for a decades-old trend. *Journal of Economic Perspectives*, *33*(2), 115–140.

Bibliography

Alesina, A., & Perotti, R. (1995). The political economy of budget deficits. *International Monetary Fund Staff Papers*, *42*(1), 1–31.

Ardagna, S., Caselli, F., & Lane, T. (2004). *Fiscal discipline and the cost of public debt service: Some estimates for OECD countries*. National Bureau of Economic Research working papers, no. w10788.

Bailey, S. (2002). *Public sector economics: Theory, policy and practice* (2nd ed.). Palgrave.

Barro, R. J. (1974). Are government bonds net wealth? *Journal of Political Economy*, *82*(6), 1095–1117.

Barro, R. J. (1979). On the determination of the public debt. *Journal of Political Economy*, *87*(5, part 1), 940–971. https://doi.org/10.1086/260807

Bernheim, B. D. (1987). Ricardian equivalence: An evaluation of theory and evidence. *NBER Macroeconomics Annual*, *2*, 263–304.

Dollery, B. E., & Worthington, A. C. (1996). The empirical analysis of fiscal illusion. *Journal of Economic Surveys*, *10*(3), 261–297.

Eichengreen, B., El-Ganainy, M. A. A., Esteves, R. P., & Mitchener, K. J. (2019). Public debt through the ages. In S. Ali Abbas, A. Pienkowski, & K. Rogoff (Eds.), *Sovereign debt: A guide for economists and practitioners* (pp. 7–55). Oxford University Press.

Eichengreen, B., El-Ganainy, A., Esteves, R., & Mitchener, K. J. (2021). *In defense of public debt*. Oxford University Press.

Eichengreen, B., & Panizza, U. (2016). A surplus of ambition: Can Europe rely on large primary surpluses to solve its debt problem? *Economic Policy*, *31*(85), 5–49.

Eichengreen, B., & Panizza, H. (2022). *Public debt: threat or opportunity?* CORE Insight. Available at: https://books.core-econ.org/insights/public-debt/00-highlights.html

Eyraud, L., Debrun, M. X., Hodge, A., Lledo, V. D., & Pattillo, M. C. A. (2018). *Second-generation fiscal rules: Balancing simplicity, flexibility, and enforceability*. International Monetary Fund.

Fatás, A., Ghosh, A. R., Panizza, U., & Presbitero, A. F. (2019). *The motives to borrow*. International Monetary Fund working papers, no. WP/19/101.

Gemmell, N., Morrissey, O., & Pinar, A. (1999). Fiscal illusion and the demand for government expenditures in the UK. *European Journal of Political Economy*, *15*(4), 687–704.

Holcombe, R. G., & Mills, J. A. (1995). Politics and deficit finance. *Public Finance Quarterly*, *23*(4), 448–466.

Hubbard, G. (2012). Consequences of government deficits and debt. *International Journal of Central Banking*, special supplementary issue, January. Available at: https://www.ijcb.org/journal/ijcb12q0a11.htm

IMF (2024). *Interest paid on public debt as a percent of GDP*. International Monetary Fund. Public finances in modern history database. Available at: https://www.imf.org/external/datamapper/datasets/FPP (accessed August 2024).

IMF (2025a). *Fiscal rules dataset, 1985–2024*. International Monetary Fund. Available at: https://www.imf.org/external/datamapper/fiscalrules/map/map.htm

IMF (2025b). *General government debt as a percent of GDP*. International Monetary Fund. Global debt database. Available at: https://www.imf.org/external/datamapper/datasets/GDD (accessed 10 October 2025).

McCarthy, D., Sefton, J., & Weal, M. (2011). *Generational accounts for the United Kingdom*. National Institute for Social and Economic Research discussion papers, no. 377.

McKee, M., Karanikolos, M., Belcher, P., & Stuckler, D. (2012). Austerity: A failed experiment on the people of Europe. *Clinical Medicine*, *12*(4), 346–350.

OBR (2012). *Fiscal sustainability report 2012: Generational and national transfer accounts.* Office for Budget Responsibility. Available at: https://obr.uk/box/generational-and-national-transfer-accounts/

OBR (2023). *Historical public finances database—Public sector net borrowing (PSNB).* Office for Budget Responsibility. Available at: https://obr.uk/data/

OBR (2025). *A brief guide to the public finances.* Available at: https://obr.uk/forecasts-in-depth/brief-guides-and-explainers/public-finances/

OECD (2021). *Financial net worth of general government—Government at a glance 2021*, Organization for Economic Cooperation and Development. Available at: https://doi.org/10.1787/fc9db6d5-en

OECD (2024). *General government deficit, %GDP (GGNLEND).* Organization for Economic Cooperation and Development. Data explorer. https://data-explorer.oecd.org (accessed 5 August 2024).

OECD (2025a). *Annual GDP and consumption per capita, US $, current prices, current PPPs.* Organization for Economic Cooperation and Development. Data explorer. https://data-explorer.oecd.org (accessed 10 October 2025).

OECD (2025b). *Public finance main indicators—Government at a glance 2025.* Organization for Economic Cooperation and Development. Data explorer. https://data-explorer.oecd.org (accessed 10 October 2025).

OECD (2025c). *Revenue statistics in OECD member countries—Comparative tax revenues.* Organization for Economic Cooperation and Development. Data explorer. https://data-explorer.oecd.org (accessed 10 October 2025).

ONS (2024). *Public sector net borrowing excluding public sector banks* (released 19 July). Available at: https://www.ons.gov.uk/economy/governmentpublicsectorandtaxes/publicsectorfinance/timeseries/dzls/pusf

Persson, T., & Svensson, L. E. O. (1989). Why a stubborn conservative would run a deficit: Policy with time-inconsistent preferences. *Quarterly Journal of Economics*, *104*(2), 325–345.

Proebsting, C., Tesar, L., & House, C. (2017). *Austerity in the aftermath of the great recession.* Centre for Economic Policy Research and VoxEU. 17 April.

Reinhart, C. M., & Rogoff, K. S. (2010). Growth in a time of debt. *American Economic Review*, *100*(2), 573–578.

Tridimas, G. (1992). Budgetary deficits and government expenditure growth: Toward a more accurate empirical specification. *Public Finance Quarterly*, *20*(3), 275–297.

UK Parliament (n.d.). *The Budget and Parliament.* Available at: https://www.parliament.uk/about/how/role/check-and-approve-government-spending-and-taxation/the-budget-and-parliament/

UNU-WIDER Government Revenue Dataset (2023). *Tax revenues as a share of GDP—UNU-WIDER* [dataset]. UNU-WIDER, *Government revenue dataset (GRD) 2023* [original data]. Retrieved 2 August 2024 from https://ourworldindata.org/grapher/tax-revenues-as-a-share-of-gdp-unu-wider

Vickrey, W. (1998). Fifteen fatal fallacies of financial fundamentalism: A disquisition on demand-side economics. *Proceedings of the National Academy of Sciences*, *95*(3), 1340–1347.

Williamson, J. B., & Rhodes, A. (2011). A critical assessment of generational accounting and its contribution to the generational equity debate. *International Journal of Ageing and Later Life*, *6*(1), 33–57.

Woo, J., & Kumar, M. S. (2015). Public debt and growth. *Economica*, *82*(328), 705–739.

Yared, P. (2019). Rising government debt: Causes and solutions for a decades-old trend. *Journal of Economic Perspectives*, *33*(2), 115–140.

17
Tax evasion and tax avoidance

Learning objectives

By the end of this chapter, you will be able to:

17.1 Explain the difference between tax evasion and tax avoidance and discuss how they can be measured.
17.2 Critically assess the deterrence model of tax evasion and explain its implications for what drives the evasion decision.
17.3 Discuss the empirical evidence on what leads individuals to evade taxes.
17.4 Critically reflect on the contribution of behavioural economics to our understanding of what influences tax evasion.
17.5 Discuss how the theory and evidence on tax evasion can inform government policy to improve tax compliance.

Introduction

Governments rely on the revenues from taxation to finance public spending, investing in essential areas such as health, education, and public infrastructure. While the majority of individuals and businesses pay their share of taxes, there are some that engage in a variety of actions to reduce their tax liabilities. This includes both legal tax avoidance activities and illegal tax evasion activities—for example, by taking payments in cash and not declaring their full value, underreporting income, overstating expenses, or investing in offshore companies and other tax shelters. According to HM Revenue and Customs, the UK government lost £6.4 billion due to tax evasion and £0.7 billion due to tax avoidance in 2023/24 (HM Revenue and Customs, 2025: table 7.1). This represents a substantial loss in revenue for the government and a significant cost to society, leading to a misallocation of resources, as individuals change their behaviour to reduce the amount of tax they pay. This then forces the government to devote resources to reducing non-compliance. Tax evasion and tax avoidance also have implications for the fairness of the tax system: if some people are not paying their share of taxes, this will shift more of the tax burden onto others. What factors lead individuals to pay—or not pay—their taxes? What tools can governments use to improve tax compliance?

We start in section 17.1 by explaining the distinction between tax evasion and tax avoidance, and discuss some of the approaches that have been used to measure tax evasion in practice and how it varies across countries. In section 17.2, we introduce the deterrence model of tax evasion and discuss its implications for what drives the evasion decision, as well as exploring some extensions to the basic model. We then review some of the empirical evidence on tax evasion in section 17.3. In section 17.4, we focus on the insights from behavioural economics for our understanding of what motivates individuals to pay their taxes (or not). Section 17.5 then discusses the implications of the theory and evidence for government policy to encourage tax compliance.

17.1 Definition and measurement

Before we can explore why individuals might not pay taxes and what governments can do to encourage tax compliance, it is useful first to clarify some key concepts. In this section, we start by explaining the distinction between tax evasion and tax avoidance, and why it matters, and introduce some related concepts, including tax compliance and the shadow economy. We then discuss some of the different approaches that have been used to measure tax evasion in practice and the challenges this involves.

17.1.1 Defining tax evasion and tax avoidance

Tax evasion is the intentional and illegal non-payment or underpayment of taxes by individuals or businesses. It arises when individuals deliberately fail to declare and pay all of the tax that they owe. Tax evasion is distinct from **tax avoidance**, which involves the reorganization of economic activity to reduce the amount of tax paid—for example, by making use of legal loopholes, or exploiting tax shelters or tax havens (see Box 17.1). Crucially, tax evasion is illegal, whereas tax avoidance is not, but in practice the distinction between the two is not always clear-cut. Examples of tax evasion include intentionally underreporting one's income, overstating deductions or exemptions, and failing to submit the appropriate tax return. Examples of tax avoidance include income splitting,[1] postponing taxes, and shifting income into lower-taxed forms. An important related concept is the concept of **tax compliance**, which refers to an individual's decision to comply with all tax laws and regulations by paying their taxes in an accurate and timely manner.

Tax evasion is one component of the **shadow or hidden economy**. There are different definitions of the shadow economy. Broader definitions see it as encompassing 'those economic activities and the income derived from them that circumvent or otherwise elude government regulation, taxation or observation' (Feige, 1989: 1). This includes illegal activities, such as drugs or people trafficking, as well as unmeasured legal activities (e.g. household production), and legal but undeclared income. Narrower definitions of the shadow economy focus only on legal market-based activities, but ones that are concealed from the authorities in order to avoid paying taxes or social security contributions, or to avoid having to meet legal labour market standards or to comply with certain administrative procedures.[2] This narrower definition excludes illegal activities such as drug dealing or burglary, as well as household production.

Although tax evasion is often associated with income taxes, other types of taxes are also susceptible to evasion. For example, individuals can evade property taxes when selling a

[1] Income splitting is a tax-planning strategy that involves shifting income from individuals who face high marginal tax rates to individuals who face low marginal tax rates within a family to reduce the overall tax burden.

[2] This definition is based on the one proposed by Buehn and Schneider (2007).

Box 17.1 Tax avoidance, tax shelters, and tax havens

There are two key principles behind most income tax avoidance mechanisms. The first involves deferring or postponing when taxes are paid. As we saw in Chapter 15, capital gains taxes are taxes levied on capital gains, the difference between the price for which an asset (e.g. a house or a piece of artwork) was bought and the price at which it is sold. The payment of capital gains taxes can be postponed by postponing the date on which the asset is actually transferred. This is based on the principle that a pound or euro today is worth more than a pound or euro in the future and, therefore, taxes paid in the future will be less costly than taxes paid today.

The second principle is income shifting, which involves taking advantage of the different tax rates levied on different types of income and shifting income from categories that attract a higher rate of tax to categories that attract a lower rate. Income can also be shifted across individuals within a family, a practice sometimes referred to as income splitting. In a progressive tax system, with increasing marginal tax rates, an individual facing a higher marginal tax rate may want to shift some of their income on to an individual who faces a lower marginal tax rate. This may, for example, influence the salaries that a family-owned business pays the various family members it employs.

A **tax shelter** is any strategy or investment scheme that allows individuals to reduce their taxable income and, therefore, the amount of tax they have to pay. This includes investing in offshore companies and certain types of trusts.[3] In many countries, some retirement saving plans are also a form of tax shelter, allowing individuals to reduce the amount of tax they pay. For example, in the Individual Retirement Accounts (IRAs) or 401(k) plans in the USA, taxes are deferred until the money is withdrawn. In the UK, individuals paying into a workplace pension are entitled to tax relief from the government: the current minimum contribution is 8 per cent, which includes 4 per cent from employees, 3 per cent from employers, and 1 per cent from the government in tax relief. There are other types of saving products that allow individuals to shelter some of their income from tax. For example, Individual Savings Accounts (ISAs) in the UK allow individuals to save or invest a given amount each year and pay no income tax on the interest or dividends earned.

Tax havens are countries which offer very low or zero rates of tax for non-domiciled investors. Popular tax havens include Ireland, Singapore, Switzerland, and the Netherlands.

property by understating its true value. Businesses can evade corporate income taxes by underreporting their income, overstating deductions, or failing to submit tax returns. Retailers can evade sales taxes by understating sales figures or by failing to register for VAT.[4] Overseas sellers can also evade VAT through online marketplaces.

[3] An offshore company is a company that is based in a different country from where it carries out most of its business, usually for tax reasons.

[4] VAT is the value-added tax. Businesses need to register for VAT, but only if their level of taxable turnover is above a certain level.

Tax evasion is a significant problem for governments and for society. Aside from the fact that it is illegal, tax evasion has implications for both horizontal and vertical equity.[5] Tax evasion affects the distribution of the tax burden: those who are paying less (or no) taxes benefit, while others have to bear the cost, in the form of either higher taxes or lower public spending. How the government decides to target resources to tackle tax evasion also has equity implications: should the government focus on combating low-level fraud, or should it focus on closing down tax shelters that primarily benefit wealthier individuals? Tax evasion has implications for economic efficiency, as the resources which are devoted to tackling tax evasion could be used more productively elsewhere in the economy. At the individual level, opportunities for non-compliance can distort the allocation of resources, as individuals may change their choices about how many hours to work, what sectors to work in, or what assets to invest in to reduce their tax liabilities.

17.1.2 Measuring tax evasion

Measuring tax evasion in practice is challenging because it is illegal. It is difficult to get reliable data on taxpayer compliance, since individuals have an incentive to keep this activity hidden. However, researchers have devised many creative ways of collecting data to analyse tax evasion. In this section, we review three types of approaches to measuring tax evasion: direct measures; indirect measures; and measures based on controlled field experiments and laboratory experiments.

Direct measures

Direct approaches to measuring tax evasion include measures based on audits of individual returns, such as the Taxpayer Compliance Measurement Program run by the US Internal Revenue Service. This programme audits a representative sample of individual income tax returns to derive an estimates of taxpayers' true income, which can then be compared with actual reported income to arrive at an estimate of income tax evasion. However, not many countries carry out these systematic audits, since they are very costly to run. These programmes also fail to account for honest mistakes individuals may make when filling out their tax returns, which are an important source of tax underpayment, as we will see below. There have also been attempts to measure tax evasion based on tax amnesty data, using the income declared by amnesty participants.[6] However, these measures will provide an incomplete picture of the extent of tax evasion, as only a subset of individuals will choose to take part in an amnesty.

Other direct approaches rely on survey evidence where individuals are asked directly about their evasion behaviour or attitudes towards tax evasion.[7] Surveys where individuals are asked directly whether they are engaged in tax evasion are unlikely to produce reliable

[5] See Chapter 2 for a review of these concepts. Horizontal equity is essentially about the equal treatment of individuals who are equal in all relevant respects. In the context of taxation, this implies that individuals who earn the same income should pay the same amount in taxes. Vertical equity is more closely aligned with the notion of redistribution and the idea that individuals with greater needs should receive more resources; or individuals with higher incomes should pay more taxes.

[6] A tax amnesty is a time-limited offer made by the government to a group of taxpayers which promises to forgive a tax liability and ensure freedom from legal prosecution in exchange for a fixed fine.

[7] One example is the World Values Survey, which we discuss in section 17.4.

results, as individuals might not respond truthfully or they might not remember what income they reported when they filled out their tax return. Some studies have made use of existing surveys collected for other purposes to derive estimates of tax evasion—in particular, large household surveys. The UK Family Expenditure Survey was a continuous annual survey that ran from 1961 to 2001, which collected detailed information on various individual socio-demographic and economic characteristics. Individuals taking part in the survey were also asked to keep a detailed record of all their expenditures over a fourteen-day period. Dilnot and Morris (1981) used the individual-level income and expenditure data available in this survey to infer the size of the shadow economy, by comparing the reported income and expenditure for different groups of individuals. They estimated the size of the black economy at around 2–3 per cent of GNP.

Indirect measures

Rather than measuring tax evasion directly, indirect methods try to infer the extent of tax evasion based on certain indicators, such as electricity consumption, labour force participation, and demand for currency. As a key input in production, electricity can be used to predict the aggregate level of economic activity in a country or region, which can then be compared with official measures of output to derive an estimate of the size of the shadow economy. In one approach, researchers used luminosity measured from outer space as a basis for estimating the scale of true economic activity, which was then compared with official income accounts to estimate the extent of tax evasion (Henderson et al., 2012). The currency demand approach relies on the assumption that most transactions in the shadow or hidden economy involve cash and therefore any increase in the size of the shadow economy will lead to an increase in the demand for cash. By establishing a relationship between the quantity of cash in the economy and the level of economic activity, it is possible to infer the size of the hidden economy. While these indirect methods focus on a single indicator, model-based approaches explicitly incorporate multiple causes of tax evasion or the shadow economy and the multiple effects of the shadow economy over time. These are used to estimate the extent of tax evasion.

Controlled field and laboratory experiments

Given the limitations with the approaches discussed above, researchers have increasingly resorted to controlled field experiments or **randomized controlled trials (RCTs)** and laboratory experiments. In an RCT, one group of individuals (the treatment group) is subject to a particular policy intervention (e.g. receiving a text message about the importance of paying their taxes on time), while another group (the control group) receives a neutral message. The impact of the policy can then be assessed by comparing the responses of the two groups (e.g. what proportion of their income they choose to report). While these types of experiments are useful for assessing the effectiveness of the different policy interventions, they do not provide a measure of the actual extent of tax evasion.

Laboratory experiments to analyse tax compliance often aim to mimic various real-world situations. For example, participants in an experiment may be given an income and asked to decide how much of this income to report to the tax authorities, bearing in mind that there is a chance they may be audited. If they are found to have underreported their income, they will have to pay a fine. This process is often repeated for a number of rounds and, at the end of the experiment, individuals receive a payment that is proportional to their earnings in the experiment. Crucially, in a laboratory experiment, individuals know they are participating in an experiment. However, participants are typically students, who may not be representative of the wider taxpayer population.

17.1.3 The extent of tax evasion across countries

In spite of the difficulties in measuring tax evasion, researchers have attempted to estimate the extent of tax evasion or the size of the shadow economy using the various methods discussed above. Table 17.1 presents estimates of the size of the shadow economy for a range of countries. These are based on the narrower definition of the shadow economy covered above, and use a combination of the currency demand approach and the model-based approach. The size of the shadow economy varies significantly across countries, with estimates ranging from less than 10 per cent of GDP in Japan and the USA to just under 69 per cent of GDP in Georgia and Bolivia. However, even these lower estimates suggest that the hidden economy is a significant problem in most countries.

More recent estimates for the UK are given in Figure 17.1, which shows how the **tax gap** has evolved since 2005/06. The tax gap measures the difference between the amount of tax that individuals should, in theory, pay to the revenue service, and the amount that is actually collected. This measure includes not only income tax, but also VAT, excise duties, capital gains taxes, corporation taxes, and other miscellaneous taxes (e.g. inheritance taxes and landfill taxes). The total tax gap in 2023/24 was estimated at £46.8 billion (HM Revenue and Customs, 2025: table 7.1), or just over 5 per cent of total tax liabilities, down from 7 per cent of total tax liabilities in 2005/06. These tax gap estimates are based on a combination of methods. The VAT and excise duties gaps are based on external data on consumption, which are used to calculate the amount of tax that should, in theory, be paid. This is then compared with the amount of tax actually paid to estimate the tax gap. Other elements of the tax gap are based on compliance checks for randomly selected samples of individuals, together with statistical methods and other data sources.

These estimates of the tax gap represent a significant loss of revenue for the government. However, the tax gap is not driven solely by tax evasion. There are various reasons why the

Table 17.1 The size of the shadow economy as a share of GDP, 2006

Country	Shadow economy (% of GDP)	Country	Shadow economy (% of GDP)
Georgia	68.7	Italy	23.1
Bolivia	68.1	Sweden	16.3
Russia	46.9	Germany	15.4
Pakistan	37.6	Singapore	14.0
Egypt	35.4	China	13.9
Mexico	32.1	Australia	13.0
South Africa	29.0	UK	10.9
Greece	26.0	Japan	8.9
India	24.6	USA	8.0

Source: Schneider and Buehn (2007).

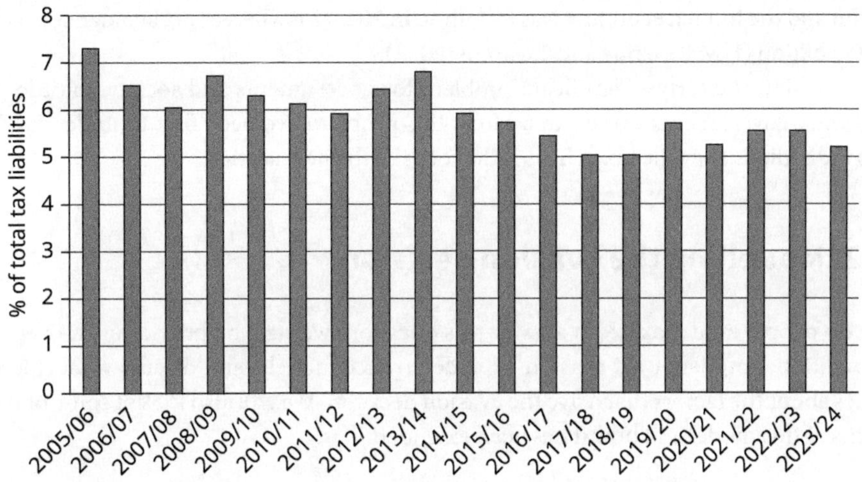

Figure 17.1 Estimates of the UK tax gap as a share of total tax liabilities, 2005–2024
Source: HM Revenue and Customs (2025).

amount of tax collected by the revenue service may be less than the amount of tax that individuals and businesses should pay. These include failure to take reasonable care, mistakes, differences in the legal interpretation of taxes owed, criminal attacks, evasion, and avoidance.[8] As Table 17.2 illustrates, failure to take reasonable care accounts for the largest proportion of the tax gap, at 31 per cent. This is followed by errors and evasion, at 15 per cent and 14 per cent respectively. The hidden economy accounts for 6 per cent of the tax gap, whereas tax avoidance accounts for only 1.5 per cent of the tax gap.[9] The combined loss from tax

Table 17.2 Share of tax gap by type of individual behaviour, 2023/24

	% share of tax gap
Failure to take reasonable care	31.20
Error	15.17
Legal interpretation	11.54
Evasion	13.68
Criminal attacks	9.40
Non-payment	11.75
Hidden economy	5.56
Avoidance	1.50

Source: HM Revenue and Customs (2025).

[8] Failure to take reasonable care refers to situations where individuals were careless and/or negligent in recording their transactions and/or preparing their tax returns. Mistakes or errors result from mistakes made in preparing tax calculations or completing returns, even though reasonable care was taken.

[9] The UK revenue service draws a distinction between the hidden economy and tax evasion. The hidden economy refers to sources of taxable economic activity that are completely hidden from the revenue service (e.g. businesses that are not registered for VAT or employees who do not declare additional sources of income beyond their main employment income). The hidden economy measures situations where individuals or businesses fail to declare an entire source of income. In contrast, tax evasion captures situations where a source of income is declared but intentionally understated. See the methodological annex in HM Revenue and Customs (2025) for further details.

evasion and the hidden economy was £9 billion in 2023/24, whereas tax avoidance accounted for £0.7 billion (HM Revenue and Customs, 2025).

Tax evasion is clearly a significant problem for governments and society. In order to explore what governments can do to address this problem, we need first to understand what leads individuals to evade taxes. This is the focus of the next section.

17.2 Modelling the evasion decision

Why do people evade taxes? To answer this question, we start by providing an overview of the traditional model of tax evasion—the deterrence model—and discuss what this model implies about the factors that drive the evasion decision. We will also look at some of the limitations of this model and how it has been extended.

17.2.1 The deterrence model of tax evasion

The deterrence model of tax evasion was originally proposed by Allingham and Sandmo (1972) and Srinivasan (1973).[10] In this model, tax evasion is essentially treated as a gamble. Individuals must decide how much of their income to declare to the tax authorities. There is a chance they will be audited, and if they have declared less than their true income, they will have to pay a fine, on top of having to pay tax on their unreported income. However, if they declare less than their true income and they are not audited, they will pay less in tax. This model is based on **expected utility theory**:[11] in deciding whether to evade taxes and how much to evade, individuals will balance their expected gains and losses, taking into account the chance of being caught and the punishment or fine they face.

Suppose our taxpayer Leni has a fixed income level Y and has to choose what level of income to declare, D, where D is less than or equal to Y, so $D \leq Y$. If $D = Y$, then Leni is honest and declares her full income. Leni's unreported income is $(Y - D)$, which must be greater than or equal to zero. For a given tax rate t, the tax owed on this unreported income is given by:

$$t(Y - D)$$

There are two possible outcomes or states of the world: Leni is either audited by the tax authorities and caught, or she is not audited. If Leni is not audited, her net income is just her total income Y minus the tax paid on whatever income she declared, D:

$$Y_{NC} = Y - tD$$

[10] This model is based on the work of Becker (1968) on the economics of crime.

[11] Expected utility theory is a model of decision-making under uncertainty which builds on the rational choice model introduced in Chapter 2. In the face of uncertainty (e.g. whether they will be caught evading tax or not), individuals choose the option that will maximize their expected utility, which is defined as the probability-weighted average of all possible outcomes.

If Leni is audited and caught evading tax, she will have to pay tax on her full income, in addition to facing a fine F on the tax that was evaded. So her net income in this case will be,

$$Y_C = (1-t)Y - F \bullet t(Y-D)$$

where the first term, $(1-t)Y$, captures her income minus the tax paid; and the second term, $F \bullet t(Y-D)$, captures the fine. We assume here that the fine is proportional to the tax rate and the level of unreported income.[12]

To derive Leni's budget constraint, it is helpful to start by identifying the two possible extreme cases: she can either be completely honest and declare all of her income, so $D = Y$; or she can be completely dishonest and declare no income, so $D = 0$. In the first case, if Leni is completely honest, her income in each state of the world is:

$$Y_{NC} = (1-t)Y$$
$$Y_C = (1-t)Y$$

So if Leni is completely honest, her net income will be the same whether she is audited or not.

In the second case, if Leni is fully dishonest and declares no income, her net income will depend on whether she is audited by the tax authorities. If she is not audited, she gets to keep all of her income and pays no tax, so her net income if she is not caught is:

$$Y_{NC} = Y$$

If she is audited and caught, her net income will be:

$$Y_C = (1-t)Y - F \bullet tY$$

which is equivalent to:

$$Y_C = (1 - t(1+F))Y$$

So Leni will have to pay tax on all of her income, as well as the fine F.

These two extremes give us the two points on Leni's budget constraint illustrated in Figure 17.2. Here, instead of measuring different goods on each axis, we are measuring Leni's income in each state of the world: on the horizontal axis we have her income if she is not audited and caught, and on the vertical axis we have her income if she is audited and caught. The budget line is the line connecting the two extreme cases, $D = Y$ and $D = 0$, since Leni is not restricted to declaring all of her income or no income—she could also declare some proportion of her income.

The budget constraint represents Leni's opportunity set—that is, all possible combinations of income in the two states of the world that are achievable. The choice of how much income to declare D determines Leni's income in each of state of the world: declaring a higher level of

[12] Some versions of the model assume the fine is only proportional to the level of unreported income and not the marginal tax rate.

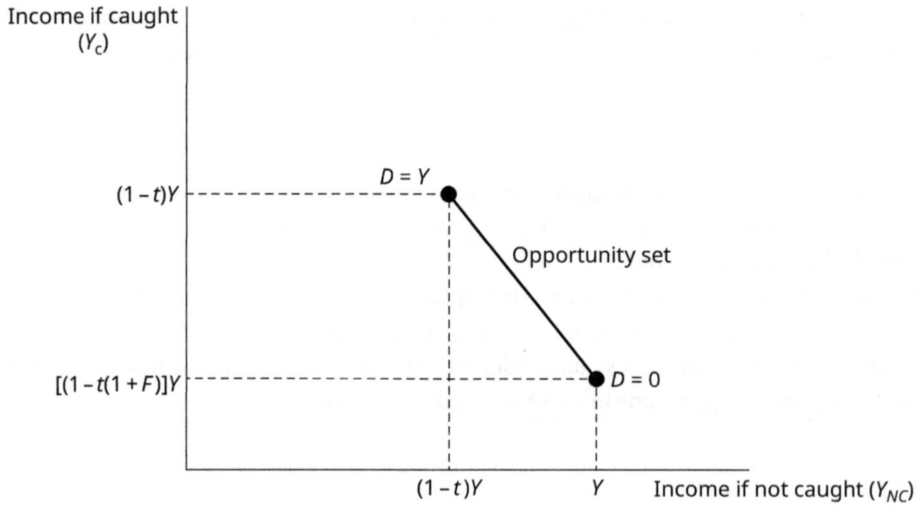

Figure 17.2 The taxpayer's opportunity set

income will provide more income if she is audited and caught; declaring a lower level of income will provide more income if she is not audited and caught. The slope of the budget line captures the price of being dishonest (or, more specifically, the price of being caught being dishonest) and is given by the negative of the fine, $-F$.[13]

Leni's utility depends on her income Y, but in this case she does not know in advance what this income will be, since it depends on whether she evades tax (and by how much), and whether she is caught. Suppose the probability of being audited and caught is given by p. This means Leni will receive income Y_C with probability p, and income Y_{NC} with probability $(1-p)$, since probabilities must sum to 1. Given the uncertainty she faces, Leni chooses the level of income to declare D to maximize her expected utility, given by:

$$EU = (1-p)U(Y_{NC}) + pU(Y_C)$$

where $U(Y_{NC})$ represents the utility Leni receives from her income if she is not caught evading and $U(Y_C)$ is the utility she receives from her income if she is caught evading. This expected utility function essentially describes Leni's preferences over her income levels in the two possible states of the world. We can derive a set of indifference curves that represent Leni's preferences, where each indifference curve represents the various combinations of income in the two states of the world that give Leni the same level of *expected* utility.[14]

One such indifference curve is depicted in Figure 17.3. Given these preferences, Leni's utility-maximizing choice is given by D^*, which is the optimal amount of income she should declare. In this example, D^* is what is known as an **interior solution**, where Leni declares some—but not all—of her income.

[13] See the appendix at the end of the chapter for details of how to calculate the slope in this instance.

[14] In Chapter 2, we saw how, in the absence of uncertainty, indifference curves represent the different combinations of goods that provide the individual the same level of utility.

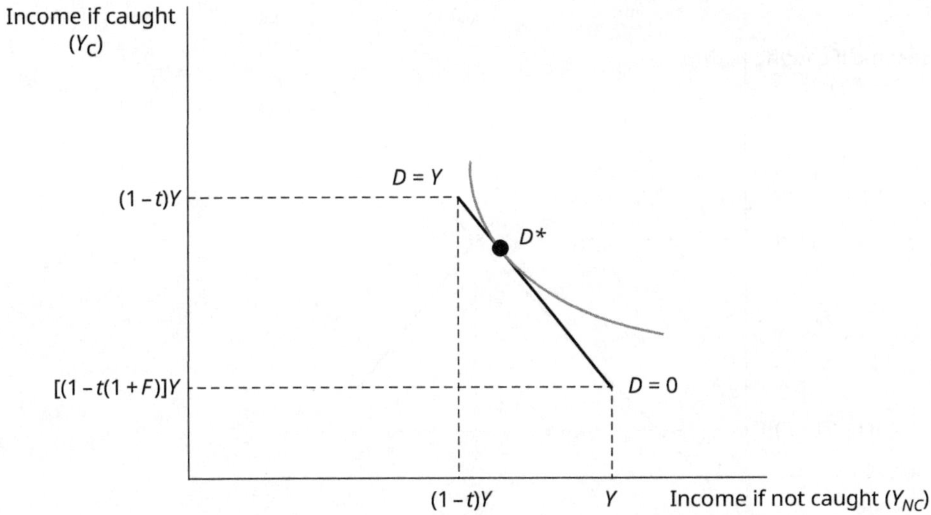

Figure 17.3 The optimal level of income to declare

What conclusions can we draw about what leads an individual to evade taxes? To answer this question, we need to take our analysis a step further. Figure 17.4 illustrates the two possible **corner solutions**—these are solutions where Leni either chooses to be completely honest and declare all her income (shown in panel (a)), or chooses to be completely dishonest and declare no income (shown in panel (b)). To understand what triggers the decision to evade taxes, it is helpful to compare these two solutions.

Looking at panel (a), we can see that Leni's indifference curve is flatter than her budget constraint at the utility-maximizing choice, where both cross the 45° line. This 45° line essentially shows all points where Leni's income in both states of the world is equal—that is, where $Y_{NC} = Y_C$. Turning to panel (b), if we were to continue sketching Leni's indifference curve upwards until it crosses the 45° line, we would see that her indifference curve is steeper than the budget line at this point. This suggests that it is optimal to evade taxes if the individual's indifference curve is steeper than the budget line where it crosses the 45° line. We know that the slope of the budget line is the negative of the value of the fine, $-F$, and we can show that the slope of the indifference curve on the 45° line is given by: $-\frac{(1-p)}{p}$.[15] Taking the absolute value of the slopes, this implies that it is optimal to evade taxes if the slope of the indifference curve is greater than the slope of the budget line:

$$\frac{(1-p)}{p} > F$$

We can rearrange this expression to get:

$$p < \frac{1}{1+F}$$

[15] See the appendix at the end of the chapter for an explanation of this result.

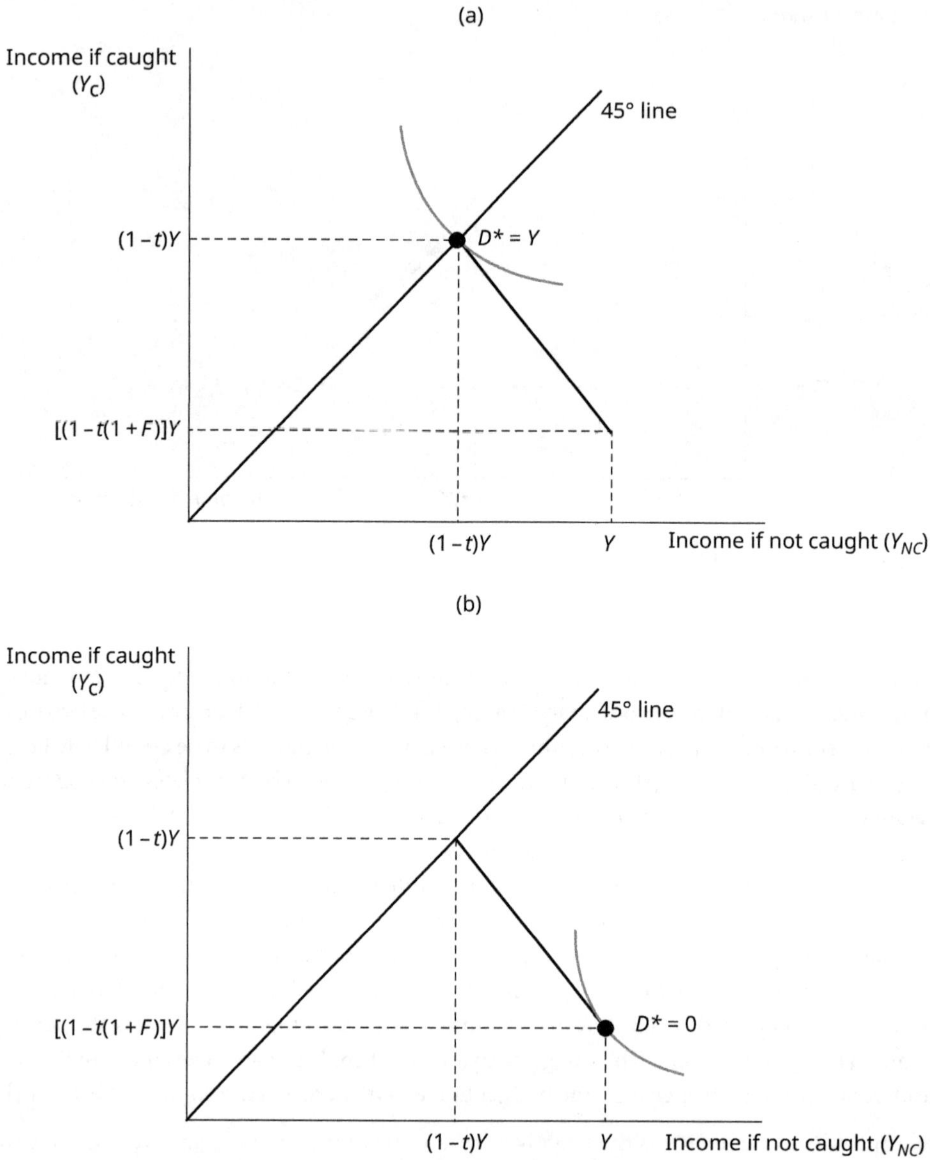

Figure 17.4 Corner solutions: declaring all income or no income

This result tells us that it will be optimal to evade taxes if the probability of being caught, p, is small relative to the fine F.

Suppose the fine is 100 per cent of the tax revenue lost, which implies a value of F equal to 1. This means that $\frac{1}{1+F}=\frac{1}{2}$. So if the fine is 100 per cent, as long as the probability of being audited and caught is less than 50 per cent, then it is optimal to evade. The probability of being audited in most countries is well below 50 per cent, which suggests that almost all taxpayers should evade at least some taxes.[16] In practice, taxpayers tend to be much more honest than

[16] The overall audit rate in the USA in 2015 was only 0.8 per cent (Alm, 2019).

this model predicts, and many individuals in most countries pay all of their taxes. Before we look into the limitations and extensions to this model, we are going to analyse in a bit more detail what this model implies about what factors drive the decision to evade taxes.

17.2.2 What factors affect the evasion decision?

In the deterrence model described above, the decision to evade taxes depends on four variables: the fine, the probability of being audited, the marginal tax rate, and income. Below, we briefly explore how changes in each of these variables affect an individual's decision to evade taxes.

- **Changing the fine, *F***: changing the fine affects the income the taxpayer receives, but only if they are caught evading. An increase in the fine means their income if they are caught evading will be lower, but their income if they are not caught will not change. This causes the budget line to rotate inwards, becoming steeper, as illustrated in panel (a) in Figure 17.5. The new utility-maximizing choice is D_2, which is closer to the point where the taxpayer is fully honest and declares their full income. So increasing the fine leads to a reduction in the level of tax evasion.
- **Changing the probability of being audited, *p***: the probability of being audited affects the taxpayer's preferences and, therefore, the shape of their indifference curves; it has no impact on the budget constraint or the taxpayer's opportunity set.[17] Increasing the probability of being audited will make the taxpayer's indifference curves flatter, as illustrated in panel (b) of Figure 17.5, where the new indifference curve is U_2 and the new utility-maximizing choice is D_2. Increasing the audit probability moves the utility-maximizing choice closer to the point where the taxpayer declares their full income, thus reducing the extent of tax evasion.
- **Changing the marginal tax rate, *t***: a change in the tax rate will affect the budget constraint and the taxpayer's opportunity set. As we saw above, the tax rate affects individual income in both states of the world—that is, if they are audited and if they are not audited. An increase in the tax rate will reduce the individual's income in both states of the world, thus causing the budget line to shift inwards, as illustrated in panel (a) of Figure 17.6. The impact on the optimal level of evasion will depend on the taxpayer's degree of absolute risk aversion. Evidence suggests that absolute risk aversion tends to fall as income increases, so as individuals become wealthier, they are more willing to take part in small bets. With decreasing absolute risk aversion, individuals will declare more of their income in response to an increase in the tax rate, thus reducing the level of tax evasion.[18] This is illustrated by the new utility-maximizing choice D_2 in panel (a). This result seems counterintuitive as we would expect a higher tax rate to provide more incentives for individuals to evade taxes. As we will see in section 17.3, it is also at odds with the empirical evidence on tax evasion, which suggests that evasion tends to increase with higher tax rates.

[17] Given the model set-up in section 17.2.1, the probability of being audited only enters into the expected utility function; it is not a variable in the individual's budget constraint.

[18] The finding that the deterrence model implies that a higher marginal tax rate reduces tax evasion was originally highlighted by Yitzhaki (1974) and is therefore sometimes referred to as the Yitzhaki puzzle.

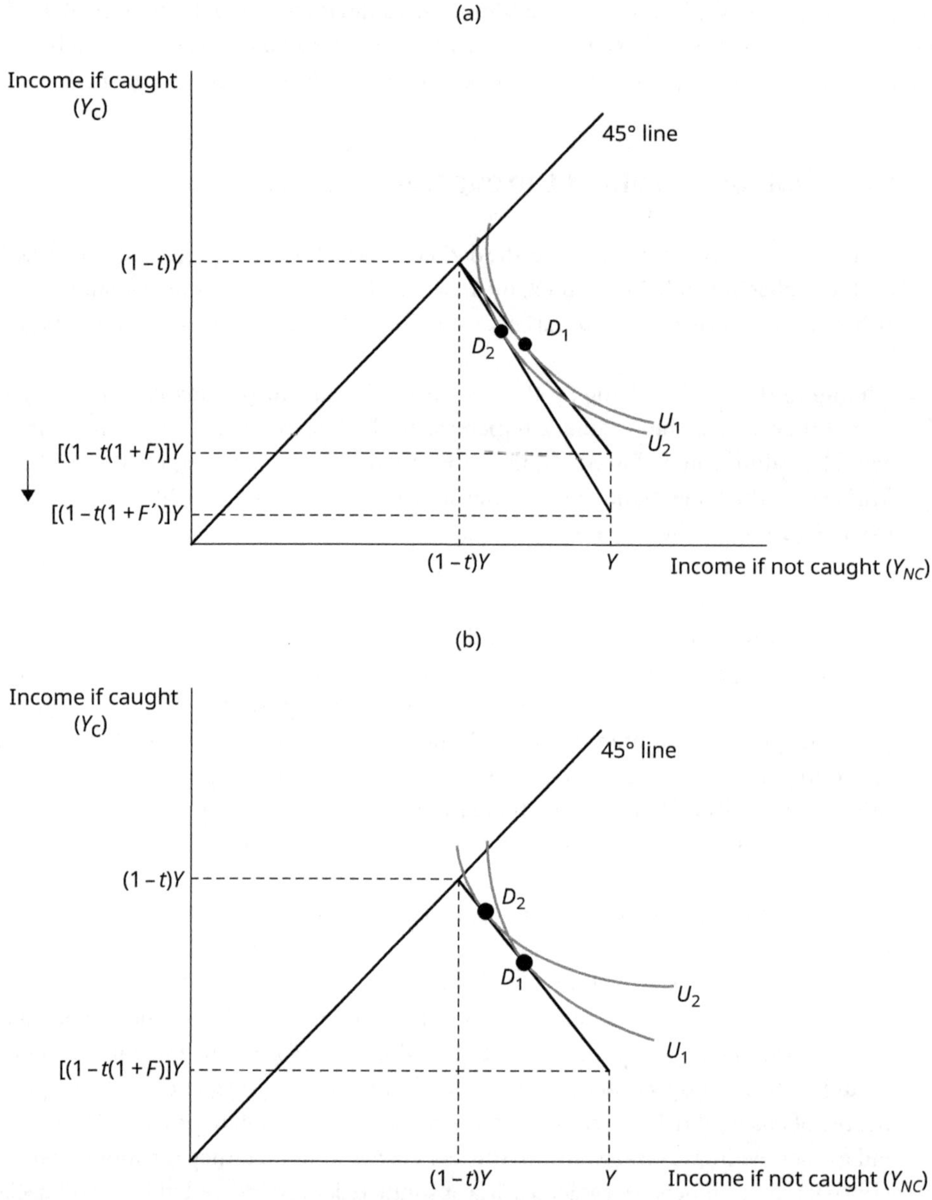

Figure 17.5 Impact of increasing (a) the fine and (b) the probability of being audited

- **Changing individual income, *Y***: a change in income affects the taxpayer's budget constraint and opportunity set. An increase in income will cause the budget line to shift outwards, parallel to the original budget line, as show in panel (b) of Figure 17.6. Crucially, the slope of the budget line does not change. The impact on the taxpayer's optimal choice will again depend on their degree of absolute risk aversion. With decreasing absolute risk aversion, increasing income will lead to an increase in tax evasion. This is shown by the new utility-maximizing choice D_2 in panel (b).

We have looked at how changes in the fine, the probability of being audited, the marginal tax rate, and income influence an individual's decision to evade taxes in the context of the

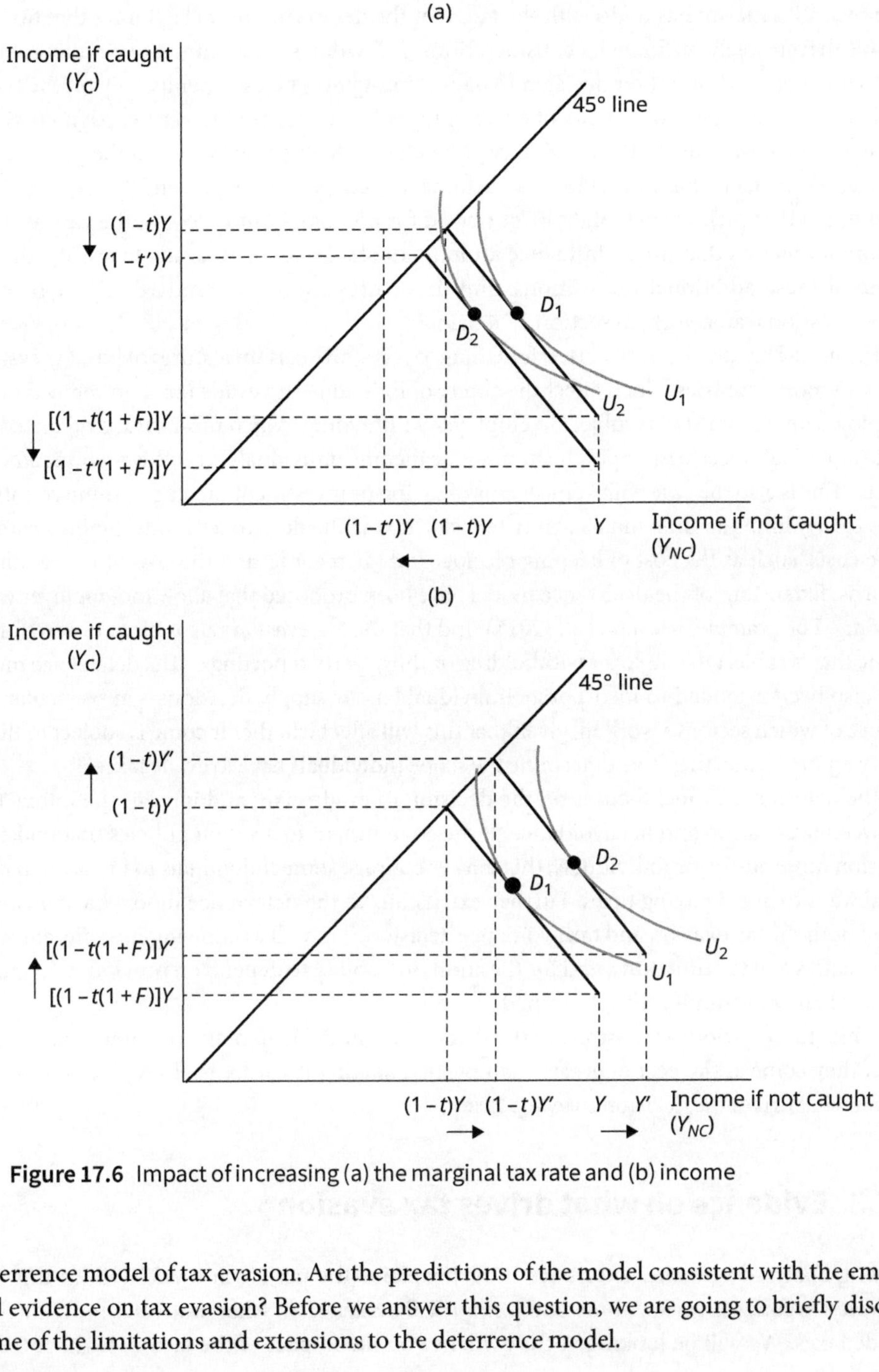

Figure 17.6 Impact of increasing (a) the marginal tax rate and (b) income

deterrence model of tax evasion. Are the predictions of the model consistent with the empirical evidence on tax evasion? Before we answer this question, we are going to briefly discuss some of the limitations and extensions to the deterrence model.

17.2.3 Limitations and extensions to the deterrence model

There are two main criticisms of the deterrence model of tax evasion. The first is the implication, noted above, that higher marginal tax rates lead to less tax evasion, which is both counterintuitive and inconsistent with the empirical evidence on what drives tax evasion.

The second criticism has to do with the fact that the deterrence model assumes that tax evasion is driven solely by financial considerations. Individuals are assumed to be fully rational and self-interested, and their decision to pay—or not pay—taxes depends only on the trade-off between the expected benefits of evading taxes (in the form of lower tax payments) and the expected costs (due to the possibility of being caught evading taxes and the punishment if caught). In fact, this limitation was acknowledged by Allingham and Sandmo (1972), who noted that their model might be criticized for not taking into account the various non-pecuniary factors that might influence an individual's decisions to evade taxes. We discuss some of these additional motivations, and departures from the standard expected utility maximization framework, in section 17.4 below.

The model has also been criticized for failing to recognize certain features of how tax systems work in most countries which affect the ability of individuals to evade taxes. In many types of employment, income tax is subject to employer withholding, which means tax is deducted before individuals receive their paycheques, so the income individuals receive is their income net of tax. This is also the case with some forms of saving or investment income in some countries. This clearly limits an individual's ability to evade taxes. The deterrence model ignores compliance costs, such as the cost of keeping receipts and tax records, and the cost of filling out tax returns. Extensions of the deterrence model have been proposed that allow for employer withholding. For example, Kleven et al. (2011) find that the tax evasion rate is close to zero for income that is subject to employer withholding or third-party reporting.[19] The deterrence model has also been extended to incorporate individual labour supply decisions—in particular, the choice of which sector to work in, given that this will affect whether income is subject to third-party reporting and therefore determine the scope individuals have to evade taxes.[20]

The deterrence model focuses on the decision to evade taxes and ignores the interaction between tax evasion and tax avoidance. If the government focuses on policies that make tax evasion more costly for individuals, this may encourage some individuals to focus on finding legal ways to avoid paying taxes. Further extensions to the deterrence model have incorporated both the tax evasion and tax avoidance decision,[21] as well as allowing for different types of penalties and tax functions, and for the audit probability to depend on previous tax returns rather than being randomly determined.[22]

While these various extensions to the deterrence model help make the model more realistic, they come at the cost of greater complexity, making it harder to draw clear-cut results about what drives the decision to evade taxes.

17.3 Evidence on what drives tax evasion

Having analysed how the deterrence model explains the tax evasion decision, in this section we are going to review some of the empirical evidence on what motivates individuals to evade taxes. We will be looking at the evidence on the impact of the factors highlighted by

[19] Under third-party reporting, employers and sometimes other organizations, such as banks, are required to report the taxable income that individuals earn directly to the government. Kleven et al. (2011) do find that tax evasion is substantial for self-reported income.

[20] See, for example, Pestieau and Possen (1991).

[21] See Slemrod and Yitzhaki (2002) for a discussion of a more general model that applies to both tax evasion and tax avoidance.

[22] See Alm (2019) for an overview of the extensions to the deterrence model that have been proposed.

the deterrence model, as well as evidence on what motivates individuals to evade taxes more generally. We will focus on the following six factors: the audit probability; the punishment or fine; the marginal tax rate; individual perceptions and the complexity of the tax system; social norms and the social context; and non-pecuniary motivations. The empirical work analysing the factors that influence tax evasion has largely relied on two approaches: econometrics analyses based on survey or administrative data, and laboratory or controlled field experiments.

17.3.1 Audit probability

The impact of the audit probability on tax evasion has been studied extensively, and the evidence suggests that higher audit rates can have a significant deterrent effect. Although the impact of the audit rate varies across studies, the estimated reported income–audit rate elasticity typically ranges from 0.2 to 0.4, suggesting that a 10 per cent increase in the audit rate increases reported income by between 2 and 4 per cent (Alm, 2019). However, the evidence suggests that the impact of increased audits is non-linear, with the deterrent effect diminishing at higher audit rates. This suggests that there are limits to how much compliance can be increased by increasing the probability of being audited. A study by Slemrod et al. (2001), based on a field experiment, also found that while the threat of an audit reduced evasion among low- and middle-income taxpayers, it did not reduce evasion among high-income taxpayers.

17.3.2 Fine or punishment

Research on the impact of the size of the fine on tax evasion is scarce and most of the evidence comes from laboratory experiments, given the practical difficulties in varying fine rates in a real-world setting. The existing experimental evidence suggests the impact is negative, which is consistent with the theory, but the magnitude of this effect is small. The estimated reported income–fine rate elasticity is less than 0.1 (Alm, 2019). There is growing evidence that non-financial punishments, such as public disclosure of known tax evaders, can also act as a deterrent.[23] Laboratory experiments also suggest that positive inducements—for example, where individuals who truthfully report their income are eligible for a lottery—can increase tax compliance (Bazart & Pickhardt, 2011).

17.3.3 Marginal tax rates

Evidence on the impact of the marginal tax rate on tax evasion has been mixed. Clotfelter (1983) analysed the tax returns of roughly 47,000 people in the USA and found that higher tax rates were associated with more tax evasion. However, Feinstein (1991) analysed individual data from the US Taxpayer Compliance Measurement Program and found that tax rates had no significant impact on the level of income reported. Geeroms and Wilmots (1985), in an

[23] See, for example, Bø et al. (2015), Coricelli et al. (2010), and Hasegawa et al. (2013).

analysis of Belgian data, found that higher tax rates actually led to less tax evasion. Most experimental studies have found that a higher tax rate increases tax evasion.[24] Research also suggests that it is not only the level of the tax rate that matters, but an individual's tax rate relative to other individuals. The amount of tax evaded tends to be higher if individuals believe their tax rate is too high relative to the tax rate faced by other individuals (Spicer & Becker, 1980).

17.3.4 Individual perceptions and the complexity of the tax system

Research suggests that it is not only actual audit probabilities that matter for behaviour, but also individual perceptions of the probability of being audited. Individuals tends to significantly misperceive these probabilities, typically overweighting the probability of an audit, which would help explain why we see less tax evasion than the deterrence model would predict (Alm et al., 1992). Knowing someone who has been audited also leads individuals to overestimate the probability they themselves will be audited (Alm et al., 1992). The complexity of the tax system and how well individuals understand the tax system also seems to have an impact on tax compliance, but the evidence here is mixed (Alm, 2019). Evidence from laboratory experiments suggests that the complexity of the tax system can affect compliance, with rates of tax compliance typically being lower in more complex tax systems.

17.3.5 Social context and social norms

Going beyond the strict rationality assumptions of the deterrence model, studies have found that the social context, social norms, and peer effects play an important role in influencing individual tax compliance. For example, experimental evidence suggests that individuals are more likely to file their tax returns and report their income when provided with information on whether their neighbours are filing returns and/or reporting their income (Alm et al., 2017). However, if individuals believe that other people are evading taxes, they may be more likely to evade themselves. Vogel (1974) found that individuals who knew other tax evaders believed they were more likely to be able to evade taxes and not get caught. The public disclosure of non-compliance has also been found to reduce tax evasion, which suggests a desire to conform with social norms. Perceptions of the fairness of the tax system, and whether individuals believe their tax rate is too high relative to the tax rate faced by other individuals, also influences individual tax compliance, as we saw above. In experimental settings, compliance tends to increase when there is a public good financed by voluntary tax payments, suggesting that individuals care about how the revenues from taxation are used.

17.3.6 Non-pecuniary motivations

Evidence suggests that individuals are not driven purely by narrow financial self-interest. A study by Baldry (1984) compared individual responses when the same choice problem

[24] See Alm (2019) for a review.

was presented as a gamble and when it was presented as a tax evasion decision, with identical payoffs. He found that in the former case, everyone gambled; whereas when the decision was presented as a tax evasion choice, some individuals never evaded tax. This suggests there are psychic or stigma costs associated with evading taxes and that some people feel bad if they do not pay their taxes. Laboratory experiments suggest that individuals who care more about the well-being of others and who engage in more prosocial behaviours have higher levels of tax compliance (Christian & Alm, 2014). Priming to elicit empathy—for example, by suggesting individuals put themselves in someone else's shoes—has also been found to have a positive effect on compliance in experimental settings (Christian & Alm, 2014).

While the evidence supports some of the predictions of the deterrence model, it is clear that tax evasion is not driven solely by narrow financial considerations—social context, social norms and non-pecuniary motivations also have an important role to play. The factors that influence tax evasion, and their relative importance, vary across countries and are also likely to change over time, particularly as technological developments change the ways in which individuals and firms can evade taxes, and the methods governments can use to enforce tax laws (see Box 17.2).

Box 17.2 Tax evasion and technological innovation

Technological and financial innovations are changing the opportunities for tax evasion. Some innovations are making it easier for governments to enforce tax laws and increase tax compliance. For example, many countries have seen a shift towards cashless payments in recent years, as debit and credit cards and smartphone payment applications have replaced cash transactions.[25] This has the potential to reduce tax evasion, particularly VAT evasion. Cash facilitates tax evasion because cash is very difficult to trace, thus allowing sellers more easily to conceal their transaction history. A study by Immordino and Russo (2018) looked at the impact of cashless payments on VAT evasion in a sample of European countries and found that electronic payments are negatively related to VAT evasion. They also found that cash withdrawals from automated teller machines are positively related with VAT evasion, by increasing the amount of cash in circulation.

However, other financial innovations pose a significant challenge for tax compliance. One example is the rise of cryptocurrencies. The first cryptocurrency, Bitcoin, was invented in 2008. Today there are more than 10,000 different types of crypto assets. Cryptocurrencies function both as an investment asset and as a means of payment, and their quasi-anonymity makes them an ideal choice for criminals. Cryptocurrency transactions have the same benefits as cash transactions because they can easily be hidden from tax authorities. While the share of purchases made with cryptocurrencies remains small, it has the potential to grow, and widespread use of cryptocurrencies could lead to widespread VAT tax evasion (Baer et al., 2023).

[25] Until relatively recently, Sweden seemed to be on track to become a fully cashless economy, but recent national security concerns have led the authorities to encourage citizens to use cash regularly and keep a minimum supply of cash.

17.4 Beyond the deterrence model: insights from behavioural economics

The deterrence model of tax evasion assumes individuals are rational and self-interested, and that their decision to pay—or not pay—taxes depends only on the trade-off between the expected financial benefits of evading taxes and the expected financial costs. The evidence discussed above suggests that while these factors are important, they only offer a partial explanation of this behaviour. In particular, rates of tax compliance are far higher in practice than the model predicts.

In assuming that individuals are amoral utility-maximizers who view the decision to evade taxes as they would a simple gamble, the deterrence model leaves no room for **tax morale**. There are different definitions of tax morale. A broad definition of this concept sees tax morale as capturing the various non-pecuniary motivations for tax compliance, as well as other factors not captured by the standard expected-utility-maximizing framework.[26] This broad definition allows for several mechanisms through which tax morale operates, which include intrinsic motivation, reciprocity, peer effects, cultural factors, information imperfections, and deviations from utility-maximizing behaviour. Narrower definitions associate tax morale specifically with an individual's intrinsic motivation to pay taxes.[27] As we saw in Chapter 8, intrinsic motivation refers to the desire to engage in an activity (e.g. pay taxes) for its own sake, because it gives us satisfaction or because we feel it is the right thing to do. This contrasts with extrinsic motivation, where our actions are driven by the prospect of external rewards or punishments.

In this section, we are going to focus on four extensions to the deterrence model of tax evasion that build on work in behavioural economics and on tax morale more generally: bounded rationality, loss aversion, non-pecuniary motivations, and social context and social norms.[28] These are not mutually exclusive and are likely to interact with one another.

17.4.1 Bounded rationality

The deterrence model assumes that individuals are fully rational, self-interested utility-maximizers, who are able to accurately collect and process all relevant information when deciding whether to evade taxes. In practice, evidence suggests that most people fall short of this ideal. As we saw in Chapter 2, bounded rationality captures the idea that individual rationality is limited by the information we have available and our ability to process that information. This, in turn, will depend on factors including the complexity of the information and individual cognitive and time limitations. Individuals might not be aware of the true costs and benefits of evading taxes—for example, they may overestimate the fine they face if they are caught evading. As we saw above, there is also evidence that individuals tend to overestimate audit probabilities, which helps explain the lower levels of tax evasion observed in practice (Alm, 2012). Spicer (1986) suggests that individual decisions are more likely to be guided by rules of thumb or heuristics, rather than utility-maximizing behaviour.[29] Individuals might also simply forget to pay their taxes or they might procrastinate in filling out their tax returns.

[26] See Luttmer and Singhal (2014).

[27] See, for example, Alm and Torgler (2006).

[28] For a more comprehensive discussion of how insights from behavioural economics have been applied to the analysis of tax evasion, see the suggested Further Reading at the end of the chapter.

[29] See Chapter 2 for a discussion of these concepts.

17.4.2 Loss aversion

The expected utility framework that underpins the deterrence model assumes that individual utility is a function of the level of income and that individuals treat gains and losses equally. However, evidence suggests that in some situations individuals may base their decisions on a value function, rather than the usual utility function. The value function depends on changes in income relative to a reference point, rather than depending on the level of income itself. The value function is also typically steeper for losses than for gains, which is consistent with the idea that individuals treat gains and losses differently in their decisions. In particular, individuals tend to prefer avoiding losses to receiving gains of the same magnitude—this is the idea behind the concept of **loss aversion**. Loss aversion can help explain why people evade taxes less than the deterrence model would suggest, as the threat of a potential audit and fine looms larger in individual decisions than the potentially higher income they would enjoy if they were not caught evading.

17.4.3 Non-pecuniary motivations

As we saw above, individuals are not only motivated by narrow financial self-interest. There are a variety of non-financial motives that influence individual behaviour, including a sense of fairness, morality, reciprocity, altruism, trust, and empathy. Individuals might be honest and not evade taxes simply because they believe it is the right thing to do, or because cheating on their taxes may lead to feelings of guilt or shame. Reciprocity captures the idea that individual willingness to pay taxes is tied to the public goods and services that the government provides, as well as individual perceptions of government and the fairness of the tax system. Evidence suggests there is a positive correlation between measures of tax morale and trust in government and the level of satisfaction with public services (Daude et al., 2012). Research has also found that if individuals perceive the tax system to be fair, this strengthens the social norm towards compliance, suggesting that honest behaviour may have intrinsic value (Fehr & Gächter, 2000).

A more complete understanding of what influences tax evasion should therefore take into account this wider range of individual motivations, as well as individual perceptions of the fairness of the tax system and how the revenues raised through taxation are used. Some of these motivations can be modelled by incorporating additional elements into the individual's utility function—for example, by including a psychic cost associated with evading taxes, which will increase the amount of income individuals choose to declare.

17.4.4 Social context and social norms

Attitudes to tax evasion and compliance behaviour vary across countries (see Box 17.3). Individual decisions are not made in a vacuum—individuals are influenced by the broader social and institutional context in which their decisions are made. Research in behavioural economics has highlighted the role of social norms and social interactions in influencing tax evasion. As we have seen, social norms are the informal, unwritten rules that define what is considered acceptable behaviour within a group or society. They can be enforced through the threat of social sanctions, such as disapproval, or individuals may feel a sense of shame

Box 17.3 How do attitudes to tax evasion vary across countries?

Evidence suggests that attitudes towards the acceptability of tax evasion vary significantly across countries. According to the World Values Survey, the proportion of people who feel it is never justifiable for someone to cheat on their taxes if given the chance ranges from 22 per cent in Tajikistan to 89 per cent in Ethiopia.[30] Among the sub-sample of OECD countries, the proportion is lowest in Lithuania and Mexico, at 46 per cent, and highest in Japan, where 87 per cent of people believe it is never justifiable to cheat on your taxes. In Great Britain, that proportion is 69 per cent. In contrast, 4 per cent of people in Spain, Mexico, and Colombia feel it is *always* justifiable to cheat on your taxes if given the chance, compared with just 0.2 per cent of people in Turkey.

These beliefs about the acceptability of evading taxes may reflect differences in individuals' intrinsic motivation to pay taxes, and can therefore have an impact on tax compliance behaviour. Research by Alm and Torgler (2006) suggests there is a strong negative correlation between whether people feel cheating on their taxes can ever by justified and the size of the shadow economy in a sample of European countries and the USA. So if more people believe it is acceptable to cheat on their taxes, more people are likely to actually cheat on their taxes.

Source: World Values Survey (n.d.).

or guilt if they fail to comply with these shared accepted standards of behaviour. If there is a social norm for tax compliance, individuals are less likely to evade taxes.

Research has found that including social norm messages in standard reminder letters, emphasizing that most people pay their taxes on time, increased payment rates for overdue tax; messages that emphasized how tax revenues were used to finance public goods and services also significantly increased payment rates (Hallsworth et al., 2017). Essentially, how other individuals behave, or how we believe others will behave, influences our own behaviour. If we believe others are cheating on their taxes, we may be more likely to cheat ourselves. How others behave can also influence individual beliefs about the consequences of evading taxes.

What does all this mean for the deterrence model of tax evasion and our understanding of the evasion decision? The deterrence model still provides a useful benchmark for understanding tax evasion, highlighting the role of important factors such as the audit probability and fine in driving tax evasion. Extensions to the model have aimed to accommodate some of the limitations and bring the predictions of the model more in line with observed tax evasion behaviour.[31] Ultimately, individuals are likely to differ in their motivations for evading or not evading taxes. Torgler (2003b) suggests that individuals can be categorized into four types of taxpayer: social taxpayers, who are influenced by social norms and social context; intrinsic taxpayers, who pay taxes out of a sense of duty or obligation; honest taxpayers, who would never evade taxes regardless of the incentives; and tax evaders, who view tax evasion as a gamble and are motivated solely by the expected payoff.

[30] However, a further 51 per cent of people in Tajikistan felt it was almost never justifiable to cheat on your taxes.
[31] See Alm (2012, 2019) for a review of some of this work.

17.5 Policy to tackle tax evasion

Having reviewed the theory and evidence on what influences tax evasion, in this section we are going to discuss what this implies for government policy to promote tax compliance. But first, we are going to focus on the question of what the optimal level of tax evasion is.

17.5.1 What is the optimal level of tax evasion?

The answer to this question might seem obvious at first: since tax evasion is illegal, the optimal level of tax evasion should be zero. However, this ignores the fact that there is a cost associated with reducing tax evasion, since this requires resources to be spent that could be used elsewhere. The optimal level of tax evasion will depend on the costs and benefits of reducing tax evasion. The government should continue to invest in reducing tax evasion until the marginal cost of doing so just equals the marginal benefit of the reduced evasion.[32]

For simplicity, assume that the only policy the government uses to tackle tax evasion is to employ more tax inspectors to carry out audits and thereby increase the probability of detection. Employing additional tax inspectors involves a cost (e.g. the cost of recruitment, paying wages, and hiring office space), and we assume here that this cost increases with the number of inspectors. For example, the government might need to offer higher wages to encourage more people to become tax inspectors as the number of inspectors employed increases. This assumption is reflected in the upward-sloping social marginal cost (*SMC*) curve in Figure 17.7. The social marginal benefit (*SMB*) of employing additional tax inspectors captures the additional tax revenue that is collected by reducing tax evasion. We assume the social marginal benefit falls as the number of inspectors increases: the first tax inspectors hired are able to significantly increase the amount of revenue collected, as tax evasion is more widespread; however, as

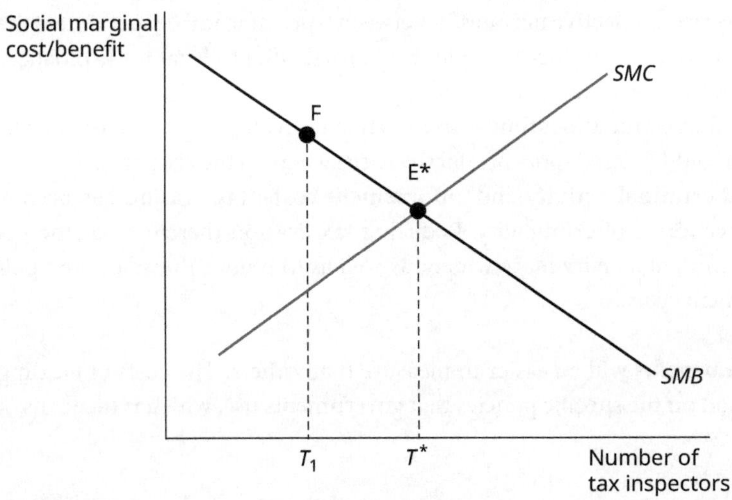

Figure 17.7 The optimal level of tax evasion

[32] See Chapter 2 for a review of these concepts and how the optimal or efficient outcome is determined.

increasingly more tax inspectors are hired, the amount of additional revenue collected will fall as there are fewer tax evaders and evasion becomes harder to detect. The *SMB* curve is therefore downward-sloping.

The socially optimal number of tax inspectors to hire is given by point E^* in Figure 17.7, where the social marginal cost and social marginal benefit are equal. If fewer inspectors are hired, at a point to the left of E^* such as point F, the social marginal benefit is greater than the social marginal cost, so hiring another inspector will bring benefits that exceed the cost of doing so. Therefore more inspectors should be hired. To the right of E^*, the social marginal cost exceeds the social marginal benefit, so it makes sense to reduce the number of inspectors employed, as the cost of employing additional inspectors in greater than the benefit of doing so.

Although this analysis oversimplifies the issue somewhat, the key message remains: from a purely economic perspective, the optimal level of tax evasion is not necessarily zero; instead, it will depend on the relative costs and benefits of reducing evasion.

What are the costs and benefits of reducing tax evasion? One obvious benefit of tackling tax evasion is the amount of tax revenue recovered, but there are other important benefits to consider:

- **Increased government spending**: by increasing the amount of revenue collected, the government will have more money available to spend. Depending on how the additional revenue is spent, this could boost investment, productivity, and economic growth. Additional revenues could also be used to reduce government borrowing. However, if taxes discourage work or work effort, then efforts to reduce tax evasion may result in lower output.[33]
- **Promoting equity**: tax evasion affects the distribution of the tax burden. Individuals who are paying low (or no) taxes will benefit, while those who do pay their taxes bear the cost, in the form of either higher taxes or lower public spending. And not everyone faces the same opportunity to evade taxes, as discussed above. Global billionaires benefit from very low effective tax rates, at between 0 per cent and 0.5 per cent of their wealth (EU Tax Observatory, 2024). While this is partly due to legal tax avoidance, it is also partly due to tax evasion.
- **Improved resource allocation**: resources that individuals and business devote to evading taxes could be used more productively elsewhere in the economy.
- **Reduced criminal activity and enforcement costs**: tax evasion has been associated with other forms of criminality. Reducing tax evasion therefore has the potential to reduce criminal activity more widely, as well as to reduce the associated policing and enforcement costs.

Some of these benefits will be easier to measure than others. The costs of tackling tax evasion will depend on the specific policies that governments use, which is the focus of the next section.

[33] See Chapter 15 for a discussion of the impact of taxes on work.

17.5.2 What policies should governments use to tackle tax evasion?

The theory and evidence on the determinants of tax evasion discussed above can help inform government policy to tackle evasion and promote tax compliance. Alm (2019) suggests that policies to reduce tax evasion should fall into one of three paradigms:

- **Enforcement paradigm**: largely based on the insights from the deterrence model, within this paradigm policies should focus on increasing the detection of tax evaders (e.g. by increasing the audit probability) and increasing the fine or punishment imposed.
- **Service paradigm**: this paradigm builds on aspects related to bounded rationality and the role of government-provided services; policies should focus on improving the provision of tax services—for example, by making services more user-friendly, providing clearer and more accessible information, providing more support with filling out forms and payment reminders, and investing in taxpayer education.
- **Trust paradigm**: this paradigm builds on the role of non-pecuniary motivations in influencing tax compliance, as well as the role of social context and social norms; policies should focus on changing the tax culture—for example, by using the media to promote a social norm of tax compliance, highlighting the benefits of taxation in terms of what they imply for publicly provided goods and services, and publicly disclosing known tax evaders.

In deciding what policies to implement, governments should weigh up their relative costs and benefits. However, identifying and measuring all costs and benefits is not always straightforward. In some cases, a simple cost–benefit approach may lead to fairly stark conclusions. For example, the deterrence model predicts that increasing the fine or punishment and increasing the probability of detection both lead to a reduction in the level of tax evasion. Increasing the probability of detection will involve employing additional tax inspectors, which involves a cost (the cost of recruitment, wages, training, etc). Increasing the fine or punishment for those caught evading taxes requires the government to pass legislation, and the cost associated with this is likely to be lower. So if the government wants to maximize its revenue, the optimal policy is to have extremely high fines or punishments (e.g. a lengthy prison sentence), but invest little in auditing to catch evaders.

However, such an extreme policy might not be optimal for several reasons. The policy assumes that the sole aim of the government is to maximize revenue. If governments care about social welfare, then a policy which involves very stringent punishments for tax evaders may no longer be optimal. Such an extreme policy might also not be politically feasible and would be difficult to implement. Different government departments are responsible for setting different aspects of tax policy. For example, the government sets the tax rate, the judiciary sets the fine or punishment, and the revenue service decides how many tax inspectors to employ. There is no single unitary authority that decides on all aspects of policy to tackle tax evasion. In addition, from the perspective of the economics of crime, the punishment for tax evasion should fit the severity of this crime, and be consistent with the punishments for other crimes. If tax evasion is deemed less severe, in terms of the harm done to society, than major crimes such as serious assault and murder, then the punishment for tax evasion should also be less severe. Lastly, imposing very high fines could potentially crowd out intrinsic motivations for tax compliance and, perversely, lead to an increase in tax evasion.

Box 17.4 Tackling tax evasion through information campaigns and prize draws

In 2012, the UK's tax authority, HM Revenue and Customs, launched an Evasion Publicity Campaign. This was designed to reduce tax evasion and increase voluntary compliance by highlighting that the government was taking action against tax evaders. The campaign involved a variety of media, including radio, posters, billboards, and digital displays, which were used to disseminate the message 'We're closing in on undeclared income', alongside an image of two eyes peering through a tear in white paper. A webpage was also set up to provide a route for individuals to access further information and an option for voluntary disclosure by tax evaders. A report on the impact of the campaign found that while awareness and recognition of the campaign was good, few people reported taking any action as a result—although this figure was higher among the self-employed (Myant, 2013). The campaign did have a positive impact on attitudes towards compliance, with the proportion of people who agreed with the statement 'It is a priority to ensure your tax affairs are in order' increasing from 74 per cent to 81 per cent (Myant, 2013).

A different approach was adopted by the Portuguese government in 2014. As part of a broad set of measures to tackle tax fraud and tax evasion, the government set up a 'Lucky Receipt' prize draw.[34] Individuals were encouraged always to ask for a receipt with their unique tax identification number on it[35] when buying goods and services for final consumption. By doing so, they would automatically be entered into a weekly prize draw. Initially, the prizes were high-end cars, but in 2016 these were replaced with government bonds worth €35,000. The aim of this policy was primarily to tackle tax evasion among retailers, by requiring them to issue receipts for the majority of their transactions. Although the policy was suspended in January 2024, the government has announced plans to reintroduce it in the near future.

Because individuals are likely to differ in their motivations for evading taxes, governments should adopt a combination of policies to promote tax compliance. In practice, countries have experimented with different approaches to tackle tax evasion, going beyond policies which focus only on detection and punishment (see Box 17.4 for some examples).

Conclusion

Tax evasion and tax avoidance impose significant costs on governments and on society. They lead to lost revenues, limiting governments' ability to invest in areas such as health, education, and social care. They also have implications for the fairness of the tax system, increasing the tax burden for those who pay taxes. If people do not feel that everyone is paying their fair share of taxes, this can breed distrust and damage social cohesion.

The deterrence model treats tax evasion as a gamble, highlighting the role of the probability of being caught and the punishment faced in driving the individual decision to evade taxes. However, as we have seen, in assuming that individuals are amoral utility-maximizers

[34] Established by Decree-Law no. 26-A/2014 of 17 February 2014.

[35] These are similar to individual National Insurance numbers in the UK.

who care only about the expected financial benefits and costs of evading taxes, the deterrence model leaves no room for tax morale. The evidence clearly shows that tax evasion is not driven solely by narrow financial considerations and that social context, social norms, and non-pecuniary motivations also have an important role to play. Extensions to the deterrence model have aimed to remedy some of its limitations, and bring the predictions of the model more in line with observed tax evasion behaviour.

Understanding what drives the tax evasion decision is crucial for designing effective policies to promote tax compliance. But individuals are likely to differ in their motivations for evading taxes: some individuals may have an intrinsic preference for honesty and never cheat, while others might view tax evasion as just a gamble. Policies to promote tax compliance need to be designed with these different motivations in mind.

Questions for discussion

1. What approaches have been used to measure tax evasion? Do you think estimates of tax evasion are reliable?
2. Is tax evasion just a gamble?
3. What may affect the optimal level of tax evasion in different countries?
4. What policies would you recommend the government should use to tackle tax evasion?

Further reading

On measuring tax evasion:

Alm, J. (2012). Measuring, explaining, and controlling tax evasion: Lessons from theory, experiments, and field studies. *International Tax and Public Finance, 19*, 54–77.

Schneider, F., & Buehn, A. (2016). *Estimating the size of the shadow economy: Methods, problems and open questions*. Institute of Labor Economics (IZA) discussion papers, no. 9820.

On the deterrence model of tax evasion and extensions to the basic model:

Slemrod, J., & Yitzhaki, S. (2002). Tax avoidance, evasion, and administration. In A. J. Auerbach & M. Feldstein (Eds.), *Handbook of public economics* (Vol. 3, pp. 1423–1470). Elsevier.

For a critical review of the deterrence model and some of the evidence on tax evasion:

Alm, J. (2019). What motivates tax compliance? *Journal of Economic Surveys, 33*(2), 353–388.

Andreoni, J., Erard, B., & Feinstein, J. (1998). Tax compliance. *Journal of Economic Literature, 36*(2), 818–860.

On the impact of technology on tax evasion:

Alm, J. (2021). Tax evasion, technology, and inequality. *Economics of Governance, 22*(4), 321–343.

Baer, K., De Mooij, R. A., Hebous, S. & Keen, M. (2023). *Taxing cryptocurrencies*. International Monetary Fund working papers, no. W/23/144. Available at: https://doi.org/10.5089/9798400246586.001

On applications of behavioural economics to tax evasion and the concept of tax morale:

Alm, J., & Kasper, M. (2023). Using behavioural economics to understand tax compliance. *Economic and Political Studies, 11*(3), 279–294.

Hashimzade, N., Myles, G. D., & Tran-Nam, B. (2013). Applications of behavioural economics to tax evasion. *Journal of Economic Surveys, 27*(5), 941–977. Provides a more theoretical discussion.

Luttmer, E. F., & Singhal, M. (2014). Tax morale. *Journal of Economic Perspectives, 28*(4), 149–168.
Pickhardt, M., & Prinz, A. (2014). Behavioral dynamics of tax evasion—A survey. *Journal of Economic Psychology, 40*, 1–19.

On policies for tackling tax evasion:

Alm, J. (2019). What motivates tax compliance? *Journal of Economic Surveys, 33*(2), 353–388.
Alm, J., & Torgler, B. (2011). Do ethics matter? Tax compliance and morality. *Journal of Business Ethics, 101*, 635–651.
Slemrod, J. (2019). Tax compliance and enforcement. *Journal of Economic Literature, 57*(4), 904–954.

On the challenge of global tax evasion and policies to address it:

EU Tax Observatory (2024). *Global tax evasion report 2024*. Available at: https://www.taxobservatory.eu/www-site/uploads/2023/10/global_tax_evasion_report_24.pdf

Bibliography

Allingham, M. G., & Sandmo, A. (1972). Income tax evasion: A theoretical analysis. *Journal of Public Economics, 1*(3–4), 323–338.
Alm, J. (2012). Measuring, explaining, and controlling tax evasion: Lessons from theory, experiments, and field studies. *International Tax and Public Finance, 19*, 54–77.
Alm, J. (2019). What motivates tax compliance? *Journal of Economic Surveys, 33*(2), 353–388.
Alm, J. (2021). Tax evasion, technology, and inequality. *Economics of Governance, 22*(4), 321–343.
Alm, J., Bloomquist, K. M., & McKee, M. (2017). When you know your neighbour pays taxes: information, peer effects and tax compliance. *Fiscal Studies, 38*(4), 587–613.
Alm, J., McClelland, G. H., & Schulze, W. D. (1992). Why do people pay taxes? *Journal of Public Economics, 48*(1), 21–38.
Alm, J., & Torgler, B. (2006). Culture differences and tax morale in the United States and in Europe. *Journal of Economic Psychology, 27*(2), 224–246.
Alm, J., & Torgler, B. (2011). Do ethics matter? Tax compliance and morality. *Journal of Business Ethics, 101*, 635–651.
Andreoni, J., Erard, B., & Feinstein, J. (1998). Tax compliance. *Journal of Economic Literature, 36*(2), 818–860.
Baer, K., De Mooij, R. A., Hebous, S. & Keen, M. (2023). *Taxing cryptocurrencies*. International Monetary Fund working papers, no. W/23/144. Available at: https://doi.org/10.5089/9798400246586.001
Baldry, J. C. (1984). The enforcement of income tax laws: Efficiency implications. *Economic Record, 60*(2), 156–159.
Bazart, C., & Pickhardt, M. (2011). Fighting income tax evasion with positive rewards. *Public Finance Review, 39*(1), 124–149.
Becker, G. S. (1968). Crime and punishment: An economic approach. *Journal of Political Economy, 76*(2), 169–217.
Bø, E. E., Slemrod, J., & Thoresen, T. O. (2015). Taxes on the internet: Deterrence effects of public disclosure. *American Economic Journal: Economic Policy, 7*(1), 36–62.
Borgne, E. L., & Baer, K. (2008). *Tax amnesties: Theory, trends, and some alternatives*. International Monetary Fund.
Buehn, A., & Schneider, F. (2007). Shadow economies and corruption all over the world: Revised estimates for 120 countries. *Economics: The Open-Access, Open-Assessment E-Journal, 1*(9), 1–66.

Christian, R. C., & Alm, J. (2014). Empathy, sympathy, and tax compliance. *Journal of Economic Psychology*, *40*, 62–82.

Clotfelter, C. T. (1983). Tax evasion and tax rates: An analysis of individual returns. *Review of Economics and Statistics*, *65*(3), 363–373.

Coricelli, G., Joffily, M., Montmarquette, C., & Villeval, M. C. (2010). Cheating, emotions, and rationality: An experiment on tax evasion. *Experimental Economics*, *13*(2), 226–247.

Cowell, F. A., & Gordon, J. P. (1988). Unwillingness to pay: Tax evasion and public good provision. *Journal of Public Economics*, *36*(3), 305–321.

Cullis, J., & Jones, P. (2009). *Public finance and public choice: Analytical perspectives* (3rd ed.). Oxford University Press.

Daude, C., Gutiérrez, H., & Melguizo, Á. (2012). *What drives tax morale?* Organization for Economic Cooperation and Development, Development Centre working papers, no. 315.

Dell'Anno, R. (2003). *Estimating the shadow economy in Italy: A structural equation approach.* University of Salerno, Department of Economics and Statistics discussion papers, no. 2003-7.

Dhami, S., & al-Nowaihi, A. (2007). Why do people pay taxes? Prospect theory versus expected utility theory. *Journal of Economic Behavior and Organization*, *64*(1), 171–192.

Dilnot, A., & Morris, C. N. (1981). What do we know about the black economy? *Fiscal Studies*, *2*(1), 58–73.

EU Tax Observatory (2024). *Global tax evasion report 2024.* Available at: https://www.taxobservatory.eu/www-site/uploads/2023/10/global_tax_evasion_report_24.pdf

Fehr, E., & Gächter, S. (2000). Fairness and retaliation: The economics of reciprocity. *Journal of Economic Perspectives*, *14*(3), 159–182.

Feige E. L. (1989). *The Underground economies: Tax evasion and information distortion.* Cambridge University Press.

Feinstein, J. S. (1991). An econometric analysis of income tax evasion and its detection. *RAND Journal of Economics*, *22*(1), 14–35.

Geeroms, H. J., & Wilmots, H. (1985). An empirical model of tax evasion and tax avoidance. *Public Finance (Finances Publiques)*, *40*(2), 190–209.

Haerpfer, C., Inglehart, R., Moreno, A., Welzel, C., Kizilova, K., Diez-Medrano J., Lagos, M., Norris, P., Ponarin, E., & Puranen, B. (Eds.). 2022. *World Values Survey: Round 7—Country-pooled datafile version 6.0.* JD Systems Institute and WVSA Secretariat. Available at: doi:10.14281/18241.24

Hallsworth, M., List, J. A., Metcalfe, R. D., & Vlaev, I. (2017). The behavioralist as tax collector: Using natural field experiments to enhance tax compliance. *Journal of Public Economics*, *148*, 14–31.

Hasegawa, M., Hoopes, J. L., Ishida, R., & Slemrod, J. (2013). The effect of public disclosure on reported taxable income: Evidence from individuals and corporations in Japan. *National Tax Journal*, *66*(3), 571–607.

Hashimzade, N., Myles, G. D., & Tran-Nam, B. (2013). Applications of behavioural economics to tax evasion. *Journal of Economic Surveys*, *27*(5), 941–977.

Henderson, J. V., Storeygard, A., & Weil, D. N. (2012). Measuring economic growth from outer space. *American Economic Review*, *102*(2), 994–1028.

Hindriks, J., & Myles, G. D. (2013). *Intermediate public economics* (2nd ed.). MIT Press.

HM Revenue and Customs (2025). *Measuring tax gaps 2025 edition: Tax gap estimates for 2023 to 2024.* Available at: https://www.gov.uk/government/statistics/measuring-tax-gaps (accessed 17 October 2025).

Immordino, G., & Russo, F. F. (2018). Cashless payments and tax evasion. *European Journal of Political Economy*, *55*, 36–43.

Kleven, H. J., Knudsen, M. B., Kreiner, C. T., Pedersen, S., & Saez, E. (2011). Unwilling or unable to cheat? Evidence from a tax audit experiment in Denmark. *Econometrica*, *79*(3), 651–692.

Luttmer, E. F., & Singhal, M. (2014). Tax morale. *Journal of Economic Perspectives*, *28*(4), 149–168.

Mason, R., & Calvin, L. D. (1984). Public confidence and admitted tax evasion. *National Tax Journal*, *37*(4), 489–496.

McCaffery, E. J., Baron, J., & Baron, J. (2003). Heuristics and biases in thinking about tax. In *Proceedings. Annual Conference on Taxation and Minutes of the Annual Meeting of the National Tax Association* (Vol. 96, pp. 434–443). National Tax Association.

Myant, P. (2013). *Evasion Publicity Campaign—Report on findings among individuals*. HM Revenue and Customs research report 278.

Pestieau, P., & Possen, U. M. (1991). Tax evasion and occupational choice. *Journal of Public Economics*, *45*(1), 107–125.

Schneider, F. & Buehn, A. (2007). Shadow economies and corruption all over the world: Revised estimates for 120 countries. *Economics: The Open-Access, Open-Assessment E-Journal*, Vol. 1, 2007–2009 (Version 2).

Slemrod, J. (2007). Cheating ourselves: The economics of tax evasion. *Journal of Economic Perspectives*, *21*(1), 25–48.

Slemrod, J. (2019). Tax compliance and enforcement. *Journal of Economic Literature*, *57*(4), 904–954.

Slemrod, J., Blumenthal, M., & Christian, C. (2001). Taxpayer response to an increased probability of audit: Evidence from a controlled experiment in Minnesota. *Journal of Public Economics*, *79*(3), 455–483.

Slemrod, J., & Yitzhaki, S. (2002). Tax avoidance, evasion, and administration. In A. J. Auerbach & M. Feldstein (Eds.), *Handbook of public economics* (Vol. 3, pp. 1423–1470). Elsevier.

Spicer, M. W. (1986). Civilization at a discount: The problem of tax evasion. *National Tax Journal*, *39*(1), 13–20.

Spicer, M. W., & Becker, L. A. (1980). Fiscal inequity and tax evasion: An experimental approach. *National Tax Journal*, *33*(2), 171–175.

Srinivasan, T. N. (1973). Tax evasion: A model. *Journal of Public Economics*, *2*(4), 339–346.

Torgler, B. (2003a). To evade taxes or not to evade: That is the question. *Journal of Socio-Economics*, *32*(3), 283–302.

Torgler, B. (2003b). Tax morale, rule-governed behaviour and trust. *Constitutional Political Economy*, *14*(2), 119–140.

Vogel, J. (1974). Taxation and public opinion in Sweden: An interpretation of recent survey data. *National Tax Journal*, *27*(4), 499–513.

World Values Survey (n.d.). *World Values Survey: Round 7, 2017–2022, question 180: Justifiable—cheating on taxes*. Available at: https://www.worldvaluessurvey.org/WVSOnline.jsp (accessed 20 October 2025).

Yitzhaki, S. (1974). A note on Allingham and Sandmo. *Journal of Public Economics*, *3*(2), 201–202.

Zhang, N., Andrighetto, G., Ottone, S., Ponzano, F., & Steinmo, S. (2016). 'Willing to pay?' Tax compliance in Britain and Italy: An experimental analysis. *PLOS One*, *11*(2), e0150277.

Calculating the slope of the budget line

The slope of the budget line is calculated by dividing the vertical distance (the rise) by the horizontal distance (the run) between any two points on the line. From Figure 17.2 we have:

$$\text{slope} = \frac{[1-t(1+F)]Y-(1-t)Y}{Y-(1-t)Y}$$

This simplifies to:

$$\text{slope} = \frac{(1-t-tF)Y-(1-t)Y}{Y-Y+tY} = \frac{-tFY}{tY} = -F$$

Calculating the slope of the indifference curve

To calculate the slope of the indifference curve, we divide the first derivative of the expected utility function with respect to the income level if the individual is not caught evading by the first derivative with respect to their income if they are caught evading.

The individual's expected utility function is given by:

$$EU = (1-p)U(Y_{NC}) + pU(Y_C)$$

The first derivative with respect to Y_{NC} is:

$$\frac{\partial EU}{\partial Y_{NC}} = (1-p)U'(Y_{NC})$$

where $U'(Y_{NC})$ denotes the marginal utility of income Y, or the first derivative of the utility function with respect to Y.

And the first derivative with respect to Y_C is:

$$\frac{\partial EU}{\partial Y_C} = pU'(Y_C)$$

So the slope of the indifference curve is given by:

$$\frac{-(1-p)}{p}\frac{U'(Y_{NC})}{U'(Y_C)}$$

By definition, on the 45° line, $Y_{NC} = Y_C$, so the marginal utility of income is the same in both cases, which means the expression above can be simplified to:

$$\frac{-(1-p)}{p}$$

Glossary

absolute measure Value determined independently of external reference points, using a fixed standard of measurement. Contrast with relative measure.

absolute poverty Poverty concept that assumes there is a fixed minimum level of consumption that constitutes poverty independent of time or place.

ad valorem tax Tax levied as a percentage of the sales price.

adverse selection Problem of hidden information which arises when buyers have more information about some of aspect of the quality of a good than sellers, or sellers have more information than buyers.

aggregate risks Risks faced by society as a whole. Also referred to as social risks.

allocative efficiency An allocation of resources is allocatively efficient if there is no way to change that allocation to make at least one person better off without making anyone else worse off. Also referred to as Pareto efficiency or Pareto optimality.

anchoring effect Anchoring effects arise when individual choices or judgements are influenced by reference points, typically pieces of information which may be completely irrelevant to the decision being made.

annuity Financial product that converts pension savings into a steady income stream that individuals receive until the end of their lives.

Arrow's Impossibility Theorem Theorem that demonstrates that there is no collective decision-making process that satisfies the properties of transitivity, the Pareto principle, unrestricted domain, non-dictatorship, and independence of irrelevant alternatives in all contexts.

asset-based welfare Welfare policies that involve providing individuals with financial assets that can provide a buffer against income shocks.

asymmetric information Situations in which one party to a transaction has more information than the other.

automatic enrolment pension scheme Eligible individuals are enrolled into a pension scheme by their employer and monthly pension contributions are deducted from their salary automatically, although individuals can opt out of the scheme if they wish to.

automatic stabilizers Features built into the tax and welfare system (e.g. income taxes and welfare benefits) that automatically dampen economic fluctuations, without requiring the government to adopt new tax or spending laws.

average tax rate Percentage of total income that is paid in tax.

Baumol's law Theory that government growth is driven by the relative rise in the cost of the goods and services provided by the public sector. The public sector will grow over time relative to the rest of the economy because it is assumed to be more labour-intensive than the private sector and less able to increase productivity by substituting capital for labour. Because labour markets in the public and private sector are linked, wage increases in the private sector lead to an increase in costs in the public sector. Also known as Baumol's cost disease or the relative price effect.

behavioural public economics Brings together insights from public economics and behavioural economics to provide a more complete understanding of individual behaviour to inform the design and evaluation of public policy.

benefit–cost ratio (BCR) The ratio of discounted benefits and costs.

Borda count method Voting rule which assigns each candidate or alternative being voted on a number of points based on their ranking, and the alternative with the greatest number of points is the one that is chosen.

bounded rationality Captures the idea that individual rationality is limited by the information individuals have available and their ability to process that information. This, in turn, depends on factors including the complexity of the information, the time horizon of the decision problem, and individual cognitive and time limitations.

bounded willpower Refers to situations in which, although individuals know what decision will maximize their welfare, they fail to act accordingly.

budget balance The difference between government revenues and expenditure over a period of time, normally a year.

budget constraint Combination of goods that individuals can afford, given their income and the prices of the goods.

budget deficit Arises when the government spends more than it raises through taxes and other public sector receipts over a given period. The budget deficit is a flow measure.

budget surplus When expenditure is less than revenues, the government runs a budget surplus.

capability approach Framework for evaluating individual and social well-being that focuses on the actual capability individuals have to achieve the sort of life they value. Well-being is not just about wealth or happiness, but about having the freedom to choose a life we have reason to value. It was developed in the 1980s as an alternative to standard welfare economics.

capital gains The difference between the price for which an asset was bought and the price at which it is sold.

capital gains taxes Taxes levied on the difference between the price for which an asset was bought and the price at which it is sold.

caring externalities Externalities that arise if individuals care about the well-being of others, so the utility of individuals who are healthy is affected by the level of healthcare consumed by those who are sick.

cash transfers Income support programmes that provide cash benefits to recipients, in contrast to transfers in kind (e.g. healthcare). Examples include old-age pensions, unemployment benefits, and sickness and disability benefits.

categorical benefits Benefits that are only available to individuals who fall within a certain category (e.g. being unemployed, retired, or having a disability).

causality Causality between two variables implies that changes in one variable cause changes in the other variable. Contrast with correlation.

centrally planned economy Economic system where decisions about what to produce, how much to produce, and how goods and services should be distributed are made by a central planner or decision-makers appointed by the government. Also known as a command economy.

certainty equivalent value The amount that, if received with certainty, would leave an individual indifferent between that certain amount and taking the risk.

citizen's pension A non-contributory basic pension. Sometimes referred to as a social pension.

club goods Goods that are non-rival but excludable.

Coase theorem If property rights are well defined and bargaining is costless, negotiations between the party generating the externality and the party or parties affected by the externality can lead to the socially optimal market quantity, and the efficient solution does not depend on who is assigned the property rights.

co-insurance In the context of health insurance, a system where patients are required to pay a percentage of the cost of their treatment.

collective defined contribution (CDC) pension schemes Schemes where contribution rates are defined in advance, as in a regular defined contribution scheme, but the risks are shared collectively between the scheme's members. These schemes also provide an income for life in retirement. Normally referred to as CDC schemes.

collectivist or socialist theories of society View society through the lens of social classes. Society is more than the sum of its individuals. Humans are social animals and the pursuit of wider social concerns should override the pursuit of individual self-interest.

command economy Economic system where decisions about what to produce, how much to produce, and how goods and services should be distributed are made by a central planner or decision-makers appointed by the government. Also known as a centrally planned economy.

common-pool resources Common-pool resources or the commons are rival but non-excludable, which means that while it would be very difficult to prevent individuals from consuming the resource once it is provided, the use or consumption of the resource by one individual reduces the amount available for others to consume.

common-property resources Common-pool resources where the right to access or use the resources is held by a group of individuals, so their use can be regulated in different ways.

competitive contracting Process in which private contractors bid to provide goods or services such as street cleaning, rubbish collection, and security. Also known as competitive tendering.

compensated demand curve The compensated demand curve measures how demand for a good changes as the price changes, assuming that money is given to or taken away from the individual to ensure their utility from buying the good is unchanged; it therefore measures the substitution effect only.

compulsory education The period of education that governments legally require all individuals to complete; typically includes primary and lower secondary education.

Condorcet paradox Describes how, when there are more than two alternatives, majority voting can lead to intransitive social preferences.

congestion charge or congestion tax Fee charged for driving in a particular area or at a particular time of day.

consumer surplus Benefit to consumers from consuming a good, measured as the difference between the price they are willing to pay for a good and the price they actually pay.

consumption externalities Externalities that arise as a result of individual consumption decisions.

contingent valuation Approach to valuing goods and services where individuals are asked to state their willingness to pay (or willingness to accept compensation) for a hypothetical change in the level of provision of that good or service.

contracting in When an in-house provider wins a contract put out to tender by the government to provide a particular good or service (e.g. rubbish collection or security).

contracting out When an external contractor wins a contract put out to tender by the government to provide a particular good or service (e.g. rubbish collection or security). Also known as outsourcing.

contract laws Laws that determine the rules of exchange and how trade is carried out.

contributory benefit Benefit where the amount individuals are entitled to receive depends on the number and level of their contributions.

contributory pension scheme Scheme where access to a pension depends on having made the requisite number of social insurance contributions.

control group Group of individuals who are comparable to the treatment group and who are not subject to the particular treatment or intervention being analysed.

convex preferences Property of individual preferences such that a combination of two outcomes which are valued equally (i.e. provide the same level of utility) is considered at least as good (in terms of providing the same or greater utility) as either of the individual outcomes.

co-payment Fixed amount that individuals are required to pay upfront to access medical services as part of their health insurance coverage. Also referred to as co-pay.

corner solution In the context of utility maximization, a solution in which the individual's optimal choice involves zero quantity of one of the goods. Contrast with interior solution.

corrective taxes Taxes designed to address the problem of negative externalities by raising the private marginal cost so it is closer to the social marginal cost.

correlation Two variables are said to be correlated if they move together. In statistics, correlation measures the degree to which two variables are linearly related. Contrast with causality.

cost–benefit analysis (CBA) Tool for policy evaluation which involves systematically identifying the costs and benefits associated with a policy or project and assigning them a monetary value in order to derive an estimate of the policy or project's overall net benefit.

cost-effectiveness analysis (CEA) Tool for comparing the relative costs and effects of different policies or interventions.

cost–utility analysis (CUA) Particular type of cost-effectiveness analysis that is often used in healthcare. In CUA, health effects are measured using quality-adjusted life years, or QALYs, which combine both the quantity and quality of life gained as a result of a particular health intervention.

cream-skimming Process whereby suppliers of services attempt to select the least costly customers. For example, private healthcare providers or insurers may choose not to take on individuals who are more likely to require treatment (the bad risks) based on their medical histories. In the context of education, schools may select students who are more likely to be high-achieving.

crowding out Situation where government intervention or increased government spending leads to a reduction in private sector spending or investment. In the context of public goods, it refers to the problem where government provision of a public good leads to a reduction in the quantity of the good provided by the market, so the total amount of the public good provided is either unchanged or not significantly increased.

current tax incidence Analysis of the incidence of a tax in the context of an individual's current resources (e.g. in a particular year).

cyclical budget deficit Temporary or short-term budget deficit that arises during economic downturns, but should disappear once the economy recovers.

cyclically adjusted budget deficit See structural budget deficit.

deadweight loss (DWL) Measure of the inefficiency or loss in welfare that arises because the market output is above or below the socially optimal level.

debt illusion Individuals are unaware of the true cost of government-provided goods and services where these are paid for through public sector borrowing rather than taxation.

debt interest-to-GDP ratio Measure of government debt interest payments relative to a country's GDP.

debt interest-to-revenue ratio Measure of government debt interest payments relative to government revenues.

debt-to-GDP ratio Measure of total government debt as a share of a country's GDP.

deductibles In the context of private insurance, where individuals have to pay the first £x of any claim.

defined benefit (DB) pension scheme Scheme where the pension provider promises to pay members a given income in retirement based on their wage and length of service. The value of the pension that will be received is defined in advance and the pension provider bears the risk of varying rates of return on pension assets.

defined contribution (DC) pension scheme Scheme where individual members pay in a proportion of their earnings, which is used to invest in assets. At retirement, the value of the pension paid to members depends on how much they paid into the scheme and how the investments performed. In contrast with a defined benefit pension, the individual bears the risk of varying rates of return on pension assets.

demand curve Relationship between the price of a good or service and the total quantity that individuals are willing to buy at that price.

denationalization The transfer of assets from the state to the private sector.

deregulation The reduction or removal of regulations and barriers to entry into markets.

direct democracy Individuals vote directly on their preferred policy alternatives.

direct taxes Taxes on individuals and corporations (e.g. personal income tax, social security contributions, and corporation tax). Contrast with indirect taxes.

discount factor The discount factor equals $\frac{1}{1+r}$, where r is the rate of interest or discount rate. This captures the fact that a pound/euro received next year is worth $(1 + r)$ times less than a pound/euro received today because that pound could earn interest of r per cent if it were received today and invested.

discount rate Interest rate used to calculate the present value of future cash flows.

distortionary tax Taxes that drive a wedge between the price that buyers pay and the price that sellers receive, distorting price signals and preventing otherwise mutually beneficial trades from taking place.

double dividend hypothesis Environmental taxes have the potential to promote economic efficiency by reducing pollution, while at the same time reducing the costs associated with the tax system, by reducing the need to rely on other distortionary taxes.

dominant strategy In game theory, a strategy that is optimal, in the sense of leading to a higher payoff, regardless of what the other player does.

duopoly Type of oligopoly market where two firms dominate the market.

economic rent Income generated by a resource in excess of its next best alternative use.

economic tax incidence Refers to who actually bears the burden of the tax or who is made worse off by the tax.

economies of scale Economies of scale arise when a firm's average cost (or cost per unit of output) falls as output increases.

economies of scope Fall in the average total cost of production when a firm produces a wider range of products or services.

effective marginal tax rate Tax rate individuals face on each additional pound or euro earned taking into account both the impact of income taxes and the withdrawal of means-tested benefits.

efficiency Ensuring that scarce resources are used to maximize total welfare given individual preferences and the production technology available. See also allocative efficiency and Pareto efficiency.

elasticity of demand The percentage change in the quantity demanded of a good in response to a 1 per cent change in the price of the good. Also referred to as the price elasticity of demand.

elasticity of supply The percentage change in the quantity supplied of a good in response to a 1 per cent change in the price of the good. Also referred to as the price elasticity of supply.

emission trading scheme See tradeable permits.

endowment effect Describes how individuals tend to value goods that they own more highly than they would if they did not own them. This leads to a mismatch between the amount individuals are willing to pay for a good and the amount they are willing to accept to give up a good.

environmental Kuznets curve (EKC) Hypothesized relationship between pollution or other measures of environmental degradation and GDP per capita.

equality of opportunity Principle that everyone, regardless of their own personal circumstances and socioeconomic background, should have fair and equal access to the same chances in life (e.g. in access to healthcare, education, and security).

equity Social objective that relates to how resources should be distributed across individuals in society. In this textbook, equity is assumed to be synonymous with social justice.

equity–efficiency trade-off Perceived tension between promoting economic efficiency and promoting a more equitable distribution of resources. For example, a policy designed to increase equity may be assumed to imply a reduction in efficiency.

equivalence scales Means for comparing household incomes across different types of households, by scaling household incomes to factor in differences in the number of adults in a household and the number and age of any dependants.

estate tax Type of wealth tax levied on the estate (property, money, and possessions) of someone who has died. In some countries, estate taxes are referred to as inheritance taxes. Estate or inheritance taxes are also a type of transfer tax.

excess burden of taxation Measure of the inefficiency or deadweight loss associated with a distortionary tax. It is the additional revenue that could be raised by an equivalent non-distortionary tax.

excludable good A good is excludable if it is possible to prevent individuals from consuming it.

exhaustive expenditures Government spending on purchasing goods and services from the private sector (e.g. labour and machinery).

expected utility theory Model of decision-making under uncertainty where individuals choose the option that will maximize their expected utility, which is defined as the probability-weighted average of all possible outcomes.

expected value Probability-weighted average of all possible outcomes. The expected value is calculated by multiplying each possible outcome by its probability, and then summing the results.

expenditure tax Type of consumption tax that is levied on the total consumption expenditure of an individual or household.

externality Externalities arise when an action by a producer or consumer affects other economic agents and this effect is not reflected in the market price.

extrinsic motivation When individual decisions are driven by external factors or rewards (e.g. payment, praise, or fame).

federal government Type of government where power is shared between a central government and state or regional governments.

financial literacy Individuals' understanding of key financial concepts, including interest compounding, inflation, and risk diversification. It is sometimes defined more broadly as having the knowledge, skills, attitudes, and behaviours that enable individuals to make informed financial decisions.

first-best economy An economy that satisfies the first-best conditions under which the market will lead to an efficient allocation of resources.

First Fundamental Theorem of Welfare Economics Under certain conditions, the operation of perfectly competitive markets will lead to an equilibrium allocation of resources that is Pareto efficient.

fiscal drag Phenomenon that arises in a progressive tax system when inflation pushes more taxpayers into higher income tax brackets, resulting in higher tax revenues for the government.

fiscal illusion Arises when individuals are not fully aware of or do not fully understand the implications of the government's tax and spending decisions.

framing effect Arises if the way in which a choice is described and how information is presented affects the choices individuals make.

franchising Process through which governments can encourage private firms to provide public services. In contrast with contracting out (or outsourcing), here provision generates its own revenue through user fees (e.g. rail passenger services in the UK).

free rider problem Problem that arises in the context of public goods if every potential consumer of the good understates their true valuation in the hope of enjoying the good more cheaply or for free, resulting in the good being underprovided or not provided at all.

free riding To consume a good without paying for it or paying less than one's true valuation of the good.

fully funded pension scheme Scheme where the value of the pension that individuals receive when they retire is tied to their contributions. Pensions are paid out of a fund that has built up over time out of individual contributions. Contrast with unfunded pension scheme.

funded defined contribution (FDC) pension scheme Scheme where individual contributions and investment returns build up in an individual account, which is then converted into an individual pension at retirement.

game theory Framework for analysing decision-making when decisions are interdependent (i.e. where the outcome of an individual's decision will depend on the actions of other individuals). The individuals or parties in game theory are normally referred to as players.

general equilibrium analysis Analysis which considers how conditions in each market in a set of related markets affect equilibrium outcomes in other markets in that set.

gift tax Type of transfer tax that is levied on assets that are given by one living individual to another.

global material footprint The total amount of raw materials required to meet final consumption demands.

government debt The total amount of money owed by the government at a particular point in time, accumulated from borrowing to cover budget deficits.

government deficit See budget deficit.

government failure Situations where government interventions cause or contribute to economic inefficiency.

general practitioner (GP) A family doctor in the UK.

Gini coefficient Measure of income inequality which takes on a value between zero (full equality) and 1 (full inequality).

gross government debt Total debt or liabilities owed by the government at a given point in time. Contrast with net government debt.

Haig–Simons income Amount that individuals could have spent over a given period without changing their net wealth position.

headcount ratio Measure of the number of households with incomes below the poverty line as a proportion of the population.

hedonic pricing Method for valuing amenities based on the implicit prices revealed by the market.

hidden economy Economic activities that are concealed (intentionally or unintentionally) from the authorities. These include illegal activities (e.g. drugs and people trafficking) and unmeasured legal activities (e.g. household production and legal but undeclared income).

horizontal equity Principle that individuals who are equal in all relevant respects are treated equally. It implies there should be no discrimination based on characteristics such as gender, race, and ethnicity.

hyperbolic discounting Hyperbolic utility functions involve a relatively high discount rate over short horizons (e.g. the present) and a relatively low discount rate over long horizons (e.g. in the future).

hypothecation In the context of taxation, process whereby revenue from particular taxes is tied to particular expenditures.

imperfect information Situations in which consumers and producers do not have all of the information they need to make an informed decision. This is different from the concept of asymmetric information.

impure public goods Goods that are rival but non-excludable, or non-rival and excludable. There are two types of impure public goods: common-pool resources and club goods.

income effect One component of the total effect of a change in price on the quantity demanded of a good or service. The income effect captures the change in quantity demanded as a result of the change in purchasing power. See also substitution effect.

income gap ratio Measure of the average normalized income shortfall among those in poverty.

increasing returns to scale Arise when output increases more than proportionately with the increase in inputs, so the firm's average cost of production falls as output increases.

independence of irrelevant alternatives Property that holds that the social choice between any two alternatives, X and Y, should only depend on the individual rankings of X and Y, and should not be affected by the introduction of a separate alternative Z.

indexation In the context of old-age pensions, where the value of the pension is tied to increases in prices to maintain purchasing power.

indifference curve Curve that illustrates the different combinations of goods that provide individuals with the same level of satisfaction or utility.

indirect taxes Taxes on goods and services (e.g. value-added tax (VAT) and sales taxes). Contrast with direct taxes.

inertia In behavioural economics, the tendency of individuals to stick with the status quo or default option rather than actively making a decision.

inflation Increase in the price of a bundle of goods and services over time.

inheritance tax See estate tax

in-kind transfers Transfers which involve the provision of goods and services directly to recipients (e.g. healthcare, education, housing, and food stamps).

insurance premium Price that individuals have to pay for insurance against adverse events.

intergenerational fairness How the costs and benefits of policies are distributed across generations.

interior solution In the context of utility maximization, a solution in which the individual's optimal choice involves positive quantities of all goods. Contrast with corner solution.

internalizing an externality Requiring those responsible for generating external costs or benefits to take these into account in their decision-making.

internal rate of return (IRR) Value of the discount rate, *r*, which ensures that the discounted benefits equal the discounted costs.

intertemporal budget constraint All possible combinations of current and future consumption that are feasible given an individual's income and the interest rate.

intertemporal choice model Economic model for analysing individual consumption decisions over time.

intrinsic motivation The desire to engage in an activity for its own sake because it gives us satisfaction or because we feel it is the right thing to do.

inverse elasticity rule Tax rates should be inversely proportional to the price elasticity of demand, so the greater the elasticity of demand, the lower the tax rate should be.

isocost Line that represents the different combinations of two inputs that producers can use for a given total cost.

isoquant Different combinations of inputs that produce the same level of output.

Kaldor–Hicks efficiency criterion Efficiency criterion which focuses on *potential* Pareto improvements (i.e. whether it is possible to reallocate resources in such a way that those who gain from the reallocation could hypothetically compensate those who lose out, and still be better off). It is also known as the potential Pareto improvement (PPI) criterion.

Keynesianism Economic doctrine based on the work of John Maynard Keynes which advocates for an active role for government in the economy.

Kuznets curve Graphical representation of the relationship between economic growth and inequality, which suggests this relationship has an inverted U-shape.

laboratory experiments Experiments carried out in a laboratory environment.

labour supply elasticity Measure of the sensitivity of hours worked to changes in the wage rate.

Laffer curve Representation of the theoretical relationship between the tax rate and the level of tax revenue raised. The Laffer curve has an inverted U-shape, suggesting that as tax rates rise, the amount of tax revenue raised initially increases, but beyond a certain point further increases in the tax rate lead to a fall in tax revenues.

laissez-faire Economic philosophy based on a belief in the efficiency of private markets and which advocates a minimal role for government in the economy.

legal tax incidence See statutory tax incidence.

liberal theories of society Theories based on the principle of individual liberty and which see private markets as an efficient mechanism for allocating resources. However, they acknowledge the need for some government intervention (e.g. to address inequalities inherent in the market system).

libertarian theories of society Theories based on the primacy of individual liberty and which advocate for private property and free markets with very limited government intervention.

lifetime tax incidence Analysis of the incidence of a tax in relation to an individual's total lifetime resources.

Lindahl equilibrium Set of tax prices which add up to the marginal cost of producing the good, such that at those prices everyone demands the same quantity of the public good.

Lindahl prices Set of personalized prices based on individuals' true willingness to pay for a public good.

lobbying Process whereby individuals or groups expend resources in an attempt to influence policymakers or politicians.

local public goods Goods that are available only within a limited geographical area (e.g. a city park).

longevity risk Risk that individuals may live longer than anticipated and therefore may outlive their retirement savings.

long-term care (LTC) Encompasses a range of personal, social, and medical services to support people who face difficulties in carrying out everyday activities over a prolonged period as a result of chronic conditions or disability.

Lorenz curve Measure of inequality which provides a graphical representation of the entire income distribution, by ordering the population in increasing order of income and plotting the proportion of income going to each proportion of the population.

loss aversion Tendency of individuals to treat losses and gains differently in their decisions—in particular, individuals tend to prefer avoiding losses to receiving a gain of the same magnitude.

lump-sum tax A type of non-distortionary, fixed tax that does not depend on any characteristics of the entity being taxed.

macro-efficiency Refers to how resources should be allocated across different areas of activity (e.g. what share of resources should be allocated to healthcare, education, defence, etc.). Contrast with micro-efficiency.

majority voting Simple majority voting is a voting rule whereby an option or policy is chosen if it is selected by 50 per cent of voters plus one voter.

marginal abatement cost (MAC) Cost of each successive unit of pollution abatement or reduction.

marginal benefit (MB) Benefit that individuals derive from buying one additional unit of a good. It is equivalent to private marginal benefit (PMB).

marginal cost (MC) Cost of producing one additional unit of output. It is equivalent to private marginal cost (PMC).

marginal damage cost (MDC) Cost of each additional unit of pollution.

marginal deadweight loss Increase in the deadweight loss when the tax rate increases by one unit.

marginal rate of substitution (MRS) Rate at which individuals are willing to exchange one good for another while keeping their utility constant. It equals the slope of the individual's indifference curve, or how much of good Y (measured on the vertical axis) an individual must give up to obtain one more unit of good X (measured on the horizontal axis), while keeping their utility constant.

marginal rate of technical substitution (MRTS) Rate at which one input can be substituted for another while keeping total output unchanged. It equals the slope of an isoquant.

marginal rate of transformation (MRT) Slope of the production possibility frontier, which measures the opportunity cost of producing one good in terms of the other.

marginal revenue (MR) Change in total revenue from selling one additional unit of a good.

marginal tax rate Percentage of the next pound/euro/dollar earned that is paid in tax.

marginal utility Increase in utility from consuming one additional unit of a good.

market economy Predominant system for allocating resources in the world today. Prices act as a coordinating mechanism, conveying information about the relative demand for different goods and services and the relative costs of producing them, thereby determining how resources are allocated.

market equilibrium Market outcome where the quantity demanded and the quantity supplied are equal.

market failure Instances where private markets fail to achieve an efficient allocation of resources. Classical types of market failure in economics include externalities, public goods, imperfect competition, and asymmetric information.

market power or monopoly power Situation where firms have the ability to influence market prices.

market testing Creation of external markets to provide goods and services that were previously provided by the government.

means-tested benefits Welfare benefits where the amount received depends on an individual or household's financial situation (i.e. their level of income or wealth).

median voter Voter in the middle of the set of voters, with exactly half of voters on either side.

Median Voter Theorem Under majority voting, the chosen outcome will be the one preferred by the median voter.

mercantilism Doctrine which advocated that governments should play an active role in promoting industry and trade, supporting domestic industries through subsidies, and restricting imports using tariffs and quotas.

merit good A good that individuals are likely to underconsume because they do not realize the full private benefits of doing so. Merit goods may also have wider social benefits associated with them.

micro-efficiency Refers to how resources should be distributed within an area of activity (e.g. education or healthcare). Contrast with macro-efficiency.

mixed economy Economic system which combines elements of free markets and government intervention. Most countries in the world today have a mixed economy.

monopolistic competition Type of imperfect competition characterized by a large number of firms which sell similar but differentiated products (e.g. different brands of toothpaste or breakfast cereal).

monopoly Market with a single seller.

monopsony Marlet where a single buyer dominates the market.

moral hazard Problem of hidden action where one party to a transaction may take actions that the other cannot observe after they have entered into an agreement, which may lead the uninformed party to trade less than it otherwise would want to.

multiple-peaked preferences Preference relation which has multiple local maxima, which means that the individual does not consistently rank the alternatives lower as we move away from the most preferred alternative.

nationalization Process whereby the government takes control of a private company or industry.

natural capital Natural capital encompasses the stock of renewable and non-renewable resources—air, water, soils, plants, animals, and minerals.

natural capital accounting Framework for measuring and reporting on the stocks and flows of natural capital in a systematic way, which can better be integrated into widely used frameworks (e.g. the System of National Accounts).

natural monopoly Monopoly market that arises when economies of scale are so significant that a single firm may be able to produce the entire output of a market at a cost below the cost if there were several firms operating in the market. This is a common feature of many public utilities (e.g. water, gas, and electricity).

negative externality When the action of a consumer or producer imposes a cost on other economic agents (e.g. pollution or second-hand smoke).

negative income tax System that integrates income support and income taxation by paying benefits to individuals whose income falls below a certain threshold and levying taxes on individuals whose income is above that threshold.

neoclassical economic theory Economic framework based on a set of assumptions about how the economy operates and what drives the behaviour of individual consumers and producers. Specifically, consumers are assumed to make decisions to maximize their utility, while producers make decisions to maximize profits and minimize costs.

neoliberalism Political and economic ideology that promotes free market competition and minimal government intervention in economic and social affairs.

net government debt Total debt or liabilities owed by the government at a given point in time, minus any financial assets the government owns. Contrast with gross government debt.

net present value (NPV) The discounted sum of future net benefits—or benefits minus costs—over the relevant time horizon of a project or policy.

non-contributory benefit Benefit where access does not depend on previous contributions. Usually financed out of general tax revenues.

non-contributory pension scheme Scheme under which a pension is awarded based on an individual's age and, in most cases, residence status. Access does not depend on previous contributions.

non-distortionary taxation A tax is non-distortionary if there is no way in which individuals can change their behaviour to reduce the amount of tax they pay.

non-excludable A good is non-excludable if it is impossible—or extremely costly—to exclude or prevent any individual from consuming the good once it is provided.

non-rival A good is non-rival in consumption if consumption of the good by one person does not reduce the amount available for others to consume.

normal good A good for which demand falls (rises) as income falls (rises).

normative analysis Analysis involving statements that are subjective and cannot be tested. It focuses on how things should be, rather than how things are.

notional defined contribution (NDC) pension scheme Scheme where individuals pay a proportion of their earnings into the scheme and a notional rate of return is applied to these contributions. Individual contributions and investment returns build up in an individual account, which is then converted into an individual pension at retirement. These accounts are notional in the sense that the balance only exists on the books of the institution that is managing the accounts.

numeraire good A good that is used as a basis for valuing all other goods and whose price is set equal to 1.

old-age dependency ratio Proportion of people aged 65 and over relative to the working-age population. It is sometimes referred to as the old-age to working-age ratio.

oligopoly Market with a small number of sellers.

open-access resources Common-pool resources that anyone can access or use and which are therefore at risk of being overexploited.

opportunity cost Value of the next best alternative forgone when a choice is made. For example, the opportunity cost of a resource measures the value of the next best alternative use of that resource.

opportunity set Set of all possible choices or consumption bundles that an individual can afford.

optimal tax theory Study of the design and implementation of taxes that will maximize social welfare subject to given economic constraints.

outsourcing See contracting out.

paradox of voting Describes how many people vote even though the expected utility of voting is likely to be negative.

Pareto efficiency An allocation of resources is Pareto efficient if there is no way to change this allocation to make at least one individual better off without making anyone else worse off.

Pareto optimality See Pareto efficiency.

partial equilibrium analysis Analysis which focuses on the impacts of changes in specific markets in isolation.

path dependence Arises when past events or decisions constrain future events and decisions. In the context of public expenditure, it refers to the theory that current expenditure is not just a function of current circumstances, but also depends on previous patterns of expenditure.

pay-as-you-go (PAYG) pension scheme See unfunded pension scheme.

pension replacement rate Measure of individuals' pension income as a percentage of their pre-retirement income.

Pigouvian tax See corrective taxes.

plurality voting Voting rule which assigns a score to each alternative based on an individual's ranking of the alternatives, so their first choice is given a score of 1, their second choice is given a score of 2, etc. The option with the lowest number of points is chosen.

points-based pension schemes Scheme where individuals earn pension points based on their earnings and contributions. Once they retire, the value of their pension equals the sum of all the pension points they have accumulated multiplied by a pension-point value.

point voting Voting rule where voters have a fixed number of points to distribute across the alternatives and the option with the largest number of points is selected.

policy capture Arises when public policy decisions consistently target particular interests rather than the public interest.

policy myopia Instances where government policy interventions prioritize short-term gains over longer-term solutions.

political economy Social science that studies how the political process affects the economy and how the economy influences the political process.

pollution permits Permits restricting the quantity of pollution that firms can emit.

positive analysis Analysis involving statements that are objective and can be tested. It focuses on how things are.

positive externality When the action of a consumer or producer imposes a benefit on other economic agents (e.g. knowledge spillovers from R&D).

potential Pareto improvement (PPI) criterion See Kaldor–Hicks efficiency criterion.

poverty gap The product of the headcount ratio and the income gap ratio, two measures of poverty.

poverty line Threshold which determines who is in poverty. A poverty line can be defined for both absolute and relative concepts of poverty.

poverty trap Problem that arises when an individual has no financial incentive to work longer hours because for every additional pound/euro earned, they are losing a pound/euro or more in means-tested benefits (i.e. they face a high implicit tax rate).

present-biased preferences Preferences that favour short-term gratification and more immediate consumption.

present value Value today of a given amount of money received in the future. The present value is generally less than the actual future amount.

pressure group See special interest group.

price controls Restrictions on the minimum or maximum prices that firms can charge (e.g. minimum wages and rent controls).

price discrimination When firms vary the price of their products depending on the consumer (e.g. charging lower prices for students) or on the quantity sold.

price elasticity of demand Measures the sensitivity of the quantity demanded of a good to changes in its price. See elasticity of demand.

price elasticity of supply Measures the sensitivity of the quantity supplied of a good to changes in its price. See elasticity of supply.

price-takers Consumers or producers in a market are price-takers if, individually, they do not have the power to affect the market price.

primary balance The difference between government revenues and government spending, but excluding net interest payments on government debt.

principal–agent problem Problem that arises when a principal (e.g. an employer) delegates a task to an agent (e.g. an employee), but cannot observe the actions of the agent, and therefore cannot ensure that the principal's objectives are maximized.

prisoner's dilemma In game theory, a thought experiment which illustrates how two individuals acting in their own self-interest can lead to an outcome that is not optimal for either of them.

private CBA Cost–benefit analysis that takes into account only private costs and benefits.

private goods Goods that are both rival and excludable.

private marginal benefit (PMB) See marginal benefit.

private marginal cost (PMC) See marginal cost.

privatization Concept usually associated with the transfer of assets from the state to the private sector, but which is in fact much broader and refers to a collection of policies designed to strengthen the market and reduce the role of the public sector (e.g. deregulation and market testing or competitive contracting).

producer surplus Benefit that producers derive from selling their goods in the market, measured as the difference between the price at which they were willing to sell their goods and the market price.

Production Efficiency Theorem The optimal commodity tax system should not distort production efficiency, which implies that intermediate goods (i.e. inputs) should not be taxed.

production externalities Externalities that arise as a result of firms' production decisions.

production possibility frontier (PPF) Set of all possible output combinations that can be produced with a given level of inputs and for a given technology.

productive efficiency When resources are allocated to ensure the maximum output is produced from a given set of inputs.

progressive tax system System where the average tax rate rises with income, which implies that richer households pay a higher share of their income in taxes than poorer households.

property rights Legal rules which establish the ownership of economic resources and how they can be used.

property tax Type of wealth tax levied on the value of real estate owned.

proportional tax system System where the average tax rate does not increase with income, so all taxpayers pay the same proportion of their income in taxes.

public choice Framework which highlights the importance of thinking about the interests and motivations of voters, politicians, bureaucrats, and other political actors. Assumes that these actors are driven primarily by self-interested utility maximization, rather than promoting the public interest.

public economics Study of the role of government in the economy. It is concerned with both government expenditures and how the government raises the revenues it needs to finance these expenditures.

public finance Study of the role of government in the economy. It is usually synonymous with public economics or the economics of the public sector.

public goods In economics, a public good is a good which is both non-rival and non-excludable. These are sometimes referred to as pure public goods.

public–private partnerships (PPPs) Agreements where the private sector is involved in both financing and providing infrastructure and services for the public sector in return for annual rental payments from the government.

public procurement Process through which the government or another public authority buys goods and services from the private sector.

pure public goods See public goods.

quality-adjusted life years (QALYs) Measure that combines both the quantity and quality of life gained as a result of a particular health intervention. One QALY is equivalent to one year of life in perfect health.

quasi-experiment Situation where a change in the economic environment (e.g. as a result of the introduction of a new policy) creates virtually identical control and treatment groups, allowing the impact of that policy to be assessed.

quasi-government agencies Public bodies set up by the government but which operate at arm's length from government departments.

Ramsey rule To minimize the efficiency cost of raising a given amount of revenue, the government should set taxes across different goods so that the ratio of the marginal deadweight loss to marginal revenue raised is the same across all goods.

randomized control trial (RCT) Type of experiment designed to test the impact of an intervention where participants are randomly assigned to a treatment group (which receives the intervention) or a control group (which does not).

rate of capital productivity Value of the additional goods which could be produced in a year's time if £1 is invested in producing them today.

rate of time preference Measure of how much individuals value present consumption relative to future consumption.

rational choice model Model of decision-making in economics that assumes individual consumers have well-defined preferences and that they make decisions to maximize their welfare or utility subject to what they can afford.

Rawlsian social welfare function Social welfare depends on the welfare of the least well-off member of society.

reciprocity Propensity to respond in kind (e.g. by rewarding generosity or punishing opportunistic behaviour).

redistribution Reallocation of resources from some groups in society to others.

regression analysis Statistical method used to establish the strength and nature of the relationship between variables (e.g. between house prices and house characteristics).

regressive tax system Tax system where the average tax rate falls with income.

regulation Use of rules, incentives, and penalties by the government to control and modify the behaviour of firms and individuals.

regulatory capture Situation where a regulatory agency (or those who work there) gradually comes to identify itself with the interests of the firm or sector that it is responsible for regulating and focuses on advancing these interests rather than acting in the best interests of consumers and society. A broader understanding of regulatory capture includes the possibility of capture by special interest groups.

relative measure Where a value is determined relative to an external reference point, so it is independent of the original units of measurement; typically expressed as a ratio or percentage. Contrast with absolute measure.

relative poverty Poverty concept that assumes that poverty depends on the prevailing standard of living in a particular society.

remunicipalization Where the process of taking back control from the private sector happens at the local or municipal level.

rent-seeking Process whereby individuals or organizations use resources to advance their own goals and gain economic benefits, rather than investing these resources in productive economic activities.

replacement rate Measure of the income individuals receive when not working as a proportion of their income when working.

representative democracy Individual voters elect representatives (e.g. members of Parliament and local councillors) who make decisions on their behalf, without consulting them on each individual issue.

returns to scale See economies of scale.

returns to scope See economies of scope.

revealed preference methods Approach that relies on using information about individual behaviour and the choices individuals make to infer a value for the good or resource being measured.

risk Situations where the probability distribution of future outcomes is known, in contrast with uncertainty. Risk can be quantified whereas uncertainty cannot. In practice, the terms 'risk' and 'uncertainty' are often used interchangeably.

rival good A good is rival in consumption if the use or consumption of the good by one individual reduces the amount available for others to consume.

rules of thumb Practical guidelines used to make a decision rather than trying to solve a complex and time-consuming optimization problem. Also referred to as heuristics.

screening hypothesis Theory that holds that education acts as a signalling device, indicating an individual's pre-existing ability level, rather than increasing individual productivity directly.

Second Fundamental Theorem of Welfare Economics Theorem that holds that if individual preferences and technology are convex, then *any* Pareto-efficient allocation can be sustained as a competitive equilibrium, for some initial allocation.

sensitivity analysis Process for checking how robust a given set of estimates are to changes in the underlying assumptions.

shadow economy See hidden economy.

shadow price Estimate of the monetary value of an intangible or non-market commodity, or a commodity for which there is a gap between its market price and its social value.

single-peaked preferences Preferences that have a single local maximum (i.e. an option that is preferred to all other options in its immediate proximity). If an individual has a most preferred option and any alternative that is further away from this most preferred option is preferred less, then these preferences are single-peaked.

sin tax Tax levied on a good that is considered harmful to individuals or society (e.g. alcohol or cigarettes).

social CBA Cost–benefit analysis that takes into account both private and social costs and benefits.

social choice theory Social choice theory focuses on the question of how to aggregate individual preferences into a social decision.

social discount rate Discount rate used for calculating the net present value of social investments.

social exclusion Concept of deprivation which encompasses low income and poor health, education, and housing conditions, among other factors.

social insurance Form of social welfare that provides protection against economic risks (e.g. loss of income due to illness, unemployment, or retirement). Participation in social insurance schemes is usually compulsory and individuals receive benefits based on previous contributions.

social justice See equity.

social marginal benefit Value to society of producing one additional unit of a good, taking into account any externalities associated with consumption of the good.

social marginal cost Cost to society of producing one additional unit of a good, taking into account any externalities associated with production of the good.

social norms Often-unwritten rules that guide the standards of what is considered acceptable behaviour in a particular society.

social pension See citizen's pension.

social preferences Individuals care not only about their own well-being, but also about the well-being of others.

social risks See aggregate risks.

social time preference rate Value that society attaches to present consumption relative to future consumption.

social welfare Level of well-being in society. Social welfare depends on both the total amount of resources in an economy and how they are distributed.

social welfare function Summarizes the welfare of society as a function of the welfare of the individuals in that society.

special interest group Group of individuals or organizations that share a common interest or goals and who work together to attempt to influence public policy in their favour.

specific excise tax Fixed tax levied on the sale of particular goods or services, in contrast to an ad valorem tax.

specific or unit tax Tax levied as a fixed amount per unit sold.

state pension age Age at which individuals are eligible to start receiving the state pension.

statutory tax incidence Refers to who is responsible for making the tax payment to the tax authorities. Also known as legal tax incidence.

structural budget deficit Takes fluctuations in tax revenues and spending over the economic cycle into account and provides an estimate of the size of the deficit if the economy were operating at a normal level of employment and activity. It is sometimes referred to as the cyclically adjusted budget deficit.

substitution effect One component of the total effect of a change in price on the quantity demanded of a good or service. The substitution effect captures the change in quantity demanded purely as a result of the change in relative prices, keeping utility constant. See also income effect.

supply curve Relationship between the total quantity of a good or service that firms are willing to produce and the price level.

taxable income elasticity Measures how taxable income changes in response to a change in the tax rate.

taxation on accrual Tax is paid on the returns on an asset as the returns are being earned (i.e. tax is paid in each period on the returns earned in that period).

taxation on realization Tax is paid on the returns on an asset when the asset is sold.

tax avoidance Reorganization of economic activity to reduce the amount of tax paid (e.g. by making use of legal loopholes, or exploiting tax shelters or tax havens).

tax base Area of economic activity on which a tax is payable.

tax compliance Decision to comply with all tax laws and regulations by paying taxes in an accurate and timely manner.

tax credits Benefit payments that are administered through the tax system, effectively reducing the amount of income tax individuals have to pay.

tax deduction Amount by which taxpayers can reduce their taxable income. It is sometimes referred to as tax relief.

tax evasion Intentional and illegal non-payment or underpayment of taxes by individuals or businesses.

tax gap Difference between the amount of tax that individuals should, in theory, pay to the revenue service and the amount that is actually collected.

tax haven Country which offers very low or zero rates of tax for non-domiciled investors.

tax incidence Analysis of who bears the burden of a tax.

tax morale Broadly defined, tax morale captures the various non-pecuniary motivations for tax compliance, and other factors not captured by the standard expected-utility-maximizing framework.

tax shelter Any strategy or investment scheme that allows individuals to reduce their taxable income and, therefore, the amount of tax they have to pay. This includes investing in offshore companies and certain types of trusts.

tax wedge Difference between the price consumers pay and the price producers receive (net of the tax).

tertiary education All formal post-secondary education, including academic and higher vocational education.

third-party payment problem Problem that arises in the context of privately provided healthcare when insurance companies are separate from doctors and patients, and doctors are paid a fee for service. If health insurance covers all patient costs, healthcare is essentially free at the point of use and patients have an incentive to overconsume healthcare. If doctors are paid a fee for service, they have an incentive to overprescribe treatments to increase the payment they receive from the insurance company. These two effects combined will lead to an overconsumption of healthcare, increasing the insurance provider's costs.

time-inconsistent preferences Preferences where individuals exhibit different degrees of patience or impatience depending on the time horizon.

total welfare Sum of consumer and producer surplus. It is sometimes referred to as total social surplus.

tradeable permits System where the government sets a limit on the total level of emissions and issues the necessary number of permits, which are then auctioned off, so firms bid for the right to pollute.

tragedy of the commons Highlights how many individuals acting independently and rationally will ultimately lead to the depletion of shared limited resources, even when it is clear that it is in no one's long-term interest for this to happen.

transaction costs Costs associated with organizing and running a market, including search costs, the costs of drawing up and enforcing contracts, and some administrative costs (e.g. costs of administering different provision schemes).

transfer expenditures Government spending on transfers to individuals (e.g. unemployment benefits, sickness benefits, and old-age pensions) and subsidies to private sector firms.

transfer taxes Taxes levied when an asset is transferred from one individual to another; these include gift taxes and inheritance or estate taxes.

transitivity Property of preference orderings that requires that, given three alternatives—X, Y, and Z—if X is preferred to Y and Y is preferred to Z, then X must be preferred to Z. Transitivity imposes a degree of logical consistency on a preference ordering.

treatment group Group of individuals who are comparable to the control group and who receive the particular treatment or intervention being analysed.

unanimity voting Voting rule which requires unanimous approval for a given alternative to be chosen.

uncertainty Situations where the probability distribution of future outcomes is not known, in contrast with risk. In practice, the terms 'risk' and 'uncertainty' are often used interchangeably.

unemployment trap Problem that arises when an individual who is unemployed has little financial incentive to look for work as the rate at which benefits are withdrawn when they start working means that the increase in their total income is marginal.

unfunded pension scheme Scheme where pensions are paid out of current contributions or current tax revenues. The current working-age population pays into the pension scheme and these payments are used to fund the pensions of the current retired population. It is also known as a pay-as-you-go pension scheme.

unitary government Type of government where power is concentrated in a single, central authority, the central government. Some authority and the implementation of certain policy decisions are often delegated to subnational units.

unitization Market-based solution to the problem of environmental externalities which involves creating a single ownership of the activities connected by an externality.

universal basic income (UBI) Flat payment provided by the government to all individuals regardless of age, gender, race, labour market status, and income.

universal benefits Welfare benefits where the level of benefit received does not depend on an individual's level of income or wealth.

Universal Credit (UC) UK-based welfare policy introduced in 2013 which aimed to simplify the UK benefits system by combining six of the previously existing means-tested benefits for working-age adults into a single benefit called Universal Credit.

utilitarian social welfare function Social welfare is defined as the sum of individual welfare or utilities.

utility Individual satisfaction or well-being.

utility function Function that represents an individual's preferences and assigns a numerical value (utility) to different bundles of goods and services.

utility possibility frontier (UPF) Describes the maximum level of utility that one individual (or group of individuals) can achieve for a given level of utility achieved by another individual (or group of individuals). All points on the UPF are Pareto efficient.

value of a statistical life (VSL) Measure of how much individuals are willing to pay to reduce the risk of death.

VAT revenue ratio Difference between the actual VAT revenues collected and the revenues that would be collected if VAT were applied at the standard rate to all consumption.

vertical equity Principle that individuals who are unequal in any relevant respects are treated unequally. For example, individuals with greater needs should receive more resources; or individuals with higher incomes should pay more taxes.

Wagner's law Tendency for the government to grow, both in absolute terms and relative to the size of the economy, as an economy develops.

welfare economics Branch of economics that focuses on defining and measuring the welfare of society as a whole.

welfare state System where the government or an established network of social institutions plays an important role in protecting and promoting the well-being of citizens by providing services such as education, healthcare, and social insurance.

willingness to pay (WTP) Maximum amount that individuals are willing to spend to enjoy the benefits of consuming a good.

X-inefficiency Situations in which a firm's costs of production are higher than necessary. This can be due to several factors, including a lack of direct competition, inefficient production processes, and poor internal organization and management practices.

Index

Please note that page references to Figures will be followed by the letter 'f', to Tables by the letter 't'.